Table of Contents

PART 1 Type, Draw, Paint

This legacy paint and rotoscoping plug-in still has its fans. Since it offers some features not supported by Paint, we demonstrate ways to use it in production.

PART 2 Animation Assistants

Diving deeper into the expression language.

PART 3   More on Effects

PART 4   Working with Audio

PART 7 Format Issues and Rendering

The Road Home

Bonus DVD Tutorials Overview

A number of tutorial projects are also included on this book's DVD. See summary on page **404**.

Afterword: CoSA Lives *(Bonus Chapter PDF on DVD)*

David Simons – one of the original creators of After Effects – takes us back in time to learn how this program we love came into being.

Learning to Play with Others

By Trish and Chris Meyer

After Effects can be applied to a dizzying variety of tasks. However, not all jobs begin and end inside After Effects – indeed, very few do. This book focuses on integrating with the rest of the world.

Imagery may be scanned, captured with digital still image cameras, created in Adobe Photoshop or Illustrator, rendered from a 3D program, or originally created as an animation for the web. Of course, a large amount of content will be recorded on videotape or film, in a variety of formats, pixel aspect ratios, frame sizes, even frame rates. Much of this footage may be used roughly as is (after a bit of color correction or enhancement, of course). However, some of it will be shot against green or blue screens, and you will need to extract the action from this background and composite it into a new scene. Some footage has objects you need to track so other objects can follow their motion; some will contain an unacceptable amount of motion or shake that you need to stabilize or remove. And not all content is visual – audio is a major portion of the motion graphics experience, as well.

Then there's output! Few of your animations will be played back only on your computer screen. Most of them will go back out to video, film, or the web, again with a large number of technical issues and workflow practices that must be observed.

Of course, there are always ways to work smarter. After Effects features a number of Keyframe Assistants plus the Expression language to help perform complex animation tasks for you. There are ways to manipulate the fabric of time itself, plus a whole host of additional plug-in effects that come with the Professional edition – and other useful ones to download or purchase. Preferences can be customized, compositions can be prerendered to save time, and renders can be split across multiple computers to meet tight deadlines.

All of this and more is what *Creating Motion Graphics, Volume 2: Advanced Techniques* is about. After you have read *Volume 1: The Essentials* and mastered the core of After Effects, we want to help you take your skills further, and enable you to tackle a wider variety of tasks – while expressing your individual creativity along the way.

Trish and Chris Meyer
CyberMotion
April 2005

As a companion book to the *Creating Motion Graphics* series, we have also created *After Effects in Production*, which puts many of the features of After Effects to work in a series of intermediate-to-advanced tutorials. It also includes a set of six broadcast case studies from award-winning studios including ATTIK, Belief, Curious Pictures, The Diecks Group, and Fido, and well as our own studio, CyberMotion. Look in the **Goodies** folder on the DVD for more information. As a set, we hope these books empower and inspire you to realize your own creativity with this wonderful program.

How to Use This Book

This book explores the more specialized portions of Adobe After Effects 6.5 – from audio to painting to keying to motion tracking and stabilization to advanced animation techniques including Expressions. We will assume you already know your way around After Effects – or at least have access to a good reference, such as *Creating Motion Graphics, Volume 1: The Essentials*.

This book also discusses how to use other programs with After Effects, including the still image applications Adobe Photoshop and Illustrator, most of the leading 3D animation packages and nonlinear editing systems, and the web animation tool Macromedia Flash MX. We also explore many of the additional features available in the Professional edition version of After Effects. You don't need to have all of these programs to use this book, but you will no doubt encounter one or more of them during your creative life – and we want to prepare you to deal with them. This book will also serve as a technical reference on video and film issues.

We suggest reading Chapter 1 on alpha channels to ensure a grounding in this core concept that touches on everything you do in After Effects. After that, you can skip around and read chapters that pertain to a particular job.

In addition to the printed pages of this book, **Bonus Chapters** on subjects including scanning, Expressions, Vector Paint, Preferences, and the creation of After Effects are included on the accompanying DVD. Additionally, there is a selection of **Bonus Tutorials** on the DVD that explore specific techniques or plug-ins, such as using expressions or enhancing 3D renders. These tutorials consist of a PDF file with instructions, a corresponding After Effects project, and a movie of the finished piece. (A summary of these tutorials starts on page 404.)

You will find that a good portion of this book is technical in nature. Like you, we're more interested in being artists than engineers, but understanding the underlying technical details of some challenges – such as dealing with film or high-definition video – makes problems go away faster, so you can get back to being an artist.

What's in a Name?

There are many elements in an After Effects project. We've tried to establish a set of typographical conventions to make it easier to understand what we are talking about and when:

• **Words in bold** refer to the specific names of folders, files, or layers you are using.

• [**Words in bold and in brackets**] are the names of compositions, as opposed to layers in a composition.

• "**Words in bold and in quotes**" are text you should enter.

• **Words and symbols in this alternate bold font** represent pieces of the Expression language.

• When there is a chain of submenus or subfolders you have to navigate, we separate links in the chain with a > symbol: for example, Effect>Adjust>Levels.

We use keyboard shortcuts extensively throughout this book. The Macintosh shortcut is presented first (followed by the Windows keystrokes in parentheses). Context-click means hold down the Control key while clicking on the Macintosh, and right-mouse click on Windows.

After Effects makes a distinction between similar keys on the normal keyboard and the numeric keypad. If we do not explicitly say to use the keypad, we're talking about the numbers and symbols in the normal portion of the keyboard. When we say the Enter key, we mean the one in the extended keypad; when we say the Return key, we mean the normal carriage return key (which also happens to be labeled Enter on many keyboards).

Iconography

The content inside each chapter is usually presented in a linear fashion. However, you will find numerous asides throughout. In addition to sidebars which focus on specific ideas or techniques, you will also see:

 Tips: Useful tricks and shortcuts, or info on optional third party products we recommend.

 Factoids: Tweaky bits of specific information that might help demystify some subjects.

 Gotchas: Important rocks you might trip over, such as special cases in which a feature might not work.

 Connects: Mini-indexes at the end of most chapters – these point out additional chapters in this book and Volume 1 that contain information related to what you just learned.

Pro **Professional edition:** After Effects comes in two flavors: the Standard and Professional editions. Subjects that rely on the Professional edition's features are identified with this icon.

Disc Access

This book and its DVD go hand in hand: Virtually every chapter has its own project file which encourages you to practice the concepts presented in these pages. Look for the Example Project box on the first page of each chapter to verify which project you are to load, and whether you also need to install any of the free third party plug-ins included on the DVD.

We recommend you copy the DVD, or at least the **Chapter Example Projects** and **Sources** folders, to your hard drive. This will speed up file access and allow you to save your own versions of the projects as you work (it will also serve as a backup if the DVD should accidentally break…you know who you are). If files become "unlinked" for some reason, they will appear in *italics* in the Project window. Simply double-click the first missing item: This will bring up a standard file navigation dialog where you can locate that item. Select the missing file from its corresponding **Sources** subfolder and click OK. Provided the folder relationship between the project and the other sources has not changed, After Effects will now search for the other missing items and link them in as well.

Installation

We assume you already have a copy of After Effects 6.5 or later installed – preferably the Professional edition. To be safe, we have included a fully-functional time-limited tryout version of After Effects Professional on the DVD. You may also download the most recent version from Adobe (www.adobe.com).

If you don't already have QuickTime installed, you can download it from Apple's web site (www.apple.com/quicktime). We assume you also have a copy of Adobe Reader on your computer. An installer is included on your After Effects CD and may also be downloaded from www.adobe.com.

There are numerous free and trial version plug-ins on your DVD. Some of these have their own installers, or must be decompressed either by double-clicking them or using StuffIt Expander (www.stuffit.com). Most of the Mac versions may be dragged directly into your After Effects>Plug-ins folder. On the Windows platform, if a plug-in ends in .aex, you may drag it directly into After Effects> Plug-ins; if it ends in .exe, it is either an installer or self-extracting archive. Copy the .exe file to your hard drive and double-click it to run it. If it is a self-extracting archive, drag the resulting .aex file into your Plug-ins folder. A Read Me summary of all these with a guide to their installation is included in the **Free Plug-ins** folder on the DVD as a PDF.

Contact the individual vendors directly for any tech support issues. If there is a problem with your DVD, contact **books@cmp.com** (with a clear subject line) for a replacement.

System Requirements

Our system requirements are similar to those Adobe recommends for After Effects. Most of the examples in this book and corresponding content on the DVD are based on 320×240 pixel images, so they take up less memory and screen real estate. The exceptions are Chapters 27 and 28, which contain large high definition video and film content which will require more RAM. In general, we recommend at least 512 Meg for After Effects; installing a gigabyte or more in your computer is considered normal in the production world.

We also recommend an extended keyboard, as many shortcuts take advantage of the function keys and numeric keypad. You don't need a multibutton mouse to use After Effects, but as many keyboard shortcuts use context-clicking, the modifier keys, and even the scroll wheel, it's not a bad idea. If you are a Mac user, Exposé takes over some of the function keys; open it in System Preferences and reassign any shortcuts that use them.

For Instructors

If you are an instructor, we hope that you will adapt this book to your specific needs and find it useful in teaching After Effects. Much of this series is modeled on the advanced After Effects classes Trish teaches, as well as sessions we've both delivered at numerous conferences and trade shows.

Recognizing the budgets and time constraints of most instructional situations, we've built 95% of the example projects using 320×240 comps and similar low-resolution sources. This requires less memory all around and results in faster demonstrations and previewing. However, the concepts are certainly from the real world, and should adapt directly to full-frame video projects.

For copyright reasons, each student must own their own copy of this book. This also allows them to review the material covered after class – without wasting valuable class time writing reams of notes. Students can open the **Chapter Example** project from the DVD, make changes to it as they practice, and save the edited project to their own folders on a hard disk or removable media. At the next class, if they mount the DVD *before* opening their modified projects, the sources should relink properly.

If your school has the available disk space, students may copy contents from the DVD to their computers, or you may place the files on a server, but again only as long as each student owns their own copy of this book. Provided each student owns the book, you are free to modify the tutorials and adapt them to your specific teaching situation without infringing copyright.

As an instructor, you no doubt appreciate how much time and effort it takes to prepare examples and class materials that both teach and inspire. If a school, company, or instructor distributes copies of the sources, plug-ins, projects, or PDFs to any person who has not purchased the book, that constitutes copyright infringement. Also, reproducing pages of this book, or any material included on the DVD (including derivative works), is also a copyright no-no. Thank you for protecting our copyrights, and those of the many vendors and studios who contributed sources – your cooperation enables us to write new books and obtain great source materials for your students to learn with.

Qualified teaching professionals can acquire evaluation copies of this book as well as our companion volume, *After Effects in Production*, by submitting the request form provided on the CMP Books web site (www.cmpbooks.com) – look under Order Info>Classroom Resources.

DVD ROADMAP

The enclosed DVD contains many useful resources for you to explore while you're reading this book. We suggest you copy its entire contents to your drive for reference and faster access. Here's what is in each folder:

▶ Bonus Chapters

Extended information on scanning, Expressions, Vector Paint, Keying, and the text Preferences. Also includes the story of how After Effects was created and has evolved over the years: *CoSA Lives.*

▶ Bonus Tutorials

Contains six bonus tutorials in PDF form that explore a variety of techniques, including using paint and expressions. All come with an After Effects project plus QuickTime movie of the final result; some contain additional source material.

▶ Chapter Example Projects

Virtually every chapter has a corresponding example project. This way, you can practice concepts as they come up in each chapter. These projects all point to the shared **Sources** folder on this DVD; some contain folders of additional content.

▶ Credits and Info

Information about the numerous stock footage houses and individual artists who contributed content for this book – we encourage you to contact them directly and see what they have to offer. Also contains the End User License Agreements that you agree to when you're using their content provided on the DVD.

▶ Free Footage & Plug-ins

Digital Film Tools, Jens Enqvist, Fnord Software, and Walker Effects have contributed useful free plug-ins for you to add to your collection. Install them; they will be used throughout this book. You'll find documentation and further information in their respective folders.

Additionally, Artbeats and 12 Inch Design have donated 1.5 gigabytes of royalty-free full-size NTSC and PAL stock footage for you to use!

▶ Goodies

A grab bag of additional content and information, including useful articles, white papers, and sample chapters, Animation Presets, Photoshop Styles, video and film safe area templates, plus information on other books, video, and music from Trish and Chris Meyer as well as CMP Books.

▶ Sources

Contains movies, music, mattes, objects, stills, and text elements used by the projects and tutorials in this book. Each file has a two-letter prefix that identifies its creator; a key is provided in the **Credits and Info** folder as well as on page 408. Make sure you read their respective End User License Agreements in the **Credits and Info** folder – many may also be used in your own commercial projects.

DVD Technical Support

Each third party is responsible for providing technical support for the products provided free on this DVD. If your DVD becomes damaged or won't load, contact CMP Books (books@cmp.com) to arrange a replacement.

1 All About Alphas

Understanding alpha channels is fundamental to understanding how After Effects works.

Alpha channels are central to working in After Effects. Every layer and every composition either has or is given an alpha, and manipulating these alphas is how After Effects combines layers. Many features and techniques – such as masking, using track mattes, stencils, and keying – create alpha channels so you can blend images together in interesting ways.

This chapter will explore how After Effects manages alpha channels internally, how to properly import sources with alpha, and the choices you have for rendering with an alpha channel. We'll spend some time demystifying *Straight* and *Premultiplied* alpha, showing you how to identify and handle footage with premultiplied alpha so you can avoid ugly fringes and halos around the edges of objects. We'll also cover a more unusual alpha channel type, *Luminescent Premultiply*. Some of the features and techniques that manipulate alpha channels (such as masking) have entire chapters devoted to them elsewhere in this series, so in these cases we'll refer you to the relevant chapters in the Connect box at the end of this chapter.

Alphas 101

An image's alpha channel is a fourth channel of information that decides the transparency of every pixel built by the normal RGB color channels. In an 8-bit per channel (bpc) file, it has 8-bit resolution for 256 possible shades of gray, which when combined with the 24-bit RGB color channels results in a 32-bit image. (16 bpc provides a far wider range of values; for the sake of simplicity, we'll stick with describing 8 bpc images in this chapter – all of the principles remain the same.) You can think of the alpha channel as a grayscale image that acts as a stencil mask for the corresponding color image: A value of 0 – black in the alpha – means the corresponding pixel is totally transparent; 255 – white in the alpha – means totally opaque. Values between these numbers mean the corresponding pixels are partially transparent.

Open the project file **01-Example Project.aep** from the **Chapter Example Projects>01-Alpha Channels** folder on the DVD, and open comp [**Ex.01-Alpha 101**]. The goldfish object is the only layer. Click on the Red, Green, Blue, and Alpha (white) channel icons along the bottom of the Comp window. Notice that the Alpha channel is white where the fish should be opaque, and black where background pixels should drop out. This allows for the fish to be composited against any color or other image (without this alpha, the fish would exist on a white background, as it appears in Photoshop).

Background Color and Alpha

It is important to distinguish between the comp's Background Color, which shows through whenever a comp's alpha channel is transparent, and filling a comp with a colored solid, which also fills the alpha channel. To see this in action, turn off any Comp window channel icons, and change the background color of the comp (Composition>Background Color) from black to blue so that the fish appears against a colored background. If you click the Alpha icon again, nothing will have changed. The background color is a display color only and doesn't affect the comp's alpha channel.

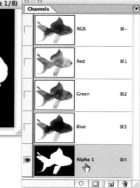

As viewed in Photoshop, the combination of RGB channels creates the color for each pixel, while the corresponding alpha channel determines the pixel's opacity. Fish object from Getty Images/Design Essentials.

Now create a new solid (Layer>New>Solid). Click the Make Comp Size button, and color it anything but blue (we made ours black). When you click OK, the solid layer will be on top of the fish, so in the Timeline window, drag the solid below the fish layer. Now click on the Alpha icon again: The alpha channel is now fully white, as the solid exists in RGB colorspace, and its alpha is all opaque.

With the Alpha icon still on, move the solid layer off-center in the comp, and you'll see the shape of the fish appear along with the solid's alpha. In other words, the alpha channel for the fish and the solid are merged together to create a single grayscale image that serves as the Comp's alpha channel. You'll see later how you can render a movie with this alpha channel embedded in it, or even render the Comp's alpha channel as a separate movie.

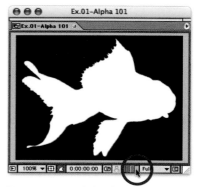

To see a comp's alpha channel in After Effects, click on the white icon at the bottom of the Composition window.

On a related note, when you nest one comp into another comp, the alpha channel of the nested comp is honored. Any background color in Comp 1 is ignored, and treated as transparency in Comp 2. If you need the background color to be visible, create a solid layer using that color.

When the solid layer is moved, you can see that the alpha channel for the fish and the solid layer are combined. (The color of the comp's background is irrelevant where the alpha channel is concerned, but a colored solid layer adds its alpha to the comp's alpha.)

Big picture time: If you're trying to create an animation that will be rendered with an alpha channel for further compositing in a video editing suite, you need to be sure that there is something interesting in the comp's alpha channel! If the alpha channel is fully white throughout the animation, there is nothing to be gained from rendering with an alpha – except a larger file.

Shades of Gray

In the case of our fish image, the shape of the fish in the alpha channel is solid white, making the fish fully opaque. In reality, the various fins of the fish would be semitransparent. If white in the alpha channel is opaque, and black is transparent, it stands to reason that shades of gray will be more or less transparent.

The original fish was fully opaque (left). By painting some gray into the alpha channel (center), the fins become semitransparent when they're composited against a background (right). Water courtesy Artbeats/Water Textures.

Open comp [**Ex.02**], where a modified version of the same fish image is composited over a water movie. Scrub the timeline and notice that the highlights from the water in the background play through the fish's fins. Double-click layer 2 to open the Layer window (this is the original source to the layer, and the Layer window also has RGB+Alpha channel icons). Click on the Alpha icon; the fins were modified in Photoshop by adding some gray paint to the white areas in the alpha channel, rendering the fins partially transparent in After Effects. (To compare this against the original image, turn off layer 2 and turn on layer 1 instead, and see how the water doesn't show through the fins in the original fish image. We think you'll agree that the composite is more believable when the layers appear to interact.) Select Window>Close All when you're done, to reduce clutter.

Without infinite resolution, a diagonal edge to an alpha channel mask resembles a staircase (left). This is *aliasing*. Mixing in intermediate gray values to form an edge, based on a percentage of how much of a pixel a theoretically perfect line would intersect (right), smoothes the edge. This is known as *antialiasing* and is another reason grayscale values in alpha channels are important.

Life on the Edge

Having gray values in the alpha channel serves another important purpose: to help smooth out diagonal edges. Video and multimedia do not have enough resolution to render edges at an angle without visible staircasing being the result, as the edge tries to decide which pixel to land on. This goes for alpha channel edges as well as any color information in a frame. This is called *aliasing*. Short of resorting to near-infinite resolution, these edges can be made to appear smoother by *antialiasing* them. In the case of alpha channels, this means mixing in intermediate shades of gray. Virtually all good alpha channels for objects that do not cover the entire frame have antialiased edges.

After Effects and Alphas

After Effects uses alpha channels to composite layers together. In fact, if footage doesn't have an alpha channel, After Effects will assign it one, as it needs to know how opaque to make each pixel. In the Project window, select the movie **DV_Pulse.mov** from the **Sources>Movies** folder. Along the top of the Project window, it will report that the movie is Millions of Colors (which means it is 24-bit, with no alpha channel). Option+double-click on Mac (Alt+double-click on Windows) the movie to open it in the After Effects Footage window. Click the Alpha icon and you'll see that the alpha channel is a simple white rectangle; it was assigned by After Effects so that it would know how to composite the movie in a composition. (Why use white and not black? Think about it…) Close the Footage window when you're done.

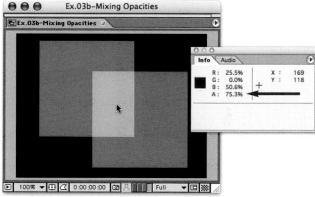

This movie on disk has no alpha channel embedded in it. The After Effects Footage window shows the alpha channel as fully white, so it will be fully opaque when it's added to a comp.

So every piece of footage that is added to a comp exists as an RGB+Alpha layer, even if the source didn't start out with an alpha. Once it's placed in a comp, there are many ways to modify this alpha channel further. Explore the following example compositions:

[Ex.03a-Opacity]: Okay, so this is an easy one… Select layer 1; if its Opacity parameter isn't visible in the Timeline window, press T to reveal it. Scrub the Opacity value and watch the layer get more or less transparent. Now turn on the Alpha icon and scrub Opacity again. When you change Opacity, you're changing the brightness of the layer's alpha, not the values of the RGB channels.

[Ex.03b-Alpha Mix]: In this example, we have a solid that is 100% blue, sitting on top of another solid that is 100% red. The Opacity for both solids is currently 50%. Click on the Alpha icon and notice that where they overlap, the alpha channel is brighter.

Make sure the Info palette is visible – if not, press Command+2 (Control+2) to open it. The Info palette defaults to displaying values in RGB 8 bpc (0–255); change this to Percent (0–100) by clicking once on the palette or by selecting it from its Options menu. Now run your cursor around the solids in the Comp window while you're looking at the Info palette. The alpha channel for each solid is 50%, which makes sense. But where the two solids overlap reads Alpha 75%, not 100% as you might expect. Alpha channel values don't add – they multiply (so 50% × 50% = 25% transparent, which is 75% opaque). The only way to have 100% opacity is for one layer to be 100% opaque (or to have so many overlapping semitransparent layers that no one will notice the tiny amount of transparency remaining). Return the Info palette to Auto Color Display when done.

The Info palette has been set to display values in Percent (0–100). Here, two squares, both at 50% Opacity, report an alpha value of 75% in the area where they overlap.

[Ex.03c-Masking]: In this comp, an oval mask is applied to a movie, making the pixels outside the mask edge transparent. When you apply a mask,

Masks create transparency on a layer by rendering pixels outside the mask shape with an alpha channel value of 0 (black). Image courtesy Digital Vision/Pulse.

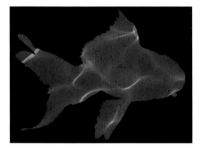

The water movie plays inside the fish's alpha channel by using it as an Alpha Matte.

the original RGB image is not changed, only the layer's alpha channel. (To see the layer and its alpha before the mask is applied, double-click the movie to open it in the Layer window and set the View popup to None.)

In Best Quality (the default), the edge of the mask is smoothly anti-aliased. In Draft Quality, the edge is stairstepped. Click on the Alpha swatch icon to view the alpha channel, then toggle the Quality switch between Best and Draft to compare results. Zoom in if you need to get a closer look.

Mask Feather should be twirled down in the Timeline window (if not, select layer 1 and press F). Scrub the Feather amount to around 80; this adds a large falloff to the edge of the mask. The appearance of this feathered edge renders differently depending on whether the layer is in Best or Draft Quality (toggle the Quality switch again if you're curious).

To see how the feathered edge composites on top of another layer, turn off the Alpha icon and add a background movie from the Project window's **Sources>Movies** folder, such as **AB_DigitalMoods.mov**. Scrub the feather amount for the masked layer – the more transparent the feathered edge, the more of the background layer shows through.

[**Ex.03d-Track Matte**]: In this example, the alpha channel of the fish image is "borrowed" by the water texture movie so that the water shows only where the fish's alpha channel is opaque. Click the Alpha icon to see the Comp's alpha channel. Change the Track Matte popup for layer 2 to Alpha Inverted – the fish shape cuts out a hole in the movie layer instead.

[**Ex.03e-Keying**]: There are various effects available to key footage, but in all cases the idea is to make a certain color transparent. This could be black or white in the case of a Luma Key, or blue or green when you're using keying effects like Keylight, Linear Key or the Color Difference Key (see Chapter 10). For instance, in this comp, the Luma Key creates an alpha channel for the **AB_FloralTwist** movie in layer 1 – it does this by making black transparent. Turn off layer 2, and click the Alpha icon to see layer 1's new alpha. Select layer 1 and press F3 to open the Effect Controls window and check out the settings.

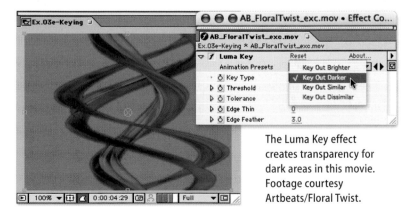

The Luma Key effect creates transparency for dark areas in this movie. Footage courtesy Artbeats/Floral Twist.

[**Ex.03f-Unmultiply**]: Free on this book's DVD is a handy plug-in from Walker Effects called Premultiply. When its Mode popup is set to Unmultiply Black, it will drop out a black background. However, it will also take dark values throughout the layer and make them semitransparent, so results are different from a Luma Key. Open [**Ex.03f**] and compare the alpha channel created (and how it composites against the background layer) with the alpha channel created with the Luma Key effect in [**Ex.03e**].

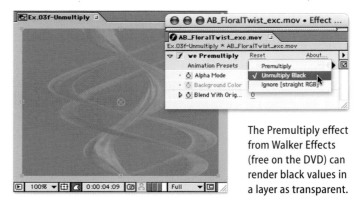

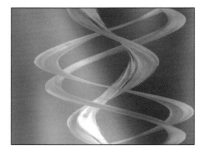

The Premultiply effect from Walker Effects (free on the DVD) can render black values in a layer as transparent.

[**Ex.03g-Blending Modes**]: There is yet another method for dropping out black backgrounds when compositing, and that is to use a blending mode for the top layer. Modes such as Add, Screen, Linear Dodge, and Color Dodge are lightening modes that work by adding pixel values from the top layer to the layers below. Black has a value of 0,0,0 RGB, so it is essentially ignored when using these modes. However, blending modes do not create transparency! Turn off layer 2 in this comp and check out layer 1's alpha channel – it's completely white, or fully opaque.

Blending modes offer different formulas for combining images together based on their RGB values – they do not affect the transparency of the alpha channel. Background courtesy Artbeats/Digital Moods.

To summarize, the Luma Key effect is better at creating an alpha for hard-edged solid objects, but it tends to leave black edges that are difficult to clean up correctly. The Walker Effects Premultiply effect is more suited to creating an alpha channel from a black background for footage such as fire and explosions, or when you need to create an alpha channel for a lens flare effect that will be composited in another application. Blending modes are great for compositing inside After Effects, but they don't create alpha channels – with one exception:

[**Ex.03h-Stencils**]: Stencils and Silhouettes are listed under Modes, but they are capable of creating transparency. In this example, the fish's alpha channel acts as a stencil for all layers below. Also, the Comp is set to display transparency as a checkerboard pattern (see sidebar, *Checkmate*).

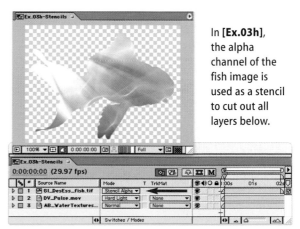

In [**Ex.03h**], the alpha channel of the fish image is used as a stencil to cut out all layers below.

[**Ex.03i-Preserve Transparency**]: The "T" switch in the Modes panel forces the layer to which it's applied to render only inside the Comp's alpha channel (because After Effects renders from the bottom up, this means the sum of the alpha channels from all layers *below* – layers above the "T" switch are not included).

Select Window>Close All before moving on.

In [**Ex.03i**], the movie layer has its Preserve Transparency switch set, so it appears only inside the comp's alpha channel. Footage courtesy Artbeats/Digital Microcosm.

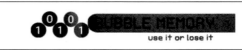

Photoshop and Alphas

When many users think of alpha channels, they think of Photoshop. (Though we hope you now have a better appreciation for how much After Effects loves alpha channels too!) If you need transparency from your Photoshop artwork when it's imported into After Effects, there are basically two approaches you can take:

[**Ex.04a-Channel #4**]: The fish image is an example of an RGB image with an alpha channel. (To view this image in Photoshop, select it in this comp and Edit>Edit Original.) There are many ways to create such an alpha channel: You could paint it, extract it, or outline the fish with a pen path then convert the path to a selection and save it as an alpha channel, among other methods. Whichever technique you use, be sure to save your file using a 32-bit file format that supports an alpha channel (for example, Photoshop, TIFF, or PICT).

[**Ex.04b-Layers**]: Photoshop layers (with the exception of the background layer) are inherently 32 bits and therefore support transparency by way of an invisible layer mask. You can also create an explicit layer mask that you can paint on or edit further. If you save this file using the Photoshop (.psd) format, you can import this layered file into After Effects. When you're importing, you can either merge the layers, or import the file as a Composition. If imported as a comp, each individual layer's mask is converted into its alpha channel. In addition, the Opacity values and modes set in Photoshop are honored by After Effects. In [**Ex.04b**], a layered image from Digital Vision was imported as a Composition; double-click a layer to isolate it in its own Layer window. (To open this image in Photoshop, select any layer and Edit>Edit Original.)

Illustrator and Alphas

[**Ex.05-Illustrator**]: Illustrator files are quite straightforward when it comes to alpha channels. Wherever the "paper" is in Illustrator will be transparency in After Effects. In addition, Opacity values set in Illustrator 10 and CS are honored by After Effects 6.5. You can merge the layers when you import, or import the Illustrator file as a Composition.

3D Applications and Alphas

[**Ex.06-3D Renders**]: When you're rendering animations that will play full frame from a 3D program, you probably won't benefit from rendering with an alpha channel. However, if you're rendering animated elements – such as this robot gizmo in [**Ex.06**] – be sure to render with an alpha. It's almost impossible to use a luma key or an "unmult" effect to drop out a black background cleanly; you also don't

This Photoshop file from Digital Vision's Rayform CD has 26 layers; it can be imported as a Composition in order to animate individual layers.

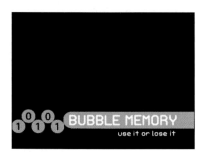

The "paper" in Illustrator becomes an alpha channel in After Effects, and Opacity values are honored.

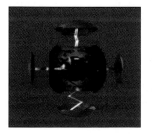
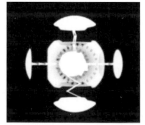

The robot animation (far left) was rendered in 3D with an alpha (left); semitransparent model pieces render as shades of gray in the alpha. Gizmo courtesy Quiet Earth Design.

want to render over green or blue and try to successfully key this color out later in After Effects. With the gizmo animation, view the alpha channel and note the subtle transparency in the robot's body; if you turn on the background layer, it will be partially visible through the body.

All 3D programs should allow you to render with an alpha channel (if not, find another app!), and you should also have the option of rendering a Straight rather than a Premultiplied alpha (see below). Some applications may create a special type of alpha channel, which is covered in the section *Luminescent Premultiplied Alpha* below.

Straight versus Premultiplied Alpha

There are two ways to save an image with its alpha channel – *Straight* or *Premultiplied* – and the theory, reasons, and correct workflow might not be intuitive at first. So make yourself a nice cup of tea, and we'll try to explain how it all works.

First off, let's get one thing straight (excuse the pun): Whether the footage has a straight or premultiplied alpha, *the alpha channel will look exactly the same* – the difference appears in the RGB channels.

Because After Effects displays images with their alpha channel already taken into account, check out the following test images in Photoshop, where the RGB and alpha channels can be viewed easily. Open Photoshop, then open the three images you'll find on the DVD in the **Chapter Example Projects>01-Alpha Channels>01_Chapter Sources>Red circles** folder (or from your hard drive, if you copied these files to your drive). This is what you should find:

• **Circle_straight_full.tif**: The RGB channels are completely filled with red. The alpha channel contains a white circle on black. When the alpha channel is used in After Effects, you'll see a red circle. The color of the RGB pixels where the alpha is black (outside the circle) is irrelevant, as these pixels will be fully transparent anyway. After Effects considers this image to have a *straight* alpha, because it can use the alpha channel as a simple "cookie cutter," and the edge of the circle is not contaminated with any background color.

This is an easy, straightforward method for creating a simple shape or solid colored logo in Photoshop. Because the artwork is created on the Background layer (not a transparent layer), you can save this image as a TIFF or PICT with alpha and it will be compatible with all video editing applications – many of which don't read the Photoshop (PSD) file format, or the TIFF format if you save with layers on.

Checkmate

Transparency in the Composition, Layer, and Footage windows can be viewed as a checkerboard pattern (just like Photoshop). To toggle on the Transparency Grid, click on the checkerboard icon at the bottom of the window (see figure below) or select it from the window's Options menu. The checkerboard is toggled on/off per window, and there is a slight performance hit when it is enabled.

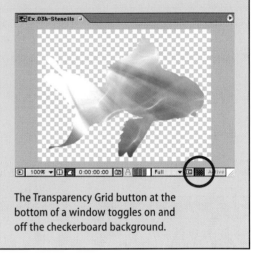

The Transparency Grid button at the bottom of a window toggles on and off the checkerboard background.

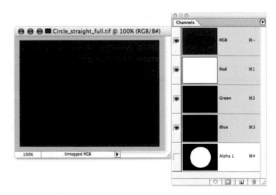

By filling the RGB channels with a solid color, and creating the circle only in the alpha channel, this image is considered to have a *straight* alpha channel.

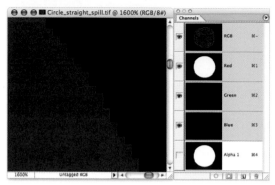

If you render a straight alpha from After Effects or a 3D application, you'll usually get an "oversprayed" edge, where the color channels are aliased and extend past the edge of the alpha channel.

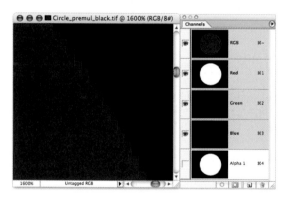

A premultiplied alpha image has the background color (in this case, black) mixed in with the color of the red circle. Unless you remove the contamination in After Effects, the edge of the circle will exhibit a black fringe.

Trick Question

View Channel #4 for all three images in Photoshop. Spot the differences? There are none! Remember – the alpha channel type is defined by how semitransparent areas appear in the RGB channels!

• **Circle_straight_spill.tif**: This image is of a red circle on a black background, but look closely at the edge of the circle (zoom in to get a better look): The edge is stairstepped, not antialiased. Toggle on/off the eyeball for Channel #4: The red pixels in the RGB channels extend to just outside the edge of the circle in the alpha channel. Despite how different these first two images appear, After Effects considers both to have a *straight* alpha, because the semitransparent pixels in the alpha channel punch through pixels that are not contaminated with any background color.

While you wouldn't normally create an image like this in Photoshop (filling the RGB channels with a flat color is an easier way to create this graphic), this is the method used by After Effects and other 2D and 3D applications when they render an image with a straight alpha channel. They "overspray" the edge so that the alpha can punch through cleanly.

• Compare these two images with our third contender, **Circle_premul_black.tif**, which is also a red circle on a black background. However, in this example, black is factored – or *multiplied* – into the color channels at the edge of the circle in proportion to how transparent the alpha is. So, in this case, if a pixel in the alpha channel registered 128 (on a scale of 0–255), then the corresponding pixel in the RGB channels would be 50% red and 50% black (a *darker* color red than the circle).

This kind of image is referred to as a *premultiplied* alpha. For After Effects to treat it properly, it needs to be told (a) that a background color has been blended into the RGB channels, and (b) what that color is. The usual color is black, but it could be white, blue, or any other color. Once After Effects gets this information, it can subtract the background color from semitransparent pixels and recreate a straight alpha image to work with internally.

You might have looked at these three images and thought that at least the premultiplied image looks like what the end result should be (a nicely antialiased red circle on a black background). So it might come as a surprise to find out that the "good-looking one" will only make your life more complicated (just like your momma said…). Having a straight image allows you to composite the red circle against any background image in After Effects (while After Effects can remove the premultiplied color and convert the image to a straight alpha channel, there is a slight quality hit to pay). Also, most video editing systems insist on a straight alpha channel, as they cannot remove a premultiplied background – the consequences of which we'll see shortly. So, whenever you're given the option, create a Straight Alpha for a more compatible render with editing systems, and also for a tiny increase in quality.

Don't Ask, Don't Tell

Now that you've dissected these three examples in Photoshop, let's see what After Effects makes of them. Some applications – After Effects included – label or "tag" their images as straight or premultiplied when they render. When you import an image that contains a labeled alpha channel into After Effects, it will report the alpha type (Straight or Premultiplied) at the top of the Project window. However, RGB+Alpha images saved from Photoshop are *unlabeled*, so After Effects normally presents you with the Interpret Footage dialog asking how it should treat the alpha channel: Should it interpret it as Straight, Premultiplied with a color, or should it take its best Guess?

You might be inclined to hit the Guess button and hope for the best. If the image was rendered by another compositing or 3D application with computer precision, chances are high that After Effects will guess correctly. Confusion reigns, though, when the alpha channel was created by a human hand, pen tool, magic wand, and so on. And when After Effects is confused, it guesses that it's Straight. So what the Interpret Footage dialog really means when it reports that "this footage has an unlabeled alpha channel" is this: *"If you know how the RGB channels were created, select Straight or Premultiplied with a color. If you don't know how this footage was created, press the Guess button – but if I'm confused, I'll guess it's Straight…"*

The lack of an "I'm not sure" answer can result in premultiplied images being misinterpreted as straight, and we'll see the problems that can cause shortly. Incidentally, you can set After Effects to automatically interpret alphas, or to always guess, under Preferences>Import. Also, when you drag and drop an image, or a folder of images, the alpha interpretation will always guess. This is handy when you're importing dozens of images at once, but don't assume the alpha channels are labeled and/or being interpreted correctly.

Straight Shooting

Most video editing systems prefer a straight alpha channel. If you're stuck with a still image or movie with a premultiplied alpha, pass it through After Effects and render it back out with a straight alpha.

The Interpret Footage dialog, when it's presented with importing an unlabeled alpha channel, asks you to help it decide whether it's Straight or Premultiplied.

Under the Hood

To see how the above works in practice in After Effects, set Preferences>Import>Interpret Unlabeled Alpha As to Ask User, and run through the following exercise:

• Select Window>Close All. Select the [**Ex.07**] folder in the Project window, select File>Import>File, and import the **Circle_straight_full.tif** image from disk. The Interpret Footage dialog will appear asking you to select an alpha channel type. Either click on Guess or select Straight, and click OK. The red circle image should now reside in the [**Ex.07**] folder and be tagged as "Straight" at the top of the Project window.

The Project window reports what type of alpha channel a source contains.

- Open the comp [**Ex.07*starter**], and add the **Circle_straight_full.tif** image to it. This is the first image you opened in Photoshop, where the RGB channels were filled with red. Once inside After Effects, though, the alpha channel is automatically factored in, making the area outside the circle transparent. The comp's background color now shows wherever the layer is transparent.

When you add the **Circle_straight_full** image to a comp, the alpha channel is factored in, showing a nicely antialiased edge (right). Shift+click on the Alpha icon to see how the color channels appear internally in After Effects (far right).

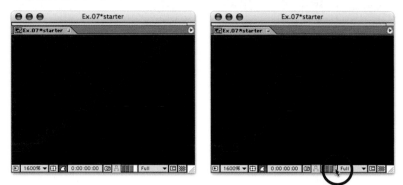

Before & After

If you double-click a movie with an alpha channel in the After Effects Project window, the QuickTime Player window opens and displays the movie *before* the alpha channel has been taken into account. Try this with the **QE_Gizmo_loop.mov** (found in **Sources>Movies**), which has a straight alpha channel. However, if you Option+ double-click (Alt+double-click) to view the movie in the After Effects Footage window, the alpha channel will be used and the edges will be clean. The Footage window does this magic by applying the settings from the Interpret Footage dialog before rendering the frame. (Other settings like separate fields, remove pulldown, looping, and so on are also taken into account in the Footage window.)

- In the Comp window, zoom in 800% on the edge of the circle; the antialiased edge of the red circle is blending with the background color. Now, press the Shift key and click on the white Alpha icon. Whoa – what's with the ugly stairstepping? What you're seeing here is the edge displayed as a straight alpha channel, with the transparency unmultiplied back out. Notice that the stairstepped edge extends *beyond* the edge of the alpha channel, but After Effects doesn't bother with the rest of the RGB image where the corresponding alpha pixel is fully black. The alpha channel itself – with all that lovely antialiasing – will cut through this stairstepped edge like a cookie cutter, creating semitransparent pixels that can be composited on top of *any* background color cleanly.

What about the premultiplied with black circle? If you're curious, turn off this layer, and import the **Circle_premul_black.tif** image. When the Interpret Footage dialog appears, click Guess, and the Premultiplied option should be selected. Click OK, and add this second circle to the [**Ex.07*starter**] comp. Repeat the Shift+click on the Alpha icon, and you'll see *the exact same result!*

In fact, all three images that looked quite different in Photoshop will look the same in the Comp window. (In [**Ex.07a-Red circles**], we've imported all three circle images if you're curious to compare them with each other.) Once After Effects is told to treat the premultiplied image as premultiplied with black, it's converted to a straight alpha channel for compositing. After Effects works internally in a straight alpha world – it just factors in the alpha channel before rendering to the Comp window.

For another peek at After Effects under the hood, open [**Ex.07b**], where a soft Mask Feather is applied to the edge of an oval mask. Shift+click on the Alpha icon and you'll see the "unmatted" image, before the alpha has been factored in. Again, After Effects doesn't bother displaying the full frame, even though these pixels are still available to it.

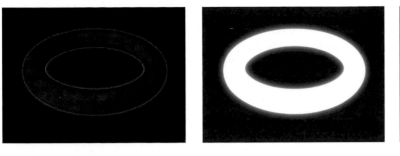

The 3D object has a white drop shadow applied (left), which renders in shades of gray in the alpha channel (center). If you rendered from After Effects with a straight alpha channel, the color channels would be unmatted (right).

Open [**Ex.07c**] for yet another example: A torus object was rendered from a 3D application with a straight alpha. Shift+click the Alpha icon to view what the image really looks like before the alpha channel is factored in. If you open this image in Photoshop (Edit>Edit External), the RGB channels will look stairstepped as you'll be viewing the "oversprayed" edges without the alpha being taken into account (just like with the **Circle_straight_spill.tif** you saw earlier).

Back in After Effects, we added a white Drop Shadow to the 3D object. Turn on the "f" switch in the Timeline to see the effect and click the Alpha channel icon. (All effects written to the After Effects plug-in specification are capable of working in 32 bits – in other words, when you apply a Gaussian Blur to a layer, it also blurs the alpha channel.) If you were to render this as a movie with a straight alpha channel, the RGB channels will render a little outside the layer's edge – preview this by Shift+clicking the Alpha icon. Yes, it's ugly, but you can learn to love ugly when you see what could go wrong...

The Fringe and the Halo

What happens if After Effects mistakenly treats a premultiplied image as having a straight alpha? Consider again the case of the bright red circle: In the **Circle_premul_black.tif** image, the red pixels along the edge of the circle are blended with the black background, resulting in pixels that are a *darker color red* than the circle itself. When the alpha channel cuts through these darker red pixels, it makes them semitransparent, but it *does not correct the color back to a bright red*. The result is that the circle will have a dark fringe around it. This fringe may not be noticeable if you happen to composite it against a dark background, but it will look ugly if you composite it against a light background. This is shown in [**Ex.07d**], where our red circle with a premultiplied with black alpha was deliberately misinterpreted as straight – zoom in and you should be able to see the dark fringe around the edge.

When you see a dark fringe in the middle of a job, you don't need to re-import the footage. Practice these steps in [**Ex.07d**]: Context-click on the layer (Control+click on Mac, right-click on Windows), and select Reveal Layer Source in Project. This will select the source of this layer in the Project window, where you can now use the shortcut Command+F (Control+F) to re-open the Interpret Footage dialog. Then click on the

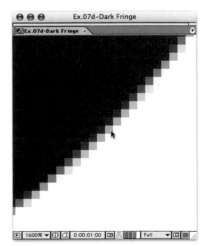

When the red circle with the premultiplied with black alpha channel is interpreted as being straight alpha by mistake, the result is a dark fringe around the edge, as seen in [**Ex.07d**].

Selective Blur

Some third-party blur effects – notably from Tinderbox and Boris – allow you to blur the RGB channels only, leaving the alpha channel untouched.

After Effects guessed – incorrectly – that this image in **[Ex.07e]** had a Straight alpha channel, a common occurrence when it's confused (right). The spaceman looks less "milky" when it's interpreted as premultiplied with white (far right). Spaceman courtesy Classic PIO/Nostalgic Memorabilia.

Premultiplied button, make sure the Matted With Color is black, and click OK. This will unmultiply black from around the edge of the circle, in direct proportion to the transparency of the alpha channel; the comp will update automatically, and the fringe will be removed. Now, no matter what you composite this red circle against, the edge will remain clean. (To compare before and after, select Edit>Undo and Edit>Redo.)

To see what a white "halo" looks like, open **[Ex.07e]**. Here, our spaceman image was imported and the alpha channel type was guessed by After Effects as being straight. It guessed wrong. The spaceman image is set against a white background in Photoshop, so the semitransparent pixels are contaminated with white. Repeat the steps above to change the **CP_Spaceman.tif** footage in the Interpret Footage dialog to Premultiplied with white (click on the color swatch and choose white).

Click OK and return to the composition. Not only does the halo around the edge disappear, but the semitransparent glass top around the spaceman looks less "milky."

Occasionally you will receive an image where the dark fringe or white halo still lingers even after the file has been interpreted correctly. If you have the Professional edition, try applying Effect>Matte Tools>Simple Choker – a half pixel choke should do the trick.

When an alpha channel is straight but incorrectly interpreted as premultiplied with black, it can appear brighter and more opaque (left) than it really should (right). This example is in **[Ex.07f]**.

Of course, mistakes can be made in the opposite direction too. In comp [Ex.07f], a render from a 3D program was misidentified as being premultiplied with black. As a result, the semitransparent object appears brighter and more opaque than it should. Select the **CM_BinarySkull.tif** footage from the **Sources>Stills** folder in the Project window, open the Interpret Footage dialog, set its alpha to Straight, and the image will now be displayed correctly.

To sum up: When After Effects makes a Guess and is confused, it will guess Straight. If you're dubious, test the image against both a dark and bright background – a correctly interpreted alpha should look good against either. If you see a dark fringe or a light halo at any time while you're working with the source, you can reinterpret the alpha channel without re-importing the file and starting over.

Remove Color Matting

Another situation you may find yourself in is when you receive a render in which the RGB channels and Alpha channel are rendered as separate movies *and* the RGB channels are premultiplied with a color. The Interpret Footage alpha interpretation process is not invoked in this case, so you're not given the opportunity to treat the color channels as premultiplied. To make matters worse, the regular Track Matte technique expects the RGB channels to be straight – so fringes and halos are unavoidable.

In this case, use the Effect>Channels>Remove Color Matting plug-in to recreate the "unmultiply" process inherent in the Interpret Footage Premultiplied option. If you use a Track Matte, you'll need to apply Remove Color Matting in a second comp or to an adjustment layer, as the Remove Color Matting effect needs to render *after* track matte has created the RGB+Alpha composite.

However, by using the Set Matte effect instead of track matte, you can follow it with Remove Color Matting all in one comp. This is shown in [Ex.07g]: The Set Matte effect takes the Luminance of the matte pass and uses it as the layer's alpha channel, but because the RGB channels are contaminated with its black background, the tire image looks darker than it should until the Remove Color Matting effect is enabled. (By the way, the Remove Color Matting effect works best for true premultiplied images, not for fixing the edges of layers that have been luma keyed or otherwise modified to extract an alpha.)

Alpha Add Mode

It is possible in After Effects to create two edges that should line up perfectly, but their alpha channels don't create a seamless result. The problem looks like a "fringe" or a "halo" issue, but the solution is different.

In [Ex.07h], a mask is applied to one layer, then the layer is duplicated and the same mask is inverted. However, if you click the Alpha Channel icon, there is slight transparency where the duplicate masks overlap. The problem is caused by the alpha channel values multiplying, not adding together (we saw this back in [Ex.03b], where a pixel with 50% opacity overlaying another pixel at 50% amounts to 75% opacity, not 100%). In [Ex.07h], set the top layer's blending mode to Alpha Add to fix the leak. You'll see the same problem not just with masks, but also with track mattes, and any other type of "seam" where two identical but inverted antialiased layers meet.

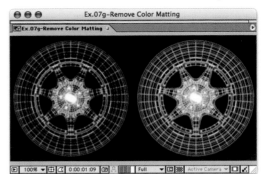

In [**Ex.07g**], the tire on the left side of the Comp window has the Set Matte effect applied to marry it with its matte pass, but because the color channels are premultiplied with black, it looks darker than the correctly interpreted tire on the right side. Apply the Remove Color Matting effect (below) to unmultiply out the black background and brighten the image.

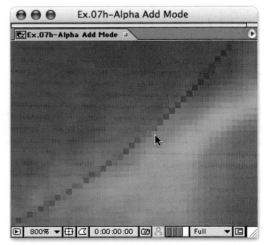

Where two layers with identical – but inverted – Mask Shapes meet, you'll see a slightly transparent seam. The fix is to set the top layer to Alpha Add blending mode.

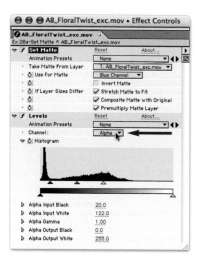

The Set Matte effect can use any channel from any layer as an alpha channel for the layer it's applied to. The Channel popup in Levels is set to affect the alpha channel only, to increase the contrast of the matte.

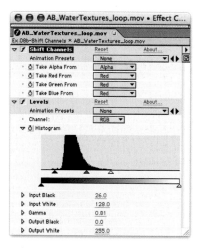

In **[Ex.08b]**, the red channel of a layer is used as a luma matte for the layer below, thanks to the Shift Channels effect, and Levels is used to increase the contrast.

Channel Effects

Remember that each RGB channel is a grayscale, 8-bit file – just like the alpha channel – so you can use effects from the Channels category to assign any of the RGB channels, or even the luminance, hue, or saturation, as a new alpha channel for a layer:

• Select Window>Close All, and open **[Ex.08a]**. Select the **AB_FloralTwist** layer and press F3 to open the Effect Controls window. The Set Matte effect is applied to the **AB_FloralTwist** movie and is set to use its own Blue channel as an Alpha channel for the layer. The Levels effect follows to increase the contrast of the new alpha; set the Channel popup to Alpha to view its histogram.

Other channel shifting plug-ins include Set Channels and Shift Channels, as well as the Channel Combiner and Calculations effects (added in version 6). These effects are generally self-explanatory, and while not particularly sexy at first glance, they come in handy for moving channels around, ignoring the alpha channel, or merging channels to create grayscale blends.

• In **[Ex.08b]**, we present a variation on this theme: The Red channel from the **AB_WaterTextures** movie is used as a luma track matte for layer 2. Turn on the Video switch for layer 1 to see the matte: The Shift Channels effect is used to move the Red channel into all three RGB channels, creating a grayscale image. The advantage to this method is that the matte is visible as a normal layer in the comp, so you don't have to click the Alpha icon to see it. The Levels effect is used to increase the contrast, but this time acts on the RGB channels, not the Alpha.

Moving channels around like musical chairs may have you headscratching at first, but the channels game can solve many matting problems or even be used to create new looks.

Output Options

When you render, you can tell After Effects to save an alpha as straight or premultiplied. Since premultiplied sources are converted to straight internally, you can even render these images back out with a straight alpha (see the sidebar, *Straightened Out*).

To render with an alpha channel, add the composition to the Render Queue, and set the Render Settings as desired. In the Output Module, choose a codec or file format that supports 32 bits, such as QuickTime Animation. Set the Channels popup to RGB+Alpha. The Depth popup will read Millions of Colors+; select Straight (Unmatted) or Premultiplied (with black) for the Alpha Channel popup.

To see how this works in practice, open the Render Queue where we've already added [Ex.09-Acme Logo] using a variety of different rendering options. Click on the Output Module to check out the settings. The first item outputs an RGB+Alpha movie, with Straight alpha. The second item in the queue outputs an alpha that is Premultiplied with black.

Straightened Out

If you have a complex layered file in Photoshop that needs to be sent to an editing system that demands a simple RGB+straight alpha channel image, it can be difficult to create this file in Photoshop. However, since After Effects converts all alphas to straight internally, you can simply pass it through After Effects to do the work in a few short steps. If you'd like to follow along, use the **Acme_logo_blue_white-glow.psd** file from this chapter's example's folder:

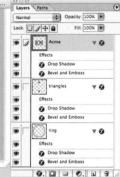

The problem: A layered Photoshop file with a white glow needs to be saved as a flattened file with a straight alpha channel.

• In After Effects, use File> Import>File and select the .psd layered file you wish to convert. Be sure to set the Import As popup to Composition in the Import dialog, and click OK. A folder and a composition will be created in the Project window.

• Open the composition. For fun, Shift+click on the Alpha channel icon – this is what After Effects will make of your color channels when you save it with a straight alpha (try doing that in Photoshop!). Turn off the Alpha channel icon, and select Composition>Save Frame As>File, and rename it.

• In the Render Queue, set the Render Settings to Best Quality.

• For the Output Module, pick a 32-bit file format that your editing application accepts (TIFF sequences are good, some Windows programs prefer Targa). Be sure to set the Channels to RGB+Alpha, the Depth to

Millions of Colors+, and the Color popup to Straight (Unmatted).

When you render the frame to disk, open it in Photoshop – but don't be surprised if it looks like a big mess! Straight alpha channels often have RGB channels that are disconcerting to look at! Turn on the eyeball for Channel #4, and the black areas in the alpha will display as a mask, previewing how nice the image will look when it's composited in your editing app. You can find our comp in the **[Ex.11]** folder, and the exported RGB+alpha file is saved as **Acme_logo_whiteglow2.tif**.

To save time in the future, create render templates: In Edit>Templates>Render Settings, set the Frame Default popup to Best Settings. In Edit>Templates> Output Modules, create a template for your favorite 32-bit file format, and set the Frame Default popup to use this template. Now when you select Save Frame As in the future, you'll need only click the Render button.

Notes: See also the Slimming Straight Alphas *sidebar at the end of this chapter. Not all Photoshop Layer Styles are supported by After Effects; more on this in Chapter 2.*

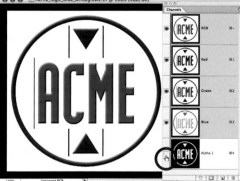

When this image is exported back out of After Effects, you will have an odd-looking but flattened RGB image with a straight alpha channel. Click the eyeball for Channel 4 to see the alpha as a mask overlay, and turn off RGB to see the alpha only.

Output Module Settings

Based on "Lossless_RGB+A straight"

Format: QuickTime Movie
Embed: Project Link
Post-Render Action: None

☑ Video Output

Format Options...   Starting #: 0   ☑ Use Comp Frame Number

Animation
Spatial Quality = Most (100)   Channels: RGB + Alpha
Depth: Millions of Colors+
Color: √ Straight (Unmatted)
Premultiplied (Matted)

☐ Stretch
Width   Height

Provided you choose a codec or file format that supports Millions of Colors+ (such as QuickTime Animation), you can select RGB+Alpha in the Output Module's Channels popup. Select Straight (Unmatted) from the Alpha popup, especially if you're sending to a system that can't deal with a premultiplied alpha.

Remember that when another application (such as a video editing system) requires an alpha channel, these applications typically prefer it be the straight variety and may not know how to unmultiply a color out of a premultiplied alpha. They may also require that the color channels and alpha channel be saved as separate movies (see the sidebar, *Two for One*).

If you render with a straight alpha channel, the Comp's background color is irrelevant. However, the background color *is* honored if you render with a premultiplied alpha. On the other hand, other editing systems that can unmultiply a premultiplied alpha may work properly only if the background color is black.

One issue with rendering a straight alpha channel is that the RGB images may appear extremely disturbing to the receiving party! If your client or the video editor were to view the movies in QuickTime player (which doesn't factor in the alpha channel), you may get a panic phone call. Explain that the RGB image (aka the "fill" or "color" channels) will look correct only when the alpha channel is used (or if you rendered the alpha as a separate movie, when the "matte pass" is applied as a luma matte).

On a related note, where the RGB channels are truly ugly, the editor or compositor will have no choice but to use the alpha. But where the RGB image is rendered against black and the stairstepped edge is subtle (as in the case of the 3D object in [**Ex.07c**] before the drop shadow effect was turned on), alpha-phobic editors have been known to reach for a Luma Key effect to drop out the black background (you know who they are). So expect to hold a few hands along the way, but do persevere in creating and rendering with straight alpha channels whenever you're given the choice – you'll run into fewer problems with this method in the long run.

Deeper Inside Premultiplied Alphas

As we've said, if a footage item is identified as having a premultiplied alpha, After Effects internally converts it into a straight alpha channel image. Let's dive into exactly how it does that, assuming for now the most common case of premultiplied with black.

To extract the "straight" color information, the color channels of each pixel are divided by the alpha value of the same pixel, and the result multiplied by 255 (100%) becomes the new color. In our red circle example earlier in

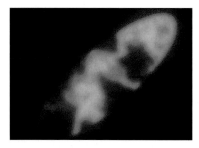

Maya can add very nice glows as a post-process to an image (above), but these make the color channels stronger than the alpha. If you interpret this image as premultiplied and composite it over a black background, the glow has lost detail (right) because the color channels were clipped when After Effects internally converted it to a straight alpha. Image by Alex Bigott of H5A5 Media AG.

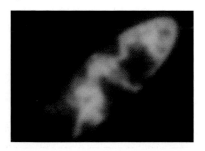

this chapter, a 50% alpha divided by a 50% red color around its edges results in 100% red in the "straight alpha" version of the color channel. The alpha itself remains untouched.

The unspoken rule is that with images that have been premultiplied against black, the value of any individual color channel for a

Two for One

When you render a movie that will be further composited in an editing suite, you may be asked to supply separate "color" and "matte" passes. The color (or "fill") pass should be the RGB channels with the "oversprayed" straight alpha appearance, and the matte pass should be the alpha channel, saved as a separate RGB movie (in other words, the grayscale alpha channel is placed in each of the RGB channels).

Remember that After Effects always renders internally a 32-bit, RGB+Alpha image for each frame. The settings used to create this frame are defined in the Render Settings. The Output Module determines how this frame is saved to disk – but you can create multiple output modules in order to save different channels or versions without having to render multiple times! So, to save separate color and matte passes, do the following:

• Add the Composition to the Render Queue, and set the first Output Module to render:
    Channels: RGB
    Depth: Millions of Colors
    Color: Straight (Unmatted)
    You will see the following warning in the bottom left-hand corner: "You should also render an alpha channel to use straight color." This is good advice, as you're about to render the ugly stuff without an alpha channel to clean it up! Click OK to close the Output Module Settings dialog.

• To save the alpha channel, select the render item and select Composition>Add Output Module. Set this second module to:
    Channels: Alpha
    Depth: Millions of Colors
    (Color popup will be grayed out.)

Create two Output Modules for the same render to save separate color and matte passes: The first saves the RGB channels, and the second saves the Alpha channel.

Select an appropriate codec, of course (if in doubt, QuickTime Animation with Quality = 100/Best should work), give both movies appropriate filenames, and make sure that all the other specifications are correct for the system that the movies will be played back on. When the render is complete, you'll have two movies that you can send to an editor for compositing. (You could also add a third output module and render just the audio, if necessary.)

We've added **[Ex.09]** to the Render Queue, and item #3 has these two output modules set up for you to explore and render. To add our templates to your preferences , click on the downward arrow and select Make Template from the bottom of the list. We named our templates so that they will sort together in the Output Module template list, and the three asterisks in their names are a reminder that these templates go together as a pair.

On rare occasions you may be asked to lay the color and matte passes off to tape so that they can be recaptured by a tape-based studio. In this case, render as above using the codec required by your hardware. Be sure to add a slate so that the two movies can be synchronized easily later on, and check whether the matte should be laid down on the same tape or to a separate tape. When you're creating these tapes, a straight alpha channel is essential, as it allows for a slight misalignment of the tape when the movies are recaptured.

Forced Premultiplied

Some images (such as light rays) have strong color channels but very transparent alpha, resulting in a wispy image. However, if you apply an additional effect, it may not react as expected to this strong color information. The Effect>Channel>Channel Combiner plug-in can convert an image from straight to premultiplied, reducing the intensity of the color channels.

Connect

pixel never exceeds the alpha for the same pixel. If it did, when After Effects went to convert it to a straight alpha, it would end up with a color strength greater than 100% – which is not possible. Is it?

Luminescent Premultiplied Alphas

Many 3D programs, such as Maya, natively calculate their images with premultiplied alpha channels. When they're left alone, they usually follow the rules above. However, many of these same programs also have post-processing effects they can apply to an image, such as glows and lens flares. And the result of some of these post-processings is that the color channel values could be stronger than their alpha channel values – which is not expected by programs such as After Effects. Other common material or surface treatments, such as partially transparent self-luminant objects, can exhibit this.

If you were to import one of these images into After Effects and interpret its alpha as premultiplied, the result could be clipping of the color values in some of the "hotter" areas (where unmultiplied colors would calculate as greater than 100%), which would alter – and often screw up – an image. But interpreting this image as having a straight alpha would be wrong as well, since the image started life as premultiplied. Neither will rendering the alpha as a separate pass and using it as a track matte work; mattes assume straight alphas, not premultiplied – again, the alpha actually is a form of premultiplied.

The workaround is to set the alpha interpretation for these images to straight, but when you composite them in a composition, choose the blending mode Luminescent Premul. This defers the "unmultiplying" of the alpha from the color channels until it is composited on top of the images underneath, where the overenthused color channels now have a chance to make it through the calculation – especially if the layer they exist in has its opacity set to less than 100%.

Where does this come up? As it turns out, Maya is one of those 3D programs that can create overly bright color channels when post-processing such as glow is applied. A sample render from Maya is included in [**Ex.10**] for you to experiment with, with all the permutations of alpha interpretation included. Note that the Luminescent Premul "cure" does not look right unless there is a background layer for it to composite over; go to the last example in the timeline and turn the background layer on and off to verify this.

In the long term, we can hope for internal color models in programs that can handle information such as this, including buffer room for extended highlights and shadows. It is also not a bad idea for 3D programs to render post-processing passes such as glows separately so you can recomposite them together later inside After Effects, with much more control. In the meantime, if your images with alphas aren't looking quite like you expect they should, try the approach outlined above: Render with a premultiplied alpha from your 3D application, interpret as straight alpha in After Effects, and set blending mode to Luminescent Premul.

Slimming Straight Alphas

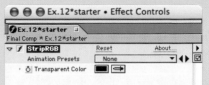

When we need to save a file with an alpha channel, we generally choose straight alphas. However, as of version 6.5, this choice usually consumes more disk space because the RGB channels are not cropped in straight alpha files, often resulting in a lot of unused picture information hanging around. A good example of this problem is when a client asks you to key some footage and to deliver QuickTime Animation movies with a straight alpha channel. The keying process creates an alpha channel, but the full, original background remains in the RGB channels – which expands the file size far larger than needed.

[Ex.12] is another example of the type of composition that causes this problem. In this case, the entire frame is filled with a background movie, then another layer (such as text) is used as an alpha matte to cut out part of it. In the final composite, the text alpha matte is filled with the background image, and the remainder of the frame is black. If you Shift+click on the Alpha icon in the Comp window, you will see what the RGB channels should look like with a straight alpha. However, if you actually render this comp as a single frame with a straight alpha (Composition>Save Frame As>File), then open it in Photoshop, you will see that the original background movie fills the *entire* RGB frame, with the text only in the alpha channel. All this extra information in the RGB channels is a disk memory hog.

To solve this in the past, we devised a number of workarounds, none of which was completely satisfactory. To the rescue comes Jens Enqvist of Cycore (of Final Effects and Cult Effects fame). Jens wrote a special plug-in (included on your DVD) to remove this redundant RGB data without adding any artifacts.

To use it, nest your comp into a new final comp. Apply Effect> Channel>StripRGB to the nested layer, and your alpha channel will now be slimmed when you render with a straight alpha channel. Try this with [Ex.12*starter].

The nifty StripRGB effect strips away redundant RGB data when rendering with straight alpha. Note that in version 6.5 you must apply it to a nested comp layer; in 5.5 it could be applied to an adjustment layer placed at the top of the original comp.

When this image is rendered to an uncompressed file format (such as QuickTime Animation, Millions+, Quality set to Best/100), this process results in a final file that takes up only 10% of the disk space as the original composition with the source material. Of course, your mileage may vary, but this gives you an idea of why we're going through this contortion.

So if you've been frustrated because a supposedly simple file won't fit on a CD you're trying to hand your client, this is how you can now save some disk space.

A very big thank you goes to Jens Enqvist for writing StripRGB for us, and to Bruce Bullis of Adobe for porting it to Windows.

When this text layer is used as a matte for a movie layer, the final result is text filled with this image (A), and the comp's alpha channel shows the transparency (B). However, if you save this frame with a straight alpha, you will see the cutout exists in the alpha channel, but the RGB channels are still filled with the entire movie frame (C). This chews up disk space.

 Working with Photoshop

Turning Photoshop art into After Effects layers.

A dobe Photoshop is the industry standard paint program many use to create their pixel-based still image artwork. It is common to take Photoshop art into After Effects to animate or treat it further. We can't teach you how to use Photoshop in one chapter; fortunately, there are many excellent books and videos available to help you expand your Photoshop skills. What we will show you are some tips and gotchas for preparing Photoshop files, and managing them inside After Effects.

Hot Keying

You can select a Photoshop file or layer in After Effects and use Edit>Edit Original to open the layer in Photoshop. (See the *Hot Keying* sidebar in Volume 1, Chapter 6 for details.)

Background to Floating

To convert a Background layer to a floating layer, Option+double-click on Mac (Alt+double-click on Windows) on it in the Layers palette.

Example Project

Explore the 02-Example Project.aep file as you read this chapter; references to [Ex.##] refer to specific compositions within the project file.

Inside Photoshop

Photoshop is an exceptionally powerful program that allows you to create complex multilayered artwork from multiple elements. That said, we tend to use Photoshop primarily to create or touch up specific elements, such as scanned artwork, digital photographs, or objects from stock footage libraries. Because After Effects is our primary tool, we find it more flexible to get these elements into After Effects as soon as possible and do our manipulation and layering there. Still, there will certainly be occasions when a client hands you a multilayered Photoshop file. Or you may find that some effects – such as type treatments using Photoshop's Layer Effects – are easier to create in Photoshop and then bring into After Effects.

There are generally three types of files you will be interested in moving from Photoshop to After Effects:
• single-layer artwork, such as photos or scans;
• objects with an alpha channel that cuts them out from their background; and
• multilayered files, where different elements of the final image exist as separate layers in Photoshop – which in turn you may wish to independently animate in After Effects.

The first type is easy. In this case, there is one layer, called Background in Photoshop. There can be only one Background layer for a file; not every file must have one. The advantage to having a single-layer Background file is that the image can be saved to virtually any file format – TIFF seems to be a favorite interchange format these days – and imported easily into any video editing application, including After Effects. If the goal is a full-screen image, there is no need for an alpha channel; if one is present, you can either use it or ignore it in After Effects after importing.

To verify that your file has only a Background layer, open it in Photoshop and check the Layers window. If there is more than one layer (or if that one layer does not have the name "Background"), click on the arrow in the upper right corner of the Layers window and select Flatten Image to convert any and all layers to a single Background layer.

The other two file types require creating and managing transparency – the subject of our next section.

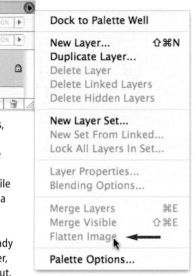

Simple scans, digital photos, and stock imagery should contain just one item in the Photoshop Layers window, called Background. If your file doesn't, and all you need is a single layer, use the Flatten Image command from the Layers window. (If you already have just a Background layer, this option will be grayed out, as it is here.)

Creating Transparency

After Effects thrives on transparency and alpha channels. This is how you cause some portions of an image to be opaque and others invisible, making them more interesting to layer with other images. A common task in Photoshop is "cutting out" shapes and objects from their background to create an alpha channel for compositing.

As Photoshop has evolved over the years, it has acquired several different methods for defining transparency, which can make this subject confusing to the casual user – especially if you haven't been keeping up with the changes from version to version. In short, there are two different types of layers, which have different ways of defining transparency:

• Most single-layer files you receive or create will consist of just a Background layer (discussed above). The Background layer does not have any transparency of its own. To create an alpha channel to use with it, you need to define a fourth channel in the Channels list. This alpha channel is visible in Photoshop only when you select Channel #4 in the Channels list. For After Effects to use this alpha, save the result in Photoshop to a file format that supports alphas (TIFF is a popular choice).

• Normal Layers – sometimes referred to as "floating" layers – each have their own inherent transparencies (in contrast to a Background layer, which does not have its own transparency attached). These layer transparencies do not appear in the Channels list; the checkerboard pattern behind your image represents where the layer is transparent.

If your file has more than one layer, or if it does not have a Background, you have to pay special attention to layer transparencies to successfully turn them into alpha channels After Effects can use.

We're going to discuss the most common ways to create and manage transparency. Central to this is the type of alpha channel that will be created: straight or premultiplied (see Chapter 1). Photoshop tends to create premultiplied alphas, whereas most video applications require straight alphas. Fortunately, After Effects can deal with both – but we're going to focus on creating straight alphas in the first place.

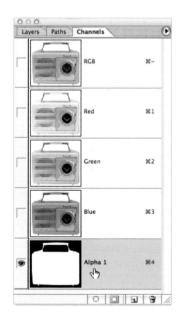

Alpha channels for simple files that contain only a Background layer are represented as Channel #4 in the Channels menu. Image courtesy Classic PIO/Radios.

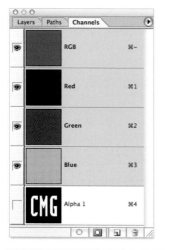

To create an alpha channel from a grayscale image (above), convert the file to RGB, copy and paste the image into a new alpha channel, then invert it. Fill the RGB channels with the color that the artwork needs to be (below).

First, let's talk about how *not* to create transparency: If you've been using the Magic Wand tool in Photoshop to select background colors such as white or black, then using the resulting selection to create an alpha channel or to fill with green or blue to key out in After Effects…please stop. *Now.* As easy as this is to do in Photoshop, it will inevitably result in bad edges and fringing around the objects you are trying to cut out. Using the Lasso or other selection tools, then filling with a solid color, isn't much better. Fortunately, there are several ways to do this correctly.

Alpha from Artwork

Quite often, you will need to use a company's logo in a job. Your first choice is to get it as an Illustrator file, as vector art like this renders cleanly with an automatic alpha channel. Your second choice is as an unflattened Photoshop file, where the alpha channel, you hope, is intact – perhaps as layer transparency. Failing that, you may need to scan the logo from a printed sample, then create an alpha channel for it:

• If the logo has good contrast against its background – such as black ink on white paper – select the RGB image and Copy. (With a color image, select and copy whichever channel has the highest contrast.)

• In the Channels palette, click on the Create New Channel button – this fourth channel will be your alpha. Paste your image into this channel; you will see a grayscale version of it.

• If necessary, use Image>Adjustment>Levels to boost its contrast so that the logo is black (0) and the paper area is white (255). Then type Command+I on Mac (Control+I on Windows) to invert it so that the logo is white (opaque alpha) and everything else is black (transparent alpha).

• If the logo is a single color, select the RGB channels and fill the entire image with the desired color (or fill with black and use Effect>Render>Fill in After Effects to apply color). This creates a straight alpha.

• If different parts of the logo should appear as different solid colors, draw selections in Photoshop's RGB channels that encompass the sections needing a specific color, and fill each region with the color you need. By extending your fill color beyond the edges of the alpha, you are creating a straight alpha channel. Save as PSD or TIFF.

For scanned logos and similar artwork, copy the image into a new Channel #4 and increase its contrast to create a good alpha (top); fill the RGB channels beyond the edges of the logo elements with the colors you need (above). The result in After Effects (right) will be a clean image with straight alpha (in this example, the background color is black).

The Mighty Pen

Most stock footage libraries save files as JPG images, which don't support alpha channels. When the images are of people or objects, quite often the object has already been cut out with the Pen tool and a Path saved with the file. While After Effects can't read these paths directly, you can convert a path to an alpha channel with a couple of clicks:

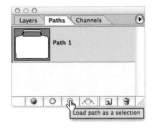

- Select the path's name in the Paths palette, then click the Load Path as a Selection button. Alternatively, Option (Alt) click this button to access the Make Selection options dialog. A selection is created from the path.

- In the Channels palette, click on the Create New Channel button to save the selection as an alpha channel.

- Be sure to resave the image to a 32-bit file format that supports alphas.

If an object needs to be cut out from its background, create a Path that outlines its shape, select the path, load the resulting selection (above), and save this selection as a new channel (below).

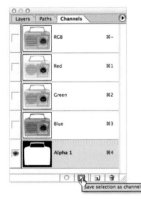

If you notice a fringe around your object in After Effects, try changing its alpha type in the Interpret Footage dialog to premultiplied, and choose a color that matches the background behind the original object. You will almost always need to do this for stock image libraries shot against a white seamless backdrop.

If you have an object that needs to be cut out from its backdrop, use Photoshop's Pen tool to create a Path for it. When you've completed drawing the path, you will see a "work path" in the Paths palette; double-click this work path and save it with a new name, then follow the steps above to create the alpha channel.

It will be tempting to create paths that exactly follow the edge of an object. If you do this, you will probably create a premultiplied alpha, as

Saving Layered Files

If you need to save a file from Photoshop that has multiple layers, non-Background layers with transparency you wish to preserve, or Vector Masks that you want to preserve as mask shapes, your best bet is to save to Photoshop's native format: PSD. You will then have several options for importing this file into After Effects, including selecting individual layers, merging all layers down to one, or importing the file as a composition, which preserves the layers and their stacking order.

If you try to save a layered file to a format that does not support layers, you will see a yellow warning icon at the bottom of the Save dialog next to the Layers option. The image will be flattened upon saving. Photoshop can save a multilayer TIFF file, but as of version 6.5, After Effects cannot access these layers.

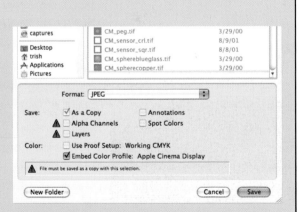

If you try to save a layered file to a format that does not support layers, Photoshop will warn you. The same is true for saving a file with an alpha channel to a format that does not support alphas.

some of the natural antialiasing around the edge of your object will be contained in the edge of your alpha. For best results, work with a high-resolution image and draw your pen path a pixel or two inside the edge – the alpha will then appear to be a straight alpha to After Effects.

Layers of Transparency

As noted earlier, when you (or your clients) create a multilayered image in Photoshop, all the layers with the exception of the one labeled Background will contain their own alpha channels, known as their transparency. These alphas will not be visible in the Channels palette. Flattening the image will *not* transfer these "hidden" alphas into a new Alpha channel in the Channels window!

To access the transparency for these layers, you need to save the file to Photoshop's native PSD format. Then in After Effects, import either a selected layer, or merge the layers upon import. After Effects will then convert the transparency for each layer (or the merged layers) into an alpha.

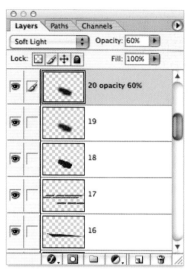

Individual layers have their own transparencies, noted by the checkerboard pattern behind them (above). These transparencies do not show up in the Channels palette (right). Layered file courtesy Digital Vision/Rayform.

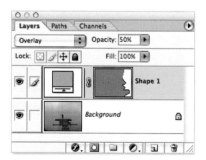

If you have a single layer with transparency that you want to convert into a conventional alpha channel, either select it in the Layers palette and use Selection> Load Selection, or Command+click (Control+click) on the layer. Then save this selection as a fourth channel, as outlined above under *The Mighty Pen* section.

Vector Masks

More recent versions of Photoshop also allow you to create Vector Masks, which are similar to creating masks on Solids in After Effects. Unlike Paths, which are drawn on normal layers, Vector Masks are drawn on Shape Layers in Photoshop. When you select the Pen or one of the Shape tools, make sure you then select Shape Layers in Window>Options. Draw your shape; a special layer will appear in the Layers window indicating that your shape is being applied to a solid fill layer.

If you want to convert these Vector Masks into After Effects masks, you need to save your artwork to the PSD format and import the resulting file as a Composition into After Effects. However, unlike applying a mask to a solid layer in After Effects, when you import a Shape layer, the

To create a Vector Mask, select the Shape Layers tool in the Options window (right) – not the regular Paths tool immediately to its right. The result will be a solid layer with a shape applied (above) that imports as a mask shape into After Effects.

RGB channels will already be cut out by the shape. If you want to animate the mask points to reveal different areas of a colored shape layer, copy and paste the mask to a full-frame After Effects solid. (Test for yourself how Shape layers import by using our example file, **02_Chapter Sources>TaiChiChuan.psd**.)

A Delicate Extraction

Not all shapes you wish to cut out and create an alpha for have sharp, well-defined edges. For example, trying to create a mask around hair is usually cause to pull your own out. Photoshop has recently added the Filter>Extract tool for this task. In the Extract dialog, draw a broad stroke over the edge that marks the transition between the area you wish to keep in an image and the area you want to drop out. Fill the area you want to keep, and Extract.

The result is a layer with transparency (if you use Extract on a Background layer, it will be converted into a normal layer). To convert the resulting transparency into an alpha channel After Effects can use, follow the same directions as outlined for layered artwork: Save as a PSD file, and import either as Comp, or import the desired layer.

The Filter>Extract tool allows you to define transition areas that are to be converted into feathered transparencies. The green brush stroke covers the edge we want to detect. Image courtesy Digital Vision/Beauty.

Importing from Photoshop

There are several ways to import Photoshop artwork into After Effects. Those options are affected by how you saved the file from Photoshop in the first place: as a single image or as a layered file.

As we've discussed, a single image would consist of only a Background layer, with an optional fourth Channel to hold its alpha. When a file has multiple layers, it must be saved as a Photoshop format file to retain those layers as individual elements. You can flatten the layers in Photoshop to merge them to a single Background layer, which can again be saved in whatever format you wish, but the layers would then lose their individuality, making it nearly impossible to edit and animate them as separate elements later.

If your goal is to eventually import the image into After Effects, there is no real reason to flatten in Photoshop as you can always import the file with the Merged Layers option on (see next page). When you're merging layers, though, it's possible to encounter a warning that your layered Photoshop file was not saved with a composite image. To fix this, go to Photoshop's Preferences and set File Handling>Maximize PSD File Compatibility to Ask or Always. Reopen the file in Photoshop and resave it. (The only reason to disable saving the composite image is if you're working with huge layered files for which saving the composite image significantly increases the file size.)

If your layered Photoshop file was not saved with a composite image and you import with Merged Layers on, you will see an error message in After Effects.

Comp and Alpha

When you import a Photoshop file as a composition, Channel #4 (normally the alpha channel) is ignored, even for the Background layer.

The type of file you save from Photoshop, and how you import it into After Effects, also has an impact on what you get and how big the image is – both in storage requirements and its size in pixels. Work through the following examples to get a feel for these different approaches:

Import Single Image: Create or open a single layer file in Photoshop (such as **AB_LifestylesMixedCuts.tif** in the **02-Example Project>Chapter Sources** folder), or open a multilayer file in Photoshop and flatten it. Save to virtually any file format: TIFF, JPEG, PICT, and Targa are the most common. Import into After Effects using the normal File>Import>File command. The result is the same size as the original image; it may have just RGB color channels or RGB plus alpha. The alpha type will depend on how you created the file (see Chapter 1).

Import Merged Image: Create a layered image and save as a Photoshop format file (or use our file **TaiChiChuan.psd**). Import this into After Effects using its normal File>Import> File command, or via drag and drop. A second dialog box will appear, defaulting to the option Footage and Merged Layers. This is what you want, so click OK. If the file included an alpha channel (Channel #4), you will be asked whether After Effects should interpret this as straight or premultiplied.

The result will be a single image in After Effects that is the same size as the original canvas in Photoshop. All layers are merged, with any Layer Effects calculated.

Under the hood: Through After Effects' version 6.5, the resulting "merged" image is actually the composite image that Photoshop saves when you enable the Maximize PSD File Compatibility option.

When you're importing a layered Photoshop file as Footage, you can select a specific layer in the file, or choose to merge (flatten) them together into one image.

Supported Features

When you import a layered file as a composition, a number of features in Photoshop are translated into equivalent features in After Effects:

Photoshop	=	After Effects
Transparency	=	Alpha Channel
Opacity	=	Opacity
Blending Mode	=	Blending Mode
Layer Mask	=	Alpha Channel
Vector Shape	=	Masked Solid
Layer Effects	=	Effects (+ Nested Comps)
Layer Sets	=	Nested Comps
Editable Text*	=	Rasterized Text

Some of this behavior changes if you save the file to a format other than PSD. We've already discussed what happens to transparency earlier in this chapter. Also, read the sections on Layer Sets and Layer Effects later in this chapter for details on these features.

* If you save text on a layer in a PSD file, it is converted to pixels in After Effects; if you save it to a PDF file, the text is maintained as vectors which you can continuously rasterize (import as layers to retain their transparency). See also *Editing Photoshop Text* later in this chapter.

Import Single Layer: Create a layered image and save it as a Photoshop format file, or again, use **TaiChiChuan.psd**. Import this file using the normal File>Import>File command. A second dialog box will appear; set the Import Kind popup to Footage, then choose the layer you wish to import. Before you click OK, set the Footage Dimensions popup to either Layer Size (automatically crop the layer to the nontransparent borders of the image in that layer), or Document Size (match the size of the canvas in Photoshop). If the layer had any Photoshop Layer Effects applied, they are ignored.

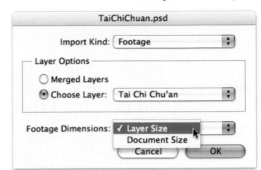

When importing a single layer, you can choose whether the layer size is automatically cropped or appears as large as the document.

Import Layers as Comp: Create a layered image and save as a Photoshop format file. Import normally (File>Import> File), but this time select Import As: Composition from the popup in the Import dialog. Note that there are two choices: Composition – Cropped Layers (which is equivalent to Layer Size in the Footage Dimensions popup mentioned above), or Composition (equivalent to Document Size).

If you accidentally import the layered file as Footage, or use the drag and drop technique to import, you can also set these options in the dialog that opens. Either way, when you click OK, After Effects will create a folder in the Project window that contains a footage item for each layer of the file, each with a straight alpha channel. After Effects also automatically creates a composition the size of the original image's canvas, with all these layers already imported – and most important, properly aligned.

When you're importing as a comp, Photoshop options that are used to blend layers – such as opacity, layer masks, and blending modes – will also be carried into After Effects. The real action occurs if you applied any of Photoshop's Layer Effects. Where possible, After Effects will add a custom Photoshop effect to these layers, which can be edited and animated just like any other effect. The catch is that some of these Layer Effects require additional trickery such as their own blending modes, preserve transparency switches, even entire precomps to recreate, so the hierarchy can be initially confusing. Also, many features of Layer Effects are not supported in After Effects, often resulting in a radically different result. We will discuss Layer Effects in greater detail later in this chapter.

To import a layered Photoshop file as a composition, select the correct Import As option in the Import File dialog (above). The result will be a folder in After Effects that contains each of the layers (left), and a composition that reconstructs their stacking order, blending modes, Opacity, and where possible, Layer Effects (below).

Pixel Aspect Ratios

A new feature in Photoshop CS (Version 8.0) is the ability to tag files as having a *pixel aspect ratio* (PAR, for short) other than square. For those unfamiliar with the subject, most standard definition video formats have pixels that are meant to be projected wider or skinnier than they are tall. This causes them to look distorted on computer displays (as shown in more detail in Chapter 21). Photoshop CS can now display properly tagged files taking this distortion into account – but at least in the initial implementation, you shouldn't assume it can do much more…

If a PSD file was saved from either Photoshop CS or from After Effects 6 or later (either through the normal Render Queue, or the Composition>Save Frame As>Photoshop Layers command), the PAR tag is saved with the file, and Photoshop CS will use it to display the image. If Photoshop does not see this tag, it will then look at the pixel dimensions of the file, and make some assumptions if it finds one of the "magic" sizes that corresponds to common video frame formats. For example, if the file is 720×480 (NTSC DV) or 720×486 pixels (NTSC D1), Photoshop CS will assume the pixels will ultimately be played back 90% as wide as they are tall – and will default to displaying those pixels on your computer screen with the same distortion. Photoshop will display a warning dialog that it is doing this as it opens the file. You may toggle this display distortion on and off with View>Pixel Aspect Ratio Correction; we turn it off immediately, because the corrected display exhibits aliasing, and it does not give us clear access to every pixel in the source image for retouching and similar work.

If the PAR tag is not present in the file, sometimes Photoshop's guess is wrong; for example, anamorphic widescreen NTSC D1 images – where the pixels will ultimately be displayed 120% as wide as they are in the file – have the same frame size (720×486) as normal 4:3 image aspect ratio frames.

If you need to create a new file in Photoshop at one of these magic sizes, select from one of the video presets and the PAR popup will be set automatically.

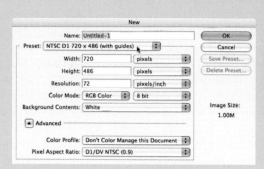

Presets designed for video users in Photoshop CS automatically set the PAR (above), or you may set or change the PAR assigned to a file (below).

You may also change the PAR being used for a file using Image>Pixel Aspect Ratio.

In addition to this ability to show files with non-square pixels "corrected" for square pixel computer monitors, Photoshop has a feature that takes PAR into account when it's pasting between files. For example, it automatically stretches a square pixel file to match the pixel distortion in an NTSC DV file. However, at least as of Version 8.0, we have not seen Photoshop CS take a file's PAR into account when it's performing any other function, such as applying a filter or a gradient. The result is a potentially distorted graphic when it's ultimately played back through a normal video chain. Therefore, we suggest you create any new files in Photoshop using the square pixel dimensions for the various video formats discussed in Chapters 25, 26, and 27, and leave it to After Effects to manage your PARs correctly.

Convert Footage to Layers

New to After Effects 6.5 is the ability to create a composition from a PSD file that was previously imported as footage with the Merged Layers option on. This saves having to reimport the file and swap layers around.

To see how this works, open the [**Ex.01*starter**] comp which contains a single layer, a Photoshop file called **TaiChiChuan.psd**. Select this layer, then select Layer>Convert to Layered Comp. The footage will be replaced with a nested comp layer called **TaiChiChuan Comp 1**, which appears in the Project window along with a folder containing the individual layers. The result is the same as if you had imported the file as a composition and nested it in the [**Ex.01*starter**] comp. To open the precomp from the timeline, Option (Alt) + double-click the nested comp layer.

In our example comp [**Ex.01_final**], we precomposed the title and its drop shadow layer, and replaced the background layer with a movie. If you find yourself working with a Photoshop artist whose job it is to design elements for you, don't forget that he or she can use frames from a movie as a guide, and you can then swap back in the real movie later on.

In [**Ex.01**], we replaced a footage item with a composition of individual layers, then swapped out the background layer with a movie from Artbeats/Lifestyle Mixed Cuts.

Editing Photoshop Text

If you create text layers in Photoshop, you can convert these layers to editable text in After Effects, provided you've imported the file as a composition. As of version 6.5, this option also supports text along a path.

To see this in action, open [**Ex.02*starter**], which consists of a PSD file imported as a composition. Layer 1 is a type layer in Photoshop, but it appears as pixels in After Effects. Select layer 1, then select Layer>Convert to Editable Text. The layer is converted to a Text layer (note the T layer icon) and the source text is now fully editable. In addition, the path the text sits on is converted to Mask 1, so you could also animate the path! For more on animating Text layers, see Volume 1, Chapter 25.

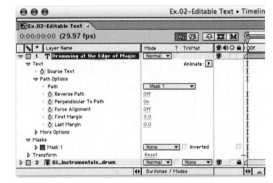

Practice converting Photoshop type layers to editable text in [**Ex.02**].

Smart Stock Footage

A welcome trend is that stock footage companies are creating highly layered Photoshop files, rather than providing a flattened image. One example is **DV_Rayform.psd** from Digital Vision, which we've imported as a comp in [**Ex.03**]. Solo the individual layers, and change the Layer Names as needed. Then think about how you might animate them to make this design move. The overall image is 1024×745 pixels; try setting the comp size to a normal video frame (such as 648×486) and using the extra pixels to animate the Position or Scale of some of the layers.

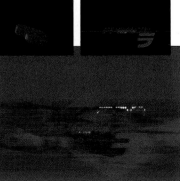

[**Ex.03**] contains a layered Photoshop file from the Digital Vision/Rayform CD.

Scanning Secrets

Bonus Chapter 2B in the Bonus Chapters folder on your DVD discusses how to scan artwork at the right size for use inside After Effects.

Sequence Cells

If you create cell-type animation, create each frame on a separate layer in Photoshop. Import Photoshop as Comp, select all layers, and use Layer>Keyframe Assistant>Sequence Layers (Volume 1, Chapter 7) to sequence them in the Timeline window.

Learning Photoshop

There are a large number of Photoshop books available. Here are the ones we personally recommend; browse these and others that catch your eye at your local bookstore.

Adobe Photoshop CS One-on-One by Deke McClelland (O'Reilly), includes two hours of Total Training videos hosted by Deke. Beginners' choice.

Photoshop CS for Nonlinear Editors by Richard Harrington (CMP Books)

Real World Photoshop CS by David Blatner and Bruce Fraser (Peachpit Press)

Adobe Photoshop CS Studio Techniques by Ben Willmore (Adobe Press)

You Can't Go Back

There are a few gotchas when you use Import As: Composition. The biggest is that you lose some of the ability to edit the individual layers back in Photoshop. After you've imported the file into After Effects, if you select one layer and type Command+E (Control+E) to "hot key" into Photoshop to edit it – say, to change its position relative to the overall image – these changes are *not* reflected in the comp After Effects already created to reassemble all the component layers.

Also, if you changed the pixels in the layer you hot keyed to edit, this layer/footage item will be updated when you return to After Effects, but if you edited another layer in Photoshop, you will need to File>Reload Footage for this layer in After Effects for the project to be properly updated.

You also cannot add a layer to your Photoshop file and expect After Effects to automatically add it to the stack – you will need to import the new layer manually or reimport the entire Photoshop file and rebuild any changes as necessary. You may want to create your layered Photoshop file with a couple of extra layers you don't need so you have placeholders to go back and use later. (Thanks to Kurt Murphy for that last tip.)

Where to Layer

Importing Photoshop files as compositions is particularly useful for those who interface with a print-based art department that creates its artwork as Photoshop layers. However, when we're starting a project from scratch, we don't create layered artwork in Photoshop; if we know we're going to build a layered image, we'll do it directly in After Effects. Many of Photoshop's functions are destructive, in that pixels are changed and resampled far too easily. With After Effects, we can change our mind on issues such as scaling and effects as many times as we want, without losing resolution.

The exception to the above rule is when we need access to image repair tools such as the Healing Brush, which After Effects does not have. We perform jobs such as photo retouching in Photoshop, then import the file into After Effects for further manipulation. We may also create some nonanimating elements such as gradients or matte layers in Photoshop to save rendering time in After Effects.

Print artists should consider creating their images in After Effects – then they can enjoy the benefits of nondestructive editing and the ability to tweak their effects and transformations after they're applied. After Effects has a composition size limit of 30,000 pixels in each dimension, which allows it to tackle all but the largest print images (assuming you have enough RAM). When you're done, you can use the menu item Composition>Save Frame As to save as an

RGB still image, with or without alpha. If you need separate layers, use Composition>Save Frame As>Photoshop as Layers. In Photoshop, to prepare for printing, change the resolution to 300 ppi (or as needed), and convert the Image>Mode to CMYK color. Showing that we practice what we preach, the covers of all of our books were created this way.

Layer Sets

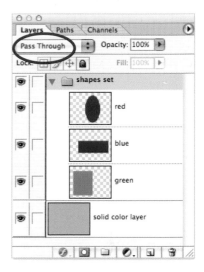

One of the newer features in Photoshop is Layer Sets. This allows you to group layers into folders in the Layer window. When you import a layered file as a composition into After Effects, these sets become nested comps. In the **Ex.04** folder in the Project window, twirl open the folder **Set = PassThrough Mode**. Open the comp [**ShapesSet_passthru**], and note that layer 1 is a comp named **shapes set**. Option+double-click (Alt+double-click) on this layer, and it will open its source comp, which contains three more layers. Back in the Project window, twirl open the folder **ShapesSet_passthru** to see these source layers and the nested comp.

In Photoshop, a Layer Set may have its own blending mode. This means the contents of the set's folder are composited together, then this composite is blended in with the other layers using this mode. However, if this set is instead assigned the mode Pass Through, this is the equivalent of enabling a nested comp's Collapse Transformations switch in After Effects: Rather than compositing this group of layers and using a new mode to blend them in, their original modes are honored as if they were all placed on the same level of the hierarchy.

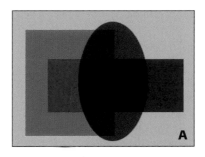
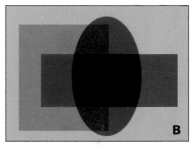

We've supplied two sample Photoshop files for you to import and compare the differences. Open **ShapeSets_normal.psd** and **ShapeSets_passthru.psd** in Photoshop. Notice how shapes blend differently against the pale yellow background, thanks to the set's blending mode: The set in the **ShapeSets_passthru** file uses the Pass Through mode.

Import these PSD files into After Effects as a Composition. In the [**ShapesSet_passthru Comp 1**], note that Collapse Transformations is enabled in the Switches column for the nested comp layer **shapes set**. In the Modes column, the blending mode popup is inactive. (Collapse Transformations was covered in Volume 1, Chapter 20.)

The same set of layers look different depending on whether the Layer Set that contains the shapes is set to a blending mode of Normal (A) or Pass Through (B). This Pass Through mode (top) passes the individual modes of each layer in the set intact to the layers below, rather than first compositing them together. To recreate this behavior in After Effects, you can enable the Collapse Transformations button (circled in red below) for the nested comp that contains the Layer Set.

Color Management

One of the great mysteries in Photoshop for many video and film artists is the subject of color management. This is an important topic in the print world, because different monitors and printers shift colors in different directions – and you need to simulate on your computer what the final output might look lIke before you splash ink on paper. By assigning color *profiles* to all devices in the chain, and having your monitor display a compensated result, you can increase the chances that images will print correctly.

By contrast, After Effects does not make any such adjustments, taking all source colors at face value. However, this does not mean you can ignore the subject of color management, as it affects all images that flow through Photoshop from scanners and digital cameras.

Our philosophy when we're creating motion graphics is that we're not necessarily after the most accurate color; we're after the *best* color. Therefore, we focus on bringing images into After Effects with the widest color space, and then adjust these colors in After Effects as needed to suit our goals.

Since After Effects is going to ignore any color profiles assigned to images, we tend to work with Color Management turned off in Photoshop. In Photoshop, type Command+Shift+K (Control+Shift+K) to open its Color Settings dialog. Select Color Management Off from the Settings popup at the top of this dialog. Under Working Spaces, set RGB to match your monitor's current profile; all the choices under Color Management Policies should be Off. The Profile Mismatches option should be set to Ask When Opening, so you can decide on a case-by-case basis how to handle images with profiles.

When we open a file in Photoshop that has not been tagged with a color profile (such as a file from a stock image library), we don't convert its color space. When we're opening a file that has a distinct color space – such as sRGB, used by most digital cameras – we go ahead and convert it to the current working space (Monitor RGB). This is particularly important with sRGB on the Mac, as it

otherwise tends to look washed out. We then resave these converted files.

If you did not have a chance to convert color spaces in Photoshop, and you use a Mac, then you should install the extraordinarily handy Übercolor plug-in from Fnord Software (www.fnordware.com) included free on your DVD. Apply this effect to your imported images, and set the Load popup under Source to match the profile of the source image. Leave the Dest profile to match your monitor.

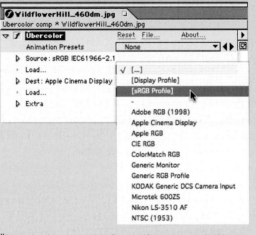

Übercolor from Fnord Software (free on your DVD) can perform color space conversion inside After Effects.

We then strongly recommend you view your work in After Effects through a monitor that represents how your work will eventually be played back – computer or video (see *Monitoring Your Work* at the end of Chapter 21). Make color corrections and enhancements while you're viewing your work through this monitor chain. For video work, if you cannot hook up a true video monitor, consider placing an Adjustment Layer above your final comp, applying Übercolor to it, leaving the Source profile to your computer monitor, and setting Dest to NTSC or PAL. Do this only for previewing how your colors might shift on a video monitor; do not render with this on.

Layer Styles

Many Photoshop users like to stylize text, logos, and other shapes using Layer Styles. These are a set of live effects, textures, and gradients that can be applied to any Layer other than the Background. To apply a Layer Style, select the layer to receive it (perhaps a Text layer with a title you need to treat), open Window>Styles, and double-click the style you want to apply. To edit a style or create one from scratch, select the layer and use the Layer>Layer Styles menu.

You can load and save Layer Styles through the Layer window's Options menu. There is a substantial number of free styles and text effects available on the Adobe Studio Exchange web site (share.studio.adobe.com; membership is free). We've also included in your **Goodies** folder a set of custom styles created by Andrew Heimbold of Reality Check (www.realityx.com), a top-notch visual effects studio in Los Angeles. Open the Photoshop files in the **02_Chapter Sources>RealityX** folder to see these styles at work.

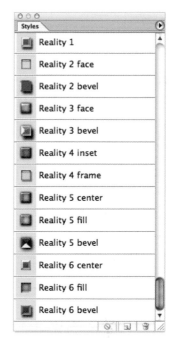

Photoshop's Styles palette.

Styles into After Effects

There are a number of different ways to load the results of Layer Styles into After Effects. Here are the two techniques we prefer:

Approach #1: If your Photoshop file contains only the styled layer(s), save to the PSD format, Import File in After Effects, and select Merged Layers. This will render the Layer Styles and the object it was applied to into a single flat layer, with alpha channel.

Approach #2: If your Photoshop file also contains other layers that you do not want to merge together with your styled layer, follow this procedure instead to rasterize the Layer Style: Create a new layer in Photoshop, place it above your styled layer, and click on the link switch for the styled layer. Then hold down the Option (Alt) key, and in the Layer Options menu select Merge Linked. This will create a duplicate of your styled layer, rendered to a flat layer, while keeping your "live" styled layer intact should you want to edit it later. Save as a PSD file, Import File in After Effects, and this time select your duplicate layer – do not select the Merged Layers option. This approach came courtesy of Richard Harrington, author of *Photoshop for Nonlinear Editors* (CMP Books); a chapter on Layer Styles from this book is included in the **Goodies** folder on your DVD.

Go Wow

Andrew Heimbold of Reality Check recommends the *Photoshop Wow!* series of books by Jack Davis (Peachpit Press) for more ideas on creating cool looks with Layer Styles.

Examples of text and logo treatments using Photoshop Layer Styles, created by Andrew Heimbold of Reality Check (www.realityx.com). These styles are included in your **Goodies** folder; the layered Photoshop files are in your **Chapter Sources** folder. (Font used for text is Adobe Copperplate Gothic.)

A great way to prepare Layer Styles to be used by any program that can import layered Photoshop files is to create a new layer, link it to your styled layer, hold down Option (Alt), and select Merge Linked. This will copy and flatten the styled layer to import.

There are a few cases in which Layer Styles may not give the same results in After Effects as you saw in Photoshop. The main culprit is if you relied on blending modes to give the styled layer a certain look over another layer in Photoshop. This is especially true for colored shadows and glows. For this reason, Andrew often leaves the drop shadow and glow layer effects off in Photoshop, and then recreates them in After Effects after he has imported the text.

Many Layer Styles were created with the idea they were going to be applied to large files, such as text for high-resolution print images. It is a good idea to create your type and shapes about four times larger in Photoshop than you expect to use them in After Effects, apply and edit your styles, then scale the result down in After Effects. If a layer style is a bit too "bulbous" or thin, in Photoshop select Layer>Layer Style>Scale Effects to tweak it.

Photoshop Layer Effects

If you attempt to import a PSD file with Layer Styles into After Effects as a composition, After Effects will recreate some – but by no means all – of the effects in the Layer Style. In general, After Effects will recreate the parameters in the Layer Styles Structure section for the Shadow, Glow, Bevel, and Emboss effects, ignoring the parameters in the Quality section – as well as all of the parameters of Satin, Gradient, Pattern, and other layer effects.

To recreate the portions of the Layer Style it understands, After Effects employs a combination of nested comps, track mattes, Transparency switch settings, blending modes, and special Photoshop effects. If you're curious, look inside the **Ex.05** folder in the Project window for this chapter's example project; it contains the comp chains that resulted from importing the styles After Effects does support.

What is more interesting are those special Photoshop effects. Some of them are very useful – such as Photoshop Drop Shadow, which can create larger, denser soft shadows than After Effects' stock Effect>Perspective>Drop Shadow. Likewise, Photoshop's Outer Glow effect creates "haloed" text much more quickly than the Professional edition's Effect>Stylize>Glow. These effects are not available in the normal Effect menu in After Effects. However, once you have imported a file that uses these layer effects as a composition, you may then copy and paste these effects to any layer inside After Effects. We have saved these as Animation Presets in your **Goodies** folder on the DVD: Look for the Presets that start with the prefix **PS_**. Note that some of these effects rely on track mattes and other transparency tricks to achieve their final results, so if they don't behave as you expect, study their corresponding comps in **Ex.05** to see what additional compositing steps you might need to take.

Buttons for Encore DVD

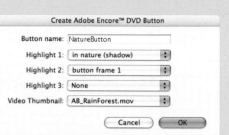

Among the many uses of layered PSD files is to exchange files between After Effects and Adobe Encore DVD. For example, PSD files are used to hold the different elements that make up a button. You can modify or create buttons from scratch in After Effects, then save each button as a layered PSD file to import back into Encore. However, it's not as simple as using Composition>Save Frame As>Photoshop Layers; Encore requires very specific naming conventions to know which layer is supposed to be which element in a button. Fortunately, After Effects can substantially automate this naming process for you.

After you design a DVD menu in After Effects, you need to save the button elements as layers with special names in a PSD file to be used by Encore DVD. Background courtesy Digital Vision/Inner Gaze; video insets courtesy Artbeats/ Rain Forest and The Orient.

Open **[Ex.06*starter]**, which contains a mockup of a DVD menu. For each button, we want to identify a video thumbnail, as well as a pair of "highlights" (color channels to be used in the button's subpicture layer): the

outline frame, and a glow for the text (which is actually an overlay that will appear on top – the text itself is an element in the final background plate). To save one of these buttons with the naming conventions Encore requires, select the layers that make up the button elements. In this example, click on **AB_RainForest**, then Command+ click (Control+click) **in nature (shadow)** and **button frame 1**. Next, choose the menu item Layer>Adobe Encore DVD>Create Button. In the dialog that opens, give your button a name (such as **"Nature Button"**); set the popups for Highlight 1 to **in nature (shadow)**, Highlight 2 to **button frame 1**, and Video Thumbnail to **AB_RainForest**.

Click OK, and After Effects will nest the selected elements into a new composition that has the button's name, with **(+)** appended to the front (the clue that tells Encore this is a button). Option+ double-click (Alt+double-click) this new layer in the current Time-line window to open the new comp, and you will see the High-light 1 layer has **(=1)** appended to the front, Highlight 2 has **(=2)**, and the Video Thumbnail has **(%)** – more clues Encore needs. The layer **xIL_GrungeDecay_matte** was also copied to this new comp, as two of the layers use it via the Set Matte effect. Now, select Composition>Save Frame As>

Select your button element layers, and choose Layer>Adobe Encore DVD>Create Button to assign these layers as Highlights or a Video Thumbnail.

After Effects automatically appends to layer names the prefix Encore needs to identify the individual button elements.

Photoshop Layers, and save the file to your drive, keeping the **(+)** at the front of the file's name. After Effects will automatically render the effects – including Set Matte – needed by each layer to create a clean PSD file. You can open this file in Photoshop for inspection, or in Encore to use as a button.

If you have already created a composition specifically for a button, you can also rename your layers directly without going through the Create Button dialog: Just select the layer in After Effects, select the menu item Layer>Adobe Encore DVD, then use the appropriate submenu item to assign a Highlight or Video Thumbnail. The required charac-ters will then be appended to the front of the layer's name.

Working with Illustrator

Illustrator survival skills, plus working with Illustrator files in After Effects.

Adobe Illustrator is a terrific complement to After Effects: Its drawing tools are powerful, and because the art is vector based, you can scale it to any size in After Effects without losing quality. Illustrator also tends to be the program of choice for print graphic designers who create company logos and titles, so even if you don't use Illustrator yourself, you'll likely receive Illustrator files from clients to use in your motion graphics projects.

This chapter covers preparing your artwork in Illustrator, importing lllustrator art into After Effects, and taking advantage of the resolution independence of vector art.

Inside Illustrator

Illustrator is a deep program that caters very well to users who create colorful illustrations for print (we're assuming that's not you). For video artists creating titles and simple vector paths and shapes, you can get a lot done knowing just the basics. If you're new to Illustrator, launch Help>Illustrator Help and concentrate for now on the following topics from the Contents list: Drawing, Working with Objects, Applying Color (basics of applying Fill and Stroke), Using Layers, and Using Type. Slightly more advanced is the Transforming and Distorting Shapes section, which covers the Pathfinder palette (indispensable for combining paths into new shapes), as well as compound paths, and warping and blending shapes. (You can probably safely ignore working with bitmap images, printing and color separations, and even effects, gradients, patterns, plus anything else which you can just as easily create in Photoshop or After Effects.)

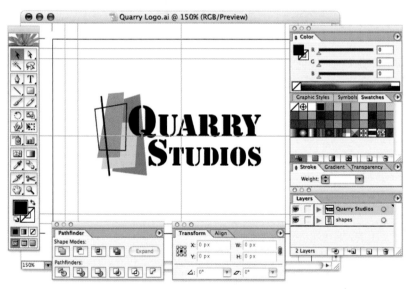

Adobe Illustrator CS offers a powerful combination of drawing and type editing tools.

Example Project

Explore the 03-Example Project.aep file as you read this chapter; references to [Ex.##] refer to specific compositions within the project file.

We also offer the following "survival tips" to help you prepare files for use in After Effects. The following steps are compatible with Illustrator CS, which is recommended for use with After Effects 6.5:

Templates: When you're preparing artwork for video's 4:3 aspect ratio, the 8.5×11-inch page that Illustrator defaults to isn't all that helpful. Therefore, we've included ready-made templates on the accompanying DVD with guides for action and title safe areas. There are four templates; these are based on the most common square-pixel video sizes (320×240 for tutorials, 640×480 for multimedia and older nonlinear editing systems, 720×540 for D1 NTSC square, and 768×576 for D1 PAL square). Use the templates appropriate for your application – Illustrator 10 or CS.

Type essentials: After Effects 6 and later include the standard Adobe type engine, as well as powerful methods for animating Text layers over time. As a result, it is no longer necessary to use Illustrator for basic typesetting tasks. However, you may need to create titles in Illustrator so your clients can use the same art in their print campaign.

If you're comfortable with using the new Type tool in After Effects, you'll be right at home in Illustrator. Most of the type tools you'll need in Illustrator are in the Character and Paragraph palettes, available from the Window>Type menu. Set the Fill color to Black and the Stroke to None (the / icon). Select the Type tool (shortcut: T), click in the center of your frame, and type away. The type style may default to a tiny size and default font, so after you're done typing, press Command+A on Mac (Control+A on Windows) to Select All and change the font, size, tracking, leading, and so on in the Character and Paragraph palettes.

Track and Kern: If you don't want your title to look like it came off a cheapo character generator, spend some time tweaking the spacing between letters. It's guaranteed to pay off in a more professional-looking title.

Kerning controls the spacing between two characters, while *tracking* adjusts the uniform spacing between more than two characters in selected type. If the overall title is too loose or tight, start by adjusting the Tracking to a good "average" value. Because type for video tends to fatten up with antialiasing, don't tighten the letter spacing as much as you might for print output.

After you set tracking, kern character pairs that are too close together or too far apart. With the Type tool selected, place the cursor between two characters and close the space by pressing Option+left arrow (Alt+left arrow), or open the space by typing Option+right arrow (Alt+right arrow). The value of each key click is set in Preferences>Type & Auto Tracing, under Tracking: We recommend a setting of 10 instead of the default 20.

RGB versus CMYK: We tend not to color simple shapes and titles inside Illustrator; instead, we give them color with effects inside After Effects. Also, After Effects ignores the color when Illustrator shapes are used as alpha track mattes. If you want to color your art in Illustrator, create colors

Selecting Layers

In After Effects, when you select a layer in the Timeline, that layer is selected in the Comp window – straightforward enough. But this is not how Illustrator works! You can have an object selected on the artboard and a different layer selected in the Layers palette. The Text, Transform, Transparency, Info, and other palettes always report the status of the *selected artwork*, not the selected layer, so watch for this when you're editing. To select a layer in the Layers palette and have it also be selected on the artboard, Option+click (Alt+click) the name of the layer in the Layers palette (a colored square will appear to the right of its name).

For Illustrator layers to be imported into After Effects as separate layers, they must reside on the top hierarchy of the Layers palette – not sublayers within a layer. You can move an object or group to a new layer by cutting and pasting, or by selecting Collect in New Layer from the Layers palette Options menu, then moving the new sublayer to the top hierarchy. See also the *Release to Layers* sidebar at the end of this chapter, which details how to use Release to Layers to convert objects onto individual layers for animation purposes.

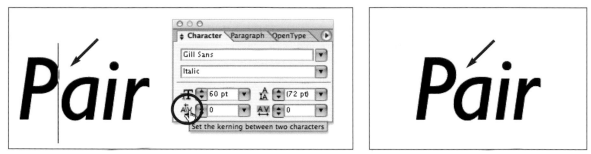

Place your cursor between any problem pairs of characters (left), then adjust the kerning until the space between all characters appears consistent (right).

Warped Shapes

If you use any of Illustrator's Distort & Transform or Warp effects, you may need to use Object>Expand Appearance to edit the shape further. See the **Warp_tip.ai** file in the **03_Chapter Sources** folder for a mini-tutorial.

When you're saving an Illustrator CS native format file, be sure to check "Create PDF Compatible File" so the file is readable by After Effects. Embed All Fonts is useful if you plan to open the file on a different computer that may not have the same fonts installed.

using RGB colorspace – not CMYK – for best results. If you need white type in Illustrator, select View>Outline rather than Preview mode to see the shapes against Illustrator's white background.

Sizing objects: It's a good idea to make your vector artwork large enough that you will not need to scale them over 100% in After Effects. If you do need to scale larger, you can turn on the continuous rasterization option (more on this later), and they will cleanly scale to whatever size you need.

Keyboard Shortcuts: Use Edit>Keyboard Shortcuts to reassign Illustrator shortcuts to taste. For instance, After Effects uses Command+L (Control+L) to Lock a layer, but this creates a New Layer in Illustrator.

Pixel Power: We like to set the Preferences>Units & Undo>General popup to Pixels so that values translate to After Effects without surprises. This also comes in handy when you need a shape in Illustrator to be an exact size in pixels – just select the object, and enter your target width and height in the Transform palette.

Set Crop Area: When you're importing Illustrator layers as a composition, the crop area sets the size of the comp. If you have not set a crop area in Illustrator, the source's overall size will be autocropped to just barely fit the sum of all the objects; see the sidebar *Defining the Document Size* later in this chapter for details. Either way, you also have the option to autocrop the individual layers or leave them full size.

Save as Illustrator: If you're using Illustrator 10 or CS, save your file using the Adobe Illustrator document format. In the Options dialog that opens, check Create PDF Compatible File so After Effects can read it. Use Compression compresses the PDF data in the file; we tend to leave it on. The Embed All Fonts option does create a slightly larger file, but it's useful if you've saved some text and then want to import the file into After Effects on another machine that does not have the fonts used in the document. (Note: There's no need to save as an EPS file as you might do for importing into a desktop publishing application. The EPS file format includes a preview image that makes for a larger file size, but After Effects ignores the preview image and uses the raw data.)

Layers: To animate individual elements in your artwork, organize elements onto Layers in Illustrator – these will become separate layers in After Effects. Save normally. When you import into After Effects, use the Import As> Composition option (more on this later in this chapter).

Type outlines: If necessary, convert type to outlines (see *The Perfect Path* sidebar). Save the outlines under a new name, then import this new file into After Effects. If you need to move individual characters to separate layers, use the Release to Layers feature (see sidebar at the end of this chapter).

Illustrator Sequences: Illustrator Sequences are handled like any other sequence format: Make a folder of same-size Illustrator files, and number them appropriately.

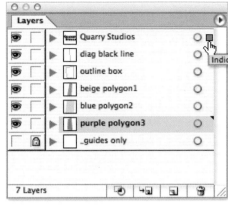

Organize elements onto separate layers in Illustrator as you would like them to be grouped in After Effects. Note that even though the fifth layer is highlighted here, the colored square indicates that the selected artwork belongs to the top layer. (Check out the *Using Layers* section of Illustrator's Help system for more on working with the Layers palette.)

The Perfect Path

More recent versions of After Effects use Adobe's CoolType technology to rasterize text. With CoolType, any fonts used in Illustrator are converted to "outlines" upon importation into After Effects. When you're saving your file from Illustrator, be sure to check the Embed All Fonts option if you're not sure the font will be installed on the machine running After Effects.

If you're still wary and want to ensure that your type in Illustrator will appear exactly the same way in After Effects, or if you will be distributing this artwork to others who may need to open it in Illustrator, you can create outlines from your text in Illustrator. This "locks in" the fonts by converting them to vector shapes, and the fonts are no longer required.

When you're creating outlines, be sure to save the original file with the font data in case you need to edit the type later. Then select the type with the Selection tool (not the Type tool) and go to Type> Create Outlines. If you then select Object>Ungroup, you'll have access to individual characters and paths

if you need to customize the outlines. Save this version using a different name. *(Note: All our Illustrator text elements are saved as outlines so they will look exactly the same if you open them in Illustrator.)*

If the file is relatively simple, duplicate the text layer(s), turn off the original layer(s), and create outlines on the duplicate. This way you have only one file to manage, and if you hotkey from After Effects to Illustrator, the original text is in the same file. *(Thanks to Michael Kelley of Idiot Box for that last tip.)*

Once a font has been reduced to outlines, you can copy and paste these outlines to After Effects as mask shapes. See the *Paths to Masks* sidebar later in this chapter for details.

In addition, After Effects has the ability to create outlines from text generated with its own Type tool, with the added advantage that the outlines can then be animated. To do this, select your text layer, then select Layer>Create Outlines. A new solid layer will be created above the text layer, and each separate outline will appear as a mask shape.

Defining the Document Size

When you import a layered Illustrator file as a composition into After Effects, the size of the comp created is determined by the document's *bounding box*. By default, the bounding box is defined by an area that just barely fits all the objects. Recent versions of After Effects also let you choose whether the component layers should each be autocropped or created at the same size as the document.

For a variety of reasons then, it's important to be able to define the size of this bounding box yourself in Illustrator. You can do this by setting the *crop area* (formerly known as *crop marks*). The crop area will then determine the size of the comp in After Effects. There are two ways to set the crop area:

• If you want the size of the document (as set under File> Document Setup) to determine the size of the bounding box, make sure nothing is selected (Select>Deselect), and choose Object>Crop Area>Make. Crop marks are placed at the corners of the document.

• With the Rectangle tool (shortcut: M), draw a rectangle that defines your intended bounding box; it doesn't matter if it's filled or stroked, though a filled rectangle will obscure your art temporarily. With the rectangle still selected, choose Object>Crop Area>Make.

To delete the crop marks, select Object>Crop Area>Release, and delete the rectangle. Because you can have only one crop area

per file, if you define a new crop area, the old crop marks are deleted automatically.

Avoiding Resampling

Back in Volume 1, Chapter 3, we discussed layers appearing softer because one or both of their dimensions consisted of an odd number. For instance, if the file was imported as 321 pixels wide, and centered in a comp that was an even number of pixels wide, the layer's center would fall on a half pixel, meaning it would be resampled (antialiased). The same is true for the vertical dimension. To avoid this problem, create crop area with even increments in the width and height:

• Switch to View>Outline and draw your bounding box rectangle around your artwork (or use no Fill so you can see the art). Resize the box as needed.

• In the Transform palette, check the size of the box, and if necessary, round it up/down to an even number of pixels wide and high.

When Illustrator's preferences are set to count units as pixels, it's easy to create a bounding box with an even number of pixels in the width and the height.

• Choose Object>Crop Area> Make.

The file size will now have even dimensions in After Effects. (Be aware that versions prior to Illustrator 10 were buggy in this regard, and may round up one or both sides by a pixel.)

The ready-made templates in the **Goodies** folder on the accompanying DVD have the crop area already set up to full-frame size.

Note: Don't confuse the crop marks you created by setting the crop area, with Filter>Create>Crop Marks in Illustrator. The latter creates visible trim marks which have no influence on After Effects.

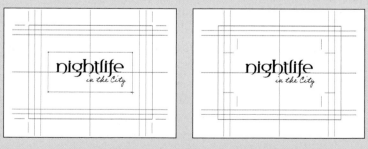

To define (or redefine) a bounding box, draw a rectangle loosely around your artwork (left); select Object>Crop Area>Make to convert the box to crop marks (right). If you press Option (Alt), you can draw a box centered around where you first click, and this point will become the center of the comp in After Effects.

Importing from Illustrator

After Effects can import Illustrator files using its regular File>Import>File menu option, or you can drag and drop from the desktop into the Project window. Single-layer Illustrator files import directly; if you import a multilayer file, a dialog will ask you whether you want to import it as Footage or as a Composition. If you select the Footage option, you can either choose an individual layer or merge the layers (which flattens all layers down to one). An additional Footage Dimension dialog allows you to set whether layers are autocropped or sized the same as the document's bounding box. We'll go through each of these options in detail below. You can also import a sequence of Illustrator files (see *More Illustrator Tricks* later in this chapter).

After Effects automatically rasterizes Illustrator vector-based files into pixels and antialiases them in Best Quality. The area considered the "paper" in Illustrator becomes transparent in After Effects, automatically creating a straight alpha channel (see Chapter 1). Illustrator layers can also be continuously rasterized so they look sharp at any size (more on this later).

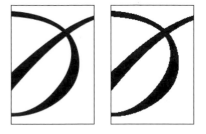

Layers in After Effects now default to Best Quality, which means they appear antialiased (left). In Draft Quality, they will look stairstepped (right). If layers are not defaulting to Best Quality, check that Preferences>General>Create New Layers at Best Quality is enabled.

Importing as Merged Footage

Let's get some practice importing Illustrator files as single layers. Open the **03-Example Project.aep** file from the **Chapter Example Projects>03-Illustrator** folder on the DVD, and follow these steps:

• Open comp [**Ex.01*starter**], which includes background footage of a city at night. The graphics department has designed a title in Illustrator that will sit above the skyline. Press Command+I (Control+I), or go to File>Import>File, and navigate to this chapter's **03_Chapter Sources** subfolder. Select the file **nightlife.ai** and click Open. If this file contained only a single layer, it would be imported directly at this point. Because it consists of two layers, you'll be presented with some options: Set the Import Kind to Footage, and select Merged Layers.

• Press Command+/ (Control+/) to add this single layer to the [**Ex.01*starter**] comp. You'll notice two things at this point: The type is black, and not necessarily positioned where you want it.

• Move the layer into a nice position above the city skyline.

• To color the title, apply Effect>Render>Fill. Click the color swatch and pick either white or a pastel color. If you got lost, compare your results with [**Ex.01_final A**].

If you'd like the Fill color to animate, we suggest you don't animate the color in the Fill effect – color swatch parameters interpolate in a straight line across the color wheel, becoming desaturated on the way. Instead, follow the Fill effect with the Adjust>Hue/Saturation effect and animate Hue (denoted as Channel Range in the Timeline window). Our version with animated color and drop shadow is in [**Ex.01_final B**].

To treat a layered file as a single piece of footage, select the Merged Layers option when you're importing.

[**Ex.01_final B**]: Our title in After Effects as a single layer. Background courtesy Artbeats/Establishments – Urban.

To import an Illustrator file as a comp, you can either set the Import As popup to Composition in the Import dialog (above) or select Footage and then Composition from the Import options dialog (below). Either way you get to choose how the layers are sized.

[Ex.05_final] is a more elaborate form of Approach A. The individual layers are pasted to an existing comp, and a null object is added to serve as a parent for the title layers.

Importing Illustrator as Comp

To animate separate Illustrator layers inside After Effects, import your file as a composition. In Illustrator, organize objects onto individual layers that should be grouped together for animation purposes, then place objects you wish to animate separately on their own layers (not sublayers). For instance, we wanted the **Nightlife** title to be animated separately from **in the City** so we created each line of type on its own layer. To import this file as a comp:

• Select the **Ex.02-Approach A** folder in the Project window (imported files will be placed into the folder that is selected).

• Press Command+I (Control+I) to open the Import dialog, and select **nightlife.ai** from the same **03_Chapter Sources** subfolder. There are two methods for importing as a composition. Either set the Import As: popup at the bottom of the Import dialog to Composition, or leave it set to Footage and select Import Kind: Composition in the next dialog. In both cases, you have the option of having layers autocropped to the dimension of each layer's content, or having all layers the same size as the document size. Unless there's a compelling reason, we would use the "cropped layers" or "Layer Size" option so that the anchor point of each layer will be centered on the layer's content.

• Once you select your options, two items will have been added to the **Ex.02** folder in the Project window: a *folder* and a *composition*, both with the same name (feel free to rename them). Twirl open the folder – it contains a footage item for each layer in the Illustrator file. Then double-click the composition: The size of the comp is 256×100 pixels, determined by the crop area we defined in Illustrator. The composition includes both layers – but they are black text on a black background. Select Composition> Background Color and change it to something bright so you can see the title. Verify that both layers are set to Best Quality.

Now that you know how to import the file as a comp, let's run through the various options available for marrying the title to the background:

Approach A: This method copies the separate layers into an existing animation. Open the comp [**Ex.02*starter**]; let's assume this comp is the start of your animation. You now want to add your title above the city skyline, but as two separate layers:

• Open the [**nightlife comp 1**] comp that After Effects created when you imported this file, press Command+A (Control+A) to Select All, and Copy.

• Bring the [**Ex.02*starter**] comp forward by clicking its tab and Paste. (Depending on the duration of the Illustrator comp, you may need to extend the duration of the layers to fill the comp.)

Note that with this approach, the original Illustrator comp is not used any longer and can be discarded. Progress at this point is saved in the **Ex.02_final** folder if you need to compare. You can now apply a different color to each layer and animate them separately.

Approach B: The second approach assumes you haven't started an animation yet, and you wish to use the comp that is created when you import the layered Illustrator file as the base for your project:

• Select Window>Close All to reduce clutter. In the Project window, select the empty **Ex.03-Approach B** folder, and repeat the steps above to import **nightlife.ai** as a comp. The **Ex.03** folder will expand, showing the resulting comp and folder of layers. Open [**nightlife comp 1**], and change the background color so you can see the black type.

• The Illustrator file was created with a crop area of 256×100 pixels, and the comp's duration and frame rate will be based on whatever settings you last used. Press Command+K (Control+K) to open Composition Settings, and rename the comp "**Nightlife Comp B**". Set the Width to 320 and the Height to 240, and the frame rate to 29.97 fps. Change the duration to 05:00, and click OK. Make sure the layers extend to the full duration of the comp; if not, extend their durations.

• In the Project window, locate the movie you want to use as a background; in this case, that's **AB_EstabUrban.mov** from the **Sources> Movies** folder. Drag this movie to the Timeline *below* the title layers.

• Select the title layers, and move them into position. The result at this point will be essentially the same as Approach A (and the same as the [**Ex.02_final**] comp). You can now proceed to effect and animate each layer separately.

Approach C: This third method takes the comp After Effects creates when it imports the Illustrator file and nests it into an existing comp:

• Select Window>Close All to reduce clutter. Twirl open the **Ex.04-Approach C** folder, and open the [**Ex.04*starter**] comp. With the **Ex.04** folder active, repeat the steps above to import the **nightlife.ai** file as a composition; when you're done, the folder of layers and the resulting comp should reside in the **Ex.04** folder.

• Select [**nightlife comp 1**] in the Project window and drag it into [**Ex.04*starter**] to nest it. The [**nightlife comp 1**] is now considered to be a "precomp" to the current layer. You can open this precomp from the Project window, or Option+double-click (Alt+double-click) on the nested comp layer in the current [**Ex.04*starter**] comp. Working across two comps can be awkward, but the advantage is that you can apply an effect to each layer separately in the [**nightlife comp 1**] precomp or apply an effect to both layers in the [**Ex.04*starter**] comp as well as animate them easily as a group. See [**Ex.04_final**] to compare with our version.

In the real world, depending on your current situation, one of the above approaches will emerge as the obvious choice. You could also use a variation on Approach A: [**Ex.05_final**] uses a null object that acts as a parent for both titles (as covered in Volume 1, Chapter 17).

Modes & More

Recent versions of Illustrator can create artwork with blending modes and transparency that are honored by After Effects. A few pointers on how this integration works in practice:

Open [**Ex.06a**]: We imported **Modes.ai** and merged the layers on import, then placed the layer on top of a background movie. Note that the blending modes are calculated only within the Illustrator layers; the composited layer uses Normal mode and 100% Opacity. While you can set a blending mode, it will apply to the layers as a group.

In [**Ex.06b**], the same file was imported as a Composition, where each layer in Illustrator appears as a separate layer in After Effects, complete with its own mode and transparency value. You can now change these values in After Effects without having to return to Illustrator.

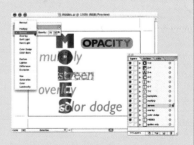

The **Modes.ai** Illustrator file has multiple layers with a variety of modes and transparency values.

If you wish to explore the settings used in Illustrator, you can find this file in the **03-Example Project> 03_Chapter Sources** folder.

Illustrator files are automatically rasterized at 100% scale (left). When they're scaled up to a larger value, such as 250%, they can look pretty soft (center). Enabling continuous rasterization causes them to be rerasterized at their current scale value, resulting in crisp outlines at any size (right).

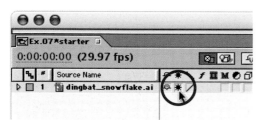

When applied to Illustrator layers, the Collapse switch in the Timeline window enables continuous rasterization. *(Note: This is not the "Illustrator switch"! Don't check it for all Illustrator layers – use it only when layers scale above 100%.)*

Illustrator in 3D

When continuously rasterized Illustrator layers are set to 3D layers, they will appear sharp when a Camera zooms in close.

Continuous Rasterization

When an Illustrator file is imported into After Effects, you can think of it as being automatically *rasterized* (turned into pixels) at 100% of its original size. As long as you restrict this layer's Scale parameter to 100% or less, and its Quality switch is set to Best, it will be treated just like any other pixel-based image and remain sharp and antialiased. However, if you scale it past 100%, things start to fall apart.

You can observe this in [**Ex.07*starter**]; make sure the comp is at Full Resolution and 100% Magnification. Notice how the artwork originally appears blocky and aliased. Set its Quality to Best; now it is antialiased. If Scale isn't already visible in the Timeline window, select the layer and press S to twirl it down. Scrub the Scale value to less than 100%, and it continues to look sharp. Now click on Scale's numeric value and enter a number larger than 100%, such as 250%: Notice how ugly the edges appear. This is because After Effects is rasterizing the art at 100%, then scaling up these pixels two and a half times.

Now for some real magic: In the Switches column of the Timeline window, click once on the Collapse Transformations/Continuously Rasterize switch (the hollow circle below the "sunburst" icon) for our layer. Surprise! The edges are rendered sharp again. Better yet, no matter what size you scale the layer, it remains crisp. This is because After Effects is applying the Scale value to the original Illustrator file, *then* converting the larger image to pixels. This process is known as *continuous rasterization*. (If you really think this is magic, read the *Rasterizing 101* sidebar to see what's going on under the hood.)

Render Order Trickery

In After Effects versions prior to 6.0, you could not apply masks or effects to layers that were continuously rasterized, but this limitation has now been overcome (and much rejoicing was heard!). So go ahead and apply any effect, such as Effect>Render>Fill to your continuously rasterized layer in [**Ex.07**]. But before you think you just got a free lunch, it's worthwhile spending a few moments understanding how the rendering order inside After Effects is being changed to accommodate this sleight of hand, as effects in particular behave differently depending on how the Collapse switch is set.

There are two points at which an Illustrator file can be rasterized, and the Collapse switch toggles between them. When the Collapse switch is off (hollow), the text is rasterized at 100%, then these pixels pass through the regular Masks, Effects, and Transform stages just like any other bitmap image or movie frame. This render order is shown in our first diagram at the right.

In prior versions, when the Collapse switch was turned on, the Illustrator outlines were passed directly to Transform, where Position, Scale, and Rotation were applied to the actual vectors. The transformed vectors were then rasterized. The problem was that the Masks and Effects stages were bypassed because they couldn't operate on vectors, and pixels were not created until later in the rendering order.

In After Effects 6.0 and later, when you continuously rasterize an Illustrator layer, the render order is rewired internally so that Transform is processed *before* Masks and Effects. This is shown in our second diagram: The Transform properties process the vectors, then the layer is rasterized, followed by Masks and Effects.

Thanks to some clever trickery, Mask Shapes are affected by Transformations so that they scale and rotate normally. Mask Feather and Effects are not quite so lucky; the following examples demonstrate anomalies you might encounter when applying masks and effects to layers that continuously rasterize.

Mask Feather Foolery

Open [Ex.08a], where a rotating illustrator layer has a vertical mask feather applied. With the Collapse switch off, preview the animation and notice that the feather behaves as you would expect (the mask feather rotates along with the object). Turn on the Collapse switch: You'll notice that while the mask shape continues to rotate properly, the feather does not.

You would normally expect the mask feather to rotate along with the object (above). But when the Collapse switch is on, Rotation is calculated before Mask Feather, producing an undesirable result (below).

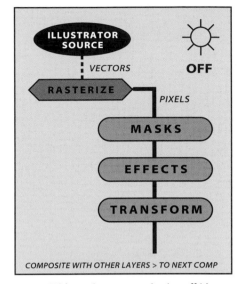

With continuous rasterization off (the default), the Illustrator file is converted to pixels at the source and is then treated like any other bitmap image.

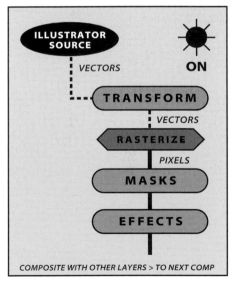

With continuous rasterization turned on, the Transform properties are calculated first, then the file is rasterized before being passed through Masks and Effects.

Paths to Masks

You can copy a path in Illustrator (or Photoshop) and paste it to a layer in After Effects as a mask; this gives you access to individual points to animate.

If you're having trouble pasting an Illustrator path as a mask, make sure to set the Copy As option in Illustrator's Preferences>Files & Clipboard to AICB>Preserve Paths in addition to PDF.

> Clipboard on Quit
> Copy As: ☑ PDF
> ☑ AICB (no transparency s
>   ⊙ Preserve Paths
>   ○ Preserve Appearan

You can also copy a path from Illustrator and paste it to any spatial property, such as Position, Anchor Point, Effects Point, Camera Position, and so on. Copy the path in Illustrator, bring After Effects forward, in the Timeline window select the individual property (not just the layer) you wish to paste to, then Paste. The middle points will be converted as roving keyframes (see Volume 1, Chapter 3); adjust the speed by moving the last keyframe.

To use Illustrator type as a mask, it must first be converted to outlines (see *The Perfect Path* sidebar earlier in this chapter for details).

These options and more are covered in the *All About Masking* chapter in Volume 1.

Eccentric Effects

If all you're doing is applying a few color correction effects, you probably won't notice whether Effects are calculated before Scale or Rotation. But many effect parameters involve values based on pixels or angle of direction, and the render order will affect how they appear.

Open [**Ex.08b**], where we've animated the rotation for an illustrator layer that has been scaled to 33%. Select layer 2 and press F3 to open the Effect Controls window: A Drop Shadow effect is applied with a Distance of 15 pixels and a Softness of 15. When the Collapse switch is off, the normal render order applies and the Effects are calculated before Transform. This means that the Distance and Softness values are being scaled by 33%, and the angle of the drop shadow is affected by Rotation (the light source appears to rotate around the frame).

Turn on continuous rasterization so that Transform is now calculated before Effects and both of these behaviors change: The Distance and Softness values are not affected by the value of Scale, and the angle of the drop shadow is consistent (since Rotation is now calculated before the effect is applied).

With the Collapse switch off, the Drop Shadow effect parameters are affected by the Scale and Rotation properties (above), and so the light source appears to rotate. When the layer is collapsed, the Transform properties are calculated first, then the Drop Shadow is applied; the shadow now renders with a consistent angle.

As you can see, it's best to make the decision to turn on continuous rasterization *before* you spend time setting effect parameters to avoid having to retweak them later. We also suggest you create Illustrator artwork at a large enough size so that you will have the option whether to turn on continuous rasterization.

Incidentally, Text layers in After Effects continuously rasterize by default, so the behavior exhibited by Illustrator layers when they are collapsed also applies to Text layers. You can explore this in [**Ex.08c**]; notice the Mask Feather doesn't rotate and Scale does not affect the Drop Shadow. Solid layers have the option of being continuously rasterized; the same caveats apply there also.

Collapsing Transformations

The same switch that turns on and off Continuous Rasterization for an Illustrator layer also doubles as the Collapse Transformations switch when it's applied to a nested comp layer.

Select Window>Close All to reduce clutter. In [**Ex.09**], the scale and position of a pointer object wiggles in Comp 1; when it's nested in Comp 2, the layer is further scaled and animated, and a Drop Shadow effect is applied. Because the Collapse switch is on in both comps, the Illustrator layer is continuously rasterized across both comps with no loss of quality.

Under the hood, the Transformations from the second comp are being added to those in the first comp, and any effects applied in either precomp are then applied to the result. Turn off the Collapse switch in the second comp; the layer appears fuzzy as you are blowing up pixels, and the effect parameters are affected by Scale and Rotation.

Collapsing Transformations is a powerful feature with other implications for render order; it was the subject of Volume 1, Chapter 20.

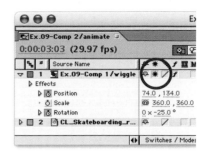

When a precomp includes an Illustrator file that is continuously rasterized, turning on the Collapse switch in the second comp (red circle) will collapse the transformations so that the layer is continuously rasterized across both comps. (This also works with 3D layers.)

Rasterize 101

If you're still a bit fuzzy on how the process of rasterization works inside After Effects, compare how Photoshop rasterizes EPS files.

When you open an Illustrator file in Photoshop, you are presented with the Rasterize Generic EPS Format dialog box (see figure) where you can enter values for the desired Width, Height, and Resolution. Once you click OK, the file is rasterized Into pixels.

At this point, were you to go into Image Size and scale up the image, you'd be blowing up pixels. This is the equivalent of increasing the Scale value in After Effects over 100% with continuous rasterization off (Figure A).

However, if instead you were to scale the file larger in the Rasterize Generic EPS Format dialog, the edges would be sharp and crisp. This is the equivalent of scaling in After Effects with continuous rasterization on (Figure B).

The Rasterize Generic EPS dialog box from Photoshop.

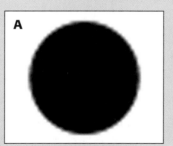

The Illustrator circle has been rasterized first at 100%, then scaled up in Image Size. Notice the degradation around the edges. This is the equivalent of scaling in After Effects with continuous rasterization off, where scaling happens after rasterizing.

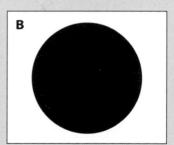

Scaling was applied in the Rasterize Generic EPS Format dialog, then the paths were rasterized. The result is a crisp, antialiased edge. This is the equivalent of scaling in After Effects with continuous rasterization on, where the paths are scaled before being rasterized.

Get Invigorated

You can create three-dimensional text and objects from Illustrator files using the Zaxwerks Invigorator plug-in.

Connect

The Anchor Point was the subject of Volume 1, Chapter 5.

Edit External (hot keying) was covered in Volume 1, Chapter 6.

Sequence Layers, see Volume 1, Chapter 7.

Motion Blur, see Volume 1, Chapter 9.

Blending Modes, see Volume 1, Chapter 10.

Masking, see Volume 1, Chapter 11.

Track Mattes, see Volume 1, Chapter 12.

Alpha Add mode was also covered in Chapter 1 and Volume 1, Chapter 13.

Parenting and null objects were covered in Volume 1, Chapter 17.

Nesting, precomposing, and collapsing transformations were explored in Volume 1, Chapters 18–20.

Adjustment Layers were the subject of Volume 1, Chapter 22.

After Effects' own Type tool was covered in Volume 1, Chapter 25.

Importing and reloading footage and the Interpret Footage dialog was uncovered in Volume 1, Chapter 28.

The Exponential Scale and The Wiggler keyframe assistants will assist you in Chapter 5.

Bonus Tutorial 1 on the DVD demonstrates using Continuous Rasterization with the Exponential Scale keyframe assistant.

More Illustrator Tricks

Here are additional techniques and tips you can use when you're working with Illustrator files. The following topics are covered elsewhere in more depth, so check the Connect box for chapter references:

Blend Shapes: Instead of using the Blend feature in Illustrator to morph between shapes, paste the initial shapes to After Effects as masks and use the Professional edition's Smart Mask Interpolation keyframe assistant (Chapter 6). It's easier to retime the resulting morph and you can better control the way the shapes interpolate.

Zooming: The Professional edition's Exponential Scale keyframe assistant makes zooming the scale of a layer look more realistic. Most footage looks bad at extreme scalings, but continuously rasterized Illustrator files retain their sharpness, making them good partners for this assistant. This technique is covered in our DVD Bonus Tutorial, *Dotcom Zoom*.

Illustrator to Photoshop Layers: To save a layered Illustrator file as a layered PSD file, select File>Export... then select Photoshop (psd) from the Format popup. Name the new file, click OK, and set the desired resolution in pixels per inch in the dialog that opens next.

Sequences: The crop area is especially critical when you're creating "cel animation" in Illustrator or making multiple files that need to be imported into After Effects in "register." To import as a sequence, select the first frame in the sequence, enable the Generic EPS Sequence checkbox in the Import dialog, and Import. Then set the frame rate in the Interpret Footage dialog. Practice this with the sequence of frames in the **DVD> Sources>Text>NumberSequence** folder.

Sequence Layers: Use this After Effects keyframe assistant to arrange multiple layers in time, and add automatic crossfades between layers.

Alpha Channels: Because Illustrator files create their own alpha channel, they make good alpha track mattes, as shown in [**Ex.10**]. White artwork, or art with shades of gray, can also be used as luma track mattes.

Alpha Add with Illustrator Layers: If you use Illustrator, you might have used the Knife tool to cut up text and other shapes. (If not, take a break and try it out – it's kind of like being in a really cheap slasher movie, but no one gets hurt…) Shapes that have been "cut" with the knife always share the same edge, but that edge is not seamless. In [**Ex.11*starter**] you'll find two sides of a broken heart shape, slashed into two pieces using Illustrator's Knife tool. Each side of the heart is on a separate layer, as the file was imported as a Composition. Set the comp's zoom level to 400% so you can see the seam, and set the top layer to the Alpha Add blending mode – the seam disappears.

Embossing: Logos and other artwork created in Illustrator can work great for embossing through video using the Texturize effect (Chapter 9).

Release to Layers

You may find you have artwork in Illustrator where shapes, text, or logo elements are all grouped on just one or two layers rather than each element being on its own layer. Illustrator offers a feature – Release to Layers – that can help when you need to move multiple elements to separate layers.

In Illustrator, open the **Quarry_practice.ai** file from the **03_Chapter Sources** folder. Let's say we want the five overlapping shapes on the left to each reside on its own layer.

In the Layers palette (Window> Show Layers), twirl open the **shapes** layer to reveal a sublayer called **<group>**. If you twirl **<group>** open, you will see the five elements, each called **<Path>**.

Step 1: Select **<group>** *(not the layer)*, and select Release to Layers (Sequence) from the Layers palette's Options menu. The five path elements under **<group>** will be converted into real layers, numbered sequentially.

Step 2: Select the newly created layers and drag them to the bottom of the Layers palette.

Step 3: When you release the mouse, the five new layers will be on the same level as the original **shapes** layer. Delete the old **shapes** layer – you don't need it.

Step 4: Rename your layers to make them easier to keep track of in After Effects, and re-order them as necessary. If you need to reverse a stack of layers from top to bottom, select the layers and choose Reverse Layer Order from the Layer palette's wing menu. Save your file under a new name. Our version is **Quarry_released.ai**. You can now import this layered Illustrator file as a

composition (as discussed earlier in this chapter).

Note: If you wish to release text characters to separate layers, you'll need to first Create Outlines (see *The Perfect Path* sidebar earlier in this chapter) before starting with Step 1 above.

Step 1: Be sure to select the **<group>** layer, not the **shapes** layer, before choosing Release to Layers (Sequence) from the Layer palette's wing menu.

Step 2: Each shape is now a layer. Select these layers and drag them to the bottom of the palette.

Step 3: The new layers now appear on the top hierarchy. You can delete the old **shapes** layer.

Step 4: Rename the new layers as needed. Note that you can re-order the layers here, or later after you import the file into After Effects.

 Paint and Clone

A painting workout in After Effects using the Brush, Erase, and Clone tools.

Vector Paint

The Vector Paint effect is covered in Bonus Chapter 4B on your DVD.

After Effects 6.0 introduced tools for painting directly on layers using an integrated Paint palette. You can use these vector-based paint tools to retouch footage and create animated graphical elements, plus use cloning to remove unwanted elements and replicate areas of a layer. The brush strokes are non-destructive and are editable in the Timeline.

The Professional edition continues to ship with the Vector Paint effect, which offers many of the same painting features; it can also automatically wiggle the brush strokes – at the cost of not having a cloning tool. If you'd like to compare both approaches to painting, Vector Paint is covered in Bonus Chapter 4B on this book's DVD.

In this chapter we'll explore using the new Paint tools and cover the basics of painting, erasing, and cloning. We will also explore the various methods for animating strokes, and walk you step by step through automating a repair task using motion tracking and expressions. Along the way we'll also present tips for incorporating other effects with Paint, as well as saving custom brushes and clone presets.

Getting Started with Paint

Open the [**Ex.01-Getting Started**] comp from this chapter's example project, where we've created a solid layer for you to practice with. Make sure the Tools palette is open (if it's not, select Window>Tools to open it). There are three paint tools that we'll be using: Brush, Clone Stamp, and Eraser. You can select and toggle between them using the shortcut Command+B on Mac (Control+B on Windows). If Auto Open Palettes is checked in the Tools palette, selecting one of the paint tools will open the

Brush Tool   Clone Stamp Tool   Eraser Tool

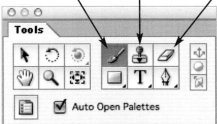

Example Project

Explore the 04-Example Project.aep file as you read this chapter; references to [Ex.##] refer to specific compositions within the project file.

If Auto Open Palettes is checked, the Paint/Brush Tips palettes will open when any of the paint and clone tools are selected. The leftmost button toggles the Paint palette open and closed.

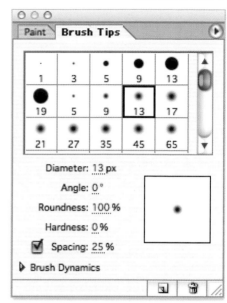

The Paint and Brush Tips palettes at their default settings. Changing any of these settings affects new strokes only; existing strokes must be edited in the Timeline window.

The Clone Options section (left) is grayed out unless the Clone Stamp tool is selected. The Brush Dynamics section in the Brush Tips palette (right) has options for pressure-sensitive tablets.

X is the shortcut for toggling the Foreground/ Background colors. Press D to reset the Foreground/Background colors to Black/White.

Paint palette; the Brush Tips palette is docked with it.

Unlike the Vector Paint effect, where you create paint strokes directly in the Comp window, the new Paint tools work only in the Layer window – attempting to paint in the Comp window will result in an error message. To create a few practice strokes, double-click layer 1 (our **Black Solid 1** layer); when the Layer window opens, select the Brush tool, check that the color in the Paint palette is something other than black (it defaults to red), verify that the Duration popup is set to Constant, then paint a stroke or two to get started. The default settings for the Paint palettes are shown in the figures above, if you need to reset any of the parameters.

Go ahead and try a few strokes using a variety of Foreground colors and brush tip sizes. You can select a new brush tip either by bringing the palette forward or by clicking on the current brush tip in

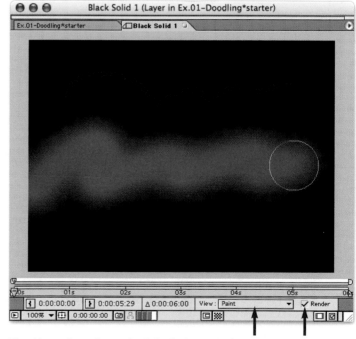

The paint tools can be used only in the Layer window. The top stroke was created with the default settings, the lower one with the 100-pixel brush tip and a yellow Foreground color. If you're having trouble seeing your strokes, make sure the View popup is set to Paint, and the Render box is checked.

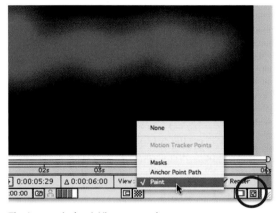

Paint is an "effect," although the only option in the Effect Controls window is Paint on Transparent; check this option to render the paint strokes only (the underlying layer will be transparent).

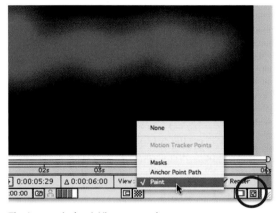

The Layer window's View menu shows the render order for this layer; other effects applied could appear before or after Paint. Make sure the Render checkbox is on to see the brush strokes. Click the Comp button (circled in red) to bring the Comp window forward.

Simple Sizing

To interactively resize the brush tip in the Layer window, press Command (Mac) or Control (Windows) and drag to set the diameter; release the modifier key and continue to drag to set the feather amount (Hardness).

the Paint palette. You can separate the Brush Tips palette from the Paint palette by dragging them apart to see both at the same time.

To resize a brush interactively, press the Command (Control) key and drag in the Layer window to set the diameter; release the modifier key and continue to drag to set the feather amount.

A few more important concepts coming up:

• Paint is considered to be an "effect," so it appears in the Effect Controls window. The only parameter you can edit there, however, is Paint on Transparent, which determines whether the underlying layer (the solid in our example) is visible or not. Because Paint is an effect, you can use multiple instances of paint as well as interleave other effects with your paint strokes. See the *Paint and Effects* sidebar later in this chapter for details.

• The Layer window in After Effects 6.x has gained a View popup and a Render checkbox. The View menu allows you to pick and choose which part of the rendering order appears in the Layer window (the original source, after Masks, or after each individual effect). The Render checkbox determines whether the current view is rendered (you will always want to render the Paint effect, but when View is set to Masks, you may prefer to view the Mask Shapes but not have them create transparency).

• Changing any of the settings in the Paint palettes affects only new strokes – if you need to edit an existing stroke, you'll need to use the Timeline window. So without further ado…

Editing Existing Strokes

Expand the solid layer and twirl down Effects>Paint to see your strokes in the Timeline window, or use the shortcut PP (two Ps in quick succession) to reveal the Paint section. Expand Paint to reveal the Paint on Transparent parameter plus a twirly for each Brush stroke created, numbered sequentially.

To the right of each brush stroke section is a popup menu for setting the Blending Mode per stroke; this mirrors the Mode popup in the Paint palette. Each brush stroke breaks down further into three sections: Shape, Stroke Options, and Transform (not to be confused with the regular Transform settings):

• The Shape is the path itself and this can be animated over time. Unfortunately, you can't reshape the stroke by manipulating handles as you can with a mask shape, but you can paste mask shapes to the Shape property (see *Random Paint Splatters* later in this chapter).

• Stroke Options allow you to edit and animate most of the brush characteristics found in the Paint and Brush Tips palettes; it also includes Start and End parameters for animating on a stroke over time. The

Channels popup mirrors the Channels menu in the Paint palette (more on this in a bit).

• You can reposition, scale, and rotate each stroke using its Transform settings.

Some of these parameters are self-explanatory; we'll explore the others as we go. The most important thing to remember is that you don't need to sweat setting up the Paint and Brush Tips palettes properly to begin with, as you can edit the mode, color, size, opacity, and so on for each stroke in the Timeline window after the fact.

Note also that each brush stroke in the Timeline window has a duration bar: A brush stroke can be moved in time as well as have its in and out points moved (without the limitations that real layers encounter). If the Duration popup in the Paint palette was set to Constant, each brush stroke will extend for the duration of the layer (we'll cover the Duration options shortly).

Managing Your Strokes

You can name brush strokes to keep track of which one is which. To rename a stroke, select its name (Brush 1, for instance), hit Return, type a new name, and press Return to accept it.

The order of the strokes in the Timeline window also sets their rendering order; brush strokes render from the bottom up. Drag strokes up and down in the stack to change their render order.

To delete a brush stroke, select it in the Layer or Timeline window and press Delete. You can also temporarily hide it by turning off the eyeball for individual strokes.

Practice editing your existing strokes by scrubbing the values in the Timeline, then create additional strokes and practice renaming and re-ordering them. Be warned that creating a new stroke while an existing Brush stroke is selected will replace that stroke; get in the habit of hitting F2 to Deselect All before creating a new stroke.

Paint on Transparent

The Paint on Transparent option can be found in both the Timeline and Effect Controls window; it determines whether the underlying layer is opaque or transparent when composited over other layers. Toggle it On and the black solid in our example comp will disappear, revealing the Background Color (blue in this case) in the Layer window. The background color is for display only; you can change this color by selecting Composition>Background Color and clicking on the color swatch. If you need to check whether the color you're seeing is transparent, toggle the Transparency Grid on at the bottom of the Layer window.

Most of the settings from the Paint and Brush Tips palettes are editable – and animatable – in the Timeline window after the fact. You can also rename strokes and change their rendering order by moving them up and down in the stack.

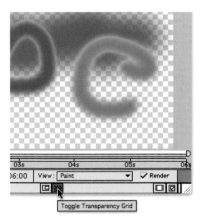

If the Paint on Transparent option is on, the solid will disappear, revealing the composition's background color. To display the background color as a grid instead, select the Toggle Transparency Grid button.

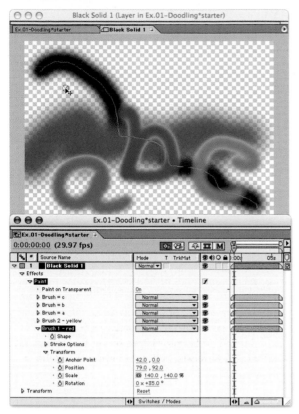

Each Brush stroke has its own set of Transform properties (not to be confused with the layer's regular Transform section).

The Channels popup in the Paint palette determines which channels are affected.

Transforming Brush Strokes

Select one of your strokes and note how it appears in the Layer window: The stroke's Anchor Point appears at the start of the stroke, and a line runs through the center of the stroke. Explore the Transform properties in the Timeline window to edit the path:

• The Anchor Point is the origin around which the stroke scales and rotates. Note that if you edit the anchor point value, the anchor point remains in the same position while the stroke offsets its position.

• You can move the Position of the stroke by simply dragging it with the Selection tool. Use the up/down/left/right arrow keys to nudge the path one pixel at a time; add the Shift key to nudge times 10.

• Changing the Scale value affects the size of the stroke path as well as the brush diameter (the width of the stroke). If need be, edit the Diameter in the Stroke Options section to counteract this. The short-cuts to edit Scale are the same as for a regular layer; select the stroke and press Option/Alt and the + and – keys on the numeric keypad (not the regular key-board) to scale in 1 percent increments. Add the Shift key for times 10.

• Use Rotation to rotate the path around the stroke's anchor point. The shortcuts to edit Rotation are the same as for a regular layer: Select the stroke and press the + and – keys on the numeric keypad (not the regular keyboard) to rotate in 1 degree increments. Add the Shift key for times 10.

Of course, all of these properties can also be animated, so you have an enormous amount of control over every single stroke.

Choosing Channels

The Channels popup in the Paint palette determines whether Brush strokes (including Clone Stamp and Eraser strokes) affect the RGB channels, RGB+Alpha, or the Alpha channel only. To compare these options, select an image with an obvious alpha channel, such as the picture frame in [**Ex.02-Frame*starter**]:

• Double-click layer 1 to open the Layer window, and select the Brush tool. In the Paint palette, select a large brush tip and a blue Foreground color. Check that Mode is set to Normal, Channels is set to RGBA, and Duration is set to Constant. Paint over the left side of the frame.

The stroke affects the RGB channels but also affects the layer's alpha. Click on the alpha channel button (the white swatch) at the bottom of the Layer to view the alpha channel only.

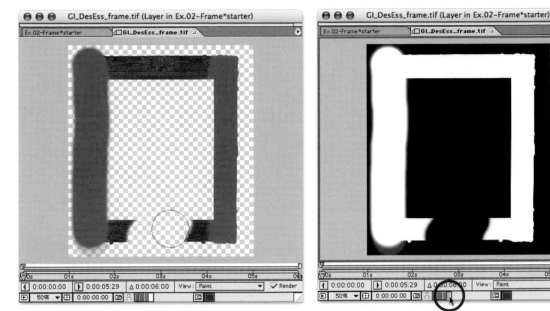

The blue stroke on the left was painted with Channels set to RGBA; the right stroke was painted in RGB mode. Painting in Alpha mode with black paint renders areas of the frame invisible. Image courtesy Getty Images/Design Essentials.

When the Channels popup is set to Alpha, only the alpha channel is affected. Select the Alpha channel button (the white swatch at the bottom of the Layer window) to view the layer's alpha. You can also paint with this button toggled on.

• Turn off the alpha channel switch so you're viewing the RGB channels again. Set the Channels popup to RGB and paint another blue stroke on the right side of the frame; the color appears only where the alpha channel is opaque.

• Set the Channels popup to Alpha; the Foreground/Background colors change to black and white, respectively. Press X to switch the Foreground and Background colors. Painting with a Foreground color of black will render the corresponding pixels in the alpha channel as transparent; painting in white will render them as opaque; shades of gray will be more or less transparent. (Alpha channels were the subject of Chapter 1.)

Painting with Modes

Each individual brush stroke includes a blending mode setting to control how they interact with the underlying layer and other paint strokes that are rendered before the current stroke. You can set the Mode popup in the Paint palette before you paint, or set it at any time in the Timeline window.

[**Ex.02_Frame_final**] shows an example of using the Color mode to colorize the frame; remember that these colors can be animated if you feel like going a little crazy.

(Blending Modes were the subject of Volume 1, Chapter 10.)

The frame was painted with different colored strokes all set to the Color blending mode.

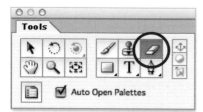

When the Eraser tool is selected in the Tools palette (above), the Erase popup in the Paint palette is active (below). *Note that the options in the Paint and Brush Tips palettes are remembered separately for each of the three tools – so be sure to select the Eraser tool first, then set options accordingly.*

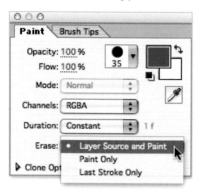

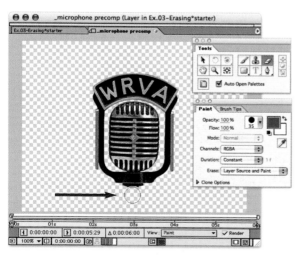

Using the Eraser tool with the Channels popup set to RGBA and the Erase popup set to Layer Source and Paint will erase portions of the image (above). The Eraser strokes appear in the Timeline window (right) just like Brush strokes.

Eraser Logic

Our next guided tour is of the Eraser tool, with which you can zap image pixels and paint strokes then unzap them at will. Erasing in After Effects is particularly stress-free because not only can you erase any unwanted paint strokes, you can also delete strokes created with the Eraser tool. Depending on how the Paint palette's Channels and Eraser popups are set, you can erase back to the background color, erase paint strokes only, or erase the last stroke only.

To explore the various options, open the [**Ex.03-Erasing*starter**] comp and double-click layer 1 to open the microphone image in its own Layer window. (Note that the original source was tall and skinny; we placed the microphone in a precomp to have it better fill the frame.)

• The Paint and Brush Tips palettes remember a separate set of options for each tool; be sure to select the Eraser tool *before* you select a brush tip or set other options in the Paint palette. We'll start by erasing the bottom portion of the microphone, so select a large brush tip, make sure Channels is set to RGBA, Duration is Constant, and the Erase popup is set to Layer Source and Paint. The Opacity and Flow settings in the Paint palette also affect the characteristics of the Eraser tool – set them both to 100%. Erase the bottom of the microphone.

• Press PP (two Ps in quick succession) to reveal the Paint section in the Timeline window; your stroke appears as Eraser 1. Although it lacks Mode and Channels popups, or a Color swatch, all other parameters of an Eraser stroke can be edited and animated just like the Paint strokes you created earlier.

• Select Eraser 1 and press Delete to remove it. Set the Channels popup to RGB, and again paint over the base of the microphone. Instead of making the pixels transparent, they erase to the Background color in the Paint palette (not the comp's background color). The alpha channel is not affected.

• Setting the Channels popup to Alpha mode with a black Background color is similar to erasing in RGBA mode; when it's set to white, you can extend the alpha channel. (You could also achieve a similar result using the Brush tool to paint in the alpha channel.)

Erasing the Paint Only

Still using the same microphone layer in [**Ex.03**], select the Brush tool and verify that the Channels popup is set to RGBA and that the Mode is Normal. Paint a few colorful brush strokes around the microphone in the Layer window; make sure some of them overlap the image itself (see figure).

Once you're happy with your paint strokes, select the Eraser tool and verify that Channels is set to RGBA; set the Erase popup to Paint Only and erase the portion of the strokes that overlaps the image. In Paint Only mode, the image is not affected – only the strokes are erased.

Erase Last Stroke

New in version 6.5 is the ability to erase a portion of the last stroke painted, which is useful when you make a mistake and the last stroke you painted overlapped other strokes you were happy with. You can erase portions of the last stroke using one of two methods:

• Select the Eraser tool, then set the Erase popup in the Paint palette to Last Stroke Only.

• Press Command+Shift (Control+Shift) when using the Brush or Clone Stamp tools; this will temporarily toggle the current brush to Erase Last Stroke Only mode.

An eraser stroke made with the Last Stroke Only option is permanent – it does *not* create an item and duration bar in the Timeline window that you can later delete, edit, or animate. On the other hand, you end up with a less cluttered stack in the Timeline window.

Remember that no matter what settings you use, you are never destroying the original RGB pixels; After Effects' painting tools create non-destructive vector paths that can always be deleted to restore the original image.

Finally, just as with brush strokes, you can rename, re-order, and delete Eraser strokes.

Our version is in [**Ex.03-Erasing_final**], where we added a Drop Shadow effect and a background layer. RAM Preview; we wiggled the microphone layer and the individual paint strokes using expressions (Chapter 6). Select the microphone layer and press F3 to open the Effect Controls window; play with changing the position and rotation wiggle amounts using the sliders in the expression controllers.

When the Erase popup is set to Paint Only, the underlying image is not affected. Note that you can erase across multiple strokes at the same time. Image courtesy Classic PIO/Classic Microphones.

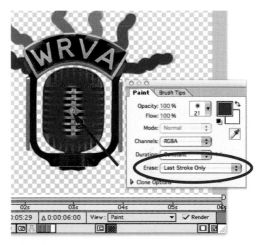

A hole was created in the orange stroke (above) by erasing in Last Stroke Only mode.

Our final version (left) includes wiggling strokes thanks to the wiggle expression (see Chapter 6).

Animating Strokes

There are various ways to animate the drawing of your brush strokes: You can animate the Start or End parameters, or you can paint in Write-on mode. You can also paint frame by frame, or use a single brush stroke and interpolate the shape of the stroke over time. And, of course, you can move the duration bar for a series of strokes to have them start at different points along the Timeline and trim their in and out points. We'll look at these options in this section.

Start Here, End There

Close all open comps to reduce clutter, and open [**Ex.04-Smoke*starter**]. An industrial smokestack belches smoke, but what color should it be? Let's say the company promised to colorize the smoke when it elected a new CEO, but Wall Street is having trouble determining the color (don't laugh, it could happen). Double-click the **AB_IndustryScenes.mov** layer to open the Layer window, and let's colorize the smoke:

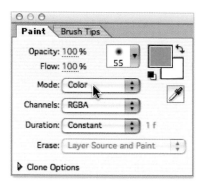

Step 1: The yellow stroke will colorize the layer when Mode is set to Color.

Step 1: Select the Brush tool, and use a soft brush tip a little larger than the width of the chimney. Check that Channels is set to RGBA, Duration is Constant, and change the Mode popup to Color (to colorize the footage). Set the Foreground color to yellow; the luminance of the color you choose isn't important, only the Hue and Saturation will be used in Color mode.

Step 2: At time 00:00, paint a swirly brush stroke coming out of the chimney (see figure). The resulting color will take on the Hue and Saturation of the Foreground color, but will retain the luminance of the underlying smoke.

Step 3: To animate on the stroke, press PP (two Ps in quick succession) to reveal the Paint property in the Timeline, and expand it to reveal Paint>Brush 1>Stroke Options. Scrub the End value to 0% and turn on the animation stopwatch.

Step 4: Move to a point later in time, like 03:00, and set the End value back to 100%. RAM Preview and the stroke will wipe on over time.

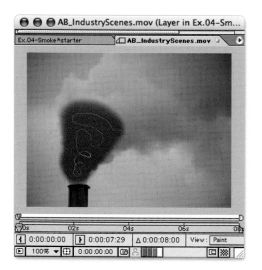

Step 2: Paint a squiggly yellow stroke in the Layer window (above). Footage courtesy Artbeats/Industry Scenes.

Steps 3–4: Animate the stroke by setting keyframes for the End parameter in the Timeline window (right). Remember that you can also change the mode, color, diameter, hardness, and other characteristics of the stroke at any time.

Using Write On Mode

Painting in Write On mode sets the End keyframes for you automatically, so let's try this alternate approach:

Step 1: With the Brush tool still selected, change the Foreground color to green and set the Duration popup to Write On.

Step 2: Press 3 to jump to 03:00 so that the new stroke starts here, and press F2 to Deselect All (if your first stroke is selected, you will replace it unless you deselect first).

Step 3: Paint another squiggly stroke coming out of the chimney over the course of about three or four seconds. When you release the mouse, the stroke won't be visible, but if you hit Play or RAM Preview, you'll see it draw on in realtime starting at 03:00.

Step 4: Press U to reveal all animated properties for the layer, and you'll see that After Effects automatically added two End keyframes to Brush 2, ranging from 0% to 100%. You can move the location of the second keyframe to retime the stroke's animation.

Note: If you were a slow squiggler, the second End keyframe may be located past the end of the comp! To gain access to the second keyframe, you can either drag the stroke's duration bar earlier in time, or temporarily extend the comp's duration.

Step 5: If you move the duration bar for Brush 2 earlier in time, the layer bar no longer extends to the end of the comp. However, unlike a movie's layer bar, you can extend the out point for a stroke's bar past its original length. Also note that when you trim the in and out points, there is no "empty bar" to show where the trimming occurred.

Whether you set the End keyframes manually or use Write On mode, the stroke itself will retain all the inherent timing nuances (speed ups and slow downs) of your hand's movement.

Step 3: **After** pressing F2 to Deselect All, paint a squiggly green stroke in the Layer window (right).

Step 4–5: Press U to reveal all animated properties. You can drag the duration bar for Brush 2 earlier in time (press Shift to have it snap to the current time), then extend the bar to the end of the comp (below).

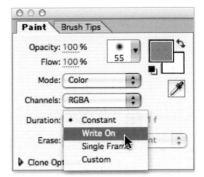

Step 1: With Duration set to Write On, paint strokes will be recorded in realtime.

Replacing Strokes

If a brush stroke is selected in the Timeline window and you paint a new stroke, you will overwrite the selected stroke. If you don't want that behavior, press F2 to Deselect All before painting a new stroke.

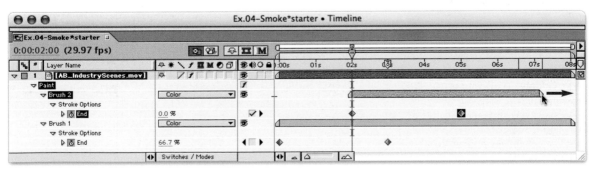

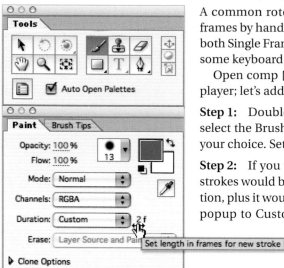

Set the Duration popup to Custom, then set the value immediately to its right to the stroke's duration. Of course, you can actually paint on any frame you like, or change the Custom frame duration value at any time. For instance, you might want to animate some sections "on 1s" and other areas "on 2s".

Rotoscoping Frame by Frame

A common rotoscoping task involves painting a series of individual frames by hand. It can be a tedious undertaking, but After Effects offers both Single Frame and Custom options in the Duration popup as well as some keyboard shortcuts to help automate this task.

Open comp [**Ex.05-Roto*starter**]. Layer 1 is a movie of a saxophone player; let's add some paint strokes emanating from the bell of the sax:

Step 1:   Double-click the movie to open it in the Layer window, and select the Brush tool. In the Paint palette, pick a brush tip and color of your choice. Set the Mode to Normal and the Channels to RGBA.

Step 2:   If you were to set the Duration popup to Single Frame, your strokes would be one frame long. This would result in a frenetic animation, plus it would be time consuming to paint. Instead, set the Duration popup to Custom; this automatically sets any stroke you create to a custom duration as set by the value immediately to the right of the popup. The default is 1 frame, so change this value to "**2**".

Step 3:   At time 00:00, paint a stroke. Press PP to see this stroke in the Timeline; note that it is two frames in duration. To advance to the next frame by the exact increment you set in the Paint palette, press:

- Command+Page Down (Control+Page down), or
- 2 (on the regular keyboard)

These shortcuts will advance the time marker to 00:02; paint another stroke then repeat to advance to 00:04, and so on. RAM Preview at any time to see how your animation looks.

No prizes for guessing that the following shortcuts will move the time marker backward by the same increment:

- Command+Page Up (Control+Page Up), or
- 1 (on the regular keyboard)

Our version is shown in [**Ex.05-Roto_final**].

In [**Ex.05-Roto_final**], we painted musical notes and flourishes at two-frame increments (above). Note that you can add multiple brush strokes at each frame (right). Footage courtesy Herd of Mavericks.

Brush Tips and Tablets

A brush stroke is actually created by many individual brush tip marks, and the settings in the Brush Tips palette control their Diameter, Angle, Roundness, Hardness, and Spacing. Furthermore, the Opacity and Flow settings in the Paint palette set the maximum paint coverage and how quickly paint is applied, respectively.

You can customize a preset brush in the Brush Tips palette and then save your new brush as a preset. These presets are saved in a Preferences file. To create a custom brush tip, select any existing brush tip and change the value for the various options: Diameter, Angle, Roundness, Hardness, or Spacing. These should be self-explanatory, but if not, check out the *Customizing Brush Tips* section in Help>After Effects Help>Using Paint Tools.

To save your customized brush tip, click on the icon at the bottom of the Brush Tips palette (see figure). Your new brush will be named automatically based on its hardness, roundness, and size.

From the Brush Tips Options menu (top right of palette), you can also Rename or Delete an existing preset, view the brushes in various ways, and Reset the palette to the default set of preset brushes.

If you use a pressure-sensitive tablet (such as a Wacom tablet), you can set how the pen's pressure, tilt or stylus wheel affects the brush's characteristics dynamically. For instance, less pressure could decrease the diameter and opacity. Expand the Brush Dynamics section and set your own preferences for how to dynamically control the Minimum Size, Angle, Roundness, Opacity, and Flow. These settings are not saved when you change from one brush tip to another, so you may want to save a set of custom brushes.

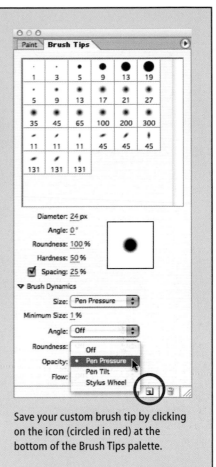

Save your custom brush tip by clicking on the icon (circled in red) at the bottom of the Brush Tips palette.

Interpolating Brush Strokes

After Effects will interpolate between different brush strokes if you animate the Shape property. To practice this technique, open comp [**Ex.06-Shapes*starter**] and RAM Preview to get a sense of the action. Let's embellish the section where the unhealthy-looking smoker takes a drag:

Step 1: Move the time marker to 02:20 where the red tip lights up, and double-click the **DV_Xposed.mov** layer to open it in its Layer window.

Step 2: Select the Brush tool, and set the Duration popup in the Paint palette to Constant. The Channels should be RGBA and the Mode set to Normal. Using a color and size of your choice, draw a fun squiggly stroke emitting from the tip of the cigarette.

Step 3: Press PP to reveal Paint in the Timeline, and twirl down Brush 1. Turn on the stopwatch for the Shape property to create the first keyframe at time 02:20.

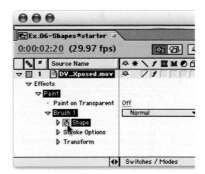

Step 3: To interpolate between brush strokes, draw the first stroke, then turn on the stopwatch for the Shape property in the Timeline window.

Wiggling and Onion Skinning

The Vector Paint effect can't interpolate between strokes, but it can wiggle individual strokes. It also offers an onion skin option (where you see a ghost of previous and future frames), something not currently supported by the regular Paint engine. For more on Vector Paint, see Bonus Chapter 4b.

Step 4: Press Page Down to advance 10 frames, and paint another quite different squiggly stroke. *Provided that Brush 1 remained selected*, the second shape will replace the first one and create a second keyframe for the Shape property. Scrub the timeline to see the first shape interpolating to form the second shape.

Step 5: Repeat Step 4 to create additional strokes as often as you like, finishing up around 06:20. If you don't like one of the shapes, return to that point in time and – with Brush 1 still selected – paint a replacement stroke. If you want to add more keyframes before 02:20, you can drag the in point in the stroke's duration bar earlier in time.

Step 6: If you change any of the settings in the Paint palette, when you create a new stroke, the new settings will apply to all previous shapes as well (think about it – all the shapes belong to a single brush stroke). The advantage, however, is that you have only one set of Stroke Options and Transform settings, so you can easily animate parameters such as Color, Diameter, and Opacity across all the interpolating shapes. Be aware that once you've turned on the stopwatch for other parameters, adding a new stroke will add keyframes to these parameters as well.

Our version is in [**Ex.06-Shape_final**], where we first created our strokes, then animated a few parameters including Scale. Note how scaling is applied after the stroke is rendered, reducing the softness of the stroke when it is scaled below 100%.

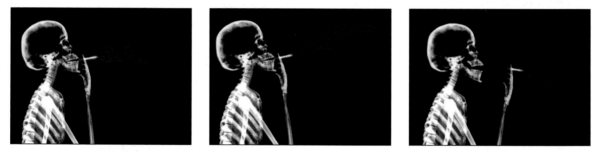

By animating Shape, a series of brush strokes appears as a single interpolating path (above). We extended the brush stroke by dragging the in point earlier in time, then animated various parameters (below). Footage courtesy Digital Vision/Xposed.

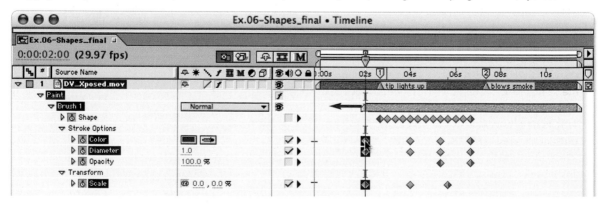

Effects and Paint

Paint is an effect that appears in the Effect Controls window. Once you've created some paint strokes, any effect you apply will render after Paint. However, you can easily re-order the effects in the Effect Controls or Timeline window, and even create multiple Paint effects.

Open **[Ex.07-FX Stack]**, where we've painted "clues" on a calendar and added various effects to tint and distort it. Double-click the calendar layer to open the Layer window, and verify that the View popup is set to Roughen Edges (the last effect in the stack). Press F3 to open the Effect Controls window.

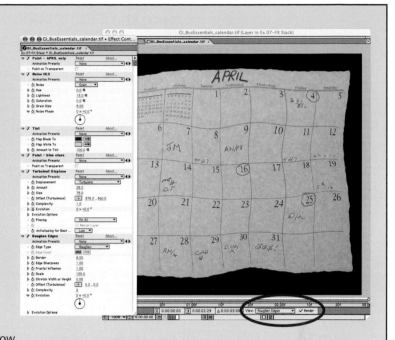

There are two instances of Paint. The first instance writes "April" at the top of the calendar; because it's first in the rendering order, it's affected by the Noise HLS and Tint effects that follow, creating a parchment look to the paper. The second Paint effect creates the clues in blue paint, then the entire composite is distorted with Turbulent Displace. Roughen Edges affects the layer's alpha channel, and would have the same effect no matter where you placed it in the effect order.

This stack of effects is also reflected in the View popup at the bottom of the Layer window; selecting any item from this list will display the composite at that point in the render order.

Try re-ordering the effects in the Effect Controls window so you get a sense of how important the rendering order is. For instance, moving Turbulent Displace to the top distorts the source image but not the paint strokes. After moving an effect, check that the View popup is displaying the desired view.

To add another instance of Paint, select a view you want to paint, such as Tint. A new Paint effect will be added directly after the current effect. (If the current view is a Paint effect, new strokes will be added to it.)

In **[Ex.07-FX Stack]** we've added a number of effects in addition to two instances of Paint: The first instance creates the word "April" at the top of the calendar, followed by Noise HLS and Tint effects to add a parchment look to the paper. The second instance of Paint adds the "clues" in blue, followed by Turbulent Displace and Roughen Edges. When you're re-ordering effects, check that the View popup is set to the desired view and that the Render switch is on.

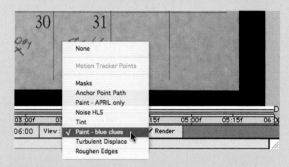

The View popup at the bottom of the Layer window determines the point in the rendering order that is being displayed. For instance, selecting the "Paint – blue clues" effect shows the layer before Turbulent Displace and Roughen Edges are factored in. If you re-order effects in the Effect Controls or Timeline windows, the View menu will immediately update to reflect the changes.

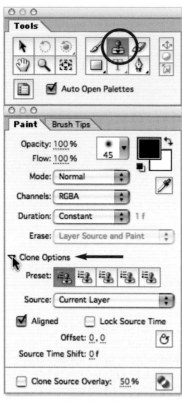

Step 1: Select the Clone Stamp tool and expand the Clone Options section.

Using the Clone Stamp Tool

The Clone Stamp tool samples pixels on a source layer, then applies the sample to another part of the same layer or a different layer in the same comp. To Photoshop users, cloning is a familiar friend for repeating sections of an image and repairing flaws; in After Effects, you can also clone from a different point in time.

In this section we'll start with the basics, including features added in version 6.5 such as Clone Presets, Overlay mode, and cloning from a different layer. We'll then cover cloning a moving source using a combination of Motion Tracking and Expressions.

We assume you've worked through this chapter from the start, as this section builds on concepts that were previously introduced. To get started, close all other comps and open [**Ex.08-Cloning*starter**].

Step 1: Our comp includes two movies; we'll start with layer 1, a clip of colorful boats in a harbor. (We'll use layer 2 in the next section.) Double-click **AB_FrenchCountryside_ex.mov** to open it in its Layer window and select the Clone Stamp tool. Twirl open the Clone Options at the bottom of the Paint palette. Choose a soft brush tip around 45 pixels in size, and verify that the Paint palette is using default values for the other parameters (see figure to the left) – particularly Mode = Normal, Channels = RGBA, and Duration = Constant.

If you've ever cloned in Photoshop, you know there are two methods of repeating the sampled area: aligned (where the first stroke you make determines the offset for subsequent strokes), and not aligned (where every stroke starts from the same origin point). We'll explore both options.

Step 2: In the Layer window (above), Option+click (Alt+click) on the red boat to set the source point, then clone a second boat. Clone strokes in the Timeline sport extra parameters (right). Footage courtesy Artbeats/French Countryside.

Clone Presets

The Clone Options settings can be saved in one of five Clone Presets. All you need to do to save a preset is first select its slot; any changes you then make will be stored in that preset. Get in the habit of picking the next Clone Preset button when you're working on a complicated job: This allows you to return to the Clone Options used earlier by reselecting that preset. The shortcuts for recalling Clone Preset 1 through 5 are the numbers 3 through 7 on the regular keyboard.

Clone Presets are convenient for storing the settings of the Clone Options section. Option+click (Alt+click) on a different Clone Preset to duplicate the current settings.

Step 2: Select the first Clone Preset in the Paint palette and verify that Aligned is enabled.

• Press the Option (Alt) key: The cursor will change to a "bull's eye" icon. Then click on the red boat to set this pixel as the clone source. The Source Layer popup in the Paint palette will update to reflect the name of this layer (we'll explore using different layers in a moment).

• Release the Option (Alt) key. As you move the cursor, the Offset value in the Paint palette updates to reflect how far you are from the source pixel. Click and paint elsewhere in the window; another copy of the red boat will appear. If you paint again somewhere else, this time you will *not* get another red boat, as the same *absolute* offset will be used.

To reset the Offset value, either repeat the Option+click (Alt+click) step to pick a new origin point, or click the Reset Offset button along the right side of the Paint palette to change the values to 0,0.

You can also scrub the Offset values directly in the Paint palette. When you do, an overlay of the offset image will appear temporarily as a guide. Press Option+Shift (Alt+Shift) and drag to reposition this overlay; this also updates the Offset value.

Step 3: Select Clone Preset 2; verify that the Source Position for this preset is at 0,0. Disable the Aligned switch.

• Press the Option (Alt) key and click on the white buoy (the ball) at the rear of the yellow boat. This sets the Source Position around X = 254, Y = 289.

• Release the Option (Alt) key and clone the white buoy behind the red boat. Try another stroke somewhere else. With Align off, every stroke you make is sampled from the original clone source, not an offset from the cursor position.

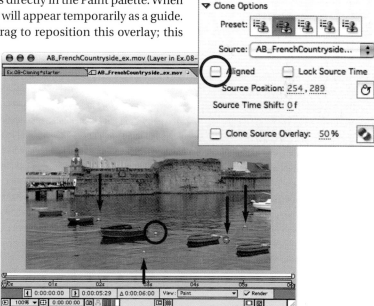
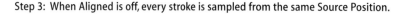

Step 3: When Aligned is off, every stroke is sampled from the same Source Position.

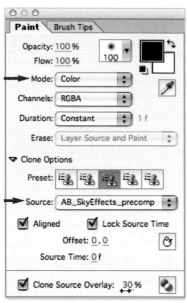

Set the Mode to Color, then set the Clone Options as shown above. The Clone Source Overlay displays an overlay of the source as a guide; set its transparency interactively by scrubbing the % value. (The button to the right toggles the overlay to Difference mode.)

By selecting a different layer to clone from (right), you can add a little color to the gray sky (above). The Clone Source Overlay helps with placement. Footage courtesy Artbeats/Sky Effects.

Clone Source Overlay

Let's add a little color to the gray clouds in [**Ex.08**] as we introduce two more features: Clone Source Overlay and Lock Source Time.

Step 1:   Double-click layer 2 – **AB_SkyEffects_precomp** –   to open it in its Layer window and preview it: It contains a big yellow sun setting over a warm sky. If you were to use this movie to colorize layer 1, the color would fade out as the sun sets, so let's clone from only a single frame.

Step 2:   Press Home to make sure the time marker is at 00:00. Bring the Layer window for **AB_FrenchCountryside_ex.mov** forward again, and with the Clone Stamp tool selected, press the third Clone Preset button.

• Set the Mode popup to Color to pick up only the Hue and Saturation of the source layer (mixing it with the luminance of the gray clouds).

• For the Source popup, select the **AB_SkyEffects_precomp** layer.

• Turn on Lock Source Time so that the same frame is used throughout, and verify that Source Time is set to 0f (the frame at 00:00).

• Check that the Aligned switch is on and that Offset is set to 0,0.

Step 3:   Turn on Clone Source Overlay in the Paint palette. The clone source will appear as an overlay when you move over the Layer window.

• Scrub the value for Source Time to pick a different source frame (if you use a later frame, the sun appears to be setting above the buildings).

• The position of the overlay is determined by the Offset value – scrub these values to get a sense of how they work. Remember that you can also drag with Option+Shift (Alt+Shift) pressed to reposition the overlay interactively. When you're done exploring, click on the Reset Offset button to set the values back to 0,0.

• Scrub the Clone Source Overlay transparency value between 0 and 100%; set to taste.

Step 4:   With a large soft brush tip (around 100 pixels), clone the sky area in one continuous stroke. There is no need to press Option (Alt) first as we want the default Offset value of 0,0.

If the color is too strong, reveal the stroke in the Timeline window and set the Stroke Options>Opacity value to taste. Note that you can change the Clone Source, Clone Position, and Clone Time in the Timeline window, but you must toggle on Lock Source Time before you paint. (If you really must do so after the fact, create a still image of the clone source frame and set the Clone Source layer popup to use it instead.)

Shifting the Source Time

Close [**Ex08**], and open [**Ex.09-CloneTime*starter**]. For your next trick, you'll clone the flag on top of the building. When you're cloning identical objects, you'll often need to also shift the timing of the duplicate:

Step 1: Double-click **AB_FrenchTowns.mov** to open it in its Layer window. Select the Clone Stamp tool, and pick the fourth Clone Preset.

• Set the Mode popup in the Paint palette to Normal.

• Set the Clone Options as per the figure to the right.

• Create a brush tip suitable for cloning the flag (we edited the soft 21-pixel size brush in Brush Tips so that it had a Hardness value of 50%).

Step 2: Zoom in 200%. Press Option (Alt) and click on the base of the original flag to set the source point. Move the cursor to the top of the leftmost flagpole; the Clone Source Overlay will follow the cursor. Clone to create a second flag, then RAM Preview to see the result.

Step 3: Notice anything odd? Both flags are flapping exactly the same, which gives the game away. Rather than offsetting the Source Time Shift in the Paint palette and redoing the stroke, it's easier to press PP then twirl until you see Stroke Options in the Timeline and scrub Clone Time Shift's value. The image will update in the Layer window. (Be aware that the footage is wrapping around itself. For instance, if you offset time by one second, the clip will wrap around to the head of the clip one second before the end.)

Step 4: This second flag is supposed to be in the rear, so reduce its size using the Clone 1>Transform>Scale value; reposition the stroke if necessary after scaling.

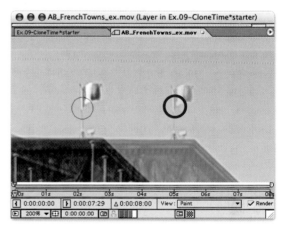

Step 2. Zoom in and sample the base of the original flag (red circle to the right), then clone a copy on top of the leftmost flagpole. Footage courtesy Artbeats/French Towns & Villages.

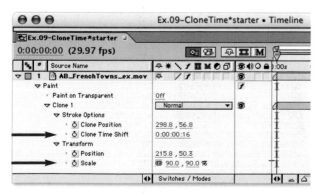

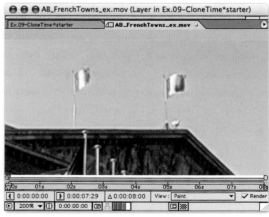

Steps 3–4: In the Timeline window (above), the cloned stroke was shifted in time and scaled down to push it to the rear (right).

The white boat in [**Ex.10**] is distracting and needs to be removed.

Step 1: Select Clone Preset 5 and pick a brush large enough to cover the boat (above). In the Layer window (below) select the water to the left of the boat (see red circle) as the clone source point, then remove the boat.

Tracking the Clone

While you can animate the position of a stroke as well as the clone source position, it's not easy to clone out an object that is moving at an irregular speed by simply setting keyframes. However, Motion Tracking (Professional edition only) excels at tracking an object from frame to frame. By combining both techniques, you can easily and accurately remove or duplicate a moving object.

Open the [**Ex.10-Tracking*starter**] comp and RAM Preview. The aerial footage of the Statue of Liberty is exactly what the clients want, but they find the white boat distracting and want it removed. In this section, you'll use motion tracking to determine the boat's location on each frame, then use a simple Expression to make the clone stroke follow the tracker data. We hope we've included enough instructions so you can follow along even if you're unfamiliar with Expressions or Motion Tracking (if not, please revisit this section after you've read Chapters 6 and 16 respectively; it should then make more sense).

Be aware that if you can't successfully remove or clone the object on a single frame, throwing the motion tracker at it won't help. The tracker excels at following a pattern of pixels – it can't work miracles and make unsuitable footage suddenly easy to clone!

Creating the Dummy Clone Stroke

In order for the Clone stroke to follow motion tracking data, you first need to create a stroke that is the right size to remove or clone your object:

Step 1: Double-click layer 1 – **AB_NewYorkCityAerials_ex.mov** – to open its Layer window, select the Clone Stamp tool, then select the fifth Clone Preset. You should know by now how to set up the Paint palette and Clone Options to create a simple clone stroke (if you don't, see *Using the Clone Stamp Tool* earlier in this chapter).

Note that the boat gets bigger before it exits the frame around 06:00, so select a brush tip that's a little larger than you need at time 00:00. We used a 50 pixel size brush with a 50% Hardness value. (Remember that you can save your current brush settings as a new brush tip by clicking on the "new layer" icon at the bottom of the Brush Tips palette.)

At time 00:00, press Option (Alt) and click on an area of clear water to the left of the boat to select a good source point, then clone some of this water over the boat. Make the stroke a little longer than you need to account for the fact that the boat will be bigger later on.

Tracking the Boat

The next step is to motion track the movement of the boat:

Step 2: Return to the Selection tool (shortcut V). Select Animation> Track Motion; this creates Tracking Region boxes in the Layer window, and the View will be set to Motion Tracker Points. The Tracker Controls palette will open, and a Motion Trackers section appears in the Timeline.

Step 3:   Track Point 1 defaults to the center of the Layer window (see **A** above). The inner box is the Feature Region (the "pattern" of pixels to be tracked); the outer box is the Search Region (the area to be searched for the defined pattern); the + symbol in the center is the Attach Point.

Zoom in, click inside the inner box (the Feature Region will zoom up), and drag the Feature Region so that it centers on the front tip of the boat (see **B** above). This takes a little practice; if you end up moving the Attach Point or enlarging one of the boxes, Undo and try again!

Step 4:   Motion tracking is normally used to attach a second layer to the footage being tracked, in which case the Attach Point (the + symbol) would be moved to where the anchor point of this second layer should be positioned. In this case, the Attach Point data will be used for the Clone Position, so move the attach point to the water to the left (see also caption for **C**). You can also set this value numerically by editing the Attach Point value in the Timeline. There's no need to resize the boxes.

Step 5:   Still at 00:00, click the Analyze Forward button in the Tracker Controls (see figures below). Although you can hit the Stop button in the Tracker Controls when the boat disappears off the bottom of the frame, we let it track to the end; you can always trim the out point for the clone stroke. When the track is done, keyframes will be created for each frame.

A: The default position for Track Point 1.

B: Moving the Feature Region.

C: Dragging the Attach Point to the left. This point will be the area of the water used for the start of the clone stroke; because the boat moves off the bottom of the frame, be sure the attach point is no lower in the frame than the tip of the boat, or it will move out of frame earlier.

Who's Up First

If you create the tracker first, the Layer window will be filled with tracker points when you try to clone. To hide the tracker interface, select Effect>Paint> Paint to preload Paint in the Layer window's View menu.

Step 5: Once the Feature Region and the Attach Point are in place, click the Analyze Forward button.

Step 5 – complete: When the track is complete, the Layer window (center) will show the path of the track (don't worry about the section at the end where the boat dipped out of the frame). The Timeline window (right) will show the data captured for Track Point 1.

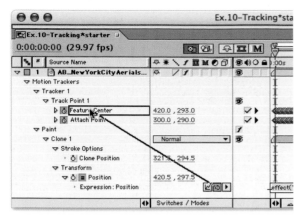

Step 6: Express the clone stroke's Position parameter to Track Point 1's Feature Center (left). Then express the Clone Position parameter to the tracker's Attach Point (right).

Hide Parameters

To simplify these figures, we hid unused parameters by pressing Option+Shift (Alt+Shift) and clicking on their names in the Timeline window.

Expressing the Clone Stroke

Step 6: Now it's time to make the clone stroke follow the tracker data. Reveal the Clone 1 and Tracker Point 1 sections in the Timeline window so you can see all of their parameters. With the Selection tool still active:

• Option+click (Alt+click) on the stopwatch for the Clone 1>Transform> Position parameter to start the expression, click on the pick whip (the spiral icon) and drag it to the Feature Center parameter in Track Point 1, then release the mouse. Press Enter to accept the expression.

• Option+click (Alt+click) on the stopwatch for the Clone 1>Stroke Options>Clone Position parameter, select its pick whip and drag it to the Attach Point parameter in Track Point 1. Press Enter to accept.

Bring the Comp window forward and RAM Preview; the boat should be removed throughout. We finished off our version [**Ex.10-Tracking_ final**] by fading out the stroke at 06:00.

Step 6 complete:
The expressions linking Clone 1's parameters to Track Point 1. The Clone stroke is faded out by animating Stroke Options>Opacity from 100% to 0%, starting at 06:00 when the boat disappears. The end of the stroke can also be trimmed.

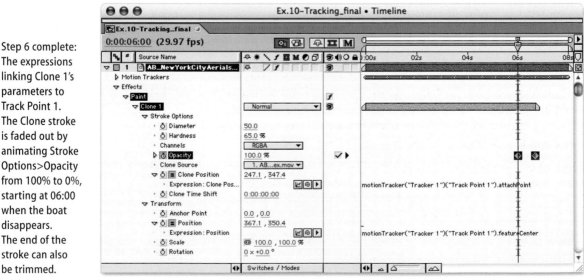

Random Paint Splatters

We'll finish our tour with a smattering of other issues and ideas for getting the best from Paint and Clone:

Painting in a straight line: To paint, erase, or clone in a straight line, click once at the start of the stroke, hold down the Shift key, move (don't drag) your mouse to where the line should end, and click again. A straight line stroke will be created. Continue holding Shift and clicking to paint additional straight line segments. Cloning in a straight line is handy for removing film scratches and so on. Practice this in [**Ex.11-StraightLine*starter**], where we've added a fake scratch at 02:00. (Tip: Set the Duration popup to Single Frame to create a one-frame stroke.)

Copy and Pasting Strokes: You can copy and paste Mask Shapes (or paths from Illustrator) to and from a stroke's Shape property. To do this, click on the Mask Shape property in the Timeline and Copy, then click on the stroke's Shape property and Paste. One example of animating a star-shaped stroke is in [**Ex.12**].

Cloning the Clone: The Clone Stamp tool samples from the cloned image. To use the original source, add a duplicate copy of your layer to the comp and select it in the Clone Options>Source popup.

Motion Tracking in Time: In [**Ex.10**], we showed using motion tracking and expressions to automate removing the boat by replacing it with the water texture. In other situations, such as removing a bird flying across the sky with a locked-down camera, you might be better off cloning from the same area of the sky but right before or after the bird flew by. To do this, in Step 6 express both the Position and Clone Position parameters to the Feature Region, then edit the Clone Time Shift value.

Revealing a Title: To use Paint to write on a layer with an alpha channel (such as a solid text layer or logo), paint over the text in Write On mode, enable Paint on Transparent, then apply Effect>Channels>Set Matte (at default settings) to reapply the original alpha channel. This is shown in [**Ex.13**], which is an excerpt from a tutorial in our companion book, *After Effects in Production*, 2nd Edition. (Note: If the text is textured, not solid, use the painted layer as an alpha track matte; see [**Ex.14**].)

Eyedropper Sampling: Option+click (Alt+click) to set the foreground color to the color currently under any paint tool pointer. To sample from a 5×5 pixel area, press Command+Option (Control+Alt). (Change this default in the text preferences file; see Chapter 31B, *Secret Preferences*.)

Opacity and Flow Shortcuts: Press a number from 1 through 9 on the keypad to set a painting tool's Opacity from 10% to 90%, respectively; press the decimal key for 100%. Add the Shift key to adjust Flow instead.

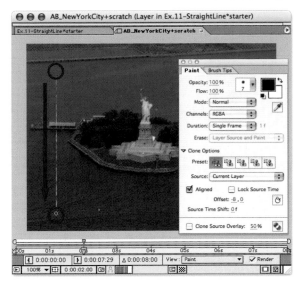

To repair this (fake) film scratch, create a straight line clone stroke with a slight horizontal Offset value or one-frame Source Time Shift.

Paint Shortcuts

For a full list of shortcuts for Paint and Clone, select Help> Keyboard Shortcuts>Using Paint Tools (6.5).

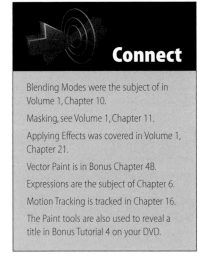

Connect

Blending Modes were the subject of in Volume 1, Chapter 10.

Masking, see Volume 1, Chapter 11.

Applying Effects was covered in Volume 1, Chapter 21.

Vector Paint is in Bonus Chapter 4B.

Expressions are the subject of Chapter 6.

Motion Tracking is tracked in Chapter 16.

The Paint tools are also used to reveal a title in Bonus Tutorial 4 on your DVD.

The Wiggler has several options over how a keyframe's parameters are randomized.

Easy Undo!

After you apply a keyframe assistant, immediately RAM Preview. If you don't like the result, you can easily Undo the new keyframes.

Simply Spatial

A common problem in getting The Wiggler to work is selecting keyframes that have position values on the X/Y/Z axes and wiggling with the Temporal option selected – try Spatial instead.

The Wiggler

The Wiggler is a nifty keyframe assistant that can impart a nervous – or, when used more subtly, a randomized or less perfect – quality to animations. It is most often used to automate the creation of jumpy titles by randomizing their position values, but it's also invaluable for creating random values or deviations for any property or effect.

The Wiggler keyframe assistant creates new keyframes between the first and last selected keyframes, randomly offset in value from where a parameter would normally be at each keyframe's point in time. You could say it adds bumps in the road as a value interpolates from one location to the next.

To use The Wiggler, make sure you select at least two keyframes (they can even be the same value), and select Window>The Wiggler (or click on its tab if it is already open). The Wiggler is not affected by the work area. Options include:

Apply To: The choices are Spatial and Temporal. Spatial is available only for properties that have an X and a Y axis: Position, Anchor Point, and Effects Point for all layers, and the Position and Point of Interest properties for Camera and Lights. All other properties are Temporal – in other words, values that change over time.

Noise Type: Choices are Smooth or Jagged. In practice, there is little noticeable difference for many parameters. The biggest change occurs with Position keyframes, where Jagged has "broken" linear path handles in and out of the spatial keyframes, compared with the more rounded motion of the tangential handles you get with Smooth. (We'll see in a moment how to change the keyframes interpolation type after the fact, so don't sweat this option.)

Dimension: Some properties, such as Opacity and Rotation, have only one parameter to change. If this is the case, the Dimension options are ignored. However, many properties – such as Position and Scale – have two dimensions (X and Y). You can choose if only one of them gets wiggled (and which one it is), if they both get wiggled The Same (same direction and same amount), or if they get wiggled Independently. All Dimensions Independently is a good default for Position, but for properties such as Scale, All Dimensions The Same is a better choice as it maintains the layer's aspect ratio.

Frequency: This is how often new keyframes are created, starting from the first selected keyframe. It can be thought of as the frame rate of the inserted keyframes. Note that if The Wiggler happens to encounter a keyframe between the first and last ones you selected (because it happened to be exactly where a new one would be created by the Frequency's timing), it will overwrite that keyframe's value. Only the values of the first and last keyframes remain unchanged.

Magnitude: How much do you want a parameter randomized by? The amount of change will fall within the range set here, with larger values resulting in bigger changes. If a property has natural limits (such as 0% and 100% for Opacity), these limits will clip the amount of change. If a property (such as Scale and Rotation) can go negative, The Wiggler will swing between positive and negative, rather than getting clipped at zero.

Wiggly Practice

• To practice some wiggler moves, open [**Ex.02a*starter**]. The layer **nervous.ai** has two Position keyframes with the same values applied at the beginning and end (select the layer and press U if these are not already visible).

• Click on the word Position in the Timeline to select both keyframes, and select Window>The Wiggler (or click on its tab if it is already open).

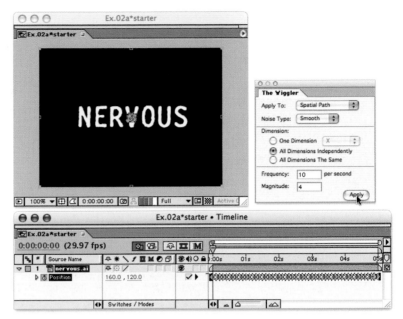

• After you have set your options, click Apply. If the Apply button is grayed out, make sure that you have at least two keyframes from the same property selected and that no other I-beams or keyframes from other properties are also part of the selection. After The Wiggler calculates the new keyframes, immediately render a RAM Preview. If you don't like the result, Undo and try again. It often takes a few tries to get it right. (Note that reapplying The Wiggler without undoing the first attempt will just further randomize the already-randomized keyframes you just created, so it's usually best to clear the first set of keyframes.)

Be sure to try out some different options. A high Frequency and low Magnitude (such as 15 and 4, respectively) are good starting points for a tight, buzzing nervousness. [**Ex.02a_final**] has some pre-wiggled keyframes for you to preview, but experimentation is the best path to understanding the effect. If layers are moving rapidly, they will benefit from some motion blur (to turn on Motion Blur, click the layer's M switch and the Enable Motion Blur button).

After you apply The Wiggler, you will have a multitude of keyframes that are difficult to edit. RAM Preview and immediately Undo if you didn't like the result, then try different settings.

Jagged Extreme

If the "jagged" Noise Type isn't jagged enough, select all the Wiggler-created keyframes and change them to Hold keyframes (Animation> Toggle Hold Keyframes).

Wiggling layers benefit from motion blur; check the layer's M switch and select the Enable Motion Blur button.

Customizing The Wiggler

The problem with The Wiggler is that the results often look too robotic. To introduce further randomness to wiggled animation:

• Consider wiggling with fairly tight values, then manually editing a few keyframes here and there to more extreme values. You can also add keyframes between those created by The Wiggler and move some keyframes in time to break up the pattern. These ideas are shown in [**Ex.02b**].

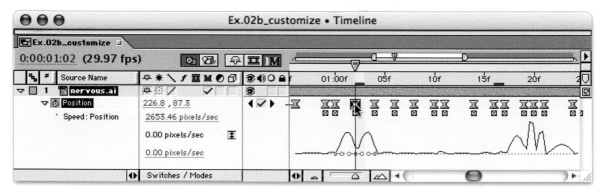

Break up The Wiggler pattern by editing select keyframes to values outside the Magnitude range, and move some keyframes in time.

You can change the keyframe interpolation type after The Wiggler has created its new keyframes. For example, if you're applying The Wiggler to Position keyframes, both the Smooth and Jagged options create Bezier keyframes for Temporal, and Continuous Bezier keyframes for Spatial. Because both options smoothly interpolate between keyframes, if you want a jagged animation, you'll need to change the interpolation type:

You're not limited to the Smooth or Jagged options for The Wiggler. Once you've applied the keyframe assistant, select the resulting keyframes and change them in the Keyframe Interpolation dialog.

• To change the Temporal Position keyframes to Linear, first select all the keyframes (click on the word Position in the Timeline), then Command+click on Mac (Control+click on Windows) on any keyframe in the Timeline to change them all to Linear. To change the spatial keyframes to Linear, use the same shortcut when you're clicking on any keyframe icon in the Comp window.

• For a really jagged animation, use Hold keyframes for no interpolation: Select all the keyframes, and Command+Option+click (Control+Alt+click) on one of them to change them all to Hold keyframes. You can also change the Spatial and/or Temporal interpolation using the Animation> Keyframe Interpolation dialog. (See Volume 1, Chapter 3 for a detailed description of each interpolation method.) Go ahead and experiment on the wiggled text you created in [**Ex.02a*starter**].

• Instead of using The Wiggler on Position keyframes, try using the Motion Sketch keyframe assistant (Volume 1, Chapter 3) – you'll usually get a more organic result since you're shaking the layer in realtime with your hand. One result is shown in [**Ex.02c**].

The Wiggle Expression

You also have the option of using an expression to do much the same thing as The Wiggler. The advantage of using an expression is that you can try out different values easily, and you don't end up with a bunch of keyframes to deal with. You can also easily toggle the expression on/off (click the = switch that appears to the right of the property stopwatch).

The disadvantage of the wiggle expression is that it defaults to continuing to randomize the layer past the last keyframe, so you need to add a fade-out to the expression to stop the layer wiggling. It's also tricky to maintain the aspect ratio when you're wiggling Scale. Refer to Chapter 7 for how to create and fade out the wiggle expression.

Quick Shakes

Remember that The Wiggler can be used to randomize values on any property or any parameter of any effect – don't limit yourself to just Position in 2D. Here are a few ideas, some of which have example comps for you to practice with:

• Close all open comps and open [**Ex.03_final**], where we've applied The Wiggler to a 3D layer. Solo and RAM Preview each layer separately. Notice that changes to the Z value of a layer make the layer move closer and farther away from the viewer, which is not unlike animating Scale in this instance. Try your own treatments with [**Ex.03*starter**].

• The alarm clock image in [**Ex.04*starter**] increases in size with two Scale keyframes; two Rotation keyframes with the same 0° values are set at the beginning and end. Try adding a little wiggle to the Scale (using All Dimensions The Same), but add a quick and larger wiggle to Rotation (the values will swing positive and negative). Turn on Motion Blur when you're done. Our version is in [**Ex.04_final**].

• In [**Ex.05*starter**], we applied a Directional Blur effect to a type layer. Select the Blur Length keyframes, and apply The Wiggler with a Magnitude of 10. If you step through the resulting keyframes, you'll probably find that many of them have a value of 0 – or no blur – which is not very exciting. With a Magnitude of 10, the values created would have ranged between –10 and +10. But since you can't have a negative blur value, any such keyframes were clipped at 0. In this case, you need to "seed" The Wiggler with different starting values.

Click the Blur Length stopwatch to delete all the keyframes. Let's say you decide that you'd like the Blur Length to range between 1 and 9. Use the center of this range (5) as your starting keyframe values, and use a Magnitude of 4 to create random keyframes within your desired range. Try this now, and compare your results with [**Ex.05_final**], where we added some Position wiggle for the full effect!

Smooth it Over

If The Wiggler result is too jagged for your taste, experiment with The Smoother keyframe assistant (see Volume 1, Chapter 3)

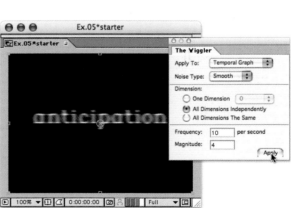

For parameters that can't render negative values, such as Blur Length, you need to "seed" The Wiggler with a value in the center of your desired range, and set Magnitude accordingly.

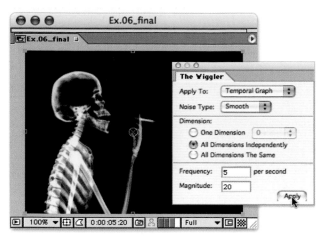

By wiggling Opacity values, you can introduce a luminance flicker to a layer. The seed keyframe values of 95%, with a magnitude of 20%, result in many keyframes that are clipped to 100%. Footage courtesy Digital Vision/Xposed.

• To apply a luminance jitter for an "old movie" effect, you could animate Opacity. Open comp [**Ex.06*starter**], set two keyframes for Opacity at 100%, select them, apply The Wiggler with a Magnitude of 50, and preview the result. Again, you'll probably find that the resulting keyframes are not random enough, with many keyframes clipping at 100%.

If you don't want any clipping, you'll need to work out a range for Opacity to span, create keyframes with the value at the center of this range, and set the Magnitude appropriately. For example, to have Opacity range from 60% to 100%, set keyframes at 80% with a Magnitude of 20%. Experiment to get a look you like.

Our example, [**Ex.06_final**], uses a seed value of 95% which causes the opacity to occasionally "clip" at 100 – an effect that makes it seem like the projector's light bulb is merely flickering. You can also apply this trick to the Intensity property of a 3D Light for another flickering effect!

Repositioning a Wiggling Layer

If you're wiggling Position keyframes for a layer, you won't be able to easily reposition this layer in the Comp window because moving the layer will likely change only one keyframe. Here are a couple of workarounds that can help:

• Select all the Position keyframes and use the arrow keys to nudge the entire layer by one screen pixel (press Shift for 10 screen pixels).

• Add a Null Object (Layer>New>Null Object), place it on top of the wiggling layer in the Comp window, and parent the wiggling layer to the null. Now when you move or otherwise transform the null object, the wiggling layer follows. [**Ex.07a**] shows this setup.

• In [**Ex.07b**], the Position parameter in the Distort>Transform effect was wiggled. This frees up the regular Position keyframes for animation.

To easily reposition a layer with wiggling Position keyframes, add a new Null Object as a parent, as in [**Ex.07a**].

• You could apply The Wiggler in a separate precomp, then do the overall animation in a second comp. This is shown in the [**Ex.08**] folder.

Keyframe Assistants from Third Parties

Digital Anarchy/3D Assistants

www.digitalanarchy.com

Digital Anarchy's 3D Assistants are designed for arranging 3D layers in cubes, cylinders, rings, matrices, spheres, and more. The 3D Assistants set includes 10 assistants along with six simplified Lite versions. Three of these Lite assistants – Box Creator Lite, Cubic Distribution Lite, and Cylinder Creator Lite – are included on your After Effects 6.5 installer CD.

To get a taste for how these assistants work, let's take a look at Box Creator Lite, which can instantly arrange layers into a cube. Open **[Ex.99*starter]**, where we've created six colored solid layers that will form the sides of a cube. We've set their 3D Layer switches on, pointed a Camera at them, and turned on the Advanced 3D Renderer (Composition Settings>Advanced tab). Select the solids (layers 1 through 6) and apply Window>Box Creator Lite, check the Scale Layers to Fit option, and click Apply. Our result is shown in **[Ex.99a]**. To animate the cube as a group, add a Null Object as a parent as shown in **[Ex.99b]**. Note that you can upgrade to the full set of 3D Assistants on the Digital Anarchy web site.

Useful Assistants can create a web gallery of images based on frames in your comp using various criteria.

Profound Effects/Useful Assistants

www.profoundeffects.com

At press time, Profound Effects had released version 1.6 of Useful Assistants, a set of over 100 keyframe assistants (with dozens more available for free from the Profound eXchange). Useful Assistants help automate dozens of tedious and time-consuming tasks related to importing, setting and editing keyframes, creating and arranging layers, exporting data, rendering, and so on. You get tools that automatically place markers where cuts in a layer are detected, reverse the direction of a mask, sequence and fade layers in numerous ways, and create a contact sheet of frames from throughout a comp (see above). You can create presets for the assistants, and assemble presets into sequences to perform more complex tasks.

Available free from the Profound Effects web site is a handy assistant called Reveal, which allows you to search for and select comps, footage, and other items in the current project that match the specified search criteria. For example, you could search through your project for all layers with a certain effect applied.

Box Creator Lite can create a cube from up to six 3D layers.

The red shape uses the default keyframe interpolation in After Effects. The green shape on top has been processed by the Smart Mask Interpolation keyframe assistant.

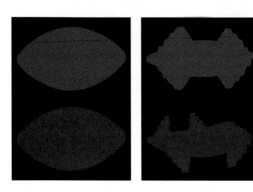

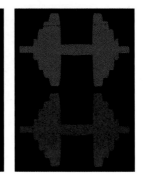

Smart Mask Interpolation (SMI)

When you animate a mask shape, After Effects guesses the best way to morph one shape into the next. The results are often not what you had in mind. The Smart Mask Interpolation keyframe assistant helps shepherd After Effects down more desirable paths.

To get a taste, close all comps and open [**Ex.09*starter**], which contains two copies of a football mask shape keyframed to change into a set of hand weights. RAM Preview; in the middle of the interpolation, the shape looks like a prehistoric fish. Make sure the Mask Shape keyframes for the **green shape** layer are revealed (if they aren't, select the layer and type U), and click on Mask Shape to select them. Then open Animation> Keyframe Assistant>Smart Mask Interpolation. Click Apply and wait for a few seconds as the keyframe assistant calculates new mask points and keyframes (progress is shown in the Info palette). Now RAM Preview: The **green shape** layer morphs through more predictable shapes, as shown in [**Ex.09_final**].

Smart Mask Interpolation yields these better results by changing the points (vertices) along the mask, creating more intermediate keyframes that use these extra points in order to keep After Effects on the desired path.

The Smart Approach

Smart Mask Interpolation's settings reside in their own floating palette, akin to The Wiggler. To open it (as of version 6), select Window>Smart Mask Interpolation. It defaults to showing a shortened set of parameters; to reveal the entire set, either click on the arrow in its upper right corner and select Show Options, or click on the up/down arrows to the left of its name until you get a taller display. The parameters generally fall into three areas of control: frame rate, interpolation, and vertex placement.

Keyframe Rate: Controls how often new keyframes are created. The default is one per frame. More keyframes mean a more controlled interpolation; if you become overwhelmed, try reducing the rate. Regardless of this setting, SMI will also always create additional keyframes just after the first and before the last keyframes you set, which it uses to establish its additional mask shape vertices (discussed below). If you're field rendering, set Keyframe Rate to the frame rate used for

Click on the up/down arrows (circled in red) to collapse and expand the Smart Mask Interpolation parameters; the full complement is shown above. The defaults often need tweaking for special cases or to improve overall quality.

rendering, and enable Keyframe Fields. Otherwise, you will get odd shape jumps at the start and end of interpolation.

There is a set of three parameters which influence whether SMI follows a curvy, organic path or a more rigid, geometric one:

Use Linear Vertex Paths: When this is enabled, SMI will move all of the mask points in a straight line between its first and last keyframes. Sometimes this is too rigid; disabling this option allows the interpolation to follow more organic curved paths. However, disabling it can cause wild swings in the mask shape; try for yourself with [**Ex.10*starter**] or RAM Preview the result in [**Ex.10_final**].

Bending Resistance: Decides how fluid the mask shape is during interpolation. Lower settings allow the shapes to bend more; higher settings maintain more rigid, geometric shapes. The default of 50% is a good compromise.

Matching Method: Leaving it at Auto works most of the time; change it only if you're having problems. Use the Curve setting for organic interpolations; Polyline for more rigid ones.

The other parameters control how many intermediate mask points (vertices) the assistant creates, and how it interpolates between them:

First Vertices Match: Keeping this enabled is crucial for having interpolations proceed in a predictable manner. Just as critical is where the first vertex is for each of your mask shapes. Set the first vertex (the one with a slightly larger square) to locations where you know you want "point A" to end up at "point B" (the first vertex tends to serve as the "anchor" for the interpolating shapes). To practice changing the first vertex for a mask shape, open [**Ex.13a_mask shapes**], select a single mask point at the base of each shape, and choose Layer>Mask>Set First Vertex.

Quality and Use 1:1 Vertex Matches: These decide how the rest of the mask vertices interpolate. Usually, you want to let SMI decide how to move one vertex to another; that means disabling Use 1:1 Vertex Matches, and if necessary, increasing Quality.

Add Mask Shape Vertices: The more mask vertices, the more accurate the interpolation (at the cost of slightly longer calculation times). Enabling this allows SMI to create additional vertices. To precisely set the number of vertices created, set the popup underneath to Total Vertices and adjust the number to its left.

Along the Curve

Having shapes interpolate in a more curvy, organic fashion or rotate as they move requires deviating from the default settings. Close all open comps, open [**Ex.11*starter**] and RAM Preview. We started with a "C" character shape (keyframe 2) and rotated the mask 180° with Free Transform

It is important to set the First Vertex (noted by the slightly larger mask point) to a similar reference point on each mask shape, such as a point centered on the top or bottom.

Inside-Out Interpolation

If a shape interpolates inside out, as in [**Ex.14**], you may need to reverse the path of the offending shape. Select the mask shape keyframe, copy, paste into Illustrator, use Object>Compound Path>Make, reverse the path direction in the Attributes palette (below), copy, and paste back to After Effects.

To allow shapes to rotate or otherwise follow more organic paths, disable Use Linear Vertex Paths. The blue shape is the result of a linear interpolation; the green shape rotates thanks to disabling this option.

Speed Shifts

Smart Mask ignores your original keyframe interpolation. To add ease in and out to the result, set the first and second-to-last keyframes to Hold, and precompose (with Move All Attributes on). Enable Time Remapping for the nested comp layer in the main comp. Use this to retime the shape morph. See **[Ex.15]** for more tips to avoid glitches.

Points (keyframe 1). With the default interpolation, it inverts itself as it animates, looking not unlike a scale animation.

• Reveal the Mask Shape keyframes for the second layer, select them, and apply Smart Mask Interpolation with Use Linear Vertex Paths enabled. RAM Preview; you get a surprisingly similar result.

• Undo until the new keyframes are gone, disable the Use Linear Vertex Paths option, and click Apply again. RAM Preview; now the shape rotates instead of inverts, but the shape spins with an offset.

• Undo again and this time set the Add Mask Vertices popup to Total Vertices (the default of 100 is fine). Click Apply; with more vertices added for accuracy, the character stays centered as it rotates. The result is shown in [**Ex.11_final**].

Straight and Narrow

When you have strong, angular geometric shapes, you need to set up Smart Mask Interpolation to be stiffer to keep these shapes intact. Open [**Ex.12*starter**] and RAM Preview. Here we've set up three copies of the letter L morphing to the letter Z. Layer 1 is our reference of the normal interpolation, and so we've locked it for safekeeping. Select the Mask Shape keyframes for layer 2 by clicking on the word Mask Shape, enable the Use Linear Vertex Paths option in Smart Mask Interpolation, and apply. Scrub the time marker; the movement is pretty good!

Now select the Mask Shape keyframes for layer 3, disable Use Linear Vertex Paths, and apply SMI. As you scrub or RAM Preview, note how the top of the blue character grows as it morphs, extending above the pale blue guide line. Undo until your new keyframes are gone, try increasing Bending Resistance or setting the Matching Method to Polyline, and reapply: These "stiffen" techniques help, but unless Use Linear Vertex paths is enabled, the top of the character still wants to grow. The three results are displayed in [**Ex.12_final**].

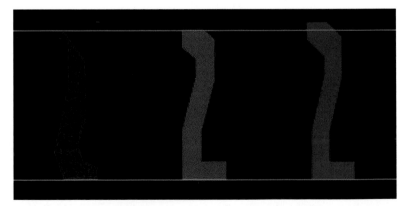

The red shape is the result of normal interpolation. The green shape uses Smart Mask Interpolation with Use Linear Vertex Paths enabled; the top of the interpolated shape does not grow beyond the height of the original shapes (the blue line). The blue shape has Linear Vertex disabled; it is more fluid, but does not stay "in bounds."

A Final Test

We leave you with a final exercise to practice with. If you have Adobe Illustrator 8 or higher, open the file **Shapes.ai** in the **05_Chapter Sources** folder, select the bell shape, and paste it as a mask shape onto **Solid 1** in [**Ex.13*starter**]. Enable keyframing for Mask Shapes, move to the end of the comp, then paste in the guitar shape. (If you don't have Illustrator, open [**Ex.13a**] where we have done this for you.) Now try to get a good morph between these shapes using Smart Mask Interpolation. Don't forget to set the first vertex in a compatible location, increase the number of Mask Shape Vertices to get a better morph, and balance off the various stiff-versus-organic parameters discussed earlier. Our result (with clues) is in [**Ex.13_final**]. In general, you may not be able to get a perfect morph, but this keyframe assistant is a big help.

[Ex.13] contains a Smart Mask Interpolation exercise for you to try: morphing a bell to the outline of a guitar.

Keyframe Assistants Roundup

After Effects 6.5 ships with a variety of keyframe assistants. Generally, assistants that include options have a floating palette interface and are available from the Window menu (these are shown with an * below). The other assistants execute when they're applied and are listed under the Animation>Keyframe Assistant menu. Assistants tend to be grayed out unless certain criteria have been met – such as selecting more than one keyframe for The Wiggler to act on, or selecting Scale keyframes for Exponential Scale to interpolate between. Here is a mini-index of where the various assistants are covered:

Standard edition:

Align & Distribute *	Volume 1, Chapter 6
Convert Audio to Keyframes	Chapter 6
Convert Expression to Keyframes	Chapter 6
Easy Ease	Volume 1, Chapter 3
Motion Sketch *	Volume 1, Chapter 3
The Smoother *	Volume 1, Chapter 3
Sequence Layers	Volume 1, Chapter 7
Time-Reverse Keyframes	Volume 1, Chapter 3

Professional edition only:

Exponential Scale	(this chapter)
The Wiggler *	(this chapter)
Maya Import	Chapter 19
RPF Camera Import	Chapter 19
Motion Stabilizer	Chapter 15
Motion Tracker	Chapter 16
Smart Mask Interpolation	(this chapter)

Connect

Animating Position was covered in Volume 1, Chapter 3, including Hold keyframes.

Rotation, Scale, and Opacity were animated in Volume 1, Chapter 4.

Motion Blur: See Volume 1, Chapter 9.

Masking – including copy and pasting mask shapes between After Effects and Illustrator – was unmasked in Volume 1, Chapter 11.

Animating in 3D, see Volume 1, Chapter 14.

Parenting and null objects were covered in Volume 1, Chapter 17.

Building chains of compositions through nesting and precomposing was covered in Volume 1, Chapters 18 and 19.

Effects basics: See Volume 1, Chapter 21.

Continuously Rasterizing Illustrator art was discussed in Chapter 3.

Expressions are covered in Chapter 6.

Time Remapping is covered in Chapter 13.

6 Express Yourself

Expressions hold the key to animating repetitive tasks or complex relationships.

Creating expressions – the ability to tell one parameter to follow another, stay at a constant value, or create new values as the result of ingenious calculations – is one of the most powerful features in After Effects. For many, it is also one of the most daunting: To get the most out of it, you have to deal with math and what looks suspiciously like computer programming. In this chapter, we'll show you how to make expressions work for you with minimal effort (and math); a bonus chapter on the DVD dives in deeper for those who want to move to the next level.

If you're an artist with an aversion to math and technical issues, you should not shun expressions because of their technical nature: They can save you time and help you avoid tedious tasks. The most common uses require no knowledge of computer programming and only the most basic math skills, such as "times 2" and "divided by 100."

If you are a programmer who can't wait to dig deeper, you will be interested to know that expressions are based on the JavaScript language – including many of JavaScript's methods – with extensions that take After Effects properties into account. As there are many books thicker than this one dedicated strictly to teaching JavaScript, it is not our intention to provide a computer programming manual here, but to explain uses for some of the more interesting pieces of the Expressions language.

Our study of expressions will be broken into three sections:

Introductory Expressions: What expressions do, how to apply (and remove) them, and some of their more common applications, presented in a tutorial manner. If you already have experience using expressions, you can probably skim or skip this section.

Deeper Modes of Expression: A bonus chapter that exists as a PDF on your DVD, this section dives into more detail, highlighting some choice sections of the expression language and demonstrating how you might use them. If you are not looking to write advanced expressions right now, you can set this section aside until later.

Expressive Tricks: A walk through several practical examples at the end of this chapter that pull together the different concepts explained in this chapter and in the bonus chapter on the DVD.

Revealing Expressions

To reveal expressions, select one or more layers, and type EE (two Es in quick succession). Typing U reveals both keyframes and properties with expressions.

Example Project

Explore the 06-Example Project.aep file as you read this chapter; references to [Ex.##] refer to specific compositions within the project file. Enable Preferences>General> Expression Pick Whip Writes Compact English while working through this chapter.

Introductory Expressions

Expressions can be thought of as an alternative to keyframes. You can apply an expression to virtually any property that you can keyframe. The expression will then create a value for this property, often by looking at the values of other properties (such as basing the Scale of one layer on its own Rotation, or on the Opacity of another layer). You can also combine expressions and keyframes – to add, for example, a slightly random wiggle to an already-keyframed motion path.

Expressions are very flexible, and are especially useful when you want to set up master/slave relationships between multiple layers – to be able to change one master color, for example, and have it affect several other layers or effect properties at once. Think of expressions as tireless assistants helping you on your project: Teach them once what it is you need done, and they copy your work or follow your instructions for as many other layers or effects as you need. In general, this is the trade-off expressions present: If you can spare the extra time up front needed to create them, they'll save you time later.

Enabling and Disabling

First, let's go through the basics of creating, enabling, and disabling expressions. Open the project file **06-Example Project.aep**, twirl open the folder **Ex.01** in its Project window, then double-click [**Ex.01*starter**]. It contains two wheels, one of which has already been keyframed to rotate. Select both layers, and type R to reveal their Rotation properties in the Timeline window – note that Rotation keyframes have been set for the **Wheel 2** layer, but not for **Wheel 1**.

Before we show you how to make **Wheel 1** follow **Wheel 2**'s rotation using an expression, first you need to learn how to apply and disable expressions, and what to do when they break.

There are three ways to enable expressions for a property. Try any of these on Rotation for **Wheel 1**. We favor the third approach:

- Select the property (not just the layer) by clicking on it in the Timeline window, and use the menu command Animation>Add Expression.

- Select the property, and type Option+Shift+= (equals sign) on the Mac (Alt+Shift+= on Windows).

- Option+click (Alt+click) on the property's animation stopwatch in the Timeline window.

After you have done any of the above, an equals sign (=) will appear between the stopwatch and the name of the property (in our case, Rotation), and the value for this property will turn red (see figure on the next page). A line will be added below this that has the words "Expression : Rotation". To the right of this in the timeline, you will see a line of text has appeared that says "rotation" – this is a default expression that says you have now made Rotation equal rotation. Press Enter on the numeric keypad to accept this expression. You can also click almost anywhere else in

Deeper Modes of Expression

For those who want to learn more about expressions, we've included a bonus chapter on your DVD called *Deeper Modes of Expression*. Look for it in the **Bonus Chapters** folder; it includes a PDF file and its own Example Project. This bonus chapter examines important sections of the expression language in greater detail. We will use many of the tricks demonstrated there in the advanced examples at the end of this chapter. Even if you don't have a desire to write code, there are a number of useful expression "modules" and Animation Presets discussed in the bonus chapter that you can reuse in your own projects. Beyond using expressions is writing scripts to control what After Effects does. This is discussed in a large sidebar at the end of this chapter.

When you first enable expressions for a property, After Effects automatically writes a default expression that makes the property equal to itself – in this case, Rotation = rotation. To accept an expression, hit Enter (not Return).

Click on the = symbol to temporarily disable an expression. The = will change to a ≠, and the property's value will revert from red to blue. Click again to re-enable the expression.

the window, and it will have the same effect. Don't hit Return; it will just start a new line for you to write a more detailed expression.

Rotation = rotation is a pretty boring expression; let's work on that. To edit an expression, select the expression's text – in this case, the word **rotation**. The text defaults to being highlighted when you create a new expression, or first click on the expression text. Type in a number that you want Rotation to equal, such as "**45**", and hit Enter. (Don't type "**= 45**" – the equals sign is assumed, and you'll get an error.) **Wheel 1** will jump to a 45° angle in the Comp window, and you will see that its value has changed to 45 in the Timeline window. Note again that the property's value is displayed in red: This is a clue that an expression is setting this parameter.

To disable an expression, click on the = sign between the stopwatch and the property's name; it changes to a ≠ symbol. As you do this for **Wheel 1**, note how the wheel jumps back to its original rotational value before you applied an expression, and that the color of this value returns to blue (or whatever color you have your Preferences>Display>Hot Text Color set to). Click on the ≠ symbol, and it's enabled again. Most expressions *replace* the value normally assigned to a layer, although it is possible to write ones that *add* to this initial value – we'll discuss that later.

You can apply expressions to properties that have keyframes, as well. Try the above tricks with **Wheel 2**. Many people like to use simple expressions just like this one to temporarily override a layer's keyframes with a single value (such as Rotation = 45° here, or Opacity = 100% for a layer that's fading in and out) to help them sort out what's happening in a complex project.

If you want to hide an expression, twirl up its property in the Timeline window. To reveal it again, select the layer and type either EE (two Es in quick succession) to reveal just expressions, or U, which reveals keyframes plus any properties that have expressions attached.

To delete an expression, do the same thing as you would to create one: Option+click (Alt+click) on either the stopwatch or = sign, select the property and use Animation>Remove Expression or type Option+Shift+= (Alt+Shift+=), or delete the expression text and hit Enter.

Breaking Expressions

Expressions are easy to break. You will encounter this often, so let's get over the shock factor now. All that happens when you break an expression is that it is disabled; you can fix it and re-enable it. You won't crash; you won't lose any work.

First, a gotcha: Still in [**Ex.01*starter**], with an expression enabled for **Wheel 1**'s Rotation to set it to 45°, try to scrub or edit its red parameter

Convert Audio to Keyframes

Before there was Expressions, the Professional edition of After Effects featured a roll-your-own Keyframe Assistant called Motion Math. Two of its most-used scripts were Layer Audio (layeraud.mm) and Comp Audio (compaud.mm), which converted the amplitude of audio in your project into keyframes. The resulting keyframes were a wonderful thing to drive expressions, creating animations that pulse in sympathy with your audio.

After Effects now features a Keyframe Assistant called Convert Audio to Keyframes which performs the same job as Comp Audio. To use it, open a composition that features audio, and choose Animation> Keyframe Assistant>Convert Audio to Keyframes. Try this for yourself in **[Ex.20*starter]**. A null object named **Audio Amplitude** will be added to your comp;

select it and press U to reveal its keyframes. It will have Slider Controls that represent the left channel, right channel, and left+right mix of the audio in your composition. If you have more than one layer with audio in a comp, and don't want to convert the audio levels of all of them, turn off the Audio switch for the unwanted layers before running this assistant.

In **[Ex.20_final]**, we've tied the resulting keyframes to the Scale of a rotating gizmo, and the Opacity of one of the background layers. You may notice that the resulting animation has a "nervous" quality from trying to follow the volume changes very closely. You can try running Window>The Smoother on the keyframes, or use Trapcode's SoundKeys (www.trapcode.com), which is a more sophisticated tool for converting sound to keyframes.

value. It appears you can edit it, but as soon as you are done, Rotation's value will change back to 45°. Guess it had no effect, eh? Not quite: Click on the = sign to temporarily disable the expression, and you will see that After Effects remembered the new value you entered. This is a feature, as expressions can modify a parameter's original or keyframed value; just make sure you don't accidentally edit a value you wanted to keep! Re-enable the expression by clicking on the ≠ symbol.

(Those who tinkered with expressions in previous versions may remember that After Effects would give you an error and disable expressions when you did this; it is more user-friendly now.)

Let's do something more problematic: Select the expression text, and instead of typing in a number, type in a word such as "**ten**" and hit Enter (not Return).You will get an error dialog, with a warning that is probably incomprehensible to most nonprogrammers. The clues to look for are words in single quotation marks (in this case, it mentions the 'ten' you just typed), and the line number the error occurred on (which will help later as you write more complex multiline expressions).

Click OK; the expression will be disabled; it can't be re-enabled until you fix your error. Either replace **ten** with a value like **45**, or hit Command+Z (Control+Z) to undo until you are back to where you were before creating the error.

Frozen Expression

Using expressions to temporarily set an animating property to a constant value is a handy tool when you're trying to sort out a complex animation.

Expression error dialogs can be baffling to nonprogrammers at first. Major hints include words inside quotes, and the line number the error happened on. You can always undo back to where you were before making the error.

Pick Whipping for Pleasure

After Effects does what it can to make writing expressions easier. The best tool for this is the *pick whip*, which allows you to literally connect one property to another.

To reduce potential confusion, close comp [**Ex.01*starter**] and open [**Ex.02*starter**], which is essentially the same composition. Select the two layers and type R to reveal their Rotation properties. Rotation has already been keyframed for **Wheel 2**; say you want **Wheel 1** to have the same animation. You could copy and paste keyframes from one to the other, or you could use expressions:

Option+click (Alt+click) on the Rotation animation stopwatch for **Wheel 1** to enable expressions (remember, the expression is applied to the layer that will be the slave, not the master). Note that three new icons appear in the Timeline window between the words "Expression : Rotation" and the expression text. The middle one (which looks like a spiral) is the pick whip tool. Click on it, and with the mouse held down, drag to the word "Rotation" for **Wheel 2** (remember you want the property name, *not* the layer name). An outline box will appear around the word "Rotation", confirming you have selected it. Release the mouse, and After Effects will write the resulting expression for you:

thisComp.layer("Wheel 2").rotation

To link one property to another, enable expressions for a layer, and use the pick whip tool (the spiral icon) to connect it to another property (below). After Effects will automatically write the correct expression to link the two (bottom).

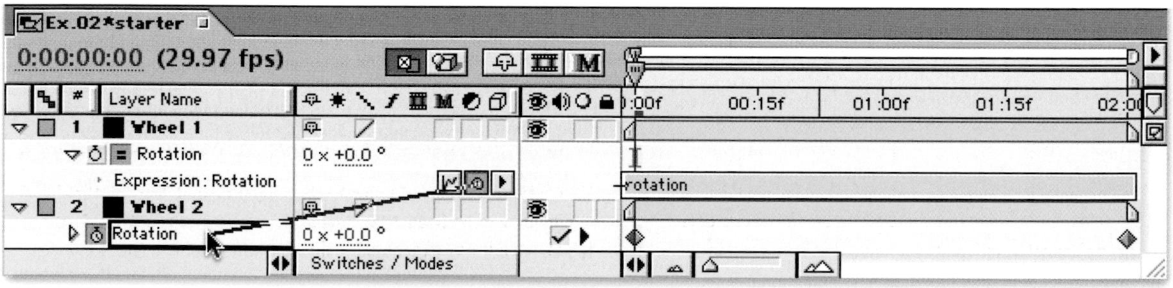

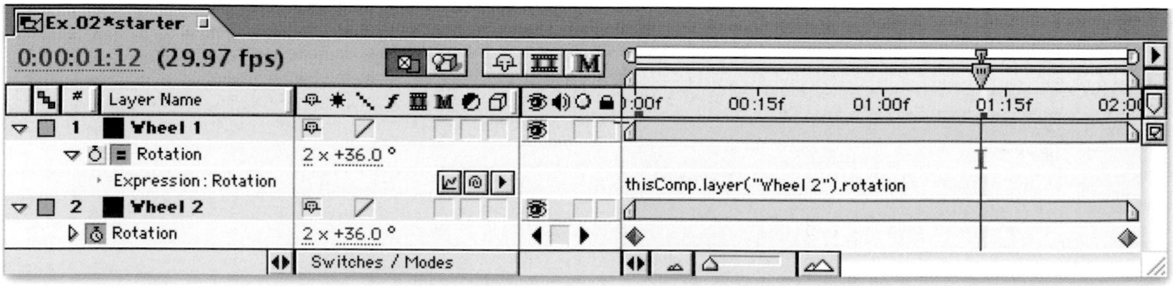

Seems like a lot of text, but actually it is quite logical: It states that in this comp, there is a layer called Wheel 2, and we want to use its Rotation. Some may find this easier to read backward: Take the Rotation, of a layer called Wheel 2, that is in this comp. Either way, the periods mark important breaks in the syntax as you read an expression. Using the pick whip tool relieves you of having to type this in yourself, avoiding both tedium and the chances for typos or other errors.

Hit Enter to accept the expression and either scrub the timeline or RAM Preview; both wheels will now rotate the same. The advantage of expressions over keyframing is you can now change the keyframe values of **Wheel 2**, and **Wheel 1** will automatically follow without needing to copy and paste keyframes again; also, editing velocity curves for the master layer will update the slave layer. Go ahead and try this yourself.

That's a nice time-saver, but there's a problem: If two wheels touched – as they do in this comp – they would rotate in opposite directions from each other. Also, because **Wheel 1** is twice the size of **Wheel 2**, **Wheel 1** should rotate only half as fast as **Wheel 2**. If you were keyframing normally, it would be time to drag out the calculator. With expressions, you can let After Effects be the calculator.

Select the expression text field for **Wheel 1**, and place the cursor at the end of the line (hitting the down arrow is a good shortcut). Then add to the end of the text:

* –1 / 2

The * –1 means times minus one, which will make **Wheel 1** go in the opposite direction. The / 2 means divided by two, which will make it rotate half as fast. Hit Enter and RAM Preview, and the resulting animation should now look correct. The finished version is shown in [**Ex.02_final**]. Again, you can edit the Rotation keyframes for **Wheel 2**, and **Wheel 1** will automatically adjust itself to match.

Math Symbols

Expressions use slightly different math symbols than those on a calculator. The first column is the standard symbol; the second is what to use for expressions:

+	+	**add**
–	–	**subtract**
×	*	**multiply**
÷	/	**divide**

More complex math operations, such as "add-and-increment" or "modulus," are discussed in **Bonus Chapter 06B** on your DVD.

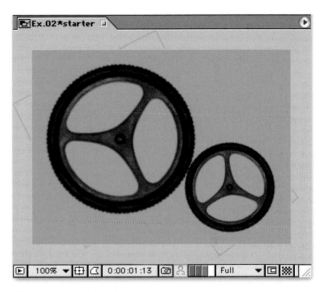

When two wheels touch (above), they should rotate in opposite directions, with their speed depending on their relative sizes. It's easy to have expressions do this math for you (below).

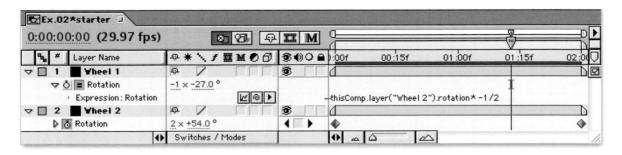

Going Backward

To reverse the direction a value proceeds in, either add "* –1" afterward (such as **rotation * –1**), or add a minus sign to the front of the value (such as **–rotation**).

To create an expression that varies Opacity as Rotation animates, we can use the pick whip to tie the two parameters together, then use additional modifiers to spread the value range of one property over the value range of the other.

Crossing Signals

Expressions may also be used to link disparate properties – for example, to have the Rotation control Opacity. To test this, open [**Ex.03*starter**] and RAM Preview: It contains one of our now-familiar wheels, rocking back and forth. Select **CM_bikewheel**, and type R to reveal its Rotation, followed by Shift+T to also reveal Opacity.

Option+click (Alt+click) on the stopwatch for Opacity to enable expressions, then use the pick whip to connect this property to Rotation. After Effects will automatically enter **rotation** as the expression for Opacity's value (there is no need for **thisComp** and the other verbiage you saw in [**Ex.02**], because After Effects always assumes you are talking about the current layer unless the expression says otherwise). Hit Enter, and either RAM Preview or drag the time marker; the wheel's opacity varies to match its rotation. Note that on frame 20, for instance, the wheel's Rotation is 57.8°, and its Opacity is 57.8% (rounded up to 58% for display purposes).

The problem is, Rotation is varying between –120° and +120°, while Opacity is restricted to a range of 0% to 100%. This won't cause the expression to break; After Effects will internally limit Opacity to not go below 0% or above 100%. But you can do a little work to make the expression more useful.

Say you want the wheel to start to become visible as soon as it rotates away from the first keyframe, at –120° (in other words, you want –120° rotation to equal 0% opacity). To accomplish this, place your cursor after the word **rotation** in the expression field, then type "+ 120" and hit Enter. At time 00:00, a value of –120 Rotation results in an Opacity value of 0%, and the wheel will be visible for a longer portion of the comp.

Before moving on, let's improve this expression just a little more. At this point, Opacity is reaching 100% well before the second Rotation keyframe is reached. Say you want to spread the 0 to 100 swing in Opacity over the entire –120 to +120 swing in Rotation. This requires a little more thought, as you are asking the expression to perform multiple modifications. You can use parentheses to tell After Effects which modification to do first. In this case, edit the expression to say:

(rotation + 120) / 240 * 100

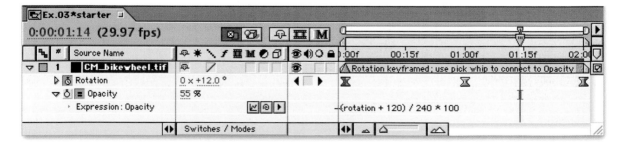

The parentheses tell After Effects to first add the 120° offset to the Rotation parameter. Then to divide the result by 240 (the total swing in Rotation), and multiply it by 100 (the total swing in Opacity). The result is shown in [**Ex.03_final**]. The careful use of parentheses is a good technique to help sort out expressions that aren't quite doing what you want.

Linking Effects and Transformations

Of course, you can link different parameters across different layers – even to layers in different comps! What gets really interesting is linking effect properties to each other, or to a layer's transformations.

Select Window>Close All to reduce clutter, open [**Ex.04*starter**], and RAM Preview. This demonstrates a common animation problem: The wheel is rotating, and a Drop Shadow effect has been applied to the wheel. However, because transformations such as Rotation are processed *after* effects, the shadow rotates as well. As it turns out, you can use expressions to cause the shadow angle to rotate in the opposite direction of the layer's rotation, stabilizing the final result.

To use the pick whip to create an expression, you have to reveal the properties you plan to pick whip between. The brute-force way to do this is to select the layer **CM_bikewheel**, hit E to reveal its effects in the Timeline window, twirl down Drop Shadow's properties, then type Shift+R to also reveal Rotation. This quickly fills up the Timeline window. If you are adding an expression to an effect parameter, try this approach instead: Select **CM_bikewheel** and type R to reveal Rotation in the Timeline window. Then hit F3 to open this layer's Effect Controls window. Option+click (Alt+click) on the stopwatch for Direction; this will enable expressions for Direction and reveal this property in the Timeline window.

In the Timeline window, drag the pick whip for Direction to Rotation. You need the shadow to rotate in the opposite direction, so type " * –1" at the end, and hit Enter. RAM Preview; the shadow remains stationary, but it's in the wrong place! This is because expressions normally *replace* a parameter's original value: in this case, 135°. To fix this, add " + 135" onto the end of the expression. Or instead of manually entering the value for the direction angle, type " + **value**" which tells After Effects to add the parameter's original value to the

Expression Offset

To have an expression add itself to a property's current value, add "+ value" to the end of the expression.

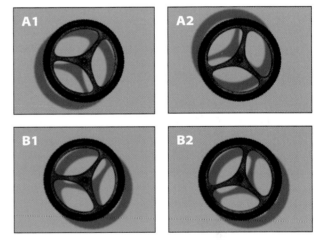

If you animate Rotation and add a Drop Shadow, the shadow will rotate as well (A1–2). To keep the shadow stationary, add an expression (below) to the shadow's Direction that rotates it in the opposite direction as Rotation is animating (B1–2).

Ex.04*starter				

0:00:00:25 (29.97 fps)

#	Source Name		:00f	00:15f	01:00f	01:15f	02:0
▽ □ 1	**CM_bikewheel.tif**						
	▽ ◎ ☰ Direction	0 x –165.0 °					
	▸ Expression : Direction		rotation *–1 + value				
	▷ ◎ Rotation	0 x +300.0 °	◆				◆

Interpolating This to That

Quite often, you will need to match up two different ranges of values, as we have in **[Ex.03]**. You can figure out the math required to do this, or have expressions do that math for you.

After Effects features a group of *interpolation* expression methods (a "method" refers to a bit of expression code that takes a set of values inside parentheses, and comes up with a new value for you). Not to be confused with keyframe interpolation, these methods make it easy to match one range of numbers to another. Take this expression:

linear(rotation, -120, 120, 0, 100)

This says "take the rotation value, and as rotation varies between –120 and +120, output a number between 0 and 100, perfectly matching together their two ranges." This is precisely the expression we created in **[Ex.03_final_alt]**. You can replace any of the numbers or properties inside the parentheses with the values you need; you can even use arrays (discussed elsewhere in this chapter).

Most of the time, you will want to use the linear interpolation method. There are also a variety of "ease" methods; these – and interpolation in general – are explained in greater detail in the bonus chapter on your DVD.

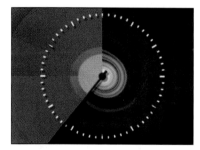

In **[Ex.05b]**, a Radial Wipe effect is tied to the stopwatch hand's rotation. This requires additional scaling to match 360° rotation to 100% effect completion. Footage courtesy Artbeats/Digidelic and Virtual Insanity.

result. This way, you don't have to remember what the original value was; you can even keyframe the value, and the expression will automatically take this offset into account. The result is shown in [**Ex.04_final**], with some parentheses added to make the expression easier to read.

Using expressions to tie together disparate properties is a great technique to make an overall animation seem more cohesive. Once you've set up a relationship between properties, you can edit the master and have the rest follow along automatically.

A few additional ideas are included in the **Ex.05** folder:

• [**Ex.05a**] ties the center of a Spherize effect applied to one layer to the location of a second layer which contains a magnifying glass. If the keyframes and expressions are not available, select **magnifier** and type U, then **background** and type EE.

• [**Ex.05b**] ties a Radial Wipe effect applied to **AB_Digidelic** to the rotating second hand on a stopwatch. Note that we had to add some simple math modifiers to scale 360° of rotation to equal 100% of transition completion. As a bonus, select **hand** and type EE: We used the trick learned in [**Ex.04**] to counter-rotate the Bevel Alpha and Drop Shadow angles as the hand revolves to keep their perspectives intact.

• [**Ex.05c**] is the classic example of tying blur amount to the tracking parameter of text (a very popular look for a while), with a Wave Warp thrown in for good measure. Note that in the case of [**Ex.05c**], the expressions link together different effect parameters; remember that Animation Presets allow you to save multiple effects – and their expressions!

In **[Ex.05c]**, expressions automatically tie blur amount and wave warp height to the tracking between characters.

Moving Between Dimensions

So far, we've discussed using expressions to link similar properties, such as a layer's Rotation and an effect's Angle. However, there are numerous occasions when you will want to link together incompatible properties. For example, if you want to link Rotation to Position, do you mean the X Position or the Y Position? This is going to require diving a bit deeper into the expression language.

After Effects is concerned about how many *dimensions* a property has. Opacity has one value, so it has one dimension. 2D Position has two values – X and Y – so it has two dimensions; 3D Position has three dimensions (X, Y, and Z). Although you may be used to thinking of Scale as a one-dimensional value, in reality it also has two or three dimensions (depending if the layer is in 2D or 3D space), as each dimension of a layer can be scaled independently. A clue that a property has multiple dimensions is if its values are separated by commas in the Timeline or Effect Controls window.

The values of a multidimensional property, taken together, are described as an *array* or *vector*. Expressions group together the values of an array inside square brackets, separated by commas: For example, a Position of X = 360, Y = 243 would be represented as **[360, 243]**.

If an expression is trying to link together two properties that have different numbers of dimensions, After Effects needs to know how to fill in the holes. One way it does this is by referring to individual dimensions inside an array: The first dimension is identified as [0], the second dimension as [1], and so forth. For example, if an expression wants to refer to the X Position value, it identifies it as **position[0]**.

The pick whip tool does what it can to help resolve differences in the number of dimensions between properties. To see this in action, close all the prior comps, and open [**Ex.06*starter**]. Select **CM_curvedarm** and type P followed by Shift+R to reveal its Position and Rotation properties. Enable expressions for Position – a property with two dimensions – and drag its pick whip to the word "Rotation", a property with one dimension. After Effects resolves this difference by creating a two-line expression that copies Rotation's value into a variable called **temp**, and then by using **temp** for both dimensions in an array for the value of Position. Hit Enter to accept the expression and scrub the Rotation value; note how Position updates: Both values (dimensions of its array) are always equal to Rotation.

Delete the expression for Position, and enable expressions for Rotation. Drag the pick whip from Rotation – a property with one dimension – to the word "Position", a property with two dimensions.

Brackets and Dimensions

When a property has more than one dimension, its value is contained inside square brackets – for example, **[360, 243]** for the position X = 360, Y = 243.

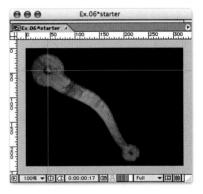

When you use the pick whip to connect Position to Rotation, Rotation is copied to a temporary variable, which is then used for both values of Position's array (below) (if needed, drag the expression text area larger to read both lines of the expression). As you scrub Rotation, both the X and Y Position take on the same value (above).

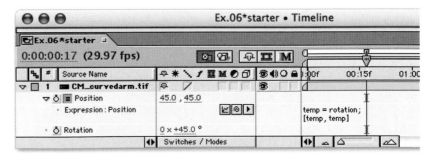

When you pick whip from Rotation to Position, the first dimension of Position – X (defined as **position[0]** in expression lingo) – is used for Rotation (left). As you alter the X Position, Rotation updates to match (right).

In this case, After Effects resolves the difference by taking just the first dimension of Position's array (the X value), as noted by the expression **position[0]**. Hit Enter to accept this expression, and scrub the Position values for **CM_curvedarm**: Scrubbing X Position causes the arm to also rotate; scrubbing Y Position does not affect the rotation of the arm.

What if you want Rotation to be tied to the Y Position, not X? There are a couple of ways to do this. You can manually edit the expression to use a different dimension – in this case, change the expression text for Rotation to be **position[1]**, and the second dimension – Y – will be used. (Many computer languages start counting at 0, not 1. Programmers are used to this, although many artists aren't.) Another approach is to use the pick whip more selectively: Delete the current expression applied to Rotation and re-enable it, and this time drag the pick whip for Rotation to one of the individual Position values in the Timeline window. A box will draw around the value to show you which one you are about to select. Drag the pick whip to the second value (Y), release the mouse button, and hit Enter – the expression will be changed to **position[1]**.

You can pick whip to specific dimensions. Here, we are connecting Rotation to the Y Position value (known as **position[1]** in expression language).

Each value inside an array is fully independent of each other; the only reason they're inside brackets is to make it clear they are part of the same property. Delete the expression for Rotation, re-enable it for Position, and again drag Position's pick whip to Rotation; After Effects will create the expression **temp = rotation; [temp, temp]**. Say you wanted just X Position to equal Rotation, but Y Position to keep its original value. Select the last **temp** in the expression text, and drag the pick whip to the Y Position value (yes, you can pick whip a property to itself). The expression will change to **[temp, position[1]]**. This means the first value in the array – X Position – equals Rotation, and the second value in the array – Y Position – equals Y Position (known in expression-land as **position[1]**). Hit Enter to apply the expression, and test it out by changing the value for Rotation.

Array Math Basics

Because each value inside an array is its own value, you can treat each one just as you would any single value you are calculating in an expression. For example, in the [**Ex.06*starter**] exercise on the previous page, you can replace either of the values inside an array with a constant, or add additional modifiers such as **rotation * 2** (demonstrated in [**Ex.06_final**]). If your calculations get complex, you might want to surround them with parentheses to make them easier to read. Just don't delete the comma that separates the values inside an array; you will get either an unexpected result or an error message.

It is possible to perform math operations on an entire array, but it is often not as straightforward as you might expect. Open [**Ex.07*starter**] where we have two arms. Select both, and type S to reveal their Scale.

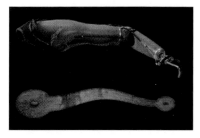

In [**Ex.07**], if we add 20 to a two-dimensional array such as Scale (below), this value is added only to the first dimension of the array (X Scale). The lower arm distorts as a result (above). Arm image courtesy Classic PIO/Medical.

Enable expressions for the Scale property of **arm 2**, and drag its pick whip to the word "Scale" for **arm 1**. Hit Enter to apply the expression. Now scrub Scale for **arm 1**; **arm 2** reacts as you would expect, scaling to match.

Click on the expression text for the **arm 2** layer, hit the down arrow to move to the end of the text, type "*** 2**", and hit Enter. As you scrub Scale for **arm 1**, both the X and Y Scale dimensions of **arm 2** change to be twice **arm 1**'s Scale – makes perfect sense.

Select the *** 2** you entered, delete it, replace it with **+ 20** and hit Enter. You might think this would add 20% to both the X and Y dimension of Scale, but it adds 20 to just the first dimension of **arm 2**'s Scale (scrub **arm 1**'s Scale to confirm this). You can multiply and divide arrays by a single number, but you need arrays with the same number of dimensions to add or subtract. For example, **position + scale** is a valid expression, but if you want to add 40 to both the X and Y Position, you need to write **position + [40,40]**. Both of these are shown in [**Ex.07_final**]. See the section *Deeper into Arrays* in the bonus chapter for more details.

Group Therapy

After Effects provides three different ways to group layers and their actions: Expressions, Parenting, and Nesting/Precomposing. They differ in how inclusive or selective they are.

Nesting/Precomposing allows you to treat a group of layers as one layer in the next comp up the chain, including adding masks, effects, and transformations to the group.

Parenting allows transformations applied to the parent layer to be reflected in the child layers. However, masks, effects, and opacity are not transferred from parent to child.

Expressions transfer only one property at a time between layers. You need to create an expression for each transform or effect property you want transferred. Expressions can be used to link different properties, such as Rotation to Scale.

Resolving Conflicts

When you pick whip from a two-dimensional property to a one-dimensional property, the one-dimensional property is repeated. When you pick whip from a one-dimensional property to a property with more than one dimension, only the first dimension is used – for example, **position[0]**.

Controlling Expressions

So far, we have experimented with using expressions to link one layer to another, or to link different parameters for the same layer. You can also link expressions to layers or effects that don't appear in the final render. This can make projects easier to organize, as it's clear who is the master controller for a group of layers.

Null Objects – which are useful as master "containers" when you're working with parenting – are equally useful as master controllers for expressions. Close any lingering comps, and open [**Ex.08*starter**] which contains the two arms we used earlier. Add a Layer>New>Null Object to this comp. Type Command+A (Control+A) to Select All, then type S followed by Shift+R to reveal their Scale and Rotation properties.

Enable expressions for **arm 1**'s Scale, drag its pick whip to the word "Scale" for **Null 1**, and hit Enter. Do the same for **arm 2**. Scrub **Null 1**'s Scale, and the two arms will follow. (Note that unlike parenting, the arms do not move closer to and farther away from **Null 1**, because you are not scaling all the layers as a group around the null's anchor point; you're using expressions to modify the Scale of each layer individually.) Now repeat the same trick for Rotation, linking **arm 1** and **arm 2** to **Null 1**.

Scrub Rotation for **Null 1**, and the two arms will rotate around their own anchor points (*not* around **Null 1**).

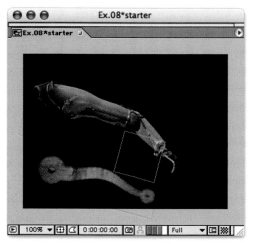

Null Objects are good masters for expressions: Using them eliminates some confusion as to which visible layer is a master and which layers are slaves.

Bonus Points for Fun: Duplicate the arm layers, and move them to another area of the comp window. Expressions are copied when you duplicate a layer, so **Null 1** will still act as a master for all of these duplicates. You can also add modifiers to the end of the Scale expressions (such as *** 0.75**) for each arm to make them different sizes, but all still controlled by the same master layer. This result is shown in [**Ex.08_final**]. Note that you can turn off the Video switch (the eyeball) for the **Null 1** layer to remove its bounding box in the Comp window – the expressions continue to work.

Now, for the heartbreak: Rename **Null 1** (select just its name, press Return, type a new name, and hit Return again): You will get an error

Expression Language Menu

In addition to the pick whip, a second way After Effects helps write expressions for you is the *expression language menu*. It exists to the right of the pick whip icon: Click on the menu arrow, and you will be presented with a hierarchical list of many of the expression properties, attributes, and methods available to you. Using this menu helps avoid typos; it also provides important reminders of the format used by expression attributes and methods.

To wit, each method (an expression piece that requires additional numbers to be entered inside parentheses afterward) contains abbreviated hints as to what values this method needs. For example, if you need a reminder as to what interpolation methods are available and how to write them, click on the expression language menu arrow, and select the submenu Interpolation. You can see that these

methods have options where you can define the minimum and maximum range for "t", or ignore it (in which case it will then use a range of 0–1).

Select the method you want, and After Effects will type this text in for you. You can then select the text for "tmin" or "value1" and either type in the number or variable you want, or use the pick whip to select another property or an Expression Control.

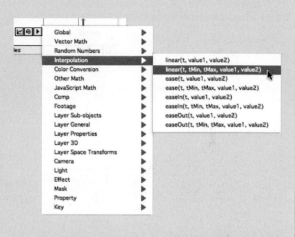

The expression language menu reminds you what attributes and methods are available, and what form they take – including hints as to what values they need. Select one, and After Effects types it in for you.

The expression language menu resides under the arrow icon to the right of the pick whip.

message from After Effects complaining that it "couldn't find layer named 'Null 1'" and your expressions will be disabled. (Note that when an expression has been disabled due to an error, After Effects displays a yellow "caution" sign next to it in the Timeline window.) When you use the pick whip, the name of the layers you point to are wired into the resulting expression. Change the name of a layer that an expression points to, and the expression breaks. You have to either change the name of the layer back to what it was before, or edit all of the expressions that refer to this layer to reflect the new name. Try to get into the habit of naming layers (and effects) *before* you hook up expressions.

Null layers are good for controlling transforms; the Expression Controls are good for nearly everything else. These effects provide basic slider, position point, angle, color swatch, checkbox, and layer selector popup user interface elements that don't do anything by themselves,

Whipping to Windows

You can drag the pick whip to a parameter in the Effect Controls window, or even to the Timeline window belonging to another comp.

but that can be used to control expressions. You can apply Expression Controls to any layer; they won't affect its appearance. We like to apply them to null objects to keep it clear who the master is.

To get a quick feel for these, open [**Ex.09*starter**]. It looks just like [**Ex.08*starter**], with a null object already added (which we've named **Master Null**). Select **Master Null**, and apply Effect>Expression Controls> Angle Control. Type E to reveal it in the Timeline window, then twirl it open. Select **arm 1** and **arm 2**, type R to reveal Rotation, and use the pick whip to hook up expressions between the Rotation properties of the arms and the Angle value of your new Angle Control. You can drag the pick whip to the word "Angle" in either the Timeline or Effect Controls window (remember to drag to the parameter name "Angle" – not to the effect's name "Angle Control"). Hit Enter, and when you scrub Angle, both arms will rotate as before. You can also rotate the Angle dial in the Effect Controls window. (For bonus points, add Effect>Expression Controls>Slider to Master Null, and hook up expressions for the Scale of **arm 1** and **arm 2** to this new controller. The result is shown in [**Ex.09_final**].)

The expression After Effects created when you hooked up these controls is a bit longer than what you've seen so far, but can still be read just the same as other expressions. Let's break it down:

thisComp.layer("Master Null").effect("Angle Control").param("Angle")

What this expression says is that in this comp, there is a layer named Master Null, which has an effect named Angle Control, and we want to use its parameter named Angle.

The Expression Controls are effects that don't render; they just provide user interface elements to hook expressions to.

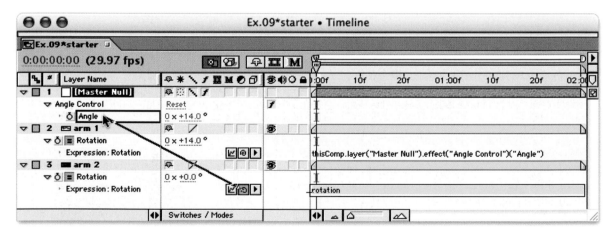

After you apply the Expression Control you want, twirl it open in the Timeline window, and use the pick whip to hook other properties to it.

Note that the name of the effect is called out explicitly: Because you can rename effects, you again run the risk of breaking expressions after they have been created. Of course, you can just go back and edit the expression text to reflect the new effect name, but your life with expressions will be easier if you can plan a little bit ahead – add the Expression Controllers, give them a short name that matches what you intend to use them for, *then* create your expressions.

We've created a pair of additional comps for you to explore, to give you more ideas of what can be done with Expression Controllers:

• [Ex.10a] contains one layer – **Master Color** – which controls the Fill effect for a number of other layers in the same comp. Select **Master Color**, press F3 to open its Effect Controls window, and edit the swatch for Color Control; note how all of the text layers update. Select any of these text layers and type EE to see their expressions. Remember that you can use the pick whip to connect expressions across multiple comps; this means one color swatch could control an entire project, making it easier to accommodate last-minute client changes.

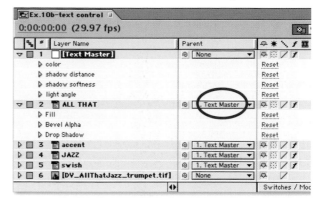

• [Ex.10b] contains a more advanced example of the master color concept. Select **Text Master** and hit F3 to open its Effect Controls: It contains Expression Controls for the color, shadow distance and softness, and the light angle for the Drop Shadow and Bevel Alpha effects applied to each of the text layers (select any of them and type EE). This is a great way to simplify control of a complex effect, even if applied to a single layer: Create Expression Controls for just the parameters you know you'll be tweaking, and twirl up the effect itself.

Also note in [Ex.10b] that we used Text Master as a parent for the text layers; this makes it easy to position and scale them. Don't be afraid to mix and match parenting, nesting, precomposing, and expressions, using the strengths of each. Just because you *can* create an expression to control a parameter, doesn't mean you *have* to!

Variables and Multiline Expressions

So far, all of the expressions we've used could be contained on one line, and are pretty explicit: Make this number equal that number. However, it doesn't take much before expressions can start getting long and messy. It is a good idea to break them down into easier-to-read chunks whenever possible. To do that, we'll add another tool to our arsenal: *variables*.

Say you wanted the width and height of a layer to be controlled by a pair of Slider Controls. In [Ex.11*starter], we've given you a head start by adding these controls to the layer **master_scale**, giving them the names "width_slider" and "height_slider". Select **master_scale** and type F3 to reveal its Effect Controls window. Then select the layer **blue_sphere** and if necessary, type S to reveal its Scale. Enable expressions for **blue_sphere**'s Scale, and do the following:

Step 1: Type "[" (open bracket, without the quotes).

Step 2: Drag the pick whip to the word "Slider" under the effect name "width_slider" in the Effect Controls window. This links the X Scale.

Step 3: Type a comma to separate the X and Y Scale dimensions in the array.

Expression Controls allow you to have one parameter control a number of layers, and to simplify effects by exposing just the parameters you need to edit. Here, a Null Object called Text Master is used as a parent (top), with Expression Controls (above) set up for color, shadow distance, shadow softness, and the bevel's light angle for a set of effects applied to a group of text layers (below). Image courtesy Digital Vision/All That Jazz.

Saving Expressions as Animation Presets

Expressions cannot be saved by themselves. Instead, you will need to copy and paste them between After Effects and a text document, or import projects that contain expressions you want to reuse.

A better way to save expressions is to use Animation Presets (originally discussed in Volume 1, Chapter 27). Expressions applied to effects – or ordinary parameters – can be saved along with the effects as Presets. Simply apply your expressions to effects, select the effects in the Effect Controls window, and use Animation>Save Animation Preset to store the result as a preset. Select a new layer and use Animation>Apply Animation Preset to recall the effects with their settings, keyframes, and expressions intact. (Note that if these expressions referred to other layers or comps, then you will need to re-enter the new layer and comp names). If you save Presets in the **After Effects>Presets** folder, they will show up in the Effects & Presets palette where they are even easier to apply.

We like to use Expression Controls and the Distort>Transform effect (which gives you a second set of Position, Scale, and Opacity controls for a layer) to write self-contained expression modules.

Expression Controls can also provide a simplified "user interface" to a complex expression or effect. Here are the naming conventions we use when we're building these expression presets:

- **in_** is used for controls that need to be pick whipped to another property – for example, the Position of a master layer.

- **set_** is used for controls that are intended to be adjusted by the user. They set parameters for an expression, such as the number of frames.

- **out_** is used for controls that contain the results of our expressions. The expressions are applied to these elements, and then we pick whip the layer properties we want to control to the **out_** elements.

We will use these naming conventions in the examples that appear in the second half of this chapter and throughout the bonus chapter on the DVD. The expression Presets we saved for you all have the prefix **exp_** and are saved in the **Goodies** folder on your DVD; don't forget to copy them into your **After Effects>Presets** folder and then reboot After Effects to see them appear in the Effects & Presets palette.

Bad with Names

When you use the pick whip to connect an expression to another layer or effect, the name of that layer or effect is used in the resulting expression. Change that name later, and the expression will break. Settle on naming conventions *before* hooking up expressions.

Step 4: Drag the pick whip to the word "Slider" under the effect name "height_slider", linking the Y Scale.

Step 5: Type "]" (close bracket).

Step 6: Hit Enter to accept the expression. If you like, scrub the two sliders to make sure they work as expected.

The result is the following none-too-short expression, appearing all on the same line:

> **[thisComp.layer("master_scale").effect("width_scale").param("Slider"), thisComp.layer("master_scale").effect("height_scale").param("Slider")]**

This long expression is hard to read; it might even extend past the right edge of your Timeline window. This also makes it hard to edit later – for example, if you wanted to select just the Y Scale portion of this expression, you need to grab a large line of text buried in the middle of an array.

Let's rebuild this expression in a friendlier way. Select the expression text for **blue_sphere**'s Scale, delete it, and with the cursor at the start of the expression text line, follow these steps instead:

Step 1: Type a name you will find easy to remember, such as "**my_X**" (again, without the quotes), followed by an equals sign. This word is a *variable*: a temporary value you can make up to store values in during an expression.

Step 2: Drag the pick whip to the word "Slider" under the effect name **width_slider** in the Effect Controls window. This links the X Scale.

Step 3: Type a semicolon; this tells After Effects you have finished one line of an expression. Hit Return (*not* Enter) to start a new line in the expression text.

Step 4: Type a second name, such as "**my_Y**" followed again by an equals sign.

Step 5: Drag the pick whip to the word "Slider" under the effect name **height_slider**, linking the Y Scale.

Step 6: Type a semicolon and hit Return.

Step 7: Type "**[my_X, my_Y]**" and hit Enter to accept the expression. If you like, scrub the two sliders to make sure they work as expected.

Field Expansion

To make the expression text area larger to read multiline expressions, click and drag on the faint embossed line underneath the text field; the double-arrow icon will let you know when the cursor is in the right position. Drag down to expand.

The result is the following multiline expression:

```
my_X = thisComp.layer("master_scale").effect("width_scale").param("Slider");
my_Y = thisComp.layer("master_scale").effect("height_scale").param("Slider");
[my_X, my_Y]
```

Although it uses more words and lines, the result is an expression that is neater and easier to read. For example, if you want to assign Y Scale to a different value, it is clearer what you need to select and edit. The last valid line of a multiline expression usually provides the final answer.

Every line or "phrase" of your expression – except the last line executed – should end with a semicolon. This tells After Effects that this piece of the expression is finished, and that the next text it encounters is a new piece of the expression. Often, a return at the end of a line works as well, but there is less ambiguity with the semicolon. We often use both to avoid errors and to make the final expression easier to read.

If you want to add comments to your expression to remind yourself later what each line is doing, type / / (two slashes), then whatever comment you want. After Effects will not try to execute anything after / / and before the next Return. When you enter a Return, this tells After Effects the line is over, and it can start executing the expression again from the start of the next line. If you want to write a long comment that requires more than one line, or sneak a comment into the middle of a line, surround your comment with the characters /* and */. To wit:

```
// this is a comment
/* this also works
as a comment*/
```

Multiline expressions that use temporary variables are often easier to break down, read, and edit. Note how we've added a comment (signified by the characters //) to the last line of this expression as well.

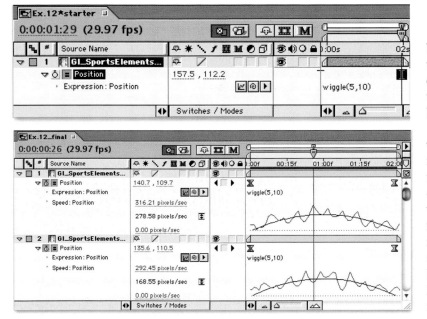

The Wiggle keyframe assistant (above) and the basic wiggle expression (below) perform the same basic function. The Wiggler's Frequency and Magnitude values correspond to the two values in parentheses for the wiggle expression.

The Wiggle Expression

Even if you believe your adventures will never wander beyond a few simple pick whips, there is one advanced expression method that is well worth learning: wiggling a value.

If you have the Professional edition, you may be familiar with the keyframe assistant known as The Wiggler, discussed in detail in the previous chapter. In short, it randomizes the values of keyframes it is applied to, yielding anything from subtle human imperfection to in-your-face jumpiness. There is an expression that creates similar effects and that in many ways is easier to control because you don't have to create new keyframes every time you want to adjust its operation.

The simplest way to add the wiggle expression to a property is to enable expressions for that property, type "**wiggle(**", enter a number for how many times per second you want the wiggle to jerk around, add a comma, enter a second number for how wide a value swing you want to wiggle by, type "**)**", and hit Enter. To try this out, close all other comps, open [**Ex.12*starter**], select the baseball layer, type P to reveal its Position, enable expressions, and enter:

wiggle(5,10)

RAM Preview, and watch the baseball wiggle in space. Change the first number to slow down or speed up the wiggling; change the second to vary how far the baseball wiggles.

The wiggle expression works with any keyframes a property may have. Click on the = symbol to temporarily turn off this expression, click on the stopwatch for Position to enable keyframing, then animate a simple movement. Then click on the ≠ symbol to turn your expression back on, and RAM Preview: Note how the baseball wiggles around the path you keyframed.

The wiggle expression wanders around any keyframed animation you have set up. The black line is the keyframed velocity curve before the expression; the red line represents the curve after the expression. Wiggles are randomized based on layer number: Note the differences between the red curves.

To get an idea of how this expression is modifying your path, click on the graph icon to the left of the pick whip tool to twirl open the *expression value graph*. In this graph, the black line is your original velocity curve; the red line is the curve after the expression has been calculated. If you have the layer selected in the Timeline window, exposing the expression graph also draws the wiggled path in the Comp window. Toggle the graph icon on/off to see the difference.

The wiggle expression randomizes its path depending on its layer number in the timeline. Duplicate the baseball layer a couple of times, and note how you now have a flock of baseballs, each wiggling independent of each other. This is shown in [**Ex.12_final**].

The wiggle expression can be applied to virtually any property, including Rotation, Scale, and Opacity – go ahead and try this in [**Ex.12*starter**] for practice; we've also included some alternate examples – [**Ex.13a**] through [**Ex.13c**] – for your perusal.

The problem with the wiggle expression is that it keeps wiggling – even if your layer is supposed to be motionless (for example, when it reaches the final Position keyframe). However, it is easy to keyframe the wiggle amount; you just need to add an Expression Control.

Open [**Ex.14*starter**]: It contains an alarm clock that we want to wiggle as if its alarm is going off. Select the clock, type R to reveal its Rotation if not already visible, enable expressions for Rotation, type in the expression **wiggle(10,30)**, and hit Enter. RAM Preview; the clock shakes for the entire comp.

With the clock still selected, apply Effect>Expression Controls>Slider Control. Leave the Effect Controls window open, placed somewhere that you can drag to it easily. In the expression text, select *just the second number* in the wiggle method (**30**, which is your wiggle amount) and drag the pick whip to the word "Slider" in the Slider Control. Hit Enter to apply. At this point the clock's not wiggling because Slider Control defaults to a value of 0, which is no wiggle amount. Increase its value, and note how it controls how much the clock wiggles.

Hit Home to return to 00:00, and turn on the stopwatch for Slider Control in the Effect Controls window. Hit U to expose its keyframes in the Timeline, and set the Slider value to 0. Move to 01:00 and ramp up the value to around 30, then at 02:00 return to 0. RAM Preview again; note how the clock's shaking follows your keyframed values. Our version is contained in [**Ex.14_final**].

This is a very handy technique for controlling how you use the wiggle expression. We will expand on this technique further in the expressions bonus chapter on your DVD – including a great little animation preset to add to all your motion control camera moves to make them look more realistic.

Applying extreme amounts of wiggle to Scale creates jumpy, nervous animations. Background courtesy Artbeats/Virtual Intensity.

To keyframe the wiggle amount, select its value in the expression text (circled in red), and use the pick whip to connect it to a Slider Control.

Expressive Tricks

We will conclude our exploration of expressions by presenting a series of examples that use combinations of the expression techniques we've discussed here, and in Bonus Chapter 06B, *Deeper Modes of Expression*, in the **Bonus Chapters** folder on your DVD.

Remember you can expose the expressions in a comp by typing Command+A (Control+A) to select all the layers, then typing EE to twirl down the expressions. If an expression is more than one line long, but only one line is visible in the Timeline window, select the expression text and it will automatically expand to show you all lines of the expression. If needed, drag on the faint embossed line below the expression text to resize its window larger or smaller. Close all other open comps as you move between examples, to reduce clutter.

[Ex.15]: Better 3D Through Science

This first example reprises a trick we showed in our companion book, *After Effects in Production*, in the extended tutorial **08B_Postcards_Bonus.pdf** – but we feel it is significant enough that we want to make sure you don't miss it.

In After Effects, many 3D effects – such as Simulation>Shatter and Zaxwerks>3D Invigorator – can be set to use the comp's camera, so they render with the same perspective as other 3D layers in the same comp. The problem is, you have to leave their 3D Layer switch *off* to do this,

Same Name Game

Most expressions refer to layers by name. When more than one layer has the same name, After Effects uses the topmost one in the Timeline window.

Other Resources

There are a number of other references available on expressions and the JavaScript language (including the bonus chapter 06B *Deeper Modes of Expression* on your DVD). Here are our personal favorites:

Web Sites:
www.motionscript.com

This web site teaching expressions and scripting was created by Dan Ebberts, a true expert in these areas (Dan helped improve this chapter, and wrote the scripting overview at its end). Dan has also written several advanced expression tutorials for the Creative Cow site (www.creativecow.net). He actively answers questions on a number of online forums, including the Adobe User to User forum on After Effects Expressions (www.adobeforums.com).

www.aenhancers.com

This community web forum includes discussions, tutorials, and a library of After Effects expressions, scripts, and Animation Presets. An international roster of After Effects power users, such as Paul Tuersley, Alexandre Czetwertynski, and Lloyd Alvarez, are regular contributors.

Book: *JavaScript – A Beginner's Guide* by John Pollock (Osbourne)

Most JavaScript books assume you want to use this language to program advanced web pages. But this book also contains some of the simplest, clearest explanations we've seen of the JavaScript language and how it works. Chris keeps it on his desk when he's working with expressions.

which means they can't interact with other 3D layers – including sorting by depth, and casting or receiving shadows.

We came up with a workaround that allows you to leave the 3D Layer switch enabled for layers with these 3D effects, and for the effects to still follow the comp's active camera. The first step is to assign the following expression to the 3D layer's Orientation property:

lookAt (thisComp.activeCamera.position, position)

This forces the layer to always look straight at the active camera. The second step is taking the angles used to orient the layer towards the camera and spinning the effect's 3D rotations in the opposite direction. This ensures the effect renders its image always facing the same direction in world space, regardless of how the camera moves around it. All this step requires is assigning the following three expressions to the effect's X, Y, and Z Rotation properties, respectively (without spaces):

–orientation[0]
–orientation[1]
–orientation[2]

Some effects (such as 3D Invigorator) may require that you leave out the minus sign at the start of the expression for X Rotation (called "Camera Tumble Up/Down" in Invigoratorspeak). Also, most effects look better if you don't use the Z Rotation expression. Run some experiments, and see what looks "right" to your eyes. Of course, you can still find ways to fool these expressions – After Effects isn't really a 3D program, and the illusion can be broken – but they will let your 3D effects intermingle more effectively with your other 3D layers.

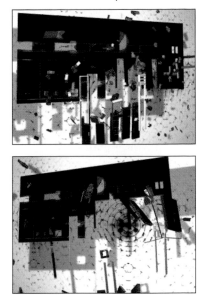

[Ex.15]: A simple set of expressions allows 3D effects to exist in 3D space, follow the comp's camera, and still cast shadows onto other 3D layers. Images courtesy Getty Images/ Discovery.

[Ex.16]: The Balance of Power

This example is based on a real-world job we had for American Isuzu Motors. Isuzu wanted us to develop a graphic to explain how its Torque-On-Demand system balanced the power delivered to the front and rear wheels of its vehicles. We visually reinforced the amount of power being distributed in three ways: with a "power bar" that shifted between the front and rear wheels; through the size of dotted lines traveling down the vehicle's imaginary driveshafts; and through the size of "swoosh" graphics that curved around their respective wheels. We needed sets of graphics for both the front and rear driveshaft/wheel groups. Plus the wheels and dotted lines had to move or rotate, matching the speed of the vehicle.

This would already be a lot of keyframes to coordinate; what made it trickier is that we would have to time changes in these elements to match a voiceover. We were provided with a scratch voiceover, but knew the timing would change again after the real voiceover was finished.

To make our lives easier and accommodate changes more rapidly, we decided to drive as much of the animation as possible with expressions. When we boiled the job down, there were only two master parameters: how far the wheels had rotated, and the current power distribution

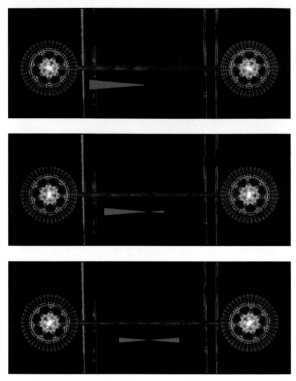

[Ex.16]: The mask for the blue bar, the size of both sets of yellow dashed lines, and the size for the red swooshes around the wheels are all driven by a single Slider Control. The rotation of the wheels, plus the speed at which the yellow dots travel, are controlled by one Angle Control. Background courtesy Digital Vision/Prototype.

Expressive Parents

Parenting is a great tool to use with expressions. A child's transforms are relative to the parent, rather than the comp, often making it easier to write reusable expressions. Null Objects also help "soak up" offsets in position, rotation, and scale.

between the front and rear wheels. We applied two Expression Controls to a null object, and drove all of our expressions from these controls. Changing the keyframes for these controls would change how the entire animation reacted.

Open [Ex.16], make sure the keyframes are visible for **Master Controls,** and scrub the Slider value for the effect **rear_drive** to see how the graphic changes. Undo to reset this value to its initial setting, then RAM Preview to see the keyframed animation. Here's how we pulled it off:

Wheel rotation was easy: We just pick whipped the Rotation property of the wheels directly to the Angle Control we created for our master rotation. The dotted lines for the front and rear wheels were created by applying Render>Vegas to a solid. These solids were parented to their respective wheels, so their rotations automatically matched. The dotted lines along the driveshafts were also created using Vegas; we just pick whipped its own Rotation parameter (which makes the dots move) to the master rotation dial. We decided this made the dotted lines travel too fast, so we added a simple "**/ 2**" at the end of their expressions to cut their speed in half.

The power balance was a little more complex. In short, interpolation methods (which say "map the range between these two numbers to the range between those two numbers") made it easier for us to translate the 0 to 100 values that represented rear-wheel power amount to all of the other parameters we needed to control.

We used a value from the master Slider Control (named **rear_drive**) to shift the X Position of a matte layer – **power_distrib_matte** – that hid or revealed the main power bar. We also used this slider to control the Width of the dotted lines. An example of an interpolation method we used is **linear(rear_drive,0,100,0,8)**, which says take **rear_drive** values between 0 and 100, and translate them linearly to Vegas Width values between 0 and 8. In the case of the front wheels, we just turned a couple of numbers around, mapping **rear_drive** values of 0 to 100 to front wheel Vegas Width values of 8 to 0, making the dotted lines for the front wheels get smaller as power to the rear wheels increased.

We were thrown a curve when we realized Vegas does not allow you to set a Width smaller than 0.5 – which means we couldn't make the dotted lines and swooshes disappear completely just by changing their width. We covered for this by creating additional expressions for their Opacity, fading Opacity down from a value of 1 to 0 as power decreased from 10 to 0.

Once we figured out this basic system of relationships, it was simple to modify these relationships for each wheel or dotted line, such as adding a minus sign if a Vegas effect had to rotate the other way.

[Ex.17]: Gearing Up

A good use for expressions is to make gears or wheels that touch rotate at the correct speed automatically, depending on their relative sizes. For example, if wheel 1 is touching wheel 2, and wheel 1 is twice as large as wheel 2, wheel 2 will rotate twice as fast, in the opposite direction (remember the example in [**Ex.02**]?).

We've set up this relationship in [**Ex.17a**]. We've keyframed the Rotation of **wheel_1**, and written the following expression for the Rotation value of **wheel_2**:

```
scale_diff = thisComp.layer("wheel_1").scale[0] / scale[0];
thisComp.layer("wheel_1").rotation * scale_diff * –1
```

The first line calculates the differences between the Scale of the two wheels (looking at just the X Scale for each: **scale[0]**); the second line multiplies the result by the Rotation value of the **wheel_1**, then multiplies it by –1 to rotate in the opposite direction. Alter the Scale of **wheel_2**, move its Position so the two wheels touch again, and RAM Preview to verify that the expression is doing its job.

[Ex.17b]: We used a combination of parenting and expressions to keep these three wheels in contact, no matter what their respective scales. Expressions keep their rotations in sync as well. Background courtesy Digital Vision/Data:Funk.

We created a mondo version of this exercise in [**Ex.17b**]. Before we detail how this works, have some fun with this comp, scrubbing the Scale of **wheel_1**, **wheel_2**, and **wheel_3** and previewing the result – the wheels always stay in contact, and always rotate at the correct speed! You can also scrub the Rotation of **null 1-2** and **null 2-3** to rearrange the wheels in the comp.

To make this work, we used a combination of parenting and expressions. We started out by lining up all of our wheels and nulls, stacked on top of each other (in other words, each with the same initial position). We then assigned **null 1-2** as the parent for **wheel_1**, **wheel_2**, and **null 2-3**. When you stack a layer and a null in this way, and parent the layer to the null, the child's Position changes to 0,0. This means we can move **null 1-2** to wherever we want, and the three children would still have an initial Position of 0,0. The layer **wheel_3** was then attached to **null 2-3**, giving it a Position of 0,0 relative to this second null.

To simplify things, let's focus first on the relationship between **wheel_1** and **wheel_2**. As you know, the radius of a circle or wheel is the distance between its center and its outer rim. If we want the outer rims of **wheel_1** and **wheel_2** to touch, they need to be offset a distance equal to the radius of **wheel_1** plus the radius of **wheel_2**. Since using nulls gave both wheels an initial Position of 0,0, we wrote the following expression to move **wheel_2** along the Y axis by the required distance:

```
wr = 92;
my_wr = wr * (scale[0]/100);
that_wr = wr * (thisComp.layer("wheel_1").scale[0]/100);
[position[0] + that_wr + my_wr, position[1]]
```

We measured a wheel at 100% scale and found its radius was 92 pixels; that's the number in the first line. To find the radius of the wheels after

Shadow Boxing

Here's a challenge for bonus points: How would you apply a Drop Shadow to the wheels in [**Ex.17b**]? If you apply the effect directly to each wheel, the shadow will spin around as the wheel spins. You could write expressions that counter-rotate the shadow's direction to compensate for the wheel's spin…as well as the Rotation of its parent null…and then two more expressions to scale the shadow distance and size based on the wheel's Scale… or, you could just select all the layers except the background, precompose them, and apply a single Drop Shadow to the precomp layer. Expressions are cool, but don't fall into the trap of trying to write an expression for every problem you may encounter!

scaling, we just needed to multiply this initial radius by their current Scale values – that's what the second and third lines do. We then calculated **wheel_2**'s new position by keeping its X position (**position[0]**), and adding together our two scaled radius values to come up with its Y Position.

To spin **wheel_2**, we used the same trick as we used in [**Ex.17a**] – take the Rotation of **wheel_1**, and multiply it by the ratio between the Scale of the two wheels. And rotate it in the opposite direction, of course.

To add **wheel_3** into the mix, we just repeated the above. The null object **null 2-3** gets the same Position expression as **wheel_2** so that they both start in the same place. We then offset **wheel_3**'s Position from **wheel_2** in the exact same way we moved **wheel_2** away from **wheel_1**. The Rotation of **wheel_3** is also found the same way – by just taking the ratio between the Scale of the wheels.

[Ex.18]: On Your Marks, Go!

In Chapter 11, we'll discuss how useful it is to "spot" important events in a soundtrack, note their locations using layer markers, then base your animation around the timing of these markers. Expressions give you the ability to automatically animate layers based on the timing of layer markers, but you need to be a bit clever about it.

Open [**Ex.18**], select all of the layers, type U to see their keyframes, and press F2 to deselect all. The only keyframes in sight perform the fade-out at the end. Now RAM Preview: Each word jumps to a new location and size every time it crosses a layer marker. We've written expressions that have these markers trigger new random values for Position and Scale. If you've peeked ahead at those expressions, you might be daunted at how long they are; as it turns out, over half the text is just bulletproofing so you can apply these expressions to other layers. The central trick isn't that complicated, so let's work from the core idea outward.

To randomize Scale values, you just need to apply the expression **random(lower_limit, upper_limit)** to the Scale property. To make the range of random values easier to adjust, we added a couple of Slider Controls

[Ex.18]: It is possible to write expressions that are triggered by layer markers. Here, we spotted important points in the audio track. We then wrote expressions for Position and Scale which use a random "seed" number that corresponds to the index number of each marker we cross, crafted so that the random number changes only when we cross a new marker.

to each layer, and pick whipped these in place of **lower_limit** and **upper_limit**. We randomized Position using a similar idea. The **random** expression method automatically gets a new "seed" to create a random number every frame. You can break that behavior by giving **random** your own seed, and setting the "timeless" flag for that seed to "true" – that means it will not change its value based on time. To do this, precede the **random** expression with a line that says **seedRandom(seed, true)**, replacing the word "seed" with any number you desire. If you want a new random number, change the value of the seed.

In this case, we decided to make the seed be the same as the number – the "index" – of the layer marker we just crossed (you don't need to give the markers numbers; they are automatically numbered starting with 1 at the beginning of the timeline). To do this, we wrote the expression **seed = marker.nearestKey(time).index**.

The problem with this brilliant idea is that the index doesn't change as we cross a marker, but *in-between* markers, taking on the value of the nearest – not most recent – marker. So, we had to add some if/then statements around our expression to figure out if we are before the time of the nearest marker (in which case, we need to subtract 1 from the seed number, because we haven't reached the next marker yet), or after the nearest marker (which means everything's okay). The expression text to do that is

```
if (time<marker.nearestKey(time).time)
{seed = seed-1}
```

(If you are not already familiar with if/then statements, they are covered in the bonus chapter on the DVD. In short, the second line of the expression is the implied "then" – if the first line is true, then do what's in-between the squiggly brackets afterward.)

Finally, we needed to add one more level of error checking, on the outside chance that there were no layer markers. We started by setting **seed = 0** (so it would have *some* value), then followed it with another if/then statement:

```
if (marker.numKeys > 0){
```

If the number of markers is greater than zero, then we go ahead and execute the bit of code just discussed above to set **seed** to equal the marker index. Otherwise, we skip around the whole mess, leave **seed = 0**, then do the random number jump. The final expression looks like this:

```
seed = 0;
if (marker.numKeys > 0)
  {seed = marker.nearestKey(time).index;
    if (time < marker.nearestKey(time).time)
    {seed = seed-1};
  }
seedRandom(seed,true);
random(effect("set_ScaleMin").param("Slider"),
effect("set_ScaleMax").param("Slider"))
```

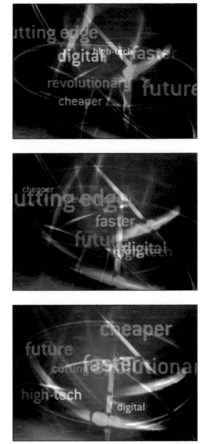

[Ex.18 continued]: As a result of our expression, each word randomly jumps to a new Scale and Position whenever it crosses one of its own layer markers.

faster • Effect Controls

```
faster
Ex.18-Markers Trigger Jumps * faster
  set_ScaleMin       Reset        About...
    Animation Presets  None
    Slider             30.00
  set_ScaleMax       Reset        About...
    Animation Presets  None
    Slider             100.00
  set_MaxPosOffset   Reset        About...
    Animation Presets  None
    Point              120.4 , 80.0
  Transform          Reset        About...
  Fill               Reset        About...
```

[Ex.18]: We saved the expression used in this example as the Animation Preset **exp_MarkTrigsJump.ffx**. It includes controls for you to set the range of Scale values, plus how far the Position can vary. In **[Ex.18]**, we then added a Fill effect to color the text.

Flush with Cache

If frames around a crossfade have been cached into memory (look for the green bar in the Timeline window), and you trim a layer, After Effects may not re-cache crossfades created with expressions (indicated by the green bar's not disappearing). Toggle the layer's Video switch on and off to reset the cache.

To make this expression easier to apply, we wrote it for the Distort> Transform effect, rather than assigning it directly to a layer's Scale and Position. A couple of other simple expressions set the Transform effect's Anchor Point and Position to be the same as the layer's Anchor Point, just to make sure the effect scales around the same center point as the layer would. As a result, we could save the entire contraption – Effect Controls and all – as an Animation Preset. And we have: It's called **exp_MarkTrigsJump.ffx**, and you can apply it to any of your own layers.

[Ex.19]: Just a Fade We're Going Through

One of our favorite keyframe assistants is Sequence Layers, which can take any number of trimmed layers you select, arrange them end to end, overlap them by the amount of time you ask for, and perform crossfades between them. However, sometimes you want to edit the length of the layers or the duration of their crossfades after the fact. Ever in search of a better mousetrap, we came up with a set of expressions that will automatically crossfade layers depending on how much they overlap. And it's not even that complex.

Open [Ex.19] and RAM Preview; note how the layers neatly crossfade into each other. The expression we've written always fades from the layer on top to the layer immediately underneath, over the amount of time they overlap. Now have some fun editing their in and out points, and sliding them along the timeline – even opening up gaps between them – just keep in mind that each layer can crossfade only to the one underneath. (For bonus points, create a full-frame black solid, and use that at the start for a fade-in from black, or at the end for a fade-out to black.)

As with [Ex.18], most of the expression we came up with is for bullet-proofing in the event something went wrong – for example, there was no overlap between layers, or the layer happened to be the last one in the Timeline stack with no layers underneath. But the final expression is still small enough to go through all at once:

```
new_opacity = 100;
if (index < thisComp.numLayers)
  {if (outPoint > thisComp.layer(index+1).inPoint)
    {new_opacity =
    linear(time, thisComp.layer(index+1).inPoint, outPoint, 100, 0)
    }
  }
new_opacity
```

Line 1: This expression is applied to Opacity (in our case, the Opacity value of the ever handy Distort>Transform effect). In the first line, we set a default value for Opacity of 100.

Line 2: We check to make sure we're not the last layer in the comp – in other words, that our own layer number **(index)** is smaller than the total number of layers in the comp **(thisComp.numLayers)**. If we are the last layer, jump ahead to Line 7. If we aren't last, proceed!

```
●●●                    Ex.19–Automatic Crossfades • Timeline
▣ Ex.19-Automatic Crossfades ◪
0:00:08:09  (29.97 fps)          ▨ ▨   ▨ ▨ M
🖿 #  Source Name             ⚟ ✱ ⟍ ∫ ▥ M ⊘ ⚏  ▨ ◀)○ 🔒  :00s   02s   04s   06s   08s   10s   12s   14s
▽ ☐ 1  📄 AB_LifestylesMixedCuts.... ⚟ / ∫          ▨             ⟨
    ▽ FadeOutOver              Reset                 ∫
    ▷ ⌖ ▤ Opacity             0.0
▽ ☐ 2  📄 AB_RainForest.mov    ⚟ / ∫          ▨                    ⟨
    ▽ FadeOutOver              Reset                 ∫
    ▷ ⌖ ▤ Opacity             57.1
▽ ☐ 3  📄 AB_TheOrient.mov     ⚟ / ∫          ▨                            ⟨
    ▽ FadeOutOver              Reset                 ∫
    ▷ ⌖ ▤ Opacity             100.0
▽ ☐ 4  📄 AB_Surfing_ex.mov    ⚟ / ∫          ▨                                    ⟨
    ▽ FadeOutOver              Reset                 ∫
    ▷ ⌖ ▤ Opacity             100.0
                              ◀▶ Switches / Modes    ◀▶ △ △      △
```

[Ex.19]: Look, ma, no keyframes – the crossfades (see image below) are performed automatically by expressions, based on how much a layer overlaps with another layer underneath (see Timeline above). Footage courtesy Artbeats Rainforest and The Orient.

Line 3: If there is no overlap between our out point (**outPoint**) and the in point of the layer underneath (**thisComp.layer(index+1).inPoint**), there is no need to crossfade, and we jump ahead to Line 6. If our out point *is* beyond the in point of the next layer, proceed!

Lines 4/5: We use a linear interpolation method to work out the crossfade. As the current time moves from the next layer's in point to our own out point, vary the resulting opacity value from 100 down to 0.

Lines 6/7: Just cleaning up the ends of our if/then statements above.

Line 8: Our final answer is stored in **new_opacity** – either our default value of 100 from Line 1, or the crossfade we calculated in Line 4.

We've saved the resulting expression as the Animation Preset **exp_FadeOutOver.ffx**. If you prefer to work bottom-up, where layers on top fade in over layers underneath, we saved this variation as **exp_FadeInOver.ffx**. If your layers have alpha channels and you need to crossfade the layers – one layer fades out while the overlapping layer fades in – we've saved presets named **exp_FadeCrossDown.ffx** and **exp_Fade_CrossUp.ffx**. Use the first of these if you've arranged your layers so that layer 1 fades to layer 2 and so forth; use the other if you have your layers stacked the other way, where layer 1 is the last layer in time. Both of the "cross" expressions use an ease interpolation method, which balances the relative opacities of the layers better as they crossfade. (For more on presets, see the sidebar earlier in this chapter named *Saving Expressions as Animation Presets*, or read Volume 1's Chapter 27.)

Note that these expressions have been bulletproofed, but not entirely foolproofed: If you have strange conditions such as the layer underneath being shorter than – and completely overlapped by – the layer above, then you're going to get strange results. We could add coating after coating of if/then statements to protect against every situation we could think of, but that would make the expression overly complex. Arrange your layers with overlaps and in a fashion that would allow you to create good manual fades, and these expressions will do it for you automatically.

Connect

Parenting and null objects were presented in Volume 1, Chapter 17.

Precomposing and Nesting were discussed in Volume 1, Chapters 18 and 19.

Animation Presets were detailed in Volume 1, Chapter 27.

The Wiggler keyframe assistant is randomized in Chapter 5.

Spotting audio, see Chapter 11.

Several of the tutorials in our companion book *After Effects in Production* – such as *Piccadilly Circus* and *Just an Expression* – also put expressions to good use.

Scripting Overview

by Dan Ebberts

Adobe introduced scripting with After Effects 6.0. Unfortunately, it had limited use and you couldn't do much with it except automate renders. If you examined it closely though, you could sense that Adobe was establishing a powerful framework for amazing things to come. The amazing part arrived with After Effects 6.5. You now have the power to create and manipulate projects, compositions, layers, cameras, lights, text, and much more. You even have access to something that has been frustratingly inaccessible to expression writers – mask shapes.

Scripting versus Expressions

Before diving into scripting, it's useful to examine some of the similarities and differences between scripting and expressions. On the surface they look very similar: They are both based on JavaScript, and they share a lot of the same After Effects-specific syntax. Although there is some overlap in use, scripting and expressions generally serve very different purposes. Expressions are live, meaning that they execute at each frame and any changes are implemented immediately. Scripts are run on demand, do their work, and exit. If you edit a script, you have to rerun it for any changes to take effect. Expressions are great for linking properties together in a dynamic way, while scripts are better suited for one-shot tasks.

Writing a script can be somewhat more complex than writing an expression. When you're creating an expression, the pick whip and the expression language menu help minimize the amount of code you have to write yourself. There's nothing like that for scripting – you have to get your hands dirty and write some code. So, if an expression will do the job, you're probably better off going that way. Use a script if you need to automate something not well suited to expressions. That would include such things as reading and writing files, creating a user interface, creating After Effects objects (such as comps, layers, masks, and so forth), adding effects, setting blending modes, and rendering automation.

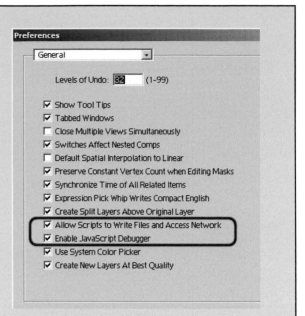

Enable these two General preferences when you're working with scripts.

Getting Started

If you plan to write scripts for After Effects, you will need to change a couple of preferences to fully enable the scripting environment. In Preferences> General, enable Allow Scripts to Write Files and Access Network and Enable JavaScript Debugger.

You create a script using a simple text editor. Don't use a word processor, because it may add header information, curly quotes, or other codes that will cause your script to fail. Save your scripts as .jsx files anywhere on your drive, using the Unicode (UFT-8) option if available. Run your scripts from the File Menu by selecting Run Script > Choose File and navigating to your script using the popup dialog.

The Object Model

Scripting in After Effects is object based. From a script's perspective, After Effects appears as a hierarchy of *objects*. Each object in the hierarchy has associated *methods* that you can invoke and *attributes* that you can examine (and often alter). Think of objects as "things" (projects, comps, layers, cameras, masks, position property, et cetera). Think of methods as actions that objects can perform. Think of attributes as characteristics of objects that you can examine and sometimes modify.

How can you tell the difference between a method and an attribute? Generally a method will have parentheses attached to it (making it like a JavaScript function in that respect). Within the parentheses may be parameters that the method will use to perform its action. Even if there are no parameters, the parentheses still need to be there.

When you write a script, you are essentially just navigating the object hierarchy, using the methods and attributes of the objects along the way to accomplish your objective.

Refer to the accompanying object hierarchy diagram which represents a solid layer with one mask and a Lens Flare effect applied. Let's examine the various levels. The top level is the application (namely, After Effects). The next level is the project. Below that is the item collection, which consists of all the items in the Project window (footage, folders, and comps). Next is the layer collection, which contains all the layers in the comp, including cameras, lights, nulls, and AV layers (an AV layer is any layer that is visible or has sound such as comp layers, footage layers, solids, text layers, and audio layers).

Finally we arrive at the level of the property groups and properties. Property groups contain properties or other property groups. For example, a layer may have several effects applied. All of the effects are contained in one property group. Within that property group, each effect is a property group consisting of the properties that make up that effect. Note that a layer is also a property group, consisting of properties (such as position, rotation, opacity, and scale) and property groups such as masks and effects.

To illustrate how this hierarchy relates to an actual script, let's examine an extremely simple, one-line script that sets the Opacity of a comp's first layer to 50%. The script assumes that the comp is the first item in the project window.

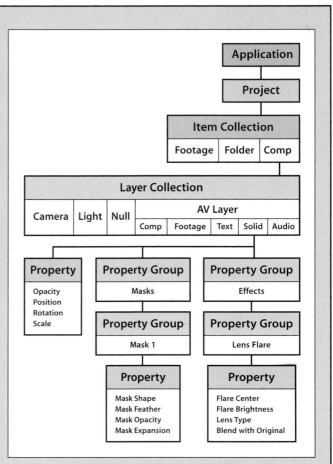

This is a simplified diagram of the After Effects scripting object hierarchy, representing a solid layer with one mask plus a Lens Flare applied.

```
app.project.item(1).layer(1).property("opacity")
.setValue(50);
```

Let's trace this script as it descends through the hierarchy. **app** selects the application (After Effects). **project** selects the project. The project's **item()** method is used to select the comp from the item collection. The comp's **layer()** method is used to select the first layer from the layer collection. Because a layer is actually a property group, the script uses the property group's **property()** method to access the opacity property, then uses the property's **setValue()** method to set the opacity value to 50.

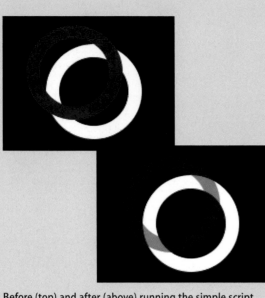

Before (top) and after (above) running the simple script **app.project.item(1).layer(1).property("opacity") .setValue(50).**

Most scripts that you encounter will have many more lines of code than the previous simple example. Usually you will see variables defined to reference objects at different levels of the hierarchy. You would be more likely to see the previous example structured like this:

```
var myComp = app.project.item(1)
var myLayer = myComp.layer(1);
var myProperty = myLayer.property("opacity");
myProperty.setValue(50);
```

Here the variable **myComp** has been created to reference the comp object, **myLayer** references the layer object, and **myProperty** references the opacity property of the layer.

One reason for creating these "intermediate" variables is to enhance the readability of the script. Another is to accommodate multiple operations at a specific level of the hierarchy. For example, in the code above, after we defined the layer-referencing variable **myLayer**, we could simply add the following line of code to set the layer's blending mode to Add:

```
myLayer.blendingMode = BlendingMode.ADD;
```

A More Complex Example

Say we want a script to create a new project, create a 320×240 comp, add a black solid, set the blending mode to Screen, add a Lens Flare to the solid, and set the center of the flare to a position of 100, 100. You could use a script like this:

```
var myProject = app.newProject();
var myComp = myProject.items.addComp
   ("Comp 1",320,240,1,4,30);
var mySolid = myComp.layers.addSolid([0,0,0],
   "Solid 1",320,240,1);
mySolid.blendingMode = BlendingMode.SCREEN;
var myEffect = mySolid.property("Effects").
   addProperty("ADBE Lens Flare");
myEffect.property("ADBE Lens Flare-0001").
   setValue([100,100]);
```

Let's examine the script line by line. Again, it will be helpful if you refer to the hierarchy illustration as you go through this. The first line establishes a variable named **myProject** that will reference the new project which is created by using the application object (**app**) method **newProject()**.

The next line establishes a variable named **myComp** that will reference our new comp. You create the comp by navigating from the new project object (**myProject**) to the item collection object (using the **items** attribute of project object). Then you use the **addComp()** method of the item collection to create a new 320×240, square pixel, 4 second, 30 fps comp named "**Comp 1**".

In the third line we use the variable **myComp** that we created in the previous line to reference the new comp and continue our descent through the hierarchy. First we establish a new variable named **mySolid** that we will use to reference the new solid. We then use the **layers** attribute of the comp object to reference the layer collection, where we then use the layer collection method **addSolid()** to create the new black, 320×240, square pixel solid named "Solid 1".

In the fourth line we set the **blendingMode** attribute of our new layer object to the value **BlendingMode.SCREEN**.

In the fifth line, we begin by defining a new variable named **myEffect** that will reference the Lens Flare effect that we are adding. We add the Lens Flare by starting with the variable referencing the new solid (**mySolid**) and using the **property()** method to descend to effects property group. Note that this works because layers are also considered to be property groups, so the **property()** method is available to them. Then we use the **addProperty()** method of the property group to add the Lens Flare effect (which is really just another property group) to the effects property group.

Finally, using our variable (**myEffect**) that references the new Lens Flare effect, we again use the **property()** method to descend to the properties of the Lens Flare effect, where we use the property's **setValue()** method to set the value of the first parameter (which is Flare Center) to [100,100].

You may be wondering why we used an equal sign to set the blending mode, but used the **setValue()** method to set the Flare Center. It's because the blending mode is an attribute and the Flare Center is a property. Generally, if you can set a keyframe for it, it's a property and you would use **setValue()** or **setValueAtTime()**.

Further Learning

In this highly condensed overview, we have barely scratched the surface of scripting. If you want to proceed further, you should be aware of some other resources that will be useful or even necessary on your journey.

You won't get very far in scripting without being fairly fluent in JavaScript. There's no way around it. You need to know about looping, conditional code, arrays, and much more. There are a number of good JavaScript references available, including *JavaScript: The Definitive Guide* by David Flannagan (O'Reilly Media).

The best resource for details about the After Effects-specific extensions to the scripting language is the After Effects Scripting Guide included on the

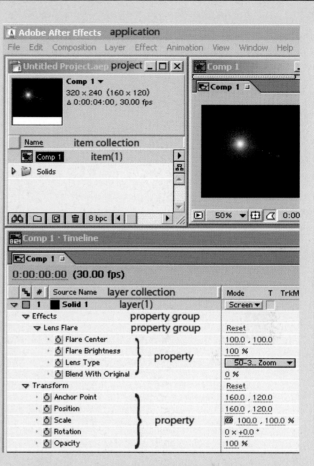

The result of running our more complex script. The various levels of the object hierarchy are noted in red.

application's CD. This reference has detailed information on all of the After Effects objects, methods, and attributes accessible to a script. It's pretty dry reading, but once you get used to the layout, it's relatively easy to navigate as a reference.

A good learning tool is to pick apart existing scripts that work and modify them to do something else interesting. There are some good sample scripts that come with After Effects, and there are other examples in the Scripting Guide. There are also some good examples at the AE Enhancers site (www.aenhancers.com). My own site (www.motionscript.com) also has additional examples and in-depth scripting information.

Professional Edition Effects Roundup

Highlights of the Professional edition, plus a discussion of 16 bpc (bits per pixel) mode and effects.

Free Plug-ins

Be sure to check out the Free Plug-ins folder on your DVD where you'll find some cool goodies, including Premultiply from Walker Effects (see Chapter 1), Übercolor from Fnord (see Chapter 2), and other effects mentioned elsewhere in this volume.

Example Project

Explore the 07-Example Project.aep file as you read this chapter; references to [Ex.##] refer to specific compositions within the project file.

Pro The Professional edition of After Effects brings to the party numerous powerful effects in several categories: 3D Channel, Audio, Distort, Keying, and Grain. Other effects included are a large particle simulation engine – Particle Playground – and useful additions such as Glow, Fractal Noise, and Advanced Lightning.

Adobe provides extensive documentation on effects in the After Effects Help file: Hit F1 while you're in the program, and then either use the Help file's Index or Search function. Also keep in mind that describing what to do with an effect is often like explaining what to do with words: They are building blocks that you can use many different ways to tell many different stories. Therefore, as with the Standard edition effects covered in Volume 1, we'll restrict our comments to effects, tips, and tricks we personally find useful – plus some common gotchas. Note that many effects are also addressed in other chapters; see the chart on the second page of this chapter for a guide.

Adjust

Color Stabilizer

This effect helps remove some of the color and luminance flickering that can occur with timelapse shots (in which the amount of light in a scene varies from frame to frame), older footage with uneven exposure, or in some cases video when a camera's autoexposure was indecisive about how bright a scene was. Color Stabilizer is not a miracle worker, but it can make mild improvements that may lessen the distractions in some shots.

The overall plan is that you can define up to three points in the frame that have representative color or luminance values you wish to keep steady. The effect will then attempt to adjust the overall color or luminance values of the clip to fulfill your wishes. You can pick a guide frame to attempt to match by locating to it and clicking on the words "Set Frame" along the top of the Color Stabilizer's entry in the Effect Controls window.

A Stabilize option of Brightness gives you one point to pick (for when the overall exposure is flickering); Levels gives you two points (for when the contrast in the clip is changing), and Curves gives you three points (to help stabilize intermediate values that are wandering). If the camera or action is not locked down in the shot, you can animate these points to chase around your representative colors. If the footage is noisy or grainy, you can increase the Sample Size to average together the color from more adjacent pixels.

To see this in action, open [**Ex.01*starter**] and RAM Preview. Note how the gradient shadows along the right hand side of the clip flicker – the mid point in particular seems to move up and down in the frame. Preview several times to burn this flicker into your memory. Select the clip, and apply Adjust>Color Stabilizer. Pick a Stabilize option of Curves, and drag the Black Point crosshair to the upper right corner. Drag the White Point to a bright area of the clip: We used the lightest part of the wall just above the doctor's shoulder for our attempt in [**Ex.01_final**]. Note that these colors do not need to be precisely white or black, just areas with good contrast between them. Then set the Mid Point somewhere in the middle of the gradient. RAM Preview again: The flicker should be reduced – although it won't be completely gone. Increase the Sample Size to smooth out the response of the effect. Feel free to experiment with the different Stabilize options and points.

Adjust>Color Stabilizer allows you to select up to three locations of representative color or luminance values; it then attempts to keep these values the same. Footage courtesy Artbeats/Retro Healthcare.

Channel

There is only one additional Channel effect included in the Professional edition, and it is…

Alpha Levels

This is just like Effect>Adjust>Levels with the popup set to Alpha, but without all the other channels to distract you – and without the Histogram as a visual aid. An example is set up in [**Ex.02**] in this project's Example Project file: Click on the Alpha swatch at the bottom of the Comp window to view the alpha, then adjust the Alpha Levels parameters. Because the ordinary Levels effect is more flexible (and comes with the Standard version), we tend to use it instead of Alpha Levels.

Distort

After Effects features several effects that are based on morphing and warping technology. Most of these are included in the Professional edition, and we'll touch on them here. We'll also cover gotchas in a few of the other more traditional distortion effects that come in this higher-end edition.

Connecting Effects

The following effects (or category of effects) are covered in other chapters throughout this volume:

3D Channel Effects	Chapter 19
Audio Effects	Chapter 12
Color Correction	Chapter 8
Compound Effects	Chapter 9
Keying & Matte Tools	Chapter 10
Paint	Chapter 4
Time-based effects	Chapter 14

Compressing Time

Many of the Distort category of effects are slow to render. In several of this chapter's examples, we have cropped our sources in a precomp to save rendering time.

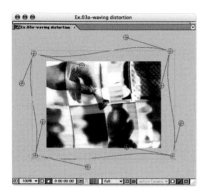

Distort>Bezier Warp is a fun tool to add organic distortions to geometric images. Select it by name in the Timeline or Effect Controls window, and you can drag its handles interactively in the Comp window. Image courtesy Digital Vision/Inner Gaze.

Distort>Corner Pin can be employed to add perspective distortion to layers, such as the text here. Background courtesy Digital Vision/Atmospherics.

We use these Distort effects to fix problems and add creative distortions to an image. As mentioned in Volume 1, Chapter 24, they work particularly well as "distortion fields" applied to nested compositions, with the animation taking place in the precomp. They are less suited to performing traditional morphs; for one, you have to perform the crossfade portion of the morph in a precomp using the Channel>Blend effect.

Common to several of the distort effects is a Quality slider, which determines how fluid the distortion is calculated. The higher the number, the higher the calculation's accuracy – each with correspondingly longer render times. (In previous versions, the Quality slider was represented by an Elasticity popup; they have the same final effect.)

Bezier Warp

This effect gives the impression of having printed your image on a rubber sheet, which you can then tug and stretch to distort the image. You can easily achieve nice, organic results. We especially like taking geometric images and warping them (such as in [**Ex.03a**]), giving the impression that they are being distorted in space, akin to cloth slowly blowing in the wind. The vertices and tangents of the Bezier Warp effect are animated to give the flowing motion. With a little more work, you can make static objects seem to flow to better match liquid backgrounds, as demonstrated in [**Ex.03b**].

You can view and manipulate the warped image directly in the Comp window: Select Bezier Warp by name in the Effect Controls or Timeline window to access its handles. If you're animating these handles, you can access the motion paths they create in the Layer window; double-click the layer, select the effect's name from the View popup along the bottom of the Layer window, and the motion paths will be visible.

It's good to set up a slightly larger image than needed so that your warpages do not cause edge artifacts and gaps to become visible in your final comp. On the other hand, warps are slow to render, which means you want to perform them on as small an image as you can get away with. In both of our examples, the image being warped is scaled or cropped in a smaller precomp to optimize rendering times. For simple distortions like these, you can set the Quality slider to a lower value, which also improves performance. If the warped object starts to display kinks and you can take the additional render time, try one of the higher Quality settings.

Corner Pin

In contrast to Bezier Warp, which is good for organic warpages, Corner Pin is used to maintain strict geometric shapes as it distorts – it skews the image into variations on trapezoids. Corner Pin is used most often to place ("pin") rectangular layers onto what should be a rectangular target that happens to exhibit perspective distortion. Two of the options in the Motion Tracker (Chapter 16) use the Corner Pin effect to "track" one layer onto another.

You can also use Corner Pin by itself to fake perspective distortion; with a bit of experimentation, you can get some quite rakish looks, as with [**Ex.04**]. In this example, we use Corner Pin in one comp as a distortion field, and scroll the text in a precomp. You may find this easier to use than manipulating a layer in 3D space. If you've installed Cycore FX (free with version 6.5), also check out Distort>CC Power Pin.

Mesh Warp

Mesh Warp differs from Bezier Warp in that instead of warping just the corners and overall outlines of a layer, it gives you a series of crosshairs laid out as a grid across the layer that you can move and twist. Unfortunately, unlike some alternate implementations of the mesh warp idea, the After Effects version does not allow you to create a custom mesh of control points *before* you start warping the image – you are stuck with an evenly divided grid as your starting point.

Here are a few less-than-obvious tips for using Mesh Warp:

• The effect needs to be selected in the Timeline or Effect Controls window before you can see the mesh.

• The crosshairs at each intersection of the mesh don't become active until you click directly on them in the Comp window.

• You can Shift+click to select multiple points and drag them as a group.

• To animate these mesh control crosshairs, you have to enable the stopwatch for the single Grid Values parameter, which will store the position of *all* the crosshairs.

• Because you have little control over where the grid lines fall beyond how many grid divisions there are, position your source layer in a precomp and warp it in the next comp in the chain. This approach is demonstrated in **Ex.05**, where we arranged and scaled the source image [**Ex.05_precomp**] while watching to see how its features aligned with the mesh in [**Ex.05*starter**]. Use this as a starting point, and have fun animating a warp yourself.

Optics Compensation

This effect is explained in detail in the After Effects online Help file, so we'll just summarize it here.

Real world imagery shot with a camera exhibits some distortion caused by the lens. This means that features that are supposed to be straight – such as the roof line of a building – are slightly bent. This distortion is more pronounced with a smaller angle or field of view (images shot with a fish-eye lens, for example, are very distorted). However, computer-generated graphics normally do not exhibit this distortion; they have perfectly straight lines everywhere you expect.

To match real and synthetic imagery, you either need to remove the distortion from the real imagery, or add it to the synthetic imagery. That's where Optics Compensation comes in. To correct a real scene, apply this effect to the source that needs correcting, overlay a straight object as a

A Banner Day

To easily create realistic flag and banner effects, check out 3D Flag from Zaxwerks (www.zaxwerks.com).

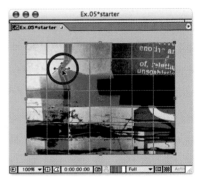

To edit Distort>Mesh Warp, click on the crosshairs where the mesh lines intersect, and drag their handles. Image courtesy Digital Vision/Naked & Scared.

Distort>Optics Compensation can be used to add or remove lens distortion from scenes, or at its extremes to create fun-house mirror effects. Footage courtesy Herd of Mavericks.

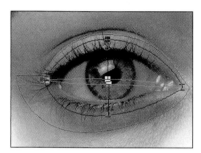

Setting up Distort>Reshape: In this example, the red mask shape captures the eyelashes and eye opening to fold down into the closed eye (the yellow shape). The blue mask shape outlines the portion of skin around the eye socket we don't want to stretch; the kink on the left side is to capture stray eyelashes. The inverted boxes are the Correspondence Points; they say "Move this portion of the image directly to this other point" (in this case, the corners of the eye). Image courtesy Digital Vision/The Body.

Different Elasticity settings obey the Boundary Mask with varying degrees of accuracy: Stiff (right) and Liquid (far right) are shown here.

reference where a straight edge should be in the scene (for example, position a thin Solid on top to use as a guide), enable Reverse Lens Distortion, and adjust the Field of View (FOV) until the edges in the image straighten out.

To add distortion to a computer-generated scene, add this effect to your render or an adjustment layer above your composite, disable Reverse Lens Distortion, and dial in the FOV you want to emulate – perhaps duplicating the value used for your camera in a 3D program or After Effects. Note that this distortion shrinks the edges of your image; make sure they don't creep too much into your Action Safe area, or start with a larger-than-full-frame source. Of course, you can also (ab)use Optics Compensation to create some "fun-house mirror" style distortions, as we have in [Ex.06].

Reshape

In our opinion, this is the most powerful and controllable of the warping-oriented Distort effects. You set up two mask shapes: one around the region you want to move, and one representing where you want to move it to and what shape you want it to take on when it gets there. A third mask shape can serve as a protection boundary that says, "Nothing (much) beyond this region should move when the objects inside it are being reshaped." You cannot cross this Boundary Mask, so make sure it encloses your other mask shapes.

How strongly the Boundary Mask is obeyed depends directly on the Elasticity settings: The higher the setting, the more strongly it is obeyed. The trade-off is increased rendering times. Be sure to give the Boundary Mask some extra distance away from the features you don't want to move. In general, you should draw your masks so they enclose – not bisect or straddle – the feature or shape you are trying to move or protect.

An example of this issue is demonstrated in [Ex.07a]. We have an image of an eye; we want to make it blink. The first thing we did is cut out an inverted mask shape for the eyeball to reveal an undistorted copy of the eye layer behind – we don't want to distort the eyeball while moving the eyelids. Next, we drew masks beyond the eyelid, trying to capture as much of the eyelash as practical, and inside the bone for the eye socket, because your bones don't slide down your face when you blink. However, the results are very sloppy with lower Elasticity settings – and the eyeliner painted around the eye socket gets dragged in anyway.

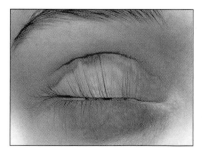

Correspondence Course

Perhaps the greatest mystery of Reshape is the subject of Correspondence Points. This is a common feature of morphing programs, in which a point along the first shape will morph directly to a certain point along the second shape. If these points are not set carefully, you may find your warp drifting as parts head in directions you did not anticipate. At the opposite end of the spectrum, you can purposely move the Correspondence Points to rotated positions in order to cause a twisting animation as you warp.

Reshape defaults to one Correspondence Point. To add more, select Reshape in the Effect Controls window and Option+click on Mac (Alt+click on Windows) on the Source or Destination Mask outline in the Comp window. When you position the cursor over one of these points, it will change to a four-way arrow. Drag the point to its new target destination. To delete an existing point, Option+click (Alt+click) on it.

[Ex.07b] has been set up for you to experiment with. Here, the telephone dial is shrunk and spun as the effect's Percent parameter animates. With the time marker at 00:00, select Reshape in the Timeline

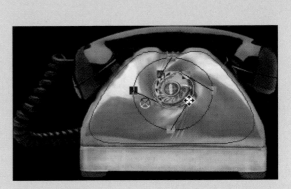

The dial on this phone is shrunken using Reshape, and twisted through manipulation of its Correspondence Points. Image courtesy Classic PIO/Telephones.

or Effect Controls window; study the Correspondence Points in the Comp window; and move, add, or delete them, observing the results.

Remember, too, that you can animate the Correspondence Points, either to follow the changing shape of an animated mask (which might be animating to follow a moving object in a movie) or to add further life to stills.

Try higher settings (and be patient while it renders) to see the difference in accuracy.

By the way, this example shows one of the most common problems with "realistic" warps: Parts of the image you want to move need to overlap parts you don't want to move. In this case, the eyelashes (which should move when we blink) overlap the eyeliner around the socket; in a real job, this photo would probably be retouched to shorten the lashes.

Through careful use of blending modes, masks, Reshape, and its Correspondence Points (left), text can be wrapped onto the surface of another layer (right). Check out **[Ex.08]**. 3D Glass by Paul Sherstobitoff.

Another good use for Reshape is to conform one shape to another. When the shape you want your selected layer to emulate exists on another layer (for example, stretching text to fit a shape on a background image), your life will be easier if you first make both layers the same size through prior trimming or precomposing. You can then draw the mask shape on the background layer, copy it, and paste it into the layer to be reshaped. This arrangement is demonstrated in [Ex.08].

The bottom is normal, boring Courier text; the top shows it eroded with Matte Tools>Simple Choker. Preview **[Ex.09]**; the Choke Matte value is animated to erode the text away to black.

Sweet Composites

The Composite Suite plug-in set (from Red Giant Software – www.redgiantsoftware.com) contains a number of excellent tools for color matching, edge feathering, and so forth.

To speed up your workflow, all three grain effects default to showing their results inside a white Preview box. Footage courtesy Kevin Dole.

Matte Tools

The two effects in this submenu – Matte Choker and Simple Choker – are most useful when you're color keying to clean up the edges of the resulting alpha channels (see Chapter 10 for more details). Matte Choker was designed to help clean up problematic color keys where there may be holes or tears in the edges. For tightening up less-tattered alpha channels, go with Simple Choker.

Beyond keying applications, the Matte Tools have some creative uses, such as "eroding" the edges of text for a grungier feel (as demonstrated in **[Ex.09]**), or providing an unusual way to wipe an object on- or offscreen.

Noise & Grain

This effect category was recently created to contain the new grain plug-ins added in version 6.5, and the noise effects that were previously in the Stylize category.

Add Grain, Match Grain, and Remove Grain

These three effects from Visual Infinity's Grain Surgery set provide a degree of instant gratification, while also being very deep. The online Help file contains many, many pages on using these effects; here we will put more emphasis on their overall application.

To combat their significant rendering time, all of these plug-ins default to creating a white-bordered Preview box that covers a fraction of the original image. To reposition the box, select the effect in the Timeline or Effect Controls window, and drag its circle-X icon in the middle of the box. For your final render, set the Viewing Mode popup for the effect to Final Output. Note that all three of these plug-ins can also be applied to masked or color-matched portions of the image; these controls are in their Blend with Original section.

Add Grain applies a noise pattern to the underlying clip. This is often done to make a computer-generated scene match filmed scenes that appear before and after it in an edit, or simply for stylistic purposes. It comes with 13 presets based on popular film stocks; you can also highly customize the character of the noise. Open **[Ex.10]**, which already has Add Grain applied to a clip. Select the clip and press F3 to open its Effect Controls window. Experiment with the Preset popup, plus the parameters in the Settings, Color, and Application sections.

Remember that film and high-definition footage have a much larger frame size than ordinary video. What seem like nice, small grains relative to a film frame can look huge when applied to a standard definition video frame. To achieve a more subtle, film-like look, consider first scaling your footage up to a film frame size, then applying Add Grain to a nested composition that contains your scaled-up footage. This processing chain is demonstrated in [**Ex.11a**] and [**Ex.11b**] (you will probably need to resize the Comp window to view these larger compositions).

Remove Grain attacks full-frame film grain, analog video noise, half-tone patterns from scanned prints, CCD noise, JPEG compression artifacts, or digital video noise; it is not designed to deal with isolated pockets of noise such as video dropouts or dirt. In addition to creating aesthetically cleaner images, the result is also often easier to compress for DVDs or the web. Open [Ex.12a], and select the **AB_RetroScience** layer which was captured on 16mm film and transferred to video. Apply Effect>Noise & Grain>Remove Grain. Make sure the effect is selected, then click and drag the icon in the center of the Preview box in the Comp window, observing its effects. Note that Remove Grain at its default settings is a bit overzealous at smoothing the image. Tweak Remove Grain's Noise Reduction Settings and, optionally, Fine Tuning parameters to trade off noise removal versus preserving detail.

As noted, Remove Grain is not just for film grain. You may have clips captured on video that also exhibit undesired grain; for instance, when shot in a dark room where the camera's gain had to be cranked up.

A common challenge for visual effects artists is blending new imagery such as 3D objects into an existing scene. A giveaway that the new object does not belong is if its grain structure does not match that of its surroundings. The Match Grain plug-in is designed for this task, analyzing the grain structure of one image, adding this grain to the image you've applied the effect to, and optionally removing any grain originally present in the new image.

Open [Ex.13*starter], and note how the clean gizmo does not blend with the grainy background. Press Shift+F5 to save a snapshot of this beginning composite. Select **QE_Gizmo_loop**, and apply Effect>Noise & Grain>Match Grain. The Effect Controls window will open; set the Noise Source Layer popup to **AB_RetroScience**. Press F5 to compare your before and after results; you can also RAM Preview to see that the new grain is animated.

Of course, Match Grain is only a portion of the battle in a composite like this. Open [Ex.13_final], and study the effects applied to **QE_Gizmo_loop**: We used Hue/Saturation to desaturate the bright yellow gizmo to better match the background, and Matte Choker to feather its edges so the gizmo would "melt" into the background.

[Ex.11b] contains a split screen showing different techniques for applying Add Noise. The video footage on the right has Add Noise applied directly; on the left, we've scaled the video up to film size in a precomp, then applied Add Noise. Footage courtesy Artbeats/Industry: Gears and Machines.

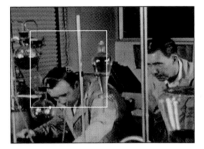

Remove Grain smoothes out the 16mm film grain in this shot – compare the shutters, wall, and skin textures inside and outside the Preview box. Footage courtesy of Artbeats/Retro Science.

To better match our gizmo (A) into our scene, we applied Match Grain (B). To finish off the composite, we also desaturated its color and used Matte Choker to feather its edges (C).

Pro Sweet 16

A major feature for professional users is the ability to process images at a color depth of 16 bits per channel (actually, 15 bits + 1; the math is more efficient and the difference compared with full 16 bits is minimal). This provides much greater resolution for processing color, maintaining more of the quality inherent in 16-bit RGB still images, 10-bit YUV video captures, and 10-bit log Cineon format files. (Note that some video codecs require you to edit the After Effects Prefs file to access their extended color range; see Bonus Chapter 31B in the **Bonus Chapters** folder on the DVD for more details.) Here are how some common values relate between the two modes:

8 bpc	16 bpc
0	0
16	2056
127.5	16384
235	30198
255	32768

What does this additional resolution buy you? Let's use a money analogy and compare rounding to the nearest dollar to rounding to the nearest cent. Say you started out with $10, and you were required to give someone 16% of it. Depending how you round, you would have either $8 or $8.40 left. Say this was followed by an 18% bonus; you would then end up with either $9 or $9.91 – a significant difference. The same happens in color space: As calculations accumulate, the

"cents" lost along the way result in a loss in the overall image quality, usually seen as posterizing (areas of flat color) in gradients, highlights, and shadows.

Setting 16 bpc Mode

If you have the Professional edition, you can place After Effects in 16 bpc mode in the File>Project Settings dialog. As the name suggests, this setting is saved per project. You can switch between 8 and 16 bpc anytime during a project: For example, you might want to work in 8 bpc mode for speed, then switch to 16 bpc for rendering. (Note that you cannot set this in the Render Settings.)

The shortcut to switch modes is to Option+click (Alt+click) on the rightmost button along the bottom of the Project window. Comp window snapshots survive this switch, so it's easy to take a snapshot (Shift+F5, F6, F7, or F8) in one mode, switch, then compare the new image with the previous one stored in the snapshot (to compare, press F5–F8 without holding the Shift key).

Cause and Effects

Effects need to be updated to process with 16-bit accuracy. You can use 8-bit effects in 16-bit projects; you just may lose some accuracy at more extreme settings. There are three ways to tell if an effect can work in 16-bit mode:

• In the Effects palette, select Show Only 16 Bit Effects from its Options menu. Change the display

To quickly switch between 8 and 16 bpc modes, Option+click (Alt+click) on the bpc button along the bottom of the Project window.

from Categories to Alphabetical to see all eligible effects at a glance.

• 16 bpc effects also have a slightly different icon in the Effects palette.

• When a project is in 16 bpc mode, any 8-bit effects will have a yellow warning icon appear next to their names in the Effect Controls window.

[Ex.99a] shows a classic example of the benefits of processing at 16 bits per channel. Two copies of the Adjust>Level effect have been applied to a grayscale gradient. The first one is set so that Output Black is 250 and Output White is 255 (on an 8-bit, 0-to-255 scale). The second copy of Levels attempts to stretch this back out, setting Input Black to 250 and Input White to 255. In 8 bpc mode, the result is a heavily posterized image – six concentric rings of different levels of gray, instead of a nice gradient – because so much information

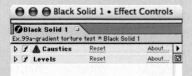

When in 16 bpc mode, effects that can process only 8 bits of color depth per channel will have a yellow warning icon next to their names.

was lost in the level compression performed by the first effect. However, when the project is set to 16 bpc mode, a smooth gradient appears again.

More useful examples are demonstrated in **[Ex.99b]** through **[Ex.99d]**. Several blending modes and color correction effects use 50% luminance as a centerpoint for their actions. However, sometimes you want these effects to focus on a different luminance range. The solution is to heavily warp this range using the Effect>Adjust> Levels, apply the blending mode or effect, then bring the midtones back where you want them with a second Levels effect (sometimes applied as an adjustment layer above a composite). In 8 bpc mode, posterization can become visible, especially in darker areas or gradients; 16 bpc mode retrieves considerably more information, smoothing the final result.

There usually needs to be at least two effects in line before enough errors accumulate for you to realize benefits from 16 bpc mode. However, some individual effects that heavily manipulate color (such as Synthetic Aperture's Color Finesse) or create gradient lighting effects (such as Trapcode's Shine or Knoll's Light Factory) are also prime candidates to benefit from 16 bpc mode.

In each of these cases, you may see benefits from the increased accuracy in color calculations in 16 bpc mode even if your video card is only displaying 8 bpc, or

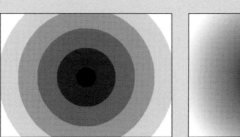

Extreme Levels adjustments on gradients can result in posterization in 8 bpc mode (left). Switching to 16 bpc often smoothes them out (right).

your final output format is 8 bpc – the potential errors are that large. You will retain even more quality if your output is to a 16 bpc RGB file format, or a 10-bit YUV codec for higher-end video cards.

In short, if you see posterizing, try 16 bpc mode. It's not a cure for all problems; for example, the 8 bpc source material used in

some of our examples limits what we can do with them, even in 16 bpc mode. 16 bpc mode also takes twice as much memory, and longer (although not twice as long) to render. But quite often, 16 bpc mode is well worth the trade-off and is almost a necessity when you're working with film sources (see Chapter 28).

The differences between 8 bpc (left column) and 16 bpc (right column) often show up in the shadows. Main images from Artbeats/Establishments: Urban and Digital Vision/The Body; textures courtesy Digital Vision/Naked & Scared.

8 Color Correction

An introduction to color correction techniques and possibilities.

8-bit Values

Throughout this chapter, we will refer to 8 bit per channel (8 bpc) color values, which range from 0 (no presence) to 255 (full value). If you have the Professional edition, and are performing radical color corrections on real projects, set File>Project Settings>Color Depth to 16 bpc for more accurate processing.

Example Project

Explore the 08-Example Project.aep file as you read this chapter; references to [Ex.##] refer to specific compositions within the project file. Make sure you install Cycore FX and Color Finesse (on the After Effects installer CD), as well as the free Digital Film Tools 55mm Warm/Cool plug-in that came with this book's disc.

Color Correction is one of the most important – and under-used – disciplines in motion graphics. The growing practice of capturing footage digitally and transferring it directly into the computer has only increased its importance, as you can no longer rely on someone else (such as a telecine colorist) to improve the footage before you get your hands on it.

In this chapter, we will give you a foundation for approaching color correction. We will start with basic contrast improvement and hue shifts, then move onto important "divide and conquer" techniques to isolate individual colors and luminance ranges. We will conclude with how to transfer these techniques to Synthetic Aperture's Color Finesse (free with After Effects 6.5). Along the way we will also discuss more fanciful color treatments. Keep in mind that color correction is as much art as science; our versions are but one idea of how to treat a scene.

Leveling the Field

The most basic form of color correction is maximizing contrast. A good tool for this job is Adjust>Levels, which also features an all-important Histogram display that helps you understand what is going on with the colors in your image.

Open [Ex.01*starter] from this chapter's project file. This was shot on a foggy day, resulting in it being "flat" without a lot of contrast between dark and light areas. Press Shift+F5 to take a snapshot of this unaltered image.

Then select layer 1, and apply Effect>Adjust>Levels; the Effect Controls window will open. First turn your attention to the Histogram display: This gives you a graphic representation of where the action is in your image. As you move from left to right, you are viewing darker to lighter values; the taller the "mountain range" is at any given point, the more these values are present in the image. Ideally, a balanced image should show some activity across the Histogram's entire width. Looking at the Histogram for this layer, we can see it has a lot of activity in the upper midtones, but the gap at the far right means it's lacking the brightest colors, such as pure white. Jump to various points in time, and notice how the Histogram changes to reflect the levels in the current frame.

The Histogram shows what's happening before you've applied any adjustments. To see what's happening after your adjustments, apply

Adjust>Levels a second time. When you adjust the controls in the first Levels effect, the second Histogram will show the results.

Now turn your attention to the triangles underneath the first Histogram: The black triangle – Input Black – indicates which value you want to be output as pure black (a value of 0), the white triangle – Input White – is for white (255), and the gray triangle – Gamma – indicates where the midpoint (128) should be. While watching the image in the Comp window, slide Input White to the left (decreasing its value) until it lines up with the right edge of the mountain range. You will see the image brighten in the Comp window. Also, the peaks in the second Histogram will now be spread across its entire width. Press F5 to compare this result with the snapshot you took of the original.

If you continue to decrease Input White, the image will "blow out" as a range of original values are output as pure white; when you release the mouse, the bottom Histogram will have its peaks crowded against the right edge. You can also increase Input Black in the first Levels effect to "crush" the blacks. You usually want to avoid extreme adjustments, unless you are going after a particular effect. Reset these sliders until they just encompass the entire range of values shown in the first Histogram.

The image looks better, but is still a bit bright and washed out. Many images benefit from altering their Gamma, which is the balance of their midtones. Drag the Gamma pointer to the right while watching the Comp window; stop when you feel you have a more pleasing balance. Our end result is shown in [**Ex.01_final**].

The Histogram display in the Levels effect (above) gives you a graphic representation of the brightness levels present in your image. Image courtesy Artbeats/Lifestyles – Mixed Cuts 1.

Rewriting History

The Histogram display does not update properly if After Effects has already cached the frame into RAM. Sometimes you will need to toggle the Levels effect on and off to refresh the Histogram.

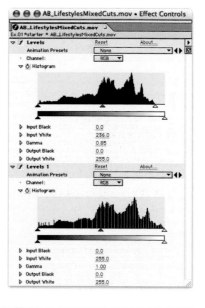

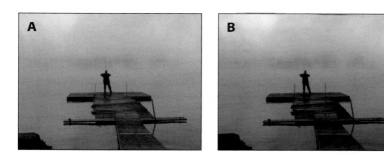

Before (A) and after (B): We made our adjustments to the first Levels effect by studying its Histogram. The Histogram in the second Levels effect displays the result, which is a more evenly spread out mix of dark areas and lights (right). The gaps in the second Histogram show where we have lost color resolution by remapping the values in an image; where possible, it is best to work with 10-bit YUV images in 16 bpc mode so these gaps do not show up as posterization in the final image.

Thrown for a Curve

Adjust>Levels is great for basic contrast adjustments, but sometimes you need more control. For example, when we were adjusting the Gamma in [**Ex.01**], we lost some of the detail in the boat in the lower left-hand corner. Adjust>Curves gives us the ability to fine-tune different ranges of values.

Open [**Ex.02*starter**], select layer 1, and press F3 to open the Effect Controls window. We've already applied a pair of Levels effects, but we're not going to adjust them; we're using them just for their Histogram displays. In-between we applied Adjust>Curves. This effect provides a "transfer function" which alters the color values of pixels as they are transferred from the input (represented by the bottom edge, or X axis) to the output (the left edge, or Y axis).

To replicate the white point adjustment we made earlier, click on the line near the upper-right corner of the Curves display, and drag slightly to the left while keeping your cursor along the top. When you release the mouse, you will see the lower Histogram spread out, indicating you've spread a narrower range of input values (left to almost all the way to the right) across the full range of output values (bottom to the very top). Tweak the position of the point you just created until you're happy. To remove it, drag it outside of the box.

Now click in the middle of this line, and drag slightly downward – this takes the midtones and outputs them darker, darkening the overall image. When you let go, watch the boat in the lower left corner of the Comp window; you will start to lose some of the contrast between its seat and bottom. To recover this detail, you need to brighten the darker areas of the image – so click along the Curves line in the lower left corner, and drag slightly upward. Likewise, we feel by lowering the center point that we've lost some of our contrast between the sky and the man; click along the curve between its center and right extreme, and drag upward to brighten the sky. Toggle the Curves effect off and on to see the results of your adjustments; our effort is saved in [**Ex.02_final**].

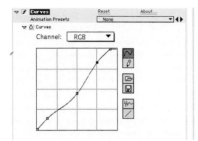

Adjust>Curves allows more control over adjusting color values from input to output (above). The extra point in the lower left corner of Curves helps us restore some contrast in the boat in the lower left portion of the image (below).

Further Reading

Color correction is a vast subject, and we only skim the surface in this chapter. To delve further, we recommend the following books:

Color Correction for Digital Video by Steve Hullfish & Jaime Fowler (CMP Books 2002 – an excerpt is included on this book's DVD)

Video Color Correction for Nonlinear Editors by Stuart Blake Jones (Focal Press 2003)

Although both are aimed primarily at editors, they include a number of case studies and tutorials that everyone can learn from. They also cover technical subjects such as reading waveform and vectorscope displays in more depth.

Gamma-Corrected Compositing: An article we wrote for DV magazine (www.dv.com) on gamma-corrected compositing for more realistic effects is included in the **Goodies** folder on the DVD.

Automatic Color

After Effects features three automatic color correction plug-ins under the Effect>Adjust category:

Auto Color attempts to neutralize color shifts in an image (especially if its Snap Neutral Midtones switch is enabled) and bend it toward a more natural – and often more saturated – range of colors with good contrast. An extreme correction is demonstrated in [**Ex.90**]; toggle the filter on and off to see its effect.

Auto Contrast performs the Levels adjustments we described earlier

in this chapter, looking to maximize the light-to-dark range of an image without shifting its color.

Auto Levels individually maximizes the red, green, and blue channels of an image. Unlike Auto Contrast, it can introduce potentially undesirable color shifts.

These three plug-ins can re-adjust their corrections on every frame of the movie. You can smooth out their response by increasing their Temporal Smoothing parameter. All are described in more detail in

Adjust>Auto Color is excellent at removing the color cast from an image, even if it changes over time. Image courtesy Artbeats/Industry Scenes.

Volume 1, Chapter 24; a "shootout" with all three applied to the same image is demonstrated in [**Ex.91**] – note the shifts in contrast and color introduced by each effect, compared with the original image. In particular, watch out for color shifts over time!

Simple Colorization

We've covered contrast; now let's talk about color. You are probably familiar with the popular Hue/Saturation effect. This allows broad shifts in color, plus the ability to increase or reduce saturation. Close any open comps and open [**Ex.03*starter**], select layer 1, and apply Adjust> Hue/Saturation. In the Effect Controls window that opens, alter the Master Hue while watching the Comp window: Increasing its value rotates the colors more toward blue; decreasing rotates more toward green. You can also increase Master Saturation to achieve a hyper-real richness, or decrease it to give an old-time feel to the footage. RAM Preview [**Ex.03_final**], where we've keyframed some of these options.

The problem with using Hue/Saturation at its default of Channel Control set to Master is that all of the colors are shifted. This can work fine for altering the appearance of stock footage or 3D renders that have one basic color, to make them blend better with the project you're working on. The folder **Ex.04** contains several comps where we've keyframed Master Hue through a full 360° of rotation (starting at 0°, or no alterna-

Shadow/Highlight

After Effects 6.5 includes a version of the Photoshop Shadow/Highlight filter, which provides an alternate way to change the apparent lighting in a scene.

Adjust>Hue/Saturation is good for broad adjustments to an image's overall color. The leftmost image is the original. Image courtesy Artbeats/Surfing.

DFT 55mm Warm/Cool (free on this book's DVD-ROM) provides a single slider approach to tinting an image warmer (orange) or cooler (blue). Image courtesy Artbeats/The Orient.

A Better Tritone

Boris BCC Tritone allows you to adjust the brightness level the midtone color maps to, giving better control over contrast. It comes free on the *Creating Motion Graphics Volume 1* DVD-ROM.

To create your own tints, place a colored Solid above your footage, and experiment with its Opacity and Blending Mode. To restore correct contrast to the final result, apply Levels to an Adjustment Layer on top.

tion); they look pretty smooth. However, if the source has a lot of colors, the result can sometimes look pretty ugly: Open [**Ex.05**], select layer 1, hit F3, and play with the Master Hue for proof! (We will discuss more discerning settings of the Channel Control later.)

Tinting

In some cases, you may prefer to add a color tint to an image. Several plug-ins can do this; here are three that quickly provide pleasing results:

Adjust>Photo Filter (new in version 6.5) simulates placing a colored gel in front of a camera lens. It comes with several presets in its Filter popup menu; you can also select Custom from this menu and create your own color. Density controls the depth of tint; Preserve Luminosity prevents the image from becoming murky. It has already been applied to a layer in [**Ex.06a**]; feel free to experiment.

DFT 55mm>55mm Warm/Cool (included free on this book's DVD) provides a very easy way to tint an image to appear warmer (more orange) or cooler (more blue). It does a better job of keeping a pleasing overall color balance than many tinting effects. It has already been applied to a layer in [**Ex.06b**]; experiment with its Temperature setting. We will discuss other creative color correction plug-ins from DFT (Digital Film Tools) in the *Third Party Magic* sidebar later in this chapter.

Image Control>CC Toner (part of Cycore FX, which comes free with version 6.5) is a very easy-to-use "tritone" effect. Its advantage over the normal Image Control>Tint plug-in is that CC Toner allows you to keep your blacks and whites pure, then tint just the intermediate colors. It has already been applied to a layer in [**Ex.06c**]; experiment with its Midtones color. Its Blend with Original parameter controls the depth of the effect.

Roll Your Own

Some users prefer to create tints using colored solids and blending modes. This is demonstrated in [**Ex.07a**], where we placed a full-frame colored solid on top of our video layer (you could also mask it to tint just a selected portion of the image). The color of the solid adjusts the color of the tint; the Opacity of the solid adjusts its depth. Use the Color blending mode as a starting point, as it replaces the colors in the underlying image stack with its own. Feel free to experiment with other modes; for example, Classic Color Dodge, Classic Color Burn, and Vivid Light work well with this footage.

The result of tinting – indeed, most color corrections – is that the contrast in the altered image may now be less than ideal. Applying Levels to the colored solid will not help much in this case, as it would adjust only the color of the solid – not of the final composite. Therefore, you will notice in [**Ex.07a**] that we added an Adjustment Layer to the top of the layer stack, and applied Levels to it. Enable the Video switch for this layer, open its Effect Controls, and experiment with using Levels to rebalance the contrast after you've picked a color you like.

Use Render>Ramp to create a color gradient (far left), and apply it on top of your footage using a blending mode such as Color (left). Skateboarding footage courtesy Creative License.

Of course, you're not stuck with just one color – many like to apply a gradient to their tinting solid so they can define a different color for the sky and ground. This is what we've done in [Ex.07b], using Render> Ramp. Again, Opacity controls the depth of the effect; different blending modes will produce different results. If you want more than one color in your gradient, consider third-party plug-ins such as Digital Anarchy's Gradient! (www.digitalanarchy.com) and Zaxwerks' GradientWerks (www.zaxwerks.com).

On the more subtle end of the spectrum, some apply a gradient to just part of the image, such as the sky. For this, use Ramp as a luma matte for a colored solid, as we have in [Ex.07c].

Divide and Conquer

The next step is adjusting individual ranges of colors. One common approach is to address the "shadows" (darker values), "midtones" (intermediate values), and "highlights" (lighter values) of the red, green, and blue channels individually. The Color Balance effect provides this level of control. Let's work through an example of using it to neutralize color casts in an image. Once you understand how to do this, you can use the same techniques to craft your own creative colorizations.

Open [Ex.08*starter]. This vintage footage lacks contrast, and has a red cast. Let's fix the contrast problem first; doing so will also give us an optimum spectrum of shadows, midtones, and highlights to work with. Press Shift+F5 to save a snapshot. Select layer 1, and apply Adjust> Levels. Note the broad gaps at the edges of the Histogram, indicating lack of contrast; drag the black and white triangles underneath it to the edges of the active display. Press Shift+F6 to remember what your Levels adjustment looks like, and apply Adjust>Color Balance.

To understand what is going on with the colors in an image, make sure Window>Info is open. Move your cursor over the areas behind the doctor that should be around 50% gray and note the R, G, and B values: They are supposed to all be around 127. Move the cursor over areas that should

Tweaking Solids

To more interactively adjust the color of a Solid, pick a good initial color, then apply Adjust>Hue Saturation, which provides real-time feedback of your adjustments.

The original footage (above) is washed out. We can fix the contrast issue using Levels (below left). This makes the red tint in the footage more obvious (below). Footage courtesy Artbeats/ Retro Healthcare.

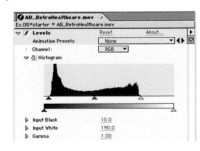

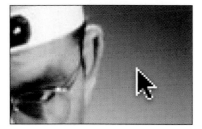

Drag your cursor around what should be black, white, and medium gray areas of the image (above), while reading the values in the Info window (right) to see if any of the color channels are particularly strong or weak.

Using our readings in the Info window as a guide, we used Adjust>Color Balance (above) to neutralize the color casts in the footage (below).

Changing Colors

To change a specific color in your image, try Image Control>Change Color or >Change To Color.

be black; all three channels should be equally low. Then move it around the white areas of the doctor's smock and headband; all three channels should be equally high.

The Shadow, Midtone, and Hilight bands overlap, so any adjustment to one will affect the readings for the others. Therefore, we're going to leave Midtone for last, as it is the most affected by the others. In the white areas of the image, you will notice that the green values are about 2 to 4 units lower than red and blue. Let's use that as a starting point, entering "4" for the Hilight Green Balance parameter. Drag your cursor around the image again to verify this correction worked.

Next, let's equalize the color channels in the shadows. You should have noticed that the green channel is weak again, this time by 2 to 6 units. Enter "6" for Shadow Green Balance, and check the black areas again. Don't be surprised if you need to tweak this a few times; we ended up with a value of 10.

Finally, move the cursor around the wall behind the doctor, looking for values that average 127. The red channel is about 15 units too high, and the blue channel about 8 units too low. Enter "–15" for Midtone Red Balance and "8" for Midtone Blue Balance, and recheck your readings, tweaking as needed; we ended up with –25 and 16, respectively.

Did we say "finally?" Oops – since these bands overlap, you will find your Shadow and Hilight adjustments may need to be retweaked. It's good to check them again at least once. We found we needed to increase the Shadow Red Balance and decrease the Shadow Blue Balance, then tweak the midtones one last time. Press F5 and F6 to compare "before" and "during" with your final. Our version is saved as [**Ex.08/intermediate**].

Our goal here was to neutralize the color cast in this footage. Of course, sometimes you may prefer to colorize an image. You can use Color Balance to create these stylings. If you're unsure how to get from one colorization to another, try applying two copies of the effect: one to remove the original color cast, and a second to introduce the cast you desire.

Secondary Correction

Sometimes, you want to adjust just a single color in an image, such as the skin tones. This technique is often called *secondary color correction* (with the overall corrections we just made being known as *primary color correction*). One way to isolate a set of colors is to return to our old friend, Hue/Saturation. Either continue with the comp you've been working on or open [**Ex.08/intermediate**], press Shift+F7 to store another snapshot, select layer 1, and apply Adjust>Hue/Saturation.

In the Effect Controls for Hue/Saturation, change the Channel Control popup to Reds. In the Channel Range bars below, you will see two small rectangles bracketing the red range of colors, with the two triangles beyond showing how the selection feathers off into the surrounding pinks and yellows. You can move these sliders yourself to set custom ranges; the default Reds selection will work fine here.

You'll notice the Master Saturation slider now says Red Saturation. Scrub it to the right

We used Adjust>Hue/Saturation, with Channel Control set to Reds (left), to increase the saturation in the doctor's skin tones (above).

while watching the Comp window until the doctor has healthy, pink cheeks (press F7 to compare your before and after results; press F5 to remember where you started!). Our version is saved in [**Ex.08_final**]. Again, we're taking corrective action here; you can use the same effects and techniques to create more fanciful effects.

Another way to isolate a color to correct is to use a keying plug-in. If you have the Professional edition, open [**Ex.09*starter**], which contains three copies of a person painting an Asian character. Say the "hand model" in this shot has older, pinker skin than the actor they are sitting in for. Press 1 to jump to a place where the hand is clearly visible. Select layer 1, and apply Keying>Color Range. In the Effect Controls window, click on the topmost eyedropper, then click in the middle of the hand in the Preview image; some of it will now turn black as it is keyed out. Then click on the eyedropper with a plus sign after it, and drag it along other portions of the hand that are still visible.

Next, you need a copy of the footage that has just the hand. Press F4 until the Modes column is visible, enable the Video switch for layer 2, and set its TrkMat popup to Alpha Inverted. You should now have the hand isolated. Select layer 2, apply Blur & Sharpen>Fast Blur, and set Blurriness to 1.0 to remove some of the wrinkles from the skin. Then add Adjust> Hue/Saturation, and adjust its parameters to make the skin, say, a paler yellow. Finally, turn on layer 3's Video switch, which is a copy of the original footage – this will fill in the rest of the image around the hand. Our version is in [**Ex.09_final**]; we've tweaked the key a bit further by adding Simple Choker. On a real job, you'd want to use a better keying plug-in such as Keylight, and use an animated garbage mask to make sure you were correcting just the skin tones – not all similarly colored objects.

Too Much Information?

You can change the scale displayed by the Info window in its Options menu – click on the arrow in its upper right corner or click the window to cycle through the options. We're using 8 bpc mode; you may prefer the Percent scale.

To color correct just the skin in this footage (A), we keyed out the hand and used the result as an alpha inverted matte for a copy of the original footage (B). We then color-corrected the hand, and placed it over a third copy of the original shot (C).

More Sex

Check out the Bonus Tutorial **Enhancing 3D** on the DVD-ROM for tips on enhancing 3D renders using Instant Sex and other techniques.

Preset Sex

An Animation Preset called **InstantSex.ffx** is included in the **Goodies** folder on the DVD. It uses the CC Composite effect (part of the Cycore FX set bundled free with After Effects 6.5) to recreate this technique using just one layer.

Adding Sex

So far, we've presented a set of traditional, by-the-book techniques for manipulating color. Next we'd like to play around with some alternate ideas using blending modes to enhance images. Hopefully these will open your mind to other experiments to perform.

Many clients want a sexy look that they associate with film. Film isn't inherently sexy, but if you light a scene well, choose a film stock to create a certain look, and take advantages of the imperfection of film – such as selectively overexposing it, causing highlights to "bloom" into surrounding colors – then you can get something better than reality. We developed a set of techniques known as "Instant Sex" to enhance 3D renders, which can often be flat; these techniques can help punch up almost any shot.

Open [**Ex.10*starter**], which contains our foggy, flat scene. Select layer 1 and type Command+D on Mac (Control+D on Windows) to duplicate it. Make sure the Modes column is visible (press F4 if it isn't), and set the copy on top to Overlay mode. Bang: You immediately have a darker, richer, moodier image. Try other modes by selecting the top layer, holding down the Shift key, and using the – and = keys to scroll through them; you may prefer a brighter mode, such as Color Dodge. Press T to reveal the layer's Opacity, and scrub its value to mix in the moded copy to taste.

Now, here comes the magic: With layer 1 still selected, apply Effect> Blur & Sharpen>Fast Blur, and slowly scrub the Blurriness parameter while watching the Comp window. The highlights will now start to blur and bloom, creating a sexier image. This is akin to the practice of spraying ProMist on a lens to make an image more magical (and to hide wrinkles, by the way).

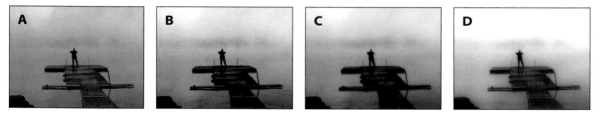

To enhance flat footage (A), duplicate the layer, use a blending mode such as Overlay (B), and add some blur to create blooming in the highlights (C). You can use two duplicates, use multiple modes, and color shift one of the layers to create richer looks (D).

To extend the technique, duplicate the layer again (make sure you've deselected the effect, or you'll duplicate it instead), and try a different mode on top. We'll often combine two different modes: one to brighten the image (such as Add, Screen, or Color Dodge), and one to add contrast (such as Overlay or Hard Light), blending their opacities to taste. Solo layer 3 to compare your result against the original footage.

Feel free to modify this technique by using different effects in place of Fast Blur, such as Box Blur or Channel>Minimax; you might also want to blur just one of the duplicate layers rather than both. Another cool trick is to perform a color shift on one of the duplicates: Add Adjust> Hue/Saturation to the layer that has your "add contrast" mode (such as Overlay) and scrub its Hue value. Our result is shown in [**Ex.10_final**].

Third Party Magic

There are several third party plug-in sets that give a large number of great preset "looks" – plus the ability to create your own.

55mm

This set of "digital optical filters" ($295 from Digital Film Tools – www.digitalfilmtools.com) covers a wide range of creative color correction needs. There are numerous "I want that look – now" plug-ins, such as Black Mist, Bleach Bypass, Fluorescent, Night Vision, Sunset/Twilight, and Ultra Contrast. There is a Rosco Gels plug-in that accurately recreates using Calacolor, Cinelux, Storaro, and Cinegels. There are a number of straightforward color correction plug-ins, such as Dual Tint (an easier way to perform the color gradient trick we showed earlier) and Color Correct, which is akin to the Color Balance effect. And there are other effects from utilitarian to highly stylized, such as Diffusion, F-Stop, Lens Distortion, Printer Points, Star, and Streaks. All have simple initial parameters; many allow you to dive deeper, including tricks like creating mattes to affect only a portion of the image.

There is some overlap between 55mm and DFT's also-excellent Composite Suite; the latter provides a set of plug-ins more focused on compositing including matte, edge, lighting, and other tools developed for their sister company, Digital FilmWorks. If you have to choose just one, go for 55mm if you're more of a motion graphics artist, and Composite Suite if you're more of a visual effects artist.

Digital Film Lab

Rather than being a package of many special-purpose plug-ins, this is a single effect from Digital Film Tools that comes with more than 135 presets (arranged into black and white, color, diffusion, grain, and temperature categories) to create a wide range of photographic looks, lighting gels, gradients, film stocks, and optical lab effects. If you can't quite find the preset you're looking for, under the hood are parameters for colorized diffusion, color gradients, gels, "lab" (including bleach, cross process, flash, and

overexposure parameters), grain, and both pre- and post-processing color correction. This means you can tweak the presets, or create your own looks, as well as save your own settings. This plug-in (with presets) also costs $295; you can get it bundled with 55mm for $495.

Magic Bullet

This suite of film-style treatment effects was developed by visual effects house The Orphanage, and is available through Red Giant Software (www.redgiantsoftware.com) for $795. Among its bag of tricks is converting interlaced video-rate footage into 24 fps progressive scan footage, removing DV compression artifacts, creating optical filmlike dissolves (including fades to black and burns to white), letterboxing, simulating damaged film, and ensuring your results are broadcast safe. However, the real attraction (from this chapter's perspective) is the Look Suite.

Enhanced contrast and reduced saturation, similar to skipping the bleaching phase of 35mm color film processing

Look Suite is broken down into four modules: Subject, which performs initial saturation, gamma, and contrast adjustments; Lens Filters, with diffusion and gradient sections; Camera, which includes several tinting options plus "3-Strip Process" (which is supposed to emulate "the classic movie look that we associate with the three-strip dye transfer color process created by Technicolor in 1932"); and Post, which includes a final set of saturation, gamma, and contrast adjustments along with warm/cool biasing. Look Suite comes with 55 presets (with previews) that recreate different film and film lab treatments; you can tweak these presets or create your own from scratch, and save them for later use.

Color Channel Tweaks

Levels and Curves both allow you to adjust the individual color channels in addition to the overall image. This is usually reserved for special effects, as it changes the color balance in the image.

Color Finesse

After Effects 6.5 comes bundled with one of the best color correctors available: Synthetic Aperture's Color Finesse (CF for short). We're going to finish by helping you translate what you've learned so far into Color Finesse's initially daunting, but very powerful, user interface. If you haven't installed it yet, do so now, and restart After Effects.

Open [**Ex.11*starter**], move the time marker to a frame you'd like to correct, select layer 1, and apply Effect>Synthetic Aperture>SA Color Finesse. Click on the Setup button in the Effect Controls window, and CF's user interface will fill your screen.

The upper left quarter of the interface contains the Analysis Window. This provides several different ways of viewing the color information in your footage; the default is the Combo view. The top two displays – a waveform monitor and vectorscope – may be more familiar to video editors. The waveform monitor shows luminance values present as you scan from left to right across an image. The vectorscope is a cross between an RGB color wheel and a histogram, with the green showing how strong each hue is. Below are expanded versions of the more familiar curves and histogram displays. Note that these display what's happening in the modified, rather than original, image.

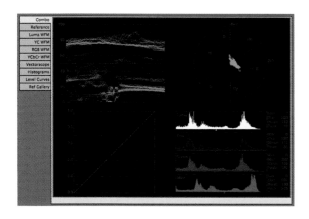

The upper right quarter of the interface contains the Image Window. It defaults to showing the result of your corrections. You can also select tabs to view the source, a reference image you may be using for comparison, and split-screen combinations of these. Especially interesting is the Luma Ranges tab, which gives a rough sketch of where the shadows, midtones, and highlights fall in your image. You can optionally edit these ranges in the Luma Range tab in the Settings window (next on our tour). Leave Image at Result for now.

The Analysis Window in Color Finesse (above). It defaults to a Combo view, which displays a waveform monitor (upper left), vectorscope (upper right), curves (lower left), and histograms (lower right). The waveform monitor displays luminance levels as you scan from left to right across the image; the hollow middle corresponds to the actor's trench coat (below). Footage courtesy Artbeats/Business on the Go.

The lower portion of the interface contains the Settings and Color Info Windows. CF allows you to attack your corrections in many different ways. For example, to alter contrast, click on the RGB tab, then the Master sub-tab. Unlike Levels' Input Black and White, here you deal with Master Pedestal – which slides the entire histogram left and right – and Master Gain, which scales the histogram. To improve the contrast in this shot, slightly increase Master Gain. You may be tempted to increase it until the Luma histogram is nicely spread out, but note the result is clipping the right edge of the Red histogram – so back off slightly. Master Gamma works just like Gamma in Levels.

CF allows individual contrast adjustments in the shadows, midtones, and highlights. If you wanted to alter the shadows in this image, click on the Shadows sub-tab, and slowly adjust the Master Gamma tab while watching the histogram. You can quickly check your corrections by enabling and disabling the checkbox for each section.

To balance the color in the image, click on the HSB tab. The Controls sub-tab gives you options similar to Hue/Saturation, again with the ability to alter the entire image, or just the shadows, midtones, and highlights. The Contrast, Gain, Gamma, and Pedestal controls in this panel also give you an alternative to the RGB tab to adjusting contrast in an image.

Now select the Hue Offsets sub-tab: This is akin to the Color Balance effect we worked with earlier, with a far more powerful interface. Click on the eyedropper to the right of the Settings Window, then click on a portion of the image that should be 50% gray – such as the highlight running down the door of the silver car. The info display underneath will show you the RGB values of that pixel before and after your adjustments (the popup allows you to change how color is displayed). We can see that the blue channel is much stronger than red and green – so go to the Midtones color wheel, click on the dot in the center, and drag it toward ten o'clock, away from the blue slice of the wheel. The histograms, Color Info, and Image will all update as you drag. Suddenly, the scene has natural colors! (Of course, you can also use these tools to create unnatural colorizations, as well…)

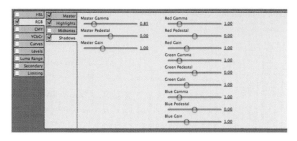

The RGB section provides Levels-like control over contrast in the image, including the ability to adjust shadows, midtones, and highlights independently of each other.

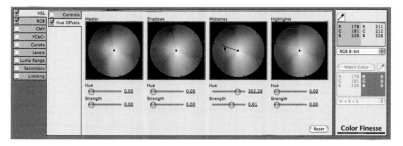  

The Color Info section (above, right section) allows you to select a color and see its before and after values. The "before" value had too much blue in the midtones, so we dragged away from blue in the Midtones wheel. We used Secondary correction to make the sky bluer and the mountains redder (right).

To end our brief tour, click on the Secondary tab. Color Finesse features six independent secondary color correctors, labeled A through F. For each secondary, you can eyedropper up to four colors, then adjust the color of the resulting selection. In [**Ex.11_final**], we used two channels to increase the saturation in the mountains, and put some more blue back into the sky. The only disappointment is that CF does not offer selective blurs or glows for these channels.

There is a lot more power inside this plug-in; we suggest you look inside the Color Finesse folder on your drive and spend some time exploring its very thorough yet easy-to-digest User's Guide. In general, the art of color correction is something that takes time and practice to master, but we hope we've given you a good head start down that road.

Connect

Blending Modes were the subject of Volume 1, Chapter 10.

Adjustment Layers were straightened out in Volume 1, Chapter 22.

Several effects – such as Levels, Curves, Hue/Saturation, Ramp, Color Balance, the Auto effects, Shadow/Highlight, Colorama, Change Color, and Change To Color – were also demonstrated in Volume 1, Chapter 24.

Keying (including the Color Range and Keylight plug-ins) is taught in Chapter 10.

Compound Effects

Compound effects may seem nonintuitive at first, but they require learning only a few simple rules.

A *compound effect* is one that looks at a second layer to decide exactly how to treat the layer it is applied to. Examples of these vary from Compound Blur – which can selectively blur one layer based on the varying luminance values of another – to Texturize, which is great for simulating those embossed station identity bugs most networks use these days, among other things.

The "modifying" layer that a compound effect points to can range from a simple gradient to a second movie or composition. In most cases, the information being passed is an 8-bit (or 256 levels of gray) image, or the luminance values of a color image. These gray levels are then used by the effect to determine which pixels in the first layer are blurred, faded, displaced, and so on.

By pointing to a second layer, compound effects side-step the normal rendering pipeline order of bottom layer to topmost layer. As a result, mastering these effects requires a little forethought in preparing your sources, and quite often requires that you create the effect using more than one comp.

In this chapter we'll focus on three of these compound effects: Compound Blur, Texturize, and the Professional edition's Displacement Map. These cover the gamut from fairly straightforward to fairly complex. Once you understand the logic behind compound effects, you should be able to adapt the techniques to any effect that uses a second, modifying layer.

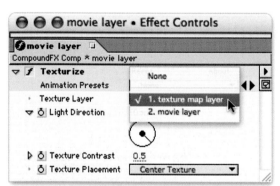

The power of compound effects comes in selecting a second layer to modify the one the effect is applied to. If the default is None, no matter how many other parameters you change, the result will still be "no effect." Don't forget to select a modifying layer.

Example Project

Explore the 09-Example Project.aep file as you read this chapter; references to [Ex.##] refer to specific compositions within the project file.

That Other Layer

Compound effects are easy to spot because they have a popup for you to select a second layer to work with. Most of these effects either default to None (which results in no effect, because no layer has been selected) or use themselves as the modifying layer. This popup menu automatically lists all layers in the current composition.

The modifier layer does *not* need to be turned on in order to be used by a compound effect. In fact, if its image is not being used directly in the comp, it's best to turn it off to ensure it does not appear accidentally.

Size Matters

The way compound effects work is to line up the modifying layer with the effected layer, pixel by pixel, and decide how to treat each pixel in the effected layer based on some property (usually luminance) of the modifier layer. If both layers are the same size, life is more straightforward. But what if the modifying layer is not the same size or aspect ratio as the layer the effect is applied to? For example, if you were to take a logo or bug that is, say, 200×200 pixels, and emboss it into a movie layer of 640×480, After Effects needs to know if it should:

- *Stretch to Fit*, which would stretch and distort the logo to 640×480 before applying it as a texture;
- *Center* the smaller logo in the 640×480 area; or
- *Tile* the logo, so that you see multiple logos, some of which may be incomplete if the two sizes do not match up nicely.

Short Circuit

While these options are often valid, they don't allow for the logo to be scaled and placed in the lower right corner of the screen à la a network ID bug.

The reason for this is the rendering order inside After Effects: When an effect is applied to the movie, and that effect is told to refer to a second "map" layer for data, it's capable of seeing the modifying layer only at its "source" – *before* any masks, effects, or transformations have been applied to it. In other words, it uses the modifying layer as it would appear in its own Layer window (with View set to None) – *not* in the Comp window. Hence, no scaling or positioning of the Logo layer is taken into account by the compound effect.

Longer (and Better) Circuit

The trick, then, is to present the effect module with a modifying layer that's the same size (or at least the same aspect ratio) as the layer being effected, and with any attributes already applied to the modifying layer. You do that by preparing the map in a precomp that is the same size as the layer being effected. You can position, scale, and otherwise transform – as well as animate and effect – the modifying source in this precomp, and the result will then be applied faithfully by the compound effect in the main comp.

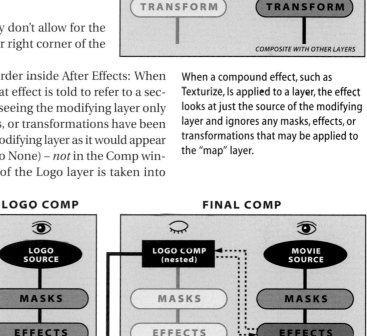

When a compound effect, such as Texturize, Is applied to a layer, the effect looks at just the source of the modifying layer and ignores any masks, effects, or transformations that may be applied to the "map" layer.

Apply any transformations (for example, scale and position the logo bug) to the modifying layer in its own precomp, and nest this into the comp with the layer that gets the compound effect (Texturize in this example). Now the effect will take the transformations applied to the bug into account when it processes.

Smooth Blur

If Compound Blur is too "boxy" for you, try the SmoothKit> Gaussian effect from RE:Vision Effects (demo available at www.revisionfx.com). It's a true compound blur with a smoother look.

even the clearest thoughts and ideas can become blurred when subjected to random disturbances from outside forces – especially when one appears to have no control over these events.

Take a text layer (left), apply Compound Blur, and direct it to use a movie of animated lines as a blur map (center). The result is selective blurring of our original image (right), based on the luminance values in the modifying layer. Animated lines created with Profound Effects' Useful Things.

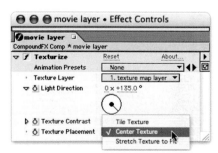

A compound effect works best when the two layers are the same size or aspect ratio. If they aren't, it needs to know how to interpret the modifier layer in order to force it to have the same number of pixels as the effected layer.

Now that we have a general understanding of how compound effects work, let's look at a few in detail:

Compound Blur

This effect can be thought of as a variable blur, with the amount of blur controlled by the luminance of the modifying layer it points to. The amount of blur is calculated on a pixel-by-pixel basis: The brighter a pixel is in the modifying layer, the more blurred the corresponding pixel will be in the layer Compound Blur is applied to.

In the **09-Example Project.aep** file (from the **Chapter Example Projects>09-Compound Effects** folder), open the **[Ex.01*starter]** comp, which contains some text and a few sources for you to use as blur maps.

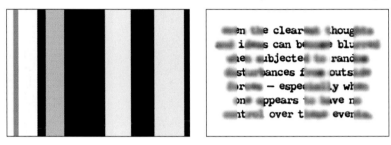

Step 1: Select the text (layer 1) and apply Effect>Blur & Sharpen> Compound Blur. The Effect Controls window will open.

Step 2: The modifying layer is set to itself (**clearideas.ai**). Change the Blur Layer popup to the **_white background solid** layer. The text will now appear at its maximum blur value, since the modifying layer is solid white. The default Maximum Blur value of 20 is usually too high – scrub it down to around 5.

Step 3: Change the Blur Layer popup to **xUT_autobars.mov**, and now the blur varies across the text in proportion to the luminance values of layer 2. Double-click the **xUT_autobars.mov** layer to open it in its own Layer window and compare how it looks with the blur pattern. Experiment with the other parameters in the Compound Blur effect, such as Invert Blur (means black areas in the modifying layer get maximum blur and white areas no blur), and the Maximum Blur amount. Try the other blur map movie **AB_SoftEdges_loop.mov** for comparison or try some grayscale images of your own.

Texturize

Many will feel this effect should have been named Emboss, because that better describes the end result: It looks like an object has been embossed into the layer it was applied to. We'll use the Texturize effect to create a bug embossed in the corner of our footage. Select Window>Close All, and open **[Ex.02-Texturize Comp]** so that you know what the end result should look like. As noted earlier in this chapter, Texturize is a prime example of a compound effect in which you may need to prepare the modifying layer in another composition so you can control the position and scale of the bug. You can take two different approaches to get there – *nesting* or *precomposing*. We'll try it both ways:

Texturizing by Nesting

If you're the type who likes to plan ahead, you would create a moving embossed effect by animating the bug in its own precomp, then nest this precomp with the movie to be embossed in a second comp. Apply Texturize to the *movie* layer, using the bug precomp as the texture map layer. If you want to recreate our [**Ex.02**] example, the steps are as follows:

Step 1:   Select Window>Close All to reduce clutter. Make a new composition and name it "**bug precomp**". It should be the same size and duration as the movie you'll be effecting (320×240 if you're using our sources).

Step 2:   Add the **Aqua2000Bug.tif** logo from the **Sources>09_Chapter Sources** folder to your comp. Our logo is a grayscale file with *white text on black*, which is ideal for the Texturize effect as it looks only at high-contrast edges, *not* the alpha channel (see the sidebar, *Texturizer Tricks*).

Step 3:   Resize and position the bug in the bottom left hand corner and verify Best Quality (the default) is selected to antialias the layer.

Step 4:   Make a second composition in which you'll create the actual effect. Do this by dragging the movie you want to effect to the New Comp button at the bottom of the Project window. We used **Sources>Movies> GI_LiquidFX.mov**. The new comp will open and contain the movie layer. Select Composition>Composition Settings, rename your new comp "**Texturize1 Comp**", check that Resolution is set to Full, and click OK.

Step 5:   Add the [**bug precomp**] from the Project window to this new comp.

Step 6:   Turn off the Video switch (the eyeball) for the **bug precomp** layer, as it is not supposed to be visible.

Step 7:   Select the movie layer (*not* the bug layer) and apply Effect> Stylize>Texturize to the movie; select **bug precomp** in the Texture Layer popup. Because the movie and precomp layers are the same width and height, the Texture Placement popup is now irrelevant. With all comps set to Full Resolution and all layers set to Best Quality, edit the Contrast slider to taste. Sharp horizontal lines may flicker when they're field rendered, so we tend to use the 0.5–0.7 range for a softer effect. (If you got lost, compare to [**Ex.02- Texturize Comp**] and [**Ex.02_bug precomp**].)

Step 8:   *Optional*: Feel free to animate the logo layer in your [**bug precomp**], and note how the Texturize effect now animates accordingly in your [**Texturize1 Comp**].

Step 7: The Timeline window of the second comp, where you can see how the Texturize effect has been set up.

Safe Bugs

When you're creating logo bugs, keep any "lower-third" graphics away from the bug zone, or verify that the bug will be placed elsewhere (such as the upper left corner).

Steps 1–3: Our bug is prebuilt in one comp, where it is sized and positioned.

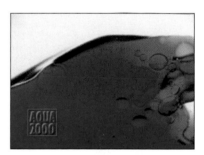

Steps 4–7: The logo bug is applied to our video layer in the second comp, resulting in an embossed effect. Background footage from Getty Images/ Liquid FX.

Texturizer Tricks

The Texturize effect also has a set of criteria as to what constitutes a useful modifying layer. In our experience, high-contrast images with sharp edges work best, so we usually use black text on a white background, or vice versa. You might think that the effect would consider the alpha channel of the logo layer, but that is not the case: It sees only the *luminance* of the RGB channels (the result of collapsing a color image to grayscale is the layer's luminance).

So if you need to use a layer's alpha, open the image in Photoshop, copy and paste the alpha channel to a new grayscale file, and use this as your source. Alternatively, use Effect>Render>Fill to fill the layer's RGB channels with white, but remember to apply the Fill effect in a precomp so that Texturize recognizes the color change in the main comp.

Another potential trouble spot appears when you're using Illustrator files. We normally create black text in Illustrator and apply color later in After Effects. The problem is that black text on a comp's background has no contrast – no matter what color you make the background, a nested comp's background is always "transparency," which is considered to be "black" by an effect.

The workaround for black Illustrator files is to place the text over a white solid in a precomp, since solids exist in RGB space. Another alternative is to change the black text to white using Effect>Render>Fill in the precomp. All in all, it might be easiest to set Illustrator to Artwork mode, and create white text or a white logo in Illustrator in the first place.

Filling with White

Make black Illustrator files white in a precomp to use them with Texturize. (The Effect>Render>Fill effect will fill the RGB channel with a flat color.)

Step 2: The **Aqua2000Bug.tif** layer is scaled down and positioned in the left hand corner, in the correct placement to be an embossed bug.

Texturizing by Precomposing

If you forgot to plan ahead and already started to create the effect all in one comp, the following steps using precompose offer an alternative to building exactly the same Texturize effect. So let's start over again with a second scenario:

Step 1: Select Window>Close All to reduce clutter. Make a new composition by dragging the movie you want to effect to the New Composition button in the Project window. Again, we used the **Sources>Movies> GI_LiquidFX.mov** in our example. The new comp will open and will contain the movie layer. Rename the comp (Composition>Composition Settings) "**Texturize2 Comp**", and check that Resolution is set to Full.

Step 2: Drag in the **Aqua2000Bug.tif** image from **Sources>09_Chapter Sources**. Resize and position the bug in the bottom left hand corner. Verify that the layer is set to Best Quality so that it is antialiased.

Step 3: Turn off the Video switch (the eyeball) for the bug layer, as it is not supposed to be visible.

Step 4: Select the movie layer (*not* the bug layer, remember) and apply Effect>Stylize>Texturize. For the Texture Layer popup, select the bug layer as the texture. The result is that the frame is filled with large bugs, as the Texture Placement popup defaults to Tile Texture. But even setting this popup to Center Texture or Stretch Texture to Fit will not show the bug scaled and positioned in the bottom left corner.

Step 5: A bit of sleuthing is in order. Double-click the bug layer to open its Layer window, which displays the layer's source. The image in the Layer window tells you what's being fed to the Texturize effect applied to the movie layer. To have the Layer window display the bug positioned in the corner, we need to precompose the bug so the Transform properties are calculated in a precomp.

Step 6: Bring the Comp window forward. Select the bug layer, and choose Layer>Pre-compose. In the Precompose dialog, name the new precomp **bug precomp** and be sure to select the *second* option, "Move all attributes into the new composition". This option will send the scale and position values down to the precomp, and create a precomp with the same size, duration, and frame rate as the current comp. Be sure to also turn on the Open New Composition switch before you click OK – that way the precomp (not the original comp) will be forward.

Step 7: The new precomp has one layer in it, the original bug layer, sized and positioned in the bottom left corner. Notice anything strange? You had turned off the Video switch for the bug in Step 3, but the precomposing step automatically turned back on its visibility (this was not true in earlier versions). After all, unless it renders in the precomp, it's not going to show up in the main comp! This precomp is nested in the [**Texturize2 Comp**], so the result is similar to nesting.

Step 8: Return to your [**Texturize2 Comp**] by selecting its tab. The logo bug will still be turned off in this comp, as desired. To summarize: The Video switch for the bug should be *on* in the precomp so that its data is sent to the main comp, but it should be *off* in the main comp as you don't want it to appear in the render.

Step 9: In the main comp, the Texturize effect should now be working correctly. (If you're using an earlier version, you need to reselect the Texture Layer in the Effect Controls window.) Verify that Best Quality is set for the movie layer so that the Texturize effect will be antialiased. At this point, the result should be the same as both our [**Ex.02-Texturize Comp**] and the nesting method you tried above.

Once you understand the logic of how compound effects work, you can adapt these nesting or precomposing steps to almost any effect that uses a modifying layer.

Additional note: When you precompose, the precomp defaults to being the same size and frame rate as the current comp, not the movie you intend to apply the effect to. You may need to resize the precomp to match the movie, or the Texturize effect may again have a placement problem. Also, if the movie has an unusual frame rate, you may wish to set the precomp's frame rate to match. However, the precomp will render at the frame rate set by the main comp and ultimately by the Render Settings. To lock in a different rate for the precomp, turn on the Preserve Frame Rate option in the precomp's Composition Settings>Advanced tab.

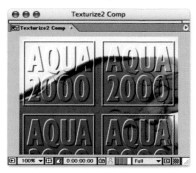

At Step 4, the Texturize effect defaults to tiling the bug across the movie layer. Not exactly what we had in mind.

Step 5: The Layer window for the bug image shows the original source layer – *before* the position and scale properties have been taken into account. This is what the Texturize effect is receiving.

When you precompose a layer that's being used by a compound effect, check that the precomp's size matches the effected layer, otherwise you may still have issues with texture placement.

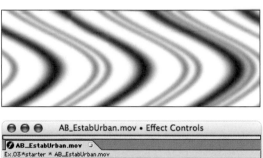

Step 5: Note the edge artifacts with Wrap Pixels Around turned off (background color set to grey). Footage courtesy Artbeats/Establishment – Urban.

In [Ex.03], the displacement map (top) is 14,440 wide by 480 high. When we applied it to the 320×240 movie, we used the Center Map setting (above).

Displacement Map

A *displacement map* displaces pixels – in other words, moves them up or down and to the left or right – depending on the luminance values of the modifying layer. It's great for creating warped effects, as well as making one layer appear as if it has been projected or painted onto an uneven surface. To see how this works, select Window>Close All to reduce clutter. Open [Ex.03*starter] comp. Layer 1 is a grayscale displacement map, and layer 2 is the movie layer that will be displaced:

Step 1: Turn off the Video switch for the map in layer 1.

Step 2: Select the movie in layer 2 and apply Effect> Distort>Displacement Map. The Effect Controls window opens automatically; resize it so you can read the full parameter names. The Displacement Map Layer popup defaults to using itself as a map, so change this to point at layer 1: CM_Displacement_map.tif.

Step 3: Choose what channel you want to use for Horizontal Displacement in the next popup; because the map is grayscale, you can use any of the Red, Green, Blue, or Luminance settings. Set the Maximum Horizontal Displacement with the slider below. The next popup and slider control the Vertical Displacement in a similar way.

Step 4: The Displacement Map Behavior parameter kicks in when the map is not the same size or aspect ratio as the movie it's displacing. Our map is 1440×480, and the movie is 320×240, so compare the Center Map and Stretch Map to Fit settings. The latter uses the entire map scaled to 320×240, so it has more extreme results.

Step 5: The final trick to Displacement Map is the checkbox for Edge Behavior. If you displace pixels away from an outer edge of the layer, what fills in the space they left behind? Checking Wrap Pixels Around borrows part of the image from the opposite edge to fill in the gaps. If the layer has a fairly consistent color around its edges, this works well, as the borrowed pixels will match.

To not displace an image, the modifying map needs to be 50% gray (RGB values 128/128/128), or its alpha channel must be transparent. Darker areas displace in "negative" directions (up and to the left), and lighter areas displace in positive directions (down and to the right), with the maximum amount controlled by sliders in the effect. You can select any number of characteristics of the modifying image to provide the map, such as the strength of a specific color. In contrast to Texturize, slightly blurred maps tend to work better than sharp ones; sharp contrasting edges result in disjointed displacements (or "tearing") along those edges.

Animating the Map

Displacement maps often look good when they're animating, and this is where the concept of preparing the map in a precomp comes up yet again, just like with the Texturize effect earlier.

Select Window>Close All, and open [**Ex.04*starter**]. Here's the same movie displaced by the same wavy high-contrast map, and if you scrub the Timeline, you'll notice that the displacement isn't moving. But turn on the Video switch for layer 1, and you'll see that the displacement map is panning from right to left (if the Position keyframes aren't visible, select layer 1 and press P). Remember that a compound effect sees the map layer at the *source* of the layer – before any masks, effects, or keyframes have been applied. Open the Layer window for layer 1 – you'll see the full still image of the map, not an animated map.

To have the map animate while it's displacing the movie, the Position keyframes need to be moved down to a precomp so that the layer is already panning by the time it hits the Displacement Map effect. Follow the steps for precomposing detailed earlier in *Texturizing by Precomposing*, to move the animated map down to the precomp. (When you're done, open the Layer window for the map precomp layer – you should see it panning and, more importantly, so should the effect.)

If you get lost, compare your results with the [**Ex.04_final comps**] folder.

Different Sizes

We've seen how you need to animate a displacement map in a precomp. But what if the image or movie you're displacing is also animating? Or what if you have a stack of layers you want to displace as a group?

In this case, you'll need to animate the movie (or group the images) together in a second precomp that's the same size as the map precomp. In the third and main comp, you nest both precomps, then create the displacement map effect.

You could think of these precomps as two sides of a sandwich. When they come together in the main composition, the Displacement Map Behavior popup will be irrelevant because both precomps are the same size. This gives you the opportunity to create the precomps a little larger than the main comp so that any edge artifacts are cropped off by the pasteboard in the main comp. Explore our sample comps in **Ex.05**.

Slice 'n' Dice

We usually suggest that displacement map sources not have sharp transitions in luminance because these could cause sudden shifts in the positions of the displaced pixels. Of course, there are exceptions to every rule. Open [**Ex.06**], and

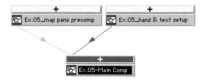

[**Ex.05**] consists of a precomp (340×260) where the map pans right to left; a second precomp (also 340×260) where the hand image and text are animated and composited as a group; and a third, main comp (320×240), where the displacement map effect is created.

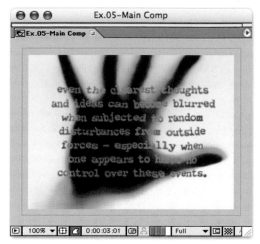

The [**Ex.05-Main Comp**] with the hand and text displaced. The edge artifacts still exist, but since they're out on the pasteboard area they won't be vIsIble in the final render. Hand from Digital Vision/The Body.

The Useful Things animated lines movie is used to both blur and displace the skyline in [**Ex.06**].

Bonus Tutorial

The "Projected Text" Bonus Tutorial on your DVD covers using a displacement map to make text on a curve ripple across a bodybuilder's back.

you'll see the same animated grayscale bars used earlier in this chapter now used to displace slices of the movie in the vertical direction.

We also applied Compound Blur to the movie so that some of the slices will be more or less blurred, and inverted the blur so that black in the map would be maximum blur, not white. (Compound Blur is best applied after the Displacement Map effect so that the blurred and displaced slices line up.)

The Mirror Cracked

Taking the sharp transitions idea to another level, [**Ex.07**] simulates a cracked reflective surface, such as a broken mirror. A painting by Paul Sherstobitoff is displaced by a map where each faux mirror shard is given a different gray value, which results in a different amount of displacement per shard.

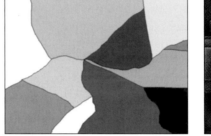

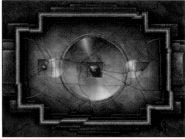

[**Ex.07**] uses a displacement map to simulate a cracked mirror effect; the lines in the map also serve as an alpha matte. Painting by Paul Sherstobitoff.

We included black separation lines to help cover for the artifacts that result along sharp displacement edges – they serve as an alpha matte to make the pieces look like they are separated slightly.

Why Isn't it Working?

The techniques you've learned in this chapter apply to all compound effects, including Card Dance, Caustics, Wave World, and others. If you're still having problems, here is a summary of the most common reasons compound effects don't seem to work initially:

• The modifier layer has been left at None, or it defaults to using itself; set the Layer popup to the desired layer.

• The modifier or map layer is not the same size as the layer the effect is being applied to, so the aspect ratio is being distorted. Solution: Place the map in a precomp the same size as the layer to be effected, and use this precomp in place of the original map layer in the Effect Controls.

• The modifier layer has effects or animation that is being ignored by the compound effect. Remember that the compound effect takes the map at its source *before* Mask, Effects and Transform. Precompose the map layer, being sure to check the Move All Attributes option.

• The precomp has a white background color, but the precomp's background color is always considered as "black" (zero alpha) by a compound effect. If this is causing a problem, use a white Solid layer instead.

Connect

Blending Modes, see Volume 1, Chapter 10.

Track Mattes, see Volume 1, Chapter 12.

Nesting and precomposing compositions were covered in Volume 1, Chapters 18 and 19, respectively.

Applying Effects, see Volume 1, Chapter 21.

Displacement mapping is also covered in Bonus Tutorial *Projected Text*.

Brain Tickler: *Walk on Water*

If you've read this chapter carefully so far, you should have a pretty good idea of what's involved in creating a displacement map effect. So now we'd like to challenge you! Select Window>Close All. Open the **[Ex.08]** folder and play the **Walk on Water.mov**: The text "Liquid" animates from right to left and appears to be at the bottom of a swimming pool. Open **[Ex.08*starter]**, and see if you can recreate this movie using the following outline:

• Layer 1 is the black text **Liquid.ai**. This needs to be animated from right to left and then displaced with the water texture.

• Layer 2 is a movie of water ripples that will be used as both a background and a displacement map. Rather than use the background movie directly as the displacement map, create a special grayscale version so you'll have more control.

• Due to the inherent video noise in the water texture movie, you'll notice some slight "tearing" when the text is displaced, so blur the grayscale version for a smoother result.

• When you apply the Displacement Map effect, make sure that the distortion in the text layer synchronizes with the highlights in the water (it's possible that they won't match if you don't build the effect correctly).

• To fool the eye into thinking the text is at the bottom of the pool, change the color of the text to a light blue (like the highlights in the water) and apply a blending mode so that the Liquid layer interacts with the water texture in an interesting way.

• Create as many precomps as you think you'll need to achieve the look of our finished movie. (Check the section *Why Isn't It Working?* if you get stuck.) When you've given it your best shot, come back here to compare results.

The Solution

How did you do? There are a few variations you could have chosen to complete the above task; our version is in the **[Ex.09]** folder. The hierarchy of comps is the most important part:

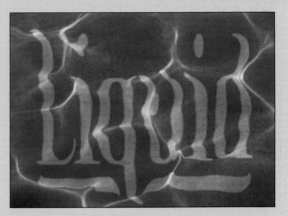

Use your newfound knowledge about displacement mapping to recreate this animation using the sources in the **[Ex.08*starter]** comp. No peeking at the solution until you've given it your best shot! Footage courtesy Artbeats/Water Textures.

• **[Ex.09_map fx_precomp]**: Using the Shift Channels effect, we used the Red channel to create a grayscale movie to use as a luminance displacement map. Adding Levels increases the contrast, and Fast Blur reduces the video noise.

• **[Ex.09_text pans precomp]**: We animated the text from right to left in a precomp, because otherwise the Displacement Map effect would render *before* the Position keyframes. In order to keep the edges of the text from appearing distorted later on, this precomp is larger than the main comp (360×270 as opposed to 320×240).

• In the main comp, **[Ex.09-Walk on Water_final]**, both precomps are nested and the background movie added. The Displacement Map effect is applied to the **text pans precomp**, and the map layer set to look at **map fx precomp**. The ripples in the distorted text line up with the ripples in the background movie even though the layer sizes differ, because the Center Map option is used. Any other strangeness at the left/right edges of the text fall outside the comp's image area. Wrap Pixels Around was turned off.

To make the type interact with the background, we used the Fill effect to color it a pale blue and then set it to Overlay mode.

10 The Blue Riders

Effectively removing a color background requires attention throughout the chain.

These two sample bluescreen shots for you to practice with are included in the **10_Chapter Sources** folder for this chapter's project: Alex and Water. Courtesy Photron (www.photron.com), creators of the Primatte keyer.

Example Project

Explore the 10-Example Project.aep file as you read this chapter; references to [Ex.##] refer to specific compositions within the project file. Some of these exercises require the Professional edition.

Compositing images shot against one background over a new background is one of the trickier visual effects tasks you will encounter. It requires separating the foreground elements from the original background they were shot against. Even if the foreground comes with its own alpha channel (the result of a 3D render), getting it to blend nicely with its new background can still be a challenge.

Time for the bad news: Not all images can be cleanly separated from their background. Neither can you assume that all images can be seamlessly blended with a new background. And the tools that come with After Effects Standard may be insufficient to do either task well. But with forethought and preparation, plus After Effects' Professional edition (which includes the Keylight plug-in from The Foundry), you should be able to produce professional results. This chapter will give you an overview of the issues, plus tips on using some of the tools.

Keying 101

The process of *keying* footage means creating an alpha channel that isolates (or "pulls") the objects or actions you want (usually referred to as the "foreground") from the background they were originally shot against. You can use a number of techniques to accomplish this separation.

The most common technique is a variation on *color keying*. The actor or object is shot against a solid-color background. This color is preferably one that does not appear in the object you want to keep – for example, blue or green backgrounds are good when people are your subject, because skin tones tend to be shadings on red. You then instruct your software or hardware to remove this background color by making the alpha channel transparent where the background is visible, and to keep whatever is not the same as the background color by making its alpha channel opaque in these areas.

In addition to keying, other terms you may hear include *chroma keying* (chroma meaning color), *Ultimatte* (synonymous with one of the oldest companies creating keying equipment), and *bluescreen* or *greenscreen* (describing the color of the background stage). A related technique is *luminance keying*, which creates an alpha channel based on the relative brightness present in a scene rather than just its similarity to one color.

Key Personality Traits

There are a number of different keying techniques, as well as a number of keying plug-in effects. Not everyone uses the same names, even when they use the same techniques. Let's try to sort it out.

Binary or Simple Color Key: The most basic color keying technique. You select a color – or range of colors – to key (usually with a definable tolerance). The keyer then decides whether each pixel matches, and it makes it transparent or opaque – usually with feathering at the transitions. It can work on simple tasks, such as solid objects against solid backgrounds, but it does not deal well with semitransparent areas such as glass, smoke, and wispy hair.

Luminance Key: Uses the relative brightness of the image or one of its color channels, with some contrast adjustments, to determine final transparency. This type of key works okay if the object was shot against solid black or white. For a do-it-yourself luminance key, copy the clip, exaggerate its contrast with Levels or Curves, and use the result as a luma

track matte for the original layer. Add Effect> Channel>Remove Color Matting in a second comp to clean up the edges. We also use the Walker Effects Premultiply plug-in (free on this book's DVD) to drop out black backgrounds from clips such as fire and explosions.

Linear Key: A refinement of Luminance keying, in which a pixel's transparency is based on its similarity to a chosen color. Preserves semitransparent areas and shadows, but does little to remove background color that is mixed into these areas. More sophisticated linear keys have additional contrast and smoothing parameters, and often the ability to "keep" a specified color (for fixing cases where holes develop).

Advanced Keys: More advanced color keying plug-ins have their own algorithms to determine the transparency of each pixel, plus additional color correction controls including suppressing any "spill" of the background color onto the foreground object.

Luminance keying works well for white text on black title cards, or for objects shot against a seamless white or black set, but it does not work well in many other cases.

Although the basic concept may sound easy, things rarely work out so neatly in practice. Real images often contain a mixture of colors rather than pure ones. It is hard to evenly paint and light a background screen or set. Chances are strong that the light hitting this background is reflecting ("spilling") onto the foreground, and as a result it will take on some of this unwanted color. Then there's the issue of how to handle semitransparent parts of an image, such as wispy hair, shadows, and smoke. And those are just the obstacles in creating a key – now you have to convincingly blend the object into another world…

That's why any keying job should be treated in three phases: shooting, keying, and compositing. We'll cover them in order, starting with some shooting advice. We will then give an overview of all the keying effects After Effects offers, focusing on Keylight (which comes bundled with After Effects 6.5 Professional), plus the Professional edition's Inner Outer Key. We'll end with techniques for reducing color spill, color correcting an image, and blending the edges more convincingly. Throughout this chapter, we'll make the assumption that you are shooting against blue; the same ideas apply to green or other colors.

Through the Keyhole

The term *key* is short for *keyhole* – creating a keyhole in the alpha channel through which you see the object you want to keep.

Unwanted Enhancements

When you're shooting for keying, turn off edge enhancement options at the camera or during the telecine transfer from film.

An Ounce of Prevention

Before you apply a single keying effect, most of the battle has already been fought: If the material has been lit, shot, and transferred correctly, your life will be much easier; if it hasn't been, you quite possibly will not be able to get an acceptable key.

It's preferable to attend the shoot, but for most of us in the trenches, that's not always an option. If the scenes have not been shot yet, encourage the producer to hire lighting and camera people with bluescreen experience. For the background, use materials designed to be keyed; not just any old green or blue will do. The lighting and shooting of the bluescreen stage is paramount: You want even lighting on the backdrop while maintaining realistic lighting (including lighting angles that match the new background you intend to use) on the foreground objects you wish to keep. You also want to minimize color spill from the background onto your foreground objects. This is greatly aided by using a deep stage, placing the bluescreen as far behind your actors as practical: You will get less spill, and the screen will be out of focus, obscuring some of its imperfections.

If the camera is locked down or under motion control, have the lighting and camera people shoot a pass of just the blue set, especially if you're using Ultimatte software. This also comes in handy when you're trying to create a Difference Matte, where you key based on the similarities between two different shots.

Shoot on the best format possible, even if the rest of the show is not being shot or posted in it. BetaSP should be considered the absolute minimum; DV and HDV's compression and reduced color space make it less desirable (see also the sidebar *Dealing with DV*). DVCPro 50, Digital S, or Digital Beta are all better formats to use. In the film world, the less grain the better, making larger formats preferable (for example, 35mm over 16mm). And turn off any automatic edge enhancement at the camera (when you're shooting on video) or during the telecine transfer (if you originally shot on film); it can make edges much harder to key.

When you transfer the footage into your computer, use an uncompressed video card such as AJA Kona, Blackmagic DeckLink, or Digital Voodoo. Use the best interconnects the deck has: analog component (YUV) at minimum, Serial Digital Interface (SDI) if you have it. Again, even if you're not doing the rest of the show this way, consider it for the bluescreen transfers. You can always recompress the composited shot later for DV or whatever format your nonlinear editing system uses.

Realtime Key

Just because you can key footage in software does not mean you always should. Keying is one of the slower effects to render. Compressed tape formats and transfers between tape and computer can also degrade the source, making it harder to key.

That is why in some cases it is good to use a hardware keyer, such as an Ultimatte system. If you have it on the set during the shoot, you can see right away if the footage will key, or if you need to adjust the lighting.

You can then record two tapes in parallel: your original footage, and a keying pass that includes a high-contrast matte to use as a luma matte for your footage. Make sure they have been properly slated or timecoded, bring them both into After Effects, line them up in a comp with the matte layer on top, and set a track matte for the second full-color layer. If you're not satisfied with the result, you can always rekey the full-color version in software.

Another option is to shoot your bluescreen footage, create your new background plate, then key and composite them together in realtime at a post house. You can then use the composited result in After Effects, or directly in your nonlinear editor.

Dealing with DV

A common question is "What should I do to key DV footage?" Our first answer is to shoot your blue-screen footage on a better format, key it, composite it, *then* transfer the result to DV. However, this isn't always possible – for example, maybe you have been handed footage that has already been shot.

The problems with DV are that it is compressed and that the color information is undersampled. Undersampling means there is less color resolution in the image to start with. Compression means it was further degraded into blocks of pixels. This combination results in tattered edges – and keying is all about preserving edges.

Some of the newer keying plug-ins, such as dvGarage's dvMatte and Ultimatte's AdvantEdge, have special algorithms that try to smooth out this blockiness. SmoothKit from RE:Vision Effects can also smooth out some of these artifacts. If you don't own these, one trick to try is to duplicate the footage, apply Channel Blur to the copy on top, blur just the blue channel (or whatever color matches your background) by one to two pixels, key this copy, then use the result as a track matte for the unblurred version underneath.

The DV format undersamples the color channels and compresses the image, making the result blocky and hard to key. Here we're looking at the blue channel of our Alex image, saved as DV.

When you shoot, see if you can use a greenscreen instead of a bluescreen – some say DV performs better keying this color. And as we've mentioned elsewhere, turn off any automatic edge enhancement your camera may have; this feature will just make the edges harder to key cleanly.

Make your selects before you start keying. Setting up and performing a key are both time consuming; you don't want to do this on footage you won't be using later. Keep together footage shot from the same camera angle or under the same lighting conditions: You may be able to share settings between these shots.

After you get the footage captured, apply a "garbage mask" around the action you want to keep so you don't waste effort trying to get a good key on parts of the frame you don't care about. If necessary, animate this mask as the action moves. For difficult shots, divide and conquer by duplicating the footage and create separate masks that isolate different keying challenges – such as a hard edge around clothing, and a softer edge around hair or motion-blurred action.

Now you're ready to start keying. But which key to use? In the next few pages, we'll give you an overview of the eight different keyers that come with After Effects. Then we'll dive into details of the bundled Keylight plug-in, and the Professional edition's Inner Outer Key.

Paint Me Down

Use paint, tape, and fabrics that have been specially formulated to be keyed, such as the Rosco DigiComp, Chroma Key, and Ultimatte lines (www.rosco.com/us/scenic/index.asp), plus fabric and lights from Composite Components Company (www.digitalgreen-screen.com/prodindex.html).

Color Difference Bonus Chapter

A tutorial on using the complex but powerful Color Difference Keyer is included on your disc as **Bonus Chapter 10B**.

Trial Run

Try to key samples of the footage before you sign on to do the whole job. Some footage simply cannot be keyed; a one-day bid for keying can easily turn into a week of rotoscoping hell…

Setting Off Fireworks

If you are compositing fire or explosions shot against black, please don't use the Luma Key. Use the free Walker Effects Premultiply plug-in that came with this book, or try a blending mode such as Add or Screen. See Chapter 1 for details.

Use the Luma Key when the action is shot against white seamless or pure black. Even small differences between the foreground (the white checks in the jacket) and background can be separated. Actor courtesy Photodisc by Getty Images/Cool Characters; background courtesy Digital Vision/Inner Gaze.

A Box Full of Keys

As the Help file that comes with After Effects contains quite a few details on its various keying effects, we're going to give just a brief overview of the two Standard and six Professional edition keying plug-ins found under the Effect>Keying menu. We will then focus on Keylight (bundled with After Effects 6.5 Professional), and the Inner Outer Key.

We've set up some examples for you to experiment with: Open the **10-Example Project.aep** file in the corresponding folder from this book's DVD, and look inside the **Ex.01** folder in its Project window to locate the specific comps mentioned. We've created a quick garbage mask where appropriate to make your life easier. Each of these comps has a pair of new background layers; turn them on and off to see how your results work in context against forgiving (**DV_InnerGaze**) and unforgiving (**Gold Solid**) images.

Color Key

The simplest of the keying effects, this is a binary key where you eye-dropper a color representative of your background, increase the Color Tolerance until enough similar colors disappear (the default value of 0 will scare you into thinking it isn't working at all), further shrink the mask using Edge Thin, then try to soften the damage with Edge Feather. This key tends to have a blobby look, which is particularly bad on wispy edges like hair. Experiment with our starter settings in [**Ex.01a**].

Luma Key

Use this tool when footage has been shot against black or white. Again, the Threshold defaults to an intolerant 0; increase it to see results, tweak Edge Thin to shrink the matte, and use Feather to expand it back out softly. Use the Tolerance parameter instead of Threshold when you're using the Key Type options Key Out Similar and Dissimilar.

In [**Ex.01b**], Luma Key works very well for dropping out the white seamless background behind the actor, even though his jacket has off-white squares in it.

In [**Ex.01c**], however, as we key out the dark background, the dark inner portion of the skateboard wheel starts to disappear as well. In this case, we placed the original layer underneath and masked just the center of the wheel; turn on layer 2 and the hole will be filled. (Layer 2 is also parented to Layer 1 so that transforming Layer 1 affects both layers.)

Linear Color Key

As we mentioned earlier, linear keys are more sophisticated than binary keys: Rather than simply keeping or matting out a color based on whether it matches a color you choose, linear keys alter the transparency of pixels based on how closely they match the color you choose. This makes them better at dealing with semitransparent areas, such as smoke.

The After Effects Linear Color Key also allows you to choose different color matching methods, and to use + and – eyedroppers to automatically set the Matching Tolerance range. More significantly, it allows you to Key or Keep Colors based on their match. This lets you apply it multiple times, using one copy to remove the background, and other copies to keep regions of the foreground that were accidentally removed by the first copy of the key. In [**Ex.01d**], select **PM_Alex.tif** and hit F3: We used one copy of Linear Color Key to remove the blue, but this created some holes in the left side of her face. We added a second copy set to Keep Colors to restore this region (switch the second effect on and off to see this in action). Once you get used to the idea of applying multiple copies of this effect, and resign yourself to removing color spill later, you may find this key the easiest to use.

Color Difference Key

This complex effect used to be the most powerful keying plug-in that came with the Professional edition. It has since been surpassed by Keylight, which we will discuss in more detail later. For old time's sake, a tutorial on using the Color Difference Keyer is included on this book's DVD as **Bonus Chapter 10B**. If you want a preview of how well it works, see the example in comp [**Ex.01e**].

Color Range Key

Color Range is an improvement on binary keyers, in that you get to define a "bounding box" in color space of what colors to remove, rather than picking just one color and adjusting a Tolerance slider. This is helpful when you have uneven color or luminance in the background.

The user interface for this plug-in is a bit different from the norm: You do your color selections in the Preview box in the Effect Controls window, and watch the results in the Comp window. Use the normal eyedropper to click once where the background is. Then use the eyedropper followed by a + symbol to select additional ranges of color to remove. You can click and drag to remove a range of colors at once. If some of the action you want to keep starts to disappear as well, use the eyedropper followed by the – symbol to put those colors back. Then increase the Fuzziness parameter until the edges crop in nicely. Don't go so far that you start to eat away semitransparent details (such as hair) that happen to be overly contaminated with your background color; you can use effects such as the Spill Suppressor later to correct the color tint in these areas.

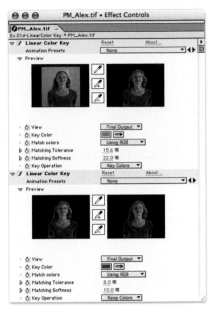

You can apply the Linear Color Key multiple times to finesse a key. In this case, the first copy removes the blue; the second copy restores the darker skin tones.

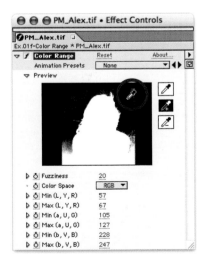

The Color Range key has a different interface: You use the eyedroppers in the Effect Controls window to add or remove from the matte, and view the results in the Comp window.

Watch the Color Space popup: It defaults to LAB, which is probably the least intuitive to work in. Try RGB first, and if you can't get an acceptable key, click on Reset and try one of the alternate color spaces. We've applied the effect and chosen our first color in [Ex.01f]; select **PM_Alex**, press F3 to open the Effect Controls window, and continue the key.

Garbage Out, Good Stuff In

Use masks outside your foreground as garbage mattes to remove unwanted areas of the background.

Difference Matte

Use this effect when you have shot two passes of your footage; a clean background plate that does not have your action present, and a normal pass that includes the action you wish to isolate from this background. If the camera is locked down, you don't need a long clip for the clean background plate; even a still will do.

In theory, Difference Matte can be used to key action out from any background – not just a solid color backdrop – as After Effects is matching the color of each respective pixel between the two passes and showing only the pixels where it finds a difference. However, anything that contaminates or adds noise to the background – video noise or film grain, dust, water, or camera shake – will make it harder to get a good key. The Blur Before Difference parameter will help reduce some of the problems caused by video noise or film grain.

Extract

This enhancement on a straight luminance keyer focuses on a single channel of information: alpha, overall luminance (good for black or white backgrounds), or just red, green, or blue (the background color you wish to remove). It gives you a visual reference of the luminance values active in this channel, and a gray Transparency Control Bar underneath where you can decide what ranges of this color to key.

In [Ex.01g], select **PM_Alex.tif** and hit F3 to open the Effect Controls window. We've chosen to work on the Blue channel, as this is the color of our background. The luminance range Histogram shows two distinct active regions: dark blue and light blue. With just a minimum of tugging on the corners of the Transparency Control Bar, we quickly figured out that we wanted to keep the dark blues, lose the light blues, and taper into the bottom of the light blue region to maintain good edge transitions. The problem is, as we remove more of the blue in the lower portion of the shot, we lose some of the hair (and even the teeth) – play around with it yourself to see the trade-off.

The Extract keyer allows you to select a specific channel to work on, then adjust the Transparency Control Bar (the gray region underneath the Histogram) to decide what luminance range of this channel to keep and remove.

Inner Outer Key

We'll go into more detail about this advanced keyer later in this chapter. It works differently than any of the keyers featured here. Instead of picking colors, you create mask shapes: an inner shape for what you want to keep, and an outer shape for what you want to lose. The plug-in then calculates transparency for the color transition between these shapes. An example is shown in [Ex.01h]; the results on a still like this are spooky-good; more work is required with moving footage.

![Pro] **Keylight**

After Effects 6.5 Professional comes bundled with a very powerful third-party keying plug-in: Keylight from The Foundry (www.thefoundry.co.uk). Keylight allows you to pull satisfactory keys very quickly and to improve them without much effort; it also contains a lot of power underneath the hood to take on challenging tasks or to further finesse the result. This one plug-in handles both creating an alpha and color correction, including spill suppression.

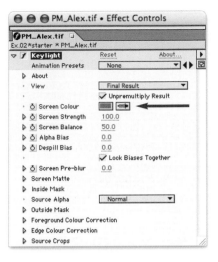

Keylight's installer is located on the After Effects installer CD. After you run the installer, you will find a very detailed, easy-to-digest PDF manual alongside the plug-in in the **Plug-Ins>Keylight** folder on your drive. For those who resist cracking open manuals (you know who you are), we're going to give a quick overview of how to apply Keylight and make quick tweaks that will cover the majority of the situations you should encounter. If you need to dive deeper, crack open that manual; it also contains a series of tutorials in the back. (Additional source material for those tutorials may be downloaded by going to The Foundry's web site, selecting Downloads>for After Effects, clicking on Keylight, then clicking on Examples under the Support & Training section to the right.)

After applying Keylight and using the Screen Colour eyedropper to select our blue background (above), we already have a pretty good key (below).

Use Window>Close All to reduce the clutter, then open [**Ex.02*starter**], which contains our now-familiar model Alex, with a garbage mask already applied around her.

• Select layer 1, and apply Effect>Keying>Keylight. In the Effect Controls window that opens, click on the eyedropper for Screen Colour, then click on the blue background between Alex and the mask. Boom – you've already got a pretty good key! But you can refine it from here…

• To see the alpha channel being created by Keylight, change its View popup to Combined Matte. You can see we have some nice grays around the hair, which indicate they will be semitransparent (as they should be); you can also see that the arm on the left side is being eaten away a bit by the key.

• To see these details more clearly, change the View popup to Status: This gives an exaggerated display where the foreground is white, the background is black, and the gray areas show the partially transparent areas. In this View, some problems that were hard to see before with noise beyond Alex's hair are now suddenly obvious.

Multiple Masks

For challenging keys, try keying multiple copies of the image, each with a different feature – such as clean-edged clothing or wispy hair – isolated with masks, so you can tweak the keyer for each feature.

• With View still set to Status, slowly scrub the Screen Strength parameter until most of the gray areas disappear; hold Command on Mac (Control on Windows) while scrubbing to change this parameter in finer increments. Increase Screen Strength until the gray noise above her head disappears; be careful not to erode too much of the semitransparent areas around the fringe of her hair. As usual, keying is a bit of a compromise; here, you may need to lose the wisp of hair trailing off to the left in order to get rid of the noise about her head.

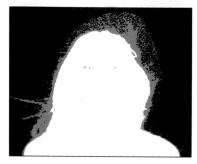

Setting the View popup to Combined Matte allows you to view the alpha channel that will be generated (top). Changing it to Status gives an exaggerated view that more clearly shows problems as gray (partially transparent) pixels where they aren't supposed to be (above).

With View set to Status, we've used a combination of Screen Strength and Clip Black to get rid of the noise above Alex's head, and Clip White to fill in her arm and eyes.

• To further tweak the alpha channel, twirl open the Screen Matte section. Clip Black provides an alternate approach to getting rid of the unwanted gray sections you see in Status view. Save your project, press Shift+F5 to take a snapshot of what the Comp window looked like using just Screen Strength to correct the problem, and reset Screen Strength to 100. Now slowly increase Clip Black to reduce the unwanted noise. Press F5 to compare your new results with Screen Strength; use File>Revert if you liked your earlier results better. Of course, you can also balance these two parameters against each other. We suggest using Clip Black to get rid of the worst of the problems, then use Screen Strength to deal with what's left. You can check your results any time by setting View to Final Result.

• Next, you need to fill in the semitransparent (gray) areas in Alex's arm and eyes. With View set to Status, slowly decrease Clip White until these areas fill in. The pale green areas that now appear in the Status view (check the arm area that used to be gray) are a warning that we may have some color issues in these fringes; we'll tackle spill suppression next.

• Change the View popup to Intermediate Result: This displays the footage with its new alpha channel, but without any color correction or spill suppression. If you like, take a snapshot of this for reference by pressing Shift+F6; you can press F6 anytime later to refer back to it.

• Change the View popup to Final Result, which shows the image with spill suppression applied. Not bad!

• If you want to remove more blue spill, increase the Despill Bias parameter. It may be tempting to keep increasing Despill Bias until all of the blue disappears from her hair, but while doing so also watch her cheek on the left side: You will start to change some of the color here too (press F6 to compare with your snapshot). You can recover the original color in the skin tones somewhat by reducing the Screen Balance value. Also, at this point it is a good idea to view the composite over its new background (in this example, enable the Visibility switch for layer 2) to see what your corrections look like in context; you may be able to get by with less Despill Bias than you initially thought.

You might have noticed that after you finish editing Despill Bias, the Alpha Bias parameter changes as well. Keylight often edits both the alpha channel and color correction to the edges in concert with each other, and therefore defaults to locking these two parameters together. If you find that editing Despill Bias is causing unwanted erosion to your edges, disable the Lock Biases Together checkbox underneath, and tweak Alpha Bias to achieve the degree of softness you want in the edges.

Now that you've had fun with this example, it's time to try a more challenging one on your own: Open [**Ex.03*starter**], apply Keylight, and tweak the parameters in the same order as you did for Alex. The water in this shot is normally a problem for many other keying plug-ins, but Keylight excels at semitransparent areas such as reflections, smoke, and water.

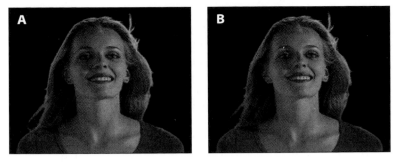

Keylight offers many other powerful features, including color correction of the foreground and edges, choosing what color to factor into the edges when they've had spill removed, the ability to select mask shapes to keep or remove areas in the original image regardless of their color, and other parameters to smooth, expand, or erode the matte. Again, we encourage you to check out its manual. Don't be intimidated by its length: The type is big, the explanations are good, and the tips are exceedingly useful. This is a very powerful keyer, and we're happy Adobe arranged to bundle it with the Professional edition.

Setting View to Intermediate Result shows the image keyed, without any color correction (A). Changing View to Final Result shows the effects of Keylight's built-in spill suppression (B). You can increase Despill Bias to remove more of the blue from the edges, but be careful you don't start altering the rest of the image – watch for brown splotches starting to appear on her cheek (C).

Other Mousetraps

In addition to the keying effects available with After Effects, numerous other companies have created their own keying plug-ins, either as stand-alone effects or as part of larger packages. Virtually all third party effects developers have demo versions online you can download and try yourself. Here are our favorite alternatives to the After Effects keyers:

Primatte Keyer (www.redgiantsoftware.com)

High-quality keying doesn't get much easier than this. Drag the mouse where you want to drop out the background, and again where you want to keep the foreground, and you're most of the way there – even with trouble areas such as hair and transparent edges. Internally it works in three-dimensional RGB space, determining which parts of that space belong to the background, the foreground, or transitions between the two. You accomplish spill suppression and other correction by selecting specific colors and offsetting them from one of these regions into another. (For information on Primatte for other programs, visit www.photron.com.)

dvMatte Pro (www.dvgarage.com)

Optimized for the tricky task of pulling keys from DV footage, this inexpensive plug-in is also at home working with footage from other sources. dvMatte is based on the techniques taught in dvGarage's excellent Composite Toolkit (hard-core real-world training for creating good keys and composites); there's a discount if you buy the plug-in and training together.

Ultimatte (www.ultimatte.com)

The standard, available as hardware for realtime keying and as software for a number of programs and platforms. The latest version of the plug-in – AdvantEdge – has probably the most complete, sophisticated set of tools out there for dealing with keys. Harnessing this power means it's not as fast or intuitive to use as Primatte or dvMatte, but the art of keying is hardly an exercise in instant gratification anyway…

'Scoping Out Alternatives

If you need to do a lot of rotoscoping work, check out silhouette+roto from SilhouetteFX (www.silhouettefx.com/roto/).

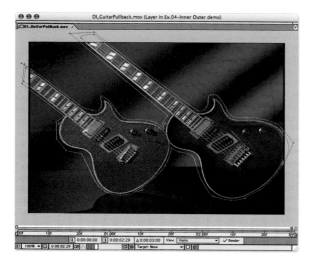

These guitars were originally shot – moving – against a blue and purple background (above). We animated rough masks just inside and outside their edges, and used Inner Outer Key to pull a matte so we could place them over a new background (below). Guitar footage courtesy Desktop Images; background elements from Digital Vision/Prototype and Light Forms.

Inner Outer Key

Clients being clients, quite often you will be asked to key or mask out an object that was not shot against green, blue, or other easy-to-key backdrop. The previous solution has been to spend a lot of time tediously hand-masking (rotoscoping) the object, being careful to trace the edges with no wander or "chatter" from frame to frame. The problem is magnified with interlaced material (potentially twice as many frames to mask), and by any motion blur or other partially transparent edges.

The Inner Outer Key plug-in provides an alternative in some situations. If there is enough contrast in color between the object and its background, it allows you to create two rough, much less precise masks: an "inner" mask that traces the inner edge of the object, and a looser "outer" mask that traces just beyond the object. Inner Outer Key will then attempt to detect the edges between these two masks and create an alpha channel. If there are areas that don't key cleanly, Inner Outer Key also allows you to create small "cleanup" strokes or masks to improve these problem areas.

In the **Sources>10_Chapter Sources** folder in the Project window, double-click **DI_GuitarPullback.mov** and play it. This shot is of a pullback from a pair of guitars resting on a purple table, with a blue background. The guitars have been sent back to the factory, but the client now decides that the background should be red and yellow like the guitars, and more "electric" (don't you just love clients).

Now open [**Ex.04**] and RAM Preview: The guitars float in space over our new background. Note that even the "teeth" along the edges (a natural artifact in interlaced video of moving objects) key out cleanly.

Hit End to see both guitars clearly, and double-click the layer **DI_GuitarPullback.mov** to open its Layer window, and set the View popup to Masks. You should be able to see the masks we created:

• The rough inner mask shape is created just inside the shape of the guitar and animated to follow the action as the guitar scales down (this shape is far rougher than we would need if we were trying to cleanly mask out these guitars).

• The outer shape mask is a looser mask drawn just outside the guitar edges, also animated to follow the motion. Close the Layer window when done.

In the Timeline window, note that both mask shapes are set to None mode so that they don't create transparency themselves. With **DI_GuitarPullback** still selected, press F3 to open the Effect Controls window and check out the settings for the Inner Outer Key effect. We've selected these two mask shapes as the Foreground (Inside) and Background (Outside). This effect then detects the edge between these masks, including creating partial transparency if the edge was soft.

There were a couple of areas of this image that Inner Outer Key had trouble detecting contrast in, such as the reflections of the guitars on the table. In this case, a few very simple two-point mask strokes were added and assigned to corresponding Cleanup Background paths (twirl open Cleanup 1, Cleanup 2, and Cleanup 3). Each of these cleanup paths have size (Brush Radius) and softness (Brush Pressure) controls to help you touch up these edges.

Inner Outer Key does not work in all situations. Cases where there is little contrast between edges and background – such as when there are excessive reflections and spillback on the object, or edges of an object fading to black against a black background – will cause Inner Outer Key to define these areas as partially transparent. However, Inner Outer Key does wonders with truly transparent areas, such as hair, which normal masks cannot. If you want to experiment more with this plug-in, try using it on our Alex bluescreen image. Inner Outer Key's parameters are discussed in more detail in the online Help file (press F1 from inside After Effects, click on Search, and enter "Inner Outer Key").

Inner Outer Key lets you choose which masks to use as the primary Inside and Outside shapes. You can also define additional cleanup shapes (which can be simple, open lines) to touch up problem areas.

A Second Opinion

There are numerous training resources and web sites out there on bluescreen history, preparation, and execution. Our two current favorites are:

dvGarage Composite Toolkit (www.dvgarage.com)

An excellent training set that shows you how to pull a difficult key step-by-step using the After Effects Color Key, Color Range, and Color Difference Key effects or their own dvMatte plug-in (an optional add-on to the Toolkit) – or by building your own keyer using standard After Effects plug-ins. It also covers spill suppression and compositing tricks. If you need to do a lot of keying, this is a must-buy.

Steve Bradford's Blue Screen/Chroma Key Page (www.seanet.com/~bradford/bluscrn.html)

This site contains a huge amount of relevant historical information on bluescreen and chroma key equipment and techniques. It will be of particular interest to those making the jump from traditional video and film compositing equipment to the desktop. Includes links to buy bluescreen supplies.

More Color

Color correction was the subject of Chapter 8; we're applying some of those techniques here.

In [**Ex.05*starter**], the water fountain footage is too green for the red sky (left) – an obvious giveaway. Color correct to taste, to better match the red sky (right). Background courtesy Artbeats/Sky Effects.

The dark statue is out of place in this snow scene (left). Applying Levels and tweaking its Gamma helps brighten it up, and Hue/Saturation helps desaturate and shift its color to better match the scene (right). Background courtesy Artbeats/Retro Transportation.

Fixing It in the Mix

If you pulled a good key, you have reason to be happy. But it's no time to quit: That final bit of polish comes in blending your newly keyed foreground into its new background image. (We've saved copies of our already-keyed footage, so you won't need the Professional edition to try these exercises.)

A dead giveaway a scene has been composited – aside from a bad key – is when the foreground and background images have different contrast and tonal ranges. You will see this sin left uncured even in feature films.

Careful use of color correction can greatly aid in compositing disparate images, or further correcting a color cast in the foreground object caused at the lighting stage.

Close all other comps, and open [**Ex.05*starter**], which contains a water-drenched statue composited against a red evening sky. The statue, although very saturated, has a different tone than our sunset. You'll need to fix that. Experiment with different color correction effects to try to push the statue's color more toward its new background. Again, there is more than one right answer; in [**Ex.05_final**], we used the Effect>Channel>Channel Mixer to reduce the strength of the green cast in the original key, then added a slight master hue shift with the Adjust>Hue/Saturation effect to move the entire foreground more toward red.

Other problems to watch out for are the black-and-white tones and the overall contrast. For example, in [**Ex.06*starter**] we took our statue and moved him out into the snow. He is way too dark for this scene, and

needs lightening. With this vintage background shot, we also have a less saturated palette of colors to match. A good place to start for these adjustments is Effect>Adjust> Levels. Gamma is usually the first parameter we grab – it leaves the black-and-white points intact and changes the gray levels between them. If the image needs more contrast, squeeze the Input Black and Input White arrows closer together; if it needs less, squeeze the corresponding Output arrows.

For additional practice, try blending the Water fountain with other backplates – the basic project is set up in [**Ex.07a**] with a pair of backgrounds to choose from. We've also placed Alex against a new background in [**Ex.07b**], but be careful when color correcting not to change her skin tone to something too sickly!

Living on the Edge

The last frontier we'll explore in this chapter is improving the edges of your keyed objects. If nothing else, you need to reduce or eliminate any leftover garbage around the edges. Ideally, you want the colors and apparent light from your new background to appear to illuminate and wrap around the edges of your foreground image. These techniques apply to compositing synthetic objects, such as 3D renders, as much as for bluescreen work.

Matte Tools

The Professional edition's Matte Choker effect was designed to help clean up problematic color keys where there may be holes or tears in the edges. The idea behind Matte Choker is to first spread the edges to fill in the holes, then choke the joined edge back in.

Unfortunately, its default parameters are not ideal for what you usually need to do. For example, if you want to spread the matte first (which is what negative choke values do), the first Choke parameter should be negative, not positive. Second, the higher the Gray Level Softness parameter, the less effect the Choke parameter has – and since the second Gray Level is set to 100%, you may think its Choke parameter is broken. Third, the Geometric Softness parameter is set a bit high for the first set of parameters (the spread pass) and low for the second set of parameters (the choke pass); try 2.0 as a starting value for both instead.

This effect can be used for softening edges, even if they are already clean. In this case, you can almost ignore the Choke parameters and treat Geometric Softness as an "amount of blur" parameter, with Gray Level Softness setting the blend. This application is demonstrated in [**Ex.09**].

For cleaning up less-tattered alpha channels, we use Simple Choker, particularly in cases where even correctly interpreting the alpha channel as Premultiplied still leaves a lingering black fringe or white halo around an object. This is a common problem with photos shot against a white background in which the alpha isn't cut quite tight enough. A value of 1.0 or slightly under is usually a good starting point for Simple Choker.

Alternative Suppression

Near the end of the Color Difference Key tutorial in **Bonus Chapter 10B** on the DVD, we discussed using the Professional edition's Spill Suppressor to reduce the amount of blue spill, bleed, or contamination around the edges of your keyed object. If you don't have the Professional edition, there are also a variety of third party plug-ins and roll-your-own solutions to this problem, such as the channel manipulation trick taught in the dvGarage Composite Toolkit.

You can also use Effect>Adjust>Hue/Saturation. This effect allows you to select a specific color range, then shift it to a new color and/or desaturate it. Select the general color range from this effect's Channel Control menu, then tweak the range sliders underneath the first color bar to center around the color you're trying to remove. Rotate the Hue setting to shift the spill color to more closely match the new background image you are compositing on top of, as if that was what was now causing the color spill. Then reduce the Master Saturation and Lightness sliders as needed to reduce how noticeable the result is. See the **Ex.08** folder for some examples.

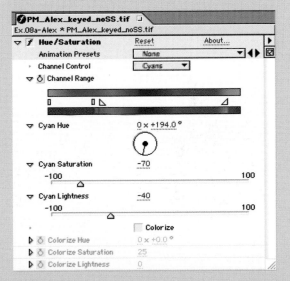

The Hue/Saturation effect can be used to isolate the spill, shift it to match the background, and make it less obvious by reducing its Saturation and Lightness.

This well-shot bluescreen footage was unfortunately mangled during the video transfer, resulting in rough edges (left). To fix this, first blur the alpha, then choke it back in size. The result is a more acceptable edge (right). Footage courtesy Artbeats.

Blurring the Lines

Another common trick for blending images into their backgrounds is to blur their edges so more of the background image will seem to leak around the foreground. This can also help repair bad edges of mattes that otherwise can't be pulled cleanly.

One tool for accomplishing this is Effect>Blur & Sharpen> Channel Blur, which can blur each color channel, as well as the alpha channel, individually. This means that we can leave the color information sharp and smear just the matte. The downside of this is that the matte usually spreads out wider as a result of being blurred, revealing more of the background. You can rein the edge back in using Effect>Matte Tools>Simple Choker – positive values shrink the matte back down in size. (If you don't have the Professional edition, use Levels, and increase Alpha Input Black to 127.) Depending on your specific problem, you might have better results by reversing the order of the effects so that you choke the edge first, then apply Channel Blur.

Backgrounds for Bluescreen

If you are creating backgrounds for keyed footage, and the key is less than satisfactory, you'll make your life a lot easier – and make the composite more believable – by designing the backgrounds using the same general color range as the color you keyed.

Let's say you're keying a talking head, and the subject is wearing glasses, has wispy hair, and there's lots of spill on the shoulders – *and* the key is less than perfect. Instead of choking the key to death, design an animated background with hues from the quarter of the color wheel centered around your screen's color. For bluescreen, you can use the range from purple to blue to blue-green. Greenscreen, unfortunately, forces you to design in the less desirable and more challenging yellow-green range.

When you add some fake lighting effects to the background, the mind is fooled into thinking that behind your subject is a live source that was casting

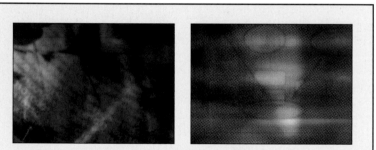

Examples of bluescreen (left) and greenscreen (right) backgrounds we created for one of our clients, Xerox Media West. We combined numerous stock library movies and stills with elements created in Illustrator and 3D programs to create something appropriate for each project.

bluish or greenish light onto the person being interviewed. Remember that unless the background looks like it emits some kind of light, the mind will find no explanation for color spill.

Volume 1, Chapter 10 includes tips for using "lighting" movies composited on top of the other layers using the Overlay or Soft Light blending modes. If possible, create looping backgrounds and animations so you can repeat them for as long as needed to go behind any shot either in After Effects or in your editing system.

Compositing Tools

If you do a lot of compositing, there are a couple of excellent third party effect packages you should check out. Composite Suite from Digital Film Tools (www.digitalfilmtools.com) is a comprehensive set which includes plug-ins for natural lighting, light wrap, color correction, blur, grain, edge treatments, and matte manipulation.

Another favorite is Composite Wizard, distributed by Red Giant Software (www.redgiantsoftware.com). This package includes plug-ins for edge treatments including repairing holes in alpha channels, color matching, color spill removal, and light wrap. Both would make excellent additions to your toolbox. (The "light wrap" effects are designed to easily create the technique shown below in *Seeing the Light*.)

Seeing the Light

Light naturally wraps around the edges of an object in a scene – such as the blue spill we've been working so hard to remove. To really sink an object into its new background, you have to make it appear as if light from this new background is wrapping around your keyed foreground or 3D render. To do this, you need to create a matte that is just a blurred edge of your foreground object, but that doesn't extend beyond your foreground's edges. You then use this as a matte for a blurred copy

The edges around Alex are too sharp to convincingly blend her into the new background image. We created a blurred matte that sits inside her edges (left), and used that to blend in a blurred version of the background, making it seem like she is affected by the colors of this image (right).

of your background. Place this blurred edge on top of your original foreground, and now the background will seem to seep around its edges.

[**Ex.10a**] shows one way to build this. It contains two copies of our already-keyed footage. The copy on top has been blurred; the amount of this blur controls how much wrap will take place. The copy underneath uses this blurred version as an Alpha Inverted matte. The result is a blurred edge that's *inside* the keyed footage's original edge. We also filled the result with white so you can see the result more clearly (and use it as a luma matte if needed), but this is not necessary.

Now open [**Ex.10b**]. It contains [**Ex.10a**] as a precomp (layer 1), which acts as a matte for a blurred version of our background (layer 2). These are then placed above our normal composite of the keyed foreground and new background. Turn the Video switch for layer 2 on and off to see its contribution; you can also alter its Opacity to blend it in more subtly.

Try different modes for layer 2: Screen makes the edges really glow; Overlay results in darker areas of the background darkening the corresponding edges of your foreground layer – almost as if they were in shadow.

Connect

Blending Modes were discussed in Volume 1, Chapter 10.

Masking (including rotoscoping moving objects) was the subject of Volume 1, Chapter 11.

Track Matte techniques were explained in Volume 1, Chapter 12.

The basics of applying effects was discussed in Volume 1, Chapter 21; common effects such as Hue/Saturation were discussed in Volume 1, Chapter 24.

Audio Basics

An introduction to handling audio in After Effects, including how to "read" audio as clues for editing and animation.

After Effects has never made audio one of its strong points. If you need to seriously rework a soundtrack, do it in a dedicated audio program. But if you just need to edit, mix, and do some basic improvement or "sweetening" to your soundtrack, After Effects already has the tools you need.

Audio is also an important guide for making animation decisions, plus it can drive some effects. But first, we need to get a handle on how sound itself works – after that, everything else makes a lot more sense.

Seeing Sound

To best handle audio, you have to become familiar with how to "read" its graphic waveform display. You can't look at a waveform and know *exactly* what the sound is, but it will give you enough important clues – such as where beats of music land, or where individual words in a sentence start.

To get some practice with this, open the project file **11-Example Project.aep** from the **Chapter Example Projects>11-Example Project** folder on the DVD, import any source footage with sound into After Effects, and drag it into a comp. If you don't have an audio file handy, open comp [**Ex.01**]. It includes a short piece of music we created called **CM_Inglemuse**.

All layers with audio, including any comps that have layers with audio, will have a little speaker icon in the Timeline window's Audio/Video switches panel; clicking on this turns the audio on and off. Twirl open the layer's parameters in the Timeline window. If the clip contains both video and sound, you will see a new category called Audio; twirl that open as well to reveal the properties Audio Levels and Waveform. If the clip contains only audio, all the normal masks and transformations will be missing, and Audio will be the only category you see.

Click on the twirly to the left of the word Waveform. See all those squiggles that appeared in the timeline? That's a visual representation of your sound. As mentioned, [**Ex.01**] contains the **CM_Inglemuse** music file for you to look at. Let's discuss where those squiggles came from, and what they mean.

The eyeball (Video switch) and speaker (Audio switch) icons in the Timeline window indicate whether a layer has image or audio data, or both. Here, the first layer has video and audio; the second has audio only (circled in red).

Example Project

Explore the 11-Example Project.aep file as you read this chapter; references to [Ex.##] refer to specific compositions within the project file.

Ex.01-waveform exposed • Timeline

Ex.01-waveform exposed

0:00:00:00 (29.97 fps)

	#	Source Name
▽ ☐	1	CM_Inglemuse.mov

▽ Audio

› Ō Audio Levels — +0.00 dB

▽ Waveform

› Waveform

Switches / Modes

Those squiggles in the Timeline window are the "waveform" of the audio, indicating how loud it is at each point in time.

Good Vibrations

For there to be a sound, something must vibrate. This vibration could be a guitar string swaying back and forth, a speaker cone pumping in and out, or pieces of glass shattering as you throw your phone through the window after the client's most recent round of changes. These motions vibrate the air, pushing it toward you and pulling it back away from you. This in turn pushes your eardrum around, causing it to flex in sympathy. This stimulates nerves in your ears, which ultimately convince your brain that a sound has occurred.

The pattern and nature of these vibrations affect the character of the sound we perceive. The stronger the vibrations, the louder the sound. The faster the fundamental pattern of vibrations, the higher the apparent "pitch" of the sound. Humans can perceive vibrations from a speed of 20 back-and-forth cycles per second to as high as 20,000 cycles per second – a lot faster than the frame rate of video or film.

Sound is recorded by intercepting these vibrations in the air with a device akin to our eardrum – typically, a microphone – which converts them into electrical signals with a similar vibrational pattern. In a computer environment, these vibrations are frozen by *digitizing* or *sampling* that electrical signal. When sound is digitized, its instantaneous level (how strongly the air has been pushed toward or pulled away from the microphone) is measured (sampled) and converted into a number (digitized) to be stored in the computer's memory. A very short instant later, the signal is measured again to see how the air pressure changed since the last measured moment in time. This process is repeated very quickly over a period of time to build up a numeric picture of what the pattern of vibration was.

The speed at which it is performed is called the *sample rate*, which is roughly equivalent to frame rate. The higher the sample rate, the more accurately high frequencies – which help make sounds more intelligible – are captured. Professional digital video cameras sample audio at

Instant Waveform

To directly access Levels and the waveform twirly, select the layer in the Timeline window and hit L for Levels. To see the waveform, hit LL (two Ls) quickly.

Waves to Keys

Animation>Keyframe Assistants>Convert Audio to Keyframes – introduced in version 6.0 – creates keyframe values that match the combined amplitude of the audio waveforms in a comp. This is great for driving expressions (Chapter 6).

Here are two simple waveforms displayed in an audio editing application, zoomed in the same amount. As the curve of the wave goes above the centerline, air is being pushed toward you; as it goes below, air is being pulled away. Time passes from left to right; the markings along the bottom of this particular display are in 10-millisecond (hundredth of a second) increments – giving an idea of how fast sound vibrates. Since the up and down excursions for the second waveform are not as tall as for the first, you know the second sound is relatively quieter; because its up and down excursions are also happening faster, you know it is higher in pitch.

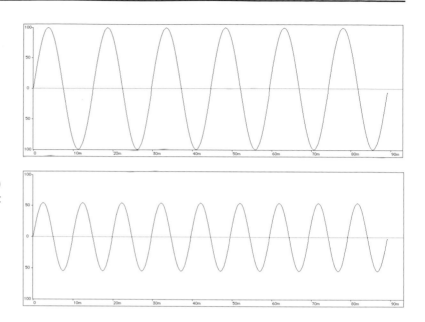

Inaccurate Waveforms

Most programs do not display every sample of a waveform, so the same waveform looks different at different zoom levels. For critical edits, zoom in to single frame view (in After Effects, hit ; on the keyboard) for the highest display accuracy.

48,000 times a second, usually expressed as 48 kHz (Hz = Hertz = cycles per second; kHz = thousands of cycles per second). Audio CDs use a sample rate of 44,100 (or 44.1 kHz); consumer DV uses a rate of 32 kHz. Professional audio can use rates as high as 96 kHz or 192 kHz; lower-end multimedia often use 22.050 kHz.

The resolution at which these samples are digitized is defined as the number of bits per sample (akin to bit depth of a color image). Higher resolutions result in less *quantization distortion*, which is often heard as noise. Professional quality gear uses 16-bit or 24-bit resolution; 8-bit resolution sounds very noisy. The special 12-bit format used by consumer DV cameras is just a bit short of the 16-bit format in quality.

This resulting *waveform* is typically displayed on a computer screen by drawing a point or line that represents the air pressure at one point in time, followed by additional points or lines that represent succeeding points in time. As a result, you can "read" a waveform from left to right to get an idea of the vibrational pattern. No one can look at the resulting squiggles and tell you what the sound was, but you can pick up some clues: Louder points in time will be drawn taller than quieter points in time; cycles that take relatively longer to fluctuate up and down are lower in pitch than ones that fluctuate more quickly.

Sample Rate Management

The final audio sample rate and resolution is determined by your Render Settings. You can combine files with multiple sample rates, and After Effects will perform the sample rate conversion automatically. Make sure you render with Best Quality for the best conversions.

If you're a real stickler for the absolute best quality, try to capture all of your audio at the final sample rate you need. If you must mix rates, before you import your audio into After Effects, use a dedicated high-quality audio program to convert the sample rates of the deviant files to be the same as your final render target.

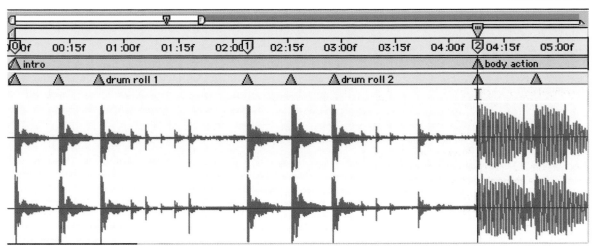

Spotting Audio

When we are animating or editing visuals to sound, the most interesting points in the audio tend to be the loudest ones: the moment a door slams, lightning cracks, a drum is hit, or a client's wails crescendo. By looking for these *peaks* – taller points in the audio waveform, going in either the upward or downward direction – we have a tremendous head start in finding the more interesting audio events, which we can then use as a starting point for visual edits and effect keyframes. Strong drum beats produce these peaks, as do syllables in words. Areas with no peaks or other visible waveform indicate pauses between words and sentences.

Comp and Layer markers can be used to mark important beats in the music or words in the voiceover. We use the 10 Comp markers to mark the major sections in the music or animation. Be warned, though, that since Comp markers are connected to the comp's timeline, the markers no longer line up if you move the audio track in time. Layer markers, on

Starting the process of spotting important points in a piece of music. We've used both numbered Comp markers along the top, plus named Layer markers. Comp markers have the advantage of letting you jump directly to them using the numbers on the regular keyboard, but you get only 10 per comp, so use them wisely. In contrast, you can have any number of Layer markers per layer, and you can type in your own notes.

Our audio after spotting. We've marked every major beat, plus added comments to a second layer that indicate where major sections of the music begin or end.

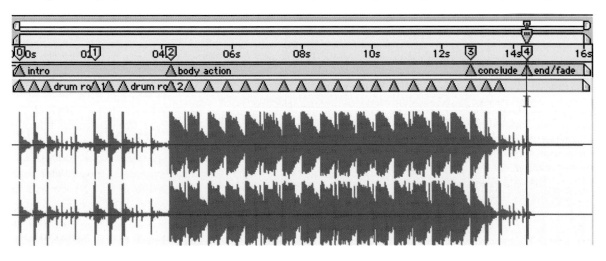

175

Audio Guide

If you are using the same audio track in a precomp as well as a later comp, click on the copy in the precomp and select Layer>Guide Layer. This will prevent it from also playing in the later comp, which may result in over-loading and distortion.

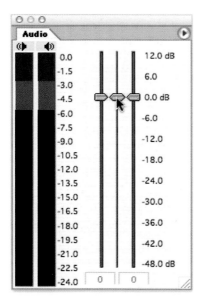

The Audio window can be resized (bottom right) for finer control. The meters display the instantaneous level of audio being previewed. If the speaker icons at the top are red, the volume was maxed out, possibly distorting. These "clip" indicators reset each time you preview; you can also reset them by clicking on them. The sliders on the right are used for setting Levels values.

the other hand, are attached to the layer. Use these to mark your musical beats and script highlights. Practice this with [**Ex.02*starter**].

If the audio layer fills up with markers, make a Layer>New>Null Object; give it a suitable name such as "**script notes**" in Layer>Solid Settings. Now you can add markers to the null layer with your more prosaic descriptions, and place markers for the music beats on the audio layer itself.

Our process is to view the waveform, locate these peaks both visually and by listening to the audio, and set Layer markers to remind us where they are. Then we twirl up the waveform display (since it has a relatively slow redraw), and animate based on the position of the markers.

For quickly adding Layer markers, use the "tap-along" method. Select the layer you want to place the layer markers on (the layer with audio, or a dummy solid layer as mentioned above), set the time marker to the start of the section you want to spot, preview the audio by pressing the period key on the keypad, and hit the keypad's asterisk key in time with the music. When the preview stops, Layer markers will appear. (You can adjust the Audio Preview Duration in Preferences>Previews.)

Don't be surprised if you tapped slightly late. When you're done tapping, study the relative location of your markers and the waveform's peaks, and slide the markers back until they line up. If the marker wants to snap to just before or just after a peak (based on the timeline's frame increments), it is usually better to err on the early side.

Once the music and script layers have markers, you can copy and paste these layers into precomps for easy animation decisions. Just make sure that only one audio layer is rendered (multiple audio layers will probably result in distortion as the combined sound is now too loud). You can either set the audio switches to off in the top comp for these nested precomps, or set the audio tracks in the precomps to be Guide Layers (Layer>Guide Layer) so that they don't render in subsequent comps.

On the Level

In After Effects, all layers with audio are assumed to be in stereo, containing left and right channels in the same layer. If the source file was mono (one channel of audio), After Effects internally duplicates the audio so that the same sound is in the left and right channels.

You can alter or keyframe the Audio Levels of a layer. These values react differently from a normal linear parameter: Most of the useful values for Level exist in a small area around the 0 mark. Unlike a parameter such as Scale or Opacity, 0 means no *change* rather than nothing rendered.

There are four ways to edit this value: Scrub it in the Timeline window, enter it directly in the Timeline window, move the sliders in the Audio window, or enter it directly in the Audio window. We'll assume you already know how to scrub or enter values in the Timeline window, so we'll focus on the Audio window.

The shortcut to expose Audio Levels in the Timeline is to select the layer and type L. The Audio window is usually tabbed together with the Time Controls palette; you can also drag it out to be its own window. If

Previewing Audio

Unlike video, audio cannot be previewed by hitting the spacebar unless you are in the QuickTime Player window. Otherwise, you will need to either preview it or scrub it.

There are several ways to perform a RAM Preview for audio inside a composition. The easiest is to set the time marker to where you want to start, then hit the decimal point key (. on the numeric keypad of an extended keyboard). Hitting any key will stop playback.

If you want to preview your images with audio playing, make sure the speaker icon in the Time Controls palette is switched on, then click on either the RAM Preview button or hit 0 on the numeric keypad. The preview will obey your work area and the Loop setting. Note that if your image is large or your video card is slow, the image may lag behind the audio; if so, the frame rate display in the Info palette will turn red during playback.

Finally, you can "scrub" audio by holding down the Command (Control) key while you're moving the time marker with your mouse. This works in the Footage, Layer, and Timeline windows. Scrubbing will play a single frame of audio for each frame you move the time marker to. If you move the cursor less than a one-frame increment in the Timeline window, After Effects instead will start playing a one-third second loop of the audio, starting at the current location of the time marker.

The quality of the sound you will hear is controlled by the audio settings in Preferences>Previews. The best choice is to use the same sample rate and bit depth as used by most of your source layers.

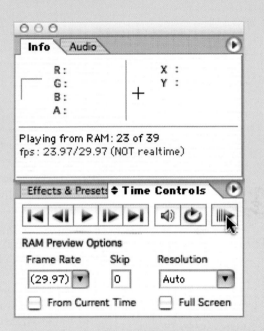

To play back audio while you're previewing your visual animation, make sure the speaker icon is turned on in the Time Controls palette and click the RAM Preview button. If playback is not realtime, the Info's frame rate display will turn red; audio and video will be out of sync.

it is currently closed, open it using the menu item Window>Audio or the keyboard shortcut Command+4 on Mac (Control+4 on Windows). To edit the Levels in this window, move the sliders: Dragging one changes just the channel it is associated with; dragging the bar between the sliders alters both the left and right channels together (keeping their same relationship). You can also directly enter values in the numeric boxes along the bottom of this window.

One of the main reasons to edit the Audio Levels for a layer is to balance the relative volume between multiple sound tracks. Focus on which is the most important sound at any given time that the viewer should be listening to – make sure that layer is the loudest, and reduce the level of the other audio layers so that they contribute but do not detract.

Maximum Viewing

After Effects draws the audio waveform after it has been processed with the Levels parameters. Spot your audio first, perhaps even with Levels set artificially high (to better see details in the waveform), then set your final Levels later.

You Edit so Fine

Audio events happen so fast, you will often need to trim audio layers with finer precision than the video's frame rate. Temporarily enter a higher frame rate in the Composition Settings, edit the audio layer, then return the frame rate to normal.

You've Got the Power

You have two ways of viewing and entering Levels parameters in the Audio window: as a *percentage* of full scale volume, and in *decibels* (units of loudness). You can switch between these two methods by selecting the Audio Options (the menu arrow in the upper right corner). These changes affect only the Audio window; the Timeline window always shows Audio Levels in decibel (dB) units.

Unless you have a background in audio, you will probably be most familiar and comfortable with the percentage scale. When we're reducing the volume of a music or sound effects track behind a narration track, we usually start at 50% volume and preview that to make sure the voice is intelligible.

Decibels is a *power* scale that more closely relates to the way we perceive loudness. When we're reducing the volume of music to help make any simultaneous narration clearer, we start at –6 dB from where the normal level was; it is not unusual to use values of –12 to –16 to really clear the way for more intelligible speech. To fully turn off the volume of a clip with audio, you need to set its Level parameter to –96 dB for a 16-bit resolution clip. When you're trying to even out the volume of a narrator that may be fluctuating from soft to loud on individual phrases, changes in the range of 0.5 to 1.5 dB are often sufficient. Since the sliders are so touchy, you might want to set the Slider Minimum to –12 or –24 dB in the Audio Options dialog, then manually type in –96 when you want to set a track to silence.

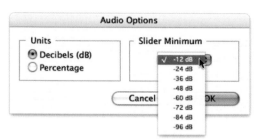

The Audio Options window is opened by clicking on the arrow in the upper right corner of the Audio palette. These affect how you enter and view Levels parameters using the palette's sliders. As most Levels adjustments take place in a small range around 0 dB, you might consider setting the visible slider range down to something like –12 or –24 dB.

You can increase the volume of clips by setting their level above 0. You may need to do this if the original audio was recorded too softly, but be careful; it is easy to scale the audio samples to the point where they exceed their maximum value and "clip" – resulting in nasty distortion. The same goes for mixing together several loud clips in a comp or project. If you preview audio for the comp and the volume meters in the Audio palette light up the top red indicator, you are clipping; reduce the volume of the audio track(s) slightly.

Speed Shifts

You cannot conform the "frame rate" of an audio file in the Interpret Footage dialog. If you conform the rate of a video file that has audio attached, the audio will *not* be altered to match. To speed up or slow down an audio layer, use Time Stretch or Time Remapping.

A better way to do this is to use a dedicated audio processing program. Many of these have dedicated time-stretching routines, with an option of preserving the original pitch of the file. If your audio program doesn't have time-stretch capabilities, convert the sample rate to a new rate that is slowed down or sped up by the speed shift you need (for example, to slow down 0.1%, increase the sample rate 0.1% – from 48,000 to 48,048), then edit the file's header info back to its original sample rate.

○○○   Ex.04c–Stereo Mixer w/ ease • Timeline

🗅 Ex.04c–Ster...xer w/ ease ◿		
0:00:03:00 (29.97 fps)	⊠ 🖾 🕀 🎞 M	◒ ▽ ▶

🦃	#	Source Name	🕀 ❋ ↖ 𝑓 🎞 M ⊘ 𝄐	🔊🕪○🔒	:00s	02s	04s	06s	
▽ ☐	1	🗅 CM_Downshift.mov	🕀 ╱ 𝑓 ☐	🔊	△ fade starts are linear		△ Ease In/Linear Out	△ Ease in	⊠
		▽ Stereo Mixer	Reset	𝑓					
		▷ 🕒 Left Level	100.00 %	◀✓▶	◆		》	》	
		▽ 🕒 Right Level	100.00 %	◀✓▶	◆		》	》	
		˒ Value: Right Level	100.00%						
				☐					
			0.00%						

     ◀▶   Switches / Modes   ◀▶   △ △   △

Often, the smoothest-sounding fades come from animating Effect>Audio>Stereo Mixer instead of Levels, using linear keyframe interpolation at the start of the fade, and Easy Ease In (or its equivalent) at the end of the fade. The Value graph shows the softened exponential fade shape that results.

Sound Advice

Remember that Audio Levels modifies, rather than sets, the volume of an audio layer. Don't get hung up on leaving its value at 0 dB, as you might leave Opacity at 100%. If the audio was recorded too soft, increase Levels; if it was recorded too loud, reduce Levels. If the volume varies in a distracting way over time, then vary its level over time to compensate. If you need to introduce a fade in or fade out for an otherwise continuous soundtrack, again, animate its level.

After Effects interpolates between audio keyframes using the power-oriented decibel scale, not normal percentage. This results in fade-downs that can range from natural to slightly abrupt. Fade-ups, unfortunately, sound very unnatural, as they seem to linger at the lower volume, then suddenly rush up when they're close to the higher keyframe. You can smooth this out a bit by easing into and out of the higher volume keyframes for fade-ups and fade-downs.

We find the Levels control so awkward to animate that we use it only for setting the overall volume of a track – not to do fade-ups and fade-downs. When we need to perform fades for a layer, we apply Effect>Audio>Stereo Mixer and keyframe this instead. By default, keyframing Stereo Mixer gives linear fades, rather than the exponential fades that the Levels parameter yields. This sounds more natural in most cases. To improve on this further, we ease into the second keyframe of a fade. To compare these, RAM Preview [**Ex.04a**] (exponential fades using Levels), [**Ex.04b**] (linear fades using Stereo Mixer), and [**Ex.04c**] (linear out/ease in fades using Stereo Mixer).

Although this may initially seem like more work, in the long run it is more flexible. If you already entered a set of fade-ups and fade-downs, then later decided the entire track needed to be louder or softer (but wanted to keep the fades), you could just alter the layer's Levels parameter. We'll discuss using the Stereo Mixer in more detail in the next chapter.

Connect

RAM Previewing was covered at the end of Volume 1, Chapter 2.

Keyframe interpolation (including the Easy Ease keyframe assistants) is discussed at length in Volume 1, Chapter 3.

Comp and Layer markers were marked up in Volume 1, Chapter 6.

Nesting and precomposing were the subjects of Volume 1, Chapters 18 and 19.

Useful audio effects – including Stereo Mixer – are discussed in Chapter 12.

Several of the tutorials in our companion book *After Effects in Production* use audio to help decide animation and edit points, as well as drive expressions. Check out *Atomic Café, RoboTV, Hot but Cool, Underground Movement,* and in particular *Just an Expression* plus the case study *ESPNDeportes.com.*

12 Audio Effects

An overview of some of the more useful audio effect plug-ins.

The Standard edition of After Effects comes with several audio processing effects; the Professional edition adds more. They are all located in the menu item Effect>Audio. We'll go over some of the more useful ones, including how they work and some suggested applications for their use. Of course, experimentation is the best way to master them.

Our personal bias is more toward audio "sweetening" than special effects creation, and that will be our focus in the effects we discuss. We've grouped together effects with similar purposes (such as those that work with echoes, or that alter the tonal balance of a sound). Of course, almost any effect can be driven to extremes to create weird sounds, and again, that's where experimentation comes in.

Trimming and Clipping

An important side effect of some common audio effects (such as Echo and Reverb) is that they produce altered versions of the sound that are supposed to exist after the original sound is finished. However, if you have trimmed an audio layer to end as soon as the original sound had stopped, the plug-in will stop there too: An effect cannot render audio that plays past the end of the trimmed layer. When you're playing around with effects that create trailing versions of the processed sound, select the layer and apply Layer>Time Remapping. You can then easily extend the last "frame" of the audio layer as long as needed by dragging its Out Point (*not* the last Time Remap keyframe). This is demonstrated in the comp [Ex.01] in the project file **12-Example Project.aep** (in the **Chapter Example Projects>12-Audio Effects** folder on the DVD).

Some plug-ins create additional copies of or boost certain portions of the original sound, potentially increasing its overall volume. Make sure you preview your audio after adding effects. In the worst case, you may now be "clipping" the signal; this is indicated by the speaker icon at the top of the signal level meters in the Audio window turning red. The result is distortion. Because Audio Levels is calculated after any effects, you can't fix the problem there; clipping has already been introduced. If an effect features Dry and Wet amounts (the level of the original and processed audio, respectively), you can reduce the level here; otherwise, place the Stereo Mixer effect first in the chain and reduce the volume there.

Audio Preview

Press . (decimal point key on keypad) to preview the audio from the current frame forward. The duration of this preview is set in Preferences>Previews. Set it to at least 15:00 for the examples in this chapter.

Example Project

Explore the 12-Example Project.aep file as you read this chapter; references to [Ex.##] refer to specific compositions within the project file. Some examples use Professional edition-only effects.

Stereo Mixer

This workhorse effect has several uses. First is as a replacement for the standard Audio Levels control, with parameter sliders on a scale that many find easier to understand. In most cases, keyframing Stereo Mixer also creates by default more natural-sounding fades than Audio Levels. (We discussed these concepts in more detail at the end of the previous chapter.) Any setting over 100% boosts the original volume of the layer; anything below reduces it. As always, watch that boosting doesn't cause clipping; preview after adjustments and watch for the red indicator at the top of the Audio window.

The downside of using the Stereo Mixer for levels adjustments is that you have to adjust both the left and right channel parameters; there is no one slider to do both. Fortunately, a simple expression (we know some of you consider that term to be an oxymoron; stick with us a moment anyway) fixes that:

Open [**Ex.02*starter**], select the audio layer that's already there, and apply Effect>Audio>Stereo Mixer. Type E to reveal this effect in the Timeline window, then twirl down the parameters for Stereo Mixer. Option+click on Mac (Alt+click on Windows) on the stopwatch icon to the left of Right Level to enable expressions. Then drag the pick whip that appears in the Switches panel for Right Level to the words Left Level. Release the mouse, and hit Enter to accept this expression. Now, as you scrub (or keyframe) Left Level, the Right Level will automatically follow. The end result is shown in [**Ex.02_final**]. We've saved this as an Animation Preset in your **Goodies** folder: **StereoMixer_link.ffx**. If you need to balance the left and right channels, use the sliders in the Audio Levels palette.

The Left and Right Pan parameters can be used to reposition a sound in the stereo field. Many sound effects and most music are recorded with a full left/right stereo spread, but you might want to narrow it down to make it seem like it is coming from a more definable location. For example, if you leave the Left control at –100 (full left) and set the Right to 0 (center), the result will be the sound still having a stereo spread, but being located a bit off to the left. As always, preview and watch for clipping; in this case, the Right audio channel is now getting added evenly

Easy Fades

Level changes with Stereo Mixer sound more natural if you ease into the second keyframe of a change. To do this quickly, select all of its Level keyframes, and use Animation>Keyframe Assistant>Easy Ease In.

A simple expression (no, really) can be used to link the left and right channels of Stereo Mixer together, so you have to adjust or animate only one parameter rather than two.

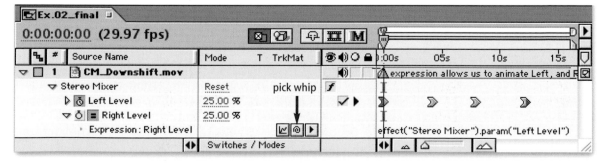

into the left and right final channels in addition to the original Left channel going 100% into the left, potentially causing clipping in the resulting left channel. Reducing their respective level parameters inside the effect will bring it back in line.

If you have a mono sound that you want to pan around, set Left and Right Pan to be the same value. As this doubles up the volume of the sound, you should reduce the Left and Right Level to 50% to avoid clipping. Again, you can use a simple expression to link the two Pan controls together so you have to animate only one. Follow the same directions as above, but instead of linking Right Level to Left Level, link Right Pan to Left Pan. As before, we have a piece of audio waiting for you to experiment on in [**Ex.03*starter**]; the result is shown in [**Ex.03_final**] (you'll need to RAM Preview through stereo speakers or headphones to hear the effect). This is saved as the preset **StereoMixer_mono.ffx**.

The Stereo Mixer effect is also a way to work around the audio-rendering pipeline. You can use it to pre-adjust the levels of different layers that might otherwise be too soft or loud compared with other clips, akin to using the normal visual Levels effect to tweak the gamma, black, and white points of source images. If another effect is causing the sound to be boosted into distortion, and you can't find a good balance of its parameters to tame it, reduce its volume beforehand with the Stereo Mixer. If you have already set up a series of Levels or Stereo Mixer keyframes, and later find that adding audio effects has thrown your volume balance off, you can again use the Stereo Mixer effect to retweak the overall level of a layer without having to reanimate your volume keyframes.

The Audio-Rendering Pipeline

We regularly discuss the "rendering pipeline" and how important it is to wrap your head around it in order to understand how After Effects processes your images. Although it's not as critical, the audio rendering pipeline is also useful to know. As with images, audio is processed in the order of the parameters you see when you twirl down an audio layer in the Timeline window:

1st:	Time Remapping
2nd:	Effects
3rd:	Audio Levels
4th:	Time Stretch

Delay	Reset
Animation Presets	None
▷ Delay Time (milliseconds)	1150.00
▷ ⚬ Delay Amount	50.00 %
▷ ⚬ Feedback	75.00 %
▷ ⚬ Dry Out	100.00 %
▷ ⚬ Wet Out	100.00 %

Delay

This plug-in is used to create echo effects. When it's rendering, it creates a copy of the original sound and plays it back delayed in time compared with the original. Delay Amount determines the relative volume of this echo. Feedback decides how much of this delayed sound to feed back through the chain, creating subsequent echoes. The higher the Feedback amount, the louder the subsequent echoes, and the longer it will take the final effect to die away. This is one of the reasons you might need to artificially lengthen sounds (as mentioned earlier in this chapter), to prevent the echoes from getting cut off prematurely.

You can time the echoes produced by Delay to specific numbers of frames for rhythmic animation. All it takes is a little math (really):

[desired delay (in frames) ÷ frame rate] × 1000 = delay time parameter (msec)

The maximum delay time is 5 seconds (5000 milliseconds), which works out to just under 150 frames at 29.97 frames per second (fps).

[**Ex.04**] demonstrates an echo trick using Delay. It also is an example of using Time Remapping not just to extend the length of a sound file, but to "freeze" the source audio at a specific point, letting the layer continue in time so the echoes generated can continue past our freeze point.

Reverb

When we hear reverberation, we're actually hearing thousands of individual echoes blending together. Instead of the archetypal echo case in which your voice bounces off a canyon wall and bounces back to you, inside more normal rooms your voice (or any sound) is scattering out in all directions, bouncing off any surface it meets, and occasionally zooming past your ears on its various ways to other surfaces to bounce off. Get enough of these echoes and reflections together, and they start to smear into an overall ambiance rather than distinct sounds. The sound loses some energy with each bounce, eventually decaying away into silence. How much energy is lost depends on the surfaces in the room – for example, reverberation takes longer to die away in a marble bathroom than in a carpeted living room with heavy drapes.

Reverb is simulated in software by setting up a number of individual echoes of varying lengths, then feeding them back on themselves to get the additional reflections. After Effects' Reverb plug-in gives you direct access to these parameters:

Reverb Time adjusts the spacing between the original reflections; longer times simulate larger rooms (where there are longer distances for the sound to travel between walls).

Diffusion adjusts how random these individual reflections are – less diffuse means a more orderly room with patterns to the reflections; more diffuse means the reflections are more ragged in timing.

Decay is how strongly, and therefore often, the reflections bounce. Use smaller decay values to simulate carpeted and draped rooms where the reverb dies away quickly, and larger decay values to simulate glass and stone where the reverb would linger much longer.

Brightness controls a very important but often overlooked parameter of reverb simulation: that imperfect real-world reflective surfaces tend to attenuate (reduce in level) higher frequencies more than lower frequencies. Crank this value up for more metallic sounds; keep it low for more realistic, organic sounds.

The default settings for Reverb are pretty good. It does not have quite the quality of a more expensive dedicated hardware or software reverb, but it can help add a sense of room (or distance) when it's used in small Wet amounts. Tweak the Reverb Time first to change the virtual room size, followed by the Decay to control how echoey it is. Varying Diffusion too much from its default quickly makes the simulation break down. Also, note that Reverb takes longer to render than most other audio effects.

▽ *f* Reverb	Reset
Animation Presets	None
▷ Reverb Time (ms)	100.00
▷ Ŏ Diffusion	75.00 %
▷ Ŏ Decay	25.00 %
▷ Ŏ Brightness	10.00 %
▷ Ŏ Dry Out	0.00 %
▷ Ŏ Wet Out	30.00 %

Sound Check

If you want to hear just what the reverb is doing, set the Dry Out to 0% and the Wet Out to around 30% to 70%, depending on how loud the original audio is. This is shown in **[Ex.05]**.

Dry Out and Wet Out

Many of the audio plug-ins feature a pair of parameters called Dry Out and Wet Out. This is because many of the processings sound best if you mix together the unprocessed sound with the processed version. The Dry Out is the original version; the Wet is the processed one. Think of it as Blend With Original, but with more control.

Most of the plug-ins sound more realistic with relatively high Dry and low Wet amounts; some, like Flange/Chorus, work better set closer to a 50/50 mix. A nice trick is to fade up the Wet Out from 0 to some nominal setting over time, causing the effect to fade in without reducing the volume of the original sound.

Flange & Chorus

A funny thing happens when an audio file is delayed only a very short amount and mixed back in against itself. Rather than hearing two distinct sounds, they start to cancel or reinforce just certain frequency components of each other. This is what the Flange & Chorus effect produces.

▽ *f* **Flange & Chorus**	Reset	About...
Animation Presets	None	▼ ◀ ▶
▷ ⟲ Voice Separation Time (ms)	50.00	
▷ ⟲ Voices	1.00	
▷ ⟲ Modulation Rate	0.30	
▷ ⟲ Modulation Depth	0.00 %	
▷ ⟲ Voice Phase Change	0.00	
·	☐ Invert Phase	
·	☐ Stereo Voices	
▷ ⟲ Dry Out	50.00 %	
▷ ⟲ Wet Out	50.00 %	

When the value for Voice Separation Time is set to roughly 10 milliseconds or shorter, as in [**Ex.06a**], the phenomenon is known as *flanging* – so called because it was originally created by playing two identical audio tapes in synchronization, then dragging your hand on the tape reel flange of one of the copies, causing this slight delay. Some describe it as a "jet taking off" effect.

Voice Separation Time values of roughly 10 to 50 milliseconds, as in [**Ex.06b**], produce a phenomenon known as *chorusing* because it sounds like more than one singer or identical instruments trying to play exactly the same note slightly out of time with each other. The result is a more watery sound. Larger values get into very loose chorusing, to the point of being called a "slap back echo" – you can hear this in [**Ex.06c**] – because it sounds like an echo bouncing off a very hard object nearby.

Typically, only one Voice would be used to create this effect, but this parameter can be increased to make it deeper and more dramatic. Note that each Voice is delayed by the Voice Separation Time, meaning the total delay is set by the number of Voices multiplied by the Voice Separation Time. To keep a flange or chorus sound, you may need to reduce the Time as you increase the number of Voices to avoid hearing a slapback echo effect. More Voices will also require you to reduce the Wet Out amount lest you start overloading. Enabling the Voice Phase Change parameters emphasizes some of the frequency cancellation effects at lower Voice Separation Time settings.

The real secret to this class of effects is a touch of Modulation Depth and Rate. This causes the Voice Separation Time to wander (modulate), resulting in a slightly watery, unstable sound. Modulation Rate values of under 1.0 are most common; higher values produce more watery or even drunken effects. A touch of this effect will help add depth and "magic" to some sound effects such as cymbal crashes and jet engine takeoffs; some also like to use it on vocals.

Bass & Treble

These are basic tone controls. They affect a broad range of frequencies: Bass affects those below 500 Hz; Treble affects those above 1000 Hz. When they're set to boost low (Bass) and high (Treble) frequencies, they have relatively subtle effects; they have a much more drastic effect when they are set to cut (negative values).

Intoxication Modulation

If you want to make your audio really sound drunken, try the Professional edition's Modulator effect. This effect is aimed more at special effects creation than normal audio sweetening. Set its Amplitude Modulation to 0 and its Modulation Depth to higher values, such as 20% on up.

Bass and treble boost effects are demonstrated in [**Ex.07a**] and [**Ex.07b**]. Boosting the highs can increase intelligibility but can also increase any hiss present; listen carefully. Decreasing highs can make sounds appear more distant, or less intelligible – which can be helpful if you have a music or sound effect track that is distracting too much from the voiceover.

Preview the Bass & Treble parameters with the Effect switch in the Timeline window toggled off and on to hear their effect. Boosting Bass gives more low-end emphasis but can also quickly result in clipping distortion; again, preview and be ready to pre-lower the volume with the Stereo Mixer effect.

If you have the Professional edition, the High-Low Pass and Parametric EQ effects have more precision and more predictable results. However, Bass & Treble is still very useful for a quick, general, subtle enhancement.

High-Low Pass

The definition of a High Pass filter is one that passes frequencies higher than a set cutoff and tries to remove any frequencies present below that cutoff. A Low Pass filter, as you would expect, does the opposite: passes all frequencies below a set cutoff.

Why is this useful? From a purely corrective point of view, unwanted sounds often exist at the extremes of the audio spectrum. For example, traffic noise, wind across a microphone, and even some ventilation system noise often exists below 100–200 Hz in frequency; a High Pass filter with a Cutoff of 100 or so can help remove this while leaving most other sounds untouched. Likewise, hiss often exists at the highest end, above 10 kHz or so; a Low Pass filter with a Cutoff of 10,000 or higher can remove some of it with minimal damage on voice.

More creatively, reducing the portions of the audio spectrum we hear can be used to mimic lower fidelity devices, such as AM radios or the telephone. In these cases, you will probably need to apply this effect twice: one copy set to Low Pass, and one to High Pass. Setting the Cutoff of the High Pass to around 800–1500 Hz and the Cutoff of the Low Pass to around 2000 is a good start at a cheap television or radio effect, as heard in [**Ex.08a**].

Most of the time, you will want to set the Wet Out to 100% and the Dry Out to 0%. If you are cutting out the frequencies you want, but otherwise find the effect too drastic, start adding in a little Dry Out until you get the desired mix.

This effect tends to reduce the volume of a sound; you may need to boost it back up again using Levels or the Stereo Mixer.

Controlled Response

If you want effects that generate graphics from audio to react only to certain portions of the audio spectrum, precompose the audio layer and apply audio effects in this precomp to focus on the desired frequencies.

1 is for Gun

By the way, the audio for [**Ex.08**] comes from an award-winning short movie by Keith Snyder and Blake Arnold called *1 is for Gun*; that's Blake's voice and Keith's music. Information on the making of it can be found at www.woollymammoth.com/gun/.

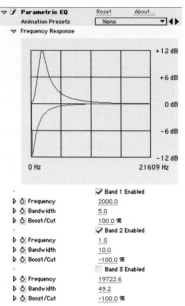

Parametric EQ

Parametric equalizers allow you to focus on specific bands of frequencies and either boost or remove them. This is the finest knife you have for altering the sound character of audio files. Examples of uses include making a voice more "present" by enhancing just parts of its range, reducing annoying harmonic peaks or *resonances* in a sound file, and cutting out specific narrow spectrum sounds such as fluorescent light buzz or other annoying sounds that are constant in pitch.

After Effects' Parametric EQ effect gives you three of these filters to work with; you can enable and disable each individually, and each is drawn on the frequency graph in its own color: red for 1, green for 2, and blue for 3. Inside the graph, pitch or frequency goes from low to high as you go from left to right; a curve that goes above the centerline is boosting a range of frequencies, while a curve that goes below that line is cutting them. Here are what the various parameters mean:

The **Frequency** parameter sets the center of the frequency spectrum range you are going to be targeting. Unfortunately, this slider (and the graph above it) has a linear range; our perception of pitch is actually exponential, meaning this effect is a bit tricky to dial in. You'll find that the lower quarter of its range has the most audible effect, getting touchier as you get farther to the left.

Bandwidth sets how narrow or wide a range of frequencies you are going to be affecting. It is defined as a percentage of the total bandwidth of the original audio. Since common audio sample rates (such as 44.1 or 48 kHz) have a bandwidth of just over 20 kHz, this means that setting the bandwidth to 1% affects roughly a 200 Hz-wide swath of frequencies. (Note to those with an audio background: This is not the same as "Q" or width on typical audio equipment.)

The problem with this parameter is that the way we perceive pitch is not linear: A 200 Hz range is perceived to be a very wide range at lower frequencies and a very narrow range at higher frequencies. As you set the Frequency parameter higher, you may find you also need to set the Bandwidth parameter higher to get the same perceptual effect.

Boost/Cut sets how much you are increasing or decreasing the prominence of the selected frequency range.

A common working practice with parametric EQs is to set the Bandwidth fairly small (such as 2) and the Boost/Cut to a moderate Boost (such as +6 or higher), then to go back and forth adjusting the Frequency and previewing the results until you have isolated the portion of the sound spectrum you want to work on. You can then adjust the Bandwidth to set

EQ Pointers

What frequencies should you use as starting points for equalization? Voice enhancement/adjustment usually takes place in the 100 Hz to 5 kHz range. Buzzes from bad dimmers and so on tend to happen around 8 kHz on up. You can also search and boost or reduce general musical instrument ranges by adjusting the range of frequencies you treat.

Ground circuit hum in the United States starts at exactly 60 Hz, and in nasty cases, also appears at integer multiples of that frequency. In Europe, the magic number is 50 Hz. Because the narrowest Bandwidth setting (0.1) corresponds to roughly 200Hz, unfortunately, you'll have trouble making surgical adjustments down that low; you will need a dedicated audio program to go after these problems.

how broad of an effect you want, and set Boost or Cut depending on whether you want to enhance it or remove it.

[**Ex.08b**] is another pass at our cheap speaker effect, this time using Parametric EQ to make it sound more akin to a telephone.

Tone

Tone can be used to create sounds from scratch: the aural equivalent of a solid. It replaces any audio that came with the layer it was applied to, including any previous Tone effects – so you need separate layers if you want to mix the results of multiple Tone effects together. A basic test tone generator is set up in [**Ex.09*starter**]; open it and experiment with the settings.

Tone can create up to five pure pitched sounds with a single master volume for all five. The layer's Levels parameter can also adjust its volume. You can disable any of the five component sounds by tuning their Frequency parameters down to 0 Hz. You can set only one Waveform, which is applied to all five component sounds. Their names describe the shape of their waves, and their general sound characters are as follows:

• **Sine** is the purest tone, containing no harmonics above the frequency it is set at.

• **Triangle** sounds just a touch brighter than a sine wave.

• **Saw** Is short for Sawtooth and is the most raucous-sounding of the waveforms.

• **Square** is strong too, but has a more "hollow" sound than Saw.

You can also set the fundamental frequency of each component sound. Waveforms other than Sine have additional higher-pitched components called *harmonics* that exist at integer multiples of the sound's fundamental frequency – 1×, 2×, 3×, 4×, 5×, and so forth – so you will often not need to set this frequency as high as you might expect to get a bright or high-pitched sound. Remember that you can hold the Shift key while scrubbing a value to make it jump by larger increments.

At its simplest, you can use Tone to create the audio portion of the bars and tone reference signals that often get laid down at the head of videotapes. Apply Tone to a layer, leave the Waveform at Sine, set Frequency 1 to 1000 and all the other frequencies to 0, and Level to 100%. Now adjust the volume of your reference tone with the layer's Levels. A common –18 dB reference tone is set up in [**Ex.09_reference –18dB**].

You can also create all sorts of sci-fi radio and electronic sounds by animating the Frequency of Tone. Again, we tend to hear pitches in a logarithmic fashion, rather than linear; that means as you keyframe Frequency to increase, it will seem to rise quickly and then slow down, even if you are using linear keyframes. When you're animating Frequency, try using Easy Ease In or Out for the keyframe with the lower value to get a more natural glide in pitch.

Sound Keys

One of our favorite plug-ins is Sound Keys from Trapcode (www.trapcode.com), which derives keyframe data from user-defined frequency ranges in audio.

▽	*f*	Tone		Reset	About…	
		Animation Presets		None	▾◀▶	
	▸	Waveform options		Sine ▾		
▹	⊙	Frequency 1		1000.00		
▹	⊙	Frequency 2		0.00		
▹	⊙	Frequency 3		0.00		
▹	⊙	Frequency 4		0.00		
▹	⊙	Frequency 5		0.00		
▹	⊙	Level		100.00 %		

Connect

RAM Previewing was covered at the end of Volume 1, Chapter 2.

Keyframe interpolation (including the Easy Ease keyframe assistants) is discussed at length in Volume 1, Chapter 3.

Effects that generate graphics from audio were mentioned in Volume 1, Chapter 24.

Expressions were covered in Chapter 6.

Basic concepts of audio, including animating fades, were the subject of Chapter 11.

Time Remapping, which can be used to pause a layer's source audio as an effect continues, is explained in Chapter 13.

13 Time Remapping

Ever wish you could make time stand still? Or just slow down at strategic points? The answer is Time Remapping.

Mixing Times

Do not combine Time Remapping and Time Stretching on the same clip – life will get too interesting…

Example Project

Explore the 13-Example Project.aep file as you read this chapter; references to [Ex.##] refer to specific compositions within the project file.

Time Remapping is another one of those concepts that seems a bit bizarre at first but is very useful and powerful once you get your head wrapped around it. With Time Remapping, you can set which frame of your source will appear at what time in your composition. You can use time remapping instead of time stretching to slow down or speed up a movie, but time remapping does so much more.

Time remapping can be keyframed: When given two or more time remap keyframes to work with, After Effects automatically interpolates between them, just as it would with any other property. Since the property being interpolated is *time*, the result is a change in the playback speed of the clip. Because you're working with regular keyframe interpolation types, you get the benefit of velocity curves for ramping speed up and down. You can also easily create freeze frames and even make a movie play backward. And did we mention that you can do all of this to nested comp layers as well?

You will not see Time Remapping listed as a default property of a layer when you reveal it in the Timeline. It needs to be enabled by selecting the layer and invoking the menu item Layer>Enable Time Remapping. It will then be the first item in a layer's list of properties, because it happens before Masks, Effects, and Transform. You can then keyframe it just like any other property. Unlike Time Stretching, Time Remapping keyframes does *not* affect the timing of other keyframes already applied to a layer – it behaves as if you time-stretched the clip in a previous composition.

Getting Started (and Stopped)

More often than not, you'll use Time Remapping to make a clip longer than it originally was. Therefore, it's a good idea to start with a practice composition that's roughly twice as long as the clip you will be working with. To get started, open the **13-Example Project.aep** file, and open the **[Ex.01*starter]** comp. It contains a movie clip of a dancer with some distinctive moves. Double-click the clip to open its Layer window and play it until you're familiar with its action.

Close the Layer window, and with the layer still selected, select Layer> Enable Time Remapping (Command+Option+T on Mac, Control+Alt+T on Windows). The Time Remap property is added to the layer (if you

twirl up the layer and twirl it back down, you'll see that Time Remap appears in the Timeline window above Transform). The shortcut to twirl down just Time Remapping is RR (two Rs in quick succession).

When you enable Time Remapping, two default keyframes are automatically created: one at the start of the clip, and another one after the clip's out point (see the sidebar *The Real Out Point*, later in this chapter). To disable Time Remapping and delete all keyframes, turn off the stopwatch to the left of Time Remap in the Timeline window. You can also select Enable Time Remapping again to toggle it off. (Remember that if you make a big mess as you learn how to time remap, toggle time remapping off and on again to start over.)

Twirling down Time Remap's own arrow to see its value and velocity graphs will also be useful; it gives you a better idea of what is being done to the clip.

Add a few new dance steps to this dancer movie using Time Remapping. Footage courtesy Getty Images/ Dance Rhythms.

Freeze Frames

With Time Remapping enabled, the layer bar is now longer than the original movie's duration. Simply drag out the triangle at the end of the layer bar to extend the layer and freeze on the last frame. Scrub the time marker around this end zone to confirm this.

To freeze on the first frame before the movie starts, click on the words Time Remap to select *both* default keyframes, then drag the first keyframe to its new time. The second keyframe will move by the same amount. For example, moving the first keyframe from 0:00 to 02:00 will produce a two-second freeze frame at the beginning of the clip. Note that you're moving its *time* keyframes, *not* the layer bar. To create only freeze frames, be certain to always move both keyframes together to keep their relationship the same as they slide along the timeline. Should they drift together or apart from each other, you will be introducing either a speedup or a slowdown of the movie, not just a simple freeze frame.

When you enable Time Remapping for a clip, it gets two default keyframes, marking its normal start and end. The ghosted area to the right of the clip's original end shows you can now extend it, frozen on the last frame.

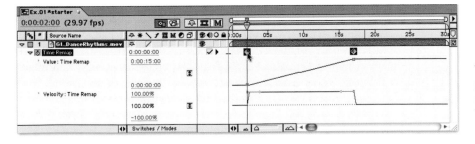

To start with a hold, then play at normal speed, make sure you drag *both* Time Remap keyframes – not just the first one.

Trimmed Time

If you have trimmed a movie, then enabled Time Remapping, immediately go to the new In point, click the TR keyframe checkbox, and do the same for the Out point. Now delete the two default keyframes. This will keep only the trimmed frames in play for freeze frames and editing.

Remapping Audio

Audio can also be time remapped. Use this for special effects and other weirdness, such as imitating DJ "scratching."

The Big Picture

Twirl down the Time Remap arrow to reveal its graphs. All these numbers may be daunting at first, but most of them are largely irrelevant. The top (underlined) number is critical: This indicates which frame of the movie or comp is being viewed at the current time. The big picture first:

• A Time Remap (TR) keyframe denotes what "frame of the source" should play at a particular point in the timeline. Time Remap keyframes have interpolation types just like other temporal properties: Linear, Auto Bezier, Continuous Bezier, Bezier, and Hold. Remember that these are just regular keyframes underneath – but instead of having a value in *percent* (as in Scale) or *degree* (as in Rotation), their values are *frames in the source*.

• By setting multiple TR keyframes, After Effects will interpolate between these values, and the movie will play fast or slow depending on how many frames of the source movie are spread across a certain number of frames in the timeline.

• Should keyframes interpolate from a higher value to a lower value, the movie will play backward.

• Hold keyframes are used to freeze on a frame, and velocity curves add ease in and out control.

• Frame blending can be used to smooth out any irregular motion: In slow motion (where frames would be duplicated), interpolated frames are created by automatically crossfading between adjacent frames. In sped-up motion (where frames would be skipped), multiples frames are blended together.

Doing Time

To add a TR keyframe, move somewhere to the middle of the clip, click on the underlined value, and enter a new frame number. To choose a new frame visually, scrub the keyframe value and watch the movie update in the Comp window. (Alternatively, you can drag the keyframe nubbin in the Value graph to edit the frame value.) After Effects will now play your chosen frame of the movie at this point in the timeline and will interpolate between keyframe values, spreading the frames in-between over time.

To give you an idea of how this might work, [**Ex.02**] is an example of a movie that has been time remapped. RAM Preview first to see how the action plays out, and make sure the graphs are visible. The Value and Velocity graphs can be read as follows:

Value : Time Remap The last frame of the movie (15:00) is at the top range of this graph, and the first frame (00:00) at the bottom. The Value line is a visual clue to which parts of the movie are used. When it ramps upward from left to right (**A**, **B**, **D**, **F**, and **H** in the figure on the next page), the movie is being played forward (the frame number is increasing); when it ramps downward (**E**), the movie is playing backward (decreasing frame numbers). A flat line (**C**) indicates it is holding on a particular frame; after the last keyframe, the movie freezes on frame 12:04.

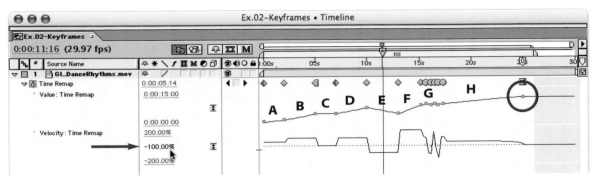

Velocity:Time Remap The middle number in this graph is the important one, indicating whether the movie is playing slowly (less than 100%), normal speed (100%), faster (more than 100%), or backward (negative value). The top and bottom numbers indicate the "range" for the graph, which defaults to a range from 0% to the fastest speed between the set keyframes. If this flat line is at 100% on the scale, it is playing forward, at normal speed. If it is flat at 0, it is a freeze frame. If it is below 0, the clip is playing backward. (When you first apply Time Remapping, this graph is a single flat line at 100%, dropping to 0% after the last keyframe.)

Now, let's analyze the implications of our keyframes in more detail:

• In [**Ex.02**], place the time marker between keyframes (KF) 1 and 2 (**A** in the figure above): the movie plays at half speed, which is displayed as 50% in the Velocity graph (it plays 1 second of source material over 2 seconds of time, duplicating each frame to do so).

• Between KF 2 and 3 (**B**), the movie plays at 100% normal speed (for every one frame of source, you have one frame in the timeline in which it plays). Note that the Value line has a steeper slope, and the Velocity line is higher – both indicators that the clip is playing faster than between the previous two keyframes.

• Between KF 3 and 4 (**C**), the movie freezes for 2 seconds, on frame 04:00 into the clip (note we're at 05:00 in the timeline because we played the first portion of the movie at half speed). The Value line stays flat, and the Velocity line is at 0%. The keyframe was changed to a Hold keyframe, which we recommend to ensure a solid freeze, especially if you're also frame blending the layer.

• Between KF 4 and 5 (**D**), the movie plays forward at 100% speed.

• Between KF 5 and 6 (**E**), the movie plays backward at –100% (one frame of source to one frame of comp). The Value line has a strong downward slope, and the Velocity line is well below 0 – both indicators that the clip is playing backward.

• Between KF 6 and 7 (**F**), the movie plays forward, this time faster at 200% speed.

• The sequence of six keyframes (7–12) (**G**) is set so that just a few frames are repeated back and forth, and Automatic Bezier keyframes help

A set of Time Remap keyframes have been set to manipulate the speed of the clip. The red arrow points to the speed at the current time.

You can edit the current source frame interactively by scrubbing the current value, just as with any regular keyframe.

Between KF 5 and 6 (E), the downward Value line indicates the movie is playing backward (a negative velocity value).

You can also drag the keyframe nubbin (circled in red) up and down to edit the keyframe value.

Time Remap Shortcut

When Time Remapping is enabled for a layer, press RR to reveal the Time Remap property in the Timeline window, or U to reveal all animated properties.

smooth out the jarring changes in direction. RAM Preview this section and then return the keyframes to Linear by Command+clicking (Control+clicking) on them, and compare the difference.

• The final keyframe has a value of 12:04, well before the last frame of the movie (14:29). An ease in was added to slow down the movie as it enters the last keyframe, at which point it holds on that frame.

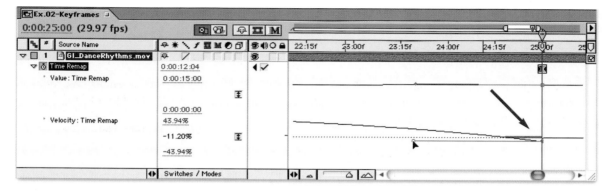

A dotted gray line (see red arrow) in the Velocity graph indicates that your clip will back up. You can stop this behavior by pressing the Shift key when you're editing handles, which prevents the velocity curve from crossing the center line.

When you're adjusting TR graphs, be careful that your velocity does not go negative, indicated by the dotted gray line in the Velocity graph – this means your clip will back up. Unless this is the intended effect, hold the Shift key down to prevent the graph from crossing the center line.

Time Remap keyframes can be dragged along the timeline as with keyframes for any other property. Dragging keyframes with the Info palette open (Command+2, Control+2) gives you feedback as to precisely which point in time you are dragging to. Start playing around with the keyframes yourself, sliding them to different points in the timeline. Observe how the Value and Velocity graphs change, and Preview to reinforce what's going on. Add some new keyframes and play around until you get a good feeling for the graphs. Now disable and re-enable Time Remapping, and start over with your own ideas for how the dancer should perform.

Time Repairing

We often use Time Remapping to alter a section of a clip to make it work better with the music or voiceover. In the following example, we'll show you how to "pad" time into the middle of a clip. Select Window>Close All, open [Ex.04*starter], and preview the **AB_LosAngelesAerials** movie of a helicopter flying around a skyscraper. At around 05:00, the view into the building is what's important to the story, but the pilot flew by these windows too fast. Let's take this section of the clip and slow it down, leaving the beginning and ending untouched:

In **[Ex.04]**, you'll use time remapping to extend the time spent circling this side of the skyscraper. Footage courtesy Artbeats/Los Angeles Aerials.

Step 1: Open [Ex.04*starter], select the clip, Enable Time Remapping, and hit U to see its keyframes. Twirl down the Velocity graph.

Step 2: Extend the layer bar's out point so that it extends to the end of the composition.

Step 3: Move to 03:00, where the helicopter is about to move around the side of the building we're interested in. Click the keyframe checkbox to add a TR keyframe at 03:00 with a value of 03:00. This anchors the first three seconds of the movie so that it will continue to play at normal speed.

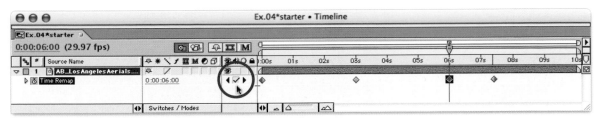

Step 4: Move to 06:00 and again click the keyframe checkbox to add a TR keyframe with a value of 06:00. This will allow the last portion of the movie, from 06:00 to the end, to also remain unaffected.

Step 3–4: Create new Time Remap keyframes at 03:00 and 06:00. The section in-between these two keyframes will be extended in Step 5.

Step 5: The idea is to take the portion of time between the two new keyframes and spread it out over a longer period of time. So the three seconds of source movie (between 03:00 and 06:00) will play from 03:00 to 08:00. To do this, move the time marker to 08:00, select KF 3 and 4, and drag KF 3 to the right. Both keyframes should move together, indicating that the speed will remain at 100% for this ending section. Press the Shift key as you approach 08:00 in the timeline, and KF 3 will snap into place. The speed should now read 60% between 03:00 and 08:00 in the timeline, and most frames will be repeated during this slowdown.

Step 6: If you RAM Preview at this point, the motion may appear unchanged while it's being cached because After Effects skips frames that repeat – the slowdown you've introduced will be visible only when the preview plays back. The motion may look acceptable, but let's add some eases to smooth out the sudden drop between the different speeds.

Step 6: Edit the velocity handles for the keyframe at 03:00 so that it smoothly ramps from 100% speed to the slower speed.

Make sure the Info palette is open; press Command+2 (Control+2) if not. With the Velocity graph twirled down, grab the outgoing velocity handle for KF 2 at 03:00, and pull it up until the Info palette reports the Velocity at 100% and the Influence somewhere around 30%. The velocity curve should now ramp smoothly from 100% to the slower speed.

Two Timelines

You can also create and edit Time Remap keyframes in the Layer window, which is useful if the key "frames" are easier to select visually than by time-code. The Layer window has additional features when Time Remapping is enabled:

With **[Ex.03]** open, double-click the **GI_Dance-Rhythms** layer to open the Layer window, and you'll notice two timelines. The upper time ruler scrubs through the movie frames and sets or edits a TR keyframe, while the lower ruler corresponds to the layer bar in the Timeline window. Play the movie (hit Spacebar) from the Layer window and watch how the top time marker scrubs back and forth (kinda spooky!) while the bottom time marker makes steady progress.

To edit an existing TR keyframe, step to a keyframe in the Timeline window. Now, in the Layer window, drag the *upper* time marker around to identify which frame of the source you want on this keyframe. To create a new keyframe, move the comp time marker (the lower one in the Layer window) to the desired point in time, then drag the upper time marker around. The timecode readout on the left is the current time in the clip; click it to enter a new Go To time. The timecode readout on the right represents the time remapped value; click it to enter a keyframe value numerically.

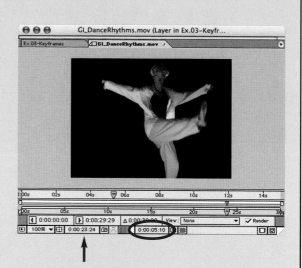

When Time Remapping is enabled, the Layer window boasts a second time marker above the regular one. The red circle highlights the time remapped frame (05:10) being displayed at the current time in the layer (13:20) (denoted by red arrow).

When Time Remapping is enabled, we suggest you create masks in a precomp or in a second comp. Otherwise, when you try to edit or animate masks in the Layer window, you'll inevitably add or edit TR keyframes accidentally as you navigate the timeline.

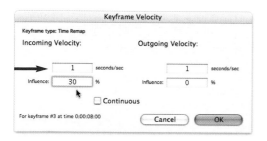

Step 7: Ease into the keyframe at 08:00 by entering values in the Keyframe Velocity dialog.

Step 7: For KF 3 at 08:00, try doing the same thing but this time do it numerically: Option+double-click (Alt+double-click) on KF 3 at 08:00 to open the Keyframe Velocity dialog. Change the Incoming Velocity to "1" seconds/sec (or, one second of source plays for one second in the timeline), and enter 30% for the Influence. Be sure to leave the Outgoing Velocity untouched, and click OK. You should now have a nice curve in the middle of your graph. Feel free to also enter the velocity for KF 2 at 03:00 numerically if you weren't happy with your first edit, remembering that you need to change the Outgoing Velocity for that keyframe. RAM Preview and adjust to taste.

So why didn't we use the Easy Ease keyframe assistants? Because they would bring the speed down to 0 seconds/sec at the keyframe – try it if you don't believe us! These keyframe assistants are still useful, however, when you need a Time Remap keyframe to slow down a clip to a smooth stop.

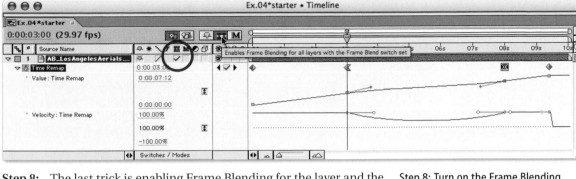

Step 8: The last trick is enabling Frame Blending for the layer and the comp. Check the Frame Blending switch for the layer, and the Enable Frame Blending button along the top of the Timeline window. Frame blending is a useful partner to "selling" time remapping, as it helps by creating artificial frames between the original ones as you vary the speed. Preview your animation again, and check out [**Ex.04_complete**] if you got lost along the way.

Step 8: Turn on the Frame Blending switch and Enable Frame Blending to help smooth out the motion.

Adding Handle

Another practical use for time remapping is to add more handle to the beginning or end of a clip by, say, stretching the first 10 frames out to 30 frames. With a longer handle, you can create a slower crossfade between clips in a sequence. The technique is similar to that shown above: Enable Time Remapping for the layer, create a new keyframe at 00:10, then drag both the new keyframe and the last keyframe 20 frames later in time. This is shown in [**Ex.05_Adding Handle**].

Because Frame Blending incurs a render hit, you might want to split your layer after remapping and turn off blending on the sections where it is playing at 100% speed, as shown in [**Ex.05_Split Layer**]. It might not be worth splitting a layer for such a short low-resolution clip, but split-ting a long clip at high resolution may deliver a handsome payback in render time saved. Also, if time remapping is affecting only a small section at the beginning or end of a layer, you can remap just this section, leaving the second layer to play the rest of the movie in its original state.

In [**Ex.05**], time remapping extends the "handle" at the beginning of the clip.

Slowing down a movie by large amounts can often get the better of frame blending. We find blending works better when the frames are more organic; prominent lines and edges, such as with the skyscraper in [**Ex.04**], can result in a "double-exposure" look. If frame blending isn't producing good results for you, there are some third-party plug-ins, such as the Twixtor plug-in from RE:Vision Effects (www.revisionfx.com), that can create completely new in-between frames.

When you're time remapping only a small section of a layer, you can save rendering time by duplicating or splitting the layer and frame blending only that section.

The Real Out Point

If you use the default Time Remap keyframes and apply velocity curves, you may not achieve a smooth entry into the last keyframe, particularly if you use a very long ease in. Because the second default keyframe is created one frame *after* the last real frame of the movie, the last real frame of the movie appears in the comp *before* the last keyframe is reached and is then repeated if you freeze the end of the movie.

For example, in **[Ex.06a]**, our 15-second movie **GI_DanceRhythms** starts at 00:00. The last frame is 14:29 and it appears at 14:29 in the timeline. But when you enable Time Remapping, the second default keyframe is created at 15:00 – one frame later.

The reason for placing the keyframe one frame after the end is that After Effects assumes your source might be an interlaced movie, whereby you would be viewing only the first field of frame 14:29 at time 14:29. If the default Time Remap keyframe was created at 14:29 also, any freeze you create at the end of the movie would freeze on the first field of this frame. As a result, you would never see the second field. By placing it at 15:00, the idea is that you would freeze on the second field of the last frame.

This is a nice feature in theory, but the reality is that not all sources are interlaced (this one isn't), so the actual image data from the last frame (or field 2 in an interlaced movie) appears *before* the keyframe icon. This is a problem only if you have a slow ease

into this keyframe. Let's say the image on the last frame is supposed to freeze at the big finale audio sound effect at 24:00. So you drag the second default keyframe from 15:00 to 24:00 and apply Easy Ease In so that the movie slows down and stops at 24:00. The problem is that the image from the last frame will appear in the comp at 23:09, well ahead of the audio, as shown in **[Ex.06b]**.

Our preference is to recreate the last keyframe so that it freezes on the first field of the last frame, as shown in **[Ex.06c]**. Now when you move the last keyframe later in time to slow it down, rounding errors are less likely to occur **[Ex.06d]**.

The workaround we used to fix this "feature" is fairly simple. Practice the following steps in **[Ex.06e]**:

• *Before* you enable Time Remapping, select the layer and press O to jump to the real out point (at 14:29 in this case), select Layer>Enable Time Remapping. Hit the ; (semicolon) key to zoom in closely in time so you can see some detail.

• Check the keyframe box to create a new keyframe for the real last frame, at time 14:29. *Note: Don't just drag the default keyframe back to 14:29.*

• Press Page Down to advance one frame and uncheck the second default keyframe created at 15:00 to remove it, or select it and hit Delete. Press the ; key again to zoom out, and continue to work normally with Time Remapping.

You can time remap a nested comp layer, which is a handy technique for retiming a complex graphical animation. Footage: Artbeats/Alien Atmospheres.

Remapping a Comp

Time remapping is not limited to movie sources – you can also apply it to a nested comp layer. For instance, let's say you have spent a significant amount of time choreographing a dozen or so layers in an animation, only to have the client ask for the entire animation to happen in less time. And could it start off slower and end a little faster? There's no need to re-do the animation. By nesting the animation into another comp and applying Time Remapping, you can adjust the timing to taste. This is shown in [Ex.07-Picasso-1/animation], where the animation takes place, and [Ex.07-Picasso-2/remap], where the speed is adjusted with time remapping.

If you're unclear how this works in practice, select Window>Close All and open [Ex.08-Practice Comp]. The layers are already animating over

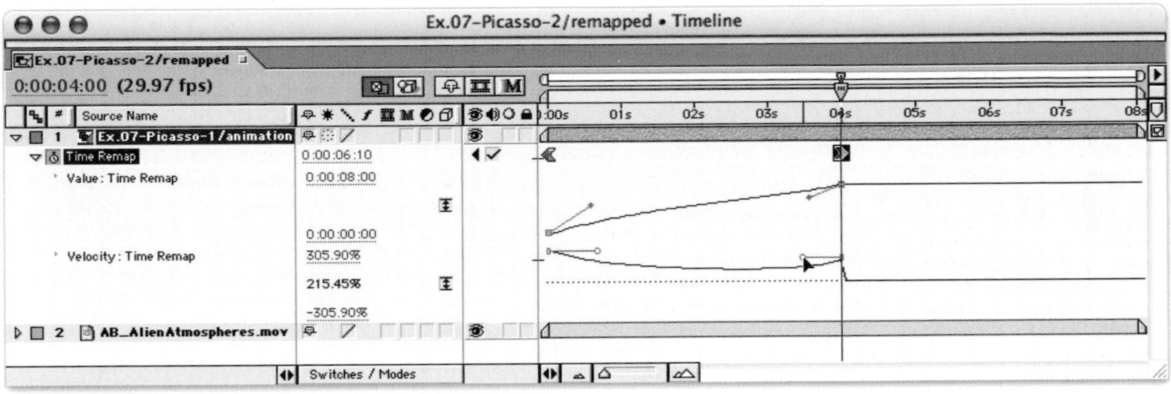

Ex.07-Picasso-2/remapped • Timeline

---

a background layer when the client delivers the bad news. Notice that the animation finishes at 06:10.

Step 1: Go to time 06:10; here the animation ends. Press Shift+0 (on the keyboard) to place Comp Marker 0 at this frame as a reminder.

Step 2: Select layers 1–11 (select layer 1 and Shift+click layer 11).

Step 3: Select Layer>Pre-compose to send these layers to their own precomp. In the Pre-compose dialog, name the new comp "**Quote precomp**". Leave Open New Composition *unchecked* – you don't need to edit this comp. Click OK. The [**Ex.08-Practice Comp**] should still be the forward comp, and the selected layers are now replaced with a single nested comp layer.

Step 4: Select Layer>Enable Time Remapping; the default keyframes should be visible.

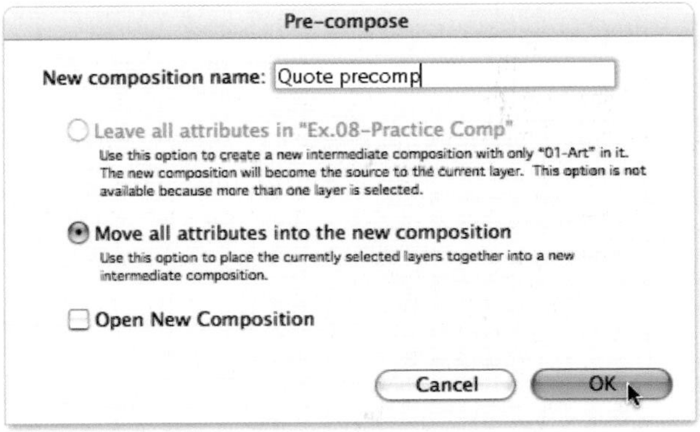

Step 5: Still at time 06:10, check the keyframe checkbox to create a Time Remap keyframe with a value of 06:10.

Step 6: Select the last Time Remap keyframe at 08:00 and delete it. There is no need to interpolate between the last frame of the animation and the end of the layer. Deleting this keyframe will save rendering time because the frame at 06:10 will be cached and repeated. If you don't delete the keyframe, the precomp will continue to be sampled at each frame, even though no change is occurring in the animation.

Above is our final time remapped title. You can practice recreating this example in [**Ex.08-Practice Comp**] by following the accompanying steps.

Pre-compose

New composition name: Quote precomp

○ Leave all attributes in "Ex.08-Practice Comp"
Use this option to create a new intermediate composition with only "01-Art" in it. The new composition will become the source to the current layer. This option is not available because more than one layer is selected.

● Move all attributes into the new composition
Use this option to place the currently selected layers together into a new intermediate composition.

☐ Open New Composition

Cancel   OK

Step 3: Precompose the selected layers (1–11) so that you will have a single layer to time remap.

Step 6: Select the last keyframe at the end of the layer and press Delete. Now the keyframe at 06:10 will be cached and repeated, saving rendering time.

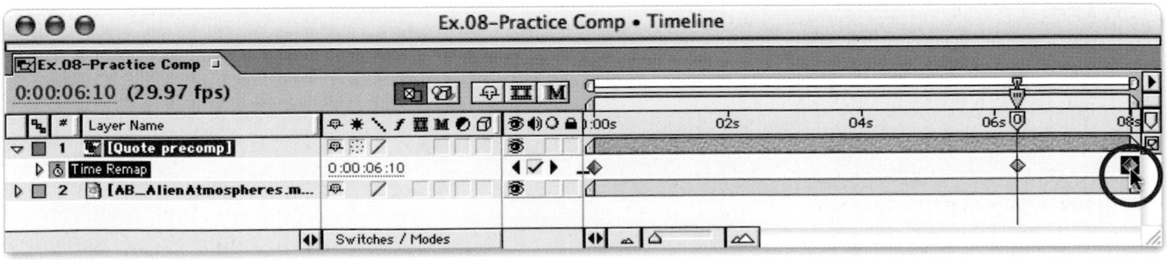

Ex.08-Practice Comp • Timeline

Simply Sequenced

If you drag multiple items to the New Composition button at the bottom of the Project window, an options dialog will open. Provided you select Create Single Composition, you can also choose to Sequence Layers (with the same options as the keyframe assistant).

After you apply the Exponential Scale keyframe assistant, the layer (above) will scale at a consistent pace, despite how the velocity controls may appear (below). You can tweak the pacing by time remapping in a second comp.

Step 7: Now you can drag the new keyframe at 06:10 earlier in time, and apply velocity curves to taste. Create a couple of variations and RAM Preview to see how easy it is to change the timing. You could even add keyframes to freeze on certain words if needed.

Of course, if the animation consists of movie layers, you probably won't be able to avail of this shortcut, as time remapping the nested comp will affect the speed of the movie sources also. But this is still a great time-saver for retiming graphical animations. Now that you know how easy it is to time remap a nested comp, let's offer a couple of variations on the theme.

Remapping Sequenced Layers

The Sequence Layers keyframe assistant can be used to distribute layers in time and create automatic crossfades between layers. In [**Ex.09-Numbers-1/sequence**], a series of 10 images (the numbers from 1–10) were trimmed to 01:20 in length, and sequenced in time with 10-frame crossfades. The end of the sequence occurs at 12:10. If you RAM Preview, you'll see that the pace of the sequence is constant.

This comp is then nested in [**Ex.09-Numbers-2/remapped**], where time remapping is applied in the same fashion as in Steps 4–7 above. A keyframe was created at 12:10 which represents where the number "10" is fully on, and then this keyframe can be moved around at will to retime the animation. By moving it to 10:00 and adjusting the Velocity graph, the numbers start counting more slowly and finish counting quickly, stopping exactly at 10:00. RAM Preview to see the difference. Now imagine trying to create this animation by carefully timing out each number! (If you'd like to learn more about this technique, check out Tutorial 1, *Atomic Café*, in our companion book, *After Effects in Production*.)

Remapping Exponential Scale

When you scale up a layer by a large amount using linear keyframes, the visual result is that the layer appears to scale quickly at first, then slow down as it gets larger. You can preview this problem in [**Ex.10a-Linear Scale**].

To the rescue comes the Exponential Scale keyframe assistant (from the Professional edition). By selecting the current Scale keyframes and applying this assistant, the scale will have a constant pace. (It does this

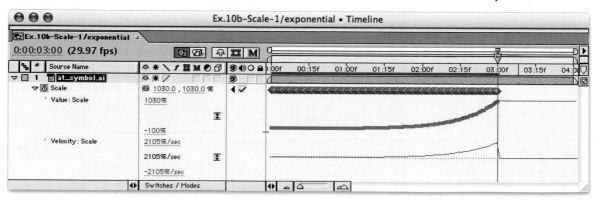

by creating keyframes at every frame, forcing a change in velocity too extreme for the velocity controls to achieve on their own.) Preview the results in [**Ex.10b-Scale-1/exponential**].

If you find that Exponential Scale is too smooth, no points for guessing that you can apply Exponential Scale in a precomp and use Time Remapping in a second comp to retime the motion. This is shown in [**Ex.10b-Scale-2/remap**]; feel free to experiment, previewing as you go.

Remapping a Sequence of Frames

Finally, Time Remapping can also be used as a "sequencer" of sorts for individual frames, such as you might have with cel animation. Import the frames as a sequence, and use Time Remapping to control how the frames play back.

Stepping Out

Chapter 14 covers a technique for using time remapping to choose particular frames from a movie and sync them to beats in a music track.

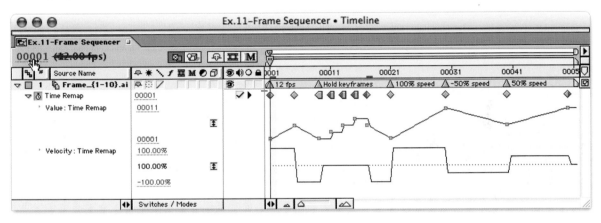

This concept is shown in [**Ex.11-Frame Sequencer**], where the comp is set to 12 frames per second (fps). The series of numbers from 1–10 has been imported as a "sequence" by selecting the first frame in the folder, and checking the General EPS Sequence checkbox in the Import File dialog. The footage is added to the composition, where it appears as one layer. By enabling Time Remapping and setting keyframes appropriately, you can force the individual frames to play forward and backward, or freeze on a frame using Hold keyframes.

When you're working with frames, you will probably want to set your project to count in frames, rather than SMPTE. You can do this from File>Project Settings, where you can also set the "Start numbering frames" to 1 if that's more intuitive to you. You can also toggle between SMPTE, Frames, and Feet+Frames by Command+clicking (Control+clicking) on the current time readout in the Comp, Timeline, or Layer windows.

To sum up, you may have considered time remapping useful only for playing movies back and forth in a fun manner, but this powerful feature has many practical uses, such as tweaking the motion in a layer so that it works better with the story, or retiming a complete animation from a precomp. Add it to your box of tricks and it will save many a day.

The current time readout is toggled to Frames in [**Ex.11**], where Time Remap keyframes control how cel animation frames play back.

Connect

Keyframe interpolation types, Velocity graphs, and Easy Ease keyframe assistants were covered in Volume 1, Chapter 3.

Split Layer and the Sequence Layers keyframe assistant, see Volume 1, Chapter 7.

Frame blending and time-stretching were covered in Volume 1, Chapter 8.

Nesting comps, see Volume 1, Chapter 18.

Precomposing, see Volume 1, Chapter 19.

Exponential Scale, see Chapter 5.

14 Time Games

Time-manipulating effects, step-time, and frame blending can create interesting new looks.

Adjusting Effects

You can apply any of these time effects to an adjustment layer (Volume 1, Chapter 22), which will affect all layers below. Depending on your hierarchy, you may then be able to create a difficult effect all in one comp.

Example Project

Explore the 14-Example Project.aep file as you read this chapter; references to [Ex.##] refer to specific compositions within the project file. Install Cycore FX, as we will be using them as well. You will need the Professional edition to use the Time Displacement examples.

In various chapters of this series of books, we cover the basics of manipulating time with frame blending, time-stretching, and time remapping. After Effects also has a few effects – Posterize Time, Echo, and Time Difference, as well as the Professional edition's Time Displacement – that can further manipulate time. This chapter explores ways to play with timing for both problem-solving and creative uses.

Preserving Time

After Effects is surprisingly fluid in how it handles frame rates. The frame rate set in a composition controls only how you step through frames in that comp. The frame rate in the final Render Settings is what really controls how often comps, and all their sources and precomps, are "sampled" as the final frames are rendered.

This is often advantageous. For instance, you can turn on field rendering in Render Settings while you're viewing full frames in the Comp window. You can also render a low-resolution, low frame rate "draft" movie without having to change the frame rate in the Composition Settings.

However, this rendering order can work against you if you are purposely trying to fake a slower frame rate by setting a nested composition (or precomp) to a lower rate. For example, open [Ex.01-Skate-1/6fps] – this includes a skateboarding movie that was captured at 29.97 frames per second (fps), but the comp is set to 6 fps to give it a step-framed look. If you RAM Preview this comp, you will see jumps in the motion compared with the original 29.97 fps movie (if you want to compare, preview the movie in the Footage window). This comp is nested in [Ex.01-Skate-2/29.97fps], which has a frame rate of 29.97 fps. Play this second comp and you will see every frame from the source movie – the frame rate of the precomp has been overridden!

As you can see, the default in After Effects is that a precomp is rendered at the frame rate of the comp it is nested into. (Ultimately, when you render, the Render Settings override the frame rate on a global basis.) However, you can force the precomp to retain its 6 fps rate up through the chain of comps. To do this:

• Bring the precomp [Ex.01-Skate-1] forward, and select Composition> Composition Settings – the shortcut is Command+K on Mac (Control+K on Windows). Select the Advanced tab, and enable the Preserve Frame Rate option. Click OK to close the dialog.

• Return to the [**Ex.01-Skate-2**] comp. RAM Preview and notice that while the type layer animates at 29.97 fps, the background skateboarding movie is running at 6 fps.

Note that if you were to animate the skateboarding movie (say, scale it up over time) in the second comp, any keyframes would be interpolated at 29.97 fps. If you animate the movie in the precomp, keyframe interpolation would be locked to 6 fps.

(Preserve Frame Rate is also covered in Volume 1: Chapter 11, *All About Masking*, and Chapter 18, *Nesting Compositions*.)

The Preserve Frame Rate option is found in Composition Settings>Advanced tab.

Posterize Time

The Posterize Time effect can also be used to lock in a frame rate for a source in much the same way the Preserve Frame Rate option can – but there are important differences. Open [**Ex.02*starter**], where the same skateboarding movie is placed in a 29.97 fps comp. Select layer 2, and apply Effect>Time>Posterize Time and set its Frame Rate parameter to 6. Even though the comp's frame rate is set to 29.97, this movie will play only every fifth frame (29.97 ÷ 6, give or take some rounding error). Note that the effect does not affect any animation you apply to the layer, as transformations happen after effects. Also, you can use Hold keyframes only for the Frame Rate, which means the frame rate can change, but it cannot interpolate between different frame rates.

The Posterize Time effect can be used to force a movie (or a nested comp layer) to render at a different frame rate than specified in Render Settings.

Preserving Random Effects

In addition to creating stutter, the Preserve Frame Rate option can also be used to "calm down" overly busy effects. Many effects that have a randomized action – such as Noise, Scatter, and Brush Strokes – randomize on every frame that is rendered, even when applied to a still. At higher frame rates (and especially during field rendering, which effectively doubles the frame rate), this randomization can turn into a buzzing distraction. RAM Preview [**Ex.04a-Fast Paint**] to get an idea of this problem.

Compare this with the chain of comps in [**Ex.04b**]. The Brush Strokes effect is applied in the first comp, and this is preserved at 10 fps. The second comp runs at 29.97 fps, and includes a background movie layer.

Preserve Frame Rate is particularly useful in conjunction with Effect>Text>Numbers. If you are randomizing this effect, it will be changing every single frame (or field). This is usually headache-inducing, as you can see if you RAM Preview [**Ex.05a**]. Compare this with [**Ex.05b**], where the numbers change at different frame rates. To achieve this effect, different styles of random numbers are created in five precomps, all of which are preserved at 29.97 fps. After they're nested in the final comp, the precomps are duplicated and different time-stretch values are applied to vary the speeds.

Applying Effect>Stylize>Brush Strokes to a still image results in its randomizing every frame – much too busy. Fish image courtesy Getty Images/ Design Essentials.

Blending Steps

It's ironic that now we've achieved full-motion playback from the desktop, we're eager to drop frames for that neat jerky look. While you can use step framing "dry," you can achieve some interesting variations if you add Frame Blending to the mix. There are two basic approaches:

• **Preblend:** In [**Ex.06a**], the **GI_CoolCharacters** movie is placed in a 10 fps comp, and frame blending is turned on. Because all the original frames are available to the comp, the blending results in multiple intermediate "ghost frames."

• **Postblend:** In [**Ex.06b**], the same movie is first prerendered at 10 fps without frame blending, then reimported and placed in a 29.97 fps comp. When frame blending is applied, the steps are more pronounced as there are fewer source frames to blend together, resulting in a harder look with fewer ghost images to bridge the gap.

Remember that you can also use Time Stretch values to speed up or slow down the movies, in addition to step framing. Experiment with some of these techniques in [**Ex.07**].

Enabling frame blending for the original movie in a 10 fps comp (top left) results in more ghost images than if you apply blending to a prerendered 10 fps movie in a 29.97 fps comp (left). Footage courtesy Getty Images/Cool Characters.

Posterization versus Preservation

Posterize Time rewires the rendering procedure somewhat, so it has a few gotchas. For Posterize Time to do its job, it needs to reach back to the source of the layer to decide which frame to display. As a result, *any masks or effects that are applied before it are ignored* (Masks render before Effects in the render order, and you can't mask a frame if its image hasn't been defined yet). This is shown in **[Ex.03a-Mask Problem]**. Verify that there is a mask – which is being skipped – by toggling the Posterize Time effect off and on. While you can drag Posterize Time to be the first effect, masks will always render before any effect.

One workaround is to use an Adjustment Layer to apply Posterize Time above the layer in question, but then the effect would apply to all layers below, as in **[Ex.03b]**. So the answer would be to precompose the layer, apply the effect in the precomp, and mask in the second comp – but if you're going to that much trouble, you should be using Preserve Frame Rate in the precomp in the first place!

Which brings us to the second major drawback of Posterize Time: It's very inefficient. When you use the Posterize Time effect, all the frames from the original footage are retrieved from disk. Then the effect says "nope, don't need that frame, or that one, or that one…" This rendering hit is compounded if you apply the effect to a nested comp with multiple layers and/or many effects. The precomp is rendered on every frame, then the second comp (where Posterize Time is applied) ignores the frames it doesn't need.

In comparison, using the Preserve Frame Rate option retrieves from disk only those frames that are being used, and a precomp is sampled only at the frame rate set. So whenever you find yourself reaching for the Posterize Time effect, precompose the layer using the Leave All Attributes option. In the precomp, open Composition Settings, set the frame rate, and turn on the Preserve Frame Rate option. Rendering times will be optimized, and you can pick and choose where masks, effects, and animation keyframes appear in the render order.

Stepping Out with Time Remap

One of the drawbacks to simple step framing is that you don't get to pick and choose exactly which frames are displayed. For example, RAM Preview [**Ex.08-Step Frame**], which has a frame rate of 2.25 fps. At this slow frame rate, less desirable frames may be held for many frames, while more attractive frames are skipped. It also took us some time to find a frame rate that worked with the music track. Close all comps and take a tour through a different technique:

Step 1: Open [**Ex.08a**]. Time Remapping was enabled for the movie in this 29.97 fps comp. Keyframes were created by stepping through the comp frame by frame, and checking the Time Remap keyframe box whenever a frame was deemed "attractive" (frames with too much motion blur or strange facial expressions were skipped). Note that the timing of the keyframes at this point is irrelevant. Also, because the keyframes interpolate, the movie plays back normally when it's previewed.

The Frame Blend Smoothie

Frame Blending can smooth the look of most of the effects discussed in this chapter. Just be aware of the render hit involved when you enable it. Frame blending was covered in Volume 1, Chapter 8.

Step 2: Open [**Ex.08b**]. The second step was to select all the Time Remap keyframes and select Animation>Toggle Hold Keyframes. This ensures that only the desirable frames will appear, with no interpolation in-between. As we didn't want the two default Time Remap keyframes (denoting the first and last frames of the movie), these were deleted.

Step 1: Time Remapping was enabled for the Cool Characters movie, and keyframes created only where frames were deemed "attractive."

Step 3: Open [**Ex.08c**]. The music track was added, and the beats were marked out with layer markers. We then dragged the Time Remap keyframes to each music beat (pressing the Shift key will make the keyframes stick to layer markers as you drag). The result is that only attractive frames are used, and the timing to the music is exact. Not only that, but by using Time Remap keyframes, you're not locked to a fixed frame rate – you can play a few frames at a faster rate, hold on one frame

Step 2: After applying Time Remapping and creating keyframes for the most attractive frames, toggle all the keyframes to Hold Keyframes so they don't interpolate.

Ex.08c–Time Remap/Step 3 • Timeline

Ex.08c-Time Remap/Step 3

0:00:07:02 (29.97 fps)

Source Name

▷ ☐ 1   🖻 TU_▼SBump1Bounce....
▽ ☐ 2   🖻 G1_CoolCharacters.mov
    ▷ 🕙 Time Remap   0:00:08:05

Switches / Modes

The final step is to drag the Time Remap keyframes to synchronize with the music beats, adjusting the animation as needed to match the music.

for longer, or play back frames out of order or backward. You can also repeat sections or change some keyframes back to Linear, as we did toward the end of the animation.

This step framing method is more work than simply applying a low frame rate, but it's worth it for those projects where you need more precision and control. Experiment with some of the above techniques in [**Ex.07**], or use your own source footage.

The Echo effect's parameters. It can be approached as a user-adjustable form of frame blending. Most unusual is the Echo Operator popup, which provides a few different forms of blending modes to blend in the echoes.

An Original Echo

For many of us, the term "echo effect" conjures images of tacky, sparkling trails following flying logos in local car ads. Fortunately, After Effects is rarely tacky. Unfortunately, the Echo effect's defaults don't really show off the strength of this effect, and you'll often need to foil the default render order to get it to work at all. First we will give an overview of using Echo; then we'll jump into some fun tricks you perform with it.

Effect>Time>Echo can be thought of as a multiframe form of frame blending, which gives you control over how many frames are blended together, and how they are blended. Echo can use frames that are either before or after the current one being displayed, depending on whether the Echo Time parameter is *negative* (frames from the past) or *positive* (frames from the future).

You can also use the Echo Time parameter to set how far apart the frames are that are used. This parameter is defined in seconds: The number of frames of spacing desired, divided by the frame rate, equals the Echo Time you want in seconds. Longer times start to give a sort of cloning effect; [**Ex.09**] gives an idea of what can be done by carefully setting Echo Time to divisions of how long it takes an object to rotate or an animation to loop.

The Number of Echoes parameter sets how many frames get used. Note that if you have a negative Echo Time, and a large value for Number of Echoes, you'll need to move to a point in the timeline where the effect has built up some momentum.

Starting Intensity decides how strongly the "original" frame is in the final blend. The Decay parameter decides how much successively weaker the following echoes appear. Decay has a smaller useful range than you might expect, as subsequent echoes get weakened by this amount – they go to being unnoticeable really quickly. The upper half of the range is best.

The power of Echo comes from its Echo Operator. These three variations show the result of different operators on the same image: Original image (left), the default Add mode (center), and Screen (right). Footage courtesy Kevin Dole.

The opacity of the original image – as opposed to the first echo of that image – is affected by the Starting Intensity parameter. If you want your original image to be 100% strong and your echoes to start at a much reduced level, you will need to duplicate the original layer on top and play with the opacity of the echoes underneath. Such an echo trail effect is set up in [Ex.10].

The most intriguing parameter of the group is Echo Operator; this is similar to "Composite Original" in other effects but with the addition of blending modes. Experiment with this parameter using [Ex.11], then swap in other sources to see how different movies react.

Echoed Animation

If you apply Echo to a layer that is getting its movement from animation keyframes, Echo may not seem to work initially. This is because effects are calculated before transformations, which yield most animation. In this case, you will need to animate the layer in Comp 1, nest this comp in Comp 2, then apply Echo. In the second comp, the animated layer looks like a "movie" with an animated alpha channel, so the effect works as planned.

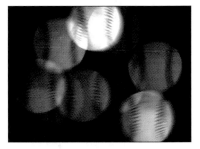

Echo following random animation can yield a complex swirl from a single still image. Image courtesy Getty Images/Sports Elements.

A lot of fun can be had with extended Echo settings and fast randomly moving objects. [Ex.12a-Echo-1] contains a simple object that was animated using The Wiggler keyframe assistant (you could also use Motion Sketch), with Motion Blur turned on. This comp is nested in a second comp – [Ex.12a-Echo-2] – with Echo applied. Be aware that render times can quickly stack up when a lot of motion blurred objects are being echoed (as is the case with this example). It also takes a while for the Echo effect to build up at the start, since the echoed frames are taken from earlier in time – and there is no time earlier than 0.

Note that because Echo reaches back to the source for data, even animating an object using the Distort>Transform effect, then applying Echo all on one layer doesn't create an echo trail.

However, you could echo multiple layers in one comp by applying the effect to an adjustment layer. An example of this is in [Ex.12b]: A null object is used as a parent to scale and rotate the three baseball objects, while an adjustment layer on top applies Echo to the result of all layers below. (Note that if you want these layers to also have motion blur, you need to turn on motion blur for the individual layers, not the null object, then Enable Motion Blur to display the results.)

A null object parent layer rotates three baseballs, while an adjustment layer on top applies Echo to the result.

Time Difference

Next we come to the Time Difference effect. It's intended as a means to calculate the color difference between two layers, which can be useful when you're matching a clean plate with foreground footage. But it also has some creative uses when you use it to compare different frames from the same movie.

To experiment with Time Difference, close all comps and open [**Ex.13a*starter**], select the movie and apply Effect>Time>Time Difference. The result will be a neutral gray image. This is because the default settings compare the original movie with itself, and there is no difference. Scrub the Time Offset parameter to the right (positive values) – a sort of embossed and ghostly image of the businessman in motion emerges. When Time Offset is set to, say, 1:00, the frame at 00:00 is being compared with the frame at 01:00. Rather than the ghost being an echo, the ghost is from a frame in the future (whoooo...sorry, couldn't resist).

The Time Difference effect (above) calculates the difference between frames in the same movie or between different layers. Similar pixels are displayed as neutral gray (below left) or, with Absolute Difference on, as black (below right). Footage courtesy Artbeats/Business on the Go.

Where there are no differences in color values between the two frames being compared, the result is neutral gray. The Contrast parameter affects the intensity of the result, while the Absolute Difference checkbox allows you to view the result as an absolute value (pixels showing no difference will appear as black).

To see the ghostly image as an echo, you need to set Time Offset to a negative value. However, if you set Time Offset to, say, –1:00, the results won't be very interesting until you scrub the time marker past 01:00 in the Timeline. (Think about it – there is no time before 00:00 to compare with.)

That's all very well so far, but the results are a little strange to say the least. However, if you remember the logic behind blending modes, you'll remember that some modes ignore values that are neutral gray and other modes ignore values that are black. In order to use blending modes with this effect, you'll need two layers to play with. So duplicate the layer, then select the background layer and remove the effect (Effects>Remove All).

In [**Ex.13a**], the time differenced layer is composited on top of the original layer using the Overlay blending mode, which drops out neutral gray.

If Absolute Difference is still on, set the top layer to a mode such as Add or Color Dodge (both of which drop out black). However, if Absolute Difference is Off, then modes such as Overlay or Soft Light should work well (these modes drop out neutral gray). Of course, there are no rules, so long as the effect works for you. One result using Overlay mode is shown in [**Ex.13a_final**].

Another way to achieve the same result is shown in [**Ex.13b**]. In this comp, an Adjustment Layer is added above the original movie, and the

Time Difference effect is applied to it, with the Target popup pointing to the original movie. You can then apply a mode to the Adjustment Layer. (The original movie layer is set to have an in point of –01:00, so setting the Time Offset to –01:00 produces a usable image from the first frame in the comp.)

In [**Ex.13c**] we go one step further. The adjustment layer also has a Hue change and uses an animated movie of grayscale bars as a luminance matte for added interest.

Of course, you don't need to use Time Difference to compare one movie with another using blending modes. In [**Ex.13d**], the original movie is composited on top of itself in Overlay mode, and offset in time by changing the in point of the top layer. However, with this method there's no way to exclude pixels that are the same color from also becoming part of the mix, so the result can be overly dark or bright. With Time Difference, you're compositing only the pixels that are different. Plus, don't forget that you can Time Difference one movie to a completely different movie for some really, er, wacky results (you know who you are…).

We leave you with [**Ex.13e**], where a movie of a hummingbird is time differenced, but this time the differences are used to create an alpha channel by setting the Alpha Channel popup to Max of Result. Having an alpha channel allows all of the blending modes to come into play, not just those that ignore gray or black.

In [**Ex.13c**], Time Difference is applied to an adjustment layer, the Hue is changed a little, and the adjustment layer is set to Overlay mode. An animated movie of random line is then used as a luma matte so that the effect is visible only through the bright bars. Footage courtesy Artbeats/The Orient.

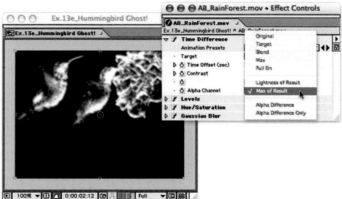

[**Ex.13e**]: By creating an alpha channel from the pixels that are different, you can select any of the blending modes to composite with, not just those that ignore gray or black. Footage courtesy Artbeats/Rain Forest.

Quality Issues

The Time Displacement effect (discussed next) often results in aliased-looking images with rough edges. This is not the effect's fault; the problem is a lack of resolution in the material it is being fed to work on.

For example, there are usually only 256 luminance values available to calculate the displacement amount (note that there are 32,769 levels in the Professional edition's 16 bpc mode, which is much better). 256 levels does not stretch seamlessly across video-sized frames which have 480 pixels or more in their shortest dimension, inevitably resulting in some aliasing or posterization. Even worse, source material frame rates are typically 30 frames per second or lower, not offering a lot of choices of where to grab new material from.

If you're shooting or rendering material specifically for a Time Displacement effect, consider using a higher frame rate (for example, shoot film at 48 or 60 fps, transfer to video frame per frame, and conform to the original frame rate in the Interpret Footage dialog). Material with less motion from frame to frame will also look smoother.

Time Displacement

This Professional edition effect is similar to its cousin, Displacement Map. It is also a compound effect (Chapter 9) that looks at the luminance values of a second layer to decide how to mess with the pixels of the layer it is applied to. But rather than displace the position of those pixels, Time Displacement grabs pixels from different points in time in the original source. The result is a strange time warpage of the layer that some might refer to as a *slitscan* effect.

There are a few rules to observe when you're using Time Displacement. Like any compound effect, it uses the source of the second "map" layer, ignoring any masks, effects, or transformations applied to the map in the current comp. If you need to edit or animate this map layer, you'll need to do it in a precomp. Time Displacement also ignores any masks created on the layer it is applied to; perform any masking in a precomp as well.

The first step is to select the Time Displacement Layer that will do the displacing.

Close all comps, and open [**Ex.14**], which has been set up as an experimentation comp for you to play with. RAM Preview the comp so you can see how the doors in the **AB_GrandOpenings** movie close. Select the layer and apply Effect>Time>Time Displacement. In the Effect Controls window, set the Time Displacement Layer popup to layer 2, which is a basic linear Ramp, and preview the result.

Darker pixels in the displacing layer reach back earlier in time to grab what pixels will be used in the effected layer; lighter pixels reach forward. Pixels that are 50% gray (RGB value 128) cause no displacement, so pixels from the current frame are used. The maximum amount of reach is determined by the Max Displacement Time parameter. Because pixels earlier in time might be needed, this effect also takes a few frames to get up to speed. Time Resolution is most effectively set to the frame rate of the source being displaced; remember that interlaced sources have twice the effective frame rate. (The default is 60 fps, which would use each field in a separated 30 fps movie.)

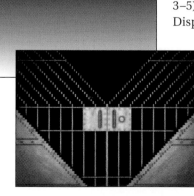

As the prison doors slam shut (above), the Time Displacement effect uses a linear ramp (center) to decide which pixels from which frame should be displayed (right). Footage courtesy Artbeats/ Grand Openings.

Feel free to try out the other maps (layers 3–5) by selecting them from the Time Displacement Layer popup in the Effect Controls window.

This effect obviously needs things to change over time in the source to have any effect. If your motion is coming from effects and animations applied to an otherwise still object, do this animation in a precomp, then apply Time Displacement in the second composition.

Displaced Affections

Here are some more examples using Time Displacement. Preview the comps to see how the displacement progresses:

• Complex maps melt and rip apart images. When you have a handle on the basics, play with time displacing some of the movies and maps in [**Ex.15**], which contains some complex maps from the Video SpiceRack and OrganicFX series from Pixélan. Maps with smoother, more gradual gray transitions give more organic results; consider preblurring your map sources if your results are too torn.

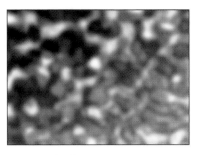

[**Ex.15**]: A complex displacement map (above left) results in a melted and oily look (above). Maps courtesy Pixélan's Video SpiceRack series.

[**Ex.16**]: A high-contrast displacement map (far left) results in a "fractured" look (left). Bodybuilder footage courtesy Getty Images/Fitness.

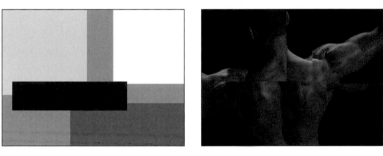

• Hard-edged displacement maps yield interesting "fractured time" visual effects [**Ex.16**]. The same thing could be accomplished by duplicating a layer, masking it, and giving it different offsets in time, but it is easier to experiment with just one layer and one displacement map.

• [**Ex.17**] uses the **AB_SoftEdges** animated grayscale movie as a map, which enhances the "I'm melting!" organic look.

• The major problem with time displacement is the tearing that results from low frame rates. In [**Ex.18**], a blur is applied to the time displaced layer. The result is then composited using the Linear Light blending mode on top of the original movie. RAM Preview (patiently) to see a fiery ghost swirling around the original dancer.

 **Fractured in 3D**

If you like the "fractured mirror" example in [**Ex.16**], try creating this look in 3D by duplicating your layer multiple times, masking each one to reveal a different section, and offsetting them in time and Z space. Then move a camera around them…

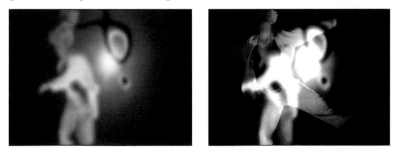

In [**Ex.18**], the dancer is time displaced using an animated map and then blurred to obscure the tearing (left). This blurred version is then composited on top using a blending mode (right). Footage courtesy Getty Images/Dance Rhythms.

Third-Party Games

RE:Vision Effects (www.revisionfx.com)

RE:Vision sells most of its plug-ins individually. It has two great time manipulation effects:

ReelSmart Motion Blur adds motion blur to footage – including 3D animations rendered without motion blur, or live action shot with fast shutter speeds – by tracking the movements of similar pixels and creating a blur vector between their positions.

Twixtor allows you to change the frame rate of your footage and creates clean intermediate frames. Unlike frame blending, which mixes together adjacent frames, Twixtor tracks the movement of similar pixels and estimates where their position would be for new in-between frames.

Boris Continuum Complete (www.borisfx.com)

This massive package includes several time manipulation effects worth checking out:

Optical Flow is a simpler version of RE:Vision's Twixtor which creates new in-between frames when varispeeding footage.

Posterize Time is a variation on the After Effects plug-in of the same name, with the advantage of creating crossfades between the final frames.

Sequencer allows you to designate up to 10 source layers that can be played back in a pattern and rhythm you define.

Temporal Blur is a flexible cross between motion blur and an echo effect.

Trails creates multiple copies of the source image, which may then be scaled, rotated, and otherwise transformed.

Velocity Remap is a twist on After Effects' Time Remapping that allows you to define playback speed by percentage, rather than which frame should play at what time.

Cycore Time Effects

The Cycore FX plug-in package (free with After Effects 6.5) includes a quartet of time-based effects:

CC Force Motion Blur & Wide Time

These effects provide ways to smear time. In both cases, animation should take place in a precomp for the effects to know how the image changes over time. Open [**Ex.19a**], and RAM Preview it. This contains a fast animation created with CC Kaleida. It's so fast it seems to strobe. CC Kaleida does not support motion blur to smooth this out.

Open [**Ex.19b**], select layer 1 (the nested [**Ex.19a**] comp), and press F3 to open the Effect Controls window. We've already applied Time>CC Force Motion Blur and increased the Shutter Angle to 360° so you can see its effect more clearly (its maximum value is 3600°, which is five times normal motion blur's limit). CC Motion Blur samples multiple points in time between two adjacent frames and blends them together. This is similar to normal motion blur, with the exception that normal motion blur works only for transformations and select effects that calculate motion blur internally. CC Force Motion Blur works on any precomp it is applied to (but not movies). The number of points used is determined by the Motion Blur Levels value – if you see distinct echoes, increase it to smooth the result (this will also increase rendering time).

CC Wide Time blends together multiple frames. It does not have the blending mode options of Echo, but it does offer the ability to select how many frames before *and* after the current frame are used. Open [**Ex.19c**], select layer 1, and press F3: We've already added CC Wide Time, with the number of Forward and Backward Steps increased from their defaults. RAM Preview and compare it with what you observed in [**Ex.19b**]. Note that CC Wide Time can be applied directly to a movie, but if you use transformations or effects, you will still need to precompose.

Both of these effects share a Geometric Motion Blur popup. When set to Off (the default), these effects will ignore the status of the normal motion blur layer and comp switches. When set to On, they will work only if the layer and comp motion blur

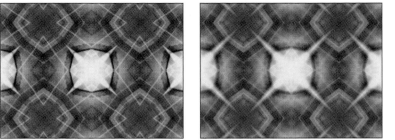

switches are enabled. At Preference Settings, CC Force Motion Blur will use the Comp Settings motion blur angle when the motion blur switches are enabled, and will use the effect's Shutter Angle when the motion blur switches are disabled.

CC Force Motion Blur takes our kaleidoscopic animation (left) and adds interframe blur to smooth it out (center); CC Wide Time blends together multiple frames (right). Image courtesy Digital Vision/Inner Gaze.

CC Time Blend & Time Blend FX

A shortcoming of Echo is that it is unable to factor in the result of other effects or transformations applied to a layer. CC Time Blend works around the inability to "see" other effects by keeping a buffer of what previously rendered frames look like. The cost is that you must go to the start of the comp, click on Clear in its Effect Controls window, then play from the beginning to build this buffer. It's rare that the benefits are worth the hassle.

More interesting is CC Time Blend FX. You apply this effect twice to a layer, with the first copy's Instance popup set to Paste, and the second copy's Instance set to Copy. You can then add any effect(s) between these two copies of CC Time Blend FX, resulting in a feedback loop. Open and RAM Preview [**Ex.20a**], which uses Distort>Transform to move our fish across the frame, followed by Distort>Twirl to introduce a wave. Then open and RAM Preview [**Ex.20b**], where the Twirl effect is sandwiched between two copies of CC Time Blend FX: The twirl now builds up over time. Select layer 1, press F3, and study the effect stack in the Effect Controls window to get a handle on how this chain is built. Note that if you make any adjustment to effect parameters, you will have to hit Home, clear the CC Time Blend FX buffers, and perform another RAM Preview.

Connect

Keyframe Assistants were covered in Volume 1's Chapter 3, and this volume's Chapter 5 (The Wiggler).

Time-Stretching and Frame Blending were discussed in Volume 1, Chapter 8.

Motion Blur, see Volume 1, Chapter 9.

Blending Modes, see Volume 1, Chapter 10.

The Render Settings are covered in Volume 1's Chapter 29; prerendering and proxies is covered in this volume's Chapter 29.

Parenting and null objects, see Volume 1, Chapter 17.

Nesting and Precomposing (and the rendering order) were the focus of Volume 1, Chapters 18 and 19.

The Interpret Footage dialog, where you can conform frame rates, is discussed in detail in Volume 1, Chapter 28.

Compound Effects, see Chapter 9.

Time Remapping, see Chapter 13.

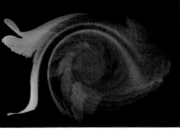

CC Time Blend FX takes a simple distortion (left) and feeds it back upon itself in successive frames (right).

15 On Stable Ground

The Professional edition includes the ability to stabilize wobbly footage. Mastering this is also the key to having one object track another.

Major Changes

The tracker/stabilizer received a major overhaul in version 6, so be prepared to re-learn what you already knew about it. The parameter defaults are much improved, it tracks much faster, and it is now easier to save and reuse your tracks inside an After Effects project.

Example Project

Explore the 15-Example Project.aep file as you read this chapter; references to [Ex.##] refer to specific compositions within the project file.

Pro **M**otion Stabilization and Motion Tracking – the subjects of this chapter and the next – sometimes seem like magic…magic that you often can't quite get to work. Some of the problems come from improper preparation of footage (not all shots can be stabilized or tracked), some with how the tracker's options have been set, and some with perhaps unreasonable expectations.

The key to both Stabilization and Tracking is learning how to track the movement of a visual feature from frame to frame in a footage item, and that's what we'll focus on here. We'll then show how to use the Stabilize option of this tool. In Chapter 16, we'll move on to having one object track the movement of another.

Stabilizing 101

The point of Motion Stabilization is to remove drift, wander, zoom, or rotation in a footage item, making it appear as if the camera and action were solidly locked down. This drift might have come from a camera that was not perfectly steady – perhaps because it was handheld – or an object that was drifting off its mark.

To stabilize a footage item, the item needs to have some feature with an identifiable edge or shape with a strong contrast in color, brightness, or saturation from its immediate surroundings that can then be recognized and followed by the software. Dots are great; sharp corners also work well. Continuous edges or lines, or otherwise indistinct features, do not work.

You point After Effects at this identifiable feature, and After Effects tracks the feature by looking for a similar feature in subsequent frames of the layer. It will then create new Anchor Point (and optionally, Rotation or Scale) keyframes to offset the apparent image center of the layer in a way that makes the overall image seem stable.

First we will discuss setting up a layer to be stabilized. We will then cover the stabilizer's all-important options, and finish by performing motion stabilization with a series of examples.

To practice motion stabilization, we will use the comp [**Ex.01*starter**] in the file **15-Example Project.aep** – if you have your computer handy, open this project and comp now. The layer you will be stabilizing is a nested comp named [**Ex.01.1 moving target**]; it contains a sphere we animated in a precomp to give us a simple "case study" to work with. Use this to practice the following concepts as we discuss them.

You can stabilize a piece of footage only if it's a layer in a composition. The user interface for the Motion Tracker and Stabilizer is a floating palette that can be opened by selecting Window> Tracker Controls. While you're in the [**Ex.01*starter**] comp, select the **Ex.01.1 moving target** layer to stabilize, open the Tracker Controls window, then click on its Stabilize Motion button. This will open the footage in its Layer window.

In the Layer window, you will see a set of Tracking Region boxes automatically named **Track Point 1**. The inner box – the Feature Region – needs to be centered and resized around the feature you have decided will make a good target to lock onto. The outer box – the Search Region – is how large an area After Effects will search beyond the inner box for each frame to find a matching feature from frame to frame.

In this example, you can choose to enlarge the Tracking Region boxes to track the entire sphere, or reduce them to track a feature of the sphere, such as one of the bright areas in its upper-left quarter. As you move the cursor around the boxes to different target areas, the cursor will change to reflect what you are about to move:

The Tracker Controls exist in their own floating window (left). In this window, select the layer in the current comp to track, the Track Type you want to perform (Stabilize, in this case), and what type of motion you want to stabilize – Position, Rotation, Scale, or any combination of these. Then click on the button Stabilize Motion. This opens the selected clip's Layer window (right) and adds a set of Tracking Region boxes, which includes the Feature Region (inside) and the Search Region (outside). Other important buttons in the Tracker Controls include Options (discussed later), a set of Analyze transport controls to track forward or backward, and buttons to Reset the Tracking Regions or to Apply the stabilization.

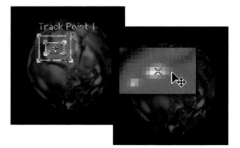

An example of making the Tracking Region boxes snugly fit our features to track, with enough room to follow its movements from frame to frame (above left). The Feature Region is automatically magnified 400% when we move the boxes, allowing you to more clearly see the detail you are tracking (above right).

Target Area	Cursor	Behavior
Region Handle		Resize Feature or Search Region
Within Track Point		Move All
Feature Region Edge, or hold Option (Alt) key down		Move All except Attach Point
Search Region Edge		Move Search Region independently
Attach Point		Move Attach Point Independently

When the tracker/stabilizer is active, a faint jagged line is drawn through the middle of the Layer window's Time Ruler.

Set the corresponding checkboxes below the Track Type popup if you want to track Rotation and/or Scale instead of Position (above). Rotation and Scale each require two Tracking Regions to calculate, called Track Point 1 and 2 (below). If you track Position in addition to Scale and/or Rotation, the Attach Point (the + symbol that defaults to the middle of Track Point 1's Feature Region) becomes the Anchor Point and therefore the center around which the stabilized layer rotates or scales. Footage courtesy Artbeats/Lifestyles: Mixed Cuts.

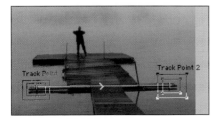

To move both boxes together, grab them in the middle of the inner box. After you start to move them, the Feature Region will appear magnified 400% to help you see details. To resize the boxes, grab their handles on their respective sides or corners. You will probably find it easiest to hold the Command key on Mac (Control key on Windows) as you drag; otherwise, the other side of the box will automatically move in the opposite direction as you drag, which can cause it to go offscreen. Dragging the Feature Region too large "bumps" the Search Region larger. The Reset button in the Tracker Controls window will return these to their default position (but will not reset the Options, which are discussed later).

The + symbol that is initially placed in the middle of the Feature Region is called the Attach Point. This point is important when you're tracking, as it says where you want the anchor point of a second layer to be placed when you're finished. It is also important when you're stabilizing position in addition to scale and/or rotation, as this is where the layer's Anchor Point will be placed, becoming the center of the layer's scale and rotation.

Minimizing the size of both the Search and Feature regions will speed up tracking, but going too small will make After Effects lose the track. Make the Feature Region just large enough to enclose the feature you are tracking, with at least a pixel of contrasting image around the edges. Make the Search Region just big enough to follow the frame-to-frame movement of the object – not how much the feature moves over the entire clip. After the software finds the feature being tracked in a frame, it will update the position of these regions to match the feature's new location. It is a good idea to preview your footage before setting this box so you have a feeling for how much your feature to track will move and change size, and in what direction.

Note that the comp's work area does not apply to this window, but the tracker will default to the layer's in and out points. Trim the in and out if you plan to use less than the entire clip in this comp; there's no point spending time tracking more of the clip than you'll need. When the tracker/stabilizer is active, you will see a faint jagged line drawn through the middle of the Layer window's Time Ruler. Trimming the Ruler's in and out points while the jagged line is visible will edit the piece of time in the clip you are stabilizing, but will not change the clip's in and out points in the composition's overall timeline.

Back in the Tracker Controls window, note the Track Type popup: Leave it at Stabilize to perform motion stabilization; the other options are for tracking (the subject of the next chapter). Beneath it are a set of checkboxes to determine what property you will be stabilizing (or tracking): Position, Rotation, Scale, or any combination of these. These choices are set with the checkboxes to the left of the property's name. To stabilize rotation or scale, you need two points to track, and you will see in the Layer window two Tracking Regions connected by a line with arrows. The arrow travels from the anchor point to the second reference to decide how much the layer has rotated or scaled. The farther apart these two regions are, the more accurately rotation or scale will be stabilized. Note that you can stabilize rotation in only two dimensions; After Effects' tracker cannot stabilize imagery that appears to tilt toward or away from you in 3D space.

Essential Options

If you never explore the Options for the Motion Tracker/Stabilizer, you will have difficulty getting a good stabilization or track in many situations. There is no one setting that works for all situations; you may need to experiment with different settings to see which gives you the best results. Let's go over each of the options and learn how to apply them to get the best stabilization.

When you're performing stabilization, you can safely ignore the Apply Motion To options; they apply only to Tracking, which is covered in the next chapter. All of the remaining options apply to both Tracking and Stabilization.

Channel helps give After Effects a better scent to track. If the detail you are tracking has a strong change in brightness compared with its surroundings (such as a white table tennis ball on a dark wall), use Luminance. Luminance is the default, but note that it is not always the best choice! For example, when the difference is more in color than in brightness (for example, a red dot against a green background), use RGB. Saturation is the option you will use the least; it comes in handy for rare cases, such as a bright red tracking point against a dull, rust-colored background. In the case of [**Ex.01*starter**], if you were tracking one of the bright highlights, luminance would be your choice. If you were to track the entire sphere, luminance or RGB should both work well (saturation might also work, but the overall saturation values for this object are a bit low, so it is less than ideal). If you were to track one of the darker islands or details in the sphere, you might use RGB, as the luminance and particularly saturation values for the ridges and such may be too close to those of the rest of the sphere to provide a good track.

Process Before Match helps occasionally with some problem footage. If the object being tracked is out of focus and therefore soft, but the footage is otherwise clean, check this box and try the Enhance option – it runs the equivalent of a "sharpen" filter on the layer just during the tracking stage. If the footage is noisy or grainy, use the Blur option (lest a speck of dust or noise gets mistaken for a detail in the image to track).

If your source material has interlaced fields (as much video does), and the feature you are tracking has sudden or unpredictable motion, try

When you have problematic tracks or stabilizations, you will need to tweak the Motion Stabilizer Options for best results. The first section to experiment with is Track Options. The Adapt Feature section is also important.

Under Lock & Key

Starting with version 6, After Effects saves tracking and stabilization data as keyframes for a layer. You can save multiple sets of tracking data for the same layer, and apply whichever one you choose later.

Stabilize, Then Move

There are times when you will want to offset or re-animate a stabilized layer – for example, to remove the effects of a shaky camera move, then reintroduce a smoother one. Here are some tips on how to do it:

Tweaking Stabilized Position

Stabilize Position animates the Anchor Point, not the Position of a layer. Therefore, you can edit or animate the layer's Position property to recenter or further animate your tracked footage.

Tweaking Stabilized Rotation

After Effects remembers the initial Rotation value of a layer before stabilizing, then keyframes the Rotation parameter as needed to stabilize it (if the 3D Layer switch has been enabled, the Z Rotation value is key-framed). Therefore, it is best to orient your layer before stabilizing. If you forgot, you can enable the 3D Layer switch and use the Orientation property to re-orient your layer, or apply Effect>Distort>Transform and use this plug-in to further offset or animate the rotation.

enabling the Track Fields option to catch this motion. If the feature you are tracking moves slowly and smoothly, try leaving this option off: Your track will run faster, and won't be thrown off by the data interpolated between fields.

You will want to leave Subpixel Positioning enabled 99.9% of the time. When it is off, After Effects will correct the position of a layer only to whole pixels, which is the equivalent of Draft Quality. Allowing a layer to be positioned on anything other than a whole pixel does soften it slightly as antialiasing kicks in, but this is a very small price to pay for smooth movement. In the previous version, you used to set how fine to divide each pixel when positioning; in version 6, the tracker/stabilizer received a major overhaul which increased its speed, so it always defaults to 1/256th of a pixel when this option is enabled.

The Adapt Feature on Every Frame option asks "Should I match what this thing looked like on the first frame of the track? Or should I match the most recent frame I just tracked?" If the feature is going to change radically over the course of the track – for example, if the object is coming toward you – then enable it (and make sure your Feature Region is large enough to capture this change in size). Otherwise, disable it, and set the popup below it to Adapt Feature: This will cause After Effects to try to match the look of the initial feature until it is too different to comfortably match (this threshold being set by the If Confidence Is Below number to its right); once the feature has changed too much, After Effects will then adapt to what the feature looked like on the previous frame and use that as a guide for the following frames. This is the combination we use most often.

The rest of the options in the popup below Adapt Feature give After Effects further instructions on what to do if it has trouble matching the feature being tracked. If the feature has changed considerably since the track started (again, the threshold being set by the If Confidence Is Below number to the right of this popup), the first two options decide whether to keep tracking regardless, or to stop so you can inspect what's gone wrong and possibly choose a new Feature Region to track. If the object you are tracking gets obscured by another object during the course of the track (for example, a car temporarily goes behind a utility pole), or the track otherwise seems to randomly jump on a few frames, try the Extrapolate Motion option: This will tell After Effects that if it is not very confident of the feature match on a given frame, it should keep moving in the same direction as the feature was previously moving, then see if it can find that feature again on a subsequent frame.

As suggested above, After Effects notes how accurately it matched the feature it was tracking in each frame; this is the If Confidence Is Below number. The default of 80% is pretty good. If you find After Effects is breaking off the track too often, try lowering this number; if you feel the track isn't tight enough, try raising it. The Confidence values are saved with each track as keyframe values in the Timeline window after a track, so you can inspect them later.

Track and Apply

Once you have set your Tracking Regions, Options, and the in and out points of the segment of time you want to track, click on the Analyze Forward or Analyze Backward buttons in the Tracker Controls (depending on whether you are starting at the beginning or end of your track). You will see After Effects walk frame by frame through your footage, attempting to follow the item highlighted in your Feature Region.

If you see the Tracking Regions wander off from the feature you are tracking, stop and re-tweak your settings. [**Ex.01*starter**] is pretty easy to track; if you are having a problem with it, your Feature or Search regions are probably too large, and After Effects is mistaking a nearby feature (such as another specular highlight) for the feature it is supposed to be tracking. Once the analysis stage is finished, you will see the motion path of your track in the Layer window.

Once the tracking is finished, you will also find the layer has a new set of keyframes in the Timeline window: Select the layer and press U to reveal them, or twirl down Tracker>Track Point 1 to reveal all of the parameters associated with the track.

Note that in previous versions, you had to go into the Options dialog to save tracking data for later, or apply the data right then and there before moving on to other work. With this new workflow, if you want to try multiple variations of a track, just create a new tracker by clicking on

Bigger is Better

If you're having trouble adjusting the Feature and Search Region boxes around small details in the image, increase the Magnification of the Layer window.

Faster in RAM

The analyze step of tracking and stabilization will go much faster if the clip has already been cached into RAM – for example, if you've recently RAM Previewed the footage.

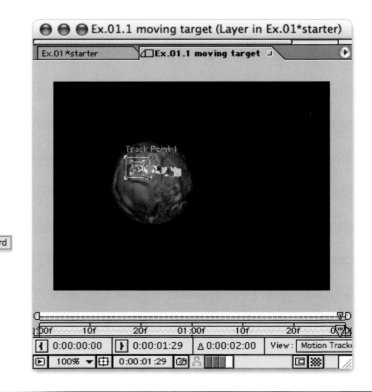

To initiate a track, click on the appropriate Analyze button in the Tracker Controls window (above). After a track is finished, you will see the motion path for the tracked feature in the Layer window (right).

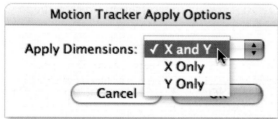

After Effects saves the results of a track or stabilization analysis as a series of parameters and keyframes attached to a layer. You can save multiple tracks per layer. This makes it easy to experiment, check on how accurate the track was (by looking at the Confidence value), and apply a track or stabilization later.

When you click on Apply, After Effects will ask you which dimensions you want to stabilize.

A Track by Any Other Name

You can rename your individual Tracker data sets, as well as Track Points, in the Timeline window by selecting them, hitting Return, typing in your new name, and hitting Enter. You can also rename a Tracker in its Options dialog.

the Track Motion or Stabilize Motion buttons: The first set of keyframes will be preserved, and a new set of Tracking Points will be created for you to experiment with.

When you are ready to apply a stabilization, verify in the Tracker Controls window that you have the right layer selected under Motion Source, and that you have selected the Tracker data you want to use under Current Track. Then click the Apply button. A dialog will appear asking you if you want to apply both the X and Y dimensions of the track, or just one of the dimensions. Applying a single dimension comes in handy in special situations such as when you want to preserve the original left-to-right (X axis) movement of an object but stabilize its up-and-down (Y axis) movement. In the case of [**Ex.01*starter**], stick with the default of applying both dimensions.

Bring the Comp window back forward by clicking on its tab: You should notice that the sphere is now in the middle of the comp, even if you are at the end of the timeline. Press U again until all of the layer's keyframes are revealed; in our example here where you stabilized just the sphere's position, you will see Anchor Point keyframes for the layer. (If you were to track Rotation or Scale, you would see keyframes for these applied as well.)

RAM Preview your stabilized comp and note that the sphere stays pretty well centered instead of wandering around (which it does in its source comp [**Ex.01.1**]). However, it does not stay completely sharp or stable. To verify this, after you have performed your track, open [**Ex.01_compare**] and RAM Preview it. This contains your stabilized animation, and a stationary copy of the sphere on top in Difference mode. The result is very dark; any slivers of color you see in this comparison comp are errors in your stabilization.

The cold, hard truth about motion stabilization is that the results are seldom perfect – so don't rely on it for absolute miracles. If the object you're tracking had inherent motion blur, the object would also appear to strangely blur in place even though it appears to be stabilized.

Masking and Motion Stabilization

When you crop footage down to a small feature – such as the head and shoulders of a person for a picture-in-picture effect – wobbles in the camera become more obvious. For example, open and RAM Preview **[Ex.02 mask only]**. This shot was filmed with a handheld camera, and the camera shake results in the head wobbling slightly inside the masked area.

After reading this chapter, you might think "no problem – I'll just stabilize the footage." But because stabilizing animates the Anchor Point, and transforms such as Anchor Point are calculated *after* masks, your mask will bounce along with the speaker, as demonstrated in **[Ex.02 wobble mask]**. It doesn't matter if you stabilize first or mask first – the render order will remain the same if you use only one comp.

To mask footage that is stabilized, you'll need to use two compositions so you can reverse the default render order. The idea is to stabilize the footage in the first comp and apply the mask in the second comp. If you want some practice:

Step 1: Open **[Ex.02*starter]**, which contains the footage to be stabilized. Consider which feature would be best to use. We tried his watch and then his eye, but realized that as he shifted his body, the wall then moved behind him. In the end, we used a corner of a book. After you Analyze and then Apply the Motion Stabilization, this layer's Anchor Point will be animated.

The original source movie is stabilized in one comp, then masked in a second comp. Now the mask is unaffected by the Anchor Point keyframes. Edge effects have been added to the picture-in-picture layer, plus a background and title layer. Footage courtesy Artbeats/Business Executives; background from Digital Vision/Electro.

Step 2: Create a new comp **[Ex.02-final]** and nest **[Ex.02*starter]** into it. Now apply a rectangular mask to the head and shoulders.

Step 3: *Optional:* You can also feather the edges or apply a bevel, drop shadow, or other edge effects to finish off the picture-in-picture effect, and add a background movie of your choice.

Our two compositions appear in the folder **[Ex.02_final versions]**.

Broken Tracks

You do not have to track an entire clip with one Tracking Region definition. For example, we once had to stabilize a several-minute-long, continuous helicopter flight that went from the clouds into the front door of a building – needless to say, the best feature to track changed during the course of the shot. Or, you might not have tracked enough of the original shot, and need to add onto a track you've already performed.

If you need to pick up a track in the middle, the most important thing is to not accidentally move the Attach Point: Otherwise, your track or stabilization will have a discontinuous jump in the middle. In case you forget, first save your project to make it easy to revert back to the track's previous state.

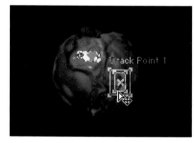

To pick up a track at a later point in time, move the time marker to the last track keyframe you want to keep (above), then carefully move your regions without moving the Attach Point. Hold the Option (Alt) key down to ensure this – you will notice the cursor changes to a white arrow (below).

Make sure that the clip you need to continue tracking is open in its Layer window (double-click it if it isn't), and that the Tracker Controls window is also open. In Tracker Controls, verify that the right layer is selected under Motion Source, and that the track you want to work with is selected under Current Track. Type U to reveal all the keyframes for this layer; you should see where the track keyframes stop. Position the time marker on the last keyframe you want to use (or the first keyframe, if you are tracking backward).

If you edit just the corners of your Feature or Search Regions, the Attach Point will not move. If you need to move the regions as a whole, hold down the Option (Alt) key before clicking and dragging. And make sure you don't accidentally move one of the previous track motion path points! (You can always Undo if you do.)

Verify your Options are set correctly, then click Analyze Forward (or Backward) to continue your track. You may notice that the motion path for the feature being tracked has a discontinuous jump where you picked up tracking again; that's okay – it's the Attach Point you don't want to jump. Apply your stabilization and verify your results.

Practice, Practice

Motion Tracking and Stabilization are something you get a feel for with experience. Here are a few real-world examples for you to practice on:

Stabilize Position 101

It is not uncommon to receive footage that has just a small amount of wobble that needs to be removed. Close all comps, open [**Ex.03*starter**] and RAM Preview it; note that this otherwise locked-down shot has a bit of camera shake. (If you can't see it, place your mouse over an identifiable point in the footage and RAM Preview; note how the reference point moves in relation to your cursor.)

Your mission is to remove this wobble. Select **AB_RetroTransportation.mov**, open Window>Tracker Controls, and click on Stabilize Motion, with the Position box checked under Track Type. The rear wheel on the airplane looks like a good candidate, as it's supposed to be stationary, and it provides good black-on-white contrast. Set up your Feature Region (the inner square) to surround it, making sure the Search Region (the outer square) is large enough to catch the small movement from frame to frame.

Click on Options and choose a set of parameters you think should work; for example, because the wheel is dark against a light background,

Where to Start

With some footage, the first frame may not be the best to start tracking or stabilizing. If you can't get a good track, try the Track in Reverse option, or retrim the in time where you start your track.

The back wheel of the airplane provides a good stationary, high-contrast feature to track. Footage courtesy Artbeats/ Retro Transportation.

set the Channel to use Luminance. Click OK, then Analyze Forward. If you're happy with your track, click Apply, using the option for both X and Y dimensions. Close the Layer window, and RAM Preview your stabilized footage. If you have trouble, compare your results with our [**Ex.03_final**]. If you need a reminder of how much the uncorrected shot wobbled, Option+ double-click (Alt+double-click) the layer to open it in the QuickTime player.

You might notice some black appears around the edges of your footage in the comp as it is repositioned to keep it stable. This "wanderlust" is a problem with most stabilized shots. You have to make a decision on how to handle this, with most of your choices involving an aesthetic compromise:

• Scale the movie larger so that edges are not visible, resulting in some softening of the image (the solution we chose in [**Ex.03_final**]);

• apply a track matte in this comp or a mask in a second comp (see the sidebar *Masking and Motion Stabilization*) to crop out the wandering edges; or

• hope these edges stay outside the Action Safe areas (which would work for this shot, but not all).

Bonus Points: Try tracking one of the headlights on the bus using the Extrapolate Motion option to help cover when people walk in front of it. [**Ex.03_final_ interp**] is our version; reveal its keyframes and note the gaps where After Effects was interpolating the motion. Note also that the result is not as good!

Motion Myths and Madness

As great as being able to track and stabilize objects and footage is, there are a number of gotchas and trade-offs:

• Not all footage can be tracked or stabilized – sorry. And every shot is its own special case. Run tests before promising the client you can do it; have a Plan B ready in the event you can't.

• It is far, far better to plan ahead than to assume you can fix it later. If you know a shot is going to need to be tracked or stabilized, shoot it with tracking markers (such as table tennis balls or other high-contrast dots) placed on the tracking points. Make sure those points stay in camera during the shot. Shoot a backup plan in the event it doesn't work.

• When you stabilize an image, its useful image area will be reduced in size. This is because it is going to get cropped off at the edges as it wanders around. If the movement is too big to hide in the overscan safe areas, plan on cropping and framing the layer in some way in the final composition. You can also scale it up, but be aware that this will soften the image.

• When you stabilize, the image will inevitably get softer. This is because you will be moving and rotating the image off its original, dead-on alignment, resulting in pixels being resampled as they are moved about.

• Beware of sudden, quick camera moves, especially with long shutter times – the resulting shot will exhibit natural motion blur that varies with the amount of movement from frame to frame, which you can't remove even if you successfully stabilize it.

• Although the tracker and stabilizer in After Effects work quite well with proper preparation and understanding, in all honesty, there may be better ones available. For tough jobs, consider using another application or plug-in, such as silhouette+roto (more information from www.silhouettefx.com).

Setting up the Tracking Region around the eye of the peacock – include some of the color outside the eye to get better edges to track. Peacock footage courtesy Harry Marks.

Stabilize Position 102

Time for a more challenging stabilization. Open comp [**Ex.04*starter**] and RAM Preview it. This close-up of a moving peacock was shot at a distance with a handheld camera at high zoom – understandably, it has a good amount of wobble that needs to be removed.

Double-click the layer **HM_peacock1.mov**, open Window>Tracker Controls, click on Stabilize Motion, and enable just Position under Track Type. As for a feature to track, the eyeball of the peacock is an obvious choice. Place your Tracking Region boxes appropriately to track this feature; keep in mind there is a lot of motion from frame to frame, so make your Search Region larger than you did for the previous example. Open the Options, and decide if RGB is the best Channel to track, or if you should try Saturation or Luminance. Turning on Process Before Match and selecting Enhance might also accentuate the edge of the eye socket for tracking; try it if you have trouble getting a good track.

Analyze, Apply, then RAM Preview. Note that the head of the peacock now stays centered in the screen. With the background moving so much, you might experience the optical illusion that your tracked object is moving. Place your cursor over the eye, then preview again to check that the tracked area is indeed stable.

Note that stabilizing this footage requires moving the layer quite a bit – too much to use the "scale up" or "rely on safe areas" solutions suggested in the previous example. In [**Ex.04_final**], we used a track matte to crop down the image to a reliably useable area.

Go ahead and experiment with alternate Tracking Regions. For example, the spurs around the large white region behind the eye are good high-contrast regions. The leftmost one sets the pivot point around which stabilization occurs further back, which results in less neck movement but more beak movement after stabilization – perhaps a better trade-off. (If you have trouble placing your Tracking Regions around this,

If an object is moving relative to its background and you stabilize the object, the background will usually move out of frame (left). To avoid seeing wandering edges, use a matte to mask the peacock down to a usable, stable region (right).

increase the Magnification of the Layer window up to 200%; hold the space bar and drag the image to center this region inside the window.) This is shown in [**Ex.04_final_alt**]. The end of the beak, on the other hand, would be a poor choice to stabilize – you don't want the entire head and body pivoting around the end of its beak as it opens and closes!

Stabilize Position & Rotation

Comp [**Ex.05*starter**] shows a different perspective on our peacock. Preview it to again note the camera wobble; also note there is a slight rotation, as the right side seems to dip down slightly toward the end. This is a good example to try stabilizing both position and rotation. Lucky for you, a male peacock in display has built-in tracking dots: the "eyes" on its feathers.

Select the layer **HM_peacock2.mov**, open Window>Tracker Controls, and click on Stabilize Motion. This time, enable the Position and Rotation checkboxes. Note that two Track Points now appear. Also note the arrow on the line that joins them: The arrow is coming away from the Track Point that surrounds the feature that will be stabilized; the other Track Point determines how much rotation correction is necessary. Select a pair of "eyes" on the feathers to track. Remember that the farther apart they are, the more accurate the rotation will be; the smaller they are, the faster they will track. For example, you might lock onto the two small eyes to the left and right above its nostrils, but feel free to experiment.

Analyze, Apply, and RAM Preview. Select the layer and hit U to note that both the Anchor Point and Rotation are being animated. As you step through the composition, note that the rotation value is changing; you can also see this from the edges of the original layer as they creep into the composition. Again, you can mask this and recenter the layer's position in the comp; just note that After Effects adds an unneeded Position keyframe at the start of the track – remove this so you can change the layer's position at any time in the composition without introducing unwanted animation.

Peacocks, fortunately, have built-in tracking dots on their feathers. Look closely and notice the Tracking Regions around them.

Our peacock after stabilizing Position and Rotation. Note from the outlines of the original layer how it has been rotated to keep the bird stable.

Connect

Subpixel positioning was discussed in the *Resample* sidebar in Volume 1, Chapter 3.

Rotation and Orientation were discussed in Volume 1, Chapter 4; the Anchor Point in Volume 1, Chapter 5.

Masking was covered in depth in Volume 1, Chapter 11; Track Mattes in Volume 1, Chapter 12.

Nesting and Precomposing were covered in Volume 1, Chapters 18 and 19, respectively.

Video overscan areas are discussed in Chapter 21.

16 Motion Tracking

Motion Tracking allows you to add an object to a scene after it was shot – if you're both lucky and good...

Pro In the last chapter, we covered the core concepts behind using the Professional edition's Motion Tracking and Stabilization engine. In this chapter, we will cover the additional features required to make one layer follow a feature in another layer, making them appear they were originally shot together, or just to coordinate their actions. We have included several real-world examples for you to practice with.

Tracking 101

Everything you learned in the previous chapter relating to Motion Stabilization applies to Motion Tracking (so make sure you read and understand that chapter first). With Stabilization, the inverse of the tracking data is applied to the Anchor Point of the layer you tracked to make it appear stable. With Tracking, the tracking data is usually applied to a second layer, hopefully making that layer move as if it were pinned to a feature in the layer you tracked. With simple tracking, the Position, Rotation, and/or Scale of the second layer is keyframed; with Perspective tracking, a Distort>Corner Pin effect is applied to the second layer, and its corners are keyframed to give it motion. You can also choose to apply the tracking data to an Effect Point of an effect.

To practice how this works, open the project **16-Example Project.aep**, and start out by opening comp [**Ex.01*starter**]. It will look similar to the first comp in the previous chapter, except there is a new layer on top. Select the second layer – **Ex.01.1-moving target** – as it is the one we want to track. Then open Window>Tracker Controls and click Track Motion. Its Layer window will open, showing a set of Tracking Regions.

Attach Point

Change the Type popup to Track while keeping an eye on the image above. You will see a + symbol appear in the middle of the Tracking Regions. This is the spot that will be used to define the Position value of the second layer. Note that the Attach Point can be moved to a location other than the middle of the Tracking Region: You might need to pin the second layer onto one particular feature, but another feature in the shot might be better to track. For our purposes here, place this "crosshair" in the middle of the blue and gold sphere.

It Takes Two to Track

To choose a Type of Track or Corner Pin, you need to have a second layer in the same comp, or an appropriate effect applied to the selected layer – otherwise, there's nothing to apply the tracking data to.

Example Project

Explore the 16-Example Project.aep file as you read this chapter; references to [Ex.##] refer to specific compositions within the project file.

Clicking and dragging somewhere inside the Feature Region (the inner square) but not on the Attach Point itself moves both the Feature and Search regions as well as the Attach Point as one unit. Option+dragging on Mac (Alt+dragging on Windows) inside the Feature Region moves the regions while leaving the Attach Point where you put it – this is very important when you're tweaking your regions. Because moving the regions can accidentally move the Attach Point – but not vice versa – get in the habit of setting your Tracking Region(s) first, then placing your Attach Point. This will help you avoid accidentally moving both of them together.

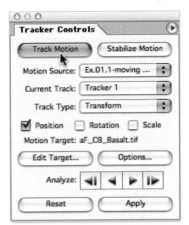

The Options dialog is the same for the tracker as for the stabilizer; refer to it for details on how to optimize its parameters. There are numerous contrasts in luminance and color to track on this sphere; go ahead and set up your Feature and Search Regions around one of these features. As the Attach Point is defaulting to the middle of this sphere – the place where we want to attach the second sphere – remember to hold down the Option (Alt) key while adjusting your regions to leave the Attach Point where it is; add Command (Control) to move the region corners and sides independently of each other.

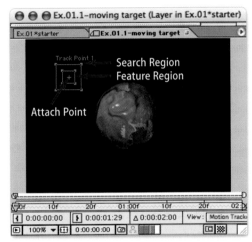

Once you have set up your Tracking Regions, Attach Point, and Options, click Analyze Forward in the Tracker Controls, and see if the track looks acceptable. Once you're satisfied you have a good track, click on Edit Target in Tracker Controls. It defaults to the layer above the one you are tracking (which is what we want in this case); you can change that default here. Click OK, then click Apply. As with stabilization, you have the option to apply either or both of the X and Y dimensions; use the default of both, and click OK. Bring the Comp window back forward, and RAM Preview. The mottled sphere (**aF_CB_Basalt**) will now follow the purple one (albeit, with some minor jitter – tracking is never perfect…).

If you realize you set up the Attach Point in the wrong place when you performed the track, you can fix it using the Motion Trackers>Tracker 1>Track Point 1>Attach Point Offset parameter. This offset is used only when you click Apply; it does not fix the motion path after you've already applied it.

To track a layer, select it, open the Tracker Controls, and click Track Motion (top). The Layer window will open with a set of Tracking Regions, given the default name Track Point 1 (above). The + symbol that defaults to the middle of the Tracking Regions is the Attach Point: where you want to pin the second layer relative to the feature you are tracking.

To tweak the position after you've applied the tracker, select the layer that has had the track applied to it (**aF_CB_Basalt**, in this case) and press U to reveal its keyframes. Click on Position to select all of the keyframes, and make sure the time marker is parked on one of them (the keyframe navigator box will have a check mark in it). Use the arrow keys on the numeric keypad to nudge the layer directly in the Comp window. You can also offset the Anchor Point of the tracked layer to change its relationship to the master layer it follows, which is important if you need to change the center around which it scales and rotates.

When you click Edit Target, you are presented with a dialog where you can choose which layer (or effect) receives the motion track data.

Averaging Tracks

You can use expressions to average together multiple tracks. For the Position of the "follower" layer, inside parentheses add together the Attach Point values of the tracks you want to average (use the pick whip to select them), then divide the total by the number of tracks you are averaging: **(track1 + track2) / 2**.

Adding Rotation and Scale

You can track properties other than Position. The Track Type popup offers choices for corner pinning (which we'll discuss in a couple of pages). Under this popup are checkboxes for Rotation and Scale in addition to Position; you can select any combination of these properties. As with stabilizing rotation or scale (discussed in the previous chapter), tracking rotation or scale requires having two features to track: One serves as the anchor point, while the other is used as a reference to decide how much the object has rotated or scaled.

To get some practice tracking Position plus Rotation, open comp **[Ex.03.1*starter]**, and RAM Preview. The goal here is to make the arrow point from one of the silver solder blobs to another as this circuit board pans past the camera. Press Home to return to the start of the comp, select the layer to track (**AB_DesktopTech_ex**), open the Tracker Controls (if it is not already visible), and click on Track Motion. Make sure the Track Type popup is set to Transform, and enable Position plus Rotation underneath. You should see two sets of Tracking Points in the Layer window. Set up one around the solder blob in the middle of the circuit board, and the other around a blob in the lower right corner. The relative luminance levels of the blobs and surrounding circuits are pretty close, so consider opening the Options and changing Channel to RGB; leave Adapt Feature off.

Click on Analyze Forward. If you're happy with the track, click on Edit Target in the Tracker Controls, and set it to **CM_arrow**. Click OK, then

Effect Track

The Motion Tracker also allows you to have an Effect Point – such as the center of Distort>Bulge – follow a feature of the layer you are tracking. First apply the effect you want to the layer, then use the Tracker.

To practice this, open **[Ex.02*starter]** where Bulge has been applied to our hapless peacock from the previous chapter. Track the peacock's eyeball using what you learned in **[Ex.01]**, placing the Attach Point at the center of the eye. After analyzing, click on Edit Target, and select Effect Point Control instead of Layer for the Apply Motion To option. Note that its popup will already be set to Bulge/Bulge Center (if you have multiple valid effects, you can choose between them here). Click OK, then Apply, choosing both dimensions. Bring the Comp window forward and RAM Preview the result. Check out **[Ex.02_final]** to compare your work.

Motion Tracking can also apply to effect points, such as having the center of a Bulge track this peacock's eye. Experiment with this for yourself in **[Ex.02]**.

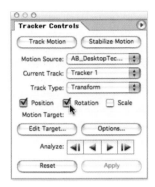

You can track any combination of Position, Scale, and Rotation (left). When you add Rotation or Scale, you will see two sets of Tracking Points in the Layer window (right): one for the anchor point, and one to measure how much to rotate or scale by. This figure shows the tracking motion paths after the analysis is done.

Apply, keeping the default of applying to the X and Y dimensions. Bring the Comp window forward, and RAM Preview: The arrow's round end should stay centered on one blob, and point at the other. However, you will notice the arrow does not perfectly reach to the other one; this is a case where you might want to track scale as well.

To practice tracking scale, open [**Ex.03.2*starter**] and RAM Preview. The camera zooms in on the motorcycle; you want the text to zoom by the same amount. In the Tracker Controls, select **CM_motorcycle** in the Motion Source popup, click Track Motion, verify Track Type is set to Transform, and below this popup, enable just Scale (disable Position). As the cycle zooms toward you, it will be better to start at the end, where the features to track will be their largest – so hit the End key, and pick two features to track that are as far apart as possible (we chose the front reflector and the rear taillight). Under Options, enable Adapt Feature on Every Frame so After Effects can keep up with the scale changes in the Feature Regions. Then click on Analyze Backward. Note that the track does not need to be perfect; we're just trying to get the Scale close.

Verify that the Motion Target is set to the type layer **terrorize your neighbors**, then click Apply. Bring the Comp window forward and RAM Preview: The type should scale up as the camera zooms in the bike. (See [**Ex.03.2_final**] for comparison.)

To track scale changes in a layer, select this property in the Tracker Controls (above), and set up two Tracker Regions. In [**Ex.03.2_final**], we made the scale of a text layer follow a camera's zoom on this motorcycle (left).

A common use for Corner Pin tracking is to paste a new message on a sign. In this example, because no trackings dots were provided, you would try tracking the corners. You would also need to mask around the fingers in a shot such as this. Faux footage from Digital Vision's Blank Message.

Corner Pinning Choices

As we mentioned earlier, there are also two Corner Pinning tracking options, found under the Track Type popup. These add the Perspective> Corner Pin effect to the second layer, and create keyframes for the corners based on the Attach Points as well as Position keyframes for roughly the center of what is being tracked.

In a couple of pages, we'll get to a pair of examples you can work through to practice corner pinning with the tracker. Before we get to them, we need to define the difference between Affine and Perspective pinning.

Normally, you will want to use Perspective Corner Pin, which tracks all four corners and does whatever is necessary to fit your new layer over your tracked points, including bending it into all manners of trapezoidal shapes. By contrast, Affine Corner Pin keeps the opposing sides of the pinned layer parallel to each other, resizing and skewing the layer only as needed – akin to using a skew filter in Illustrator or Photoshop. To accomplish this, only three of the four corners are tracked, as the fourth corner has to be calculated in a way to keep the sides parallel. Use this option only if the layer is not supposed to take on an angled, perspective look.

Select Window>Close All before moving on to the real-world examples.

Motion Blur

One of the secrets to making motion tracked objects work in a scene – particularly when there is a lot of movement – is to use Motion Blur. Most footage of moving objects captured on film or video tape exhibit motion blur; you will need to have After Effects add blur to objects tracking a feature in your footage to make it appear as if they were shot at the same time.

To add this blur to your objects, enable the Motion Blur switch for the "applied to" layer, enable the Motion Blur switch in the Timeline window, and RAM Preview to see if it helps. The Motion Blur Shutter Angle has a large effect on how well it works: too much angle, and the object will seem to overshoot its movements, even if the shot was tracked perfectly. You can change this in Composition>Composition Settings under the Advanced tab.

If you need this angle to be different for every other layer in the rest of your comps, consider using the Distort>Transform Effect for your movement.

It has its own shutter angle, which can override the program's default. Copy and paste your Anchor Point, Position, and/or Rotation keyframes from the normal layer properties into the Transform effect's properties. Of course, remember to go back and delete the original keyframes and reset their values to a good starting point, or else you will get twice the motion.

Each composition also has its own motion blur shutter angle, so another method for getting different motion blur values per layer is to select the tracked layer and the layer that's following it, Layer>Precompose, then set the desired motion blur shutter angle in the precomp.

Note that Motion Blur often does *not* work well when you use one of the Corner Pinning options. This is because Motion Blur is only looking to the Position keyframes to decide how to blur the layer, but the layer itself is being "moved" by a combination of Position and the Corner Pin effect. You may need to manually keyframe a blur effect to get the best final result.

Real-World Examples

Every motion tracking case is different; that's why it is better to work through some actual examples. Here are three examples of projects you could expect to be asked to do.

Two-Part Track

You're working on a commercial. The cameraperson has taken some nice continuous pans across a product, and the clients decide it would be cool to have their slogans track the camera move as if hanging off of or attached to the product. And they want them to start offscreen, track across onscreen, then continue offscreen in one smooth motion. Of course, there's no way to track a single point this far – you can't accurately track something that's no longer in the camera's view. Therefore, you will need to track it in two parts, using one tracking region for half the move to pull the object onscreen, and another to push it offscreen.

Open [**Ex.04*starter**], and RAM Preview. This contains footage of a continuous camera move along the neck of a guitar (**DI_guitarneck.mov**) and the slogan that is supposed to follow the shot (**PerfectFeel.ai**). Shuttle around the first half of the shot (00:00 to 03:00) by dragging the time marker, and look for good details of the guitar to track that stay in camera during this time – some of the fret ends and corners of the fretboard inlays appear to be candidates. Then shuttle around the second half of the comp (03:00 to 05:29), looking for a second point that stays in camera for this second half of the clip. Now position the time marker in the middle of the comp (03:00) and position the slogan to a place that looks good to you, select the layer **PerfectFeel**, and press P to reveal its Position value.

Select **DI_guitarneck**, verify Window>Tracker Controls is open, and click Track Motion: The Layer window will open, with one set of Tracking Regions visible. (If you see more than one set, verify that just Position is enabled.) Twirl open the parameters for **DI_guitarneck** in the Timeline window until you can see the value for its Attach Point.

The first Tracking Region (A) is set up at time 03:00 and will be tracked backward. Note that the Attach Point + icon is in the lower right of the frame, where we want the slogan to be. After tracking (B), note that the Attach Point has been pushed off the top of the screen at time 00:00 – this means it will start offscreen. Go back to time 03:00, and set up a second Tracking Region (C) for the rest of the clip. After tracking (D), the Attach Point has been pushed off the bottom of the screen by the end of the clip. Footage courtesy Desktop Images.

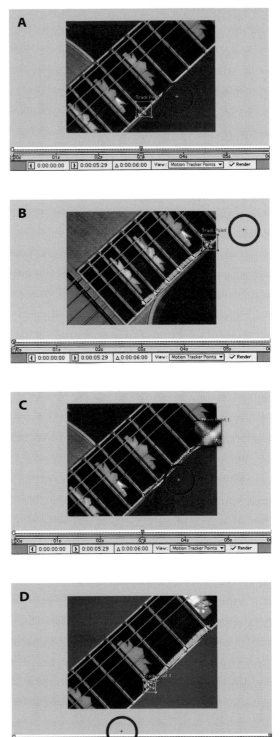

Let's do the first half first. Because we're going to start offscreen, this is a good candidate to track backward, starting where we want to end up. Set the time marker in the Layer window to 03:00. Open the Options, verify that Adapt Feature is off (you don't need it, as the guitar does not change size or perspective during the shot), and consider if it would be better to track RGB or Luminance. Click OK.

Since we're tracking backward, 03:00 is the start of the track; therefore, this is the time to place your regions and points. Place the Tracking Regions around that first detail you wanted to track. Then copy the Position value for **PerfectFeel**, and paste it into the value for **DI_guitar-neck**'s Attach Point: This will ensure the text is placed where we want at 03:00 as a starting point.

Parental Tracking

To have several objects track the same feature, first apply the track to a Null Object, then use Parenting to have other layers follow this null. (See *Parenting Skills*, Volume 1, Chapter 17.)

Click on Analyze Backward and watch After Effects track the first half of the movie. By the time it reaches 00:00, you should see that the Attach Point has been pushed off onto the pasteboard, meaning the slogan will start offscreen just as the client wanted.

Now let's do the second half. Set the time marker back to 03:00. Hold the Option (Alt) key and drag your Tracking Regions to a new feature in the footage that will stay onscreen for the second half of the movie. You can also press Command (Control) and resize the boxes by dragging their handles. Be careful not to move any of the keyframes from the first track's motion path; increase the Magnification of the Layer window if you're having trouble. Also verify that the Attach Point has not moved: This will happen if you forgot to hold a modifier key while you were dragging. As you're picking up the track from 03:00 again (where we had originally trial-positioned the text), you can always paste **PerfectFeel**'s Position value back into **DI_guitarneck**'s Attach Point.

This time, click on the Analyze Forward button; note that the Attach Point is now pushed off the bottom of the screen by the end of the clip. Verify that the Motion Target is set to **PerfectFeel**, and click Apply, choosing the default of both dimensions. Bring the Comp window forward and RAM Preview your result. The text should move like it was stuck to the guitar. If you're not happy with the text's position, edit the Anchor Point for the **PerfectFeel** layer to offset its location: Select the layer, press A to reveal this property, and scrub its values in the Timeline window. Our result is saved in the comp [**Ex.04_final**].

The slogan Perfect Feel now has Position keyframes that track the guitar neck, from start to finish, offscreen to onscreen to off again. The secret was tracking in two segments.

Tracking with Dots

For motion tracking jobs, you really want to consider placing tracking dots on the object to be tracked – even if the object is a 3D render. Many 3D programs can now export their camera data for use in After Effects (discussed in Chapter 19), but for those that don't, you can still use this tracking trick.

In [**Ex.05*starter**], we rendered a 3D videowall box on a virtual stage with a simple camera move around it. The face of the wall was left blank so we could apply different movies later in After Effects; this renders much faster than having to render the video directly in the 3D application. To make this easier, we rendered a second pass in 3D, with virtual table tennis balls stuck on each corner of the face of the box. This technique gives us a far cleaner set of features to track than trying to follow the corners of a gray box against a gray backdrop. If you are doing a live shoot with a motion control camera that can automatically perform the exact same move over and over, you might consider shooting a separate take for just the tracking dots; this will come in handy as any other activity (such as an actress walking across a stage) might obscure the dots during the shot.

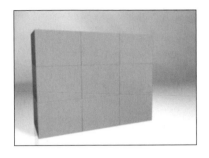

A virtual stage rendered in 3D (left), along with virtual tracking dots that were placed on the corners of the box and rendered as a second pass (right). This is a good technique to use with real sets and motion control cameras as well.

Select the layer **CM_stagedots** (layer 3), and click on Track Motion in the Tracker Controls window. Set the Track Type popup to Perspective corner pin; you should now see four Tracking Regions in the Layer window. The order of the regions is very important! Place Track Point 1 on the upper left dot, 2 on the upper right, 3 on the lower left, and 4 on the lower right – otherwise, the wrong corners will be pinned. There seems to be a bug in version 6.5 where occasionally these four regions will appear in scrambled order (for example, 2 in the upper left and 1 in the lower right); if this happens, delete the Tracker in the Timeline window and click Track Motion again.

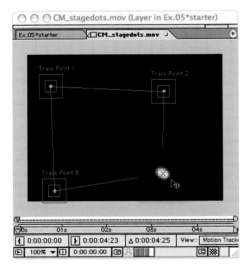

Leave the Attach Points at their default positions of centered in their respective Feature Regions. As you adjust each Feature Region, place the X icon in the middle of the dot. Where you place these points is where the corners of your video will be pinned. Check the Options (Luminance is an obvious choice for Channel; you can leave Adapt Feature off), and click Analyze Forward. Click on Edit Target and choose **AB_EstabUrban** as the target layer, click OK, and then click Apply. Bring the Comp window forward and RAM Preview: The movie layer will now be pinned onto the videowall front.

The final trick in a job like this is to clean up the edges. Most motion tracks still end up with some jitter, which gives the game away – particularly as the edges wander in relation to their frame. Layer 1, **CM_stage-face.mov**, is a matte for just where your tracked image is supposed to end up. To use it, set the TrkMat popup for layer 2, **AB_EstabUrban.mov**,

Select Perspective corner pin for Track Type; set Motion Target to **AB_EstabUrban** (left). Then center each Tracking Region over its respective dots, centering the crosshair in the dots (above). After Effects will automatically magnify the Feature Region as you drag.

After tracking the dots, the video is perfectly pinned onto the front of our virtual videowall (A). To clean up the edges, we rendered a separate 3D pass of just the front face of the wall (B) and used that as a track matte for the video, as shown in **[Ex.05_final]**. We also used a Hard Light transfer mode to allow the creases and shadows of the wall to show through the video. Footage courtesy Artbeats/Establishments: Urban.

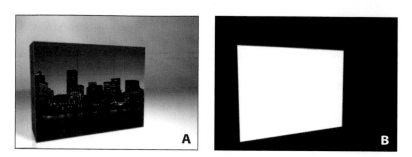

to Luma Matte, as we did in [**Ex.05_final**]. Of course, in 3D, it's easy to render a separate high-contrast pass of just the face that is supposed to receive the tracked image; on a video shoot, perhaps paint this surface green or blue and key it later as your matte. In either case, set your Attach Points slightly outside the area where the image will get matted to so you have some spill to crop off.

A Challenging Replacement

A common motion tracking task, from corny in-house videos to serious feature films, is to replace a sign or billboard in a shot with something more appropriate to the storyline. This requires using the Perspective Corner Pin option for the tracker.

This shot of the sign changes from a close-up to a zoom-back, adding to our challenge. (By the way, the reason the sun and shadow patterns are so strange on the wall is that this was taken during a solar eclipse, turning the gaps between a tree's leaves into numerous pinhole cameras.) Footage courtesy Kevin Dole.

In comp [**Ex.06*starter**], we have a rather challenging example for you: motion tracking an interlaced DV NTSC shot of a street sign in France we want replaced. Problem is, it's a handheld shot (lots of wobble), and the camera also zooms out – so the features we want to track change over the course of the shot.

Fortunately, the sign practically has tracking dots built in: the blue dots of paint in its corners. The sign corners are also fair game, though the sunlight patterns occasionally wash them out in contrast to the pale wall.

The biggest challenge is the camera pullback during the shot, because this means the size of the features we want to track is going to change during the track. You can try tracking the shot in multiple segments (such as before, during, and after the pullback), enabling Adapt Feature on Every Frame, or leave Adapt off and set the popup below it to Adapt Feature.

3D Tracking

After Effects can track in 2D only. It fakes 3D perspective by using the Corner Pin effect to warp the layer that is being applied on top of another. However, there are applications that can track a scene and derive 3D movement information from it. For example, Boujou 2 from 2d3 (www.2d3.com) can transfer this info directly to After Effects through

a plug-in it provides. Slightly less straightforward, MatchMover from REALVIZ (www.realviz.com) exports its information to 3D applications, including Maya, Cinema 4D, and 3ds max. You will need to then export camera data from these applications into After Effects. See Chapter 19 for more on integrating with 3D programs.

While you're in the Motion Tracker Options, you may consider enabling the Track Fields option. However, the upper and lower fields of deinterlaced video interpolate into slightly different images from each other, which can confuse a highly adaptive track. To see for yourself, try this track with and without the field option checked, and render an interlaced movie for playback. You will have other decisions to make, such as whether to try either of the Process Before Match options, and whether to set the Channel to RGB or Luminance.

Expect to need to make several attempts before you get an acceptable result! Don't forget you can save multiple track attempts per layer, and to set the Attach Points just beyond the outer corners of the sign (so that it will be completely covered by the new sign). If you become exasperated, consider hand-tracking the sign by manually keyframing the Corner Pin effect – sometimes this is your only choice.

After you have successfully tracked the old sign and corner-pinned on our new one (which says "Your Name Here" in French), you might notice it looks a bit flat and artificial. The unspoken second half of every motion tracking job is making the new object look like it actually belongs in the original scene.

For clues, look at the sign on the original video clip. Notice it has some thickness and a shadow where it does not mount perfectly flush against the wall. Perhaps it would be best to simulate these in the new sign. Try a couple of the Perspective effects, such as Bevel Alpha and Drop Shadow. Eyedropper colors from the original scene and adjust intensities to help improve the blend. A little blur might help as well, to match the camera focus. Our attempt is included as [**Ex.06_final**]. As you can see, there's no one answer to making a tracking shot "work." But start to view these tasks with an artist's eye, and it will be easier to solve their puzzles.

In addition to setting up the Tracking Regions, think about where to place the Attach Points. The exact corners of the sign might not be a good idea, as the color of the sign bleeds into its surroundings (caused by the color undersampling inherent in DV). Remember to set the Attach Points out far enough that your new sign will cover this bleed.

Our improved version of this shot is in [**Ex.06_final**] and includes Bevel Alpha and Drop Shadow to help make the new sign look more real. Place them before the Corner Pin effect so they get the same perspective distortion as the shot animates. Good luck trying to duplicate the lighting effects...

Connect

The Anchor Point was first discussed in Volume 1, Chapter 5.

Motion Blur, which helps match an object with the natural camera blur in the original shot, was the focus of Volume 1, Chapter 9.

Blending Modes, which can help a tracked image appear to be "projected" onto another layer, were covered in Volume 1, Chapter 10.

Track Mattes, see Volume 1, Chapter 12.

The basics of animating effects were described in Volume 1, Chapter 21.

Setting up the Motion Tracker/Stabilizer engine was covered in Chapter 15.

Techniques for integrating 3D renders with After Effects are discussed in Chapter 19.

 Integration 101

Going beyond the simple exchange of rendered movies and images.

After Effects can read and write a large variety of movie and still image file formats. Beyond this, After Effects has the ability to import a number of other project files, often converting them into compositions. These comps contain the sources that made up the original project, arranged in the same order by layers or in time.

Once you're inside After Effects, you can alter, tweak, and enhance this arrangement. This allows you to use other tools to extend what After Effects can do, or use After Effects to offload some of the work you might otherwise have to redo in another program. It also allows you to shift the workflow to the best tool for the job. For example, you may find it quicker to use a dedicated editing package to edit together a sequence of clips, but you can then use After Effects to come up with composites and effects that would be difficult or impossible to achieve in your editing package.

What's Possible

Unfortunately, there is no one universal file format for media creation that covers editing, compositing, 3D, and everything else we creative types may want to do. Even more unfortunate is that there usually is not a dominant project file format inside any one field, such as a universal 3D project. As a result, integrating After Effects with other applications is mainly a case-by-case affair. That said, here's an overview of what can be done (and why you might want to do it):

Layered Artwork: Adobe Photoshop and Illustrator allow users to separate elements or groups of elements onto their own layers, and to save this arrangement. After Effects can import these layered files and create a composition that maintains this arrangement. You can then turn individual layers on or off, process them with effects, and animate them inside After Effects. This was also discussed in Chapter 2 and 3.

Editing Timelines: You can export projects from several major nonlinear editing (NLE) systems as well as Apple's Motion, and import this into After Effects. The resulting comp maintains all of the layering, timing and trimming of your edit, and in some cases reconstructs the simpler transitions and effects. This allows you to create a rough cut in the other

QuickTime Integration

When a company mentions that it features "QuickTime integration" with After Effects, what it usually means is it can read and write QuickTime files…and that's it – no special project files are supported.

system, then use After Effects to create more complex composites and animations. You also get access to the full untrimmed media so you can tweak the edit in After Effects without needing to go back to the NLE.

3D Camera Moves: It is often possible to get camera data from a 3D program into After Effects. This allows you to add layers in After Effects on top of an already-rendered 3D scene, and have these new layers experience the same perspective distortion as the camera flies around them. In some cases, it is also possible to get individual render properties or mattes into After Effects, making it easier to modify or color-correct a specific item in an overall scene without making a trip back to 3D.

Web Integration: Vector-based layers (for example, type, solids, masks, and Illustrator layers) can be exported to the Macromedia SWF format as vectors, with unsupported features exported as JPG. After Effects can also import and rasterize a SWF file.

DVD Buttons: After Effects can save layered PSD files – with special layer name prefixes – to be imported as buttons in Adobe Encore DVD. (This was discussed in Chapter 2.)

Importing Projects

The most common way After Effects integrates with other programs is by importing their projects. But before you can import, you have to export.

Inside the other applications, you will usually need to export to a special file other than the app's normal project format: For example, from Avid you need to export an OMF file; from Maya you need to save a .ma file. These options usually exist in a special Export menu or submenu item, rather than as an option in the normal Save dialog. Some applications do not normally export a format After Effects can read, so you need to purchase a third party plug-in or script. Examples of this include Automatic Duck's Pro Import AE to save an XML file from Apple's Final Cut Pro.

You can't count on all the information you need being saved in the project you export – for example, the OMF format does not contain Avid keyframes, and not all 3D applications save their camera's Angle of View information. Research the integration procedure ahead of time as described in the next three chapters, and make a list of additional information you will need to transcribe by hand before closing the donor app.

Some formats can be imported by all versions of After Effects (such as layered Photoshop and Illustrator files); some are supported only by the Professional edition (such as Maya projects); Premiere Pro is supported only in the Windows version. In many cases, you will need to get a

Half-Baked

There are occasions when you need to prerender or "bake" portions of your project before importing into After Effects, such as creating a keyframe for every frame of a camera move, or prerendering otherwise realtime effects in your NLE.

Click on the Enable popup in the Import dialog to see a list of supported file formats. If you've installed any special import plug-ins from a third party, they should appear here as well.

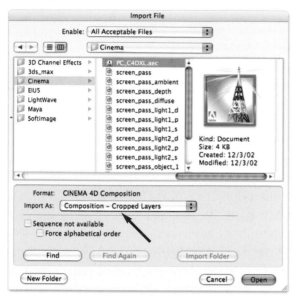

When After Effects recognizes a format it can import as a composition, the Import As popup can be set to Composition. Make sure the Show popup at the top is set to All Acceptable Files to prevent supported formats from being blocked.

special import plug-in from a company's web site or its installer CD. And again, there are times when you will need to buy a third party plug-in to read additional formats (such as Automatic Duck's Pro Import AE for OMF project files).

To import a project, in most cases you will use the normal File>Import>File dialog. Make sure the Enable popup at the top of the dialog is set to All Acceptable Files; for confirmation of whether you have the correct import plug-in installed, click on this menu and see if your project format is mentioned on this list. When you have selected a supported file, the Format line below will change to the name of the file, and the Import As popup will either automatically change to Composition, or offer it as an option. Then click Open.

After Effects will then typically create a comp that contains its best shot at recreating the project or layered file, and a folder that contains all of the individual files used by that comp. This folder may also contain additional files not used in the comp but that nonetheless were saved as part of the project from the other application. (If you don't want to import these files, remove them before exporting the project.) There are some exceptions to this in the 3D world: For example, when you import a Maya project, all that comes in are the camera data and specially named nulls, with no other model pieces. It is also up to you to import the rendered 3D scenes.

In some cases, such as when you're combining After Effects and Adobe's Encore DVD in a production workflow, importing a project will be combined with the use of layered Photoshop PSD files. One suggested workflow is to start a DVD menu design in Encore, then from inside that program use Menu>Create After Effects Composition. Encore will save a layered PSD file of the menu elements and create an After Effects project that has these layers already imported and arranged in a composition. You could then animate these elements to create a movie that plays before the menu elements settle into place. Render this movie and bring it back into Encore, resolving into the menu's layout.

The Codec Chase

When you're importing editing projects, quite often the media used will require its own special codec so you can view it. If you don't have compatible hardware already installed on your After Effects workstation, you may need to obtain these codecs. You can usually download them from the hardware manufacturer's web site (be prepared to do some hunting). Check back often, as these codecs are often updated to match new versions of hardware, software, and operating systems, as well as provide bug fixes. The same holds true for project import plug-ins: New versions of an NLE or 3D application often require updated plug-ins to enable After Effects to read their new project files. Keep the old versions archived, in the event you need to read older media or project files.

High-End File Exchange

You cannot transfer projects between After Effects and high-end workstations such as those from Discreet and Quantel. However, you usually can exchange footage in the form of image sequences. In most cases, these files have the same dimensions as you would expect for D1 NTSC (720×486 pixels, lower field first) or PAL (720×576 pixels, upper field first).

An exception to this rule are Quantel NTSC systems. Their frames have an unusual format of 720×488 pixels, upper field first. When you're sending files to a Quantel, it is a bad idea to send it a different number of lines than it expects, as it might stretch the frames to match its desired size – messing up your fields in the process. A better approach is to use the AFX2VPB plug-in from FAN (www.fandev.com), which translates the Quantel's native .VPB files to 720×486 pixel lower-field-first media on the way in, and translates 720×486 lower-field-first renders to 720×488 upper-field-first VPB files on the way out.

Importing Data

There are occasions when integration does not come through a project file, but as data embedded in a render file or exported by a script. The primary need for this is importing camera data from 3D programs. For example, the 3D package 3ds max embeds its camera data inside each frame of a rendered RPF sequence. To get at this data, you need to import the sequence (not the 3D project) into After Effects, add this footage item to a comp, then use the Professional edition's Keyframe Assistant> RPF Camera Import on the resulting layer. If you are using LightWave 7.5, you need to use a third-party script to export the camera keyframes to a text file, which can then be opened, copied, and pasted into an After Effects camera. In yet another example, a third-party script for Softimage|XSI saves camera and light data as a Cinema 4D format .aec file, which can then be imported as a project into After Effects.

Exporting

There are a few cases in which After Effects can export useful data or projects as well. For example, you can create a set of transform keyframes in After Effects (as the result of a motion track, keyframe assistant, or expressions), select and copy them, then paste these into a bin in Media 100's 844/X to create a "filter stack" of keyframe data. This keyframe data can then be used inside its system.

After Effects can also export some file formats not otherwise supported in the Render Queue's Output Module, such as MPEG 4. These formats are found under the File>Export menu item. One of the more interesting file formats is SWF, which is often used for scalable web animations. This is discussed in more detail in Chapter 20.

Integration, by its very nature, is imperfect: If one program could do everything another could, there would be no need to integrate them; you would just pick one to work in. Rather than bang your head against what you can't do in the middle of a project, plan out ahead of time what you *can* do, and take advantage of that as the project progresses.

The SWF Settings export dialog.

Connect

Layered Photoshop files (including Encore DVD integration) was discussed in more detail in Chapter 2; importing layered Illustrator files was discussed in Chapter 3.

Integrating with nonlinear editing systems is the subject of Chapter 18.

Integrating with various 3D packages is covered in Chapter 19.

Exporting SWF files is the subject of Chapter 20.

PART 6
CHAPTER

Integrating with Nonlinear Editing Systems

Importing the timeline from Avid, Final Cut Pro, Media 100, and Premiere – as well as Motion – into After Effects.

...and Motion, too!

Timelines from Apple's motion graphics tool Motion may also be imported into After Effects. Although not an "NLE," it is also covered in this chapter.

Example Project

Explore the 18-Example Project.aep file as you read this chapter; references to [Ex.##] refer to specific compositions within the project file.
Note that this project also references the free Artbeats footage on this book's disc; copy this to your hard drive as well.

Although After Effects' editing tools are nothing to sneeze at, many still prefer a workflow in which they or a separate editor perform a rough edit in the nonlinear editing system of their choice (or perhaps start a project in Apple's Motion), then enhance this arrangement of clips inside After Effects. We'll discuss how to get your edit out of Adobe's Premiere Pro, Media 100's i, HD, and 844/X, various Avid systems, or Apple's Final Cut Pro and Motion into After Effects, including what will and won't come across in the translation.

Overview

Here's an overview of what you will need to do to get a timeline from your nonlinear editing system (NLE) or compositing software into After Effects:

• You will need to save the project from your software. In many cases, you will export a format that is different from its native project file.

• You then import the project into After Effects. In most cases, you will need to add a plug-in to After Effects to recognize this new project file format.

• The result in After Effects will be a composition that attempts to recreate your other software's timeline, and a folder that contains pointers to the source files it uses. This comp will have the clips in the right order with the correct in and out points, as well as handles for the unused portions of the media so you can retrim your edit points. Indications of transitions between clips will also be in the timeline, although quite often you will need to rebuild these transitions yourself.

Sounds easy. But of course, there is also a list of gotchas for you to be aware of as you go about this process:

• Don't forget to move all of the media used by your source project to the computer you are running After Effects on. This includes any rendered transitions (which are easily left behind). As many other programs use an absolute file reference system, once you move the clips to another computer, the correct links to them will be broken; be prepared to have to manually relink your footage in After Effects.

• If you try to load this project into After Effects on a computer that does not have your editing hardware installed, you will need a matching codec to read the media files that go with the project. You can usually find a link to these codecs on the support pages of the company that made the video card you are using; occasionally you may need to email them to get it (or copy it over from the computer that had the NLE installed).

• Don't expect any advanced transitions, titling tricks, realtime effects, behaviors, or other processing to make it across. In most cases, all that can be recreated automatically are dissolves, pushes, and in some cases simple transforms plus blending modes.

Overall, this workflow is not suited to finishing an edit in your NLE, and then adding a touch of fairy dust in After Effects. In all cases, you cannot load your After Effects project back into your NLE. This work-flow is better suited for projects you know you are going to execute in After Effects, but want to do a rough pass of first in your NLE. It is also helpful for occasions when you have a section of an overall edit that could use enhancement – export just that portion of your timeline, work your magic in After Effects, and render a movie or series of frames to import back into your NLE.

Adobe Premiere Pro

As you might expect, some of the best integration available is between Adobe's own applications: After Effects 6.5 and Premiere Pro 1.5. If you use the Mac platform, you're out of luck, as Premiere Pro runs only on Windows, and the Mac version of After Effects cannot import its files. If you're on the Windows platform, you're in for a treat. Numerous features are supported or translated, including:

• Premiere Pro sequences are translated into Adobe After Effects compositions, including nested sequences.

Codec Conundrum

If you run After Effects on a computer other than the one that has the NLE installed, you will need a codec that matches the NLE's hardware to read its files. Through lack of foresight, some companies make this available only to registered owners of their hardware; try to get a copy from the NLE computer or owner.

AAF Import

A new standard is emerging for exchanging timeline and sequence information: AAF (Advanced Authoring Format). After Effects 6.5 has the ability to import AAF files; Premiere Pro can export AAF (select the sequence and use Project>Export Project as AAF); there is also a plug-in for Final Cut Pro to export as AAF.

AAF is an evolving specification, and support within After Effects will no doubt evolve over time. If you have another path – such as OMF files from Avid or XML files from Final Cut Pro (both used through Automatic Duck's Pro Import AE), or import-ing a Premiere Pro project into the Windows version of After Effects – use it, as you will probably find

more features supported. On the other hand, AAF is the only way to get a project from the Windows-only Premiere Pro into the Mac version of After Effects.

To try AAF for yourself, type Command+I on Mac (Control+I on Windows) and select **AEImport.aaf** from the **18_Chapter Sources** folder. Relink the missing footage in the **AEimport.aaf** folder that appears on the Project window, open **[simple edit]**, and compare the results with **[simple edit]** inside the **Ex.01** folder: You will find that some features, such as project folders, layer markers, text layers, and solids are not supported, and that all layers are left at Draft Quality (rather than Best), but simple transforms and crossfades are indeed imported successfully even at this early stage of AAF implementation.

When you import a Premiere Pro project into After Effects, the project folder hierarchy is maintained. Color mattes and type layers are converted into solids in After Effects.

- Project folder hierarchies are maintained (good if you organize clips into bins).

- Photoshop layers and PSD sequences convert as if you had imported them directly into After Effects.

- Clip markers are translated to layer markers.

- Motion properties in Premiere Pro (such as Position, Rotation, Anchor Point, et cetera) translate to their corresponding transform properties in After Effects.

- Cross Dissolves translate to Opacity keyframes for the affected layers.

- Volume and Channel Volume audio filters in Premiere Pro are converted to the Stereo Mixer effect.

- Frame Hold in Premiere Pro is translated to Time Remap keyframes.

- The Crop video filter is converted to a layer mask.

- After Effects plug-ins applied to clips in Premiere Pro are maintained when imported into After Effects.

The normal procedure to bring a project from Premiere Pro into After Effects is to save it as normal in Premiere Pro, then use Control+I to import it into After Effects (again, Windows version only). After Effects will then present you with a dialog asking if you want to import an indi-

Individual sequences in Premiere Pro (above) are converted into After Effects compositions (below). Edits, transform properties, and After Effects plug-in effects come across intact; text layers are replaced with solids and must be recreated inside After Effects.

vidual sequence or the entire project. The dialog also has an option for whether to import audio.

To see an example of a project imported from Premiere Pro, in this chapter's Example Project file twirl open the folder **Ex.01-Premiere Pro Import**. The **Sources** folder contains a series of subfolders we created for our media in Premiere Pro; twirl these open and relink the footage by double-clicking on the clips and finding them on your drive (the video content is in the **Free Footage>Artbeats>NTSC>Clips** folder). Type and Color Matte clips (which we originally stored in the **Generators** folder) are translated into solids and placed in the folder with the same name.

The comp [**simple edit**] relates to the single sequence we had created in Premiere Pro. Double-click it to open it; if the layers are not already twirled open, select all, type U to see their keyframes and Shift+E to reveal their effects. On the plus side, Position and Opacity keyframes came across fine, as did the markers on the audio track. On the downside, the text layer – **as night.prtl** – was translated into a simple black solid (albeit with its Position and Opacity keyframes intact); you need to recreate the text, as well as any fancier transitions or Premiere Pro-specific effects. (If you have Premiere Pro 1.5 or later, open **AEimport.prproj** to compare.)

The integration between After Effects 6.5 and Premiere Pro 1.5 goes beyond just importing a project: Essentially all the features supported for project import are also supported for copying and pasting between the two applications (yes, you can also paste from an After Effects timeline into a Premiere Pro sequence), including transform properties and After Effects-compatible effects. Clips edited in a Premiere Pro sequence can be copied and pasted directly into an After Effects comp, allowing Premiere Pro to be treated as a capture-and-trim module for After Effects.

Media 100 i/HD

Media 100 i and HD software has an Export to After Effects menu option, which creates a special .M1A project file. To import this file, first you need to get the free M100ProjectImporter plug-in for After Effects from Media 100 (available at support.media100.com). The installer should place it in the folder **After Effects>Plug-ins>Standard>Format>fpf**. Make sure you get the latest version of this plug-in, as it is updated with each major release of the Media 100 i or HD software. Also install the Media 100 Transcoder to ensure you have the special Media 100 QuickTime codec.

When you import a .M1A file, a comp and a folder will be created in your After Effects Project window with the same name as the .M1A file. The folder holds all of your footage pointers. The comp reconstructs the Media 100 sequence by placing all of the edited clips end to end in the After Effects Timeline window, then places on top of this layers for the prerendered Media 100 transitions. This means if you don't change the edit points, you don't need to recreate the transitions; if you do, the entire length of each source clip is available in After Effects to slip edit or retrim. However, the Media 100 system will not automatically prerender any clips that have realtime ColorFX applied to them; the manual gives

Missing Link

Double-click any missing item (*italicized name*) in the Project window and relink it to the source on your drive – other missing footage in the same folder or hierarchy should be found at the same time.

Reference Copy

Many transitions, text elements, and effects will not translate from your NLE into After Effects. Ask to get a rendered version of the project for visual reference, in addition to the project file.

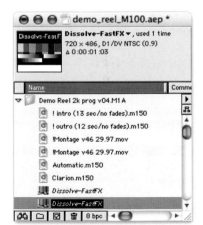

When After Effects loses the link to footage files, they appear as color bars. Use File>Replace Footage>File to relink each item manually. This is made trickier by Media 100's naming convention for transition items.

Demo Reel 2k prog v04.M1A • Timeline

Demo Reel 2k prog v04.M1A

0:00:41:28 (29.97 fps)

Layer Name
▷ ☐ 1 Dissolve-FastFX
▷ ☐ 2 Dissolve-FastFX
▷ ☐ 3 Sun JavaOne 3D.m150
▷ ☐ 4 Swarm.m150
▷ ☐ 5 TwoWayTV room.m150
▷ ☐ 6 QAD 2k data1.m250
▷ ☐ 7 QAD 99 Auto2.m150
▷ ☐ 8 Xearth out.m150

Switches / Modes

Mask ▶
Quality ▶
Switches ▶
Transform ▶
3D Layer
Guide Layer
Blending Mode ▶

Effect ▶
Keyframe Assistant ▶

Open Effect Controls
Open Footage
Reveal Layer Source in Project
Reveal Layer in Project Flowchart View
Reveal Expression Errors

Create Outlines

Track Motion
Stabilize Motion

Invert Selection
Select Children

To relink the correct transition footage file, look at the Timeline window to verify the names of the layers it is transitioning between, context+click on them, and select Reveal Layer Source in Project (right). Then find the file that has the transition's source layers in its name (below).

Replace Footage File (Dissolve-FastFX)

Enable: All Footage Files

_demo reel Media

Name	Date Modified
Greatest w/intro audi.M1QA.a1.2	6/12/00
OmegaCode/D1(lossless).mov.M1QV	4/19/01
PromoClosev1.17 D1/L.voo.M1QV	4/19/01
PromoOpenv1.19 D1/L.voo.M1QV	4/19/01
QAD 2k /QAD 99 –Dissolv–100KB	4/19/01
QAD2001 liftoff proff v10..M1QV	4/19/01
QAD2001 puzzleproof v14.vo.M1QV	4/19/01
RoboTV@final.voo.M1QA.a1.1	4/19/01
RoboTV@final.voo.M1QA.a1.2	4/19/01
RoboTV@final.voo.M1QV	4/19/01
Simptopia (w/ credit).M1QA.a1.1	6/12/00

Format: QuickTime Movie
Import As: Footage

☐ Sequence not available
☐ Force alphabetical order

Find   Find Again   Import Folder

New Folder   Cancel   Open

Illuminating Footage

The Media 100 i, HD, and 844/X codecs use the reduced "601" luminance range, not the full range After Effects expects. You may need to stretch the luminance range of these clips on input, and compress it again upon rendering. See Chapter 24 for more details.

you instructions on rendering just these clips and swapping them into the After Effects project.

The tricky part comes in linking the footage back in. If you moved the project to another machine, its links will probably be broken (exhibited by appearing as color bars in the After Effects project); you will need to relink all of the source clips one by one. And then come the transitions: The After Effects project shows a missing file named after the Media 100 plug-in that created the transition (such as **Dissolve-FastFX**), but the file's name on the hard drive is whatever the Media 100 system autonamed the transition when it prerendered it (such as **QAD 2k/QAD 99-Dissolv-250KB**). To resolve these names, you have to follow this procedure for each transition in the comp:

• Check the names of the layers this transition layer is creating a transition between (in our example in the figure on the next page, layer 6 is called **QAD 2k data1.m250** and layer 7 is **QAD 99 Auto2.m150**).

• Context+click on this transition layer (in this example, that's layer 1, **Dissolve-FastFX**), and select the option Reveal Layer Source in Project, which will select the corresponding footage item in the Project window.

• To relink this footage item, type Command+H on Mac (Control+H on Windows) to open the Import File dialog, navigate to the folder that holds the transitions, and find a file that contains the names of the clips this transition bridges followed by the name of the transition (such as **QAD 2k/QAD 99-Dissolv-250KB**).

If the person who gave you the Media 100 project and media forgot to also give you the transition files, you will have to rebuild them manually in After Effects. The other main gotcha to watch out for is that if you had two mono audio tracks panned left and right to create stereo in the Media 100, you will need to repan them in After Effects using the Audio Levels controls or Stereo Mixer effect.

Media 100 844/X

Media 100's high-end system offers some of the best integration of any NLE with After Effects. It is also currently the only one that gives you a path to get keyframes from After Effects back into their NLE.

When you install the 844/X software, you have the option of also installing a special project import plug-in for After Effects. If you intend to read these projects on a computer other than the one the 844/X is installed on, you will need to copy this plug-in to the **After Effects>Plug-ins>Standard>Format** folder on your After Effects workstation. Save a program (your current timeline sequence in a session), and import that program – not the entire session – into After Effects. A folder will be created in the Project window that contains the footage used as well as a comp that reconstructs the edit.

As with the Media 100 i and HD systems, all clips with their in and out points will be brought in, as well as rendered transitions to bridge them. However, realtime effects will not be recreated in After Effects; you will need to prerender them in the 844/X.

With the 844/X, a number of advanced features are also successfully imported into your After Effects project:

• Subcomps in the 844/X are linked as nested comps in After Effects.

• Blending modes are honored (although keyframed changes to blending modes are not; you get the first one selected).

• Alpha channels in the 844/X are actually separate luminance matte files. Importing a program that has alpha channels will be reconstructed in After Effects using Luma Track Mattes. They are even parented together for you.

• Transform keyframes (Anchor Point, Position, Rotation, Scale, and Opacity) come across from the 844/X into After Effects keyframes.

Dual Mono

If you import a stereo audio track into an NLE (such as Media 100 or FCP), it will often be separated into two mono tracks, panned left and right. When you import this into After Effects, you may get two copies of your original audio clip, without panning applied to its Levels – resulting in signal overload as the audio gets doubled up. To deal with this, set the Left Level on one and the Right Level on the other to –96dB (0%) as we have in **[Ex.03]**.

When you import an 844/X project into After Effects, edit points as well as nested comps, transform keyframes, blending modes, and alpha channels (in the form of track mattes) are maintained.

After you create keyframe data in After Effects – say, as the result of a motion track – copy it from the Timeline, and paste it into an 844/X bin to create a Filter Stack. Then drag this Filter Stack to the Geometrics property of a clip in the 844/X. Footage courtesy Hot Lemonade Productions and Media 100.

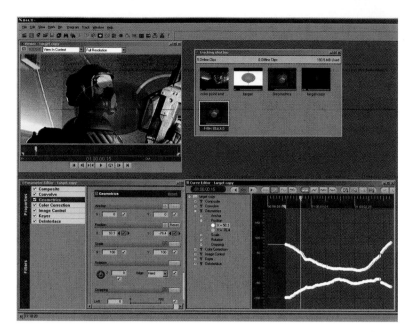

In the Details...

Detailed instructions on using the 844/X and After Effects together – including viewing your Comp window through the 844/X's hardware, and other tricks – may be found in a white paper on Media 100's web site (www.media100.com/pdf/workingwithae.pdf).

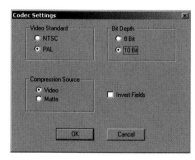

When you're rendering a movie with an alpha channel for the 844/X, save it as separate video and matte passes by using two Output Modules for the same render. Make sure you set the Compression Source in the Codec Settings to match, and append "**-v**" or "**-m**" to the file name for video and matte passes, respectively.

- If you are working on an anamorphic widescreen project, all footage will be properly tagged in their Interpret Footage dialogs; the comp will also be tagged with the correct pixel aspect ratio.

Giving Something Back

What sets the 844/X apart from other NLEs with regards to After Effects is the ability to transfer something more than QuickTime movies from After Effects back to the NLE. If you create transform keyframe data in After Effects – such as the result of a motion track or stabilization, keyframe assistant, or "baked" expression – select them in the Timeline window, and Copy. Then switch to the 844/X, context+click in the Bin window, and Paste. This will create a new Filter Stack that contains the keyframe data. You can then drag and drop this Filter Stack onto the Geometrics property of a clip in the 844/X.

When you render a file with an alpha channel from After Effects to be imported back into the 844/X, it is best to do it as two separate files: one for the RGB information, and one for the alpha channel, which will serve as a luma matte. Do this by using two Output Modules for the same render (as originally discussed in Chapter 1). When you're choosing the 844/X codec, click on the Options button, and in the Codec Options set the Compression Source button for Video or Matte, depending on which pass you are setting up. Set the Channels popup in the Output Module for the matte pass to RGB (not Alpha as you might expect). Render these two passes to the same folder, and give them the same name with the addition of "**-v**" for the video pass and "**-m**" for the matte pass. This way, when you import one into the 844/X, it will automatically find the other and treat it as one clip with an alpha channel.

Pro Import AE

If you want to import timelines from Apple's Final Cut Pro (FCP) or Motion, or an Avid ABVB, Meridien, or Xpress DV system, there is an excellent one-stop solution: Automatic Duck's Pro Import AE plug-in set.

A single installer places the plug-ins you need in their respective folders on your drive. After exporting a project from Avid, FCP, or Motion, don't use the normal import shortcut in After Effects; use File>Import> Automatic Duck Pro Import. This presents you with a special import dialog with additional options such as whether to automatically separate fields, and how to handle audio. Pro Import AE will build you an After Effects comp that attempts to create the timeline as closely as possible, including the ability to retrim the footage if you had any handle left over. Layer names are also typically preserved.

Speed Blender

Pro Import AE translates clip speed changes into Time Remapping keyframes in After Effects. Enable Frame Blending for these layers for smoother motion.

A very nice feature in Pro Import AE is the ability to partially translate the Avid's Title Tool (MC 10 or later) and Marquee, or text in FCP or Motion, into a Text layer in After Effects. Stylings such as the font, position offsets, point size, and the like won't make it across, but at least all the words will. Also note that some features may require After Effects Professional: For example, Distort effects in FCP are recreated using the Professional edition's Corner Pin effect.

Pro Import AE does the best job we've seen of any of the importers of finding and automatically relinking the source media for you, even after they've been moved to different drives and folders. It will also transcribe across markers, and add its own markers to give hints about transitions and the like which it might not support.

For the remainder of this chapter, we will discuss individual details of how Pro Import AE 3.0 handles Avid, FCP, and Motion files. We encourage you to visit Automatic Duck's web site – www.automaticduck.com – to keep up on its ever-expanding list of supported features; its documentation is also excellent.

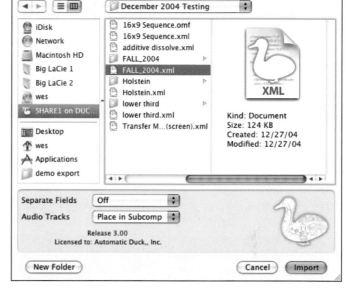

Pro Import AE has its own import dialog, accessed under File>Import> Automatic Duck Pro Import. It contains additional options on handling video fields and audio.

Avid

Avid systems are able to import and export Open Media Format (OMF) files. Although After Effects can read OMF media essence files, it cannot read OMF project files. Install Pro Import AE, and remove the OMF plug-ins that come with After Effects (Automatic Duck's documentation tells you how), and now you will be able to import OMF projects. To maximize compatibility, save your projects using OMF 2.0. Also, digitize your files as OMF media, not MXF.

Automatic Duck's Pro Import AE can take an Avid project (above) exported as an OMF project file and import it into After Effects, recreating its Timeline (below) and many of its basic transitions and layered effects.

Avid Codecs

Avid's QuickTime codecs can be hard to find on Avid's own web site. Automatic Duck keeps links to them at www.automaticduck.com/support

Pro Import offers a lot of niceties for Avid users. For example, collapsed or nested layers in the Avid are translated into nested comps in After Effects. Many Avid effects are also recreated in After Effects, including Dissolves, Superimpose, 3D Warps, Flops and Flips, X, Y, and Z-Spin, Matte Key, Submaster, Freeze Frames and Motion Effects. An improvement in Pro Import AE 3.0 over the earlier Automatic Composition Import plug-in is that PIP (Picture in Picture) and Superimpose effects get much better treatment, with Scale, Position, Opacity, Crop, Feather, and Rotation (in the 3D case) being translated.

Although OMF files traditionally have limitations in how they remember keyframes, Pro Import AE does a good job recreating proper keyframes inside After Effects for dissolves, PIP, 3D Warp, and several other effects. Also, if you have set up blending modes using the Profound Effects Transfer AVX plug-in (www.profoundeffects.com), Pro Import AE will preserve those modes in After Effects.

Final Cut Pro

Pro Import AE's support for Final Cut Pro is exceptional. After installing the plug-ins and building your sequence in Final Cut Pro 4.1 or later, use the command File>Export>Automatic Duck XML Export. Then in After Effects, use File>Import>Automatic Duck Pro Import (again, *not* the normal File>Import>File command), and select the XML file you just saved.

A good number of effects as well as the Motion tab's transform properties are translated successfully from Final Cut Pro to After Effects, including Dissolves, Flops and Flips, Crop, Feather, Scale, Position, Rotation, Opacity, and (if you have After Effects Professional) Distort – including their keyframes. Audio levels and keyframes are supported, as well as time-stretching and freeze frames. Final Cut Pro Composite Modes are converted to After Effects Blending Modes. Nested sequences are recreated as nested compositions inside After Effects. Layer names assigned in Final Cut Pro will come across into After Effects; pixel aspect ratios and alpha channel settings are also maintained.

As with Avid and Motion, Text Generators in FCP are translated into After Effects Text layers. You will lose styling details such as font and size, but you get the words; also, animation performed under the Motion tab

OMF File Support

After Effects 6.5 can import and export OMFI media essence files, as well as import AAF projects that reference OMF media files (but not OMF projects – you need Automatic Ducks' Pro Import AE for that). The OMF codecs Uncompressed, Avid AVR, Avid JPEG, JFIF, and DV are supported.

Silence!

Pro Import AE will not set Audio Levels in After Effects any lower than –48dB. If you want to fade an audio layer to silence, manually enter –96dB.

Embedded Projects

After Effects has an option in its Output Module that allows you to embed a copy of the project into the QuickTime movie it creates. That means if you later need to make changes to the movie After Effects rendered, at least you have a copy of the correct version of the project that rendered it (just the project file is embedded, not the sources).

This additional data is so small in comparison with most renders, it is not a bad idea to change your Output Module templates to always embed this file, rather than relying on your memory and good naming conventions to keep track of which version of your project created which movie. If file size is a consideration, at least choose the Link option, which will save a pointer back to the project (assuming you still have it on your hard drive).

When you render a QuickTime movie, you can embed a link to the project file that created it, or embed the project itself.

If you need to open an After Effects project that has been embedded in a rendered movie, make sure you set the Import As popup in the Import File dialog to Project; it defaults to Footage. Also, programs that have Edit Original commands – such as Premiere Pro – can use this feature to reference the project that created the movie.

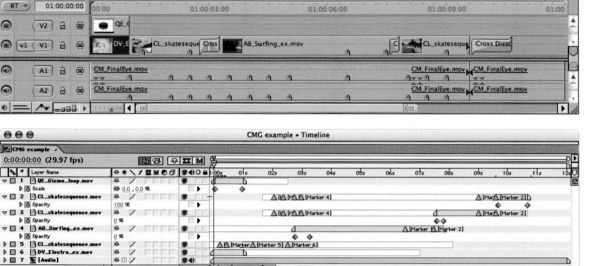

Automatic Duck's Pro Import AE does a very good job recreating a Final Cut Pro sequence inside an After Effects comp, including transform keyframes and blending modes.

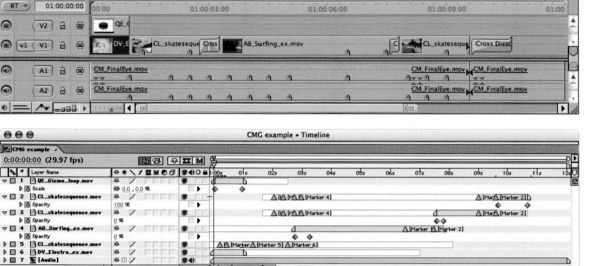

Motion 2

If you have Motion 2 installed, you can import a Motion 2 project file into After Effects, use it as if it were a rendered movie, and later use Edit>Edit Original to re-open the Motion project. To do this, either add .mov onto the end of your Motion project file before importing, or in the After Effects Import dialog, set Enable to All Files, select the Motion project, and then set Format to QuickTime Movie.

will come in just as if the text was a normal clip. You will still need to rebuild some effects such as fancier transitions. Final Cut Pro color mattes are replaced with After Effects solids without any color animation.

A significant new feature is that After Effects plug-ins applied in FCP will be translated into the After Effects project – with some restrictions, of course. The main limitation is that plug-ins must have their parameters in the effect tab; those that require custom user interfaces (for example, to enter text or crop a source) are not supported. Synthetic Aperture's Color Finesse is the exception to this rule.

To give you an example of what you might have to deal with in a real-world translation, a project that includes Scale animation, crossfades, and a blending mode has already been imported in the **Ex.02** folder. The **as imported** version has two issues: It lacks the Color Balance effect applied in FCP, and the dual mono tracks in FCP come in as doubled-up stereo files (see the sidebar *Dual Mono*). We've corrected these in the **fixed comps** folder.

Motion

One of the most intriguing new features introduced in Pro Import AE 3.0 is the ability to import projects from Apple's Motion. But before you get too excited, you have to accept that Motion and After Effects – although both motion graphics applications – are indeed very different animals, with different approaches to creating graphics.

First, the good news: Transformations such as Opacity, Position, Scale, and Rotation come across; so does Motion's Crop and Four Corner warp (the latter requiring After Effects Professional's Corner Pin effect). Markers are preserved, as are playback ranges and trimmings. If you

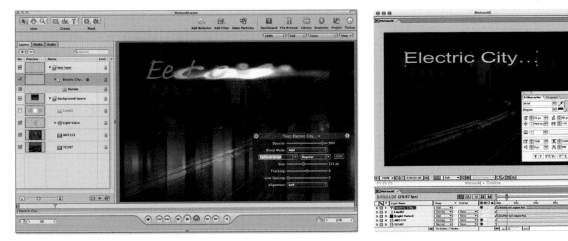

change the playback speed of a layer in Motion, the frame rate will be changed to match in its Interpret Footage dialog in After Effects. If you apply an After Effects compatible filter to a layer in Motion, this will also be preserved in the resulting After Effects project.

As with Avid and Final Cut Pro, if you create a text layer in Motion, you will get the same text in After Effects, but none of the stylings such as font, position offset, drop shadows, outlines, or glows. And this is where the difference between the two programs starts to rear its head. For example, it is common to apply a Behavior in Motion to create interesting text animations; these will not be translated into After Effects. If a Behavior affects a simple transform property in Motion, try using its Object>Convert to Keyframes option and save it under a new name to see what you can salvage. In most cases, you may be better off isolating the affected layers in Motion, rendering them with an alpha channel, and bringing this render into After Effects instead of trying to recreate the animation.

Likewise, the Particle Generator in Motion is not supported in After Effects – again, render the layer in Motion and import it into After Effects (this is one approach to creating elements for use in After Effects projects). Fortunately, Pro Import AE gives you a warning dialog during the import process for every unsupported behavior or particle. It also adds comments to stand-ins for these layers inside your comps so you know what you're missing, and where to swap in your pre-rendered effects.

Finally, layer arrangements in Motion are honored in After Effects, although Pro Import AE 3.0 has a tendency to flatten projects whenever it can (see its documentation for details); we expect to see the hierarchy more slavishly preserved in future versions. The biggest gotcha in 3.0 is that if you applied a Blend mode other than Composite to an overall Layer, in addition to the clips inside a layer, this combination will not be accurately recreated inside After Effects – you may need to do some pre-composing yourself. Otherwise, Pro Import AE does a great job preserving modes across the translation.

Pro Import AE allows you to import projects from Apple's Motion (left) into After Effects (right), but of course it cannot translate Behaviors and Particles unique to Motion – you will need to render these effects in isolation in Motion, and swap them in for their corresponding layers in After Effects. Footage courtesy of Artbeats, included in the **Free Footage** folder on your disc.

Connect

Relinking footage, see Volume 1, Chapter 6.

The Slip Edit tool, see Volume 1, Chapter 7.

Frame Blending, see Volume 1, Chapter 8.

Embedding project files into your renders, as well as other Output Module settings such as codec choices, were discussed in Volume 1, Chapter 29.

How to render separate RGB and Alpha at the same time was detailed in Chapter 1.

The Wiggler, and other Professional edition keyframe assistants, were in Chapter 5.

Mixing audio was discussed in Chapter 11.

For the Motion Stabilizer and Tracker, see Chapters 15 and 16, respectively.

Integrating with 3D Applications

Techniques to get more information from your 3D program into After Effects to aid with compositing, and the overall production flow.

Documentation

Search for "3D channel" in the online help file for additional information about 3D channel effects and files.

Example Project

Explore the 19-Example Project file as you read this chapter; references to [Ex.##] refer to specific compositions within the project file. Many of the examples require the Professional edition, but you can still view the others with the Standard edition.

3D programs are great, but they are often slow. This can become a source of frustration when you're accommodating client changes, or just trying out different looks. Offloading portions of the work from your 3D program to After Effects will save valuable time (and sanity).

In version 4.1, After Effects introduced the Professional edition's 3D Channel effects, which took advantage of additional information embedded in files rendered from certain 3D programs. With the introduction of 3D space in version 5.0, it became possible to import camera information (and in some cases, information about lights and null objects) from some 3D programs into After Effects for use by its own 3D layers.

In this chapter, we will explore strategies for integrating a variety of 3D programs – including Alias Maya, Autodesk 3ds max, Electric Image Universe, Maxon Cinema 4D, NewTek LightWave 3D, and Softimage|XSI – more tightly with After Effects. We'll start by covering the Professional edition's 3D Channel effects, providing Standard version alternatives where possible, and for 3D programs that are not directly supported. Quite often, the alternative is even more powerful!

We will then present a sample task – compositing video in After Effects onto a 3D videowall – and demonstrate different ways to tackle it, including specific instructions for a variety of 3D programs. This section will place particular emphasis on importing camera data from 3D programs into After Effects; it will also reinforce the techniques discussed in the 3D Channels section. Along the way, we'll uncover a whole host of gotchas and suggest ways to avoid them.

3D Channel Effects

Some 3D applications let you save information beyond just color and alpha channel when they render. For example, it is common to be able to save a *Z-depth* map which represents the distance of each rendered pixel from the 3D camera. You may save this as a separate file, or in the case of the RLA or RPF formats (supported by 3ds max and more recent versions of LightWave), embed it in the main render file. Other programs can save additional channels of information, such as what object or texture material is visible per pixel in the frame. You may hear these referred to as *auxiliary* or *G-buffer* information.

After Effects Professional's 3D Channel effects can access this information to allow additional processing such as selective proportional blur (for "depth of field" camera focusing simulations) or synthetic fog, or create a variety of mattes that can then be used for other effects.

3D Channel effects work only with specific file formats. The most flexible ones are RLA and RPF, which should contain color, alpha, and a large number of additional channels of information in one file. These files should be identified with the suffix *.rla* or *.rpf*.

Softimage and Electric Image users have direct access only to Z-depth information, which must be rendered into a file separate from the normal color + alpha render pass. In both cases, the resulting files should have the same main name, with different suffixes. For Softimage, the normal file must be tagged *.pic* while the Z-depth render must be tagged *.zpic*; for Electric Image, the main render is an Image file with a suffix of your choosing (normal is *.img*); the Z-depth file must use the suffix *.eiz*. When you import these files, make sure both are in the same folder, and import only the normal 3D render – After Effects will find the Z-depth file automatically.

When these files are imported and selected in the Project window, the additional channels they contain or reference will appear along the top of this window, just under the bit-depth information. (The exception is RPF sequences, although individual RPF frames display correctly.) They behave as normal color plus alpha footage items until you apply one of the 3D Channel effects to them. At that point, highlighting the effect in the Effect Controls window allows you to click on their image in the Comp or Layer windows and have the additional channel information displayed in the Info palette, which can be opened by typing Command+2 on Mac (Control+2 on Windows).

This information is very important: You will often have to set parameter ranges based on the information displayed in the Info palette, because it will vary from render to render. Set the ranges incorrectly (or leave them at their defaults), and most of the 3D Channel effects won't work very well. Z-depth is the most critical in this regard. Note that this feature works even if the effect is turned off (provided the effect's name is selected in the Effect Controls window), meaning you can view the uneffected image in the Comp window while you explore its 3D Channel values in the Info window. While the effect is enabled, leave the layer at Best Quality and view the Comp window at 100% or larger to get the best idea of what's going on.

3D Channel Extract

This effect creates a grayscale or simplified RGB image based on information in the 3D channels. This image can then be used as a luma matte to isolate a portion of a scene or blend in an effect, or as a "seed" for compound effects such as Blur & Sharpen>Compound Blur or third-party camera blur effects.

When a file has 3D Channel information attached, selecting it in the Project window displays the additional channels that are available underneath the Color information (with the exception of RPF sequences). This RLA file has numerous additional channels.

To find the range of a 3D Channel parameter, add the footage to a comp and apply any 3D Channel effect. Select the effect in the Effect Controls window click, and hold the mouse down on the footage in the Comp window. The active channel's parameter will be displayed for that pixel along the bottom of the Info window while the mouse is down.

The 3D Channel Extract effect can create a grayscale map from a variety of auxiliary channels.

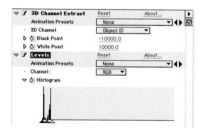

The defaults for Z-Depth Black and White Points results in a low-contrast matte (top). Find the lightest and darkest values, and type these values into the White and Black Points to maximize contrast (above).

Following 3D Channel Extract with Levels (top) allows you to more clearly see Object and Material IDs by spreading them across the full range of luminance values (above). Image by Shelley Green of Shetland Studios.

To practice using this effect, open the file **19-Example Project**, then the comp [**Ex.01a*starter**]. It contains one layer: a render from Electric Image named **CM_metropolis.img** which was imported with its associated Z-depth file **CM_metropolis.eiz**. Study the image in the Comp window, with an eye toward remembering which objects seem to be the closest to and farthest away from the viewer. Select this layer, and apply Effects> 3D Channel>3D Channel Extract. The Effect Controls window will open automatically. Note that the 3D Channel popup defaults to Z-depth, with the White and Black Point parameters active. The Comp window will show a washed-out grayscale version of the image; this is a default attempt to map out the different Z-depths present in this render.

With 3D Channel Extract selected in the Effect Controls window, and the Channel option set to Z-Depth, click once on various places on the image in the Comp window and note the readings in the Info window to find the nearest and farthest objects of interest. Enter these values as the White and Black Points, respectively (traditionally, white is used for nearby objects). We typically set the Black Point a little bit "farther back" than the last object so that this last object will be dark gray and stand out a bit from any holes in the background that might have distance of infinity (and therefore will be black); a good result is shown in [**Ex.01a_final**], where the Black Point is set to 1000 and the White Point is at 45.

The other options under the 3D Channel popup are for isolating additional information that may be embedded in RLA or RPF renders from 3ds max and LightWave. Open [**Ex.01b**], select the layer **SH_stairs**, and hit F3 to open its Effect Controls window. Experiment with the different 3D Channel options. With the 3D Channel Extract effect selected, click around the Comp window and note the values displayed in the Info window.

Unfortunately, you do not have Black and White Points available with these other options – they are translated directly to grayscale or raw RGB values. Still in [**Ex.01b**], select the 3D Channel option Object ID. This represents specific ID numbers you can assign to different objects in 3D programs such as 3ds max. The Comp window will display a very dark image; as you move the mouse over it, you will see luminance values in the range of 0 to 16 displayed in the Info window. Click in the image, and the Info window will display matching Object ID values. If this seems like probing around in the dark, turn off the effect (the stylized "f" icon); as long as the effect is still selected, you can still click on the image and see the corresponding 3D Channel values in the Info window.

How do you turn this information into a useful grayscale matte? By using a combination of Adjust>Levels and >Curves. Open [**Ex.01c**], select **SH_stairs**, and press F3. You will note that the 3D Channel Extract effect is followed with Levels. Note that in the Levels Histogram, all of the values are crowded down to the left. Drag the Input White arrow under the Histogram to the left and watch the Comp window: The gray values will now spread out across the entire spectrum. Change the 3D Channel popup to Material ID (which isolates textures, as opposed to objects) and repeat your experiments.

If you need to select a specific ID, you'll use the ID Matte effect which we'll look at later. However, if you need to select a range of IDs, you can follow 3D Channel Extract and Levels with Effect>Adjust>Curves. Now "peak" the curve to make your selected objects white and the rest black. [**Ex.01d**] is an example of creating a matte out of two sequential IDs. Select **SH_stairs**, hit F3, and look at the Curves effect, turning it on and off to get an idea of what it is doing. If you need to select multiple discontinuous IDs, you will need either a trickier Curves setting or multiple copies of the layer with different settings, along with the Add blending mode to blend them together to create your composite matte.

Some of the 3D Channel options you played around with in [**Ex.01b**] gave multicolored images. In these cases, each color channel – R, G, and B – represents the strength of a different parameter, such as the X, Y, or Z surface normals (the directions the polygon faces are pointing) respectively of your model pieces. To see this in action, back in [**Ex.01b**] set the 3D Channel popup to Surface Normals, and click (or Shift+click) on the individual red, green, and blue switches along the bottom of the Comp window.

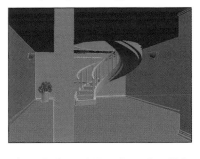

When 3D Channel Matte is used on RLA files and set to show Surface Normals (above), each color channel (see figures below) shows an axis of which direction the surface of an object is pointing – red is the X axis, green is the Y axis, and blue is the Z axis.

Blending this raw information can help you add extra lighting in After Effects to come from a particular angle and to fall "properly" on your rendered 3D object. For example, open

[**Ex.01e**], select layer 1, and hit F3 to open its Effect Controls. To add lighting that appears to come from above a scene (positive Y), we set 3D Channel Extract to display Surface Normals, isolated the green (Y) channel using Channel>Shift Channels, and used the resulting grayscale image (toggle the layer's Video switch temporarily on to see the matte). We used this as a luma matte for a cool blue solid (layer 2), which is composited onto a copy of the original image (layer 3) using Overlay mode. (Toggle the Video switch for layer 2 off and on to compare the scene with and without this treatment.) Scrubbing the Opacity of layer 2 adjusts the amount of blue light cast down on the original scene. Note that we added a Levels effect to layer 1; adjust its Gamma to alter the balance of how much light "spills" onto the side walls as well.

We used 3D Channel Extract to create a matte based on how much the surface of an object is pointing up, or in the Y direction (below left). This allows you to take an already-rendered 3D scene (below center) and selectively brighten it after the fact (below right) – in this case, down onto the floor, spilling onto the walls.

Apply Directly

3D Channel effects do not work when they are applied to precomps or to solids used as adjustment layers. Apply them directly to RLA, RPF, ZPIC, or EIZ format files.

When you're trying to composite a 2D layer – such as the gizmo here – into a 3D scene (left), use the Depth Matte effect to create an inverted alpha matte (right) to cut out the portions of the 2D layer that is supposed to be obscured by pieces of your 3D render. Gizmo by Lachlan Westfall/Quiet Earth Design.

A Focused Slider

With Depth of Field applied, click around the Comp window to get a feel for where your nearest and farthest objects are. Context+click on the Focal Plane value, select Edit Value, and set the Slider Range to match these limits. This slider will now be nicely responsive.

 **Depth Matte**

This effect looks at the Z-depth of a layer, and creates a binary on/off (as in front/behind) matte based on a Z distance you can set or animate. Think of this effect as creating a matte that can be used to cut out portions of an image to give it the illusion of being inserted in the middle of your 3D render, even though your new layer is being placed on top of the 3D scene.

To accomplish this, have an unaltered version of your 3D render as the back layer of a comp, then place on top of it the layer you want to insert in the "middle" of this render. Add a duplicate of your 3D render on top of that, and apply Effect>3D Channel>Depth Matte to this topmost duplicate. Set the Depth parameter to the distance you want your new

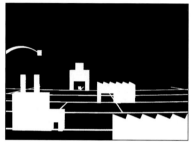

layer to appear. Whether you need to enable the Invert option depends on how your 3D program measures Z (do larger values mean closer to the camera, or farther away?). Then set that new, middle layer to Alpha Inverted Matte mode – it will now have sections matted out of it to make it fit into the layer underneath. This is illustrated in [**Ex.02a**]. While you're there, play around with the Depth parameter on the topmost layer to reposition the new, inserted layer.

If you have sharp eyes, you might notice there are some issues with aliased matte edges where the buildings overlap darker areas of the gizmo. This can be improved by using a double-resolution Z-depth render: see the next page's *Oversampling* sidebar. An example of this is demonstrated in [**Ex.02b**]. Note that the matte layer – **CM_metropolis_2z** (a double-sized Z-depth matte we rendered) – has been scaled 50%. But there is still some white fringing between the buildings and sphere, and Depth Matte's Feather parameter does not seem to help this. This fringe can be cleaned up by applying Effect>Matte Tools>Simple Choker to the topmost layer (the one with Depth Matte applied), and setting Choke Matte to somewhere around 1.0; try it yourself with this comp.

Depth Matte Alternative

If you are not using Electric Image, Softimage, or a program that can render an RLA or RPF file, or if you do not have the Professional edition, there is another way to get the same result. To do this, you must render a separate Z-depth matte for your scene. Then use this separate render as an inverted luma matte, rather than as an inverted alpha matte. Instead of 3D Channel>Depth Matte, apply Adjust>Threshold to the matte layer. The threshold value now works the same as your Depth parameter. This has been constructed in [**Ex.02c**] for your inspection.

Oversampling

3D channel information gives an absolute value for each pixel, such as material #1 or #2. This often results in an aliased edge for the resulting matte. Rendering an image at least double size and scaling down in After Effects greatly improves these edges, at the cost of rendering time and disk space.

One strategy is to render your main color + alpha channel pass at normal size. Then render the special file with the additional 3D channel information at 2× or 4× size, using the fastest render options your 3D program offers. This will take less time to render than a full-quality image at this increased size. Import both into After Effects, apply 3D Channel effects to this second render, and scale it down (keeping Best Quality enabled) to match your normal render so the resulting images line up. This is essentially the same as when your 3D program oversamples the main render.

If you want to keep your normal render and your oversampled 3D channel render together and treat them as one file, there is a tricky procedure to do so using proxies. First, import your oversampled 3D

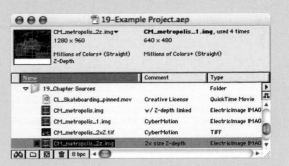

Channel render. With this file selected in the Project window, select File>Set Proxy>File. Choose your normal render as the Proxy. After Effects will scale up your image render to match the size of your special 3D channel render, but will still access the 3D channel information in your special render. You can treat the result as a single file; just remember to keep it at Best Quality and scale it down to fit your comp size.

An example of this is shown in this chapter's Example Project. Inside the **Sources>19_Chapter Sources** folder, you will see a file called **CM_metro-polis_2z.img**. Select it, and read the top of the Project window to see how they are linked together. The black square to its left turns the Proxy on and off.

Depth of Field

This effect creates selective "focus" based on the Z-depth information for a file, which can be animated to add drama. Open and RAM Preview [**Ex.03a**] to get a feel for the possible results.

Depth of Field will seem to do nothing when you first apply it to your own image. You have to set the Maximum Radius (blur amount) parameter to some number above 0. Also set the Focal Plane Thickness parameter to some number that represents a good slice of your total effective Z-depth range, or the effect will seem touchy, with only one value of Z-depth in sharp focus. Note that the Maximum Radius parameter directly relates to how large the source file is: If you created an oversampled Z-depth map and had to scale it down to 50%, you would now need twice as much blur for the same visual result.

Depth of Field can fake camera focusing effects on files with embedded Z-depth maps.

Whenever you're using a literal Z-depth map, aliased edges and the effect they have on the final image are always an issue. As always, using a higher-resolution Z-depth map helps. Compare the differences between the images in [**Ex.03a**] and [**Ex.03b**]: The latter uses a double-resolution map, resulting in the grid's metal bars looking sharper. (See the sidebar *Oversampling* for more details on how to create a higher-resolution map.)

Matte Edge Cleanups

A common problem you may have with the black and white mattes that result from slicing operations such as Threshold is that their edges won't be clean or smooth, or will extend slightly wider than you want, creating some unwanted fringing. The general solution is to "choke" the edges to erode away artifacts and reduce fringing. There are a couple of ways to go about this.

If you own the Professional edition of After Effects, the preferred approach is to use the Simple Choker effect. If your matte already has an alpha channel (possibly the result of applying Depth Matte), you can add on the effect Matte Tools>Simple Choker directly. If your matte is based on luminance information, first apply Channel>Shift Channels. Set the Take Alpha From popup to Luminance. The result is an alpha channel based on luminance information; this is important, because Simple Choker works on the alpha, not luminance. Then apply Effect>Matte Tools>Simple Choker. We've already built this chain for you in **[Ex.99a]**.

Positive Choke Matte values shrink the edges; negative ones expand the edges. Use the result as an alpha (not luma) matte for the layer you want to set into your final scene. To compare results, make sure the Threshold Level value is the same in **[Ex.02c]** and **[Ex.99a]**. In **[Ex.02c]**, press Shift+ F5 to save a snapshot. Then return to **[Ex.99a]**, using F5 to compare results. The images are similar, but if you study the building's peaks, you'll see an aliased fringe in **[Ex.02c]** (your snapshot) that is smoothed out in **[Ex.99a]**.

If you don't have After Effects Professional, an alternate approach is to apply Adjust> Levels to the matte layer, and increase the Input Black point until the fringe goes away. This approach blacks out the semi-transparent portions of the matte, starting with the darkest areas first, giving a choking effect. If you need to go the other direction and spread the matte out wider, decrease Input White instead. To further clean the edges, you can try increasing the amount of a blur effect placed before Levels,

Mattes derived from Z-depth renders tend to have aliased edges, even if you used a double-resolution map (above). Using a touch of blur followed by Matte Tools>Simple Choker helps clean this up (below).

and bringing both Levels' Input Black and Input White points inward to shape the edges. This is demonstrated in **[Ex.99b]**, and saved as **DepthSliceChoke.ffx** in the **Goodies>CMG Presets** folder. Note that you can use this result as a Luma Matte, rather than Alpha Matte.

Depth of Field Alternative

If your 3D program of choice does not create an embedded Z-depth map, you can achieve a similar look by rendering a stand-alone Z-depth file, treating it with Image Control>Colorama and Channel>Minimax, and using the result as a map for Blur & Sharpen>Compound Blur. This is demonstrated in [**Ex.03c**].

Open [**Ex.03c-DOF-1**], select **CM_screens_depth**, and press F3 to open the Effect Controls window. Turn off the Colorama and Minimax effects for now. What you see in the Comp window is a raw Z-depth map, in this case rendered from Cinema 4D. In this map, white equals the closest pixels, and black equals the pixels farthest away. We need black to equal the pixels that are to be in focus, and white to equal the pixels most out of focus.

Turn on the Colorama effect, and twirl open the Output Cycle section. We have set up a cycle with white (out of focus) at the extremes, and black (in focus) in the middle. The spacing between the two black arrows defines the focal plane thickness. Click on the black and white arrows and drag them around the Output Cycle wheel, noting how the display changes. You can enable keyframing for Output Cycle, allowing you to animate your focus map.

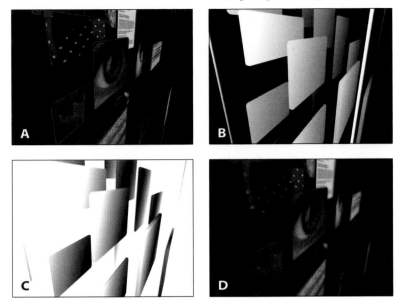

To add a depth of field blur to a 3D render (A), we need to take its Z-depth map (B), process it with Image Control>Colorama and Channel>Minimax (below) to remap black to the area to be in focus and white to the areas to be out of focus (C), and use the result to drive Blur & Sharpen>Compound Blur applied to the original image (D). Inset images courtesy Getty Images.

The black fringes around the objects are caused by remapping the color values of antialiased edges. Turn on the Minimax effect: When its Operation popup is set to Maximum (the default), it chokes in the black edges. We have saved this chain as Animation Preset **Z_to_DOF.ffx** in the **Goodies** folder on this book's DVD.

Now open [**Ex.03c-DOF-2**]. Our depth of field map in [**Ex.03c-DOF-1**] has already been imported as a precomp, but its Video switch is turned off – we don't want to display the image; we just need the grayscale information it contains. Select **CM_screens_rgba** and hit F3; note that Compound Blur has been applied, and that its Blur Layer popup has been set to **Ex.03c-DOF-1/map precomp**. Turn Compound Blur on and off to see the result of this effect. If you have enough screen real estate, drag these two Comp windows to be side by side (setting their Magnification to 50% may help), and play around with moving the Output Cycle arrows in [**Ex.03c-DOF-1**] while observing the results in [**Ex.03c-DOF-2**].

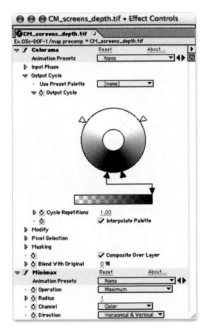

Frankly, we don't like the quality of the Compound Blur effect; it looks smudgy to our eyes. Better alternatives include SmoothKit's Gaussian from RE:Vision Effects (www.revisionfx.com), or Composite Wizard Super Rack Focus and Image Lounge TrueCamera Rack Focus available from Red Giant Software (www.redgiantsoftware.com). Note that you need to use three to five times higher blur values in these third-party effects compared with Adobe's Compound Blur to get the same amount of blur in the final image.

The Fog 3D effect allows you to choose a gradient (top) to use as a luma matte for the resulting fog (above). Procedural map from Pixélan's OrganicFX.

Fog 3D

Fog is another effect that relies on Z-depth information embedded in or linked to by a 3D render. In short, what it does is take a color of your choice and blend it into the 3D image with increasing strength as the Z-depth values increase in the file. The Fog Start Depth defines where the fog is at its thinnest; the Fog End Depth defines where the fog is at its thickest. Scattering Density can be thought of as a gamma correction curve that controls how quickly the fog thickens or thins along the Z axis. You can define the Fog Color; Fog Opacity acts as a "fog amount" control.

Open [Ex.04a], select **SH_stairs**, press F3, and experiment with these parameters to get a feel for how Fog 3D works (press the Shift key as you scrub Fog Start and End to edit in large increments). Atmospheric effects tend to add a very pale sky color to objects, not pure white; consider choosing a Fog Color that is tinted slightly.

This effect in its basic form can look very synthetic. To make it look more realistic, you need a Gradient Layer, which acts as a luma matte for the fog. Still in [Ex.04a], double-click **VS_oc Fog2 large** to open its Layer window: This is a complex gradient that travels from white at the top to black at the bottom, with a cloudy pattern in-between. Back in the Effect Controls window, change the Gradient Layer popup for Fog 3D to **VS_oc Fog2 large**, and note how the fog in the scene takes on a much more complex character. The Layer Contribution slider controls how strongly the gradient layer is used to matte the fog.

Even better is when this gradient layer animates. Consider using stock footage of drifting fog or smoke from companies such as Artbeats. Or you can use various fractal noise effects such as the Professional edition's Render>Fractal Noise. This has been animated in [Ex.04b-fog-1] to create a thick swirling fog matte (if its keyframes are not already visible in the Timeline window, select **fog solid** and type U to reveal them). Open [Ex.04b-fog-2], select **SH_stairs**, and if necessary type U to reveal its own keyframes. In addition to using an animated fog matte, we're animating the Fog 3D effect itself to make the fog (or smoke, in this case) appear to flow into the room. RAM Preview to see this in action; if the preview is too slow, type Command+Shift+J (Control+Shift+J) to go down to Half Resolution, and/or press Shift+RAM Preview to skip frames.

Unfortunately, like all 3D Channel effects based on Z-depth, the edges can appear a bit aliased – in this example, look at the cutout above the spiral staircase. Also, Fog 3D gets cut by the layer's alpha, which may give unexpected results – such as holes where there should be fog. The effect has a Foggy Back option, but it affects objects that are an "infinite" distance from the back – not objects that are cut out by the alpha. If you are using Fog 3D, you may need to make sure you render without an alpha channel, or at least plug up any "holes" in your models.

In Search of Z

For programs that won't render a Z-depth file directly, here's a time-honored workaround: Change the texture of all your objects to 100% matte or self-luminant white. Then fill the scene with black-colored fog, if possible set to start around the face of the nearest object, and reaching maximum density just beyond the back of the last visible object. Render this as a separate Z-depth map for your scene.

Fog 3D Alternative

The point of fog is to obscure objects as they get farther away from the camera. To simulate this, you can mix in a second layer using a Z-depth map as a luma matte. As noted previously, this second layer can vary from something as simple as a white solid to footage of actual swirling smoke and fog.

Recreating this is easy with standard effects, once you have your Z-depth layer. This is demonstrated in [**Ex.04c**]. Layer 1 – the Z-depth map – acts as an inverted luma matte for the "fog" layer (in this case, a pale blue solid – layer 2). The Opacity of the fog layer controls the maximum density of the fog. To recreate the controls available in the Fog 3D effect, apply Effect>Adjust>Levels to the Z-depth map: Input White Point becomes Fog Start Depth, Input Black Point becomes Fog End Depth, and Gamma becomes Scattering Density. All the caveats mentioned before about cleaning up the edges of the Z-depth matte apply here as well.

Unmultiply Black

When you're using footage shot against black for the fog texture, try Effect>Walker Effects> WE Premultiply (provided free on the DVD) with its Mode popup set to Unmultiply. This will create transparency where the footage is dark.

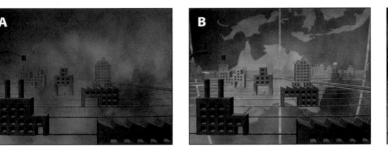

A separate Z-depth map can be used directly as a luma matte for a fog texture. Try different blending modes to blend the fog into the scene – here, we used Normal (A), Screen (B), and Color Dodge (C). Fog texture from Artbeats/Alien Atmospheres.

If you replace the fog solid with stock footage or an animated fractal, you may have issues with the darker portions of your fog layer darkening the underlying scene – as if you were mixing in black fog. One solution is to try different blending modes to apply the fog. In [**Ex.04d**], make sure the Modes panel is visible in the Timeline window (F4 toggles it). Double-click the fog layer – **AB_AlienAtmospheres** – to open its Layer window; note it is very dark overall. When it is blended into the scene using Normal mode, the continents in the background are obscured by these dark areas. Try Screen mode for layer 2; the continents become more visible, and the fog more luminescent. For a more vivid look, try Color Dodge, or experiment to taste.

Of course, you can extend this technique of treating the fog to get more stylized looks. An eerie glow effect based around a fog map is demonstrated in [**Ex.04e**]. Here we heavily blurred the Z-depth map (layer 1) to get the colored fog to wrap around the edges of the foreground buildings, rather than just sit behind them. We chose a deep gold color for the "fog" and blended it in using the Classic Color Dodge blending mode, which preserved the black background. Feel free to experiment with the amount of blur, color of the fog, and blending mode used. This will hopefully get you to start thinking about 3D not just to reconstruct reality, but to create some cool abstract or hyperreal looks.

Fog maps can be used for creative effects as well. Here, the fog map is blurred out, and gold "fog" is applied with the Classic Color Dodge blending mode, creating the progressive glow effect.

ID Matte

Imagine if a client, upon viewing your 72-hour render of a complex animation, told you, "It looks great, but could our logo be a little more blue?" One of the real powers of the RLA/RPF formats comes in tweaking colors of objects after the render. ID Matte allows you to isolate pixels in a render based on either their Object or Material IDs. Rather than creating a matte, it creates a new alpha channel for the layer it is applied to, leaving just the isolated material or object. If you need just a matte, use this layer as an alpha track matte for a layer underneath.

Comp [**Ex.05a**] contains our now-familiar room with the spiral staircase; it has a lot of IDs for you to practice with. Experiment with scrubbing the ID Selection value with the Aux. Channel popup set to Object ID, then Material ID; hold down Command (Control) while scrubbing for more control. Note how different parts of the scene are isolated when you do this.

The Use Coverage checkbox often helps clean up color fringing of selected objects. Still in [**Ex.05a**], toggle this option on and off while you're looking at different IDs. Be careful, though; you may find that some models actually introduce artifacts when this is turned on. For example, set Aux. Channel to Material ID and ID Selection to 3, and note how the edges along the ceiling and spiral staircase cutout become aliased when you toggle Use Coverage to On. Also be aware that, unfortunately, the Feather parameter can often cause more problems than it solves because it spreads the alpha channel beyond the object you are trying to isolate. Try using Matte Tools>Simple Choker to tame unruly edges.

[**Ex.05b**] shows one potential use of Material IDs: in this case, isolating and tweaking the colors of the walls and floor by applying Effect> Adjust>Hue/Saturation after a material has been isolated. Don't forget that you will need a copy of the original image behind everything, to fill in the spaces that are not altered.

The original room is nice (top), but the clients decide they prefer rosier tones. To accomplish this, we isolate the floor and walls using ID Matte and colorize them using Hue/Saturation (above) without having to rerender the image.

Reflecting ID

When a material reflects other objects in a scene, most 3D programs will assign the area of reflection to the ID of the reflected material – not the underlying material. This may require hand-masking the matte to fix.

ID Matte Workaround

Only a few programs – such as 3ds max and LightWave – offer the ability to embed Material and Object IDs in RLA or RPF files. And as noted, the edges in these files often have problems with aliasing. Therefore, quite often you will need to render your own special matte passes if you want to cleanly isolate a specific object or ID.

The best approach is to duplicate the objects or project file, set the texture for the object(s) of interest to 100% self-luminant or "matte" white, and everything else to 100% non-reflective or "matte" black. Render this scene, without raytracing or shadows, and use the result as a luma matte. Some programs (such as Maya and Electric Image) have the ability to set objects to cut holes in the alpha channel created by that object, which can in turn be used as an inverted alpha matte. A bonus with either of these techniques is that the edges should be pretty smooth – at least as good as your 3D program creates. We will discuss how to execute these techniques for different 3D packages in detail later in this chapter.

Real-World 3D Integration

To give a better idea of how you would integrate the workflow between your 3D application of choice and After Effects, the rest of this chapter is devoted to tackling a sample project, and showing how you might tackle it in different 3D programs. (Incidentally, you don't need to own any of these 3D programs to complete the following exercises, though you will need the Professional edition for some of them as noted by the Pro icon.)

For this project, we have chosen the common task of having to map video in After Effects onto a 3D videowall or other similar surface. We have already created a scene in our 3D programs which consists of a videowall, the client's logo in front of the videowall, and additional logos behind. The camera animates around this scene. Because the job calls for us to map many different pieces of video onto this wall (to try out different edits, accommodate client changes, and produce a series of bumpers or promos with this same basic scene later), we will save a significant amount of time changing this video in After Effects rather than rerendering the 3D scene with a different texture map every time the video needs changing. To accomplish this, we need to figure out how to do the following:

• Match the 3D camera move so our video will move in After Effects as if it were originally rendered into the scene.

• Composite, matte, or mask the video so that it appears "between" the main logo and the videowall's face.

• Blend the video onto the face in a way that allows it to pick up the lighting and surface cues that appear in the 3D scene.

• Perform selective adjustments to the rest of the scene, such as blurring the logos in the distance.

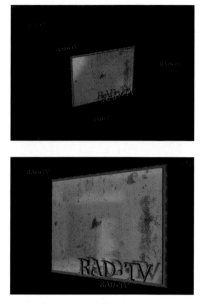

Our task is to map video onto the screen of this videowall, taking into account the camera move, shading that falls on the screen, and the fact that the main logo partially obscures it.

Importing a Camera Move

If you can't get the video in After Effects to follow the videowall's face, you won't be able to composite your new video in After Effects – which means you're stuck with long renders every time the video changes. Therefore, we'll tackle this problem first. We'll detail the procedures program by program, ending with what to do if your 3D program is not directly supported by After Effects. For each program, we'll break the process down into these steps:

Step 1: How to get the camera data out of your 3D program.

Step 2: How to get the camera data into After Effects.

Step 3: What else you need to do in After Effects to have your new video match the camera move in your 3D render.

In general, you will render a movie or sequence of frames as normal, import this into After Effects, create a comp, and add your render to this comp. A 3D camera will then be added to this comp – either manually by you, or automatically by the camera data import procedure. You can then add a footage item to this comp, enable its 3D Layer switch, and the

Free Textures

The surface textures and reflection maps used in many of these examples are included in the **Sources>Maps_Mattes_Spices** folder on your DVD. They are excerpted from dvGarage's Surface Toolkit and Reflection Toolkit texture libraries (www.dvgarage.com).

An Army of Help

Invaluable help in researching the various 3D programs discussed in this chapter was provided by the Pixel Corps: the training, research, and "think tank" arm of dvGarage (www.pixelcorps.com). The primary work was performed by Chris Bator, Dave Carness, Mike Kelleher, Fred Torres, and Tim Schaller, with additional contributions from Terrance Holmes, Zack Klinger, and Scott Krehbiel. Thanks to old friend and dvGarage founder Alex Lindsay for coordinating this.

Also, a huge tip of the hat to Bill Hinkson and Jim Altier of Reject Barn (www.rejectbarn.com), who provided the Softimage expertise; Shelley Green of Shetland Studios (www.shetlandstudios.com), who created the original RLA test files; Rob Birnholz of Absolute Motion Graphics (www.absolutemotiongraphics.com) for exposing some Electric Image issues; and René de la Fuente and Will Scates of The Cellar Door Experiment (www.thecde.com) for Maya import advice. Scripting guru Al Street (www.ats-3d.com) provided solutions to LightWave-specific problems.

camera will fly around your new layer. Note that you leave the 3D Layer switch *off* for your 3D renders: They have already had the camera move rendered into them, so there is no need to fly around them a second time.

If you can plan ahead, there are several things you can do that will make life easier while you're trying to match the camera move:

- If possible, construct your 3D set so that the face of the videowall has the same dimensions in "world units" as the video you intend to apply to it later in After Effects. It is good to err on the small side so you can have some extra pixels outside the safe areas in the video to crop off later. This has been done for some of the examples in this chapter; that's why we can leave the video at 100% in most cases. If this didn't happen in your project, write down the size of the videowall's face so you know how big you need to make your video layer in After Effects.

- Unless you have Maya and remembered to set up a null where your new video is supposed to go, also write down the position of the object in your 3D application that you wish to replace with a 3D layer in After Effects. Detach this model piece from all nulls or effectors to get its true position in world space.

- Note the camera's angle or field of view (FOV): Again, unless you have Maya, this information does not always come across during camera data import. This is usually measured horizontally; be careful to note this as well, and set the Measure Film Size popup in the After Effects Camera Settings dialog to match.

There are also significant issues with frame rate, frame size, and pixel aspect ratio we'll discuss as we go along. In short, you're better off if you can render to a square pixel file, at the exact rate you will need later for playback – 29.97 fps (frames per second) for NTSC video.

Alias Maya

After Effects can import camera data as well as the position of any properly named nulls in a Maya project. Therefore, a good working practice is to create a "locator" null that has either **NULL** or **null** in its name, place it exactly in the center of the object that will eventually receive your video (such as the face of our videowall here), and attach that object to your new null. Also make sure you create and animate a "rendering" camera in Maya, as After Effects ignores orthographic and perspective cameras.

Step 1: Render your scene as an IFF sequence. Select Edit>Keys>Bake Simulation to create keyframes for every frame of your animation. To save space and import time, streamline the project by removing any geometry you don't need to bring into After Effects (anything not connected to the camera or your specially named nulls), as well as any static channels. Save this file as its own .ma (*not* .mb) project file.

Step 2: Import your render into After Effects, and if necessary conform its frame rate in the File>Interpret Footage>Main dialog to your final output frame rate (in our case, 29.97 fps). We have already done this for you; we have also placed the files inside the Project window folder **Ex.11-Maya**.

Select this folder and Import the Maya camera data as a composition: Type Command+I (Control+I) and navigate to the file **19-Example Project>19_Chapter Sources>Maya>Maya_camera.ma** on your DVD. Note that below the file list in the Import File dialog, the Format is listed as Maya and the Import As popup has been automatically set to Composition. Click Open, and a comp will be created named [**Maya_camera**]. Double-click it to open it.

There will be three layers: **nullShape**, **cam_null**, and **camera_Shape1**. If the Parent panel is not visible in the Timeline window, type Shift+F4 to reveal it. Note that **camera_Shape1** is parented to **cam_null**; the depth of this parenting chain depends on how you have set up your camera in Maya (for example, as a one-node or two-node camera). Select all the layers, and hit U to reveal keyframes: Note that **cam_null** is doing the animating; the camera (**camera_Shape1**) is going along for the ride.

Step 3: Back in the Project window, select the sequence **PC_Maya_main** from the **Ex.11** folder, and type Command+/ (Control+/) to add it to your comp. Then locate the footage item **Sources>Movies>CL_Skateboarding _ramp**, select it, and type Command+/ (Control+/) again.

In the [**Maya_camera**] composition, enable the 3D Layer switch for **CL_Skateboarding_ramp**, and note how it snaps to the videowall – but isn't quite lined up. Select **nullShape** (the null in the Maya project that represents the videowall face), type P to reveal Position, click on the word Position, and Copy its value. Then select **CL_Skateboarding_ramp** and Paste, transferring the null's position to the new footage. (If you forget to create this null in Maya, you will need to write down its coordinates in Maya's world space. Units in Maya 6 and later should translate directly to After Effects units in pixels; earlier versions of Maya may require some translation, such as dividing by 2.8346, with an optional multiplication by 10 to make up for centimeters/meters differences.)

To Null or Not

Many Maya users parent their cameras to a null, and animate the null. However, some have reported better camera matches in After Effects if the camera was animated directly.

Steps 2–3: The comp created by importing the Maya project contains a null to show where the screen is positioned (layer 3), a null which is the parent for the camera (layer 4), and a camera (layer 5). Add to this your 3D render (layer 2) and your new footage (layer 1), enable the 3D Layer switch for your footage, and copy the screen's Position to your new footage (below). The result is the new video tracking the rendered videowall (above). Footage courtesy Creative License.

```
●●●                    Ex.11a_Maya camera • Timeline
 Ex.11a_Maya camera
 0:00:00:00  (29.97 fps)                    ⊠ ⊘  ⊕ ☰ M
  ▏ #  Source Name          Parent          ⊕ ✱ ＼ ƒ ☰ M ◉ ⊡  ◉ ◁ ○ ⌂  :00f    10f    20f    01:00
 ▽ □ 1  ▤ CL_Skateboarding_ramp....  ◎ None  ⊕  ╱        ⊡   ◉
    ›  ⏱ Scale                        ◎      ◎ 3.5 , 3.5 , 3.5 %      I
 ▷ □ 2  ▤ PC_Maya_main_[1–30].iff ◎ None    ⊕  ╱           ◉
 ▷ □ 3  □ nullShape          ◎ None          ⊕ ⬚ ╱       ⊡   ◉
 ▽ □ 4  □ cam_null           ◎ None          ⊕ ⬚ ╱       ⊡   ◉
    ▷ ⏱ Position                     -10.0 , 0.0 , -13.8        ◀ ✓ ▶
    ▷ ⏱ Scale                        ◎ 100.0 , 100.0 , 100.0    ◀ ✓ ▶
    ▷ ⏱ X Rotation                   0 × +0.0 °                 ◀ ✓ ▶
    ▷ ⏱ Y Rotation                   0 × +25.8 °                ◀ ✓ ▶
    ▷ ⏱ Z Rotation                   0 × +0.0 °                 ◀ ✓ ▶
 ▷  5  ☇ camera_Shape1       ◎ 4. cam_null   ⊕                  ◉
                              ◀▶              Switches / Modes         ◀▶  ▵ ◭       ◿
```

AOV = FOV

Most 3D programs use the term Field of View (FOV) to define their camera's zoom; After Effects uses the term Angle of View (AOV). The two are interchangeable; we tend to use FOV.

Alpha Interpretation

Most 3D programs generate Premultiplied alpha channels. Electric Image generates Straight alphas; some programs give you a choice. When in doubt, the File>Interpret Footage>Main>Alpha "Guess" button usually picks correctly.

Step 2: Camera data is embedded in RPF files. To access it, context+click on the layer in the Timeline window and select Keyframe Assistant>RPF Camera Import.

Scrub the time marker or RAM Preview, and note how the new video layer tracks the videowall in the render. The result is saved in the **Ex.11_Maya prebuilt** subfolder as [Ex.11a]. We'll deal with other issues such as cropping its edges and compositing the logo later. If you edited the start frame in Maya to be 0, remember to also set the Render Globals to start at frame 0 as well. If you didn't, the 3D render may start at frame 1, causing a mismatch between the render and the camera move. As a result, you might need to slide the camera layer back a frame in time to line up with the render.

Autodesk 3ds max

This program pioneered the practice of saving numerous channels of information beyond Z-depth in RLA format files. It then extended these capabilities further with the Rich Pixel Format (RPF files), including embedding camera data into each rendered frame.

Step 1: Make sure you write down your camera's Field of View setting (50° for our scene); this vital bit of information is *not* saved in the RPF file. Also write down the location of the object you want to map your video onto – in our case, the videowall's face, which was placed at 0,0,0.

When you are ready to render, open the Render Scene Dialog. In the Output section, click on Files. In the resulting Render Output File dialog, change the "Save as type:" option to RPF Image File, and hit Save. In the subsequent RPF Image File Format dialog, you can set 3ds max to Store Alpha Channel (if you need one), and enable the Optional Channels of your choice (which we will discuss later in the section *Creating a 3D Matte*). Render your animation.

Step 2: Import the image sequence into After Effects, and conform the frame rate as needed in the sequence's Interpret Footage dialog (see the sidebar *The Frame Rate Dance*). If you open the Project window's folder **Ex.12_3ds max**, you will see that we have already done this for you. Drag the file **PC_3dsmax_main** to the "Create a new Composition" button at the bottom of the Project window; After Effects will create a comp with the same dimensions, duration, and frame rate as your file. Context+click on the layer **PC_3dsmax_main** in the resulting comp, and select Keyframe Assistant>RPF Camera Import. A layer named **RPF Camera** will be created; select it and hit U to see the properties that have been keyframed.

Step 3: Back in the Project window, locate the footage item **Sources>Movies>CL_Skateboarding_ramp**, select it, and type Command+/ (Control+/) to add it to your comp as the top layer. Enable its 3D Layer switch…and it won't line up with the screen. We know the videowall face

Importing Sequences

Many 3D programs save their renders as sequences of individual frames rather than self-contained movies. Quite often, multiple 3D renders will also be saved to the same folder, creating some confusion. Here's how to sort them out.

When you want to import a specific sequence into After Effects, press Command+I (Control+I) to open the Import File dialog, and select one of the files in the sequence you want. Make sure the Sequence option is checked underneath the file list; otherwise, only one frame will be imported. However, *don't* check the Force Alphabetical option: If you check it, the entire contents of the folder will be imported as one sequence. Click Open; only the sequence you selected will be imported.

Sequences import at the default frame rate set in the Preferences>Import dialog. If you need the sequence to be a different rate, select it, type Command+F (Control+F), and conform the Frame Rate as needed.

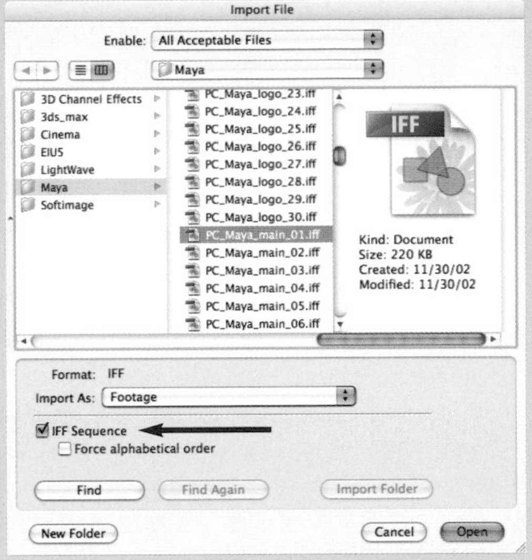

When you're importing sequences of images, select one of the files in the sequence and enable the Sequence option switch. If more than one sequence has been saved to the same folder, do *not* enable the Force Alphabetical option.

was located at 0,0,0 in 3ds max, so select **CL_Skateboarding_ramp**, type P to reveal its Position, and enter these coordinates (remember you can tab between parameters).

Close, but it still doesn't fill the screen; the animator assured us he made the screen the correct size. Oops – we forgot to also set the camera's Field of View. Double-click on **RPF Camera** to open its Camera Settings dialog, make sure the Measure Film Size popup is set to Horizontally, and enter 50° for the Angle of View. Click OK, and now the video nicely fits the videowall. (If the 3D artist had made the screen a different size in world units than the video, you would then need to adjust your video's Scale until it fits.) RAM Preview to verify the result. Our version is saved in [**Ex.12a**] in the **Ex.12_3ds max prebuilt** subfolder.

Step 3: When the video is added in After Effects and set into 3D space, it doesn't line up with the videoscreen (A). Entering the position of the videowall's face from the original 3D project centers it, but it doesn't fill the screen as planned (B). Entering the correct Angle of View for the camera completes the match (C).

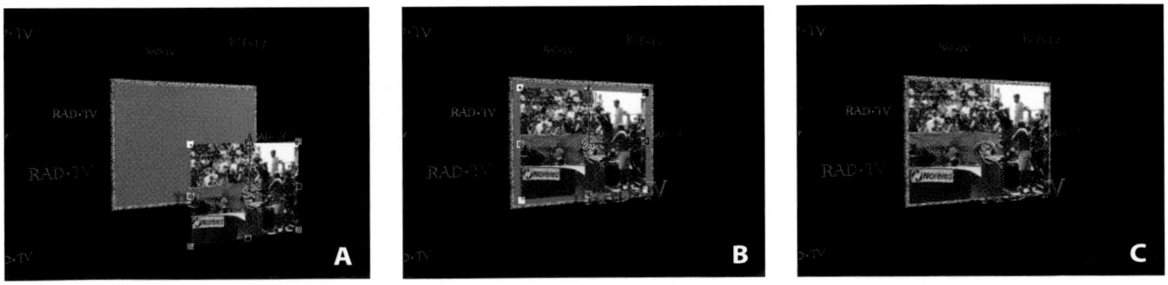

A

B

C

The Frame Rate Dance

NTSC video runs at 29.97 frames per second (fps). Most 3D applications, however, do not support this value; they force you to animate and render at 30 fps. It falls on you to correct the frame rate of your 3D elements back to 29.97 fps in After Effects:

• After importing your renders, open their File>Interpret Footage>Main dialogs, and conform their frame rates to 29.97. Then create your comps at 29.97 fps. As a bonus, if you are extracting the camera move from an RPF sequence, its keyframes will now be spaced at 29.97 fps because you already conformed the sequence's frame rate to this number.

• If you import a Maya or Cinema 4D project that automatically creates a comp with a camera for you, the keyframes for that camera are also probably at the wrong frame rate. Select the camera layer in the comp (or the null that controls the camera, in the Maya case), select the menu item Layer>Time Stretch, and set the Stretch Factor to 100.1%. This slows down the 30 fps keyframes to be respaced at 29.97 fps.

Make sure Layer In-point is set to Hold In Place, and click OK. You will also need to do this if you pasted in camera keyframe data from a project that originated at the wrong frame rate. If you want to be extra sure the keyframes line up correctly with the frames in After Effects, select the camera layer, type U to reveal its keyframes, and increment the time marker a frame at a time, selecting and dragging the nearest keyframe until it snaps to the time marker. Beware of an imported project having a completely incorrect frame rate. For example, if you create a project in Electric Image at 59.94 fps, export its camera move as a Maya project, and import this into After Effects, the resulting project will have a frame rate of 30 fps! To fix this, hit Home, select the camera layer, Time Stretch it to the correct speed (in this case, 30 ÷ 59.94 x 100% = 50.05%), copy all its keyframes, delete the keyframes, restore the layer's Time Stretch to 100%, then paste back in the speed-adjusted keyframes you just copied.

Motion Blur

If you rendered your 3D scene with motion blur enabled, enable Motion Blur in After Effects for the layers you map onto your render. Don't forget to note and match the blur's shutter angle.

Electric Image Universe

There are several ways to get animation data out of Electric Image Universe Animator (EIU for short). Currently, the most direct path is to export it as a Maya project. Follow these steps (given for EIU version 5); you can also refer to the earlier section on Alias Maya if you want more background:

Step 1: Render your scene as normal. Back in EIU, write down the location of the object you want to map your video onto (in our case, the video-wall's face, which was placed at 0,0,80). Also write down the camera's Field of View (FOV) setting: 36.87° for the render we're working with here. Sometimes this data does not come across correctly, so it's best to be safe.

Open EIU's Render Information dialog, and select the Resolution tab. *Make sure* the Aspect Ratio popup at the top is set to the same aspect as your final frame (for example, 1.333 for normal 4:3 aspect video). The absolute safest approach is to set it to Custom, and enter the square-pixel values of your final render size.

Then select the active camera, and go to the menu item Animation>Export Motion>Maya ASCII Motion. In the dialog that opens, enter the duration of your animation in frames (it defaults to 0 frames duration – duh). Click OK, and EIU will save a .ma file.

Step 2: Time to import the camera data into After Effects. Select the folder **Ex.14-EIU** in the Project window, and import the file **19_Chapter Sources>EIU>CM_EIU_cam_Maya.ma** from your DVD. This will create a comp named **CM_EIU_cam_Maya**. Double-click it to open it; you will find an already-keyframed camera inside. Even though our EIU project had a frame rate of 29.97 fps, the comp was created with an incorrect rate of 30 fps. Open the Composition Settings and set it to 29.97; select the **Camera2Shape** layer and Layer>Time Stretch it by 100.1% (see the sidebar *The Frame Rate Dance*).

In the Project window, select the footage item **CM_EIU_main** (which has already been imported into this folder), and drag it on top of the icon for the comp [**CM_EIU_cam_Maya**] to add it to this comp.

Step 3: Still in the Project window, locate the footage item Sources>Movies>**CL_Skateboarding_ramp**, select it, and either drag it onto the icon for [**CM_EIU_cam_Maya**] or type Command+/ (Control+/). Enable its 3D Layer switch, and type P to reveal its Position. Enter 0,0,80 which corresponds to its position in the EIU project. (The Y dimension in After Effects is flipped compared with the Y dimension in EIU; if the Y coordinate of the video screen had been, say, +20 in EIU, we would need to enter –20 in After Effects.)

At this moment, the video will look far too large. When you bring in EIU camera data through .ma files, After Effects divides all of the coordinates by 10. To resolve this, you have two options. One is to divide the Position and Scale values for the video layer by 10 to match this division. Another is to use an expression to multiply the camera's Position values by 10. Even if you're a little scared of expressions, this is the easier path, as you don't have to keep translating coordinates for all of your other layers. Select **Camera2Shape**, press P to reveal its Position, and Option+click (Alt+click) on the stopwatch icon next to Position. Then, in the expression field enter **value * 10** and hit Enter (not Return). The video should now be centered on your screen, filling it nicely. RAM Preview and enjoy the animation. Our result is saved in the **Ex.14_EIU prebuilt** subfolder as [**Ex.14a**].

Step 3: EIU camera moves translated through .ma files result in coordinates being divided by 10. You can use the expression **value * 10** to restore these original values (below). Place the video screen at the same coordinates as in the EIU file, and they should track nicely (top and above).

● ● ●		Ex.14a_EIU_camera ● Timeline					

Ex.14a_EIU_camera

0:00:00:00 (29.97 fps)

	#	Layer Name			Stretch	0:00	00:15f	01:00
▽ ☐	1	[CL_Skateboarding...			100.0%			
		○ Position	0.0 , 0.0 , 80.0					
▷ ☐	2	[CM_EIU_main.mov]			100.0%			
▽ ☐	3	Camera2Shape			100.1%			
		▽ ○ = Position	–560.0 , –540.0 , –994.0	✓ ▶				
		› Expression : Position				value * 10		

Switches / Modes

Auto-Orient Off

When you're importing camera keyframes, make sure the camera's Layer>Transform> Auto-Orient property is Off, or it may face the wrong direction as it animates.

Auto-Orientation

Auto-Orientation
- ⦿ Off
- ○ Orient Along Path
- ○ Orient Towards Point of Interest

[Cancel] [OK]

Maxon Cinema 4D

This 3D package (version 7.303 or later) has the best integration with After Effects, hands down. It has a "multi-pass" option with which it can render individual properties of the final render (such as diffuse, specular, and reflection passes), the individual contributions of each light (including their shadows), and special channels you request such as mattes for specific objects – all in one pass. It can also create a special After Effects project that reassembles all of these passes into a final composite, and it can create a camera and lights in After Effects that match their partners in the original Cinema scene.

Step 1: In Cinema, open the Render Settings dialog, and choose the Multi-Pass pane. Enable the Enable Multi-Pass Rendering option along the top of the window, as well as the Save Multi-Pass Image option below. Click on the Path button and set the destination for your multipass renders, then click on Options to set the file format (a QuickTime format that supports alpha channels is good). Leave the Layer Name as Suffix option checked, to help identify the individual layers when they are imported into After Effects.

Which Channels you want saved depends on how much control you want over the final composite in After Effects. We'll discuss some of the specific options later, but for this project we clicked on the Channels button, selected Add All, and then deleted channels we didn't think we would need until we were down to RGBA Image, Shadow, Depth, Ambient, Diffuse, Specular, and Reflection, and then added Object Buffer 1 (discussed in the next major section of this chapter). For maximum control, set the Separate Lights popup to All, with the Mode popup underneath set to 3 Channels. (If you want separate passes for specific lights only, set Separate Lights to Selected in the Multi-Pass pane, then go into the Details section of the Attributes palette for each light you wish to break out, and enable its Separate Pass option.)

When you render, these individual properties will be saved as their own QuickTime movies in the same folder with an .aec file: a special After Effects project that also contains the camera information. You can also save the .aec file by itself in the Save pane in the Render Settings dialog.

Before you leave Cinema, jot down the coordinates of your target object (here, the face of our videowall, which was placed at 2.281,0,–0.292), as well as any details of the lights you wish to recreate inside After Effects (such as their cone angle). Note that lights in After Effects are much more limited than in 3D programs such as Cinema; they don't have glow or falloff, among other characteristics. But having their basic positions brought into After Effects still goes a long way toward helping you better blend layers in After Effects into your final scene.

Render Settings

General
Output
Save
Antialiasing
Radiosity
Caustics
Effects
Options
Multi-Pass
QuickTime VR

☑ Enable Multi-Pass Rendering   ▲▼ Channels ▶
  ☑ RGBA Image
  ☑ Shadow
  ☑ Depth
  ☑ Object Buffer: 1
  ☑ Ambient
  ☑ Diffuse
  ☑ Specular
  ☑ Reflection

☑ Save Multi-Pass Image   Separate Lights | All   ⬍
☐ Multi-Layer File
☐ Shadow Correction   Mode | 3 Channels: Diffuse,Specular ⬍

Path... | CheesyPoofs:Users:cbator:Desktop:Render_Pass:screen_pass
Format | QuickTime Movie   ⬍   [Options...]
Depth | 8 Bit/Channel ⬍ ☑ Layer Name as Suffix

Step 1: In the Cinema 4D Render Settings dialog, go to the Multi-Pass pane, and check the option Enable Multi-Pass Rendering. You can then define which properties of your render are saved as individual files. A special .aec project file will also be created; this contains the camera information.

Step 2: Go to the Maxon web site (www.maxon.net), pick your language, then click on Downloads, then Updates, then Cinema 4D R9. Here you should find the latest version of the After Effects/Cinema 4D Composition Import plug-in. Download it, move it to the Plug-ins folder inside your After Effects application folder, and relaunch After Effects.

Re-open this chapter's example project. Select File>Import>File and navigate to the folder **19_Chapter Sources>Cinema 4D** on your DVD, and select the file **PC-C4D.aec** (if you can't select it, you don't have the Composition Import plug-in installed correctly). Note in the Import File dialog that the Import As popup below changes to Composition. Click Open, and two folders will be added to the Project window: **CINEMA 4D Composition** and **Special Passes**.

To keep things neat, drag these into the folder named **15_Cinema 4D**, twirl open this folder, then twirl open the **CINEMA 4D Composition** folder. This folder contains a comp generated by Cinema and all of the layers used by the comp, including subfolders for the contribution of each light in the scene. (The **Special Passes** folder contains additional render passes that are not needed to reconstruct the original Cinema render, but that you might have other uses for, such as object mattes – the subject of the next section.)

Open the comp [**CINEMA 4D Composition**]. Note that it contains not only an animating camera (with the correct Angle of View), but also two light objects to replicate those in the Cinema project. Feel free to solo the individual layers to see which components of the final image they contain. Make sure the Modes panel is open in the Timeline window (F4 to toggle) and note the blending modes used – typically Multiply for shadows, and Add for reflections, speculars, and lights. Normally, the main visual information is carried in the bottommost layers: shadow, specular, and diffuse. Since we requested each light to be rendered out separately, these layers are black, as all of the basic visual information is provided by the [**Light 1**] and [**Light 2**] subcomps.

Step 3: In the Project window, locate the footage item Sources>Movies> **CL_Skateboarding_ramp**, select it, and press Command+/ (Control+/) to

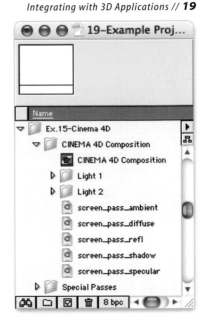

Step 2: After you import the .aec project file, you will find two folders: CINEMA 4D Composition, and Special Passes. The first folder contains all you need to reconstruct your render out of the individual passes you requested.

Step 3: Cinema 4D creates a comp that contains the individual render passes, in the correct stacking order with the correct blending modes, as well as camera and light objects that mimic those set up in the Cinema project. All you need to do is add your new video layer, enable its 3D Layer switch, and set its Position coordinates correctly. Don't forget to set all of the comps and footage items to the correct frame rate!

Cinema.mov

The Mac version of Cinema 4D does not automatically add the .mov extension to QuickTime layers it renders. This means the Windows version of After Effects will not recognize these files. Add the .mov extension to these files yourself, then re-link the footage as needed in the After Effects project.

3D Renders in 2D

Remember that your 3D renders must be left in 2D space inside After Effects; they already have the camera move built in.

Mo' is Better

MoCon (in beta at the time this was written) is a new plug-in developed by visual effects artists that will import and export object and camera data from a variety of formats, including Maya, LightWave, Electric Image, Kuper, Biovision, and others. It is available from 3Dmation Visual Effects (www.3dmation.com).

add it to [**CINEMA 4D Composition**]. Press F4 to toggle back to Switches, enable its 3D Layer switch, and type P to reveal its Position. Enter the Position coordinates you jotted down from your Cinema project: In this case, 2.281,0,–0.292. RAM Preview; your new video tracks the videowall's face perfectly. (If you got lost, check out the **Ex.15_Cinema prebuilt** sub-folder, and comp [**Ex.15a**].) Note the lighting falloff across your video, courtesy of the lights Cinema added to the comp. We'll discuss how to polish off the rest of the composite later in this chapter.

NewTek LightWave 3D

LightWave 8 will embed its camera data in RPF files; see the earlier section on 3ds max on how to extract it (Professional edition required). If you do not have the Professional edition, or are still using LightWave 7.5, all is not lost; the TransMotion Utilities Pack (www.ats-3d.com) gives the LightWave user several ways to get camera – and other – data from LightWave to After Effects. We used these scripts to create the data for the following exercise, but you don't need them if you'd like to follow along:

Step 1: Render your project as normal, using the file format of your choice. Write down your camera's FOV setting (45.24° × 34.71° for us), as well as the world space location of the object you need to map your video onto (0,0,0 for this scene). Then duplicate your camera or save your project under a new name, as you are about to modify your camera animation.

You need to create explicit keyframes for every frame of your animation, to make sure any curves you've applied to the camera's motion make it into After Effects correctly. If you have set up the camera in LightWave to target another object – such as a null placed where you want the camera to focus – you have to go through an extra step to encode the camera's actual rotational values in world space (otherwise, they may not reflect the additional rotation required to make the camera face the targeted object).

First, select the camera in LightWave, and type m (lower case) to open the Motion Options. Under the IK and Modifiers tab, select Add Modifier> Motion Baker. Enable only the Rotation channels (we've observed strange results when Motion Baker processes Position curves), and set the New Key Mode to Use Existing. Make sure Overwrite Keys is *not* enabled. Step through the animation; now you have rotation values for every frame of the animation.

Next, with the camera selected, click on Graph Editor. When the Graph Editor opens, Shift+select the Position-oriented Channels down the left side of the dialog. Click on the Keys popup along the top of the dialog and select Bake Selected Curves.

Then (in version 8) select the Utilities tab and click on LScript/RT. Locate the TransMotion script **LWcam2ae.lsc** and open it. This script allows you to save the camera motion as a set of After Effects keyframes in a text file. Make sure you have the AutoCamera option turned *off* (this is for matching a background plate, not a 3D object as our task is here). Under Windows, this script will automatically open Notepad and place the keyframe data there; on the Mac, before you run the script you first need to select a file inside the folder where you want your camera data to end up, then enter a new name for the script to save it to (otherwise, it will overwrite the file you selected).

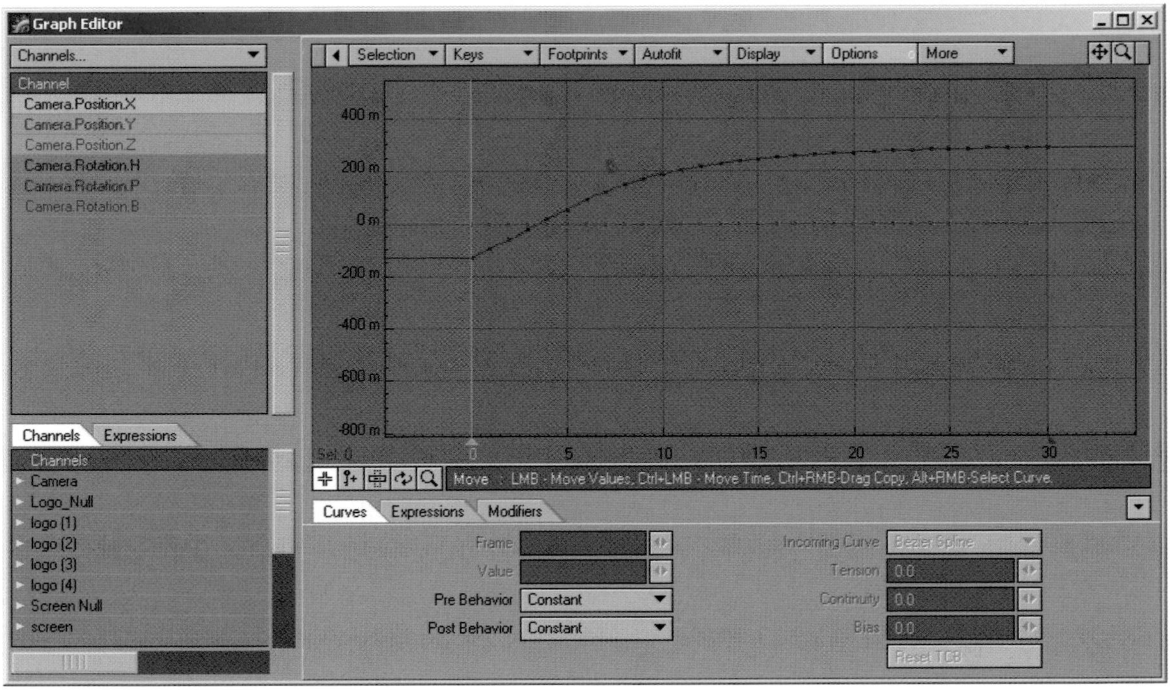

Step 2: In After Effects, get a comp ready to receive the camera data. Import your render, create a new comp that is the same size, duration, and frame rate as your render, and place your render in it. If you open the Project window's folder **Ex.16_LightWave**, you will see we have already done this for you. Open [**LW composite**], and use Layer>New> Camera to create a fresh camera. Enter the FOV value you wrote down earlier (45.24° if the Measure Film Size popup is set to Horizontally, 34.71° if set to Vertically) for the Angle of View. With this camera selected, go to Layer>Transform>Auto-Orient, and set it to Off: The camera data we are about to paste for this example is for a "one-point" camera, not the normal "two-point" camera After Effects defaults to that uses a Point of Interest.

In a text editor, open the camera data that was exported by the LWcam2ae script; we've saved a copy of it for our camera as the file **19_Chapter Sources>LightWave>PC_LW_cam.txt**. Select all the text in this file and Copy. Return to the After Effects comp [**LW composite**], make sure the time is still at 00:00, select the camera you created, and Paste. Press U and observe the new keyframe data for your camera.

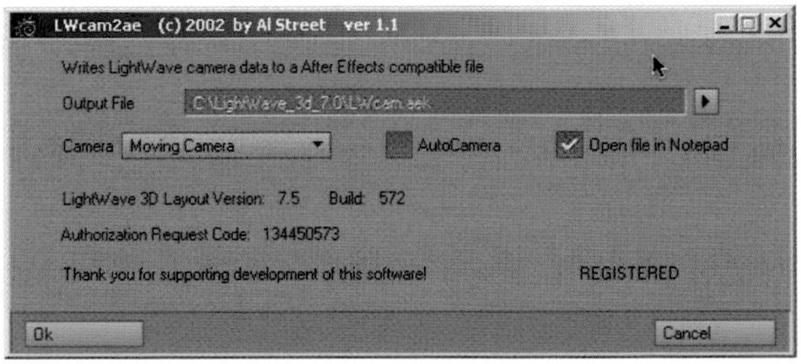

Step 1: If your camera targets another object (such as the videowall's screen), in LW 7.5 two steps are required to create the necessary keyframe data. First, use the Motion Baker modifier to convert the Rotation channels to keyframes. Then use the Graph Editor's Keys>Bake Selected Curves function to convert the Position channels. If you do not have the camera targeted to another object, you can select all the curves and bake them In the Graph Edltor.

The TransMotion Utilities Pack (www.ats-3d.com) contains scripts that allow you to get camera and other object motion data out of LightWave and into After Effects.

Step 3: If you believe you entered all the parameters correctly but the video still doesn't line up (above), see if setting the camera's Layer>Transform>Auto-Orient feature to Off fixes it (below).

Step 1: Download and open Helge Mathee's XSI script, edit the FPS parameter to match your project (highlighted here), and click on Run (circled). Save the resulting .aec file, which will include your camera and light data.

Step 3: Back in the Project window, locate the footage item **Sources> Movies>CL_Skateboarding_ramp**, select it, and type Command+/ (Control+/) to add it to your comp. Enable its 3D Layer switch, then hit P to reveal its Position, and enter the coordinates of the original 3D object (0,0,0). It should now line up with the videowall's face; RAM Preview to double-check. If the video lines up on the first and last keyframes but wanders in the middle, you probably forgot to bake your camera data back in Step 1, and only the first and last keyframes are making it across. If the move doesn't match at all, make sure you set the camera's Auto-Orient property correctly in the previous step. Our result is saved in [**Ex.16a**] in the **Ex.16_Lightwave prebuilt** subfolder.

Softimage|XSI

This 3D package does not directly support camera data export. However, a clever user – Helge Mathee – has created an XSI script that allows users to transfer camera and light data through, of all things, a Cinema 4D plug-in…

Step 1: Render your scene normally. If you like, you can use the .pic and .zpic formats discussed early in this chapter to preserve Z-depth information, or to another format of your choosing. In XSI's Camera dialog, note the Field of View angle, and the way it is measured (vertically or horizontally); for this project, it is 53.638°, measured horizontally. Also write down the location of the object you want to map your video onto – in our case, the videowall's face, which was placed at 0, –2.0, –7.8.

Go to Helge's web site at www.mindthink.de/ohm/aftereffectsxsi, click on Download, and provide your email address; you will then receive the link to download the script. Once you have it on your drive, open your project in XSI, click on the Script Editor, select File>Open, and locate the script **aeexport.vbs** on your drive. After the script has been loaded, scroll down and change the FPS parameter to match the frame rate of your render and resulting After Effects project. Then click Run in the Script Editor, and save the resulting .aec file to your drive – preferably in your project's folder.

Step 2: Go to the Maxon web site (www.maxon.net), pick your language, click on Downloads, then Updates, and then Cinema 4D R9. Here you should find the latest version of the After Effects/Cinema 4D Composition Import plug-in (you may need to hunt in other folders for it; Maxon regularly updates its web site). Download it, move it to the Plug-ins folder inside your After Effects application folder, and relaunch After Effects.

Re-open this chapter's example project. Select File>Import>File and navigate to the folder **19_Chapter Sources>Softimage** on your DVD, and select the file **RB_camera_XSI.aec** (if you can't select it, you don't have the Composition Import plug-in installed correctly). Note in the Import File dialog that the Import As popup below changes to Composition. Click Open, and a folder will be created in the Project window named

XSI Composition. To keep things organized, drag this folder into the **Ex.17-Softimage XSI folder**.

Twirl open the folder XSI Composition. It contains two comps – [**Camera+Light**] and [**XSI Composition**] – and placeholders for three files: **bg.0**, **rad_tv.0**, and **screen.0**. These three footage items correspond to three object groups the 3D artist (Bill Hinkson of Reject Barn) created in XSI's Explorer window. If needed, to view these in your own XSI project, change Scene to Passes.

Select **bg.0**, then choose the menu item File>Replace Footage>File. In the dialog that opens, navigate back to the **19_Chapter Sources> Softimage** folder, and click on **RB_XSI_bg_0.pic**. Enable the Softimage PIC Sequence option in the lower left portion of this dialog (but leave Force Alphabetical Order disabled), and click Open: This sequence will now replace the placeholder file. With this new file still selected in the Project window, type Command+F (Control+F) to open its Interpret Footage dialog, set Alpha to Premultiplied, change the frame rate to 29.97 fps, and click OK.

Now do the same thing for the other placeholders, replacing **rad_tv.0** with the sequence **RB_XSI_logo** (you will need to scroll down the Softimage folder's contents to see this; select the first one and enable PIC Sequence as before), and replacing **screen.0** with **RB_XSI_main**. Don't forget to edit the Interpret Footage settings for these sequences as well!

Now open the comp [**Camera+Light**]. It contains a camera and several lights, all corresponding to their counterparts in the original XSI scene. All are keyframed at 30 fps. Select all the layers, then open Layer>Time Stretch. Enter a Stretch Factor of 100.1% and click OK: This will slow all of them down to 29.97 fps. Type Command+K (Control+K) and change the comp's frame rate to 29.97 fps. Finally, double-click the **Camera** layer, verify that the Measure Film Size popup at the bottom is set to Horizontally, and enter the XSI Field of View value you wrote down (53.638 for this project) into the Angle of View field. Then click OK. Ignore the warning message about not having a 3D layer; you're about to add one.

Step 3: With the comp [**Camera+Light**] still forward, select **CL_Skateboarding_ramp.mov** in the Project window's **Sources>Movies** folder, and type Command+/ (Control+/) to add it to the top of your comp. Enable its 3D Layer switch, and type P to reveal its Position. Then in this comp, look for the light named **screen_tracker**: Bill Hinkson cleverly attached a dummy light to the videoscreen's face, so we would know where it was located (and could follow it in the event it was animating). Type P to reveal its Position, click on the word Position to select its value, and copy; turn off its Video switch while you're at it, as it is unneeded. Then select **CL_Skateboarding_ramp.mov** and paste. RAM Preview; you will see the video swivel around, reacting to the camera move.

Now open [**XSI Composition**]: It contains the 3D renders, as well as the video, which may be looking a bit tall (a small bug). If that's the case,

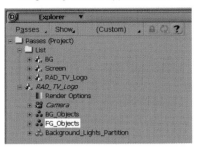

If you organize your XSI project into groups in the Passes>List folder, these will be represented by placeholders when you import the corresponding .aec project into After Effects.

Using the Cinema import plug-in allows you to bring both cameras and lights from XSI into After Effects (top). The animator placed one light – **screen_tracker** – on the face of the videoscreen in XSI; this allowed us to paste its position into our new video layer in After Effects to place it correctly (above).

Make a duplicate of the object that is supposed to receive the video, and give it a unique name. Apply a texture map to it that has tracking dots or boxes in its four corners. Give these a flat shading so they keep maximum contrast when you render. Then turn all of the other objects off, and render this special motion tracking pass.

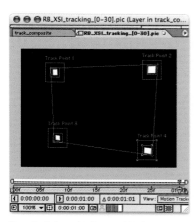

Step 2: Select the layer with the tracking dots, open Window>Tracker Controls, click on Track Motion, then select Perspective Corner Pin. Press Home or End depending on where the tracking dots are the largest, then set up the four tracking regions around them. Move the Attach Points out to just beyond the corners you are tracking.

select Camera+Light, type S to reveal its Scale, click on the Constrain Proportions chain link icon to disable it, and enter 100% for both X and Y values. Finally, change this comp's frame rate to 29.97 fps as well. RAM Preview: The video tracks the 3D renders perfectly. We've saved our results in [**Ex.17a**] and [**Ex.17b**], rearranging the 3D renders to their correct stacking order.

If you want to simplify your life, you could ignore the comp [**XSI Composition**], and instead import the 3D renders yourself (rather than use the Replace Footage routine we outlined). Place these renders in the comp [**Camera+Light**] in the order you need for your composite.

Pro Corner Pinning

What if your 3D program of choice does not support a way to directly import camera data into After Effects? One approach is to see if you can write a script that will allow you to extract that data, perhaps to be further massaged in an Excel spreadsheet into the After Effects keyframe format. Another approach is to fall back on the time-honored technique of not using 3D space, but corner pinning the 2D video in After Effects onto the desired object in the 3D footage. We will give an overview of the latter technique here; the screen shots are from Softimage|XSI but the same general concepts can be applied to any 3D program.

Step 1: Render your project as normal. Now you need to create a special pass that focuses on the four corners of the object you want to apply video to (such as our videowall's face), making it easier for After Effects to track. There are several approaches to this, including creating four small objects and placing them at the corners of the screen, or duplicating the screen object and applying a texture to it with dots or boxes in the corners. The smaller you can make these spots, the more accurately you can track them later in After Effects.

Make sure these tracking dots are textured in a way to make them highly visible, such as 100% self-luminant white. Turn off all of the other geometry in the scene, and render a special pass of just these tracking boxes or dots, adding a special suffix to the file name such as "**_mt**".

Step 2: In After Effects, import both your normal render and your special motion tracking pass. If necessary, conform both to the correct frame rate (29.97 fps for us). Then create a comp that has the same size, frame rate, and duration as these renders. Add these two renders, plus the footage you want to map into this scene, to your comp. This has already been done for you in the chapter's example project: Look inside the Project window's folder **Ex.18-tracking**, and open the comp [**track_composite**].

With only layer 3's Video switch turned on, RAM Preview or scrub the time marker through the comp to get an idea for the videowall's motion. Then turn on layer 2, which contains the motion tracking dots. Note how the white boxes follow the corners of the videowall's motion. Turn off layer 2 (we don't want to see those dots in the final composite), and turn on layer 1: the video that will be mapped onto the wall. Unlike the procedures for the other 3D programs, this one needs its 3D Layer switch turned *off*. We don't have a 3D camera in this scene, because we couldn't get the camera data out of this particular 3D program. Instead, we're going to corner pin the video onto the videowall.

Select **RB_XSI_tracking** (layer 2), then open Window>Tracker Controls. Click on the button Track Motion: This will open **RB_XSI_tracking** in its Layer window, with one set of tracking regions. Then set the Track Type popup to Perspective Corner Pin; four sets of tracking regions will appear. It's easier to track objects when they start off at their largest; in this case, this is at the end of the camera move, so hit End.

Place each of the inner Feature Region boxes around its nearest white tracking square. Reduce the size of each box to just contain its square. Then take the four + icons in the middle of the window (the Attach Points), and place them just beyond the outside corners of each tracking square – this will give us a little "slop" or safety margin that we will matte out later. The lines connecting the crosshairs will show the outline of the video we will be pinning. (If you need a refresher course on setting up the Motion Tracker/Stabilizer, review Chapters 15 and 16.)

In the Tracker Controls, click on the Analyze Backward button (as you want to start at the end where the regions are their largest). When you're done, verify that the Motion Target is set to the video you want corner pinned onto your screen (**CL_Skateboarding_ramp** for us); if necessary, click on Edit Target and select this layer. Then Click on Apply.

Step 3: At this point, the Effect Controls window should open, with Corner Pin applied to the **CL_Skateboarding_ramp** layer. Select this layer and press U to see its keyframes. In the Comp window, the video should be distorted to cover the face of the videowall. (You can close the Layer window now; you're done with it.) To verify the track of the video to the screen, reduce the Opacity for **CL_skateboarding_ramp**. RAM Preview; if the video seems to jump around in relation to the screen, you will need to re-do the track. Our result is in **Ex.18_tracking prebuilt>[Ex.18a]**, where we also used Overlay mode to check the composite. We'll discuss how to crop the edges of the video in the next section.

LightWave Pinning

The plug-in CornerPin in the TransMotion Utilities Pack (www.ats-3d.com) allows LightWave users to export motion data from four nulls placed at the corners of an object, which in turn can be pasted directly into the Corner Pin effect without having to run the Motion Tracker.

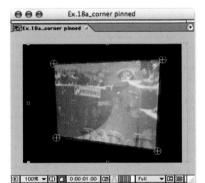

Step 3: After applying the Perspective Corner Pin track, the video layer should have the Corner Pin effect applied, keyframed for every frame of the animation.

Nonsquare Pixel Issues

If you plan to import camera data from your 3D program into After Effects, you will save yourself a lot of grief by rendering at a square pixel size and compositing in a square pixel comp inside After Effects. Then do the necessary stretch or squash as your last stage before final output.

When you're field rendering from 3D, choose a size that has the same number of horizontal lines as your final output so you don't accidentally rescale your interlaced fields. For example, if your final destination is 720×486 D1 NTSC output, render a frame size of 648×486 pixels from your 3D program, and composite at this square pixel size inside After Effects. If you are not field rendering at all, and you want to maximize your quality, render and composite at a size of 720×540 pixels. Then conform these to a 720×486 pixel frame in the Output Module's Stretch dialog. If you are field rendering, render from 3D at 720×540 at 60 fps, conform the frame rate of the 3D render to 59.94 fps in After Effects, and work in a 720×540 square pixel comp. Before you render, nest this comp into a 720×486 D1 comp, and scale the layer to fit. (These techniques are discussed in detail in Chapters 25 through 27.)

If you render at a nonsquare pixel size and try to import camera data into After Effects, you will have grave difficulty trying to get the camera's angle of view to match, as it is distorted by the pixel geometry. One 3D program that has this sorted out is Alias Maya. Say you created your project in Maya with a frame size of 720×486 pixels, and a pixel aspect ratio of 0.9. When you import the corresponding .ma file into After Effects, two comps will be created: **[Square Camera]** with a size of 648×486 pixels and a square pixel aspect ratio, which will be nested into a second comp called **[Camera]** that has a size of 720×486 pixels with a 0.9 pixel aspect ratio. You composite your new video in **[Square Camera]**, which contains the 3D camera move. You then place your nonsquare pixel 3D render into **[Camera]**, where it should be composited behind the results of the nested comp **[Square Camera]**. This is shown with half-size images in **[Ex.11b]**.

By the way, the corner pin trick we outlined has the added bonus of working regardless of the pixel aspect ratio: After Effects doesn't care how the pixels are being displayed; it just knows it has to stretch your new video to cover the screen you tracked.

OpenGL Off

OpenGL does not always render mattes, effects, and other tidbits accurately. Set Fast Previews (along the bottom right edge of the Comp window) to Adaptive Resolution or Off when working with these composites.

Creating a 3D Matte

At this point, the new video layer you added in After Effects should track its corresponding object (the face of the videowall) in your 3D render. But life's not perfect yet; there may be some ragged edges to clean up, and there is the matter of the main logo which is supposed to appear in front of the new video. Your next task is creating a matte that cuts out the video so that the edges are clean, and the logo shows through.

In general, the solutions fall into two categories. Some programs (such as 3ds max, Cinema 4D, and LightWave) allow you to include object- or material-specific matte information as part of the normal rendering process. If your program does not support this feature, you need to figure out a way to create this special matte yourself. One approach is to create a texture that renders the areas you want to keep (our videowall's face) as 100% self-luminant white and everything else as 0% non-reflective black. Another is to have model pieces that may obscure your target object punch a hole through the target's alpha channel.

As with importing camera data, there are almost as many solutions as there are 3D programs. Although the following instructions are program-specific, we suggest you go ahead and read the sections that apply to programs you don't own, as they might give you ideas for alternate approaches in your own program. The format we will follow for each program is:

Step 1:   Creating the matte in the 3D program.

Step 2:   Using the matte in After Effects.

Alias Maya

There are several ways to get Maya to render the matte you need. One is to apply the surface material Use Background to all of the model pieces you need to cut a hole in the alpha – such as the logo in front of the videowall's face.

Step 1:   In Maya, open the Hypershade window, then double-click Use Background – it will appear in the Work Area. Then drag and drop it onto the objects you want to cut holes in the alpha (namely, everything except the videowall's face). Render out this sequence with a special name. The result is an image of just the visible portion of the videowall face (which we don't need right now), with everything else cut out of the alpha channel – a perfect alpha matte for your new video layer.

Step 2:   We've imported this sequence – **PC_Maya_screen** – into the Project's folder **Ex.11-Maya**. Add it to either [**Ex.11a**] in the **Ex.11_Maya prebuilt** subfolder, or to the comp you created following the Maya camera import instructions earlier in this chapter. Make sure it is placed above the **CL_Skateboarding_ramp** layer, and hit Option+Home (Alt+Home) to make sure it starts at the first frame of your comp. Open the Modes panel in the Timeline window (F4 toggles), and set the Track Matte popup for **CL_Skateboarding_ramp** to Alpha Matte. Voilà – your video clip is now perfectly trimmed to fit inside your videowall's frame, and it now appears "behind" the main RAD•TV logo. The result is shown in [**Ex.11c**].

Step 2: The result of rendering a special pass with Use Background applied to everything except the videowall's face is a sequence in which the face of the video screen appears in the RGB channels (A), but any object that might obscure it is cut out of the sequence's alpha channel (B). The skateboarding footage appears in front of the logo (C) until you apply this as an Alpha Matte to the video – now it fits perfectly inside the frame and "behind" the main logo (D).

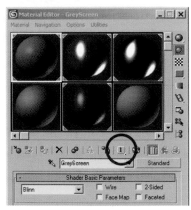

Step 1: To assign a Material Effect ID, click on the small number underneath the display grid in the Materials Editor (above). To assign an Object ID, change the G-Buffer Object Channel in the Object Properties dialog (below).

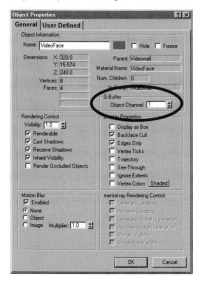

Step 1 *continued*: Render to the RPF format, remembering to enable Material Effects and/or Object as needed.

Autodesk 3ds max

This program lets the user tag specific objects or materials with IDs, which can then be used to derive a matte that shows just where this object or material is visible in a frame.

Step 1: To assign a Material Effect ID, open the Materials Editor, and assign an Effect ID by clicking on the number in the row of icons just under the material display grid. To assign an Object ID, in the Object Properties dialog change the G-Buffer Object Channel from its default of 0 to the number you want. In both cases, beware of unintentionally having two different materials or objects with the same ID; you'll have trouble sorting them out later in After Effects.

Render as an RPF sequence. When you select RPF Image File as your Save As type and click Save, you will get the RPF Image File Format dialog where you choose which Optional Channels of data to save. Enable Z depth, as well as Material Effects and/or Object (depending on what you want to use as a matte). Also enable the Coverage option, as this improves the matte edges in many cases.

Step 2: Open the comp you created earlier when you were importing the camera data, or [Ex.12a] in the **Ex.12_3ds max prebuilt** subfolder. Select the 3D render layer – **PC_3dsmax_main** – and duplicate it. Drag this duplicate above your video layer, **CL_Skateboarding_ramp**. Solo the layer (the raised button icon to the right of the Video switch), and view the alpha channel in the Comp window (the white icon along its bottom).

Then apply Effect>3D Channel>ID Matte to this duplicate layer. The Effect Controls window will open. Note that the default Aux. Channel type is Object ID, which is what we used in this render. The default ID Selection of 0 matches 3ds max's default ID. Change the ID Selection value in the Effect Controls window to 1; notice that just the visible portion of the videowall's face is shown in the Comp window – this can be used as an Alpha Matte for the video layer underneath. Change it to 2; just the main logo is visible – this can be used as an Inverted Alpha Matte for the video layer, cutting it out just where the logo is.

If you look closely, you should notice that the edges of these mattes are very blocky – they're not antialiased. Layers now default to Best Quality in After Effects, so that's not it. Enable the Coverage option for ID Matte; the edges are a bit better now – although still not perfect. This is where the idea of creating an oversized matte pass comes in (see the sidebar *Oversampling* earlier in this chapter). Or, you might want to manually create your own matte using one of the techniques described for the other 3D programs later in this section.

Set ID Selection to 1, enable Use Coverage, and turn off this layer's Solo switch as well as the Comp window's Alpha switch. Press F4 to reveal the Modes panel in the Timeline window, and set the Track Matte popup for **CL_Skateboarding_ramp** to Alpha Matte. The Video switch for the matte layer will turn off automatically, and in the Comp window

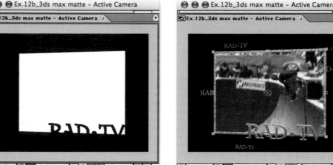

the video will now be cut out to make it appear "behind" the main logo. You can also scale up the video layer if you like; it will still be cut out by the matte from the video-wall's screen. The final result is demonstrated in [**Ex.12b**].

Electric Image Universe

A favorite approach of Electric Image users to create a matte is to edit the Material for any object that should be invisible or cut out so that they cut a hole in the alpha channel. The result then works as an Alpha Matte.

Step 1: Select Material>Add Master Material. Select this new Material in EIU's Project window, rename it something like "**alpha punch**" and double-click it to open it. Select its Diffuse tab, and set the Mask value to 1.0 (fully Transparent). Then select the objects that are supposed to obscure the surface getting the new video in After Effects (in this case, the main logo, and to be safe the frame around the videowall's face), and duplicate them. Select Material>Assign Master Material, and click on your new **alpha punch** material. Turn off any objects that are safely behind the screen; plus the originals of the objects you duplicated. Re-render your scene to a format that saves the alpha channel, such as EIU's native .img format. To save rendering time, you can use a lower-quality rendering engine such as Flat. Don't reduce your Anti-Alias or Sampling Levels; you still want clean antialiased edges for your render.

Step 2: We've imported this render – **CM_EIU_matte** – into the folder **Ex.14-EIU5**. Add it to either [**Ex.14a**] in the **Ex.14_EIU prebuilt** subfolder, or to the comp you created following the Electric Image camera import instructions earlier. Make sure it is placed above the **CL_Skateboarding _ramp** layer, and hit Option+Home (Alt+Home) to start it at the first frame of your comp.

Press F4 until the Modes panel is visible in the Timeline window, and set the Track Matte popup for **CL_Skateboarding_ramp** to Alpha Matte. The main logo will now appear in front of the skateboarding video. If you look very closely at the screen, you might notice some gray fringing where the video's edge meets the screen's edge. You can easily cover this by selecting **CL_Skateboarding_ramp**, hitting S to reveal Scale, and increasing this value a few percent. This will also clean up any ragged edges in the original video capture. The result is shown in [**Ex.14b**].

Step 2: Apply Effect>3D Channel>ID Matte to a duplicate of your RPF file (above left). In our case, we want to focus on Object ID 1, which corresponds to the videowall's screen. Solo this layer and view the alpha channel in the Comp window (center) to verify it is creating the matte shape you need. Then apply this as an Alpha Matte to the video layer (right).

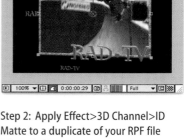

Step 1: By increasing an object's Material>Diffuse>Mask value to 1.0, it will cut a hole in the alpha channel wherever it otherwise would have been visible.

Step 2: The new matte pass cuts out the video to reveal the logo in front.

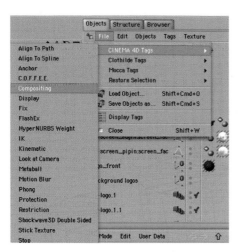

Step 1: To render a matte for an object, select it, and in the Objects Manager, add a Compositing Tag to it (top). In the Compositing Tag dialog, Enable a Buffer, and assign it an ID number (above). Then Add this Channel to your Multi-Pass render options.

Maxon Cinema 4D

As mentioned earlier, the Save Multi-Pass Image option in Cinema offers the best integration with After Effects. It also allows object mattes to be saved at the same time as your main render.

Step 1: In the Cinema project, select the object you need to create a matte for (for example, our videowall's face) in the Object Manager, and add to it File>Cinema 4D Tags>Compositing. Open the Compositing Tag, and turn your attention to its Add to Object Buffer section. Enable one of the Buffers, and assign it a number.

Then in the Render Settings dialog, choose the Multi-Pass pane, and set it up as described back in the Camera Move section of this chapter. Click on the Channels menu in the upper right corner of the dialog, and select Object Buffer. Render, and import the resulting project as described earlier (you'll need the .aec import plug-in for this also).

Step 2: When you imported the Cinema project into After Effects, a folder was created called Special Passes – twirl it open. (If you did not work through the camera import section yourself, you will find a copy already in the Project window's **Ex.15-Cinema 4D>Ex.15_Cinema prebuilt** subfolder.) In it is a footage item called **screen_pass_object_1**; double-click it and play it – this is the matte pass. Add this either to the Cinema composition you were working on earlier, or our comp [**Ex.15a**]. Open this comp, set **screen_pass_object_1** to start at the beginning, and make sure it is placed above the video layer (**CL_Skateboarding_ramp**).

Press F4 until the Modes panel is visible in the Timeline window, and set the Track Matte popup for **CL_Skateboarding_ramp** to Luma Matte (not Alpha Matte). The main logo will now appear in front of the skateboarding video. If you like, you can scale up the skateboarding video to clean up its edges; the matte pass will keep it contained to the video screen. (The white border you see in the Comp window is just a highly reflective material bordering the videowall's face.) The result is shown in [**Ex.15b**].

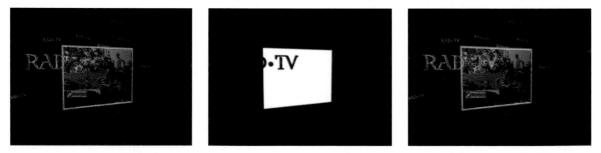

Step 2: Previously, the video added in After Effects blocked part of the main logo (left). A special object matte added to the Cinema multipass render (center) cuts a clean luma matte for the video, revealing the logo again (right).

NewTek LightWave 3D

The addition of RLA and RPF support to LightWave 7.5 would make you think its integration with After Effects would now be on par with 3ds max. Unfortunately, there are some significant problems in both version 7.5's and version 8's implementation:

Gotcha 1: The user currently cannot pick Material and Object ID numbers; they are assigned automatically. Compounding this problem, LightWave 7.5 assigns Object IDs with numbers above 32,000 – which is out of the range where After Effects can access them (this is fixed in LightWave 8). Both versions fortunately place Material IDs in a "legal" range.

Gotcha 2: Even after you have successfully created a matte using a Material or Object ID, the Coverage option for improving the quality of the matte's edges does not seem to work.

Gotcha 3: In LW 7.5, we've seen Material IDs for the same project change from render to render; this is a problem for assembling the final sequence when you're rendering patches or distributing a render.

Gotcha 4: If a material or object shows a reflection of another material or object, that reflection will cause an additional hole in the matte. (To be fair, this reflection problem is also exhibited by other 3D programs such as 3ds max.)

At the end of the day, we suggest you look at a path other than RPF channels to extract a good matte out of LightWave; refer to the next section on *Generic Matte Creation* for some ideas on how to proceed. If you still are curious about working with RPF files rendered by LightWave, you can experiment with comp [**Ex.16b**]: It contains a few of these gotchas including out-of-range Material IDs created by LightWave 7.5.

LightWave 7.5 automatically assigns Object IDs when it writes RPF files, starting at numbers over 32,000 (above). Unfortunately, the After Effects 3D Channel plug-ins recognize only IDs 0 through 32,000 (below).

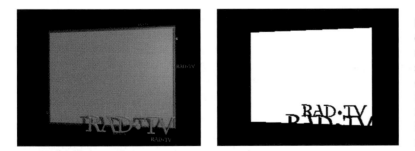

LightWave – like other 3D programs – counts reflections of an object or material as being the same as the source when creating mattes. This causes unwelcome holes in the mattes: Note where the slight reflection of the main logo on the screen (far left) creates holes in the alpha channel in the resulting matte's alpha channel (left).

Generic Matte Creation

In many cases, trickier isn't better. Here's a slightly labor intensive but straightforward method that creates clean mattes in any 3D program:

Step 1: Duplicate the object you want to create a matte of, as well as any objects that directly border it, or that cross in front of it during the course of your animation. Turn off all other objects.

Select the duplicate of your object to be matted (in our case, the video-wall's face), and give it a new material that is 100% self-luminant or "matte"

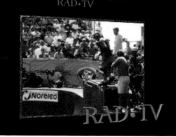

white. Then select all of your other duplicate objects, and give them a material that is pure or "matte" black, with absolutely no reflections, diffuse value, or specular highlights. (These are textures you will use again and again in future projects; consider saving material presets for them. There's a chance your 3D package already has them.) Render this scene as a special matte pass. An alpha channel is not necessary; you will be using the luminance values in this scene.

Step 2: Import this pass into After Effects. Add it to your comp as the layer above the video you are compositing onto your render. Press F4 until the Modes panel is visible, and set the Track Matte popup for your video to Luma Matte. This is shown in [**Ex.16c**] in the LightWave subfolder.

Step 2: Import your special matte render (above left), and place it above your video footage in the Timeline. Set the video footage's Track Matte popup to Luma Matte (top), and your video will be neatly trimmed at the edges with any objects in front neatly cut out (above right).

To avoid the hassle of creating a special matte, you can render the objects to be inserted behind the new video as one layer (left), and all objects that go in front of the video as a second layer (center). Then place the video added in After Effects in-between (right).

Multilayer Composite

Yet another solution is to not worry about cutting a matte: Instead, break the scene into layers and render these as individual passes, so you can place new layers in After Effects between 3D render layers. This is demonstrated in **Ex.12_3ds max prebuilt>[Ex.12c]**. Note that the logo layer – **PC_3dsmax_sep_logo** – was also rendered with its shadow, which falls nicely on the video placed in-between.

If you have the Professional edition, another example of this multipass approach is demonstrated in **Ex.18_tracking prebuilt>[Ex.18b]**. Note that in this case, even though we had the logo as a separate layer, we still created a matte of the videowall's screen to make sure the video's edges were clean. The smaller logos in the background were also rendered as their own layer, and placed behind the other three. This allows even more flexibility in altering their appearance, which we'll explore at the end of this chapter.

Compositing Tricks

The previous two sections – getting camera data from a 3D program into After Effects, and generating mattes to selectively obscure portions of a layer to be composited into a 3D scene – were the difficult, technical portions of our real-world task. What remains – making video added in After Effects blend more pleasingly into the scene, and further tweaking the result – are more creative challenges. We'll close out this chapter with a few tricks to accomplish this.

The Blending Mode Shortcut

To make the video you add in After Effects appear as if it were rendered as part of the original 3D scene, you would prefer that the video pick up all of the shading – the diffuse values, specular highlights, shadows, and reflections – that appeared on the blank videowall. The multilayer composite we were working with in [**Ex.12c**] shows a first step toward this, by rendering the logo – with the shadow it casts – as a separate layer that can be placed in front of the new video layer.

However, the best way to make this happen is to take advantage of the blending modes feature in After Effects. Instead of just stacking layers on top of each other, blending modes blend them together by looking at color values and deciding how they should mix. To optimize this mix, edit the material applied to the videowall's face so that it averages 50% gray. The so-called Lighting Modes – such as Overlay, Hard Light, and Soft Light – will then make it appear as if your video has been projected onto this surface.

Open **Ex.14_EIU prebuilt>[Ex.14b]**. Turn off the Video switch for **CL_Skateboarding_ramp**, and RAM Preview. Note all of the detail on the videowall's face: a "stained mirror" texture, lighting falloff, shadows cast by the logo, and global reflections. Hit End to go to the end of the comp (where you can see these details the clearest), and turn **CL_Skate-boarding_ramp** back on – all of those details are now obscured.

Reveal the Modes panel (shortcut: F4), and change the Mode popup for **CL_Skateboarding_ramp** to Overlay: Note how all of these details are revealed through the video layer. RAM Preview and note how the movement in the shadows and global reflections are visible again. With **CL_Skateboarding_ramp** still selected, hold down the Shift key and

The videowall's face in [**Ex.14b**] has a lot of texture and detail (below left), which is obscured when you insert a video layer in front of it (center). However, because the face was textured to be roughly 50% gray, we can use blending modes to blend the video onto this face as if it was originally rendered into the scene (right).

press – or = to scroll through the various modes; see which one you like best. Examples of this blending mode trick are illustrated in [**Ex.11d**], [**Ex.12d**], [**Ex.14c**], [**Ex.16d**], and [**Ex.17d**] (the last in particular having another combination of stained-mirror texture, shadows, and reflections that blending modes reveal nicely).

What if the blank video screen wasn't exactly 50% gray? Then the result with modes might turn out lighter or darker than expected. In particular, you can use Hard Light instead of Overlay to get a darker composite, as we did in [**Ex.16d**]. Or, you can adjust the gray point of just the screen.

Open [**Ex.17c**], hit End to move to its last frame, and press Shift+F5 to take a snapshot of its current appearance. Then turn off layer 1 (the video precomp). With Window>Info open, move your mouse over the Comp window, and note the values in Info: They seem to start at 50% gray (128 on a 0–255 scale) and get brighter from there. Because you want to correct just the screen itself, you need a layer whose alpha channel outlines this screen. **Select Ex.17-Softimage XSI>RB_XSI_matte** and add it to [**Ex.17c**], starting at 00:00. Drag this layer to be just above the screen layer, **RB_XSI_main**.

The videowall's screen has a great stained-mirror surface (above), but it is a bit bright on average, which can cause our video to appear blown out. Duplicate the screen's matte layer, drag it just above the main screen layer, and turn on its Video switch as well as its Adjustment Layer switch (right).

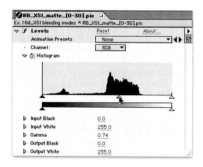

Apply Effect>Adjust>Levels and play with the Gamma slider until you have a nice gray level balance (above). The final composite now has an optimal luminance range (below).

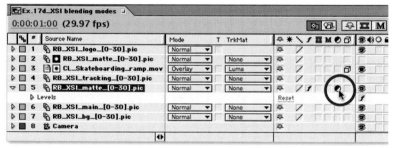

Then reveal the Switches panel (F4 toggles), and turn on **RB_XSI_matte**'s Adjustment Layer switch (the half-moon icon); the image will disappear, but any effects you apply to this layer will be applied to all layers below where its alpha channel is opaque. With **RB_XSI_matte** still selected, apply Effect>Adjust>Levels. In its Effect Controls window, drag the gray Gamma slider under the middle of the Histogram to roughly the middle of the fattest portion of the display – this is the screen's gray levels. If you remembered to turn this layer's Video switch on, you should see the Comp window update as you do this. When you feel you have a good gray balance, turn **CL_Skateboarding_ramp** back on, and toggle F5 to compare the original composite with yours – it should look less blown out in the middle. The final result is shown in [**Ex.17d**].

There will be cases in which the matte you already rendered may not have an alpha channel as required to use it for an adjustment layer. This is easy to cure with just a few additional steps: The first step is to duplicate the matte layer, turn on its Video switch, apply Effect>Channel>Shift Channels, setting the Take Alpha From popup to Luminance. To use the new alpha channel as an adjustment layer, it must first be precomposed, so type Command+Shift+C (Control+Shift+C) to precompose it, selecting the Move all Attributes option. Click OK, and you now have a layer with an alpha channel based on the matte's luminance – drag it above your main screen layer, enable its Adjustment Layer switch, and apply Levels as outlined above. You can practice this by using [Ex.16c] as your starting point; the result is shown in comps [Ex.16e-1] and [Ex.16e-2].

Multipass Compositing

Many 3D artists like to render individual aspects of their scene – for instance, diffuse color, specular highlights, shadows, reflections – as "passes" to independent files to be reblended in After Effects, often using a combination of the blending modes Multiply to darken the composite (shadows) and Add or Screen to lighten it (lights, highlights, and reflections). This allows a large amount of additional control, such as being able to change the strength of a reflection map or darkness of a shadow without having to go back into the original 3D project.

Most 3D programs require you to set up and render each of these passes individually. If you are trying to isolate specific properties perhaps on just a few objects in your scene, you can tweak your project file as needed between renders – such as save a much stronger specular highlight than you think you'll need, knowing you can reduce its strength later in After Effects by reducing this pass's Opacity.

However, the current king of making it easy to create and work with multipass renders is Maxon's Cinema 4D: As mentioned earlier in this chapter, you can specify which properties you want, have them rendered to separate files all at once, and save an .aec project file which tells After Effects how to reassemble the passes into comps and layers.

We're going to take advantage of this feature to improve our video composite in this sample project. Open **Ex.15_Cinema prebuilt>[Ex.15b]** and press End to see the videowall more clearly.

More on Multipass

For a detailed tutorial on multipass rendering and compositing, see the *3D Mechanic* tutorial by dvGarage's Alex Lindsay in our companion book *After Effects in Production*. Also check out dvGarage's Multi-Pass Render Lab (www.dvgarage.com) for a set of in-depth training materials.

Another great multipass trick is called Channel Lighting, in which you render two passes from your 3D program: one with the normal materials applied to your objects and 100% ambient light, and a second with a plain white material applied to your objects and each light given a primary color of red, green, or blue. (If you have more than three lights, you can render additional passes.) The contributions of these colored lights to the scene can then be isolated, recolored, and blended inside After Effects without having to return to your 3D program to change the lights. The Walker Effects Professional Edition plug-ins (visit www.walkereffects.com) make this easy, including documentation on how to pull it off.

Solo the individual layers to see what they contribute to the scene. The nested comps [**Light 1**] (left) and [**Light 2**] (center) provide the basic illumination to the scene; **screen_pass_ambient** adds a very strong reflection map (right). We need to brighten the screen and attenuate the reflection map.

Time Remapping 3D

If your 3D scene does not need to animate for the duration of the final spot, render only the section that does animate, and use the Time Remapping feature (see Chapter 13) to extend its duration. In this chapter, all of the 3D camera moves ease into a hold on their last keyframe, meaning we can hold this last frame of the render to extend the final movie.

Open **[Ex.14c]**, select **CM_EIU_main**, and select Layer>Enable Time Remapping. Hit End to move the time marker to the end of the comp,

press U to view the keyframes. Repeat this for layer 1, **CM_EIU_matte**.

Next, type Command+K (Control+K) to open Composition Settings, change the Duration to 05:00, and OK. Zoom out to see the full duration (pressing – a few times should do it), press End again to jump to 04:29, type Command+A (Control+A) to select all of the layers, then Option+] (Alt+]) to trim all of them to the new comp duration. RAM Preview, and you finally get to see the skateboarder complete his drop-in. Our result is shown in **[Ex.14d]**.

Currently, the video we added in After Effects covers the videowall's face. If you set the **CL_Skateboarding_ramp** layer's Mode to Overlay as we were just suggesting, the result is very blown out, with the details of the video obscured. Turn off the Video switch for **CL_Skateboarding_ramp**, and you'll see that the videowall's face is overwhelmed by a global reflection in the scene, as opposed to 50% gray as we recommended.

Solo layers 6, 7, 8, and 9 one at a time to get a feel for what each is contributing to the scene. The nested comp [**Light 2**] shows the result of a strong spotlight off the left side of the screen, while the nested comp [**Light 1**] is the result of a weak omnidirectional light used as an overall fill. The layer **screen_pass_refl** is the metallic reflection on the edges of the videowall's frame and the logos. The layer **screen_pass_ambient** is what's contributing the overpowering reflection map image. (Layers 10, 11, and 12 are not contributing anything and can be deleted; their normal roles are replaced by [**Light 1**] and [**Light 2**].)

Since each of the properties of this scene were rendered as separate passes, it is easy to use Adjust>Levels to rebalance the contribution of each light and weaken the ambient reflection by reducing its Opacity. Now when the video is composited using Overlay mode, the results are more even.

Turn off all of the Solo switches, and temporarily turn off the Video switches for **screen_pass_ambient** in addition to **CL_Skateboarding_ramp**. With the reflection turned off, the underlying screen is darker than the 50% gray that is optimal for using blending modes. Because we have the contributions of the two lights isolated as separate layers, we can alter their strengths. Apply Effect>Adjust>Levels to [**Light 1**] and [**Light 2**], and adjust their Input White Point and/or Gamma settings to rebalance your lights and brighten the image (remembering that [**Light 1**] was the overall fill and [**Light 2**] was the strong spotlight off to the side).

Turn the video layer **CL_Skateboarding_ramp** back on: It should blend onto the screen nicely now in Overlay mode. Then turn **screen_pass_ambient** back on, and press T to reveal its Opacity. Scrub its Opacity value down until you get a pleasing blend of the video, with a bit of the reflection map visible. RAM Preview, and feel free to tweak the Levels effects applied to the light layers as well as **screen_pass_ambient**'s Opacity until you're pleased with the blend. Our version is shown in [**Ex.15c**].

By using ID Matte and Hue/Saturation applied to multiple copies of the 3D render, we can shift its color scheme from chrome + primary colors (far left) to something more pastel (left) without having to go back to the 3D program itself.

Tweaking Individual Objects

We close out this chapter by looping back to where we started: using the Professional edition's 3D Channel effects to isolate and tweak individual features of a 3D render. In the Project window, open the **Ex.12-3ds max** folder and select **PC_3dsmax_xtra**. This was rendered from 3ds max 5 to the RPF format. In the top portion of the Project window, you can see that Z-Depth, Material Effects, Object ID, and Z coverage information was saved in the file.

Inside the **Ex.12_3ds max prebuilt** folder, open the comp [**Ex.12e**]. Select layer 4 (the bottommost copy of **PC_3dsmax_xtra**), duplicate it, and with the duplicate selected type Command+Shift+] (Control+Shift+]) to send it to the top of the layer stack. Turn on its Solo switch. Apply Effect>3D Channel>ID Matte, and enable Use Coverage. The default Aux. Channel selection should be Object ID. Press Command (Control) and scrub the ID Selection parameter while watching the Comp window, noting that each ID selects a different group of objects. Change the Aux. Channel popup to Material ID and repeat. Select an Object or Material ID you would like to experiment with – such as Object ID 6, the green bands.

Turn off the Solo switch for the duplicate layer so you can see it in the context of the rest of the composite. Then apply Effect>Adjust>Hue/Saturation to this layer. Rotate the Master Hue control until you get a new color you like. You can duplicate this layer and continue to alter other pieces in the scene – for example, select Object ID 0, and use the Colorize option in Hue/Saturation to add a tint to the videowall's chrome frame. One possible set of tweaks is demonstrated in [**Ex.12f**].

Of course, as discussed earlier in this chapter, you don't need to use RPF files to get the same flexibility. For example, in [**Ex.17d**] the background, main screen, and main logo have been rendered in separate passes, allowing you to color-correct each pass individually – go ahead and give it a shot. Or you can combine techniques: In [**Ex.17e**], we applied Image Control>Tint to **RB_XSI_bg** to add color to the background logos, then 3D Channel>Depth of Field to selectively blur the logos that were farthest away.

Of course, just because you *can* do all of this post-production work in After Effects doesn't mean you *should*. The closer you get your original 3D render to the way you want your final scene to look, the easier life will be later. However, it's great to have all of this power inside After Effects, so you can improve upon your work later without having to dive back into 3D.

Connect

Blending modes, see Volume 1, Chapter 10.

Track Mattes, see Volume 1, Chapter 12.

3D space in After Effects was explored in Volume 1, Chapters 14 (3D basics), 15 (cameras), and 16 (lights).

Parenting and null objects were covered in Volume 1, Chapter 17.

Nested comps, see Volume 1, Chapter 18.

Applying effects was covered in Volume 1, Chapter 21; some of the most often used effects such as Levels, Curves, Hue/Saturation, Colorama, and blurs were demonstrated in Volume 1, Chapter 24.

Adjustment Layers were the subject of Volume 1, Chapter 22.

Importing sequences of files, linked Z-depth renders, and project files was discussed in Volume 1, Chapter 25.

Alpha channels are unmasked in Chapter 1.

Fractal Noise effect, see Chapter 7.

Color correction was the subject of Chapter 8.

Simple Choker effect, see Chapter 10.

Chapters 15 and 16 give a thorough overview of using the Motion Tracking and Stabilization tools.

Working with NTSC's frame rate of 29.97, as well as dealing with its nonsquare pixels, are the main focus of Chapter 25.

Assigning proxies, see Chapter 29.

20 Integrating with Web Applications

After Effects is being used more and more as a tool for creating – and repurposing – web content.

The World Wide Web has become pervasive. As a result, many companies who previously needed video content now also want web content – and are asking their graphic designers if they can use the same assets for both. Although you won't be creating web pages in After Effects, recent versions can read and write some of the most common web file formats – including the Macromedia Flash format, SWF. First we'll discuss import issues, then export ones.

Importation Tax

Importing common web file formats into After Effects is a mixed bag. JPEG images come in fine. However, GIF files will lose any embedded transparency, with transparent areas being filled with white. This is related to After Effects' inability to recognize transparency in any file that uses indexed color (where a color lookup table is used in place of individual color channels). You will have the same problem with PNG files that have been saved using "8-bit" or indexed color.

If you need to preserve the transparency in GIF or PNG files that use indexed color, first open them in Adobe Photoshop, and change their Image>Mode to RGB color. Keep the image as a transparent layer; do not flatten it. Save using a new name, selecting either PNG or the native Photoshop PSD format. Import this new file into After Effects, and its transparency will appear as a normal alpha channel.

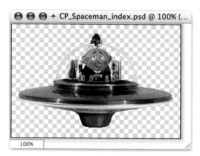

If a GIF or PNG file is saved using indexed color, its transparency (the checkerboard pattern in the image above) will not be honored by After Effects. Spaceman courtesy Classic PIO/Nostalgic Memorabilia.

You can also import animated GIFs, with the same warning about transparency being lost. However, keep an eye on the frame rate; it may be incorrect, with a corresponding change in duration. Select the file in the Project window, type Command+F on Mac (Control+F on Windows) to open the Interpret Footage dialog, and enter the correct rate in the Conform to Frame Rate box.

Flash Flood

There is a lot of interest in web animations created using Macromedia's Flash and its associated SWF ("swiff") file format. Most SWFs consist of vector artwork (akin to what you create in Adobe Illustrator), resulting in small file sizes. These vectors can be resized cleanly upon playback. The "flat" look of Flash has also become a major trend in broadcast design.

Example Project

Explore the 20-Example Project.aep file as you read this chapter; references to [Ex.##] refer to specific compositions within the project file.

If you have a SWF file, you may import it directly into After Effects 6.5. These files are rasterized by QuickTime into pixels, and After Effects treats the result like any other footage item. However, if you want the smoothest possible workflow – including compatible image sizes and frame rates and access to an alpha channel – some preplanning is in order.

Frame Size

Flash does not deal with nonsquare pixels, so you should create animations at one of the popular square sizes for video (see the sidebar *Video Sizes*), and rescale the result to fit your video comps in After Effects. If your SWF has the same vertical dimension as your target video format (such as 768×576 square pixels for the 720×576 pixel PAL format), After Effects will automatically rescale the footage to fit the video comp without any additional work on your part – as long as your animations are tagged in their Interpret Footage dialog as having square pixels, and your video comps have the correct nonsquare pixel aspect ratio set. For all other sizes, use the shortcut Command+Option+F (Control+Alt+F) to scale your square-pixel SWF layer to fit the video size comp.

If you have been given a Flash project that was created at a size smaller than a video frame, and the animation consists of vector artwork, you can cleanly rescale the file to your desired size upon exporting from Flash. You might consider exporting at a larger size than needed: The extra pixels will give you the opportunity to zoom or pan on the overall animation in After Effects, or tilt it in 3D space while still filling the frame. Note that you cannot cleanly rescale a SWF file beyond 100% in After Effects; it has already been converted to pixels before you get a chance to change its scale.

Frame Rate

Those who are familiar with Flash know it is inconvenient to change the frame rate and maintain the same "per second" timing after you have already created keyframes. Therefore, you should think about what frame rate you want your animation to move at before you start animating. Macromedia's documentation suggests 12 frames per second (fps) for web work, and many cartoons are animated at this rate, but you will probably find this too choppy for video work. Choose 24 to simulate film, 25 for PAL, and 15 or 30 for NTSC.

The correct frame rate for NTSC video is 29.97 fps, but Flash currently does not support this. Even though you can enter 29.97 fps in Flash's Property Inspector, you will

---

Video Sizes

As Flash does not currently deal with nonsquare pixels, create or export your animations at one of the following sizes, and scale the result to fit your video comps inside After Effects:

Format	Working (Square) Size	Video Size
NTSC DV 4:3	648×480 or 720×534	720×480
NTSC D1 4:3	648×486 or 720×540	720×486
PAL DV or D1 4:3	768×576	720×576
NTSC DV 16:9	864×480	720×480
NTSC D1 16:9	864×486	720×486
PAL 16:9	1024×576	720×576

Decide on your frame size and rate before starting an animation in Flash. These are set in the Document Properties dialog; click on the Size button in the Property Inspector to open. The graph paper pattern in the Background Color swatch shows we have set it to be transparent, which is important for exporting QuickTime movies with alpha channels.

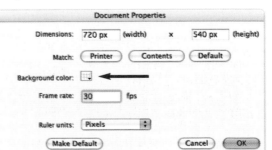

Smooth Going

To get the best antialiasing from a Flash file, enable the Smooth option upon exporting. Also set the Compression for all of your bitmapped assets in the Library to Lossless (PNG/GIF), and enable Allow Smoothing.

PNG Pong

If you read or write PNG files, check out the free SuperPNG plug-in for Photoshop and After Effects from Fnord (www.fnordware.com). It supports 16-bit color, lossless compression, and transparency.

The easiest way to save Flash animations with alpha channels is to Export Movie to a PNG Sequence (top), setting the Color popup to 24 bit with alpha (above).

notice that its timeline will still say 30 fps, and the exported movie will be tagged as 30 fps. Therefore, remember to conform the frame rate of 30 fps animations down to 29.97 fps in the File>Interpret Footage dialog in After Effects. If you used 24 fps, you might want to conform the rate to 23.976 fps; this way, After Effects will nicely add pulldown to this footage when you field render at the NTSC rate of 29.97 fps (see Chapter 23 for more details).

Flash animations do not have interlaced fields. Despite what you may have read elsewhere, do not separate fields for Flash-generated animations when you import them into After Effects; you will end up with crunchy images that lose half of their vertical resolution.

If you want very smooth field-rendered motion, animate at 50 fps (PAL) or 60 fps (NTSC) in Flash, import into After Effects without separating fields, and field-render your output. In the NTSC case, remember to conform your 60 fps animations to 59.94 fps.

If your SWF files have audio as well, conforming them to a different frame rate may cause synchronization issues for longer animations, as conforming frame rates in After Effects does not change the audio playback speed. In this case, add two copies of the footage to your Timeline window, disable the Audio switch for one, and disable the Video switch for the other. For the copy with the Video switch turned off, set its Layer>Time Stretch speed to a value that compensates for the difference between the animation's original frame rate and the rate you conformed it to in After Effects. For example, if you are slowing 30 fps animations down to 29.97 fps (or 24 fps to 23.976 fps, or 60 fps to 59.94 fps), set the Time Stretch value to 100.1% to bring the audio back in sync with the video.

Alpha Dog

When you import a SWF file into After Effects, the alpha channel will be completely opaque and will not cut out your objects. Open this chapter's example project, **20-Chapter Project.aep**, and in the Project window, twirl open the folder **Ex.01**. It includes an imported SWF – **SB_TV.swf** – placed in a comp; notice that the alpha is opaque. Select the SWF file in the Project window and then open the Interpret Footage dialog (File>Interpret Footage>Main): The Alpha options are grayed out. There are ways to get alpha channels out of Flash and into After Effects, however; you just need to use another file format.

Method 1: The most foolproof method is to use Flash's File>Export Movie command, and in the Export Movie dialog select a Format of PNG Sequence. Then in the Export PNG dialog, select 24 bit with alpha channel for your Colors option (see figures to the left). In After Effects, import the resulting sequence, remembering to enable the PNG Sequence option near the bottom of the Import File dialog. Any area outside your objects (symbols) in Flash will be transparent, and the background color will be black in After Effects. Remember to conform the frame rate as needed in the Interpret Footage dialog; frame rates of sequences default to the number set in Preferences>Import. In our tests, After Effects initially interpreted the Alpha as Straight (Unmatted), until we asked it to Guess again, whereupon it changed its mind to Premultiplied (Matted with Black). When in doubt, check your edges carefully.

Method 2: You can also export your art as a QuickTime movie, but you must first create a custom background color in Flash. In the Color Mixer, create a new color with Alpha set to 0%, and click along the bottom of the Color Swatches window to add this color to your palette. It will be identified with a graph paper pattern. Then in the Properties Inspector, select this transparent swatch for the Background color.

Next, use the Mac version of Flash's File>Export Movie command, and choose QuickTime Video (not the choice directly above, QuickTime). In the subsequent Export QuickTime Video dialog, select a Compressor that supports alpha channels, such as Animation. Don't forget to set the Quality slider below as well – drag it all the way to the right to create a lossless Animation file. Then in the Format popup, select 32 bit color (alpha channel). Click OK; the resulting file can be imported into After Effects with a useful alpha.

Flash saves premultiplied alphas, so check that it is not interpreted as straight by mistake. In After Effects, select the file in the Project window, then open the Interpret Footage dialog and click on the Guess button. The Premultiplied option should be selected automatically, and the Matted With Color swatch assigned to a color that matches your Background in Flash (even if the Background Color's Alpha is set to 0, the custom color you made in the Color Mixer has a color in its RGB channels). You may also want to Conform your footage to 29.97 fps.

Method 3: Some Windows users have an alternate workflow in which they have their Flash animator export using the QuickTime option (not QuickTime Video, which is unavailable in the Windows version of Flash MX 6 or 2004), setting the corresponding Alpha popup to Alphatransparent. The result is a Flash animation embedded inside a QuickTime wrapper, which creates a small file

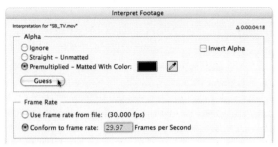

When you're importing a PNG Sequence, be sure to conform to the desired frame rate in the Interpret Footage dialog, and click the Guess button for the Alpha channel type (above).

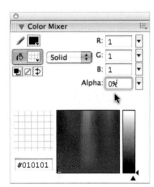

Making a custom color in Flash's Color Mixer with Alpha set to 0% (right).

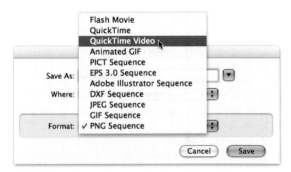

To save a QuickTime movie with an alpha channel, export to QuickTime Video – *not* QuickTime (above), choose a codec that supports an alpha channel, and set the Format popup to 32 bit color (below).

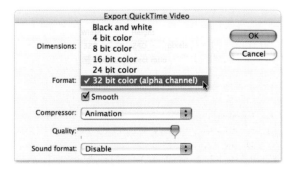

To composite a Flash animation with video and stills in After Effects (above), we exported from Flash with an alpha channel (A), and used a second file containing just the screen (B) as a track matte. TV animation courtesy Wernher Goff of Spot Box; inset video courtesy Photodisc by Getty Images/Cool Characters.

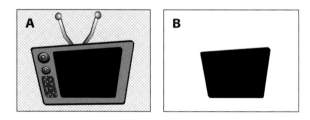

Blurring the Facts

Flash animations do not have motion blur, and enabling the Motion Blur switch in After Effects will not help as the movement has already been rendered in Flash. One solution is to use ReelSmart Motion Blur from RE:Vision Effects (www.revisionfx.com).

that is easy to email. They then open this file in QuickTime Player Pro, and File>Export it to a QuickTime movie using the Animation codec set to Millions+ Colors. (Mac OS X users should be aware that as of QuickTime 6.5, the alpha is not exported correctly with this method. If you receive such a movie from a Flash animator, try to get the original Flash file, open it in your own copy of Flash, and export as a PNG Sequence or to QuickTime Video.)

We have imported a Flash animation saved as a QuickTime movie with alpha into the folder **Ex.02**, and placed it over a background in the comp [**Ex.02**]. To create a cutout for the TV's screen, we exported a second SWF file of just the screen symbol, and used it as an inverted luma matte for our picture-in-picture video (because we used the luminance – not alpha – for this cutout, we could save it as a normal SWF). We also added some shadows in After Effects to finish off the composite. The original Flash files – courtesy of Spot Box – are saved in the **20_Chapter Sources** subfolder on your DVD for you to experiment with.

Export Duties

After Effects is capable of rendering to a number of file formats commonly used by the web, including QuickTime, Windows Media, RealMedia, GIF, and PNG. Each of these choices typically has its own set of Format Options in the Output Module. For example, if you render to GIF, you can select what color is used for the transparent areas.

In addition to going through the normal Render Queue and Output Module, After Effects also can render a selected comp or Project window footage item through the File>Export submenu. This menu includes a number of formats not supported in the Output Module, such as AVI and MPEG-4. As you (or Apple) add components to QuickTime, look for them under this submenu if they don't appear as a Format choice in the Output Module.

Creating SWFs in After Effects

The most interesting Export option is the Macromedia Flash format, SWF. SWF files can contain audio, bitmapped artwork (the normal type of image After Effects creates), and vector artwork (akin to Illustrator outlines). Clients sometimes ask, "Can you export my animation as a SWF as well?" The answer is yes…but in most cases, the result is a very large, inefficient SWF that contains bitmapped images. In this case, SWF provides no advantage over using a format such as QuickTime.

To make the most of SWF, you really want to export your artwork as vectors: They are far more space efficient, and can be cleanly rescaled on playback. Unfortunately, only a small subset of features in After Effects export as vectors. Virtually everything else is either ignored, or if you request, rendered to pixels and saved as a bitmapped image inside the SWF. In addition to the Type tool (see sidebar to the right), these are your choices:

Illustrator Artwork: Stroked or Filled paths in Illustrator footage items will be exported as vectors. You can animate the Transform properties (such as Position, Rotation, Scale, and Opacity) of these objects; you can also enable the Continuous Rasterization switch without fear.

Illustrator files are the most efficient source you can use in After Effects to create a SWF file. If you duplicate an Illustrator layer multiple times, it will be treated as multiple instances of the same "symbol" in the SWF file, which saves space. (By contrast, if you duplicate Solids or Masks, they will create new symbols.)

Note that you cannot apply most effects to an Illustrator file without it needing to be converted to a bitmapped image upon export. We normally advise you to create black text in Illustrator and color it with Effect>Render>Fill in After Effects, but if you intend to export it to a SWF, choose your colors in Illustrator (or change them later in Flash).

Path Text: Now that animated text created with After Effects' new Type tool can be exported as SWF, it's unlikely you'll need to use the Effect> Text>Path Text effect. But just in case you inherit such a project, do know that Path Text can be saved as vectors. The only exceptions are the Fill Over Stroke option, the Difference mode, and the Composite on Original switch; you can have only one copy of Path Text applied to each layer. Also, enabling Motion Blur will cause Path Text to be rasterized into pixels. Each character in Path Text is converted into its own object in the SWF file.

Audio Spectrum and **Audio Waveform:** These two graphical effects can also be saved as vectors. However, there are some limitations; for example, only the Inner Color is honored, and the Softness parameter is ignored (again, unless you request that unsupported features be rendered as bitmaps).

Solids: Create a Layer>New>Solid to make simple shapes that will be exported as vectors. Set the Solid's color in Solid Settings – don't apply an effect to set the color. You can animate the Transform properties of these solids, and apply expressions to them.

SWFing Textacy

As of version 6.5, text created with After Effects' new Type tool can be exported as a SWF. This includes support for text Animators so the sky is the limit for creating dynamic text animation. You can also use any of the hundreds of Text Presets that ship with the program, but be aware that some of them also apply effects (such as blurs and Echo) to the Text layer, which will force it to rasterize when exported as a SWF. Note that as with any layer, enabling Motion Blur will also cause the text to be rasterized into pixels. Each character in the text layer is converted into its own object in the SWF file.

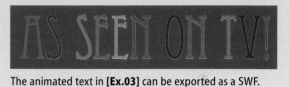

The animated text in **[Ex.03]** can be exported as a SWF.

No Precomps Please

Nested comps are always processed as pixels when exporting to SWF, even if the precomp contains vectors and the nested comp is collapsed. Try to work in one comp, using nulls as parents for grouping.

[Ex.04] contains an animation that can mostly be exported to SWF as vectors – the exception is the still image, which has a few effects applied. Photograph courtesy Digital Vision/All That Jazz.

Masks: Masks will be exported as vector shapes, as long as a few rules are followed. The Feather value must be set to 0. Only Add and Difference modes are supported; if you have multiple masks applied to a layer, they must all have the same mode. If a mask is set to Difference, avoid Mask Opacity values less than 100% or inverting the mask. If you have more than one Add mask on a layer, each will be converted into its own object in the SWF file.

Everything else will either be ignored, or rendered and converted to bitmapped artwork. You also need to composite your layers in one comp, as nested comps are not supported, even if collapsed. If you are placing objects in a precomp in order to animate them easily as a group, parent them to a null object instead so you can work in one comp.

[Ex.03] is a simple animation using several objects that can be exported as vectors – plus one that cannot (the still image on top, which has several effects plus a blending mode applied). Use it for practice in the next section.

SWF Export Options

To export a comp as a SWF file, select it, and use the menu command File>Export>Macromedia Flash (SWF). Note that it is sorted at the top of the Export submenu; don't look for it alphabetically under Flash, Macromedia, or SWF. In the SWF Settings dialog, the most important setting is the Unsupported Features popup. A feature is considered unsupported if:

- After Effects must convert a vector-based layer to pixels (such as applying a Drop Shadow effect to an Illustrator file); or

- After Effects must change the pixels in a layer beyond simple transformations.

Note that pixel-based layers – such as still images and movies – are considered to be supported, even if you animated their Position, Rotation, Scale, Anchor Point, or Opacity. However, virtually anything else – such as applying a track matte or enabling the 3D Layer switch – makes them "unsupported."

If you want to keep your SWF file a lean, mean, vector-based machine, set this popup to Ignore. If you want everything saved, even if it means creating less efficient JPEG-compressed bitmaps, select Rasterize. The JPEG quality is set by the slider and popup above.

SWF Settings

┌─ Images ──────────────────────────────┐
JPEG Quality: 5 Medium

Smaller File   Larger File

Ignore
✓ Rasterize   Unsupported Features
Choose Ignore to skip all features that are not supported by the SWF format.
Choose Rasterize to rasterize all frames that contain unsupported features.

☑ Audio

Sample Rate: 22.050 kHz
Channels: Stereo
Bit Rate: Auto

┌─ Options ─────────────────────────────┐
☐ Loop Continuously
☐ Prevent Import
☑ Include Object Names
☐ Include Layer Marker Web Links
☑ Flatten Illustrator Artwork

Cancel   OK

When you export a SWF file, you are asked how to handle the resulting images and audio. There are also a number of useful options, such as forcing the animation to loop continuously.

Next is the Audio section. SWF files use the same audio compression as MP3 files. Here you set the quality for the saved audio, balancing size against quality.

The Options section offers several useful choices:

Loop Continuously decides if the resulting animation should play once and stop, or loop.

Prevent Import won't allow the file to be imported into a program such as Flash. You will probably want to be able to import your SWFs into Flash, to add other elements or to optimize them (for example, by swapping symbol assignments to make sure all identical objects point to the same master).

Include Object Names means the names of layers and effects in After Effects are used in the SWF file.

Include Layer Marker Web Links includes embedded marker information (see sidebar *Make Your Mark*).

Make Your Mark

You can add Web Links in Layer markers that will be included when you export to SWF. When the animation plays past this point in the timeline, the URL and Frame Target included in the marker will be used. One use is to go to a home page after an animation has played.

Marker
Comment: go to home page
Time: 0:00:01:00 is 0:00:01:00 Base 30non-drop
Options
Chapter:
Web Links
URL: http://www.cybmotion.com
Frame Target:

Note: Web Links and Chapters only work with output types that support them.

Cancel   OK

Flatten Illustrator Artwork decides how semi-transparent shapes are rendered. If you have an Illustrator layer with several shapes, and set the layer to 50% Opacity in After Effects, the objects are composited together and the result is then made semitransparent. If you uncheck this option, each shape has its opacity set to 50% and is then composited, resulting in the SWF file potentially looking different from the After Effects comp.

Upon exporting, After Effects creates the requested SWF file, plus an HTML document that contains your SWF and a report of your settings and what unsupported features, if any, were rasterized on each frame. Practice exporting [**Ex.03**] with both the Ignore and Rasterize choices, and open the .htm files in your web browser. You should be able to see subtle differences: The still image is tinted differently, and Ignore loses the second color in the Audio Spectrum effect. But the difference in file sizes is huge! In the Rasterize version, the image on top causes the entire composite to be converted into pixels, which also affects quality when attempting to scale the result larger.

After Effects is certainly not the ultimate web content creation tool, but the fact that it is such a great compositing and animation tool makes it very useful for creating bits and pieces to include in a web design.

Thanks to Richard Fenton and Wernher Goff of Spot Box, Jonas Cox of Soup2Nuts, Jeff Butler of Cabin One Productions, and Jim Tierney of Digital Anarchy for their help in researching this chapter.

Connect

Layer markers were discussed in Volume 1, Chapter 6.

Masks – including details on using Photoshop and Illustrator paths as masks – can be found in Volume 1, Chapter 11.

The Type tool is the subject of Volume 1, Chapter 25. The Path Text effect was Bonus Chapter 25B.

Photoshop was discussed in Chapter 2; Illustrator in Chapter 3.

An overview of video issues such as frame rates, frame sizes, nonsquare pixels, and broadcast safe colors is presented in Chapter 21. Additional rate and size details are included in Chapters 25 through 27.

Our companion book *After Effects in Production* contains a detailed tutorial (Tutorial 12: *Flamingo 4*) on creating animations to export to SWF.

21 Video Issues

An overview of all those pesky technical issues you need to keep straight when you're working with video.

Just because we can edit and create video content on our computers doesn't mean video is like any other computer artwork. There are a number of nonintuitive technical issues – including interlaced fields, frame rates, frame sizes, pixel aspect ratios, safe image areas, and color spaces – that differentiate video and that must be handled properly to ensure your final work appears on television as you intended. We will give an overview of these topics here, and elaborate on them in the next six chapters.

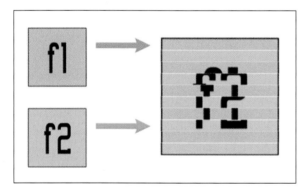

A video frame often contains two fields – subimages captured at different points in time – that have been interlaced into a full frame. Fortunately, After Effects knows how to pull these fields apart and reassemble them later.

Fields and Interlaced Frames

Most video employs a trick in which each frame of the image contains visual information from two different points in time. The two subimages that represent these different points in time are known as *fields*. These two fields are combined into a single *frame* through a technique known as *interlacing*: The first horizontal line for the full frame is taken from the first line of one field, then the next horizontal line for the full frame is taken from the first line of the other field, then the next line for the full frame is taken from the second line of the first field, and so forth. Which field comes first is known as the *field order* of the footage, which is important to know in order to keep time straight when you pull the lines apart again.

Whenever an object in the frame is moving, that object will be in two different positions at the two different times the individual fields were captured. This often results in a visual "comb teeth" effect in a whole frame that was built from interlaced fields. To see this, open this chapter's project file **21-Example Project.aep**, and in the Project window look inside the folder **Ex.01**. Option+double-click on Mac (Alt+double-click on Windows) on the file **CL_skateboarding_fields.mov** to open it in its Footage window; you should see this comb effect. With the file still open and selected, type Command+F (Control+F) to access its Interpret Footage dialog. Set the Separate Fields popup to Upper Field First and

Example Project

Explore the 21-Example Project.aep file as you read this chapter; references to [Ex.##] refer to specific compositions within the project file.

click OK; note in the Footage window that the teeth have disappeared, and that you see the skateboarder in one position in the air. Open the Interpret Footage dialog again, set Separate Fields to Lower Field First, and click OK again; the skateboarder will now be in a different position in the air, earlier in time.

When you have set the Interpret Footage dialog correctly, After Effects is able to pull apart ("separate") the lines of a frame to reform the original fields. After Effects can then work internally at the field rate of the footage (double the frame rate), and reinterlace these fields back into frames when saving a render to disk. When the resulting file is played back through a matching video system, motion will be smoother, as it has been sampled at twice the overall frame rate.

A side effect of the interlaced nature of video playback is that thin horizontal lines are more prone to flickering. Working with interlaced footage, and dealing with these flicker issues, are discussed in Chapter 22.

Interlaced video frames that contain motion often appear to have "comb teeth" – this is caused by fields showing two different points in time being interlaced on alternating lines. Footage courtesy Creative License.

Frame Rates

Typical frame rates for computer-only animation are 10, 12, 15, 24, or 30 frames per second (fps). However, NTSC-spec video – the standard in North America and Japan – runs at 29.97 fps: 0.1% slower than 30. The difference sounds tiny, but it adds up to a frame every 33.3 seconds (or a field every 16.7 seconds), which quickly becomes noticeable. Mismatches in frame rates between 30 and 29.97 can cause audio/video synchronization errors, as well as skipped or repeated images.

Therefore, when you're working with NTSC video on input or output, you should make a point of conforming all of your 30 fps footage to 29.97 fps in the Interpret Footage dialog, set your comps to 29.97 fps, and render at 29.97 fps.

Along with the oddball frame rate of 29.97 comes two different ways to number the frames: *drop-frame* timecode and *non-drop* timecode. Drop-frame alters the counting sequence so that for long continuous pieces of video, the number assigned to the frames in an editing program or on tape matches a normal realtime clock. To do this, it skips the first two frame numbers (not *frames*; just the *numbers* assigned to frames) every minute, except for the multiples of 10 minutes.

Confusing? Yes. That's why most After Effects users (us included) use the non-drop counting method: Every frame is given a sequential number, and you rarely will have a project long enough in After Effects for the running time versus realtime discrepancy to become an issue. The subjects of 29.97 fps and timecode are discussed in more detail in Chapter 25, which focuses on NTSC issues.

The Real 29.97

The frame rate of NTSC video is actually 30,000/1001 fps, not 29.97 fps. However, After Effects uses 29.97; conform NTSC footage to this number.

Hi-Def
Frame Rates

The Advanced Television Standards Committee (ATSC), which set the rules for high-definition video in the United States (also adopted by Canada, South Korea, Taiwan, and Argentina), decided to make 23.976, 24, 29.97, 30, 59.94, and 60 fps all valid rates. It turns out that most production to date is being done at 23.976 and 29.97 fps, therefore perpetuating this hell we have been forced to live in since we got color TV (black-and-white originally ran at 30 fps). A grand opportunity has been missed to standardize on a more sensible rate such as 30, which would have been close enough to 29.97 to painlessly repurpose old material and still have the dreamlike motion characteristics of 24 fps film that many favor. Oh well.

Those who live in places where PAL-spec video is the norm (virtually everywhere outside North America and Japan) have life easier, as they use a clean 25 fps as their standard. We here in NTSC-land are jealous of you.

Film usually runs at 24 fps. When film is transferred to NTSC video, it is slowed down by 0.1% to 23.976 fps, and every four frames of film are distributed across five frames (ten fields) of video through a process known as *pulldown*. When film is transferred to PAL video, it is either sped up to 25 fps, or transferred through a more complex pulldown sequence that distributes 24 frames of film across 25 frames (50 fields) of video. These processes are described in more detail in Chapter 23. Also note that film can be shot at virtually any rate, including 25, 29.97, or 30 fps; this is not a bad idea if you know a project is going to end up only on video.

Frame Sizes

There are two overall image aspect ratios you will be dealing with: normal television, which has a 4:3 width/height relationship, and widescreen or high-definition television (not always the same thing), which has a 16:9 image aspect ratio. The frame sizes in pixels that different video formats use to fill these overall images are often different from the computer monitor resolutions you are used to.

When you are working under the NTSC standard, the professional D1 frame size is 720×486 pixels; the DV frame size is 720×480 pixels – the same as D1, but with six lines cropped off. (You might occasionally see the numbers 720×483 and 720×488, especially if you have Quantel experience.) These same sizes are used whether the overall image is to be displayed at a 4:3 aspect ratio or a 16:9 aspect ratio; the individual pixels are scaled horizontally as needed to fill the frame. (We'll get to the issue of non-square pixels next.) Some older video cards may also use a size of 640×480 or 648×486 pixels.

When PAL is the standard you are working under, both D1 and DV frames are 720×576 pixels. As with NTSC, this same size is used whether the overall image is to be displayed at a 4:3 aspect ratio or a 16:9 aspect ratio; the individual pixels are scaled horizontally as needed. Some older PAL video cards may also use a size of 768×576 pixels.

The ATSC standard for hi-def video in the United States supports several frame sizes. When the final image is supposed to have a 4:3 aspect, the frame size may be 704×480 or 640×480 pixels; these are the "standard def" sizes inside the ATSC standard. When the final image is supposed to have a 16:9 aspect, the recognized sizes are 704×480 (standard def), 1280×720 (hi-def), or 1920×1080 pixels (also hi-def, and the most common of the two hi-def sizes).

Those who have already whipped out a calculator will have noticed some discrepancies by now, such as whereas $4 \div 3 = 1.33$ (the overall aspect ratio of a normal television image), $720 \div 486 = 1.48$. Why? The difference is that in most video formats, not all pixels are intended to be perfect squares. We'll discuss that little piece of mental torture next.

Nonsquare Pixels

Up until now, all that's been special about video are a few relatively trivial technical details, such as its frame size or frame rate. But now we have to tackle a subject that's not at all trivial or intuitive: nonsquare pixels and pixel aspect ratios.

In a computer, each picture element (pixel) that makes up a file is assumed to be square. Create a file that is 100 pixels tall and 100 pixels wide, and the computer assumes it will be displayed as a perfect square on your computer monitor. These same assumptions are made when the computer processes an image – for example, rotate this file 90°, and it should still be displayed as a perfect square.

For reasons far too convoluted to bore you with here, professional digital video systems *don't* treat pixels as perfect squares. In the case of 4:3 images, D1 and DV pixels in NTSC systems display their pixels to be roughly 90% as wide as they are tall. If you look at a D1 or DV NTSC capture on a computer monitor that displays pixels as squares, your video captures will look about 10% wider than normal. D1 and DV pixels in the PAL world are distorted in the opposite direction, intended to be displayed about 7% wider than they are tall. To get an idea of what this looks like, open the folder **Ex.02** inside this chapter's project, and double-click on the two files inside – **AB_IndGearMach_NTSC** and **AB_IndGearMach_PAL** – to view them on your computer monitor. They will look out-of-round.

You can get used to viewing out-of-round images on your computer monitor. (If you can't, we'll get to a couple of workarounds.) However, problems can arise when you don't pay attention to the pixel aspect ratio of your sources versus how they will be displayed. For example, if you send a computer-native square pixel image out through a D1 or DV NTSC video card or converter, the square pixel image will appear on the video monitor about 10% skinnier than you would expect.

p and *i*

When a frame rate or frame size is followed by the letter *p* – for example, 24p – it means it was captured with progressive scan, with no interlacing of fields. When it is followed with an *i* – for example, 1080i – it means the frame has two fields that have been interlaced.

HDV & DVCPRO HD

These new HD formats use non-square pixels. HDV stretches a 1440x1080 source frame size to fill a 1920x1080 image (with a pixel aspect ratio of 1.33:1); DVCPRO HD uses a 1280x1080 source frame to fill 1920x1080 (PAR = 1.5:1) and 960x720 to fill 1280x720 (PAR = 1.33:1). The **Interpretation Rules.txt** file in the **Goodies** folder will add popups to After Effects for these new PARs.

A round wheel appears correct when it's displayed in the environment it was created for. If you correctly tag both the image and the composition you place it in, the wheel will be distorted as needed to stay round when it's displayed in either world.

Nonsquare D1 and DV NTSC pixels make round objects appear "fat" when they're displayed on a square pixel computer monitor. This is okay; they will be round again when they're displayed on a video monitor through a D1 or DV chain.

Images captured using PAL D1 or DV systems will look skinny when they're displayed on a computer monitor – this is correct. (By coincidence, *improperly* tagged square pixels will look like this when they're displayed in NTSC.)

This skateboard wheel, shot using the DV NTSC format, looks out-of-round on a computer screen. However, as it rotates it doesn't wobble – it remains stretched horizontally. With nonsquare pixel sources, the image itself isn't distorted; just the way it is being displayed. Footage courtesy Creative License.

To view your nonsquare pixel comps as square pixels while you're working, enable the Pixel Aspect Ratio Correction switch along the bottom of the Comp window (below). You will see a warning dialog that your final render will not use this pixel aspect correction (bottom).

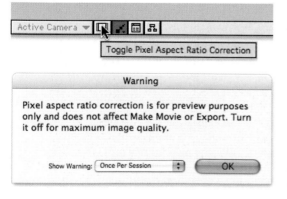

This would all be reason for despair…if After Effects didn't have the capability to track these pixel aspect ratios throughout a project and make adjustments under the hood as needed to translate between them. You just have to do two things for this to happen:

• Set the Pixel Aspect Ratio (PAR) popup correctly for all your sources in their respective Interpret Footage dialogs (see Chapters 25–27). This means keeping track of the system they came from – NTSC, PAL, or a computer.

• Set the Pixel Aspect Ratio popup in the Composition Settings dialog to match the way the output of this comp will be displayed. For example, if you are working in a 720×480 pixel comp that will be rendered and played back on an NTSC DV system, set the comp's PAR to D1/DV NTSC (0.9).

If you want to verify this piece of magic, open comp [**Ex.02**]. The comp has been set up to the DV NTSC frame size and pixel aspect ratio; it also contains DV footage of a skateboard wheel. The wheel looks out of round on a computer monitor because these pixels expect to be displayed through a chain that will eventually show them skinnier than this. RAM Preview; note that the rotating wheel doesn't wobble – it keeps the same distortion. With nonsquare pixels, *it's not the original image that's distorted – just the way it is being displayed.*

Now turn on the Video switch for the layer **CM_bikewheel** – it looks stretched, just like the skateboard wheel. Double-click it to open it in its Layer window; it now looks perfectly round. This is because it was created in a 3D program using square pixels. Since it has been tagged as such, After Effects knows to stretch it when it's placed in a D1/DV NTSC comp. Scrub its Rotation value in the Timeline window, and note that just like the skateboard wheel, it doesn't wobble; it remains stretched horizontally regardless of its angle of rotation.

We will work through more examples of these stretches in the NTSC and PAL chapters (25 and 26, respectively).

Working Square

If viewing slightly distorted images drives you mad, and you don't have a way to preview your comps through a real video monitor (discussed in the section *Monitoring Your Work*), After Effects provides a fix. You will find the Pixel Aspect Ratio Correction switch along the bottom of the Comp window, to the right of the 3D View popup. Click on it to toggle correction on and off. When on, it will now rescale the *display* of your comp window to simulate square pixels. Don't worry – sources still aren't being altered, and this feature is ignored during rendering. However, this feature employs a draft quality "nearest neighbor" algorithm, which can produce visually crunchy images. It is up to you to decide which is the lesser evil.

Generally, when we're designing for a 4:3 image, we work at the native D1/DV sizes with Aspect Ratio Correction turned off, and view our work through a native D1/DV display chain – or just live with the distortion on our computer screen, compensating mentally. If we find there are some graphic elements that beg for straightforward square pixels (creating graphics on grids, using certain effects that work only in square pixels, and so on), we'll create these elements at their square pixel sizes (as discussed in the respective NTSC and PAL chapters), then nest this comp into the final D1 comp, scaling the nested layer to fit. If we are designing for anamorphic 16:9 playback, we tend to do all of our work in square pixel comps, as the pixel aspect distortion is too great to ignore on a computer screen.

View Options

Another way to access the Pixel Aspect Ratio Correction switch is inside the View Options, found in the Comp window Options menu (click on the arrow in its upper right corner).

Anamorphic Widescreen

High-definition television has adopted a *widescreen* overall image aspect ratio of 16:9, and usually square pixels. However, there are many who want the widescreen look without having to upgrade to hi-def equipment. Therefore, devilishly clever video engineers figured out a way to give us widescreen images using our current equipment: They take a widescreen image, squish it horizontally until it fits into a standard 4:3 frame, and save that image to tape or DVD. On playback, compatible televisions or video monitors can be set to restretch the image back out to fill a 16:9 aspect ratio. This technique is referred to as *anamorphic widescreen*.

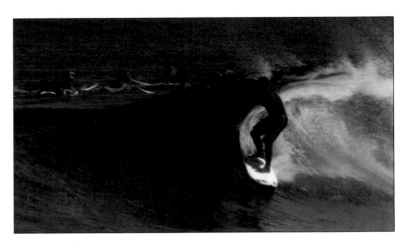

The anamorphic widescreen technique takes widescreen images (above) and squishes them horizontally to fit into a standard 4:3 frame (below). Note that you cannot always tell footage has been squished just by eyeballing it! Footage courtesy Artbeats/Surfing.

This widescreen footage is trickier to handle inside After Effects, as it has the same frame size as normal 4:3 footage – so in most cases, After Effects cannot automatically tell the difference. This often leaves it up to you to manually tag the Pixel Aspect Ratio of widescreen footage in the Interpret Footage dialog. Look at the image and see if something strikes you as funny – like the unnaturally thin surfer in the

Truth in Aspect Ratios

Almost all software (and these days, video hardware) uses the same numbers for translating between nonsquare and square pixels. Unfortunately, these de facto standard numbers are arguably not the precisely correct ones. Most of the time, you won't notice. Occasionally, you will.

This round wheel was shot on DV, tagged as such by After Effects, and placed in a square pixel comp. On a well-adjusted monitor, it will look slightly skinny, because the default PAR After Effects (and most other software) uses is very slightly wrong.

For example, open **[Ex.04]**. This skateboard wheel was shot straight-on (to eliminate perspective distortion) using an NTSC DV camera. After Effects tags it as having a pixel aspect ratio (PAR) of 9/10. But when you place it in a square pixel comp – as we have here – and view it through a properly set up monitor with no distortion, you may notice that the wheel ends up slightly skinnier than perfectly round. (If you want verification, layer 1 contains a perfect circle the same height as the wheel. Set the Track Matte popup for the wheel movie to Alpha to see the wheel inside this circle, and note the tiny slivers to the left and right.) This is because D1 and DV NTSC pixels really have a PAR of 10/11. You will need to rescale this wheel by the difference between these two ratios – 101% wider than tall – to get it to look closer to perfectly round.

For those who notice such things, here is a list of arguably more correct pixel aspect ratios for working at standard definition sizes:

D1/DV NTSC (4:3 image):   10/11
D1/DV PAL (4:3 image):   59/54
D1/DV NTSC (16:9 image):   40/33
D1/DV PAL (16:9 image):   118/81

Even though the ATSC hi-def standards define square 1:1 pixels, several of the older hi-def formats had very odd pixel aspect ratios. Also, some of the new HD capture formats have nonsquare pixels – for example, HDV spreads 1440 pixels across a 1920 pixel frame (for a ratio of 4/3); DVCPRO HD also uses non-square pixels.

To make these ratios available as options in the Pixel Aspect Ratio popups in the Footage and Comp Settings dialogs, we have provided instructions on how to edit the **interpretation rules.txt** file in the **Goodies** folder on your DVD. For example, to add the NTSC and PAL ratios discussed above, enter:

0, 0, 0, "0000", * = 10/11/"Correct NTSC 720", *, *, *
0, 0, 0, "0000", * = 59/54/"Correct PAL 720", *, *, *
0, 0, 0, "0000", * = 40/33/"Correct NTSC 720 16:9", *, *, *
0, 0, 0, "0000", * = 118/81/"Correct PAL 720 16:9", *, *, *

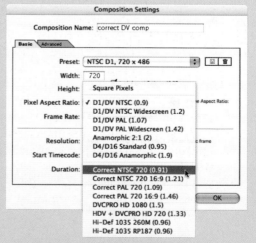

You can add your own pixel aspect ratios to the **interpretation rules.txt** file, which will then show up in the Interpret Footage and Comp Settings dialogs.

footage inside the [**Ex.03**] folder in this chapter's project. (Both NTSC and PAL widescreen will look skinny, just by different amounts.) If you're not sure, ask the cameraperson who shot the footage. Once you tag it correctly, again, After Effects will handle the rest. More details on handling widescreen footage are discussed in Chapter 27.

Safe Areas

When television was first being worked out, there was a lot of concern over the quality and repeatability of the image that would be projected on the screens. Picture tubes were prone to shift the image off-center, shrink the size of image they were projecting with age, and cause visible blurriness and distortion around their edges. Therefore, television was defined as an *overscan* system: The image frame extends beyond the visible portion of the television screen, cropped by the bezel that runs around the picture tube. This is in contrast to the typical computer display, which is *underscanned* – there is a black border around the edge of the picture before you reach the bezel to make sure no important information is cut off.

A region inset 5% from each edge of the frame is defined as the *action safe* area. It is assumed that any action beyond this area could be cut off by a television set's bezel. Therefore, 10% of the height and width of the frame could potentially not be seen by the viewer. You should still put some image (such as an extension of your background) in this area, because you have no idea how much of it will truly be visible or will be cut off by any given TV set. But don't put anything in this region that you expect your viewer to see.

A second region inset an additional 5% along each side from action safe (taking another 10% overall from the edges, consuming a total of 20% of the width and height of the frame) is referred to as *title safe*. It was assumed that picture tubes would distort the image too much for text to be readable beyond this area. Therefore, it is common practice to keep all text you expect your viewer to read inside the title safe area.

As television picture tubes have improved through the years, you see many news and sports broadcasts using the lower portion of the action safe area to display stock market tickers, sports scores, and news updates – although it still gets cropped off by some older sets, particularly if they have an overly oval-shaped bezel.

The design implications of this are that you have far less area of the screen you can use for supposedly visible elements than if you were designing for multimedia or other computer-based playback. Design using the entire screen, and your compositions will appear zoomed up and cropped off when they're played back on a video monitor.

Solid PAR

Solids may ignore the pixel aspect ratio in their Interpret Footage dialog – you must set their PAR in the Solid Settings dialog. Issues with solids, PAR, and effects are discussed in Volume 1 in the sidebar *An Important Aspect,* found inside the chapter *Applying Effects 101.*

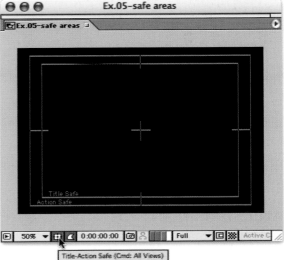

Action and title safe areas – shown here as the white lines inside the borders of the image area – reduce the cumulative width and height of the frame you can work with by 10% (for design elements) to 20% (for readable text). In After Effects, they are toggled on and off with the crosshair icon along the bottom of the Comp window, or with the apostrophe key.

Viewing the Comp window on a computer monitor can lull you into a false sense of security, as it will show you more of the image (right) than will eventually be visible on TV (far right). Footage courtesy Artbeats/Industry: Gears and Machines.

Compression Artifacts

Be aware that if your video card or format of choice compresses the image too much, synthetic graphics – such as text – can have chewed-up edges. This is common with the DV format. DV also undersamples the color, resulting in banding on color gradients.

DV Out...of Luck

Not all DV devices work with After Effects Video Preview – for example, some DVCPRO decks will not work, while a consumer DV camera will. Although this situation has been improving over time as QuickTime is updated, test before you buy!

Open comp [**Ex.05**], and make sure the safe area overlays are turned on (click on the crosshair icon along the bottom of the Comp window, or hit the apostrophe key). Notice how much of this image would be cropped off outside the Action Safe area, and would potentially be distorted in the region outside the Title Safe area. On the bright side, the bezel of the TV crops off a lot of junk – such as black borders and half-field scan lines – that reside outside the Action Safe area in many video captures.

Safe areas are one of the reasons we strongly recommend that you add a video card capable of NTSC or PAL output to your After Effects workstation (discussed later). This way, you can get a better idea of what will truly be visible as you animate and design. Failing that, take advantage of the safe area overlays in After Effects. Preferences>Grids & Guides allows you to adjust where these safe area grids appear, if you want to tweak them. For example, it is generally accepted that the safe areas are much smaller on hi-def sets (although no one seems to know where they really are!).

Safe Colors and Video

Images viewed on a video monitor will appear different from those on your computer monitor. One reason is that video uses a different gamma curve for luminance than most computers, often appearing brighter on video than on the computer screen. In particular, areas that appear buried in black on your computer monitor may be quite visible once they hit video. This is why we strongly recommend that if you are working in video, you should add a card or DV converter with NTSC or PAL video out capabilities to your After Effects workstation – it really is the only way you'll get an accurate idea of how your highlights, shadow, and overall scene brightness are working.

Another reason is that video uses a different color space – YUV – than computers, which prefer RGB. The two color spaces do not completely overlap, so it is possible to create RGB colors that do not translate directly into YUV. Also, video has certain restrictions in that it must be encoded for broadcasting or recording on tape, which creates a further restriction in what colors are wise to use. For example, it is advisable to stay away from deeply saturated pure colors, such as hot reds and yellows. Reds are particularly notorious for "blooming" and smearing on NTSC VHS tape.

Multimedia Resize

When you're designing for "real" video, the good news is that your images will play full screen, probably on a large monitor. The bad news is, you shouldn't really use 20% of the height and width for important elements, because of safe areas. When you design multimedia for computer playback, the bad news is that the window will usually be a fraction of the total monitor's size. The good news is, you can see all of it – and you should use all of it, since it's so small.

If you're repurposing your video creations for multimedia, consider cropping off at least the action safe areas as you scale your video to its new size so that the entire "usable" video area fills your entire multimedia window. For example, if you built a 640×480 video comp and observed safe areas, when you place this comp inside a 320×240 comp for multimedia output, it should be scaled 55% instead of 50% to take into account the 10% "lost" due to the action safe area. This is demonstrated in [**Ex.06**].

The 640×480 video comp is designed so the type stays inside title safe (top right). When we're repurposing for 320×240 multimedia, we size the video 55%, not 50%, to crop off images beyond the action safe area, eliminating dead space around the edges (right). Background image from Digital Vision/Inner Gaze.

Chapter 24 discusses strategies for checking and correcting colors to make sure they are broadcast safe. There are also more third party tools emerging to help you manage your colors, such as the excellent Color Finesse from Synthetic Aperture (www.synthetic-ap.com).

Composite Dot Crawl

Related to the "safe color" issue are artifacts that can appear when certain colors are placed side by side, then displayed through composite video systems (the lowest common denominator, and how most television sets receive their signal from VCRs and the like).

When you're viewing a video image sent through a composite connection on a video monitor, you might notice a series of dots crawling

Free Color

Synthetic Aperture's Color Finesse comes bundled free with After Effects 6.5. Look for it on your installer CD. See Chapter 8 for tips on using it.

Color bar test signals show a weakness of the composite video format: Contrasting colors can cause dots to appear along their borders.

vertically along high-contrast edges at a rate of about one line per video field (roughly 60 pixels a second for NTSC). This artifact is caused by the way composite video is encoded. Reducing the amount of contrast on sharp vertical edges – for example, by feathering or blurring the edge – will reduce this artifact.

Similarly, sharp transitions between saturated colors that have large differences in YUV colorspace can also cause a dot pattern to appear along a shared horizontal edge (from scan line to scan line), especially on higher-resolution studio monitors. Ironically, lower-quality consumer TVs and VTRs may not show this particular flaw; record a VHS tape (if that is your intended playback target) and play it back on a normal TV before completely freaking out or changing the color scheme of your design. (Note that this problem is *not* related to the field flicker issues discussed in Chapter 22.)

Monitoring Your Work

Many of the issues raised in this chapter – nonsquare pixels, interlaced fields, safe areas, color spaces, and the such – are the reasons we suggest you strongly consider adding real NTSC or PAL output capabilities to your After Effects workstation. Viewing your work through an actual video chain is the only way to really see how it will look in the real world. Looking at a computer display and trying to make judgment calls about how much pixels will stretch, thin lines will vibrate, colors will shift, and how much of the image will be chopped off, just doesn't cut it.

Our preferred path is to add to our computer a display card that features direct video output. We highly recommend cards such as the AJA Kona, Blackmagic DeckLink, or Digital Voodoo D1 Desktop. These act as a second entire monitor screen working at either 720×486 or 720×576 (depending on the video standard you need). Drag and center (Command+Shift+\ on Mac, Control+Shift+\ on Windows) your composition window to this screen and view it on an NTSC or PAL monitor to get a correct idea of colors, safe areas, and pixel aspect ratio. If you have a fast computer and a slick card (such as the Deck-Link), you will even be able to RAM Preview to this second screen at full frame rate. As these cards provide a true second dis-

You can set up Preferences>Video Preview to echo your Comp window through a compatible video device.

Preferences

Video Preview

Output Device: Blackmagic Video O...

Output Mode: Blackmagic NTSC – ...

Frame Size: 720 x 486

Output During: ☑ Previews
☐ Mirror on computer monitor
☑ Interactions
☑ Renders

OK
Cancel
Previous
Next

Note: To show the current frame on the output device, press the forward slash '/' on the numeric keypad.

play, you can also take advantage of them in other programs such as Photoshop or a 3D application.

Another option is to add a FireWire device (such as a deck, camera, or FireWire-to-analog video converter) to your computer. You can then use the Preferences>Video Preview feature in After Effects to echo your current Comp window out to this device. If you have a compatible video card (such as the DeckLink), you can also override its second desktop feature and use it to echo the Comp. This is perhaps helpful if you prefer to keep your Comp window on your main computer display, but want to blast its image out to video every now and then as a confidence check. (This technique was discussed in detail at the end of Volume 1, Chapter 2.) The main trick is usually setting the Output Device popup properly – for example, you usually want the RGB option, not YUV.

The next step up from Video Preview is using Synthetic Aperture's EchoFire software suite (www.synthetic-ap.com). It adds a host of useful features to the equation, such as deciding how odd-sized comps are scaled to fit the video display, providing transport controls, playing from disk (instead of just RAM), a stand-alone video previewer, optionally overlaying a waveform monitor and vectorscope, and previewing Photoshop documents or the computer's desktop to video through devices that don't support independent desktop display. EchoFire also tends to support additional video cards the stock Video Preview function doesn't.

Video Monitor ≠ TV

When you're choosing a monitor to view your video output on, seek out a true video production or broadcast monitor – not a normal television set. Believe it or not, normal televisions are not set up to display the most accurate image – they are purposely misadjusted at the factory to provide a brighter, darker, more saturated, or color-shifted image (depending on the manufacturer's theories of what you would prefer to watch). Any trip into a store that has two or more different brands showing the same image side by side will illustrate this fact.

By choosing a professional monitor (one that uses SMPTE C phosphors, for best color accuracy), you have a good baseline to work from when you're choosing colors. Most newer professional video monitors also have a 16:9 switch that changes the way they draw the picture on their screen, so you will see a widescreen image in its correct aspect.

Hi-def video cards are also available from the likes of AJA, Blackmagic, and Digital Voodoo. True hi-def monitors, however, are a very expensive proposition. The current trend is to use a flat-panel screen that has enough pixels to show a hi-def frame (such as an Apple 23″ Cinema display) and a conversion box such as a Blackmagic HDLink to translate HD SDI – serial digital hi-def signals – to the monitor's DVI input. The colors will not be perfectly accurate, but it will give you a good idea of how your image will look at the final resolution.

One of the many features of Synthetic Aperture's EchoFire is the addition of transport controls (that replicate tape deck controls). These work while you're previewing comps inside After Effects or playing rendered files from the desktop.

Useful Links

Most of the information presented in this chapter will be elaborated on in the next several chapters. If you are interested in additional technical information, here are some excellent web sites:

lurkertech (www.lurkertech.com) – Contains the now-legendary *Lurker's Guide to Video* that Chris Pirazzi wrote while at SGI, including an update for those writing Linux drivers. Also contains a pointer to the Apple specification for uncompressed video (which Chris also wrote).

Adam Wilt (www.adamwilt.com) – Highly useful ruminations on a wide assortment of video gotchas, particularly in the area of the myths and realities of dealing with the DV format, as well as color and text issues.

Synthetic Aperture Tips and Articles (www.synthetic-ap.com/tips/index.html) – Articles on selecting a FireWire-to-Video converter, choosing and calibrating a video monitor, and using QuickTime and AVI codecs.

High Definition Specifications (www.atsc.org/standards.html) – ATSC document A/53 describes the ATSC specs for hi-def television; Table A3 is the money box with the frame size and rate specs.

22 Playing the Field

A video frame is more than it seems to be: One frame can represent two different points in time, known as fields.

Fields and interlacing are among the most foreign video concepts a graphic artist has to deal with. Understanding them results in improved smoothness of motion. Getting them wrong results in all sorts of unpleasant visual side effects. Even on their own, fields can introduce flicker artifacts that call for some careful blurring to hide. In this chapter we'll cover the theory, input, output, and flicker aspects of fields.

Two Faces

When you shoot footage with a video camera, it usually does not record whole video frames at a time. Instead, it captures half the lines of an image (and these lines alternate – lines 1, 3, 5, and so forth). It then goes back and captures the remaining lines (lines 2, 4, 6, and so on) to fill in the blanks. These two sets of lines are called *fields*.

Fields are placed one after the other on videotape. When this tape is played back to a video monitor, the monitor draws one set of lines – again, skipping every other line – then uses the next field of information to draw in the remaining lines. Most important, these fields come from (and are played back at) different points in time, at a speed that is twice the frame rate. In other words, the field rate of NTSC video is roughly 59.94 fields per second (29.97 × 2); it is 50 fields per second for PAL (25 × 2).

Individual fields – half frames – of an image are captured and placed one after the other on videotape.

Example Project

Explore the 22-Example Project.aep file as you read this chapter; references to [Ex.##] refer to specific compositions within the project file.

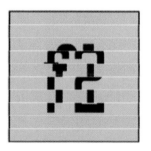

Pairs of fields are interwoven, or *interlaced*, when they are captured as a frame inside the computer.

Although each field has only half the resolution (number of lines) of a whole frame, this doubled rate makes motion appear much smoother.

For better or worse, most computer software and file formats do not think in terms of individual fields, but in terms of whole frames. When video is captured into a computer, two fields are woven or *interlaced* into a whole frame. This may initially seem easier to handle, but because alternate lines are from different points in time, it is dangerous to treat an interlaced frame as being the same as a whole frame.

To best handle these images, on input we must separate the frames back into their individual fields. We then render a field at a time, and reinterlace the fields back into frames before we save them to disk. After Effects is capable of doing both. The tricky part of both procedures is knowing which field in a frame comes first in time.

A video frame with interlaced fields (left) often exhibits a comblike effect around moving objects. This is a result of the difference in motion between the two different points of time (fields) an interlaced frame holds. When we separate these fields, two distinct images appear (center and right). But which came first in time?

Upper, Lower, Even, and Odd

After Effects names the field order of frames according to which comes earlier in time – the first or *upper* line, or the second or *lower* line. If the first line came first, the frame is considered to be *upper field first*. Most 720×486 systems – as well as both NTSC and PAL DV 720×480 pixel systems – are *lower field first*; all of the older 640×480 pixel NTSC systems, non-DV PAL formats, and US ATSC video formats that have interlaced frames are *upper field first*.

Some systems use the terms *even* and *odd* instead of *upper* and *lower* to define field order. Unfortunately, this is ambiguous, as some systems consider the first line to be number 0 (an even number) and some consider it to be 1 (an odd number). In applications such as Adobe Photoshop and Apple Final Cut Pro, "even"

Field Dominance versus Field Order

Many systems use the terms *field dominance* and *field order* interchangeably. Unfortunately, this is not accurate.

Dominance refers to where video editing systems consider frames to start on tape for the sake of editing between them – between field 1 and field 2, or between field 2 and field 1 of the next frame.

Order refers to which set of lines comes before the other set of lines in time in an interlaced frame that has already been captured from tape into a computer. Therefore, when a video capture/playback system says it is lower field *dominant*, it probably meant to say it was lower field *first*.

Known Field Orders

The following table contains – to the extent of our personal experience and of rumors from people we otherwise consider to be reliable – the field order for several video hardware systems. (ATSC stands for Advanced Television Standard Committee, which set the standards for US high-definition video.)

640×480 NTSC	upper
640×480i ATSC	upper
648×486 NTSC	lower
704×480i ATSC	upper
720×480 DV NTSC	lower
720×486 NTSC	usually lower*
720×576 DV PAL	lower
720×576 non-DV PAL	upper
768×576 PAL	upper
1920×1080i	upper

Note that some systems, such as some Abekas DDRs (digital disk recorders), have the ability to flip the field order on playback.

* The Aurora Igniter, Mac-based Avid systems without Meridien hardware, and very early Digital Voodoo D1 Desktop cards are known to be upper; Media 100 software-only transcoders prior to version 6 also would incorrectly interpret this footage as upper field first. 720×488 Quantel .vpb files are also upper field first.

Tell After Effects how to separate the fields in interlaced footage in its Interpret Footage dialog.

is the *lower* field. In ElectricImage, Apple's JPEG-A and JPEG-B codecs, and some Autodesk products, "even" is the *upper* field. If you are not sure, try both settings with a known file (such as DV, which is always lower field first) and see which looks correct. On output, run tests using the same hardware that will be used for final layoff to tape before committing to a long render. Later in this chapter, we'll discuss how to make a test file to check field order of hardware.

Degrees of Separation

When After Effects imports an interlaced movie, it looks to see if there is a resource saved with the file that already indicates the correct field order (After Effects adds this resource to movies it renders, and some NLEs such as the Media 100 insert it as well), or if it has an Interpretation Rule script (see the **Goodies** folder on your DVD) that tells it how to separate the fields for this kind of file. If it finds neither, it then treats the video as if it were noninterlaced, meaning all the lines in the frame belong to the same point in time.

If the source was interlaced, but After Effects does not separate the fields, and you were to then scale or rotate this source in a composition, you'll most likely mix information from the two different fields – and therefore two different points in time – onto the same new line. Even if you field render on output, a mixture of these different fields would end up on each field in the output movie. The result is a shuddering mess, often referred to by a highly technical term we coined: *field mush*.

To avoid field mush, every time you import an interlaced movie, select the footage in the Project list, go to File>Interpret Footage>Main, and choose either Upper or Lower Field First for the Separate Fields popup. This tells After Effects to separate each frame into two separate fields and space them 1/59.94th of a second apart (1/50th of a second for PAL). Then it constructs a full frame out of each field (using field interpolation at Best Quality, or field doubling at Draft Quality), which is then displayed in the Comp window.

Now when you field render your animation, interlaced source footage will be processed correctly: pixels from the first temporal field of the source will end up on the first field of the output movie, and pixels from the second field of the source will be routed to the second field on output.

If you don't separate fields correctly (above), motion will seem to stagger back and forth – for example, look at the position of the basketball. Separate correctly (below), and motion will progress as expected.

Before you can separate fields, of course, you'll need to know whether the source is upper field first or lower field first. If you're not sure of the field order, guess Lower Field First, and click OK. Then open the movie in After Effects' Footage window by Option+double-clicking it on Mac (Alt+double-clicking on Windows) from the Project window. The Footage window displays the source after the Interpret Footage has done its job, so it will display each field, interpolated to a full frame. (If you merely double-clicked on it, you would open the standard QuickTime player, which does not take field separation into account.) Use Page Up and Page Down to step through the fields. If your guess was correct, a moving object will make steady progress as you step through or play the movie; if you guessed wrong, the object will appear to stagger back and forth as the fields play out of order.

To try this out, open the file **22-Example Project**. Inside folder [**Ex.01**], you will find an interlaced footage item called **CM_interlaced.mov**. Option+double-click (Alt+double-click) on it, and you will notice it looks slightly messy – the rightmost digit seems like a mixture of a 1 and a 2; the bar at the bottom is divided into thin lines. These are normal artifacts of viewing interlaced footage. Step through it using the page up/down keys, and you will notice these artifacts persist.

Select this movie in the Project window, type Command+F (Control+F) to open the Interpret Footage dialog, and set the Separate Fields menu to Lower Field First. You will notice the text looks a bit crunchy; this is a natural side effect of seeing only one field, with every other line being interpolated. Use Page Up and Page Down to step through the movie frame by frame: You will notice the bar along the bottom moves in a jerky fashion, and the numbers don't count in the right order. Change the Separate Fields option to Upper Field First, and now all the elements

Post-Interpretation

Press Option (Alt) when you double-click a movie in the Project window to open the source in the After Effects Footage window. Unlike the QuickTime Player, the Footage window takes the Interpret Footage dialog settings into account.

Get an Edge

The old Motion Detect option in the Interpret Footage dialog has been replaced with a Preserve Edges option, which improves the interpolation of fields into frames.

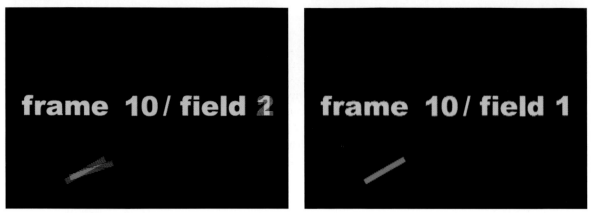

When you initially open the field rendered movie in the **[Ex.01]** folder (left), the interlaced fields are obvious in the mixed 1/2 and the red bar underneath. When you separate its fields (right), it looks crunchier because you are seeing only one field; notice, however, that we also see only one field number, and the red bar is whole now.

Between the Lines

If you want a parameter, such as Position, to jump cleanly from one frame to the next, don't place normal linear keyframes one frame apart. When you field render, there is an extra field in time that gets rendered between these two keyframes, which will expose your move. Use Hold keyframes instead.

will progress as you would expect as you step through it. This smoother progression is how you know you separated the fields correctly.

3:2 Pulldown and Progressive Scan

You may receive a piece of footage in which some frames have field interlacing and others don't. When you step through them field by field, sometimes the same field appears twice; sometimes it appears three times. There's nothing wrong – it just means this footage originated on film and was then transferred to video with "pulldown" added (discussed in more detail in the next chapter). Look past the repeated fields and just make sure the motion is correct – rather than staggering back and forth – when there *is* a change.

If you don't see any scan line artifacts in the QuickTime Player or before the fields are separated, or if you see a pattern of nothing but repeated fields after separation, perhaps your movie was shot or rendered in progressive scan mode. This means field separation is unnecessary – switch it back to Off in the Interpret Footage dialog.

Composition Frame Rate

A composition's frame rate does not affect the source material's frame rate. If you separate fields, resulting in a field rate of 59.94 per second, there is no need to increase a comp's frame rate to 59.94 – you can continue working at 29.97 fps (frames per second). Just remember that as you step through a comp, you will now be seeing only the first field of each frame (which has a lower resolution, because every other line is interpolated). Likewise, you will still be placing keyframes at the start of every frame; there will just be two fields inside each of those frames.

Open [Ex.02] and step through the timeline. You will see only Field 1 of the interlaced movie we played with above. The second field isn't missing; you're just stepping through time a frame at a time, temporarily leaping over every other field. Compare the difference between Draft and Best Quality by toggling this switch for the layer **CM_interlaced.mov** – the field is doubled in Draft, and interpolated in Best.

If you want to see every field, you can double your comp's frame rate to 59.94 (50 for PAL) frames per second. In [**Ex.02**], type Command+K (Control+K) to open the Composition Settings, and type in "**59.94**" for the Frame Rate. Now as you step through the comp, you will see both Field 1 and Field 2 of our movie. Although this is not essential, this can be a good confidence check that nothing is slipping by you as you step through a comp, and it is useful when you're editing mask keyframes for accurate rotoscoping (discussed in Volume 1, Chapter 11).

Note that the act of doubling a comp's frame rate does not increase the temporal resolution of your source material. If your footage's rate was 29.97 and you did not separate fields (or there were no fields to separate), you will not magically get a new image every 1/59.94th of a second: You will only see each frame duplicated as you step through the comp at this finer increment of time. More than one user has *not* field rendered from their 3D program to save time, assuming they would get fields by then field rendering the same material in After Effects. Sorry – After Effects cannot create the missing motion all on its own. Use a plug-in such as Twixtor from RE:Vision Effects (www.revisionfx.com) if you need to create new temporal information in existing source material.

Rendering with Fields

How can you take advantage of the extra temporal resolution of fields when you render? By *field rendering* your output. This makes After Effects double the rate at which it renders a composition. It will render an image at the beginning of a frame and temporarily store this image. It will then forward its internal clock one-half of the frame rate asked for when rendering – 1/59.94th of a second when it's working in NTSC – and render another image using information at this point in time. If you have any footage at this frame rate with separated fields, one field will get used in rendering the first image, and the other field will get used in rendering the second image. These two rendered images are the two fields of the newly rendered frame.

After Effects will then combine these two images into a final frame, using the interlacing method described earlier in this chapter: Every other line is kept from one image, with the remainder thrown away; these lines are replaced with the corresponding lines from the second rendered field and the interlaced frame is saved to disk. Which field starts on the topmost line is set by the Field Render menu in the Render Settings dialog (discussed also in Volume 1, Chapter 26).

When you field render your output, After Effects separates the fields in any properly tagged footage into two frames. It then renders two entire frames at two different points in time, and throws away alternating lines of each image to interlace them into the final frame that is saved to disk (above). Which field comes first in time is set by the Render Settings>Field Render menu (below).

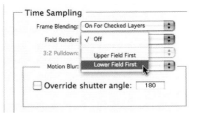

Progressive Scan

A feature gaining popularity in many cameras is a *progressive scan* mode, in which the entire frame is captured at one point in time rather than one half at one point in time and the other half slightly later. This approach better simulates the look of film, which does not have fields, and which also typically has a lower frame rate than video.

If the camera's shutter is kept open for the same portion of time per frame, and the frames are on screen longer (either because of a lower frame rate or because only whole frames – not two fields per frame – are being shot), then it follows that more motion is being captured per frame. This results in an increase in natural motion blur, which also

contributes to what some feel is a more "filmic" look. However, note that switching a video camera from interlaced field mode to progressive scan mode does not necessarily double its shutter time. Many cameras keep the same shutter time when you make this switch, resulting in more strobed motion rather than increased motion blur. Learn how to override the automatic shutter time on your camera if you want to get more motion blur.

Progressive scan playback is also an option in all of the Advanced Television Standards Committee (ATSC) digital video formats. If you work entirely in progressive scan, you can blissfully ignore this chapter. We should all be so lucky.

Best Fields

To get better field interpolation, leave the Quality switch for interlaced layers to Best (the default). With Draft quality, separated fields are merely duplicated.

Testing Output

There can be uncertainty about the field order of the hardware you will eventually play back your renders through. For example, Mac-based 720×486 Avid systems with AVBV hardware are upper field first; PC-based Avids and Meridien hardware 720×486 Avids on either platform are lower field first. You may also be sending a rendered file out of your studio to another, which uses hardware you don't have personal experience with. Although the world has stabilized somewhat since the early days of desktop video when field order almost seemed to be a random decision made by each manufacturer, it is still a good idea to check beforehand to see what the field order of the hardware in question is. If no one knows for certain, create a test file and output that first – *before* you waste time on your actual final render.

To do this, take any simple object – such as a solid or piece of text – and animate its position in a comp, such as from upper left to the lower right of your visible image area over a short period of time. Render it out using your best guess for field order for the intended hardware – upper field first for 640×480; lower field first for most 720×486 systems. When you play it back through your video hardware, it will quickly become obvious whether you guessed right: If you guessed right, motion will be smooth; if you guessed wrong, the motion will have a nasty stutter to it.

[**Ex.03**] includes a simple test set up for a variety of formats, already configured in the Render Queue as upper and lower field first. Select the ones that match your system's frame size, change the Render Settings to use your codec (they default to using the Lossless template, which can also be imported by virtually any system), render, and test.

Problems with Field Order

If your source footage has the same field order as your final render, and you remembered to separate fields, everything works fine. If your sources are the same size as your final render, and are always used centered and full screen, the lines that got separated into individual fields will be the exact same lines kept during field rendering and reinterlacing on output. If any scaling, rotation, effects, or other treatments were performed on the footage, you are still okay, as long as you told After Effects in the Interpret Footage dialog to separate the fields into two new "frames" to process individually.

That's a lot of "ifs" – and if one of them proved not to be true, then your image can degrade in quality. A common complaint from people working with interlaced footage is that it seems to get softer from input to output. There are several possible reasons for this, virtually all correctable.

Reason 1: It's Just Fields

When you separate fields for a footage item, After Effects is now effectively doubling its frame rate. To come up with two frames for one, it takes half the lines from each field and interpolates the rest. It looks softer and jaggy; this is what you now see in a composition or when you Option+double-click (Alt+double-click) on a footage item and step through its fields.

Don't worry – this is a natural, temporary artifact. If you correctly field render your output, the fields will be reassembled, and the image will sharpen back up to match the original.

Reason 2: Field Misalignment

A subtle gotcha creeps up when you're working with full-frame material and the field order of your source material is different from your render, or if the frame sizes or positions don't line up.

Say you separated fields for a piece of upper-field-first footage. The first field now contains, from the top down, line #1 from the original source material, line #2 consisting of pixels made up by interpolating between the lines above and below (because the original line #2 belonged to another field in time), followed by another line of original source material, and so on.

If you were to render out the same footage item full frame, but *lower* field first, on the first rendered field you would skip the first line, grab the next line (line #2, the interpolated line), skip the third line, and so on. The result is a softened image.

In this chapter's project, open [**Ex.04-field softening test**] which consists of our interlaced movie already separated as upper field first. Open the Render Queue (Window>Render Queue), and look at the last two entries in the list. You will notice that [**Ex.04**] has already been placed in the render queue twice, with names already specified as "test upper" and "test lower" – they have been set to render this comp to two

Field Medic

If you need to make better-looking whole frames from interlaced material, check out ReelSmart FieldsKit from RE:Vision Effects (www.revisionfx.com).

Flipping Fields

To permanently change the field order of an interlaced source (from upper to lower or vice versa), import it and *don't* separate fields. Drag it to the New Comp icon in the Project window, move it up or down one pixel in the comp, and render again with field rendering *off*.

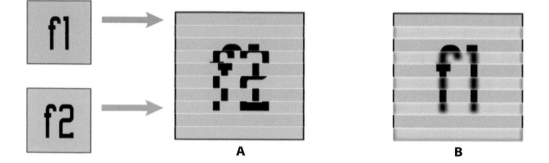

A   B

As shown earlier, a video frame often consists of two interlaced fields, as with alternating the yellow and blue lines above (A). When they are separated into two individual frames, the lines that belong to another field are recreated by interpolating between the lines that are kept. These interpolated lines are shown as gray (B) and are softer in focus than the original lines because they are inter-polated. If you field render, but use a different field order on output, *only the interpolated lines are kept during the interlacing process,* resulting in a softer final image overall.

different field orders in Render Settings. Click on the file names, select where you want to save the movies to, and click on Render. (If you opened the project directly on the DVD and try to render both movies at the same time, you'll get an error because After Effects won't be able to write its log file back to the DVD; either move the project to your hard drive or simply render one movie at a time.)

We have set the Output Module>Post-Render Action for both so that when they are finished, both movies will have automatically reimported themselves into your project. Double-click (not holding Option or Alt) to open them and step through them – you will notice the "test lower" movie is fuzzier than the "test upper" movie.

A similar softening can occur when you mix D1 and DV footage. Most NTSC D1-size footage is 486 lines tall, lower field first. All NTSC DV footage is 480 lines tall, lower field first. If you set up a 486-line-tall comp that you intend to render lower field first, then center a piece of DV footage in this comp, there will be three blank lines at the top and bottom, meaning it got shifted down three lines – an odd number. The lower field of the DV footage now lines up with the upper field of your intend-ed final render, resulting in your using only the softer, interpolated fields. Move it up a line, and the fields line up again. The same applies to PAL footage: DV and D1 sources have the same number of lines, but oppo-site field orders; you need to shift one a single line relative to the other.

To summarize, these are the points to keep in mind with field alignment:
• If a full-frame movie of the same size is rendered out with a different field order than it came in with, the result will be softer compared with the original.
• If a full-frame movie is rendered out with the same field order as it came in, but it was shifted vertically an odd number of lines in-between, it will also get softer.
• If a full-frame movie is rendered out with a different field order than it came in with, but was shifted an even number of lines from in to out, it will get softer.
• Moving an unscaled image up or down an even number of lines keeps its field order.
• Moving it an odd number of lines reverses its field order.

Note that all of this is not an issue if you are scaling and otherwise altering the source footage, since there is no longer a clean one-to-one correspondence between fields in and fields out.

Reason 3: Frame Rate Mismatch

You may have noticed that we tend to save our footage and build our comps at 29.97 fps, which is the frame rate for NTSC footage. Say you've built your comps and set up your renders at 29.97 – but when you play back the results, your video footage seems to alternate between sharp and soft, roughly every 16.7 seconds. What's going on?

Chances are, your original interlaced source material (perhaps an interlaced 3D render, or some interlaced stock footage libraries) was tagged at 30 fps. This is slightly faster than 29.97, resulting in a field being slipped every 16.7 seconds as the fields fall out of alignment with each other. As we mentioned above, slipped or reversed fields look soft. Go back and make sure you have set the frame rate for all these items to 29.97 fps.

If you always work at NTSC rates, and you like your software to do the worrying for you, add the following lines to the **interpretation rules.txt** file which resides in the same folder as After Effects (for more details, see the **Interpretation Rules** folder inside the **Goodies** folder on your DVD):

 # conform all near-NTSC rates to NTSC

*, *, 60, *, * = *, *, 59.94, *

*, *, 30, *, * = *, *, 29.97, *

*, *, 24, *, * = *, *, 23.976, *

We personally work on a wide enough variety of projects that we don't use these rules, as we're afraid they may autocorrect a piece of footage we meant to be left alone. But if your main use for After Effects is to post-process 3D renders – which often default to 30 fps – these might save you some labor (and grief) in the long run.

Finally, there may be some footage that comes in tagged as 29.97 fps but actually has a small deviation from this number, causing other drifts that result in the image going soft. To force all "29.97" footage to be After Effects' precise idea of 29.97, add the following line to your **interpretation rules.txt** file:

 # NTSC frame rate forced conform

– fixes some rate roundoff issues

*, *, 29.97, *, * = *, *, 29.97, *

This same strobing between soft and sharp frames can also occur if you set up your comps and renders at 30 fps, when your input and output are really 29.97 fps video. But you wouldn't do that, would you?

The Real 29.97

The frame rate of NTSC video is actually 30,000/1001 fps, not 29.97 fps. However, virtually every video program – After Effects included – uses the latter approximation.

24 or 23.976?

The most common rates for hi-def production are either 24 fps or 23.976 fps (both progressive scan) – the cameras often support both. Triple-check the frame rate before progressing too far on a hi-def project.

Odd Pixel Out

Footage items that are an odd number of pixels tall or wide are likely to end up on fractional pixels, since their centers are on half-pixels (for example, 243 ÷ 2 = 121.5). This causes them to be resampled and to appear softer.

If you need to convert a 486-line D1 render to a 480-line DV output file, *don't* use Stretch in the Output Module (above). Instead, crop an even number of lines off the top and bottom (below) to reduce its size while maintaining field order.

Reason 4: Scaling Vertically After Interlacing

If you scale a movie with interlacing *without* separating the fields, the results are more disastrous than just softening; the time order will also be confused, as fields will be moved to other fields, reversing their order in time. There are three common ways this mistake can occur:

• Someone forgot to separate fields in the Interpret Footage dialog, then transformed the footage in a comp.

• Someone scaled the footage vertically in the Output Module dialog, when fields have already been introduced in the Render Settings.

• When someone imported a file into a nonlinear editor, the file's height did not match the editing project's height, and the NLE scaled it to make it fit.

These problems are to be avoided at all costs. If you need to resize your render vertically (say, to change 486 lines to 480), instead use the Crop feature in the Output Module to add or trim off pixels from the Top and Bottom (again remembering that moving by an odd number of lines vertically reverses the field order).

Reason 5: Transformations

The final reason is a natural result of manipulating footage: If you scale it, rotate it, distress it, or even just place it on anything other than an exact whole pixel position increment, the resulting pixels will be changed from the originals. And these changes are often perceived as softening and lost resolution (although occasionally, scaling a layer down will make it appear sharper). This rule of nature applies to virtually all footage items – video, film, stills, and text.

If you need to animate footage, these results are inevitable. However, there is one avoidable miscue: If you are simply placing or relocating a footage item that has not been scaled or rotated, try to make sure the Anchor and Position values are on whole pixels. Any fractions will result in antialiasing taking place, and therefore potential perceived softening (although this *is* a technique some use to reduce interlace flicker, which we'll discuss in just a moment). This problem was also discussed in detail in Volume 1, Chapter 3, in the sidebar *Resample: The Good, the Bad, and the Avoidable*.

Managing Interlace Flicker

One side effect of the interlaced, field-based nature of video is that adjacent horizontal lines are drawn on true video monitors and television sets at different points in time. Coupled with the tendency of the illuminated picture phosphors on a screen to decay (go dim), high-contrast horizontal lines or detail in an image tend to *flicker* (or vibrate) on video screens, even if no movement is happening. Similar objects that are moving slowly in a vertical direction might also exhibit an odd *crawling* effect, seeming to get shorter and taller as they move – particularly annoying for credit scrolls. This is a different issue from the field mush described earlier and is a problem inherent in video. To fix it, you will need to selectively blur parts of your image.

First, let's look at the problem. These examples will be more evident if you have a video card in your computer that can drive a video monitor directly, or are previewing through FireWire and a DV camera or deck to a video monitor. Open the comp [Ex.05] and display it through your video out – either by dragging it to the desktop display on a AJA Kona, Blackmagic DeckLink, or Digital Voodoo video card and typing Command+Shift+\ (Control+Shift+\) to center it. Then use Preferences>Video Preview or Synthetic Aperture's EchoFire to echo your Composition window to video (these setups are discussed in the previous chapter).

Layers 6 and 7 – **grid 1** and **grid 2** – should be the only ones turned on right now. Look closely: Notice how the vertical lines of the grid don't vibrate, but the horizontal ones do. Interlace flicker affects only horizontal lines. Then turn on the Video switch for layer 3: **Flicker.ai**. Again, vertical lines do not flicker, but horizontal lines – such as the bars that connect the bottoms of the characters – do. The text is antialiased, so the flicker isn't as bad as with the grids, since antialiasing smears the edges enough to reduce some of the flicker artifacts – but it still has a slight nervous or unstable quality to it.

For additional subtle examples with text, turn on layer 4, **Flicker/sans serif**, created using the sans serif font Arial, and layer 5, **Flicker/serif**, which uses the serif font Times Roman. (To try some of your own fonts, select either of these layers, choose the Type tool, and change the font in this tool's Character palette.) In addition to high-contrast horizontal lines, areas that tend to flicker are slightly angled lines (such as the top of the "e" in layer 3, **Flicker.ai**).

Turn off the text layers and turn on layer 8: **CP_Radio.tif**. Again, note that the round portions of the dial and speaker opening don't vibrate, but you should notice that the horizontal lines of the speaker grill and dial

Interlaced Footage Flickers

Footage items that have fields and lots of motion, and that have not had their fields separated, will flicker on video monitors. Do not soften this footage; the flicker will disappear when you separate fields or field render.

High-contrast horizontal lines – such as the grid patterns in the corners, or the speaker grill on the radio – are prone to flickering when they are displayed on interlaced video monitors. Radio courtesy Classic PIO/Radios.

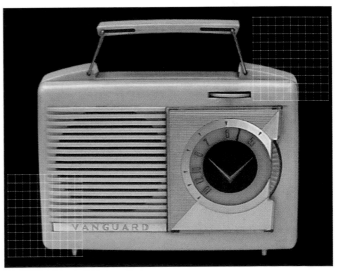

Reduce Interlace Flicker • Effect Controls

Reduce Interlace Flicker
Ex.05-interlace flicker 2 * Reduce Interlace Flicker

▽ ƒ **Reduce Interlace Flicker**	Reset	About....
Animation Presets	None
▽ Ŏ Softness	1.0
0.0		3.0

Directional Blur • Effect Controls

Directional Blur
Ex.05-interlace flicker 2 * Directional Blur

▽ ƒ **Directional Blur**	Reset	About....
Animation Presets	None
▽ Ŏ Direction	0 x +0.0 °
▷ Ŏ Blur Length	0.5

Reduce Interlace Flicker blurs images in just the vertical direction (top), or you could just as easily use the Directional Blur effect (above) set to 0° direction. You can also use Fast or Gaussian Blur with the Blur Dimension popup set to Vertical (not the default of Horizontal and Vertical).

Crawling Titles

When you're scrolling credits and titles, avoid any speed in pixels per second that is an odd multiple of the field rate of your video. These speeds cause details of the text to be displayed on only one of the two fields, resulting in a loss of half your resolution. See the sidebar *Credit Roll Issues* in Volume 1, Chapter 26.

detail do vibrate. If you were to open any of these sources on your normal computer monitor (double-click to open their Layer windows), they would look fine.

There are several ways to solve this. After Effects has a Reduce Interlace Flicker plug-in (Effect>Video> Reduce Interlace Flicker) designed to blur images in just the vertical direction, resulting in less contrast between horizontal lines (since pixels are now being blurred between them). Turn on layer 2, which is an adjustment layer with this effect applied. Notice how the vibrating suddenly stops. Go ahead and enable the various image layers (3 through 6) to see the effect this filter has on them. Select Layer 2 and hit F3 to open its Effect Controls window and set this filter to taste, balancing blur against flicker; as little as 0.5 to 1.0 can kill most problems.

We've noticed that in some circumstances the Reduce Interlace Flicker effect introduces some visible artifacts of its own. Therefore, we prefer using Effect>Blur & Sharpen>Directional Blur set to a Direction angle of 0° (to keep the blur vertical). To see the Directional Blur effect, turn off layer 2 and turn on layer 1 (an adjustment layer with Directional Blur effect applied), and again play around with different values. A blur length of 0.7 roughly corresponds to 1 in the Reduce Interlace Flicker effect.

To see how much better the grid and type layers can appear with a little vertical blur, turn off layer 8, and turn on layers 3 through 7. Now toggle either layer 1 or 2 on and off to compare the results.

Blurs and Scaling

You can apply a selective vertical blur directly to the offending images, rather than an adjustment layer that affects all layers underneath. This is preferable if only a few elements in a composite are flickering; why soften the entire image? However, keep in mind that scale and rotation take place *after* an effect is applied. If you scale an image down, you are also scaling down the amount of blur – and therefore might need to increase the blur amount to compensate.

Still in [**Ex.05**], turn off all layers except layer 8, **CP_Radio**. Select layer 8, apply Effect>Blurs & Sharpen>Directional Blur, and set the Blur Length to 1 in the Effect Controls window. If you've been viewing this comp on a video monitor, the flickering should stop. With **CP_Radio** selected, type S to reveal its Scale parameter in the Timeline window, and set Scale to 25% – notice that the flickering returns! You need to increase the blur length accordingly: 1 (blur length) ÷ 0.25 (scale) = 4 (new blur length to try). This can become tedious to calculate every time you change the scale of a layer. As a result, we often perform our deflickering with an adjustment layer on top of the layer stack, as it is unaffected by the scalings applied to the individual layers underneath.

Selective Blurring

When only part of the image is causing a flicker problem, you might want to consider selectively blurring just that part of the image. Open comp [**Ex.06**]; only layer 2 should be turned on. Output this comp to your video monitor as you did with [**Ex.05**] and observe the flicker. Now, turn on layer 1. This is a copy of the radio, masked down to just the most offensive areas of flicker – the speaker grill and dial detail. You can temporarily solo layer 1 if you wanted to see what areas have been masked. Directional Blur has been applied to just this layer. The result is blurring just the worst areas of flicker, while keeping the rest of the image sharp.

If you need to animate the radio, you could Parent the masked face to the original radio to keep them together as a group. Or, as this is a still image, you could selectively blur the offensive areas in Photoshop and replace the original image in the Project.

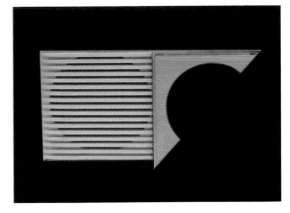

If blurring an entire object to reduce interlace flicker is overkill, mask out the portions that have been causing flicker and blur just these areas.

Fields, Stills, and Multimedia

Broadcast and videotaped video often have fields, but still images and animations created to play back on a computer monitor don't – or at least, they shouldn't.

When you're using interlaced video captures or 3D renders while you're creating content for multimedia and the web, separate the fields of this footage in the Interpret Footage dialog. This will take only the first field from each frame of the source movie and interpolate the single field out to a full frame. This is the same effect you would get with Photoshop's De-Interlace filter on a single frame. Draft Quality in After Effects equals Photoshop's Create New Fields by Duplication option, while Best Quality is akin to the Interpolation setting. If this does not give you sufficient image quality (after all, you're throwing away half your visual information), check out ReelSmart FieldsKit from RE:Vision Effects (www.revisionfx.com): It recovers lost resolution by looking for the pixels that are moving and those that aren't, and keeping whatever pixels it can.

No matter what you might have read elsewhere, *don't* separate fields for still images or computer-specific multimedia – such as Flash animations – on input into After Effects. These sources didn't have fields to begin with, so there's nothing to separate – you would just be throwing away useful pixels. If these images are too sharp and are flickering, try the deflicker techniques discussed in the last few pages of this chapter. And whatever you do, if your destination is the computer screen, don't field render your output! Same goes for still images for print. Fields and interlacing are only for "real" video.

When you're converting a full-frame interlaced movie to half size for playback on a computer monitor, don't just render the full-frame comp at Half Resolution as you may introduce some unpleasant aliasing artifacts. For the highest quality, bring the rendered movie back into After Effects, separate fields, create a comp that matches your target output size, *scale* the movie to fill the comp, and render that. Alternatively, render the original at full size without field rendering and scale down in the Output Module. Either way, remember to set the Render Settings to Best Quality for smoother, interpolated fields.

The Half-Pixel Solution

Sometimes you can exploit the natural antialiasing After Effects performs to kill your flicker problems. If a layer's Position or Anchor Point values are placed on a half-pixel in the Y dimension – for example, Y = 240.5 instead of 240 – After Effects has to antialias the image to make it straddle pixels. This re-rendering causes a slight blurring to the image, which is often enough to fix flickering images.

Re-open [**Ex.05**], displaying it on your video monitor. Turn on just layers 6 through 8; return the **CP_Radio** layer to 100% Scale. Select these layers, type P to reveal their Position values, then hit F2 to deselect them. Click on the Y Position value for any one of these layers, and add 0.5 to it. Its image will become slightly blurred vertically, and the interlace flickering will stop. We use this trick occasionally on illustrations, boxes and lines that are flickering, and other graphics we create in After Effects.

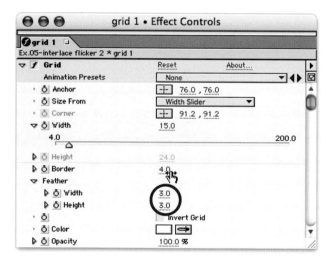

Some effects that create graphical elements that might flicker – such as Render>Grid – have parameters to help combat interlace flicker without having to apply an additional blur effect. In this case, Grid has built-in Feather controls.

Blurring the Effect

If interlace flickering is being caused by graphics created by a plug-in you applied in After Effects – such as Render>Grid – sometimes changing the parameters of the effect will cause the graphics to antialias enough to remove the flicker.

Back in [**Ex.05**], turn your attention to the layers named **grid 1** and **grid 2**. These were created with Render>Grid. Make sure their Video switches are turned on, select **grid 1**, and hit F3 to open its Effect Controls window. Twirl down its Feather parameter, and note that it has separate controls for Width and Height. Hold the Command (Control) key down and scrub the Height value while you're watching the results on your video output. The flickering should pretty much go away by the time you reach a value of 3. If this makes the lines too thin, set the Width value to match, and Command+scrub (Control+scrub) the Border value by fine increments until you thicken them back up to a look you can live with.

Indistinct Edges

Quite often, problems with interlace flickering do not occur within an image but around its outside edges, or when you're shrinking an image down for a picture-in-picture effect. Sometimes, this flicker can be fixed by adding a glow or shadow around the object, softening the contrast between its edges and the background. This technique is also helpful when you're animating objects with thin lines that might otherwise appear to alias on video output. As a result, you can reduce or eliminate the amount of blur you might otherwise need to apply to an object.

If the object is continuously moving vertically – for example, a typical credit scroll – you might also see if normal motion blur, rather than the

Ex.07–credit crawl example • Timeline

Ex.07–credit crawl example

0:00:00:00 (29.97 fps)

Enables Motion Blur for all layers with the Motion Blur switch set

| # | Source Name |
| | 1 | "FLICKER" text |

Switches / Modes

applied effect, blurs the edges enough to reduce flickering. With the animation keyframes already set, enable motion blur for the layer and in the composition. Remember, you can alter the shutter angle amount under the Advanced tab in the Composition>Composition Settings dialog. In comp [**Ex.07**], toggle the Enable Motion Blur switch in the Timeline window (the large M) on and off to see this potential effect; RAM Preview the results to your video output to see this trick in action. Make sure you have enabled During RAM Preview in Video Preview>Video Preview. If your video card cannot preview at full frame rate, consider getting Synthetic Aperture's EchoFire and using its Rapid Preview function.

Enabling motion blur for continuously animating layers – such as credit scrolls – can add enough blur to counteract interlace flickering.

Preferences

Video Preview

Output Device: Blackmagic Video O...

Output Mode: Blackmagic NTSC – ...

Frame Size: 720 x 486

Output During: ☑ Previews ←

☐ Mirror on computer monitor

☑ Interactions

☑ Renders

OK

Cancel

Previous

Next

When you're RAM Previewing to check the results of your antiflicker measures, make sure you enable Output During: Previews in Preferences>Video Preview.

It's a fact of life: Standard definition video does not have enough resolution to hide all the artifacts of a pixel-based medium. You may have to compromise to work around these shortcomings. Some images will simply give you trouble. For instance, computer screen dumps come to mind, as interface designers tend to use thin lines on a contrasting background. If the intention is that the viewer will be able to read the information being displayed (and therefore blurring it is not an option), this is a case in which a multimedia-based presentation may better serve the job than doing it on video.

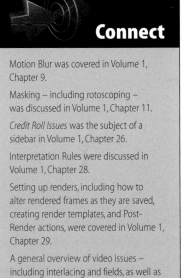

Connect

Motion Blur was covered in Volume 1, Chapter 9.

Masking – including rotoscoping – was discussed in Volume 1, Chapter 11.

Credit Roll Issues was the subject of a sidebar in Volume 1, Chapter 26.

Interpretation Rules were discussed in Volume 1, Chapter 28.

Setting up renders, including how to alter rendered frames as they are saved, creating render templates, and Post-Render actions, were covered in Volume 1, Chapter 29.

A general overview of video issues – including interlacing and fields, as well as how to preview your work on a real video monitor – was provided in Chapter 21.

3:2 pulldown is covered in Chapter 23.

NTSC-specific issues such as frame rate are the subject of Chapter 25; PAL-specific issues are the subject of Chapter 26.

More information on Interpretation Rules is in the **Goodies** folder on the DVD.

23 3:2 Pulldown

Film and NTSC video run at different rates. To transfer film to video, some trickery is required.

Footage originally shot on film and transferred to video using the *3:2 pulldown* process can be used just like regular video. However, there are situations – such as frame-by-frame masking and rotoscoping – in which reverting back to the original film frames can be a big time-saver, as well as improve the smoothness of speed changes and frame blending. In this chapter we'll discuss what this process is and how to remove it.

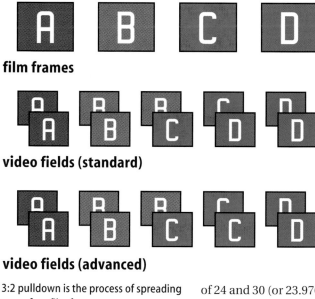

film frames

video fields (standard)

video fields (advanced)

3:2 pulldown is the process of spreading every four film frames across a sequence of ten video fields.

Example Project

Explore the 23-Example Project.aep file as you read this chapter; references to [Ex.##] refer to specific compositions within the project file.

Film to Video

A good deal of film (and high-definition video) is shot at 24 frames per second. NTSC video runs at 29.97 frames per second, and PAL runs at 25 frames per second. How are these differences in frame rates resolved?

In countries that use PAL, the footage is often just sped up from 24 to 25 frames per second (fps), with the audio either sped up or time-stretched to match. However, the difference between 24 and 29.97 is too large to simply varispeed between them. Instead, the film frames are parceled out among video fields to make their average effective frame rates match.

First of all, film is slowed down 0.1% to 23.976 fps – the same difference as between 30 and 29.97 – to keep the math simple. The rates of 24 and 30 (or 23.976 and 29.97) have a fairly simple math relationship between them: 4 to 5. The simplest pulldown method, *repeated fourth frame*, does exactly that – it transfers the first four frames of film to four frames of video, repeats the fourth film frame for the fifth frame of video, then repeats this overall sequence. You rarely see this method employed, except with government and military video. Although it's simple, the motion is not exceptionally smooth.

Five video frames can be thought of as ten fields of video. The standard method of 3:2 pulldown takes the first film frame and spreads it over two video fields. The next film frame is spread over three video fields. Likewise, the third is spread over two fields, and the fourth over three fields, yielding four film frames to ten video fields – or five video frames. This sequence is then repeated for as long as necessary. There is also an "advanced" pulldown method (sometimes referred to as 24Pa) with a different sequence that uses a two/three/three/two cadence for spreading frames over fields; the overall effect is the same. In this chapter, the examples will all use the standard pulldown method.

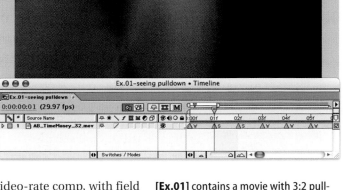

Just a Phase

Open the file **23-Example Project.aep** from the **Chapter Example Projects** folder on the DVD; open example composition **[Ex.01]** and step through it in the Timeline window. This example simulates footage shot on film at 24 fps, slowed down to 23.976 fps, with 3:2 pulldown added to

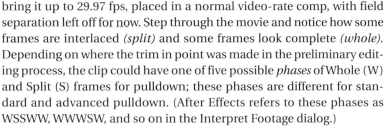

[Ex.01] contains a movie with 3:2 pulldown. We've marked which frames are whole (W) and which are split (S). This frame is split; you can see the interlaced lines in the image. Original footage courtesy Artbeats/Time & Money; we specially modified it to simulate a source exhibiting 3:2 pulldown behavior.

bring it up to 29.97 fps, placed in a normal video-rate comp, with field separation left off for now. Step through the movie and notice how some frames are interlaced *(split)* and some frames look complete *(whole)*. Depending on where the trim in point was made in the preliminary editing process, the clip could have one of five possible *phases* of Whole (W) and Split (S) frames for pulldown; these phases are different for standard and advanced pulldown. (After Effects refers to these phases as WSSWW, WWWSW, and so on in the Interpret Footage dialog.)

The vast majority of primetime television in the United States originates as film or hi-def video and is transferred to video through this process before we see it – so obviously, it works well enough. However, there are some gotchas for those of us working in the production stages. A film editor working in video has to consider many issues to later conform the edit decisions back to the actual film. Our points of concern are simpler: Video fields are being redundantly padded out (we'll call them *bonus fields* for short), and the footage has an irregular motion stagger that shows up when it's time-stretched.

Removing Pulldown

When a video clip requires rotoscoping, it's common to expand the roughly 60 video fields that occur during a second to 60 interpolated frames for editing. In this case, you would separate the fields of a 29.97 fps clip and add it to a 59.94 fps comp, where you could now step through and edit the clip field by field.

But if the footage originated on film and has had pulldown added, only 24 of these 60 frames are "real," and reverting back to the film frames can save hours of tedious masking. To remove the pulldown,

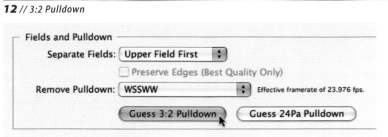

Under Fields and Pulldown in the Interpret Footage dialog, click on either the Guess 3:2 Pulldown or Guess 24Pa Pulldown buttons (depending on the footage), and After Effects will attempt to discern the field order and pulldown phase of your file.

Varispeed and Audio

There may be times you want to revert back to the absolute original film rate of 24 fps. You would do this by conforming your 29.97 fps footage to 30 fps, then removing pulldown. However, if the file also had audio attached, After Effects will give you a warning that "audio may not synchronize." As of version 6.5, After Effects *still* won't conform audio.

You have a few options to keep the two in sync. One is to not conform the file in the Interpret Footage dialog, just remove the pulldown. Place the movie in a 24 fps comp, and time-stretch the layer by 99.9%, undoing the 0.1% telecine slowdown. Another option is to conform the footage to 30 fps and time-stretch just the audio as its own layer – but make sure you keep the original in points lined up, or you could drift out of sync.

select the clip **AB_TimeMoney_32** in the **Ex.01** folder of the Project window and type Command+F on Mac (Control+F on Windows) to open the Interpret Footage dialog. In the Fields and Pulldown section, click on Guess 3:2 Pulldown. (If you knew the footage was captured using advanced pulldown, you would click on Guess 24Pa pulldown instead. If you don't know, try both!) After Effects will scan the first ten fields of the clip, figure out the field order and the phase, and revert the footage to its original 23.976 whole frames per second. Step through either the clip in the Footage window or its associated [Ex.01] comp, and you will see only whole frames now.

You will notice that a message indicates that the 29.97 fps video clip now has an "Effective frame rate of 23.976 fps" rather than 24, which accounts for the slowdown that occurs during the telecine process. (Just to confuse you a little more, After Effects may display the 23.976 rate truncated to 23.97 or rounded up to 23.98 – rest assured that the internal frame rate is accurate enough that no rounding of frames is taking place.) If you're working on a project in which the output is not NTSC video, you might want to Conform Footage to 30 fps – removing the pulldown will now produce an effective frame rate of an even 24 fps (which divides in half to a web-friendly 12 fps).

Pulldown Miscues

After Effects will beep if it can't guess the pulldown phase. One way to help After Effects guess is to trim the start of the clip before importing so that the first ten fields are clean, do not contain a fade-up from black, and have some obvious motion.

To check that the footage has reverted correctly to the original film frames, Option+double-click (Alt+double-click) the clip in the Project window to open it in the After Effects Footage window, which shows the clip *after* it's processed by the Interpret Footage settings. Play or scroll through the entire clip – *there should be no interlaced frames visible*. If interlacing is visible, manually select different phases until you arrive at the correct one. Occasionally we've encountered a single clip with a mixture of phases, and can only assume that it was time-stretched during editing (which means you're hosed). Also, when a comp is at Half Resolution, don't panic if you see interlacing – it will disappear at Full Resolution. (If it bothers you, you can prerender the source at 23.976 fps and permanently remove the pulldown.)

If a footage item has an edit in it, the pulldown phase might change at the edit point. If so, edit the video capture so that each scene is a separate footage item to After Effects, and apply Remove Pulldown to each clip separately. If that is not an option, import the unedited source clip multiple times and manually set the phase for each segment you plan to use.

Advantages of Removing Pulldown

There are two areas where removing pulldown from telecined footage will make your life much easier: masking and time-stretching.

Problem Unmasked

When you're masking a moving object in interlaced video footage, you often need to set your comp rate to 59.94 fps, and either mask on every field, or at least check every field to make sure the mask isn't wandering as it interpolates between keyframes. If the footage was originally shot on film and has pulldown added, the pulldown pattern will add an irregular temporal stagger which makes smooth mask shape interpolation even more difficult. However, if you can remove this pulldown, you'll have only 23.976 frames per second to mask (less work!), and each frame will progress in even increments.

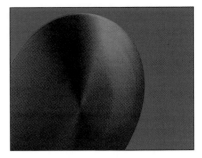

If the mask is not locked down with the Preserve Frame Rate option set, it will look correct when the frames align (above), but will slip (below) when you field render the footage that you originally removed pulldown from.

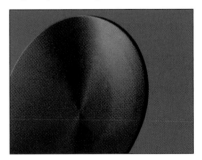

Life is good if you render this comp at 23.976 fps. But if you don't take precautions to lock the mask down, its alignment will slip if you render at the 29.97 fps video rate. This is because After Effects looks at the comp rate only for display and setting keyframes; when it renders, it uses the frame rate in Render Settings to sample the sources. Similarly, if you nest the 23.976 comp into a comp running at 29.97 fps, the mask will also slip.

Comp [Ex.02-masking-1] contains a swinging pendulum, from footage with pulldown removed, masked at 23.976 fps. If you step through it, you will see that the mask follows the motion correctly. This masking comp is nested into [Ex.02-masking-2], which is running at the video field rate (59.94 fps); we will use this comp to simulate what would be sampled if you rendered at 29.97 fps with fields. As you step through this simulation comp, the mask now slips in relation to the pendulum, because the mask shape is now interpolating at a different frame rate than it was designed to run at.

One fix is to prerender the masked layer in its precomp at 23.976 fps with an alpha channel and to reimport – this locks down the mask to each frame. The "Preserve frame rate when nested or in render queue" option offers an even better way, as it doesn't require more disk space and keeps the precomp "live." Open [Ex.02-masking-1], and type Command+K (Control+K) to open its Composition Settings. Click on the Advanced tab, enable the Preserve Frame Rate option, and click OK. Then return to [Ex.02-masking-2]: As you step through the frames, the mask should not slip because the precomp is sampled only at the frame rate it's set at.

Mask the **AB_TimeMoney** movie in a precomp at 23.976 fps, and enable the Preserve Frame Rate option under the Advanced tab in the Composition Settings dialog.

PAL Pulldown

When the speed-up from 24 to 25 is not tolerable, there is a system in which the 12th and 24th film frames get spread across three video fields each instead of two, making 24 equal 25. This yields a huge number of potential phases; plus, half the video frames will appear split in a program such as After Effects.

Transfer Savings

To save time, money, and disk space, have your telecine film-to-video transfers done at 30 fps (one film frame to one video frame). Capture or import the video, and Conform the footage to 23.976 fps in After Effects' Interpret Footage dialog. This way, you can avoid the hassle of removing pulldown.

Stretching by Numbers

When telecined footage is time-stretched to run slower, the "three fields, two fields" staggered pattern can be slowed to the point where it becomes distracting. Comp [**Ex.03**] again has our pendulum, with pulldown removed. Make sure only the first layer is turned on; this features the pendulum time-stretched 300%. RAM Preview (Composition>Preview> RAM Preview, or hit 0 on the keypad). Notice the stagger, even with Frame Blending turned on.

You can smooth the motion with a little math (we know; we keep saying that – but a *little* math isn't bad). You want to use a time-stretch value that will evenly place one film frame every certain whole number of video frames. For instance, if you time-stretch a one-second clip (24 film frames) to 80%, the new duration of 00:24 will place one film frame per one video frame. A value of 160% will place one film frame per two video frames. In short, multiply the amount of stretch you want by 80% to account for the difference between 30 and 24. For example, to stretch eight times: $8 \times 80\% = 640\%$. Using similar logic, since there are two fields per video frame, you can stretch by 40% increments and have a film frame every whole number of video fields.

The other layers in [**Ex.03**] feature these different stretch amounts. Solo and preview a few; note that their pattern is a little smoother.

Stretch
80.0%
160.0%
240.0%
320.0%
400.0%
480.0%
560.0%
640.0%
720.0%
800.0%

Time-stretching by multiples of 80% on footage that has had 3:2 pulldown removed will result in smoother motion.

Removing Repeated 4th Frame

After Effects does not remove Repeated 4th Frame pulldown automatically. We've personally used several different techniques to do this, including hand-removing the repeated frames from a movie or still sequence. Our current favorite 5:4 removal recipe is to carefully line up a 29.97 fps movie in a 23.976 fps comp until we find an arrangement where it naturally skips the redundant fifth frame. The steps:

Step 1: Import the movie, making sure field separation is turned off and the frame rate is conformed to 29.97.

Step 2: Drag it into a new comp with a frame rate of 23.976.

Step 3: Step through each frame of the movie, looking for repeated frames. If you find one, slide the movie one frame later in the timeline (or earlier, if you can afford to lose some of its head), and step through the timeline again.

Step 4: Once you find the offset that results in no repeated frames, render back out at 23.976 fps, without fields. You now have a clean film-rate movie to work with.

Rendering with 3:2 Pulldown

Now that you've been working happily at the film rate on whole frames, how do you get back to video? Very simple: After Effects can add pulldown during rendering on the way to creating a video rate movie.

The easiest procedure is to just render at 29.97 fps, with fields, and After Effects will naturally introduce pulldown as it samples 23.976 fps source material during the rendering process. If you have been mixing video and film sources, or want additional sources to render with smoother motion, this is the way to go.

However, it is often stylistically a better match if all the sources are rendered with the same frame rate of motion. To do this, set up your compositions at 23.976 fps, and use this rate to keyframe your additional elements such as titles and other graphics. Add this comp to the Render Queue. You can then add pulldown during rendering: In the Render Settings, set the Field Render popup to Upper or Lower as your hardware requires, and select any standard (not advanced) phase from the 3:2 Pulldown menu (unless you are specifically matching back to edits in film, where you might need to match a specific phase). The comp will be sampled at 23.976, but a 29.97 fps movie with an overall 3:2 interlaced pattern will be created, using the same process as a telecine.

The advantages are faster rendering (since you are sampling the comp at 23.976 fps, not 59.94 for normal field-rendered video), and all your video having a matching look. The disadvantage is that the lower frame rate of 23.976 fps can cause visible strobing with faster movements. If this is a problem, you might try cranking up the Motion Blur Shutter Angle in the Render Settings to higher than its default 180°.

(Note that if your footage and comp are set to 24 fps, and you render with pulldown and a frame rate of 29.97 fps, the comp will be sampled at 23.976 fps – slightly slower than your sources are running at.)

A Grand Compromise

There is a middle ground between the smooth motion (and long render times) of interlaced video, and the fussiness of working with 24 fps film with pulldown added: Work at 29.97 fps, with no fields. For instance, film can be shot at 30, not 24, and transferred to video a frame to a frame. Create 3D animations at 30 fps as well. Conform this footage to 29.97 fps as needed. Some video cameras also have a 29.97 fps "progressive scan" (no fields) mode. Composite and render at 29.97 fps with field rendering left off. Rendering goes faster, and motion will be more filmlike without quite the tendency to strobe as 24 fps sources can.

Filmlike 3D Motion

A popular trick among 3D animators is to render at 24 fps to better simulate the motion characteristics of film. Import these renders into After Effects, conform them to 23.976 fps, and render with pulldown added, resulting in a rate of 29.97 fps. To smooth the motion, render your 3D with motion blur, or postprocess in After Effects with ReelSmart Motion Blur from RE:Vision Effects.

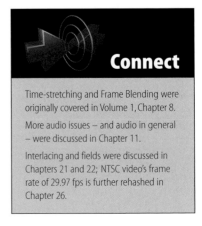

Connect

Time-stretching and Frame Blending were originally covered in Volume 1, Chapter 8.

More audio issues – and audio in general – were discussed in Chapter 11.

Interlacing and fields were discussed in Chapters 21 and 22; NTSC video's frame rate of 29.97 fps is further rehashed in Chapter 26.

Time Sampling

Frame Blending: On For Checked Layers

Field Render: Lower Field First

3:2 Pulldown: WSSWW

To add 3:2 pulldown to a 23.976 fps comp, and raise it to 29.97 fps interlaced at the same time, queue it up to render, set its Render Settings to set the field order you want, then select a phase in the 3:2 Pulldown popup. The frame rate will automatically change to sampling the comp at 23.976 fps and rendering a movie to disk at 29.97.

Luminance and IRE Issues

A not-so-simple matter of black and white, plus making your colors "broadcast safe."

Some video systems use different internal representations for defining "black" and "white" points in their files. It is important to track these differences throughout a project – although few users do, as they don't realize these issues exist. Ignore these issues, however, and your sources may shift in relative brightness and contrast for no apparent reason, resulting in either washed out or oversaturated images. You will need to do a little sleuthing to understand what is going on, but once you do, many mysterious problems will disappear.

This chapter also covers the issue of "broadcast safe" colors, including approaches for reducing the chance that a video engineer may turn his or her nose up at your finished graphics – for technical, not aesthetic, reasons.

Black and White

Different video hardware and codecs present different luminance ranges to computer-based applications such as After Effects. It comes down to a definition of what is black and what is white.

Most computer software – After Effects included – defines black as having an RGB value of 0,0,0 (or an overall luminance value of 0), and white as having an RGB value of 255,255,255 (or an overall luminance value of 255). These are the extremes of brightness you can pick.

However, the ITU-R 601 digital video specification has a different approach. For starters, it divides grayscale luminance out into its own channel, separate from the color information. It then defines black in this luminance channel as having a relative value of 16, not 0, and white as having a value of 235, not 255. Systems based around this spec – which include virtually all video hardware, from DV to high-definition cameras and decks as well as nonlinear editing systems – use this compressed luminance range internally so that they may have some internal values that go "blacker than black" and "whiter than white" for special purposes.

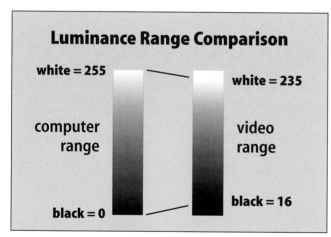

Luminance Range Comparison

white = 255

computer range

black = 0

white = 235

video range

black = 16

Computers and many video systems use different numeric definitions for black and white. It is your job to keep them lined up throughout a project.

Example Project

Explore the 24-Example Project.aep file as you read this chapter; references to [Ex.##] refer to specific compositions within the project file.

Problems occur when these systems encode and decode files in a way that they present this unaltered 601 luminance range to a computer program such as After Effects, instead of the full range After Effects is expecting. On the input side, footage items appear washed out and lacking contrast, as they do not use the full luminance range available to After Effects. On the output side, by using the full range available to you but then saving to a format that expects a more limited luminance range, you could create images that have "illegal" luminance values.

An image that displays its internal 601 luminance range will look a little washed out (left) when compared with the same image displayed using the full computer luminance range (right). Image courtesy Perception Communications and American Isuzu Motors Inc.

Although there are trade-offs, it is usually desirable to work inside After Effects with the full 0-to-255 luminance range. This is because virtually none of the plug-in effects or other processing steps in After Effects know about potential 16-to-235 limitations, and therefore can create luminance values that would end up illegal in some systems – especially if you use glows or blending modes that can brighten part of an image, or create images from scratch with pure colors. Therefore, we prefer to work in a way that we convert any 601-range footage to full luminance range on the way in, and convert our final graphics back to 601 range on the way out if the system we're delivering to requires it.

Input Conversion

Some video codecs automatically convert their internal 601 luminance range to full computer range before they hand a frame over to After Effects. Examples of this include Avid (at its default settings), Blackmagic, and Digital Voodoo; they require no further processing or thought on your part. However, some systems – such as Media 100, Aurora Igniter (at its default settings), most file sequences saved from dedicated digital disk recorders (DDRs), and some DV codecs – pass on to After Effects their internal 601 luminance range without conversion. Therefore, footage items that use these systems need manual conversion in order to take advantage of the full luminance range After Effects has to offer.

8 bpc versus 16 bpc

For simplicity, color values in this chapter will be presented using 8 bit per channel (bpc) ranges. Some video formats use a 10-bit range for the luminance channel, and the Professional edition version of After Effects has an optional 16 bpc mode (which is really 15 bpc, plus 1 extra value – see *Sweet 16* in Chapter 7). Here is the conversion between these systems for some common luminance values:

8 bpc	10 bpc	16 bpc
0	0	0
16	64	2056
235	1880	30198
255	1023	32768

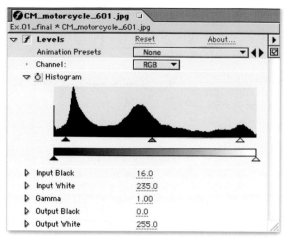

To stretch 601 footage to the full luminance range, apply Levels and set Input Black to 16 and Input White to 235.

To practice expanding the luminance range of 601 standard footage, open this chapter's example project, **24-Example Project.aep,** then open the composition **[Ex.01*starter]** by double-clicking it in the Project window. Layer 1 – **CM_motorcycle_601** – shows a scene originally captured on DV with the internal 601 luminance levels intact. Layer 2 – **CM_motorcycle_full** – shows the same scene, with the internal 601 levels stretched to fill the full luminance range. Toggle the Video switch for layer 1 off and on to compare it with layer 2 underneath.

To expand the luminance range of a layer, select it (**CM_motorcycle_601** in this case), apply Effect>Adjust> Levels, and set the Input Black point to 16 and the Input White point to 235 while leaving the default values of Output Black at 0 and Output White at 255. Try this with layer 1 in **[Ex.01*starter]**; notice how this treated clip

QuickTime Curveball

The Apple QuickTime DV codec automatically converts between an internal 16–235 luminance range and an external 0–255 luminance range for programs like After Effects. This is normally a good thing, as it is one less source for you to worry about converting.

However, this codec also introduces a gamma curve as part of its translation, making images appear darker after decoding. If you want to undo their gamma correction so that footage that uses this codec looks the same in After Effects as the same shot captured through a non-DV full luminance range system, you need to add Effect>Adjust>Levels to your footage on input and set the Gamma to approximately 1.228, as shown in comp **[Ex.09a]**.

If you then render to another format (like Blackmagic or Digital Voodoo, which are always full range), use the levels adjusted footage as is. However, if you render back to the Apple QuickTime DV codec, you should consider redoing the gamma correction: Apply Levels to the final comp, and set Gamma to about 0.824, as shown in **[Ex.09b]**. We used an adjustment layer, because we want our entire composition to get this curve. These two Animation Presets have been saved as **QTDV_gamma_undo.ffx** and **QTDV_gamma_redo.ffx** and saved in the **Goodies** folder on the DVD.

The Apple QuickTime DV codec adds a gamma correction to files as it decodes them, causing them to look darker (above) than they would if they were processed through another full luminance range workflow (below).

now looks virtually identical to layer 2, which is the full-range clip (toggle layer 1's Video switch to compare). If you have trouble getting this to work, compare your results with [**Ex.01_final**]. We have saved this setting on the DVD for you in the **Goodies** folder as Animation Preset **601_remove.ffx**.

If you are using a clip more than once in a project, you might want to give that clip its own composition with the luminance adjustment applied, then use this comp throughout your project to avoid having to remember to apply effects to each copy of your source. If you have several video clips – all from the same 601-range source – that you have already edited together in a comp (such as when you import a Media 100 project as a composition), another approach is to go to time zero (0:00:00:00), create a Layer>New>Adjustment Layer, and apply Levels to it to stretch the luminance of all layers underneath. This technique is demonstrated in [**Ex.02**].

Hidden Switches

Some codecs have switches that change how they process luminance levels. They might reside in their QuickTime codec options when you select them to render (Avid and Aurora), or may be in a control panel.

A Whiter Shade of Pale

The potential downside of normal-izing all of your luminance ranges to 0–255 inside After Effects is that any blacks below 16 and whites above 235 will be clipped off, possibly causing some posterizing around shadows and highlights. This is more of a problem for the

latter, as many cameras can capture levels above 100 IRE (the upper limit for legal white, which is supposed to map to luminance 235), and flattening these hot spots out can be noticeable. We've had this problem with a fair amount of DV footage we've received, particularly if it was shot on a lower-end camera.

This problem is demonstrated on a simple black-to-too-white gradient in [**Ex.03**] and an actual image in [**Ex.04a**]: Turn the Levels effect (which we've renamed **601 removal**) on and off and watch the details in

Some DV cameras have a tendency to shoot illegal whites when they're left in Auto mode. This shot contains a lot of detail in the bright white areas (above left), which also happen to have been shot over 100 IRE (brighter than legal white). If we apply our simple Levels adjustment to this clip, detail is lost in these areas (above right). Using a Curves profile (below left) that rolls off rather than clips these highlights results in a more gentle alteration of the image (below).

the white areas disappear and reappear. In this event, you might want to use the Adjust>Curves effect instead and gently roll off rather than clip the white point. A Curves preset that does just this is saved in the **Goodies** folder as **601_remove_curve.ACV** and is used in [**Ex.04b**]. Know that at this point, you are no longer accurately treating your video through the processing chain; you are trying to make the best of footage that was shot or transferred incorrectly before it found its way into After Effects.

16 bpc Color

If you are performing any color alterations and you have the Professional edition, you will get better results if you set File>Project Settings>Color Depth to 16 bits per channel.

Of course, the best approach is to take more care in shooting footage, dialing back the brightness at the camera if needed. Most cameras can display a "zebra" pattern to show you when you are going out of legal range. You can also adjust the input processing amplifier on your non-linear editing workstation when you capture footage from other sources to compensate for these whites. If you shoot or transfer legally, you don't need to go through all these extra gyrations with the Curves effect.

If losing details in these extended black-and-white areas is a deep concern to you, you can always keep your video in its original 601 luminance range; just make sure you don't create blacks darker than 16 or whites brighter than 235 in After Effects. This means watching the color values of your "black" and "white" text and carefully monitoring the results of any effects that overly darken or brighten the image – you may need to use Levels to bring them back into 601 legal range. Also, if you wish to composite a photograph or 3D render into your scene while you're working with a 16–235 luminance range, you will need to reduce the luminance range of these items to match. You can use the same effects as you would to convert your entire render to a 16–235 luminance range (the subject of the next section).

The 16–255 Approach

An alternate technique some employ when they are presented with footage that uses a 16–235 luminance range and has white values over 235 is to stretch just the black point down to 0, but leave the white point temporarily untouched. To do this, apply Levels to the footage in question with Input Black set to 16, but leave the Input White alone.

After you are done processing and compositing the footage, raise its black point back up to 16 (apply Levels, and set the Output Black to 16 while leaving Output White alone).

Then decide how you are going to deal with your illegal white values (those over 235): Apply Curves and gently ramp them down to a maximum of 235, or use a more sophisticated tool such as the Limiting section of Synthetic Aperture's Color Finesse (www.synthetic-ap.com) with its Preferences>Video System>Video Coding Level popup set to 16–235.

Credit to Adam Wilt (www.adamwilt.com) for suggesting this technique.

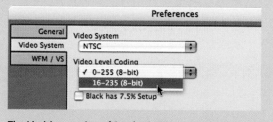

The Limiting section of Synthetic Aperture's Color Finesse is a good tool for taming too-hot whites. Remember to set its Preferences to reflect the luminance range of the image you are feeding it.

Output Conversion

Just as some codecs don't convert luminance from 601 to computer ranges when they decode a frame, neither do they make the inverse conversion when they're saving the frame. However, many possible processing steps in After Effects – such as adding glows and using blending modes – can result in illegal black and white values in the 601 domain, even if you are careful to otherwise track the colors you pick for all your other elements. Plus, elements rendered in other programs (such as 3D animations) are probably using the full luminance range, rather than the restricted 601 range, as well.

Therefore, when you are saving to a codec or file format that expects 601 luminance ranges (16–235), you will need to convert your normally full-range luminance values to this restricted range before the file gets saved to disk. The best way to do this is to place a full-frame adjustment layer as the topmost layer in your final comp, and apply your luminance range correction effect to this adjustment layer.

The easiest way to compress full-range luminance down into the 601 range is to apply Levels to an adjustment layer that sits above all of your full-range footage items. Open [**Ex.05*starter**], hit Home to make sure the time marker is at the beginning of the comp, and create a New>Layer>Adjustment Layer. With this layer still selected, apply Effect> Adjust>Levels. In the Effect Controls window, set Output Black Point (*not* Input Black) to 16, and Output White Point to 235. This is saved in your **Goodies** folder as Animation Preset **601_addition.ffx**. The result is demonstrated in [**Ex.05_final**].

One of the main advantages of using an adjustment layer is that you can view (and render) either an adjusted or unadjusted image, depending on your needs. Turn this adjustment layer off when you're viewing on a computer monitor or rendering to a codec that does not need conversion (Avid, Blackmagic, Digital Voodoo, et cetera), and turn it on when you're viewing through a video card that mirrors your Comp window without performing a luminance range correction, or rendering to a codec that needs this adjustment (Aurora and Media 100 are examples).

If the comp you are rendering has areas where you see the black Composition Background Color, these areas remain RGB 0,0,0 black – even if you have an adjustment layer in place to convert the visible blacks from 0 to 16. Place a black solid behind all your layers in your final comp, then make the level change with an adjustment layer or in a later comp. This is demonstrated in [**Ex.06**]: Turn the black solid in layer 3 on and off, and run the eyedropper around the black areas in the Comp window while noting the values in the Info window – they'll read 16 when the Solid is on and 0 when it is off, even when the adjustment layer on top with Levels applied is still on.

What if you applied our highlight-preserving Curves preset mentioned above on some footage – should you use a complementary curve on output? No. The purpose of that curve was to tame illegal whites into the legal range; we don't want to re-expand them back out into the illegal range.

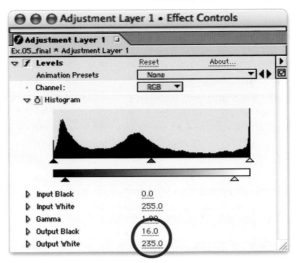

To compress a full luminance range down to the 601 range, apply Levels and set Output Black to 16 and Output White to 235 (above). To do this to an entire composition, apply Levels to an adjustment layer that resides at the top level of the layer stack (below).

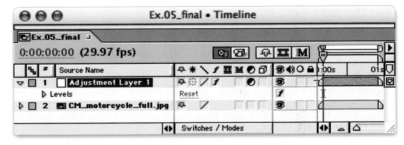

Video on Fire

EchoFire from Synthetic Aperture (www.synthetic-ap.com) is an excellent utility for working with video. It lets you mirror your Comp window, play back video, and display color bars; plus, it has a built-in waveform monitor and vectorscope. It also understands different luminance ranges.

What's My Luma?

If you don't know what luminance range your codec is handing you in After Effects, digitize a tape that has a proper set of SMPTE-style color bars with PLUG (picture line-up gradient) bars in the second square from the right along the bottom. If you see three skinny bars inside this square, your footage is probably a 16–235 range. If you see one wide bar and one skinny bar, it is probably a 0–255 range (the two bars that merged together represent black, and blacker than black – which is the same as black in a 0–255 world). Clean examples of these bars, generated with Synthetic Aperture's free Test Pattern Maker (www.synthetic-ap.com), are inside the **Goodies** folder on your DVD.

If you can see three distinct PLUG (picture line-up gradient) stripes in your digitized color bars, you probably have a 16–235 luminance range – assuming the bars were recorded and digitized properly in the first place.

NLE Luminance Fix

If you accidentally rendered footage for a 601-based system with the incorrect full range of 0 to 255, you may be able to fix it on the fly if the system has realtime color correction. For example, in a Media 100 i or HD, apply ColorFX, with Contrast set to roughly –16 to bring the white and black points closer to legal.

Workflow Summary

The point of applying these corrections is to keep all of your footage in the same luminance range. Our goal is to make sure all incoming footage is in the computer's (and therefore, After Effects') luminance range; if it isn't already, only then do we apply these input adjustments. Likewise, if we're rendering out of After Effects to a codec or video card that does not directly accept the computer luminance range, only then do we apply these output adjustments, to bend our computer ranges into what these codecs expect.

Here is the workflow to use if you want to maximize the luminance range in After Effects:

• Convert any footage that uses the ITU-R 601 luminance range (Media 100, Aurora Igniter default settings, most file sequences saved from DDRs, and some DV codecs) to full luminance range using one of the techniques outlined in *Input Conversion* or *Whiter Shade of Pale*.

• Do not convert any footage that either naturally uses the full luminance range (photos, Illustrator art, 3D renders, elements created inside After Effects) or has a codec that does the luminance range conversion for you (such as Avid at its default settings, Blackmagic, Digital Voodoo, or QuickTime DV).

• Work at full luminance range in After Effects: Black text can be 0, white text can be 255, plus no worries about glows, blending modes, and similar treatments, making your luminance ranges illegal.

• If you're rendering back to a codec that does luminance range conversion for you automatically, do nothing special on output.

• If you're rendering back to a codec that expects native 601 luminance ranges, place an adjustment layer above the final comp, and convert the luminance range using one of the techniques outlined in *Output Conversion*.

Admittedly, this is a lot of extra fiddling to keep track of. We keep hoping that someday, After Effects will allow these conversions to take place in the Interpret Footage and Output Module dialogs, which is cleaner, and their proper place. In the meantime, keep track of the luminance ranges of your sources and targets, and compensate accordingly – that way, your luminance values will stay consistent from input to output, resulting in better video and fewer headaches.

But just because your luminance ranges are legal, doesn't mean your colors are too. We'll get to Safe Colors in a bit. But first, we need to clear up some confusion about how video hardware does or does not affect luminance ranges inside After Effects.

IRE, Setup, and Luminance

Many confuse the issues of luminance ranges inside your software, with "setup" or "pedestal," which affects the electrical representation of a video signal. These are separate issues: The luminance ranges we've discussed before this point are strictly *digital* issues, whereas IRE is an *analog* issue. Setup does determine how black-and-white values will be mapped between the digital and analog worlds upon conversion, but one should *not* be adjusted to compensate for the other unless you have a very good reason and know what you are doing.

The IRE scale is used to measure the relative brightness of an analog video signal. "Full legal white" is typically defined as 100 IRE; "full legal black" is defined by most systems, *except those most common in North America*, as 0 IRE. Video capture and playback cards then map between digital luminance values and these IRE values. If you are using hardware based on 601 luminance ranges, 235 will be translated to 100 IRE, lining up white to white. Many video cameras capture higher than legal white, which means a video signal higher than 100 IRE; this is part of the reason the 601 luminance range puts white at 235 – so it still has some headroom to represent these whiter-than-white signals. But the potential presence of these illegal luminance values in the original video does not change how your video card or DV deck interprets black and white.

The most confusion arises in the definition of black. In North America, NTSC composite video has an additional *setup* or *pedestal* added to the black point, so that it now measures 7.5 IRE instead of 0 IRE. If setup is present in the composite signal, it is present in the Y/C or "S-video" signal as well; this pedestal is also occasionally present in component video.

Personal Adjustments

You can rename Adjustment Layers – they're just Solids. Select them, and type Command+Shift+Y on Mac (Control+Shift+Y on Windows) to open their Solid Settings dialog.

Superblack

On rare occasions, you might be asked to output an animation over "superblack." Some video systems pull a key or matte from areas of an image that are blacker than black – in other words, below the normal legal black point.

To do this, you will need a video system that operates in the 16–235 luminance range and a hardware interface that can be set to 7.5 IRE setup. The goal is to place the black in your animation at 16 so it will go out of the hardware at 7.5 IRE (legal black), then fill the background around it with a luminance value of 0. This background will then come out of the hardware around 0 IRE, which is illegal, or blacker than black: superblack.

Assuming you have the above hardware, on the After Effects end you will need to set up your final comp the same as in **[Ex.07]**: Set your Composition> Background Color to black, and do not fill in areas that are supposed to be keyed later (in other words, the opposite approach as shown in **[Ex.06]**). This will ensure that any transparent areas in your image will go out as superblack.

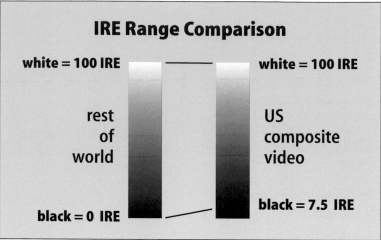

IRE Range Comparison

white = 100 IRE   white = 100 IRE

rest of world   US composite video

black = 0 IRE   black = 7.5 IRE

Different IRE setups use different voltages over analog video to define black and white. White is almost exactly the same, but black is considerably higher with 7.5 IRE setup.

The computer file has no knowledge of this analog setting, *nor should it care* – it is just a switch or adjustment in hardware on how to map digital black to an electrical video signal's representation of black. However, if the IRE setup is wrong, then wrong values will end up in the computer file.

Just as it is important to manage luminance levels inside your computer, it is very important to keep the setup consistent throughout your signal chain outside the computer. For example, if a videotape was recorded with 7.5 IRE setup, you need to set your video card the same; otherwise, your black points will no longer line up, making you think you've got problems elsewhere with luminance ranges when in fact the problem happened further upstream. If you are using SDI/analog converters, make sure they have been calibrated for your decks – for example, you can order AJA SDI/analog component converters (www.aja.com) that have been calibrated to mate up to Sony BetaSP decks, which use a 7.5 IRE setup even for their component signals.

The same goes for playback: Find out if your client wants setup added to the tape you're delivering and set your video card or NLE accordingly. PAL and Japanese NTSC do not use setup, therefore black is 0 IRE; in North America, if it's analog, black is probably at 7.5 IRE. (The vast majority of prosumer DV decks use 0 IRE as the black reference point, so setup is not an option. More professional decks do offer setup as an

sRGB versus RGB

Another area where you may see washed-out images is with digital photography on a Mac. Consumer digital cameras capture images using the sRGB colorspace, not the regular Apple RGB colorspace that After Effects expects. Photoshop 7 and later recognizes these photos as sRGB, and asks you how you would like to manage these images in Photoshop; for instance, work in sRGB colorspace, or convert sRGB to your working colorspace. However, After Effects ignores color profiles and assumes they are the equivalent of Apple RGB. This results in washed out, lower-contrast results for sRGB images. There are two approaches you can take to fix this problem:

• Open the sRGB image in Photoshop, and select Mode>Convert to Profile and select Destination Profile: Apple RGB. Resave and import this image into After Effects.

• Import the sRGB images into After Effects, and use the Übercolor plug-in from Fnord Software (www.fnordware.com) which is included free on this book's DVD. Apply the plug-in to your layer, set the Source to sRGB, and the destination to Apple RGB. (See Chapter 2 for more info.)

optional setting. Beware a "7.5% setup" option on DV camera such as the Sony PD-150; they improperly boost the digital luminance values rather than change how the analog interface works.) When you deliver the tape, mark on it whether black is at 0 or 7.5 IRE in the event it's being recaptured or duplicated.

Note that IRE applies only to analog video; digital video by definition does not have setup added. However, when you have an analog-to-digital video conversion somewhere, setup becomes an issue again – to map black between the analog and digital worlds.

Also make sure that the video monitor you're previewing your work on has been calibrated to the same setup as your video card; otherwise, you'll get confused about how dark is dark while you're working. All of our video monitors are calibrated for 7.5 IRE setup, because that's what our BetaSP deck uses for its component connections, and also what all of our composite connections use. We became very confused when we bought a new monitor that happened to come from the factory set to 0 IRE setup – things just didn't look right on it until we changed it to match our video card. Many monitors don't have their black points adjusted properly; it is worth investing in a color bar generator (about $300) or software that can output proper bars through your video card just to set up the black point on your monitor if nothing else.

Safe Colors and Video

As alluded to throughout this chapter, video uses a different color-space (YUV) than computers (RGB). These two colorspaces do not completely overlap. Also, it is possible to create combinations of color and luminance values that, when they're modulated together to travel down a video cable or to be broadcast by a transmitter, would create out-of-range electrical values. Therefore, we need to be concerned about so-called *broadcast legal* or *safe* colors.

In general, it is advisable to stay away from deeply saturated pure colors, such as hot reds and yellows. Reds are particularly notorious for "blooming" and smearing on NTSC VHS tape. The color shifts involved in translating from RGB to YUV space might also not be aesthetically pleasing. That's why we recommended back in Chapter 21 that you have some way to preview your compositions to a real video monitor, and check your colors as you work. If your delivery format is VHS, record proofs out to tape to see how bad the damage is. Tailor some of your color choices based on what you see.

Aesthetics aside, quite often the engineering department of the facility that will duplicate or broadcast your final project will check your colors to make sure they stay within proper ranges. You can leave it to them to color-correct your imagery after you're done with it – many do, feeling that ignorance is bliss. Or, you can pre-emptively try to correct the colors yourself before you hand over your final work.

We've Been Set Up!

An excellent article by Adam Wilt (www.adamwilt.com) on setup from *DV* magazine (www.dv.com) appears in the **Goodies** folder on your DVD.

Blind Rules

You should not apply the same rules blindly – such as always reduce saturation, or always reduce brightness – to correcting colors. Remember that reducing saturation moves a color toward gray; reducing its brightness moves it toward black.

To our eyes, yellows usually correct better if you desaturate them rather than reduce their brightness (the latter can look "dirty"). In fact, we often will shift primary yellows toward the yellow-gold/orange range lest they move toward green-yellow on tape. Conversely, reds usually look better if you reduce their brightness closer to a blood-red than reduce their saturation (which can shift them toward a salmon pink).

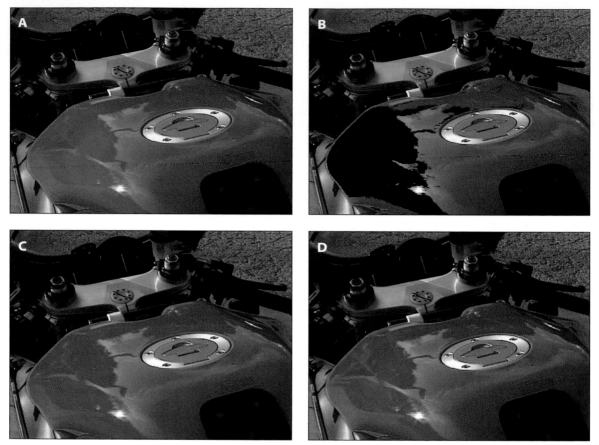

Footage with bright, saturated colors, such as the motorcycle we've been using throughout this chapter (A), might possibly not be "legal" or "safe" for broadcast. By applying Broadcast Colors and selecting Key Out Safe, we can easily see (B) which colors are going to cause us problems. Notice the aliased edges around these unsafe areas: This is the selection mask Broadcast Colors will use to apply its own corrections – which can be rather harsh (C). To tackle this case, we focused on the yellows, shifted them very slightly toward orange (a safer color), and reduced their saturation (D).

To help you be legal, After Effects has a Broadcast Colors effect (Effects>Video>Broadcast Colors) that you can apply directly to suspected offending layers, and have it automatically reduce either the saturation and luminance of the offending areas of an image. However, we don't recommend you use it that way – aesthetic control is taken out of your hands, and there can be a bit of posterization as you transition from legal colors to the selectively treated illegal colors.

Instead, we prefer to place an adjustment layer at the highest level of our final comp, and apply Broadcast Colors to that. We use one of the Key Out options in the How To Make Color Safe popup: Key Out Safe, which will then leave only the regions where colors are unsafe, or Key Out Unsafe, which will cut holes in the image where the unsafe colors are. The comp's Background Color will show through the keyed areas; it may be helpful to set the background to a garish color not otherwise in your image if you select the Key Out Unsafe option – that way, the holes where the colors aren't legal will be really obvious. Which colors the Broadcast Colors effect decides are unsafe depends on the video system you are working within (NTSC or PAL), and how hard you want to push the limits of legal colors (the default of 110 IRE is a good compromise).

Once you've set this up, stare at your image and decide which layers the illegal colors are coming from, then tweak just those layers to bring them back into legal range. When no more unsafe areas are being highlighted (indicating that you've changed the offending colors to make them legal), turn off the Video switch for the adjustment layer that contains Broadcast Colors – you don't want this filter to take effect during rendering.

To practice this process, open [**Ex.08*starter**] – it has our motorcycle clip already in it. Add a Layer>New> Adjustment Layer, and apply Effect>Video>Broadcast Colors to it. Set the How To Make Color Safe popup to Key Out Unsafe; notice large swaths of the fuel tank key out as being illegal. Select the **CM_motorcycle_full** layer and apply Adjust>Hue/Saturation to it. Tweak until your colors are safe and you're pleased with the result (yes, this will require quite a compromise from the original color). Note that this effect allows you to target specific color ranges rather than adjust an entire image; this allows more selective correction. Turn off the adjustment layer when you're done. One potential solution is in [**Ex.08_final**].

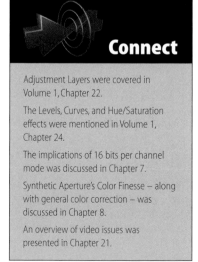

The Adjust>Hue/Saturation effect allows you to target a specific color range to alter.

There are more powerful tools available from third parties to help you make your color safe, as well. We particularly like Color Finesse from Synthetic Aperture (bundled with After Effects 6.5, see Chapter 8), as it lets you tackle the luminance separately from the color. As their excellent documentation explains, they are two separate signals as far as video is concerned, each capable of causing its own problems.

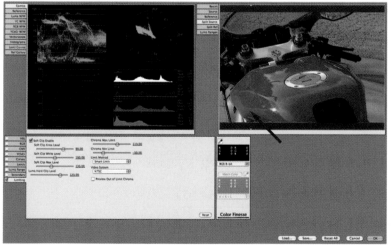

Synthetic Aperture's Color Finesse has a section dedicated to making your video broadcast safe, including processing the luminance and color separately. The split-screen feature (see red arrow) allows you to see before and after comparisons – it's shocking how much adjustment the yellow fuel tank needs to make it safe!

Connect

Adjustment Layers were covered in Volume 1, Chapter 22.

The Levels, Curves, and Hue/Saturation effects were mentioned in Volume 1, Chapter 24.

The implications of 16 bits per channel mode was discussed in Chapter 7.

Synthetic Aperture's Color Finesse – along with general color correction – was discussed in Chapter 8.

An overview of video issues was presented in Chapter 21.

25 Working with D1/DV NTSC

NTSC and 525 Lines

We're using the term *NTSC* for video that will eventually be broadcast in this format. Some would refer to this as *525-line* video, which includes the blanking interval lines you don't see.

Example Project

Explore the 25-Example Project.aep file as you read this chapter; references to [Ex.##] refer to specific compositions within the project file.

The video standards used for DV and professional "D1" NTSC video have a few important quirks – the most significant being that, in contrast to a computer, video's pixels are not square. Another is field order: Although most NTSC video is lower field first, DV and D1 have a different number of lines, which makes aligning their fields tricky. Finally, NTSC has an unusual frame rate – roughly 29.97 fps (frames per second) compared with the 30 fps many try to round it to – and two different ways to number those frames. We'll show how to deal with these quirks inside After Effects.

Square and Nonsquare

The most common image aspect ratio (IAR) for a television image is four units wide to three units high, or, as many shorten it, 4:3. Many computer monitors also have a 4:3 image aspect ratio, which is reflected in their screen resolution choices – 640×480, 832×624, 1024×768, et cetera – with 640×480 being a common frame size for early video hardware. The pixels that make up this image are supposed to be square: as wide as they are tall. As a result, most computer software works natively with a 1:1 pixel aspect ratio (PAR).

The most common digital video specification – ITU-R BTU.601-4 (often shortened to just 601) – has a different idea about the size of an image. The aspect ratio of the viewed screen is still 4:3. However, this standard defines 486 scan lines for NTSC video (the standard for North America), not 480. It also defines 720 pixels across, not 640. Of course, 720:486 ≠ 4:3; what's going on?

In 601-land, the pixels that make up an image do not have a 1:1 aspect ratio. When they are seen on a video monitor, they are drawn skinnier than a perfect square. They are captured this way, as well as displayed this way, so everything works out.

However, our computer monitors – and a lot of our computer software – can only conceive of pixels as being square, and as a result, display and think of these 601 images as being wider overall than we would expect. Not only is this visually confusing, it creates real problems when we try to combine the two worlds – such as when we try to add square pixel text on top of a nonsquare image.

For those few who actually like math, you can derive the pixel aspect ratio for 601 NTSC video: 486 lines × 4 ÷ 3 = 648 for a square pixel image; 648 ÷ 720 = 0.9 for the pixel aspect ratio After Effects uses. (At least, that's what revisionist history has decided. See the sidebar *Truth in Aspect Ratios* in Chapter 21 for a more pedantic perspective.)

The world has been further complicated by the introduction of the DV format. Its NTSC size is 720×480 pixels. Fortunately, it can be treated like a 601-size image, just with six lines missing (four from the top and two from the bottom). Its pixel aspect ratio is the same as for 601. Likewise, one of the specifications for standard-definition ATSC (digital) television is 704×480 pixels; it too uses the same pixel aspect ratio as D1 and DV.

We covered the basics of nonsquare pixels in the section *Nonsquare Pixels* in Chapter 21. What we'll go into now is how to deal with these nonsquare pixels when you're working on NTSC-spec D1 and DV video.

Pixels are displayed on computer monitors as square (left). However, when they are displayed through an NTSC D1 card or DV converter, they are projected skinnier than perfect squares (right). As a result, images intended for computer playback appear skinny on video, and NTSC D1 or DV images appear fat on a computer.

Tracking Aspects

Fortunately, After Effects can compensate for different pixel aspect ratios. Whenever a footage item is set to have a D1/DV NTSC pixel aspect ratio in its Interpret Footage dialog, After Effects knows those pixels are intended to be displayed 90% as wide as they are tall. If you use this footage in a composition that has been set to Square Pixels, After Effects will automatically scale the width by 0.9, in essence converting the footage item to square pixels. This way it will mix naturally with square pixel footage.

The Composition>Composition Settings dialog has the same pixel aspect ratio menu as you see in the Interpret Footage dialog. This tells After Effects how to preprocess the footage items inside it, considering that it will eventually be displayed with this pixel aspect ratio. As it is easy to forget to set this menu, get in the habit of selecting a composition preset (the top popup menu) when one is available; these presets automatically set the pixel aspect ratio for you.

If you drag a properly tagged D1/DV NTSC pixel aspect footage into a comp that has been set to also have D1/DV NTSC aspect pixels, no scaling will take place. However, if you drag a footage item tagged as having square pixels into this same nonsquare comp, the square pixels will get stretched wider to match the pixel aspect ratio of the composition (and the D1/DV NTSC footage also in that comp). When they're played back on an appropriate monitor, the pixels will get resquished and appear at their original proportions.

Each footage item has its pixel aspect ratio defined in the Interpret Footage dialog; many preset sizes trigger the popup to be set automatically, otherwise the default is Square Pixels.

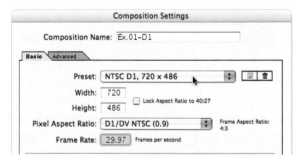

The preset popup in the Composition Settings dialog (where the cursor is pointing) sets the size and pixel aspect ratio automatically. Using the presets avoids mistakes, such as creating a 720×486 square pixel comp.

Comp Window Aspect Correction

If viewing slightly distorted images drives you mad, and you don't have a way to preview your compositions through a real video monitor (discussed in Chapter 21), After Effects provides a fix. Along the bottom of the Comp window to the right of the 3D View popup is a Pixel Aspect Ratio Correction switch (a corresponding option resides in the comp's View Options). Toggling it on will rescale the *display* of your Comp window to simulate square pixels. Don't worry – sources aren't being altered, and this feature is ignored during rendering. However, the image quality will be slightly reduced while you're working, so we recommend you use this as a confidence check only, and revert back to viewing all the pixels when you're done.

Toggle Pixel Aspect Ratio Correction

To check your nonsquare pixel comps as square pixels while you're working, enable the Pixel Aspect Ratio Correction switch at the bottom of the Comp window.

The great thing is that After Effects will do all of this automatically – as long as you have your footage, and your comps, tagged correctly and you didn't incorrectly prepare any footage items before you brought them into the program. Make sure that you never mislead the program about what the aspect ratio of the pixels really is! And to do that, you need to keep track of where images came from, and where they are going.

Comps and Footage

In the example project that goes with this chapter, we've started three comps for you to experiment with – [**Ex.01-D1**], [**Ex.01-DV**], and [**Ex.01-Square**]. Select them individually and type Command+K on Mac (Control+K on Windows) to see what their settings are:

• The DV comp has been set up for 720×480 and for nonsquare D1/DV pixel aspect ratio.

• The D1 comp is 720×486 in size, and is also nonsquare D1/DV pixel aspect ratio.

• The Square comp has been set up for 640×480 square pixels, which is a common size for older and lower-end video cards and editing systems, and is another one of the standard definition sizes specified by the ATSC for digital television.

Another common square pixel size to work at is 648×486, following the math outlined earlier. This is actually a good compromise size for NTSC work: You lose a little horizontal resolution, but you keep your comps square and with the correct number of lines, which makes designs easier to visualize on a computer display. You can change [**Ex.01-Square**]'s Composition Settings to this size (the NTSC, 648×486 preset) if you like.

Double-click the footage item **CL_wheel** in the Project window's **25_Chapter Sources** subfolder. This is a DV 720×480 movie. Notice how the wheel looks stretched horizontally compared with what you might expect; this is because it was captured with nonsquare pixels but is being displayed on your square pixel monitor with no compensation. Close the QuickTime Player window, open either the [**Ex.01-D1**] or [**Ex.01-DV**] comps, and drag this footage item into them. Notice that it looks the same: This is because the footage item and these comps both have been set up to the same nonsquare pixel aspect ratio, so After Effects does not perform any adjustments.

Now open the [**Ex.01-square**] comp and drag the skateboard wheel footage into it: Notice how it squishes horizontally and the wheel looks more round. This is because After Effects is correcting the pixel aspect ratio of the image to match the comp, which is square. If you have both it and one of the nonsquare comps open at the same time, click back and forth between the two tabs and note the difference.

A special note about DV footage: Because it has lines missing compared with D1-sized images and has a different field order than 640×480 captures, in most cases it needs to be moved down one pixel so that its Y Position = 244 in a 486-line comp (rather than its center 243). Similarly,

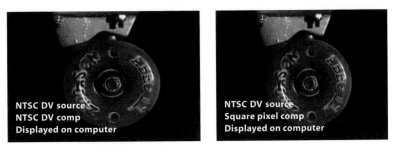

When DV NTSC footage is placed in a DV NTSC comp and viewed on a computer monitor, round objects – such as this skateboard wheel – look fat (far left). When the same footage is placed in a square pixel comp (which matches the computer monitor), it looks more round (left). Footage courtesy Creative License.

you would place a lower-field-first D1 source at Y Position 239 in a DV comp, rather than its center (240). This aligns its field order so it will render more sharply. More on this concept later in this chapter.

Square Sources

Now, let's play around with how our square pixel, computer native images interact with our nonsquare footage and comps. In the **Sources>Objects** subfolder in the Project window, you will find a few round objects such as a wireframe car wheel. All were created with square pixels. Drag them into the [**Ex.01-square**] comp: They keep their normal round shape, as you would expect. Now drag them into one of the nonsquare comps, and notice that they stretch horizontally. Rotate them, and they stay stretched horizontally. It is important to understand that the source footage item itself has not changed; just the way it is being used in the comp has changed.

This may initially look wrong, but it is actually right: These square pixel footage items are getting pulled into the same "world" that our nonsquare footage exists in. When they are played back later, they will get squished back again automatically and appear round on a TV monitor.

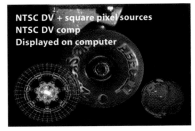

The wireframe car wheel and golden sphere are actually round; they are just displayed on a square pixel computer screen as being wider because the pixels in this nonsquare comp are intended to eventually be displayed skinnier than the computer displays them.

Stills, Scans, and Vector Art

Virtually every source file other than video that you will be using will be created with a square pixel aspect ratio. This includes scans, still image stock footage libraries, square pixel Photoshop files, and Illustrator artwork including text and logos. So the next question becomes: What size should you be creating new images at?

The size you should *not* be creating square pixel artwork at is 720×486 or 720×480 pixels. Even though these match D1 and DV image sizes for NTSC, remember that these sizes imply nonsquare pixels, while your artwork is being created using square pixels. Import these images into After Effects, and it will assume they have been prestretched horizontally by the 9:10 ratio discussed earlier – and therefore tag them to be treated this way. The fact that they appear round in a nonsquare pixel comp (such as [**Ex.02-wrong-1**]) leads you to believe that you must have done something right. Don't be fooled. When they are displayed later on a video monitor, they will then get squished and look out-of-round (this is simulated in [**Ex.02-wrong-2**]). The difference is noticeable – especially to clients who happen to like nice, round circles, rather than squished

Best Stretch

When you're mixing square and nonsquare footage items and compositions, make sure to render in Best Quality (the default), even if you don't scale them – After Effects is scaling them internally to make up the difference in pixel aspect ratios.

Square pixel sources tagged as nonsquare
NTSC D1 or DV comp
Displays correctly on computer…

…but gets squished on video monitor

Intuition may tell you to create your artwork at a D1 or DV size such as 720×486 or 720×480 (left). However, when they are displayed later on a video monitor, they will be squished horizontally (right), because the pixels were assumed by After Effects not to be square in the first place. Background image from Digital Vision/ Naked & Scared.

Create your artwork at a square pixel size that matches the overall aspect ratio of your final image, such as 720×540 (below left). Then scale it to fit your final comp – 720×486 for D1 size. It will look stretched on a computer monitor (below right) but will look correct when it's displayed on a video monitor later. Background image from Digital Vision/ Naked & Scared.

egg shapes, in their logos. The rule is that when you add square pixel artwork to a D1 comp, the images *should* look wider than normal.

A common size to create still artwork for D1 NTSC is 720×540 pixels (720×534 for DV, since it has six lines missing). After Effects will treat this as a square pixel size and rescale the image horizontally as necessary to mix with nonsquare footage. Uniformly scale these images to 486 pixels tall in your D1 compositions (480 for DV), either manually or by using the handy fit-to-comp shortcut Command+Option+F (Control+Alt+F).

To try this yourself, select Window>Close All to reduce clutter. Open [**Ex.03-right-1**], select the image **NTSC_rightsize** in the Project window's **25_Chapter Sources** subfolder, and hit Command+/ (Control+/) to add it to the comp. It will stretch wider, and you will notice from the white lines in the pasteboard region of the Comp window that it is bigger than the comp. Scale it to fit the comp, and it will look stretched – but that's okay, as this is a nonsquare comp. If you preview this comp on a D1 monitor, the circles will look correct. If you don't have such a video pre- view, open [**Ex.03-right-2**], which is a 648×486 square pixel comp, with [**Ex.03-right-1**] nested inside. This comp simulates how the final image will look on playback when the pixels are projected skinny, and you can see that the circles are round once more.

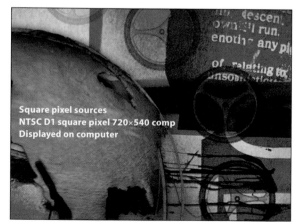

Square pixel sources
NTSC D1 square pixel 720×540 comp
Displayed on computer

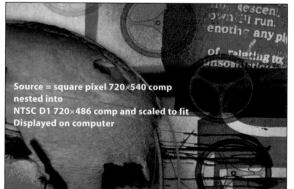

Source = square pixel 720×540 comp nested into
NTSC D1 720×486 comp and scaled to fit
Displayed on computer

There is no rule that says your square pixel sources have to be the exact same width as your composition; just remember they have square pixels, and don't use one of the sizes After Effects automatically assumes to be nonsquare, such as 704×480, 720×480, or 720×486 (or any of the other special aspects highlighted in Chapter 21). Quite often, we create images, crop pictures, and render animations at 800×600 or even 1024×768 pixels, which still have an image aspect ratio of 4:3, but also have extra resolution to allow us to scale or nudge their position slightly in the composition.

The 720×540 and 648×486 Routes

There are ways to work in square pixels all the time. When working on a design that *does not* incorporate full-screen video, some artists like to set up their compositions at 720×540 pixels (720×534 for DV final output) so they can see everything "normally" on their computer monitors and keep maximum resolution. If you are incorporating video footage, you may find it easier to work at the alternate size of 648×486 pixels (648×480 for DV): It has a little less horizontal resolution, but you keep your field lines at their sharpest.

When you are ready to render the final, nest your square pixel final comp into a 720×486 (or 720×480) comp, use Command+Option+F (Control+Alt+F) to scale it to fit, and enable Collapse Transformations to maximize image quality. This chain of comps is shown in [**Ex.04**].

If you are working at 648×486 (or ×480), you can also just scale it horizontally to 720 pixels wide in the Output Module. However, you should *never* scale field rendered material vertically in the Output Module (such as 540 lines down to 486): You will destroy your fields, causing severe motion artifacts.

Generally, we work at D1 720×486 when there is any D1 video involved in the project, using the 720×540 method only when the job is pure graphics and effects. When we're working in D1, though, we might find that there are some graphic elements that beg for straightforward square pixels (creating graphics on grids, using certain effects that only work in square pixels, et cetera). In these cases, we will create a precomp at 720×540 for the graphics only, then nest the precomp into the final D1 comp, scaling the nested layer to fit (as detailed above).

There are many ways to mix and match footage and comps of various aspect ratios, but we try to preserve the native pixel aspect ratio of video sources as much as possible, and adapt to each project's requirements on a job-by-job basis.

Out-of-Round Effects

It is possible for effects to be aware of the pixel aspect ratio of the layer they are applied to, including solids. However, not all effects do! Most of the Adobe effects do; exceptions include Cell Pattern and Advanced Lightning, as well as just the user interface of a select few effects such as Bulge. However, as of the time this was written, several third-party packages such as Cycore FX 1.0 – bundled free with After Effects 6.5 – do not. (Note that Cycore FX HD – an upgrade available from www.cycorefx.com – does indeed take aspect ratios into account.)

When a plug-in does not recognize a layer's pixel aspect ratio, some effects for which shape matters – like Perspective> CC Sphere – can appear out of round on final playback if you're not careful. In cases like this, apply these effects to square pixel layers that have the correct square pixel dimensions (such as 720×540 or 648×486 for an NTSC D1 comp), then scale the layer to fit the comp. If you must apply an effect directly to footage with nonsquare pixels, see if the effect gives you separate height and width parameters, and if it does, set the height to be about 90% or 91% of the width value to keep it symmetrical on output.

	Width		Height		
Rendering at:	648	x	486		
Stretch to:	720	x	486		Custom
Stretch %:	111.11	x	100.00		Stretc

☑ **Stretch**

☐ Lock Aspect Ratio to 40:27

You can stretch 648-pixel-wide renders to NTSC's 720 pixels in the Output Module. But if you field render, don't stretch 540-line-tall comps to 486 lines – you'll destroy your fields.

Conform to 29.97

The frame rate of NTSC video is actually 30,000/1001 fps, not 29.97 fps. Even this slight difference can result in slipped frames. To be absolutely safe, reconform all NTSC footage to 29.97.

When you're rendering a D1 486 line comp to a 480 line DV format, use the Crop section in the Output Module to remove 4 pixels from the Top and 2 pixels from the Bottom. (Note: If you're going from 480 lines to 486 lines, do the opposite: Crop the Top by –4 pixels and the Bottom by –2 pixels.)

Fit to Comp Size

The Command+Option+F (Control+Alt+F) shortcut will stretch any layer to exactly fill the size of a comp, regardless of aspect ratio. To preserve the image's aspect ratio, use Command+Option+Shift+G (Control+Alt+Shift+G) to fit vertically, or Command+Option+Shift+H (Control+Alt+Shift+H) to fit horizontally.

Field Orders and Frame Rates

Pixel aspect ratio is one of the biggest trip-ups when you're working with DV or D1 video. However, there are still a few other issues to worry about:

Field Order Flipping

Both DV and D1 NTSC footage tends to be lower field first. But DV has 480 lines, compared with 486 for D1. If you center DV footage in a D1-sized comp, the result will be three blank lines top and bottom. Offsetting an image an odd number of lines vertically aligns it with the wrong field. If you were to render this comp out lower field first, it would become visually softer, because you would be using only the interpolated pixels.

To keep maximum sharpness, you will want to shift DV footage items down one line (to Position value 360, 244) in a D1 NTSC comp. Conversely, if you are using full-size lower-field D1 footage in a DV comp, shift these footage items up one line from center (to Position 360, 239) for maximum sharpness. This is demonstrated in [**Ex.05a**] and [**Ex.05b**] respectively.

You can also convert between 480 and 486 lines using the Output Module's Crop options, as long as you observe the "even line offset" rule. If your final comp is 486 lines tall and you are saving to the 480 line DV format, Crop the Top by 4 pixels and the Bottom by 2 pixels to safely remove six lines. If your final comp is 480 lines tall and you are saving to a 486 line file format, crop the Top by –4 pixels and the Bottom by –2 pixels to pad out six extra lines.

The 704×480 standard definition size for ATSC (Advanced Television Standards Committee) digital video is actually upper field first, not lower. This means that when you're working with full-frame footage, you can center it in a D1 720×486 composition and vice versa. However, again: DV 720×480 footage – because it's lower field first – will need to be shifted down one line in a 704×480 comp, and 704×480 footage will need to be shifted up a line in a DV comp.

These little shifts are of no relevance if the footage is being moved or scaled vertically, is rotated, or is otherwise mangled by effects, as pixels are getting moved around between fields anyway. You can also ignore these one-pixel shifts if your footage is noninterlaced (30 fps film or DV shot progressive scan), since there are no fields to separate and interpolate.

Frame Rate Wrangling

As you know by now, NTSC video runs at 29.97 fps, not 30. Unless you are specifically playing with alternate rates, it is a very, very good idea to make sure all of your footage is conformed to 29.97 in the Interpret Footage dialog and to set up your comps at 29.97 – this will greatly reduce headaches later when you're playing your final renders through a video card or importing into an NLE.

Working with D1/DV NTSC // 25

We discussed the potential problems that result from a frame rate mismatch between 29.97 and 30 fps in Chapter 22, but it bears repeating: If you mix 30 fps material with 29.97 fps material, you will be slipping one frame every 33.3 seconds, or one field every 16.7 seconds. This can result in audio synchronization problems, stutters in motion, and flickering between soft and sharp images as fields become misaligned.

To Drop or Not to Drop?

When you're working at NTSC rates, you want to set your Timecode Base in File>Project Settings to 30 fps. You will then be presented with an additional menu called NTSC with a choice of either *Non-Drop Frame* or *Drop Frame*. This affects how the numbers in the Timeline window are counted in this timebase. It also is the source of almost as much confusion as the rate 29.97 fps. There is no such thing as a 29.97 fps counting timebase, because there is no good way to count with fractional frame numbers (1/29.97, 2/29.97, and so on) – that's why we use 30. However, 29.97 is slightly slower than 30. If we count at 30 and run at 29.97, when we're running in realtime, eventually the frame numbers in a long composition will drift behind the "clock on the wall."

That's why SMPTE created an alternate counting method known as Drop Frame. Contrary to the belief of some, this does not mean any frames are actually "dropped" – just that certain frame *numbers* are skipped so that for longer projects, the frame count and realtime (the clock on the wall) match more closely.

To pull this off, the first two frame numbers of each minute – for example, 0:01:00:00 and 0:01:00:01 – are skipped, meaning in this case the counter in the Comp and Timeline windows would jump straight from 0:00:59:29 to 0:00:01:02. The exception is every whole tens of minutes (00, 10, 20, and so on), where we would count normally.

Confusing? You bet. That's why most people use the Non-Drop counting method, unless the duration of the program is over a half hour or so, and they need to carefully track running time for commercial breaks, and so forth. Unfortunately, After Effects defaults to Drop Frame; set it to Non-Drop and all new projects will then default to this setting.

An exception to this practice is when you're trying to compare the timeline in After Effects with the timeline in your video app. You may need to use the same counting method in both for numbers to stay in sync – for example, DV uses drop frame counting. Also, if you are burning in timecode for a long piece, note on the tape whether the counting is non-drop so that others (musicians, perhaps) can set their software to match, avoiding potential sync issues later.

When movies are imported into After Effects, whether they were captured from tapes that were numbered with drop frame or non-drop frame is irrelevant – After Effects doesn't receive this information from QuickTime. And at the end of the day, when you render your movie, it is not "tagged" as drop or non-drop frame – the Time Preferences affect only how frames are counted inside After Effects' own Timeline.

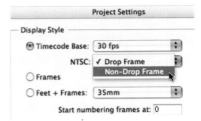

The Time Preferences allows you to count in Drop Frame or Non-Drop Frame timecode. This is applicable only when your comp is set to 29.97 fps.

Connect

Nesting comps was studied in Volume 1, Chapter 18.

Collapse Transformations was the subject of Volume 1, Chapter 20.

The Interpret Footage dialog – where you can set pixel aspect ratio and conform frame rates – was the subject of Volume 1, Chapter 28.

The Render Queue – including the Output Module – was dissected in Volume 1, Chapter 29.

The basics of frame rates, nonsquare pixels, common pixel and image aspect ratios, and previewing your comps to a real video monitor were discussed in Chapter 21.

Fields and interlacing, known field orders for several video systems, as well as the importance of working at 29.97 fps, were covered in depth in Chapter 22.

Preferred preferences are proffered in Chapter 31.

Working with D1/DV PAL

Like NTSC, PAL has nonsquare pixels – but in a different direction.

Déjà Vu

You may notice that this chapter is largely similar to the previous one on NTSC; the difference is that PAL stretches pixels in a different direction, and by a different amount. Read the chapter that pertains to the format common in your country.

Example Project

Explore the 26-Example Project.aep file as you read this chapter; references to [Ex.##] refer to specific compositions within the project file.

PAL – the most common video format outside of North America and Japan – has several advantages over NTSC. Its frame rate of 25 frames per second (fps) is much cleaner mathematically and close enough to film that pulldown is often not used. The three most common PAL digital formats – square pixel, D1, and DV – also have the same number of scan lines (although field order is still an issue). The big gotcha is that the D1 and DV variants still use nonsquare pixels, which are ultimately displayed wider on a video monitor than on most computer monitors. Therefore, it requires a little thought and planning to mix nonvideo elements with PAL footage.

A Different Size, a Different Squish

The most common image aspect ratio (IAR) for a television image is four units wide to three units high, or, as many shorten it, 4:3. Many computer monitors also have a 4:3 image aspect ratio, which is reflected in their screen resolution choices: 640×480, 832×624, 1024×768, et cetera. The pixels that make up this image are supposed to be square: as wide as they are tall. As a result, most computer software works natively with a 1:1 pixel aspect ratio (PAR).

PAL standard video has 576 lines of image area that we're interested in. Therefore, early PAL digital video systems took $576 \times 4 \div 3 = 768$ pixels across as a good size to work at. However, the most common digital video standard – ITU-R BTU.601-4 (601 for short) – has a different idea about the size of an image. The overall image aspect ratio is still 4:3. But it decrees that there should be 720 pixels across, not 768. Of course, $720{:}576 \neq 4{:}3$; what's going on?

In 601 land, the pixels that make up a PAL image are not square. When they appear on a video monitor, they are drawn wider than they are tall (compared to D1/DV NTSC, where pixels are drawn skinnier than tall). Because they are both captured and displayed this way, everything works out.

However, our computer monitors – and most of our computer software – can only conceive of pixels being square, and as a result, display and think of these PAL 601 images as being skinnier overall than we would expect. Not only is this visually confusing, it creates real problems when we try to combine the two worlds – such as when we try to add square pixel text on top of a nonsquare image.

For those few who actually like math, you can derive the pixel aspect ratio for 601 PAL: 756 ÷ 720 ≈ 1.0667 for the pixel aspect ratio, which is what After Effects uses (it rounds this number to 1.07 in its dialogs; we will use that shortened number ourselves for the rest of this chapter). Because video standards are often expressed as ratios of whole numbers – such as 4:3 rather than 1.333:1 – you might also see this ratio described as 16:15. (This precise ratio is the subject of some debate; see the sidebar *Truth in Aspect Ratios* in Chapter 21 for more numbers.)

We covered the basics of nonsquare pixels in the section *Nonsquare Pixels* in Chapter 21. What we'll go into now is how to deal with these nonsquare pixels when you're working on PAL-spec D1 and DV video.

Tracking Aspects

Fortunately, After Effects can compensate for different pixel aspect ratios. Whenever a footage item is set to have a D1/DV PAL pixel aspect ratio in its Interpret Footage dialog, After Effects knows that those pixels are intended to be displayed 1.07 as wide as they are tall. If you use this footage in a composition that has been set to Square Pixels, After Effects will automatically scale the width by 1.07, in essence converting this footage item to square pixels. This way it will mix naturally with square pixel footage.

The Composition>Composition Settings dialog has the same pixel aspect ratio menu as you see in the Interpret Footage dialog. This tells After Effects how to preprocess the footage items inside it considering it will eventually be displayed with this pixel aspect ratio. It is easy to forget to set this menu, so get in the habit of selecting a composition preset when one is available; these presets automatically set the pixel aspect ratio for you.

If you drag the same piece of tagged D1/DV PAL pixel aspect footage into a comp that has been set to also have D1/DV PAL aspect pixels, no scaling will take place. However, if you drag a footage item tagged as having square pixels into this same nonsquare comp, the square pixels will get squished horizontally to match the pixel aspect ratio of the composition (and the D1/DV PAL footage also in that comp). When the pixels are played back through a PAL-compatible D1 card or DV converter to a video monitor, they will be stretched horizontally

Pixels are displayed on computer monitors as square (left). However, when they're displayed through a PAL D1 card or DV converter, they are projected wider than perfect squares (right). As a result, images intended for computer playback appear fat on video, and PAL D1 or DV images appear skinny on a computer.

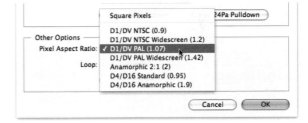

Each footage item has its pixel aspect ratio defined in the Interpret Footage dialog. Many preset sizes trigger this popup to be set automatically; otherwise the default is Square Pixels.

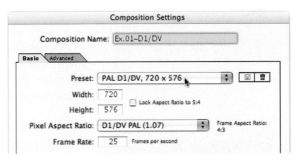

The preset popup in the Composition Settings dialog (where the cursor is pointing) sets the size and pixel aspect ratio automatically. Using the presets avoids mistakes such as creating a 720×576 square pixel comp.

Comp Window Aspect Correction

If viewing slightly distorted images drives you mad, and you don't have a way to preview your comps through a real video monitor (discussed in Chapter 21), After Effects provides a fix. Along the bottom of the Comp window to the right of the 3D View popup is a Pixel Aspect Ratio Correction switch (a corresponding option resides in the comp's View Options). Toggling it on will rescale the *display* of your Comp window to simulate square pixels. Don't worry – sources aren't being altered, and this feature is ignored during rendering. However, the image quality will be slightly reduced while you're working, so we recommend you use this as a confidence check only, and revert back to viewing all the pixels when you're done.

To check your nonsquare pixel comps as square pixels while you're working, enable the Pixel Aspect Ratio Correction switch at the bottom of the Comp window.

and appear at their original proportions. (Again, the reasons behind this are explained in the section *Nonsquare Pixels* in Chapter 21.)

The great thing is that After Effects will do all of this automatically – as long as you have your footage and your comps tagged correctly, and you didn't incorrectly prepare any footage items before you brought them into the program. (Make sure that you never mislead After Effects about what the aspect ratio of the pixels really is!) For this magic to happen, you need to keep track of where images came from and where they are going.

Comps and Footage

In the example project that goes with this chapter, we've started a pair of comps for you to experiment with – [**Ex.01-D1/DV**] and [**Ex.01-Square**]. Select them individually and type Command+K on Mac (Control+K on Windows) to see what their settings are.

• The D1/DV comp has been set up for 720×576 and for a nonsquare PAL D1/DV pixel aspect ratio.

• The square comp has been set up for 768×576 square pixels, which was a common size for older video cards and editing systems and is still a good size to work at (as we'll explain later).

Double-click the footage item **AB_IndGearsMach_PAL_L** in the Project window's **Sources>26_Chapter Sources** folder. Notice how it is squished subtly narrower horizontally; this is because it was captured with nonsquare pixels but is being displayed on your square pixel monitor with no compensation. Close the QuickTime Player window, open the [**Ex.01-D1/DV**] comp, and drag this footage item into it. Notice how it looks the same. This is because the footage item and the comp have both been set up to the same nonsquare pixel aspect ratio, so After Effects does not need to perform any adjustments.

Now open the [**Ex.01-square**] comp and drag either one of the gear movies into it – notice how it stretches horizontally and the gears look more round. This is because After Effects is correcting the pixel aspect ratio of the image to match the comp, which is square. If you have both it and the nonsquare comp open at the same time, click back and forth between the two tabs and note the difference.

Square Sources

Now, let's play around with how our square pixel, computer native images interact with our nonsquare footage and comps. In the **Sources>Objects** subfolder in the Project window, you will find a few round objects such as a wireframe car wheel. All were created with square pixels. Drag them into the [**Ex.01-square**] comp – they keep their normal round shape, as you would expect. Now drag them into [**Ex.01-D1/DV**], and notice that they squish horizontally. Rotate them, and they stay squished horizontally. It is important to understand that the source footage item has not changed; just the way it is being used in the comp has changed.

PAL DV source
PAL DV comp
Displayed on computer

PAL DV source
Square pixel comp
Displayed on computer

The gears look squished horizontally when they're placed in a PAL comp and displayed on a normal computer monitor (left). This is okay; tagging the comp as PAL tells After Effects they will be stretched later on playback. When they're placed in a square pixel comp (right), After Effects stretches them to match this new world. Footage courtesy Artbeats/Industry: Gears and Machines.

This may initially look wrong, but it is actually right: These square pixel footage items are getting pulled into the same "world" that our nonsquare footage exists in. When they are played back later, they will get stretched back automatically and appear round on a video or TV monitor.

When you're mixing square and nonsquare footage items and compositions, make sure to render in Best Quality, even if you don't scale them – After Effects is scaling them internally to make up the difference in pixel aspect ratios.

Stills, Scans, and Vector Art

Virtually every source file other than video that you will be using will be created with a square pixel aspect ratio. This includes scans, still image stock footage libraries, square pixel Photoshop files, and Illustrator artwork including text and logos. So the next question becomes: What size should you be creating new images at?

The size you should *not* be creating square pixel artwork at is 720×576 pixels. Even though these match the D1/DV image size for PAL, remember that these sizes imply nonsquare pixels, while your artwork uses square pixels. When you import these images into After Effects, it will assume they have been presquished horizontally by the 16:15 ratio discussed earlier – and will therefore tag them to be treated this way. The fact that they appear round in a nonsquare pixel comp (such as [Ex.02-wrong-1]) leads you to believe that you must have done everything right.

Square pixel sources
PAL DV comp
Displayed on computer

The objects in this comp are actually round; they are just displayed on our square pixel computer screen as being skinnier, because the pixels in this nonsquare PAL comp are intended to eventually be displayed wider than the computer displays them. Background courtesy Digital Vision/Data:Funk; clocks courtesy Photodisc by Getty Images/Business Essentials and Classic PIO/Sampler.

If you design artwork at a size of 720×576, After Effects will misinterpret it as having nonsquare pixels. It will look "right" in a PAL comp on your computer screen (left), but will be stretched horizontally when it's played back to video (right) – note how all of the elements are fatter, and the sphere is no longer a perfect circle. Background image courtesy Digital Vision/The Body.

Don't be fooled: When they are displayed later on a video monitor, they will then get stretched and look out-of-round (this is simulated in [Ex.02-wrong-2]). The difference is noticeable – especially to clients who happen to like nice, round circles for their perfect-circle logos. The rule is that when you add square pixel artwork to a PAL D1 or DV comp, the images *should* look skinnier than normal.

Instead, create your artwork at 768×576. After Effects will treat this as a square pixel size, and when this artwork is added on top of nonsquare footage in a nonsquare comp, After Effects will rescale the image horizontally as needed to mix. These images will look skinny on your computer screen when you're working in a 720-wide comp (assuming you remembered to set the comp's pixel aspect ratio correctly, or let the PAL preset frame size menu do it for you), but they will be restretched when they are later displayed on video. This process is simulated in the two example comps in the [Ex.03] folder.

Out-of-Round Effects

It is possible for effects to be aware of the pixel aspect ratio of the layer they are applied to, including solids. However, not all effects do! Most of the Adobe effects do; exceptions include Cell Pattern and Advanced Lightning, as well as just the user interface of a select few effects such as Bulge. However, as of the time this was written, several third-party packages such as Cycore FX 1.0 – bundled free with After Effects 6.5 – do not. (Note that Cycore FX HD – an upgrade available from www.cycorefx.com – does indeed take aspect ratios into account.)

When a plug-in does not recognize a layer's pixel aspect ratio, some effects for which shape matters – like Perspective>CC Sphere – can appear out of round on final playback if you're not careful. In cases like this, apply these effects to square pixel layers that have the correct square pixel dimensions (such as 768×576 for a PAL D1 comp), then scale the layer to fit the comp. If you must apply an effect directly to footage with nonsquare pixels, see if the effect gives you separate height and width parameters, and if it does, set the height to be about 106% to 107% of the width value to keep it symmetrical on output.

Square pixel sources
PAL D1 square pixel 768×576 comp
Displayed on computer

Source = PAL D1 square pixel 768×576 comp
nested into PAL D1/DV 720×576 comp and scaled to fit
Displayed on computer

The 768×576 Route

There is a way to work in square pixels all the time: Set up your main comps to be 768×576 using square pixels. After Effects will automatically rescale properly tagged, 720-pixel-wide D1 or DV PAL footage to stretch across this entire width.

When you are ready to render your work, nest your square pixel final comp into a 720×576 comp, where it automatically scales to fit, and enable Collapse Transformations to maximize image quality. This chain of comps is shown in [**Ex.04**]. If you have video preview capability (as discussed in Chapter 21), you can also send the second comp out to your monitor to verify safe areas and colors.

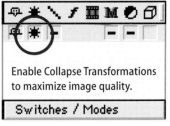

Enable Collapse Transformations to maximize image quality.

Create your PAL full-screen artwork in square pixels at 768×576 pixels (left). After Effects will automatically scale it horizontally to fit in your PAL D1/DV compositions. Circles will look squished on a computer monitor in these comps (right) but will look correct when displayed on a video monitor later. Image courtesy Digital Vision/Music Mix.

Field Order Flopping

D1 and square pixel PAL video are both upper field first, and fortunately have the same number of lines, which greatly simplifies mixing together footage from different sources. However, there is one kink in the system: PAL DV has the same number of lines, but a different field order. Mix D1 and DV full-frame footage together, both centered in a composition, and one of them will go soft due to field interpolation (this side effect is explained in greater detail in Chapter 22).

How do you avoid this? If your output will be PAL D1, shift any full-frame DV footage up one line (Position value 360,287) in a full-size comp to keep it sharper, as demonstrated in [**Ex.05a**]. Conversely, if your output will be to DV, shift any non-DV full-frame PAL captures down one line (Position value 360,289) in full-size comps, as demonstrated in [**Ex.05b**]. These shifts are of no relevance if the footage is not interlaced, is being moved or scaled vertically, is rotated, or is otherwise mangled by effects, because pixels are getting moved around between fields anyway.

Connect

Nesting comps, see Volume 1, Chapter 18.

Collapse Transformations was the subject of Volume 1, Chapter 20.

The Interpret Footage dialog – where you can set pixel aspect ratio and conform frame rates – was the subject of Volume 1, Chapter 28.

The Render Queue (including the Output Module), see Volume 1, Chapter 29.

The basics of nonsquare pixels, common pixel and image aspect ratios, and previewing your comps to a real video monitor were discussed in Chapter 21.

Fields and interlacing, see Chapter 22.

# 27 Working with Widescreen

The many roads to widescreen – including high definition, anamorphic widescreen, and letterboxing.

Future Proofing

If you are creating standard definition compositions today that might be repurposed for hi-def in the future, try to use vector art whenever possible. This allows you to continuously rasterize it, maintaining resolution at larger sizes.

Example Project

Explore the 27-Example Project.aep file as you read this chapter; references to [Ex.##] refer to specific compositions within the project file.

Motion picture film started out having a 4:3 image aspect ratio. When television – a perceived threat to film – appeared with the same aspect ratio, film differentiated itself by adopting a wider aspect. Today, television is chasing film by moving to widescreen aspect ratios – typically, 16:9.

The hitch is, right now several different concepts of "widescreen" exist, and will probably co-exist for the next several years. We will discuss each of these in this chapter, in the following order:

• High-definition television
• Standard definition anamorphic 16:9 widescreen
• Repurposing 4:3 content to play back on 16:9 television
• Formatting 16:9 content to play back on 4:3 television
• Creating content for both 16:9 and 4:3 playback
• Giving the impression of widescreen using normal 4:3 video

High-Definition Television

The members of the Advanced Television Standards Committee (ATSC), in their infinite wisdom and the spirit of grand compromise, settled on not one but an entire list of standards all deemed legal for digital television. These include the standard definition sizes of 640×480 and 704×480 pixels, and the high-definition (hi-def) sizes of 1280×720 and 1920×1080 pixels. The two hi-def sizes specify a 16:9 widescreen image, using square pixels.

The distressing part of the equation comes in the interlacing and frame rate choices. According to the ATSC's documents, the 720-line format uses progressive scan (no interlaced fields), but the 1080-line format can be progressive or interlaced. The 720-line format can run at 23.976, 24, 29.97, 30, 59.94, or 60 frames per second (fps); 1080 progressive can run at 23.976, 24, 29.97, or 30; and 1080 interlaced can run at 29.97 or 30 fps.

Although technically you may need to deal with any of these combinations of frame sizes and rates, in reality the following combinations are the ones you are most likely to come across for production work in the United States:

• 1280×720 pixels, progressive scan, 30 or 60 fps (often called 720p)
• 1920×1080 pixels, interlaced fields, 29.97 fps (often called 1080i)
• 1920×1080 pixels, progressive, 23.976 or 24 fps (often called 24p)

We have specimens of the first two formats for you to play with. Open the example project that goes with this chapter, and in the Project window twirl open the folder named **Ex.01**.

Select **AB_Surfing_720p**; note that the info display above says it has a size of 1280×720 and a rate of 30 fps. Option+double-click on Mac (Alt+double-click on Windows) to open its Footage window. While you're viewing at 100% Magnification, look closely and note that you don't see any of the "comb teeth" effects that indicate interlaced footage: This clip uses the progressive scan method, in which each frame is whole and represents just one point in time. Use Page Up and Page Down to step through the frames. (If you cannot view the entire frame on your video monitor, position your mouse over the image, hold down the spacebar until a hand icon appears where your cursor was, then click and drag the image to pan it inside the Footage window until you're satisfied you don't see fields.) If you need to, zoom back to a Magnification of 50% or less to see the entire frame at once; note its widescreen aspect.

Then select **AB_coast_1080i** and note its parameters along the top of the Project window: 1920×1080 pixels, 29.97 fps, with field separation currently turned off. Option+double-click (Alt+double-click) on **AB_coast_1080i** to open it in the Footage window; for now, set this window's Magnification to 100%. Assuming you can't view this entire frame plus the Footage window controls on your monitor, place your mouse over the image, press the spacebar until the Hand tool appears, then click and drag up and left until you can see the bird in the lower right corner of the frame. You should notice the familiar "teeth" along its edges that indicate the presence of interlaced fields.

This illustrates the relative sizes of 720×486 (A), 1280×720 (B), and 1920×1080 (C) frames. Footage courtesy Artbeats, from Industry: Gears and Machines, Surfing, and a title in development.

Quite often, when you import hi-def footage, the fields will not automatically be separated – meaning you may need to do this yourself. Select the footage in the Project window and type Command+F (Control+F) to open the Interpret Footage dialog (also found under File>Interpret Footage>Main). Interlaced ATSC-spec hi-def footage is upper field first. Set the Separate Fields popup to Upper Field First and click OK. Then use the Page Up and Page Down buttons to step through the individual fields of the footage – the bird should fly smoothly. If you want to verify what happens when you separate fields incorrectly, go back into the Interpret Footage dialog, choose Lower Field First, and repeat the experiment – the bird's flight pattern will now be jerky.

A frame size of 1920×1080 pixels, progressive scan (no fields), at a frame rate of 23.976 or 24 fps, has become a popular production format, as the frame size and rate are very similar to that of scanned film. These similarities have allowed many to apply film production techniques when working on hi-def programs. This format is often transferred to standard def 4:3 aspect video running at 29.97 fps, with 3:2 pulldown introduced – just like a telecined film dub. Offline edits are performed using this dub, which is then reconformed back to the hi-def masters.

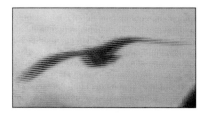

The common 1080i hi-def format is interlaced, as you can see by the "comb teeth" lines along the bird's wings in the After Effects Footage window.

HDV & DVCPRO HD

These new HD formats use non-square pixels. HDV stretches a 1440x1080 source frame size to fill a 1920x1080 image (with a pixel aspect ratio of 1.33:1); DVCPRO HD uses a 1280x1080 source frame to fill 1920x1080 (PAR = 1.5:1) and 960x720 to fill 1280x720 (PAR = 1.33:1). The **Interpretation Rules.txt** file in the **Goodies** folder will add popups to After Effects for these new PARs.

A common approach to widescreen video production is to take a 16:9 image (below left) and squeeze it horizontally to fit a 4:3 NTSC D1 video frame (below right). Background image from Digital Vision/Naked & Scared; foreground 3D scene by CyberMotion based on icons designed by Ridgley Curry for QAD Inc.

However, since you have a flexible tool like After Effects, you can work directly with these 24p frames if you so desire.

When you create a new comp, After Effects has presets for 1280×720 and 1920×1080 sizes, but it makes assumptions about frame rates that may not match your footage. The better idea is to drag a clip to the Create a New Composition icon along the bottom of the Project window, to ensure you get the correct frame rate.

Working with hi-def footage is in many ways easier than working with D1 or DV NTSC or PAL: The pixels are square; there's no odd distortions to worry about. The hitch is, the frames are *huge*, requiring a lot of RAM and processor power to move around. This is certainly a case where you will want to set your comp to a lower Magnification and Resolution for the sake of speed, or create lower resolution proxies of your footage.

Anamorphic Widescreen

How do you represent widescreen 16:9 images on standard definition tape formats such as BetaSP, DigiBeta, or DV, which may have been originally designed to carry 4:3 images? Simple: You squeeze the image horizontally until it fits. Upon playback the image is stretched back out to its original width. This technique is referred to as *full-height anamorphic widescreen*.

The side effect of this approach is that during production on a square pixel computer screen, the images look far skinnier than they are intended to be displayed. Because the pixel dimensions of widescreen anamorphic frames are the same as normal 4:3 frames, it's not always obvious whether a frame is 4:3 or 16:9. Stare at the footage and figure out if objects look extremely squished horizontally (which means it was recorded anamorphic), or if they look slightly skinny (D1/DV PAL) or something between normal and just slightly wide (typical NTSC D1/DV pixel aspect ratio).

This anamorphic approach is really just a variation of the nonsquare pixel examples of the previous two chapters. For D1, DV, and ATSC NTSC, the pixel aspect ratio used by After Effects is 6:5 (1.2); for D1 and DV PAL, the aspect ratio is 64:45 (~1.4222). (These precise numbers are the subject of debate; see the sidebar *Truth in Aspect Ratios* in Chapter 21.) However, as the frame sizes for anamorphic 16:9 and normal 4:3 footage are the same, After Effects assumes this footage is 4:3 unless the file has been

16:9 image (864×486)

Squeezed to NTSC D1 720×486

specially tagged as widescreen. You may well need to set the Pixel Aspect Ratio popup in the File>Interpret Footage>Main dialog for these footage items to be treated as widescreen.

Whenever a footage item is set to have this widescreen pixel aspect ratio, After Effects knows those pixels were intended to be displayed much wider than they are on the computer's screen. If a comp has also been set up to use a matching widescreen pixel aspect ratio, no scaling will take place. However, if you drag a footage item tagged as having square pixels (such as scans, stock photos, vector art, and so forth) into this same nonsquare widescreen comp, the square pixels will get squished to match the aspect ratio of the composition (and the widescreen footage in the comp).

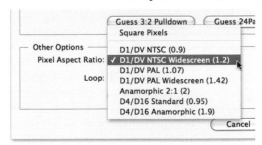

To see this in action, open [**Ex.02**], and type Command+K (Control+K) to view its Composition Settings. Although it has the familiar D1 NTSC frame size of 720×486 pixels, note that the Pixel Aspect Ratio popup has been set to D1/DV NTSC Widescreen. Close this dialog, and look at the Comp window: It contains anamorphic footage of our surfer. At first glance, you might not notice the footage is anamorphic; the surfer merely looks skinny, or slightly contorted.

Anamorphic widescreen footage is often not tagged as such. Because the overall frame size in pixels is the same between 4:3 and 16:9 footage, this means After Effects may not know a source is actually widescreen. In these cases, you'll need to set the Pixel Aspect Ratio yourself in the Interpret Footage dialog.

Back in the Project window, locate the **Sources> Objects** folder, then the **CM_wireglobe** item inside it. This is a 3D render that was created using square pixels. Drag it into [**Ex.02**]; notice how it squishes into an egg. Double-click it to reveal the original source image in its Layer window, and you see it really is a perfect globe.

Widescreen comps and footage will look skinny on your computer monitor, but when they are played back on an appropriate monitor, the pixels will get restretched and appear at their original proportions. Working in this artificially skinny world can be disconcerting, especially when you're adding nonvideo elements such as text and photos. Next we'll discuss different strategies for viewing your work with a normal aspect ratio.

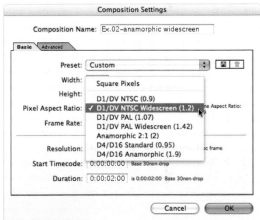

Comps can be set up to use the anamorphic widescreen pixel aspect ratio (above). When you drag square pixel artwork into these comps, they look squished (far left). To view sources with their native pixel aspect ratio, open them in their Layer window (left).

Working Wide and Square

There are three approaches to viewing your anamorphic widescreen projects as they would be seen on final playback: have the Comp window compensate for the pixel aspect distortion, view the comp through a widescreen monitor, or work in an enlarged square pixel comp.

To view a nonsquare pixel aspect comp as "square" pixels on a computer monitor, enable the Toggle Pixel Aspect Ratio Correction checkbox along the bottom of the Comp window. (Note that you can also enable Pixel Aspect Correction for individual Layer and Footage windows.)

After Effects includes a feature that can stretch or squash the Comp, Layer, or Footage windows' displays to reflect how a nonsquare pixel image would look through its proper final display mechanism. To enable, click on the Toggle Pixel Aspect Ratio Correction switch along the bottom of these windows (in the Comp window, it's between the 3D View and Fast Previews popups). In the case of anamorphic widescreen comps, the image will now be stretched to a 16:9 aspect ratio. The downside of this feature is that the stretching is done with a lower-quality algorithm, which means your images will look a bit crunchy. Don't panic; this feature is only for display – the original images at full quality are used for rendering.

Another option – which you should consider regardless of what format you are working in – is to view your Comp window through a real video monitor. Details for this are described in Chapter 21. In short, you will need a compatible video card or FireWire converter. Depending on which solution you choose, you can then either echo your Comp window out to this using the built-in Video Preview feature or Synthetic Aperture's EchoFire software, or in the case of cards that offer a second desktop display (such as AJA Kona, Blackmagic DeckLink, or Digital Voodoo) drag your Comp window to this screen and hit Command+Shift+\ (Control+Shift+\) to size it to fit this window. You will then need to connect this card or converter to a widescreen video monitor, or a 4:3 monitor that has a widescreen switch (which most modern high-quality monitors now have).

Shooting PAR

The secret to having After Effects manage your pixel aspect ratios for you correctly is to make sure all of your sources are labeled with the correct pixel aspect ratio in their Interpret Footage dialog.

Hi-Def Desktops

The DeckLink HD as well as the Digital Voodoo HD Fury and Vengence video cards also function as additional desktop monitor outputs on the Mac, allowing you to drag your hi-def comp window to them.

The third option – which we personally prefer – is to work in After Effects using square pixels with a comp that has a 16:9 aspect ratio. This is a more intuitive way of working, as what you see in your comp is what you will get upon playback through an appropriate monitor. This path maximizes resolution and reduces the chances of unwanted pixel aspect ratio distortions creeping in. For example, not all third party effects take pixel aspect ratio into account when they're creating their own graphics. You then perform the anamorphic squeeze at the render stage. The images that you save (and that will be recorded to tape) will then be artificially squished just like your anamorphic captures, but they will be restretched to their correct aspect upon playback through a proper widescreen monitor. The comp and render sizes for the different formats are as follows:

D1 NTSC:	Comp: 864×486 square	Output stretch:	720×486
DV NTSC:	Comp: 864×480 square	Output stretch:	720×480
ATSC SD:	Comp: 854×480 square	Output stretch:	704×480
D1/DV PAL:	Comp: 1024×576 square	Output stretch:	720×576

The advantage of these sizes is that they have the same number of horizontal lines as the final output format, so there are no issues with stretching fields. (Some use a size of 960×540 for 16:9 NTSC work, as an extension of using a square pixel size of 720×540 for 4:3 NTSC work. However, in the 16:9 case, using this larger size is a waste of pixels, and runs the risk of messing up your fields.)

To see this in practice, open [**Ex.03**], which has been created at the D1 NTSC size with square pixels. Then select the footage item **AB_Surfing_NTSC_ D1_wide** from the **Sources>Movies** folder in the Project window, and type Command+/ (Control+/) to add it to this comp. Because this movie has already been tagged as having D1/DV Widescreen pixels, when you add this movie to a square pixel 16:9 comp, After Effects will perform the pixel aspect correction for you, and this anamorphic source will automatically be stretched to fit the comp. Conversely, as you drag square pixel sources into this comp (such as **Sources>Objects> CM_wireglobe**), they will maintain their normal aspect.

When you render, you'll need to reintroduce the anamorphic squeeze. After you've added your square pixel comp to the Render Queue, but before you've hit the Render button, open the Output Module for your queued comp. Enable the Stretch option, disable the Lock Aspect Ratio button, and type in the Width you need for your destination format using the table we just gave. To save mouse clicks (and potential errors) later, you might want to save some Output Module templates with common squeezes already entered.

This method means that the image you save to disk – and that you will record to tape – is artificially squished again. But that's okay; that's how they're supposed to be on tape when you're using the anamorphic format. If you view the result through a normal 4:3 monitor, it will look wrong, but when it's viewed through a proper widescreen monitor, it will be stretched back out to the correct overall aspect ratio.

Click the disk icon in Composition Settings to save your custom settings as a preset. This is particularly handy for the common size "NTSC Widescreen 864×486 square" which is not currently provided as a preset.

Queue your square pixel widescreen comp to render, then in the Output Module use the Stretch dialog to re-impose the anamorphic squeeze on your file. You should change only the Width setting – any time you stretch the Height, you run the risk of messing up interlaced fields.

4:3 in a 16:9 World

Sometimes it happens that people decide to execute a project using the widescreen format, shoot original footage using the widescreen mode of their cameras, and only during editing realize that they have normal 4:3 footage that they have to cut in somehow (you know who you are). Since it is often too late at this stage to start over and execute the project using a 4:3 format, what do you do?

What you absolutely do *not* do – under any condition – is stretch the 4:3 footage horizontally to fill the widescreen frame (or intercut 4:3 and 16:9 footage in your NLE, which will usually treat them both the same –

When you need to mix 4:3 footage (above) in a 16:9 project, *don't* stretch it to fill the screen (below) – it will just display wrong, embarrassing everyone.

with one getting displayed wrong on output). Oh, the number of fat faces, oval-shaped-formerly-round logos, and other strange things we've seen displayed on fancy 16:9 plasma screen displays at trade shows…it's really quite sad, and makes everyone involved look quite unprofessional.

To see how bad this looks, first open [**Ex.04a**], which contains 4:3 footage inside a square pixel 4:3 comp, then [**Ex.04b**], which contains the same 4:3 footage stretched to fit a square pixel 16:9 comp. Although the footage may look "right" when you're working with it on a computer screen (as it does in [**Ex.04a**]), it will display horribly wrong once it hits widescreen projection (as shown in [**Ex.04b**]). Playing around with the pixel aspect ratio settings for the footage or comps may fool you into thinking you've got it fixed, but you really don't – you need to design your way out of this one.

There are several ways to try to resolve this problem. One is to merely center the 4:3 footage in the 16:9 frame and hope the black "pillars" down the left and right aren't too offensive (trust us – they're less offensive than stretching the footage abnormally). You can try blowing up the footage slightly to reduce the size of the vertical pillars at the cost of losing some of the top and bottom of the original image. These choices are demonstrated in [**Ex.05a**] and [**Ex.05b**], respectively.

Another way is to justify the 4:3 footage to the left or right side of the 16:9 frame, then try to find a good use for the remainder of the frame. One common trick is to use repeated or treated versions of the original footage to fill out this bar, as shown in [**Ex.06a**]. Another is to use this area for the client's logo, text that might otherwise go in a lower third or over the footage in a normal 4:3 layout, or just an interesting abstract background image. This is demonstrated in [**Ex.06b**]. (Of course, keep an eye on your action and title safe areas while you're doing this.) You've heard the saying: When life gives you lemons, make lemonade. Make very good lemonade, and the client will reward you.

Worst case is you can center the 4:3 footage in the 16:9 frame, with a "pillarbox" result (left). You can scale up the footage to reduce the size of the bars (right), with the tradeoff of a possibly softer image.

There are numerous creative solutions to filling a 16:9 frame when you have 4:3 sources – from simply repeating the source down the side (left), to using the extra space for logos, text, or other interesting imagery (right). Background from Digital Vision/Naked & Scared.

Widescreen in a 4:3 World

It is very common to need to find an artistic (or at least, expedient) way to cram a widescreen image into a normal 4:3 frame. For example, most motion pictures are composed for widescreen display, but are then later broadcast on standard definition 4:3 network television. Today, with networks having to broadcast hi-def 16:9 and standard def 4:3 versions of the same program simultaneously, this has become even more of an issue. We're going to discuss a few ways to make this conversion, then explore artistic solutions to what might otherwise be a choice between bad compromises.

Solution 1: Protected for Full Aperture

As mentioned at the beginning, most film has a raw aspect ratio of roughly 4:3. Many are careful when they're shooting film to frame the action vertically in the center for widescreen, but also to keep the top and bottom of the frame clear of props, microphones, lights, and so forth (a practice sometimes referred to as *protected*) so they can use the full aperture of the film later for 4:3 broadcast without resorting to the other tricks we're about to suggest.

This is a good technique to keep in mind if your footage is originating on film: Shoot full frame, but frame your shots so the action happens inside the smaller vertical widescreen area. (Likewise, when we design film title sequences, we ask our clients if they would like us to create it protected for full aperture, crafting a 4:3 frame but keeping the text and more important imagery centered inside a widescreen area.) This approach is less practical for production that

originates as 4:3 standard definition video, since it would mean shooting at 4:3 and using fewer lines (and therefore, less resolution) to fill out a 16:9 frame for the widescreen version.

16:9, 14:9, and 4:3

The Mill has devoted several excellent pages on its Web site to the subject of shifting between 16:9 and 4:3 worlds, including the BBC-standard 14:9 compromise. Check out www.mill.co.uk/widescreen/.

It is common practice to frame shots based on widescreen presentation but to protect the areas above and below (tinted white in this photo) for clean 4:3 playback as well.

Solution 2: Letterbox Presentation

A common approach is to scale down the widescreen image to fit inside a 4:3 frame, filling the top and bottom with black bars. This is commonly referred to as *letterboxing* the image.

There are several schools of thought about how to scale an image for letterboxing. The most straightforward approach scales the 16:9 image evenly so that its width just fits into 100% of the width of the 4:3 image. The result is a 75% overall scale. This is demonstrated in [**Ex.07a**]. This means that the 4:3 version does not contain any more or any less image than the widescreen version.

To some, this leaves too much black area above and below the image. So some users won't scale the 16:9 image down quite as much. The result is that some of the original 16:9 image gets cropped off the left and right

The most aesthetically pure approach is to take a widescreen image and rescale it to fit inside a 4:3 frame, with black bars above and below (A). This is known as a 16:9 letterbox. Other approaches scale the footage less, ending up with a 15:9 (B) or 14:9 (C) letterbox. Notice the yellow lines on the pasteboard to the left and right; this means some of the original image is getting cropped off.

sides, but with smaller black bars above and below. The most common approach is to aim for a 15:9 or a 14:9 final aspect ratio of the image to be fitted inside the 4:3 final (working out to an overall scaling of 80% and 85.7%, respectively). These are shown in [**Ex.07b**] and [**Ex.07c**]. Hit the apostrophe key to toggle the safe areas on and off; remember that some of the frame outside the Action Safe zone will also be cut off by the television's bezel.

[**Ex.07**] demonstrates scaling down standard definition widescreen footage. Of course, you can also scale down hi-def captures: [**Ex.08**] shows the same framings using 1080i source material.

Frank Capria of Kingpin Interactive, who has worked on *The American Experience* and was one of the first to tackle hi-def for PBS, notes that the way the footage was shot often determines the letterbox format more than how much black they are willing to tolerate on screen. "If the material was shot in 16:9 protecting for 4:3 (meaning the action was centered in the 4:3 area), then we are more likely to settle on 14:9 or 15:9. If the material was shot using the full 16:9 canvas, then we are most likely to use 16:9 letterbox."

Whether you choose to present a 16:9, 15:9, or 14:9 aspect of your original image inside a 4:3 image will be determined by anything of visual interest that may appear at the left and right edges. Meanwhile, the top and bottom will be fully visible – overscan and all. It is also best to choose your compromise as early as possible so materials can be shot and created with these croppings in mind.

Solution 3: Pan and Scan

Another potential conversion technique is to keep the full height of the image, chopping off part of the sides to make it fit. Depending how the action is framed, it might be best to cut more off of one side than the other, or to vary which portions get chopped during a scene. This is the *pan and scan* technique often used for transferring motion pictures to a 4:3 video format. In some extreme pan and scan cases, the image might even get scaled horizontally.

This is demonstrated in comp [**Ex.09a**], where we're trying to keep the surfer somewhat centered in the screen as he cuts across the wave. Select the layer **AB_Surfing_NTSC_D1_wide** and hit P to reveal its Position keyframes, if they are not already visible.

Also drag the Comp window larger so you can see the yellow outline of the layer that's left over on the Comp window's pasteboard. Scrub the time marker through the timeline, and note how the layer slides across the visible part of the frame.

Solution 4: Crop the Sides

An increasing amount of primetime network television in the United States is being shot using hi-def equipment, which means a 16:9 image. However, the network knows in most cases it will be viewed on a 4:3 set. When you're cranking out a new show every week, it's hard to find the time to reframe every scene using pan and scan techniques – but not all networks think their viewers are comfortable with widescreen letterboxing.

Therefore, they just chop the left and right sides off the image when they dub it down from hi-def to standard def, with no panning. We've given an example of that in [**Ex.09b**], using a 720p version of the surfer. This requires that shows be carefully shot in 16:9 protecting for 4:3. The important action is restricted to a 4:3 box in the middle of the frame, while making sure the left and right edges of the set are still fully dressed for those who will see the full width of the frame on hi-def. Welcome to reality during these awkward years while we convert from old-fashioned to high-definition television.

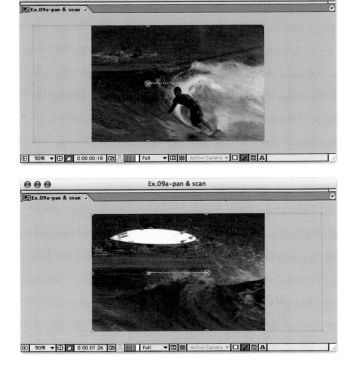

Panning and scanning means taking a widescreen image and animating its Position in a 4:3 frame to keep the action centered. Note the yellow outlines in the Comp window's pasteboard area; this is the area of the widescreen frame we're chopping off.

If you are creating titles or graphics for hi-def television, you will need to find out how your client is going to derive the 4:3 standard def version – crop or letterbox – and design accordingly. It's best to design two versions: 16:9 and 4:3. And that's what we're going to discuss next.

Designing for 16:9 and 4:3

During the next several years, as we transition to various advanced and digital television standards, the chances are strong that your title sequences and graphics will need to be shown on both 4:3 and 16:9 systems.

The two formats have quite different aesthetics. A title that is a comfortable width in widescreen suddenly becomes large – possibly even encroaching on safe areas – when it's cropped down to 4:3. On the other hand, if you design with safe areas of 4:3 in mind, you'll have large unused areas to the left and right in widescreen. There will be many occasions when artistically it will just be better to design and deliver two different versions. The consensus so far seems to be that it is easier to design the widescreen version first, then figure out how to create a 4:3 version.

Clean Edges

When you're letterboxing, it's a good idea to slightly cover the upper and lower edges of the video with a solid to clean up partial scan lines and other artifacts.

After you design a nice widescreen frame (above), you may find you have difficulty getting it to fit into a 4:3 frame in a pleasing manner using traditional panning (below). Of course, you could always letterbox it, but don't be surprised if the best solution is to build a new 4:3 version. Model from Digital Vision's The Body; textures from their Naked & Scared CD.

The simplest path to creating a widescreen look is to add black letterbox bars to the top and bottom of an image. This job for American Isuzu Motors Inc. and Perception Communications was played back at a trade show through a normal 4:3 projector, so the black bars also helped crop the projection.

Open [**Ex.10a**]. This is an example of a graphic that was designed for the widescreen format. Now open the currently empty 4:3 comp [**Ex.10b**], and drag [**Ex.10a**] into it. Try to find an acceptable position ("pan") for this widescreen title that looks pleasing in its new 4:3 frame. And watch those safe areas! You might even try squishing it slightly horizontally to get more image to fit; just make sure the globe icon doesn't become too obvious of an egg shape. If you're not happy with this look, instead try a letterbox framing as described in **Solution 2** earlier in this chapter.

If you're not satisfied with the results you're getting, you'll need to rebuild the graphic. To practice this, open [**Ex.10a**], type Command+K (Control+K) to open its Composition Settings, and choose the NTSC, 648×486 preset (for this example, it's easier to stick to square pixels – normally you would select NTSC DV or D1 which have nonsquare pixels). Now slide around the layers until you have something that works better in a 4:3 framing (keeping safe areas in mind). One solution is presented in [**Ex.10c**].

If you are curious to see if your (or our) 4:3 version would have also worked as a widescreen version, open the Composition Settings again, change the Width back to 864, and see if you like the result. Too often, after designing a nice title-safe 4:3 version, you will find your elements unacceptably crowded toward the center of the resulting 16:9 version.

That Widescreen Look

The widescreen look tends to come across as being classier: It implies film, hi-def video, or hi-tech in the form of flat widescreen plasma monitors and the like. However, quite often your final product will be displayed using an ordinary 4:3 television or video projector. So instead of a technical challenge, you have a creative one: How to give the *impression* of widescreen in a 4:3 frame?

Letterboxing

The easiest way to fake widescreen is to overlay a letterbox mask on top of normal 4:3 video. After all, when film production switched to a widescreen approach, in which the image is anywhere from 1.85 to 2.35 as wide as it is tall, the film often did not get wider; the projection cropped off the top and bottom of the 4:3 (1.33) image to make it appear wider.

Letterboxing is easy to achieve in After Effects by simply creating black solids to obscure the top and bottom. We've included several prerendered 16:9 letterboxing masks for common frame sizes in the **Goodies>Templates** folder on this book's DVD – just add the appropriate image to the top of your layer stack. An example is shown in comp [**Ex.11a**].

Another approach is to make your composition's Background Color black and place a solid on top of the layer stack that is the size of the image you wish to reveal. Then set its Mode popup to Stencil Alpha, to cut out all of the layers underneath. This is demonstrated in [**Ex.11b**]. In either case, you may need to reframe the final image by shifting the underlying video layer(s) up or down slightly.

What size should this letterbox hole be? In reality, any size you like – you're faking the look anyway; crop off enough to give the impression you want without obscuring important areas of the original image. If you want to calculate the size of a box to use for a specific image aspect ratio, take the square pixel dimension of a full-height video frame (such as 648×486 for D1 NTSC), multiply its width by the fraction that represents the aspect ratio you want (such as 9/16), and use the result for your height of your mask or solid (in this case, 364.5 pixels), rounded to the nearest even number to have the same number of whole pixels above and below the mask in a comp.

In this faux widescreen look for a trade show video, we placed song lyrics overlapping the letterboxed bars and normal image area. Images courtesy Xerox Media West and Getty Images.

Outside the Box

If you know your work is going to be projected with the top and bottom cropped off (in other words, a physical mask is placed over the monitor, or a video is being projected onto a "widescreen" aspect surface), you will probably want to fill the top and bottom with black bars. However, if you know the viewer will still see the full 4:3 frame, take this as a creative opportunity to put the normally wasted letterbox bars to good use.

On this page, you will see a couple of ideas. For example, in a trade show booth video for Xerox, we again restricted our imagery to a widescreen stripe, but then used the additional space to overlay song lyrics and other text. We particularly like the Hallmark Channel design executed by TAG, in which they used the letterbox bars to hold the client's logo, then had action cross the line out of the widescreen stripe into and out of the entire overall frame, giving the impression of coming out of and going into your television set.

Connect

Stencil Alpha, see Volume 1, Chapter 13.

The Collapse Transformations switch was expanded upon in Volume 1, Chapter 20.

The all-important Interpret Footage dialog was dissected in Volume 1, Chapter 28.

The Render Queue, Render Settings, and Output Modules were explained in detail in Volume 1, Chapter 29.

A basic primer on nonsquare pixels was included in Chapter 21. That chapter also contains sections on how to view a comp through a video monitor, plus the subject of overscanning and safe areas.

Interlaced footage and field flicker were treated in Chapter 22.

3:2 pulldown, see Chapter 23.

A common production flow for hi-def mimics that of film, see Chapter 28.

Proxies are covered in Chapter 29.

A great example of putting letterbox bars to creative use from a branding design done by TAG (www.tag.com) for the Hallmark Channel (Creative Director Jim Kealy, Executive Producer Anne White, Producer Toby Keil, Designer and Director Alan Douglas; the agency was 3 Ring Circus; post performed at Stargate Digital).

28 Working at Film Resolution

***The Big Screen requires
big hard drives – and
lots of planning.***

O nce you've mastered working with video in After Effects, it's not much of a leap to want to work with film. What's obvious is that you will need more RAM and disk space. What's not obvious is the additional project management skills needed to both receive and deliver what is required. We will focus on working with the most common "2K" film resolution – 35mm Academy Aperture – as well as the popular Cineon file format with its log-based color space.

An Academy Aperture film frame as it might appear on a contact print for projection. (The optical audio track is added for clarification only.) The grayed-out area at the top and bottom, though captured on film and rendered, will not be seen in the theater (resulting in a projected aspect ratio of 1.85:1), but it may be used when the film is later transferred for TV and video (1.33:1 aspect). Image courtesy Cinesite Los Angeles (www.cinesite.com).

Film Flavors

It's easy to be overwhelmed by the number of aspect ratios, formats, and film systems that are available. What makes it even more confusing is that quite often the entire film frame is exposed, but only a portion of it is projected, with bits on the top and bottom masked upon projection. We're interested in the aspect ratio of this projected area, although quite often the rest of the frame – which fits a 4:3 aspect ratio – will be used later for video.

Just to add another layer of confusion, part of the film frame is usually also reserved for an optical soundtrack. The bible on film systems, the *American Cinematographer Manual* (published by the ASC Press) differentiates between the full frame and the area minus soundtrack as follows:
- *Full Aperture* (also known as *camera aperture* or *silent aperture*) refers to the total area between the 35mm perforations, including the area normally reserved for the soundtrack.
- *Academy Aperture* refers to that area of the negative excluding the soundtrack area.

Example Project

Explore the 28-Example Project.aep file as you read this chapter; references to [Ex.##] refer to specific compositions within the project file.

Which Road to Travel

Different types of jobs, such as film titles or live action visual effects, can all be done on the desktop, but they require different approaches to achieve the best results with the minimum amount of pain. The pivotal decision is whether it is best to work in your computer's normal linear color space, to get comfortable with a log color space such as the Cineon format, or to do the composite outside the computer.

Option 1: Pure Graphics

If you are creating graphics from scratch – such as a 3D render – that are not composited over any previously shot film, the simplest approach is to work in normal linear color space. Then, the file format you will output is typically a series of stills saved in SGI-RGB format. This format has an RLE (run length encoding) option, which means it can use a lossless compression scheme that is essentially the same as PICT files.

Note that there is a small advantage in saving your graphics out to the Cineon log color space and file format instead (discussed later), because it will give the operator who's doing your final output to film some additional flexibility in exposure control.

Option 2: Composited Images

If you are treating previously shot footage or adding graphics on top of footage, you will want to do everything possible to retain the color range and detail that was in the original film. Therefore, you should consider working in the log space native to the Cineon file format developed by Kodak.

In this workflow, you keep the source footage in log space throughout, and convert any computer-generated graphics from their native linear space to log to composite them with the film footage. You can temporarily convert the final image to the linear space for checking your work on a computer monitor or making video proofs, but you will ultimately render to the Cineon log format.

Fortunately, After Effects has built-in support for this format, and we'll discuss how to manage this process in this chapter. The **Goodies** folder also has additional papers from Kodak on the Cineon format.

It is not required that you perform these jobs in log color space; for example, we composited titles over the opening footage of the movie *Now and Then* in linear color. However, this puts a lot more pressure on the film scanning operator to aesthetically fit the extended dynamic range of film into the reduced linear range (occasionally requiring costly rescanning).

Option 3: Optical Composite

If your contribution consists of relatively simple solid-colored titles to be overlaid on a film scene, it might work out faster and cheaper to build the graphics just as white images on black and save them to the SGI-RGB format (as with Option 1). These images would then be composited over the film using an optical printer; the operator can even color your titles at this stage and add fades. We won't be covering this method here, as it's more often used for stills as opposed to animation, but keep it in mind as an option.

Option 4: Resizing Video

With the advent of relatively inexpensive, high-quality digital video cameras, an increasing number of people are shooting on video, working at video size, then scaling the result up to film size for output. As images can degrade seriously when they're scaled up beyond 100%, you will want this scaling to be done by a film house that specializes in this technique, or use a program such as Apple's Shake which has exceptional scale-up algorithms. Additional video-to-film tips include using progressive scan (interlacing and film do not get along), working in PAL since its frame rate is much closer to that of film (25 versus 24 frames per second), or working with high-definition video.

The most common aspect ratio in the United States is 1.85 or Academy Aperture, while in Europe, 1.66 is more popular. This ratio is determined by dividing the width of the image by its *projected* height. (In reality, an Academy Aperture image *as shot* has a 1.37:1 aspect ratio, but the top and bottom are cropped upon projection.) You'll often see these ratios written in formats like 1.85:1, but it's referred to as "one-eight-five." Before you start work, confirm the projected aspect ratio with the client.

Pixel Dust

Film is usually scanned to fit the final output: If you plan to output Academy Aperture, have the film house scan only the Academy area. Most of the time, you won't need the additional image that appears in the Full Aperture area, and your scans will be properly centered without worrying about where the optical soundtrack is. (Of course, there are exceptions to every rule; occasionally you will want some extra image to play with to reframe shots or perform other adjustments. In these cases, assuming the shot was not cropped with a hard matte as it was filmed, you may need to request a "Full Ap" scan and reframe yourself for Academy.)

If you're outputting computer-generated animation to Academy Aperture, it's a waste of render time and disk space to create files at Full Aperture size – no one will see that extra image in the soundtrack area.

While recommended pixel sizes can vary slightly between different post houses, the standard Cineon sizes are below:

Academy Aperture:	1828 W × 1332 H
Full Aperture:	2048 W × 1536 H

(Some scanners/recorders use 2048 × 1556; ask to be sure.)

Note again that the usable area of the film is close to a 4:3 aspect ratio, not the 1.85 (or 1.66) you thought you were getting. The reason to render the extra pixels is in case the movie won't be letterboxed when it's eventually transferred to video or shown on TV. Make sure that any important action happens in the vertical center and that titles are safe for the 1.85 aspect ratio (not just the TV title safe area). Examples of both Full Aperture and Academy Aperture, with templates overlaid to show title safe areas, are demonstrated in this chapter's example project, in the Project window's [**Ex.01**] folder.

With that advice given, occasionally you will be asked to design only inside the widescreen film window. It is very important then to establish if the 4:3 video version will be presented letterboxed (so you'll see the entire widescreen area, minus a small amount off the sides for video safe areas), or if it will be "panned and scanned," which means substantial portions of the sides will get chopped off. This latter approach has serious implications on how you design your titles or images, as discussed in the previous chapter in the sections on going between 16:9 and 4:3 worlds. Ask early, ask often, and get it in writing.

Thumbs Down

When you're working with film res sources and comps, the Project window will bog down as it draws thumbnails. Speed up redraw by checking the Disable Thumbnails in the Project Window preference (Preferences>Display).

The Real Center

When you're designing for one-eight-five (Academy), titles should be centered across their 1828 pixel area, not 2048. If you center for 2048 (Full Ap) but you really wanted Academy, they will be offset to the left when they are projected.

If you designed your animation at Full Aperture size (2048×1536) when you really just need Academy output, make sure that the film house can scale your animation to fit the Academy image area, and that you clearly tell the film house to do so – otherwise, your animations will appear off center, since the Academy "window" is offset to the right to make room for the optical soundtrack.

Occasionally a film house will ask you to render a Full Aperture frame, with your Academy Aperture animation positioned inside it. You can do this by nesting and offsetting your 1828×1332 animation into a second comp created at 2048×1536 for output, as demonstrated in [**Ex.02**].

The same scene as earlier; Academy Aperture size (1828×1332 pixels), overlaid with 1.85 and TV safe zones.

Timeless Templates

Film frame sizes are often referenced in inches, in relationship to the film – for example, Academy Aperture is typically 0.864×0.630 inches. Obviously, that's not very helpful in the digital world. Over the years, various service providers have obliged us with their definitions of how inches relate to pixels. After collecting quite a few templates, we built our own versions in Illustrator.

Check out the **Goodies>Templates** folder on the accompanying DVD for these Film Templates. The Academy Aperture templates at 1828×1332 fit the common Cineon size, and there are also templates that place this frame inside Full Aperture (2048×1536). They are supplied as white TIFFs with alpha channels – drag them on top of your design and turn them on temporarily when you're placing or sizing graphics. Make them a Layer>Guide Layer and they will not render; see the comps in [**Ex.01**].

If you need to design your film titles in Illustrator, we've included an 1828×1332 Illustrator template, with not only guides but also a 12-field chart that divides the frame into 12 even increments in all directions from the center. When the editor makes a request for you to "move the title up one field,"

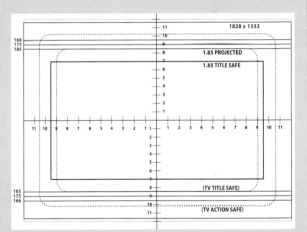

Templates included on the DVD will help you visualize the safe areas for a number of common film formats.

he or she is referring to a "field" (grid line) in the 12-field chart – not a video field. We've also included a separate 12-field chart template, which you can overlay in a comp as a handy guide when you're repositioning or measuring titles.

Note: *As far as we know, these templates are as accurate as anything currently out there, but we make no guarantees as to whether they are pixel-accurate for what your specific film house desires.*

Film Preferences

There are a number of Preferences in After Effects that are made for working with film:

- Since you'll be creating Comps at 24 fps, also set the Display Style to 24 fps (File> Project Settings). You can also set the Display Style to Feet+Frames, or just Frames.

- Change the default frame rate for newly imported sequences to 24 fps (Preferences>Import> Sequence Footage). (Don't forget to reset this to 29.97 or 25 when you're working on a video project again.)

- Be aware that the "Start numbering frames at" value controls both Feet+Frames and Frames. Film scans usually come in frames starting from 1, while a film editor using an Avid Film Composer counts in feet+frames starting from 0. However, since the preference sets the starting number for both Frames and Feet+Frames, you'll need to be on the ball when you're cross-referencing numbers and switching back and forth.

- Despite the large sizes, you can work efficiently with film res comps set to quarter resolution and 25% zoom, which is slightly smaller than full-frame video.

- You might also want to "Disable thumbnails in project window" to speed up the Project window's reaction times (Preferences>Display).

Sizing Up the Job

A 2K Academy SGI-RGB frame of 1828×1332 pixels requires about 7 megabytes of RAM when it's opened in an 8 bit per channel (bpc) project – twice that in 16 bpc mode. Because of the noise inherent in film grain, it is usually not much less when it's saved on disk. Since film runs at 24 frames per second (fps), one second of film takes up nearly 170 megabytes of disk space. One minute of film – 1440 frames – takes up about 10 gigabytes. If your design calls for working with the 10-bit Cineon file format, which requires a 32-bit file per frame (two bits are unused), a 1828×1332 frame will consume 9.3 megabytes each.

Working at film resolution usually leads to a shopping spree for cheap, fast, and large hard drives, which fortunately continue to fall in price. To process film resolution frames, you'll also need a generous amount of RAM. The amount will depend on the number of layers you're rendering and the effects being used. An individual film frame requires seven to nine times as much RAM as a video frame, but you're usually using fewer layers and applying fewer effects, so the RAM requirements don't scale up proportionally. As a general guide, dissolving between two frames while overlaying a title is no more taxing than a moderately complex video project, but a minimum of 512 megabytes is recommended for special effects with nested compositions. (Fortunately, modern operating systems such as OS X can overflow into virtual memory as needed, but at the cost of speed.) Make sure to test that you can render your design at Full Resolution and Best Quality well before the deadline, which should also give you a good estimate of how long rendering might take.

For title sequences, plan on also creating at least one *textless* version, which is used for international distributors. Try to plan how this can be achieved without rerendering the entire sequence – for example, rendering "patches" just for the frames or scenes where the titles came up in the *texted* version. You could also render the textless version first, then use this render as a backplate for the texted version. Either way, it's best to give the film house an entire linear sequence for both versions, and not expect them to correctly assemble frames from different renders where some frames are common for both versions.

Scanning the Horizon

In order to have film scanned, or your animation output to film, you'll need some heavy-duty equipment – your slide scanner won't cut it. This means working with a post house with a film scanner and a film recorder. (Make sure you're sitting down when you get the estimate…)

Film is typically scanned and recorded by a device connected to an SGI (Silicon Graphics) computer. While most film houses have integrated desktop computers into their production environment at some level, be prepared to spend a little time working out the optimum method for transferring files to and from your desktop. Your service bureau will prefer file formats that the SGI reads quickly, such as SGI-RGB (8-bit or 16-bit linear) or Cineon (10-bit log). Targa or TIFF (both 8-bit linear) are other options, although they are accepted less. Fortunately, After Effects can read and write all of these formats. If you insist on a file format not on their preferred list, expect a delay and a possible extra charge for format conversion.

As more film houses have become desktop-friendly, you should be able to use FireWire drives to receive and deliver files (check to see what OS the drive must be formatted for). There may be some cases in which they will insist on using backup tapes (such as DLT), using the Unix TAR (Tape ARchive) format. That means you'll need a compatible drive and a utility that can read or write TAR to that drive. Budget for this extra time and equipment (and media – DLT tapes in particular can add up fast).

When you decide on a film house, test the entire production path at the beginning of the job – make sure you can read their files, make sure

A Switch in Time

Command+click on Mac (Control+click on Windows) on the frame number display in After Effects to toggle it between the three different counting methods: SMPTE, Frames, and Feet+Frames.

TAR and Feathered

An increasing number of film houses are able to handle Mac- or PC-formatted media such as FireWire drives. However, there may still be occasions when they'll prefer a tape format such as DLT, written as a Unix Tape ARchive (TAR).

On the Mac platform, when we had to use DLTs we used the OS 9 application Backup, which is part of the QuTape set (available from CyberComp – email cybercomp@earthlink.net). On the PC side, we've heard that WinTAR-SCSI from SpiralComm Communications (www.spiralcomm.com) was a cost-effective choice.

TAR has a set of options concerning how large the data chunks written to tape are: the block size and number of files per archive. Check with the film house you are working with to get its preferred block size; 16 sectors (8192 bytes) is common. If no one can give you this information, ask for a sample tape. Many TAR programs have an auto-detect option during reading; write back the tapes using the same setting as detected while reading.

TAR's one-file-per-archive option is convenient, because each frame will become its own archive, making locating individual frames easier. That said, your film house may prefer that you save all the files in one archive, because they read and write much faster than the one-file-per-archive option.

Speaking of which, don't forget to leave lots of time not just for rendering, but also for transferring to tape. In fact, the faster computers get, the more the tape transfer becomes the bottleneck. For long projects, we set up a production pipeline where frames are rendered to a hot-swappable hard drive. This drive is then moved to a second machine that transfers them to tape, while the first machine continues rendering the next section.

Macintosh users have a couple of additional issues to be aware of:

• On the reading side, Mac files require a file type and creator to be set when using CyberComp's Backup utility; in the Preferences, *before you read the tape*, enter SDPX for the Type and either 8BIM (Photoshop) or FXTC (After Effects) for the Creator.

• On the writing side, After Effects tags each frame with a preview icon for viewing in the Finder. This additional icon can show up as a separate file when it's saved to TAR, which can be confusing to the service bureau. To disable this feature, you need to quit After Effects, locate the After Effects 6.5 Prefs file (under OS X, look for it inside Users>(your name)> Library>Preferences), and edit its text. Search for the line that says "Pref_WRITE_THUMBNAIL_ICONS" and change the value that follows from 01 to 00.

More Resolution

When you're working with film, we strongly recommend you use the Professional edition's 16 bpc (bits per channel) color space, discussed in Chapter 7. This will maintain more resolution in the colors, yielding fewer problems with banding. To get a wider range of available contrast or "dynamic range" while preserving details such as overbright whites, use the Cineon format (discussed later in this chapter).

An alternative to Cineon is OpenEXR (www.openexr.com). Created by Industrial Light & Magic, OpenEXR files come in 16-bit floating point, 32-bit floating point, and 32-bit integer flavors that encompass a far wider dynamic range than Cineon. Special effects house The Orphanage has released a free plug-in that reads OpenEXR files and converts them to a logarithmic color space, allowing you to use a Cineon-style workflow with OpenEXR images. For more details, see www.theorphanage.com/tech/OrphEXR/.

Tops is working in a floating-point color space. As of version 6.5, After Effects does not support "float," but you can cheat it using The Orphanage's eLin plug-in set (www.redgiantsoftware.com/elin.html), which remaps floating point into a log space inside After Effects. An advantage of eLin is that it performs gamma-corrected compositing (see the **Goodies** folder), which allows more realistic mixing of imagery.

they can read yours, and work closely with them during the project. Once you have the flow sorted out, you'll need to settle on what size the film frames are to be scanned and output at. Again, there are a lot of choices, and film scanning and output are both very expensive to redo, so make sure everyone involved agrees on formats in advance.

Getting What You Want

When you're completing an order form for scanning or recording, you'll need to know the frame size (Full Aperture, Academy Aperture, and so on), color depth (10-bit log, 8-bit linear, or 16-bit linear), file format, and what media you'll use for the file exchange. If there's a checkbox for Resolution, Full Resolution refers to 4K frames; Half Resolution to 2K (which means either 2048 or 1832 pixels across, depending if the scan is Full or Academy), and Quarter Resolution would be 1K. You also specify what film stock to print to and the number of prints required, both of which will normally be dictated by the film's editor or production office. Obtain an order form in advance of output so you can verify that you have an answer for every checkbox.

Scanning In

The biggest issue on the scanning side, after general issues of frame size, file format, and precisely which frames you want (see the sidebar *Telling Time*), is color correction. Film is a lot more subjective than video, with each film stock looking different, and a wide range of adjustments available on both input and output.

Most desktop computer monitors do not look like projected film – the gamma does not match, and they are typically set to a much higher color temperature than film (9000K or 6500K versus 5400K). And, chances are, the person who shot or edited the footage is already in love with the way it already looks. Therefore, we take the approach of making the absolute minimum amount of color correction to the original footage in our computers, pushing the task of making it "look right" onto the scanning stage. We then match our graphics to look good when they're composited with the footage we received.

To achieve this end, ask the film's production department to supply the scanning room with a sample, either in the form of a *match clip* or a *guide clip*. A match clip is a handful of the exact frames being scanned in, with a color gamut the Powers That Be are already happy with. A guide clip contains frames that aren't from the exact scene being scanned, but that can serve as an overall color guide. Then ask the scanning operator to match these colors.

If the scan at the default settings doesn't match, the operators can either re-adjust their scanners, or if they're using the Cineon format, color correct the frame digitally in 10-bit log color space on monitors that are expertly calibrated, then supply color-corrected Cineon frames to you for compositing. If the frames were scanned into the linear format, chances are good that the film will have to be rescanned, since this format does not contain any real latitude for post-correction. If you get saddled with color correcting a scene or two anyway, try to isolate a clip you know the client is happy with, and match the tonal balance of the clip you are correcting to this reference. Another approach is to get a match clip or guide clip yourself, tape it over a white area on your monitor, and compare it with a linearized image in After Effects – either to calibrate your monitor or to create an adjustment layer that will bring your footage around to match. If you do any correcting, outputting a wedge (discussed later) becomes even more important.

Finally, don't assume just because the scanning equipment costs more than your house that any problem with the supplied scans is your fault. If the color looks odd, question it before you composite the titles and record it back to film. Several film projects we've worked on have had to be rescanned – we even received a shot in which the film was loaded into the scanner backward…

Telling Time

In addition to the differences in frame rates, film does not count time using SMPTE; instead it counts the physical measurement of feet+frames. With 35mm film (the most common format), there are 16 frames to a foot and typically 24 frames to a second. Similar to SMPTE, the frames are counted 0 to 15, not 1 to 16.

There are occasions when you may deal strictly in the number of frames since the start. For example, when your film is scanned, each frame will have a unique number – not a feet+frames indicator – that usually counts from the beginning of the clip. In this case, be aware that most film scanning facilities count the first frame as 1, while many computer people count the first frame as 0.

In any case, you can set the counting method in After Effects in the File>Project Settings. Calculators are available that convert between the two; you can also Command+click on Mac (Control+click on Windows) on the frame number display in After Effects to toggle it between these different counting methods.

Each individual reel of film stock is identified by a unique keycode (or Keykode™) number. This is printed along the edge of the film stock in a format readable by both humans and machines. Video dubs of film should have these numbers "burned in" along with the feet and frames timing; they may also have the video SMPTE timecode burned in.

When you receive a video dub of the footage, it should have a variety of numbers burned in over the image. In this case, the numbers along the bottom from left to right indicate the video dub's timecode, the keycode numbers (two letters followed by six numbers), and the feet+frame measurement from the start of the reel.

When you're ordering a segment of film to be scanned, you will need to provide both the keycode number and the feet+frames readings for the in and out points. Also add a few frames of handle on to the front and back for safety, and clarify whether the in and out points requested include or exclude the handle. You cannot go back and ask for just a few more frames later on; you will inevitably experience slight shifts in color and position from scan to scan.

Bits and Pieces

If you deliver your animation on multiple tapes, drives, or cartridges, but need continuous output, be sure to specify this – otherwise it may be output in pieces. If you built in break points, note these as well in case there's a problem while recording out.

Saving Templates

To save the Output Modules in our example project for use in your own projects, select Make Template from the bottom of the Output Modules menu. This will add them to your Prefs file.

Computer Black

You may be asked to output a number of "black" frames at the head of your animation, especially if your titles fade up from black. Rather than render a sequence of black frames, render a single black frame and ask the film house to output it multiple times. Also, if fading up from black, add a tiny white dot in the corner of frame 1 so the editor can sync to the first frame.

Recording Out

In After Effects, render to a sequence, at 24 fps, with field rendering off. In the Render Settings, if you feel that not all of your frames are going to fit onto one drive or piece of media, enter a Custom Work Area to render only enough frames to fit (1000 Cineon frames will fit on a 10-gigabyte DLT, for example), and queue up multiple renders as needed to do the entire comp. By setting a Custom Work Area, you can easily rerender the section by simply duplicating the render queue item. In the Output Module, make sure you set Starting # to match the frames being rendered for each render item.

The common file path for film files (especially TAR tape archives) is a folder with the movie's name, which then holds a folder with the frame size as its name (1828×1332, for example). Place the frames inside that folder. End the frame's name with an underscore, the frame number, a period, then the file type code (cin for Cineon, rgb for SGI-RGB). An example as it appears in the Render Queue would be **titleseq_[####].cin** – note that the number of pound symbols denote how many digits the frame number will have. Examples of this naming convention are also already loaded into the Window>Render Queue in the example project.

You can create a video proof at the same time by selecting the item in the Render Queue and choosing Composition>Add Output Module. Edit the output module to "Stretch" (actually, squeeze) this movie to 720×486 (or whatever your video card supports). Select your hardware's codec, or render to a QuickTime Photo-JPEG movie. Then render both the film and QT versions simultaneously. You'll now be able to quickly step through the QuickTime movie to check for any problems. Note that this render will be at 24 fps; if you want a 29.97 fps version, you will need to import this movie and rerender at the higher frame rate.

Before you output a large sequence of frames, it is best to order a trial output of a few frames or seconds at different exposures. This is commonly called a *wedge*. Call the clients in to view it projected at the film house. Have the clients pick which exposure they like best; if they couldn't pick one, go back and tweak your graphics based on their feedback.

If you have a long sequence to record, ask if the film house can output the entire job continuously, and note this on your order form. If you provide a long sequence over multiple tapes or drives, make sure that the frame numbers are sequential and that you specify Continuous Output. Otherwise, you may find that each tape will be output and processed separately, rather than as one piece of film. Note that you cannot easily "insert edit" on film; you might see color shifts. If there's a mistake, you have to output a section again between two hard cuts. If it's a long title sequence, design the animation with *break points* (hard cuts at major scene changes). If there's an output problem, or a credit needs changing later, these break points give you and the film house the option of re-outputting between two break points rather than starting over from the very beginning.

Offline/Online Workflow

So far, we've discussed getting film frames in and out, but we've not discussed the real-world nitty-gritty of working on a film project such as an opening title. Quite often, it is not as easy as just ordering up a bunch of frames, being creative, then sending a drive off to the film house – you will often first have to create an offline version of your work using video dubs of the film footage. We will focus on the case of working with 24 fps film and 29.97 fps video (which includes 3:2 pulldown); most of the principles carry over to the PAL world as well. Note that many of the workflow issues discussed here apply to hi-def video production as well as film.

Hi-Def and Film

Much hi-def production follows the same general workflow as a film project. Therefore, this section on workflow applies equally to hi-def and film.

The Video Edit

A good portion of your film work will not consist of creating all-new graphics from scratch, but of using footage from the show as your main elements. In this case, you may be doing anything from editing together shots and adding text on top to performing more extreme treatments and compositing tricks.

The first task is creating the rough edit. If that task falls in your domain, this means getting video dubs of clips from the production, probably working with the client to select favorites, then building an edit. You will need to have a solid path to relate your video clips back to the original footage: either a window burn with the timecode and/or keycode numbers, or sheets detailing what timecode on the video dub you received relates back to what frame on the original film or 24p hi-def master tapes.

You may be creating titles over an edit that will be performed by someone other than you. In this case, you need to get a video dub of the edit, dubs of all the source clips that went to build that edit, and an Edit Decision List (EDL) or Assemble List that provides a roadmap of how these individual clips were put together to create the edit. You will then need to recreate the edit – either directly in After Effects, or in your own non-linear editing system (NLE), in which case you can then import your NLE's timeline into After

Often, an edit of the footage to be used will be created by someone else, and you need to recreate it from the EDL or Assemble List. In this case, all times are in feet+frames; the Footage column is the running time of the edited piece. The First/Last Ink column are the times from each individual source clip, followed by the clip name.

```
REVISED TITLES SCANNED 8-16      58 events        handles = 0
Picture 1                        0 dupes          total footage: 733+04
New Assemble List                3 opticals       total time: 00:08:08:24


        Footage      Duration    First/Last Ink      Clip Name

   1.    0+00         12+00      (NO EDGE NUMBERS)    HEAD&FOCUS LEADER
         11+15

   2.    12+00         2+00           LEADER
         13+15

Add    1+00   Dissolve here.

   3.    14+00        25+11        502-0120+03        LOGO-1
         39+10                       0145+13

         14+00   LOCATOR            502-0120+03
       9001

Add    1+00   Dissolve here.

   2.    39+11         0+03           LEADER
         39+13
         WARNING: short cut

Add    1+00   Dissolve here.

   5.    39+14        19+12        502-0149+02        LOGO-2
         59+09                       0168+13

   6.    59+10        13+15        Opt 1-0000+00      OPTICAL #1
         73+08                       0013+14

   7.    73+09         9+03        356-0826+00        1032-5
         82+11                       0835+02
```

Audio Rate

If you are using the audio from a video dub as your guide, verify if it has been slowed down 0.1% from the original in order to make the video dub (it probably has). If this is the case, place the captured audio on its own layer, and Time Stretch it to 99.9% to recreate its original speed, or your 24 fps edits will be off.

Composition Settings

Composition Name: reel 1/clip 3 – enters bedroom

Basic / Advanced

Preset: Cineon Half, 1828 x 1332

Width: 1828
Height: 1332 ☐ Lock Aspect Ratio to 457:333

Pixel Aspect Ratio: Square Pixels   Frame Aspect Ratio: 457:333

Frame Rate: 24 Frames per second

Resolution: Half   914 x 666, 4.6 MB per 16bpc frame

Start Frame: 127+01 ⬅

Duration: 0003+12 Frames @ 24 fps

Cancel   OK

To keep better track of source frame numbers, we give each clip its own comp, and set the comp's Start Frame to match the clip's starting timecode or keycode number.

Effects (see Chapter 18). Compare your version with the edited version you received frame by frame to make sure you rebuilt it correctly.

Since you will eventually be ordering film frames to be scanned, it is best if you can work with accurate representatives of those film frames in your offline video proof. To do this, you will need to convert the video dubs back to the original film frames by conforming the frame rate of each clip from 29.97 to 30 fps (reversing the slowdown that occurs in the telecine process), then removing the 3:2 pulldown in the Interpret Footage dialog for each clip (see Chapter 23).

Tracking Times

Again, we cannot stress enough how important it is to be able to track the frames you use in your creations back to the source frames on film. This is what you are going to be ordering the film house to scan – and scanning film is expensive, usually costing in the area of a dollar or more per frame. However, After Effects does not automatically track the timecode or keycode of clips you import. Therefore, you need to go through some extra steps to re-attach the source timecode to each clip.

Rather than use the video clips directly in the same comp to perform the edit, we give each clip its own comp (running at 24 fps, after the pulldown has been removed). These precomps contain the entire running length of each source clip, "flash to flash" (slate to slate) if possible. In the Composition Settings dialog for each clip, we set the Start Frame to match the timecode of the clip, as far back up the chain as we know it: worst case, the in point for each clip on the video dub; best case, the feet+frame number from the original reel, derived from the window burn on the dubs.

Edit using these precomps as if they were the clips. After the final offline design proof is signed off, you can go back and read the timecode ranges used for each clip's comp. Transcribe these into a shot list for the film house (or for the post house capturing the hi-def video frames for you), including shot durations and descriptions of each scene for confirmation, in the event a number was mistranscribed. Add at least two frames to the head and tail for safety; add a full second if you can afford the extra scanning fees or if you think the client may want to tweak an edit later. Tell the film house whether you've already added handle to the frame numbers you've given them.

If you have the original keycode numbers, you're ready to scan. Occasionally, you will have the "ink" numbers from a work print that has been made of the original film. In this case, you need to rely on the production staff to translate these ink numbers back to the original film's keycode numbers. If you have only the timecode number on an intermediate dub, hope that the place that made the dub has its own sheet to conform those numbers back to the master reels or hi-def tapes.

Scaling Up

When it comes time to recreate your offline proof with the original film or hi-def frames, you don't have to start from scratch; with a bit of thought and preplanning, you can just scale up your After Effects comps and get very close.

First, change the size of each of your comps to match the film or hi-def frame size. In the individual comps which were dedicated to each raw video-size clip, set the time marker to equal the timecode value you requested for the original segment, and add this partial full-resolution clip to the comp. Eyeball the video clip to make sure it lines up with the full-res version; if needed, slide the full-res clip to match, then turn off the video clip.

If you create your text elements using the Type tool in After Effects, you can use a larger font size when you're creating the high-resolution version. (To figure out how big to make it, calculate the ratio between the number of lines in your offline and online versions: For example, 1080 lines ÷ 486 lines = 2.22 times larger in the case of hi-def production.) We prefer to create film titles in Illustrator at the correct size (or a little larger, for safety) using the template included on the DVD, and then size them down in After Effects for the offline. When we're creating the online version, we just change the layer's Scale to 100% (or a little less if they are too large) in After Effects. The advantage of using Illustrator over the built-in Type tool is that it is easy to print out the credit pages from Illustrator to fax to the client to check spelling and layout – essential!

Many effects have parameters based on pixels: this many pixels of blur, that many pixels of offset for the drop shadow effect. You can use the same multiplication factor you calculated for the text as a starting point for scaling up your pixel-dependent effect parameters, but indeed treat it only as a starting point. Even if they're mathematically correct, effects can look subjectively different in the context of the larger frame size and increased resolution. Be prepared to tweak values to get the same aesthetic result you originally intended.

The Cineon File Format

Throughout this chapter, we've been referring to Cineon files and log color space. Kodak designed this format to better mimic the characteristics of film so that film could be copied digitally without losing any of its detail. This format is probably new to users with a video or multimedia background, and its logarithmic response is not native to the way most desktop computer software displays color. However, After Effects has a set of tools that allow you to work in this truer-to-film space.

The Cineon file format can represent each color channel as a 10-bit range, with 1024 possible values. When neutral test cards are shot on film and scanned into this format, 2% reflection (black) is set at a Cineon value of 180, 18% reflection (neutral gray) at 470, and 90% reflection (stark white) at 685. Since the entire range of values of 0 to 1023 is not used for

Four Lumps, or Five?

After Effects defaults to five digits for the frame number. However, many film houses prefer four. Delete one of the # symbols in the default filename to save with four digits.

Quick Video Proofs

To create a quick video proof, in the Render Settings dialog set the Frame Rate to 23.976, enable Field Rendering (set the field order to match your hardware), and enable 3:2 pulldown (any phase will do). The result will be a 29.97 fps movie that renders more quickly than rendering your final comp at 29.97 fps.

Cineon for Techies

The **Goodies** folder on the DVD includes white papers on the Cineon file format, courtesy Cinesite Los Angeles (www.cinesite.com).

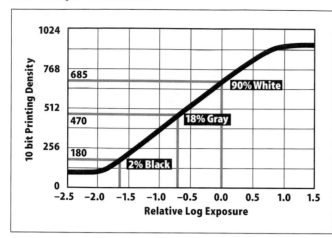

Film is typically exposed just above the "toe" where the darker luminance values round off, allowing lots of headroom for specular highlights. This nominal luminance range is usually mapped to values 180 to 685 inside Cineon's 1024 potential values per color channel.

nominal black to white, there is extra room left to capture (and recover) darker or brighter than normal portions of a scene. In the case of film that was purposely overexposed to trade off reduced highlights for less noise in the shadows, increasing the exposure on the film one "stop" raises all these values by 90.

Cineon in After Effects

When you import a properly tagged Cineon file in After Effects (suffix is .cin), the program will by default spread Cineon's 1024 internal values per color channel across either the 256 possible values in an 8 bpc project, or (if you have the Professional edition) the 32769 possible values in an After Effects 16 bpc project. (By the way, when you're working with Cineon files, we highly recommend working in 16 bpc mode; otherwise, you will be throwing away some of the resolution inherent in the Cineon format. Set File>Project Settings>Color Depth to 16 bits per channel, or Option+click (Alt+click) on the 8 bpc / 16 bpc switch at the bottom of the Project window.)

Using the Full Range default, the resulting image will look washed out – this is because you are viewing the full range of log color values in a linear color space (your computer's monitor). To view a Cineon file in linear color space, you will need to remap its internal color values. There are two ways to do this:

Method One: Select the file in the Project window and type Command+F (Control+F) to open its Interpret Footage dialog. Click on More Options, and set the Preset popup to Standard. This gives the same results as applying the Cineon Converter at its default settings, which we will explain next.

Method Two: Instead, leave the Cineon Options in the Interpret Footage dialog to its default Full Range. Then add the Cineon file to a comp, and apply Effect>Channel>Cineon Converter. The default parameters convert Cineon log space to the After Effects linear space. We prefer this method, as it leaves the conversion controls exposed in the Effect Controls window where we can interactively change them while we're watching the results in the Comp window. Try this with the Cineon file in [**Ex.03**].

The Cineon Converter dialog looks like an enhanced Levels effect – but in this case, you are remapping log color space to a linear space, not manipulating values already inside a linear space.

The Cineon Converter effect can perform three basic types of conversion: Log to Linear (to view Cineon files in the linear space native to After Effects); Linear to Log (to remap linear color space stock footage, 3D renders, and the like to Cineon's log color space); and Log to Log (to convert a 10-bit log file to an 8-bit log file – used sometimes to render proxies in order to save disk space). The other "obsolete" choices are to accommodate older projects that used an earlier version of the Cineon Converter.

From here, this plug-in looks a bit like a Levels effect, but with a few important differences. To get a better understanding of what the controls are doing, go ahead and apply Adjust>Levels after the Cineon Converter; we'll use its Histogram to give us additional insight.

In the Cineon Converter, the 10 bit Black Point and 10 bit White Point parameters define what is "black" and "white" in the Cineon

The full logarithmic color space of a Cineon file looks washed out when it's viewed in linear color space on your computer (A). A Levels Histogram shows how the colors are bunched in the middle of the available values (B). Apply Effect>Channel>Cineon Converter to remap the log values to linear values (C). The resulting Histogram (D) gives an idea of how the colors have been stretched and remapped.

file. It is common to map a value of 95 (1% black or "Dmin" in a normal Cineon file) to the darkest color you will be using in After Effects: This is the Internal Black Point value, which is normally 0. Likewise, it is common to map a Cineon value of 685 (nominally 90% white) to an Internal White Point of 255 for 8 bpc, or 32768 for 16 bpc. You can alter these values creatively if you are trying to extract a nonstandard color and contrast range from the film, or scientifically when you're compensating for specific effects (for example, knowing the original film was overexposed by a stop, which means the 10 bit Points need to be shifted upward by 90).

The Cineon format was created to help preserve "whiter than white" values, such as hot spots caused by direct lights or harsh reflections. Our sample file here has an issue where the walkway behind and to the right of the actress is hit hard by the glare of the sun: If you move your mouse over this area of the Comp window while looking at the Info window, you will note the Blue channel is pegged at 100%, with the other channels not far behind. The Highlight Rolloff parameter can be used to bend just these bright spots back into a color range where they are not posterized. For this image, increase it from its default of 20 up to 40, and note the changes in the Histogram in the Levels effect you applied, as well as the values you are seeing in the Info window.

Note that this Highlight Rolloff parameter changes the overall luminance curve of your images. This is fine for just viewing Cineon files on your monitor, or if you know you are going to make a new image out of this footage. However, if the scene you are treating is supposed to match up exactly with similar scenes that you are not treating, you will have a brightness shift in the highlights. If matching other shots is essential, instead you should set Highlight Rolloff to 0, increase the 10 bit White Point until you feel you have captured all of the whites you want to keep, and make sure you use this same 10 bit White Point Value later when you're converting back to log space.

The Gamma parameter is ideally set to match that of your computer monitor (1.7 for Mac, 2.2 for Windows). Again, if you change this, either do it for strictly artistic reasons, or remember to use the same value when you convert back to log.

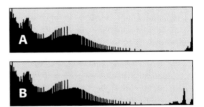

If the original footage contains bright spots that posterize after conversion to Linear, you can use the Highlight Rolloff parameter to curve them back into an acceptable range. Note how just the highest values change in these before (A) and after (B) histograms, and how the sidewalk is now slightly duller (C).

Film Movement

To make your video look more like film, shoot progressive-scan at 24, 25, or 29.97 fps. If your source already has fields, try removing them with RE:Vision Effects' FieldsKit (www.revisionfx.com).

To keep scanned film in its Cineon color space, you need to convert your added graphics into log space (A). The Adjustment Layer (layer 2 in Timeline, below) converts everything underneath back to linear space (B) for proofing on your computer monitor or to video.

Log Logic

You can use the Cineon Converter to move Cineon files into the linear color space you know and love, and do all of your compositing and effects in this space. However, often the preferred path is to keep all log scans in the log format and to convert your linear space, computer-created images into log space. This preserves maximum color resolution and gives more flexibility to perform color corrections when you print back to film. To work this way, you need to organize your layers as follows:

• The background Cineon file is the bottom layer. There is no need to apply the Cineon Converter, as this source is already in log space.

• Non-Cineon graphics layers, such as titles, are layered on top of this. Apply the Cineon Converter after any other effects applied to these layers (such as Tint or Fill and Drop Shadow for text), with Conversion Type set to Linear to Log. Your graphics will now be in the same log color space as the film layer underneath, complete with altered black-and-white points.

• On top of this goes a Layer>New>Adjustment Layer, also with the Cineon Converter applied, set to Log to Linear. Turn this layer on only when you want to see your comp in linear color space – such as while you're working at your computer, or rendering a video proof. *Do not render your film output with this layer on!*

• An option is to apply any overlay grids on top of this, remembering to also turn this layer off when you render.

An example of this working method is included in [**Ex.04**]. Turn the various layers on and off; note in particular how the colors change when the adjustment layer is toggled. Try changing the color of the type (set by the Tint effect applied to **FilmTitle_example**) with **Cineon Adjustment Layer** turned on, and you will see the "mind warp" part of working in log color space: You cannot directly pick colors, because they will be changed by the linear to log color space conversion. There are a few exceptions to this; for example, if you need pure white text, you can create or tint the text using the color Cineon white (67% white, which is

🔲 Ex.04-mixing in log space ▫								
00001 (24.00 fps)			🔲🔲 🔲🎢🔲 M					
🔲 🔲 # Source Name	Mode	T TrkMat	🔴🔲○🔒 0001	00006	00011	00016	00021	00
▷ 🔲 1 ☐ 1828x1332_Acad Ap_EZa.tif	Normal ▼		🔴					
▽ 🔲 2 ☐ Cineon Adjustment Layer	Normal ▼	None ▼	🔴					
▷ Cineon Converter ◀—	Reset		*f*					
▽ 🔲 3 🖼 FilmTitle_example.ai	Normal ▼	None ▼	🔴					
▷ Tint	Reset		*f*					
▷ Drop Shadow	Reset		*f*					
▷ Cineon Converter	Reset		*f*					
▷ 🔲 4 🔲 color bar solid	Color ▼	None ▼	🔴					
▷ 🔲 5 🖼 CineonGirl_1828x1332_0001.cin	Normal ▼	None ▼	🔴					
	Switches / Modes		🔲 △△	△				

21974 in 16-bit linear), with no need to apply the Cineon Converter to this layer. This is demonstrated in [**Ex.05**].

Overall, though, you'll have to get used to repeatedly nudging colors in the direction you need to make the linearized display look right. Instead of making repeated trips to the color picker, you could interactively set the color while watching the Comp window by applying a default Fill color, then using Hue/Saturation to interactively offset the color.

Also, whereas some simpler blending modes (such as Multiply and Add) will still behave pretty much as you expect, others will composite differently in log versus linear color space because the 50% gray point is no longer where they expect it to be. This usually leads to the result being brighter than anticipated. You will either need to live with these modes behaving differently, or switch your work flow to build at least some of the final imagery in linear color space.

Rendering to Cineon

To render out to the Cineon format, in the Output Module dialog you must select the format Cineon Sequence. Make sure the Color is set to RGB; you'll note the Depth defaults to Trillions of Colors. This repacks the data into a 10-bpc Cineon file.

In the Output Module, click on the Format Options button to view the Cineon Conversion parameters. Fortunately, the conversion Presets cover the most common cases: If your comp is in log space, choose Full Range; if it is in linear space, choose Standard. The Presets change all of the parameters except for File Format; for this, FIDO/ Cineon 4.5 is far more common than DPX.

Since [**Ex.04**] is a log comp, we want to use the Full Range preset. Open the Window>Render Queue, and verify this setting in the Output Module options. If, on the other hand, you have a comp that is in the linear color space, you need to convert it to log at this output stage. To do this, select the Standard preset, and tweak the conversion parameters only If necessary (for example, if you want to print an overexposed or "heavy" negative). This is the case with [**Ex.06**]; check the Output Module options for the second item in the Render Queue.

Of course, if you're going out linear you don't have to save to the Cineon format. Make sure your comp is in normal linear space (as in [**Ex.07**]) and save to the SGI-RGB format. This is demonstrated in the third item in the Render Queue. This file format is particularly useful if you're only saving titles against a black background or rendering animated mattes – the SGI-RGB format includes an RLE option, which losslessly compresses frames to as little as 300 kilobytes, instead of more than 9 megabytes! In the Output Module, set the Color Depth to Millions of Colors for 8 bpc, or if you have the Professional edition and need the resolution of 16 bpc, set this popup to Trillions of Colors (though you should first check that the film house can take a 16 bpc SGI-RGB file). *Thanks to Tim Sassoon of Sassoon Film Design for his help in compiling the information in this chapter.*

If your comp is already in log color space, use the Full Range Preset to save a Cineon format file. If you need to convert a linear color space comp to Cineon's log space, use the Standard preset.

Connect

16 bit per channel (bpc) mode was introduced in a sidebar in Chapter 7.

Color Correction was the subject of Chapter 8.

Importing sequences from NLEs was outlined in Chapter 18.

3:2 Pulldown – including adding pulldown in the Render Settings to ease making video proofs – was the subject of Chapter 23.

Considerations for working in both widescreen and television aspects, as well as working with hi-def footage, were covered in Chapter 27.

29 Prerendering and Proxies

Planning ahead can save time later.

One of After Effects' strengths is that you don't have to prerender anything: All of your sources, layers, and manipulations are "live" all the time, allowing you to make unlimited changes. However, calculating everything all the time can slow down both your work and your final render.

In this chapter, we'll explain how prerendering complex comps can speed up your workflow, and using proxies for footage and comps can streamline that process further. Then we'll work through an example so you can see this in action.

Prerendering

Prerendering is the practice of creating a movie or still of an intermediate composition, or one that you intend to reuse as an element. You then swap this rendered movie into a project in place of the comp that created it. The reason is you save processing time while you're working, as well as rendering time later on. You can create prerenders for various reasons and purposes, but you should be clear on whether the prerendered element is temporary, or whether it could be used to speed up the final render:

- When you're satisfied that a precomp is final, you could render it at this point to save processing time later. This really adds up if it is nested multiple times, or if you expect to be rendering a lot of proofs. This precomp might contain, say, a stack of background movie layers with blending modes, masks, and blurs; when it's nested it might be colorized or manipulated further, but the basic precomp design is locked down. Once you've prerendered this comp and swapped in the resulting movie, only one movie needs to be retrieved and no further processing is needed. If you're prerendering a logo or element that will be manipulated further in other comps, be sure to save the prerender with an alpha channel.

- You might have one layer that has a very slow effect applied (such as a particle system or a large radial blur). Prerender this one layer, with an alpha channel if needed, and reimport the movie. Turn off the original layer (don't delete it), and use the prerendered layer instead.

- You could also create a still to stand in for an animated composition. For instance, say you created animated wallpaper or other background elements that change from frame to frame, but it is not important to see

Temporary Freeze

If you don't have time to prerender a slow precomp that's not changing much, apply Time Remapping to the nested comp layer. Find a representative frame and create a time remap keyframe here, then delete all other time remap keyframes. A single image will be rendered and cached as you work along the timeline. Just don't forget to remove Time Remapping before you render!

Example Project

Explore the 29-Example Project.aep file as you read this chapter; references to [Ex.##] refer to specific compositions within the project file.

these changes while you're working on the foreground elements. This is particularly useful if you don't have time to prerender the comp, but you need to work a bit faster.

• Likewise, you could export one frame from a source movie and use that in place of the original footage while you're designing the rest of the project. Since this still image will be cached in RAM, no slowdown will occur in retrieving frames from disk as you move about the timeline.

In all cases, you can import the prerendered element normally and use the prerender in place of the original. To swap in the prerender where the original comp was nested, use the Replace Source technique covered in Volume 1, Chapter 6. However, there is a slicker way to manage these stand-ins: Proxies.

Proxies

A *proxy* is a file that is designed to stand in for a footage item or an entire composition. It can be used temporarily to speed up editing, or as part of the final render. It is easy to turn proxies on or off on an individual basis, or on a project-wide basis when you render. After Effects will also automatically scale a lower resolution proxy to match the size of the footage or comp it is standing in for. When it comes time to archive the project, you can trash the proxies without ruining your hierarchy – just remove the proxies to return the project to its original structure.

There are several situations where we use proxies, some of which are the same as the reasons we create prerenders:

• Prerender a composition, to save time during both working and rendering. This prerender is created at the full size of the composition, interlaced if necessary, and referred to as a *Comp Proxy*.

• Prerender a still of a comp, to save time while you're working. This is also considered a Comp Proxy, though you would not use it during final render.

• Create reduced resolution versions of movies, to save time while working; these are referred to as *Footage Proxies*. You can prerender footage proxies in After Effects or another program, taking care that they are the same length as the original movie. The original footage would be used during final rendering. Creating smaller-sized versions of movies is recommended only when the original footage is at hi-def or film resolution, where the savings would be significant. Otherwise, the comp's Resolution setting is designed to drop all footage to Half or Quarter Resolution on the fly.

• If you have an extremely large background still image that's slowing you down, create a low-res proxy for just the background layer (open the hi-res image in Photoshop, scale to 25%, and save under a new name). Now you can work at Full Resolution to design the foreground layers, while the background layer alone is at "quarter resolution."

• Export one frame from a "talking head" movie and use it temporarily as a footage proxy. Now, instead of retrieving frames as you move about the timeline, this single frame is used and cached.

Lossless Prerenders

If you prerender elements that will be used in the final render, you do not want to lose any image quality in the process. A good choice is a QuickTime movie, using the Animation codec set to Best (Quality = 100) with the keyframing option turned off. This uses the same color space as After Effects (RGB) and is lossless. If you have the Professional edition and want that last ounce of quality, set File>Project Settings>Color Depth to 16 bits per channel, and save to a codec that supports Trillions of Colors. Note that most uncompressed video cards use the YUV color space, and the inevitable translation between RGB and YUV can result in a slight loss in quality, especially if the codec does not support 10-bit YUV.

For the highest quality, render without fields at double the frame rate (59.94 frames per second for NTSC). This way, you'll have the extra visual information you need when you transform later. If you are prerendering a full-frame layer that will not be scaled or animated further, and your output will be field rendered, you can safely field render the prerender; there is no point in rendering and saving more data than you need.

After you have assigned a proxy, a black box (the proxy on/off switch) appears to its left, and two sets of information appear overhead – the right one is for the proxy. The item whose name is in bold is the one that's active.

Layer Proxies

After Effects cannot create or assign a proxy for a single layer in a comp – proxies apply to entire compositions only.

Applying Proxies

After you have prerendered your proxy, in the Project window select the footage item or composition it is supposed to stand in for, select File>Set Proxy>File, and locate your proxy file. Two things will change in the Project window: A black box will appear next to the comp or footage item in the list, and when you select this item, two sets of information will appear along the top of the window. The left one is for the original file/composition; the second one is for your proxy. (You may need to widen or scroll the Project window to see both.)

If you rendered the full length of a selected comp to create its proxy, their size and duration will match. If the proxy's size was smaller, After Effects would automatically scale it up so it appears to be the same size as the original. If you need to change any of the Interpret Footage settings for the proxy (for example, to separate its fields or set it to loop), select File>Interpret Footage>Proxy.

The black box next to the item is the Proxy Switch. Click on it to toggle usage of the proxy off and on. The current status is echoed in the top of the Project window: The source being used – proxy or original file/comp – will have its name in bold. To change the proxy file, use Set Proxy again; don't use File>Replace Footage. To remove a proxy, use File>Set Proxy> None. When it comes time to render, the Proxy Use menu in the Render Settings determines whether proxies are rendered at their current settings, globally turned on or off, or set to render Comp Proxies only.

Placeholders

If you know a footage item is coming, but it hasn't been provided yet, After Effects allows you to create a Placeholder object: File>Import>Placeholder. You can set its dimensions and duration; it will default to the frame rate set in Preferences>Import under Sequence Footage. After Effects will create an image of color bars, which you can now animate, mask, and add effects to as desired. When the footage arrives, use File>Replace Footage, and this new file will be swapped in for the color bars.

That said, you're free to use any dummy image – even a Layer>New>Solid – as a placeholder. It is a good idea to use an image that is visually more representative of the footage you expect. However, Placeholders have the advantage of having "fixed" durations, which make them more like movies to handle and edit once they're in a comp.

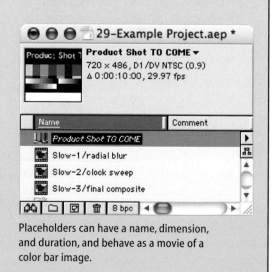

Placeholders can have a name, dimension, and duration, and behave as a movie of a color bar image.

Proxy Behavior

When a proxy is assigned to a footage item or comp, it is as if you replaced that item. The exception is that low-res proxies will be scaled to the original dimensions of the item they are standing in for. Low-res proxies may look a bit pixelated, but the autoscale feature has a great advantage in that all your transformations and effects settings will work the same for the proxy as for the original file. If you had simply replaced the file with a smaller one, this would not be the case as you would have had to scale up the stand-in (perhaps in a precomp) to match the original's size.

When a proxy is used for a comp, stepping through time in the comp steps through the prerendered proxy. Editing layers in the comp the proxy is applied to will not change what you see in the Comp window, which can be disconcerting. A yellow border around the Comp window tips you off that you are viewing a proxy, not the comp's contents. Of course, further comps that use this comp won't care if the layer they are accessing is a comp or a prerendered image or movie, and navigating higher up the chain will be much faster.

You can, of course, turn off the proxy in the Project window, which will now make the comp "live" again. Make your changes, and observe the effects downstream in the comps that use this comp. If you prefer your new variation, render a new proxy and swap it in, or simply remove the proxy and work normally.

Working with Proxies

Let's get some practice creating and using proxies. We'll take advantage of the Post-Render Action option in the Output Module Settings. Originally discussed in Volume 1, Chapter 29, these make creating prerenders and proxies much easier.

Open the project file **29-Example Project.aep** that goes with this chapter; you'll find it in the **Chapter Example Projects>29-Example Project** folder on this book's DVD. It contains a chain of three comps that nest into each other. Open Preferences>Display, and enable Show Rendering in Progress in Info Palette. Then make sure the Info palette is visible (if not, select Window>Info). Open **[Slow-3/final composite]** and move the time marker around – notice how slow the Comp window updates. Watch the Info palette to figure out what's slowing you down: If you have a slower computer, you may notice the motion blur applied in **[Slow-2/clock sweep]** triggering a Transform & Compositing delay; the Radial Blur effect applied in the first comp **[Slow-1/radial blur]** is also a major factor.

Archiving Proxies

Because proxies are just stand-ins, you could archive your project without saving the proxies.

Drafty Proxies

You can also select a comp in the Project window and use the menu command File>Create Proxy, which will automatically set the Post-Render Action option to Set Proxy. However, the default Render Settings for proxies in 6.5 is the Draft Settings template; change this default under Edit>Templates> Render Settings to Best Settings.

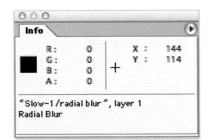

When Preferences>Display>Show Rendering Progress option is enabled, the Info palette lets you know what's taking so long as you move from frame to frame. Here, the Radial Blur effect is slowing down **[Slow-1/radial blur]**. Images from Digital Vision/Inner Gaze and Getty Images/Business Essentials.

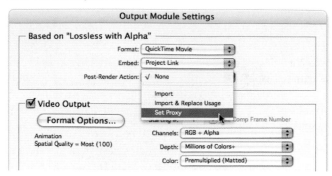

Set the Post-Render Action popup in the Output Module Settings (above). Using Set Proxy means After Effects will automatically assign the rendered file as a proxy for the comp you are rendering. You can also access these options by twirling open the Output Module in the Render Queue (below), which has the added feature of allowing you to pick whip to another footage item or comp in the Project window to assign this proxy to.

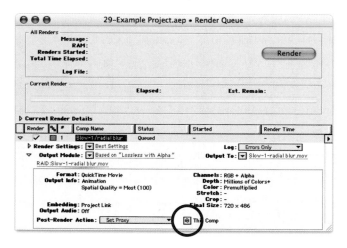

Collapsing and Proxies

The one instance where behavior of a comp and a comp proxy differ is if you enabled Collapse Transformations for this comp layer in another comp. Collapse looks beyond the frame size of a nested comp and can access images on the pasteboard; a comp proxy does not have this information anymore. If you're depending on using Collapse Transformations, you may not be able to use a comp proxy.

Now open the nested comp [**Slow-2/clock sweep**]. Move the time marker; this comp is almost as slow, as After Effects is still calculating motion blur and Radial Blur. You can turn off the Motion Blur switch in this comp's Timeline window to temporarily disable this calculation, but the Radial Blur in [**Slow-1/radial blur**] is still making things sluggish.

Open the nested comp [**Slow-1/radial blur**], and move its time marker or RAM Preview to get a feel for how slow the Radial Blur effect is. This precomp is a good candidate for a proxy. If you are in a hurry, you can make a still image to stand in for this comp. Type Command+Option+S on Mac (Control+Alt+S on Windows) to render the current frame. Bring the Render Queue forward, give the file a name that you will be able to find later, and twirl down the Output Module section. At the bottom of this section is a popup labeled Post-Render Action: Change its setting from None to Set Proxy. This means After Effects will automatically assign the rendered file as a proxy for the comp you are rendering. Click the Render button and a single frame will be rendered and saved to disk.

When the render finishes, look at the Project window: The item [**Slow-1/radial blur**] has a black box to its left, indicating a proxy has been assigned. Select this comp, and the Project window will display details of the comp and its proxy (you may need to drag the window wider).

Return to [**Slow-1/radial blur**]. A yellow box is drawn around its Comp window, with the words Proxy Enabled in the lower left corner. Move the time marker or RAM Preview, and note how quickly it responds: All After Effects is doing is displaying the still image you rendered, rather than calculating Radial Blur. You can even toggle the Video switch for **DV_InnerGaze** off and on; the image will still be visible in the Comp window. Toggle the Proxy switch off in the Project window, and [**Slow-1/radial blur**] is back to its ol' sluggish self. Turn the Proxy switch back on for now.

Open [**Slow-2/clock sweep**] again, and RAM Preview. It should be more responsive now – especially if the Motion Blur switch is still off!

But there's a slight problem: The Radial Blur effect was animating in [**Slow-1/radial blur**], and we don't get to see that progression now, as a still image is standing in for the animation.

Return to the Project window, select [**Slow-1/radial blur**], and select File>Set Proxy>None. This removes the link to the proxy (but does not delete it from your hard drive – you can File>Set Proxy>File and use it again later if you wanted). With this comp still selected, type Command+M (Control+M) and this time render a movie of it. In the Output Module, set the Post-Render Action popup to Set Proxy. As [**Slow-2/clock sweep**] does not rely on this precomp's alpha, you don't need a file format that saves an alpha channel. If disk space is more precious than perfect image quality, try QuickTime using the PhotoJPEG codec with its Quality set somewhere between 70 and 99. Click the Render button, and go make yourself a nice cup of tea while you're waiting… When the render is done, the new proxy will automatically be assigned. Return to [**Slow-3/final composite**]. It should be much more responsive, especially if Motion Blur is still turned off for [**Slow-2/clock sweep**].

You can use a proxy for [**Slow-2/clock sweep**] as well – just queue it up to render. Remember to set the Post-Render Action to Set Proxy. Also open its Render Settings, verify Motion Blur is set to On For Checked Layers, and change the Proxy Use popup to Use Comp Proxies Only to take advantage of the proxy we already rendered for [**Slow-1/radial blur**]. Since we need an alpha channel for this precomp, choose a file format that saves one, such as QuickTime Animation Millions+. After the render, note how much zippier [**Slow-3/final composite**] is.

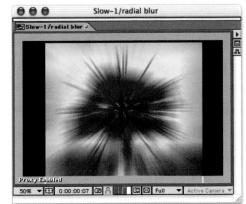

When a proxy has been assigned to a comp and is enabled, the Comp window has a yellow outline. Edits to the comp's layers will not be visible in the Comp window, as After Effects is looking to the proxy instead.

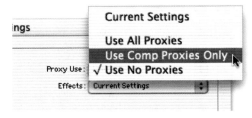

You can override your proxy switches in the Render Settings dialog.

Rendering with Proxies

When it comes time to render, you can use or ignore proxies. This is determined in Render Settings under the Proxy Use menu. You want to ignore proxies if they were low-resolution versions of your footage; you want to render the proxies that are prerenders standing in for computationally intensive compositions.

The normal choice is Current Settings, which means obey the current status of the proxy switches in the Project window. This means the final comp will render exactly as you are viewing it. The other choices override the Project window settings.

If you were using low-resolution footage proxies, but the prerendered comps were final versions, choose Use Comp Proxies Only for your final render. This will use the original footage, but still use any composition proxies you may have prerendered to save time. This is our usual default.

If you used stills to stand in for comps, remove these proxies in the Project window before the final render, or select Use No Proxies. Of course, if you've already prerendered horribly slow comps, Use No Proxies will start rendering everything again from scratch (been there, done that…).

Connect

Collapsing Transformations was the subject of Volume 1, Chapter 20.

Importing Footage was originally covered back in Volume 1, Chapter 28.

Rendering in general was covered in Volume 1, Chapter 29.

Fields were deinterlaced in Chapter 22.

Working with film and hi-def footage was discussed in Chapter 28.

30 Advanced Rendering

Network rendering and project management features, including Reduce Project, Collect Files, Render Engines, and the Watch Folder.

When projects get big, you need help. That help may come in the form of cleaning up your project by removing duplicate or unused sources. Or stripping out everything except what is needed for selected comps so you can pass a portion of your project onto another artist. Or collecting all of your source footage to one folder for backup or transport. Or even enlisting the aid of other copies of After Effects to help you render a particularly intense comp.

After Effects can provide all of these forms of help, and we'll review them in this chapter. We're going to start with general file management issues, then proceed to the Professional edition's ability to distribute a render across a network of machines (plus discuss some other network rendering options, including GridIron X-Factor).

Spring Cleaning

After Effects offers several commands to help you reduce the clutter in a project:

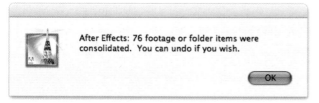

Consolidate All Footage removes duplicate sources in a project and relinks comps to use the consolidated sources that remain.

Consolidate All Footage looks for duplicates of footage in a project, and removes the duplicates. If a comp used one of the duplicates, these layers will be relinked to use the single copy of the footage item that remains. This feature comes in handy when you've imported multiple projects or folders or source materials, and there are overlaps in the sources. (Note that if footage doesn't consolidate, chances are that the interpret footage settings are set differently for each item.)

Remove Unused Footage looks for source items that are not used by any of the comps in your project and deletes them. This is particularly helpful when you've imported a large number of source files early on during a job while you were still deciding which sources to use, and now want to reduce a project down to the sources actually used.

Reduce Project looks at the comps you have selected in the Project window, keeps these comps, any precomps and source material used by those comps, then deletes the unselected comps and all other unused footage. This is good for reducing a complex project just to the comp or comps a co-worker may need to work on. The one occasion when this function can trip you up is if an expression in a comp you kept referenced a comp you did not select before running Reduce Project: The referenced comp will still get deleted.

All of these commands exist under the File menu. Fortunately, all can be undone. Still, it is a good idea to save your project to a new name *before* performing one of these commands, in the event you accidentally hit Save instead of Save As.

> After Effects: 185 items that were not used by the selected items have been deleted. You can undo if desired.
> WARNING: items referenced ONLY by expressions are not preserved.
>
> OK

Reduce Project keeps only the comps you selected in the Project window along with any sources used by those comps.

Collect Files

The Collect Files command has several uses. One is to take a project that may reference source items spread out across several folders and drives, and consolidate all of this footage into a single new folder, complete with a new copy of the project file that links to these copied sources. This is handy for archiving, or moving a job and all of its assets to another computer. Note that in the Collect Files dialog, the Collect Source Files popup has options to either collect just the sources used in the project (akin to running Remove Unused Footage, mentioned above), or copy all sources whether or not a comp currently uses them.

Another way to use Collect Files is as a variation on the Reduce Project command discussed above. First, you select the comps you want to collect, then select Files>Collect Files. Set the Collect Source Files popup to For Selected Comps, and click Collect. Rather than delete the unused comps and sources from your project (which is what Reduce Project will do), all of the comps and source files referenced are left in the project, but only the sources used by the selected comps will be copied to their new location.

A third use for Collect Files is to set up a multimachine network render, which we'll discuss later in this chapter.

Be aware that Collect Files does not collect everything you need to recreate a project: Fonts, effects, and codecs are *not* copied. Instead, Collect Files creates a text file named xxxReport.txt (xxx is the name of your project) which gives you statistics on which files are used by the current project or the selected comps in that project, plus a list of fonts and effects used. If you are archiving a project, or moving it to another machine, it is up to you to make sure a copy of the fonts and effects you need make the trip as well. Note that you can also add your own hints, reminders, and comments to the Report file; just click on the Comments button in the Collect Files dialog before collecting.

Collect Files

Collect Source Files: ✓ **All**
    For All Comps
    For Selected Comps
    For Queued Comps
    None (Project only)

☐ Generate Report Only
☐ Obey Proxy Settings
☐ Reduce Project
☑ Change render output to 06–final renders folder
☑ Enable "Watch Folder" render
    Maximum Number of Machines: 5

    2 single-machine render items.
    0 multiple-machine render items.

31 file(s) (38.1 MB) will be collected.
17 effect(s) are used.

Comments...   Cancel   Collect...

Collect Files allows you to be selective in deciding how much source footage you want to copy to a new location. A Report file is also generated listing the fonts and effects used.

Frozen in Time

When we're backing up a major project, we will often back up our entire After Effects folder as well. This ensures we have a copy of the same version of the program that created the project, as well as the correct version of the plug-ins.

Name Templates

A new feature introduced in version 6.5 is the ability to use a file name template when you're naming a render. This helps you keep your renders organized, particularly when you will be handing them off to another person. You may select a new file name template from a popup menu in the Render Queue's Output Module section – look between the words Output To: and the file name. Selecting a new template automatically renames your render.

Adobe provides a number of useful templates, many of which are based on the Comp's name (which in turn relies on you giving your comps meaningful names – no more Comp 1, Comp 2, et cetera). You can also create your own templates: Select Custom from the popup, string together whatever properties you want (such as frame number or field order) from the popup menu next to the Template dialog, and add your own characters – such as dashes – between these properties.

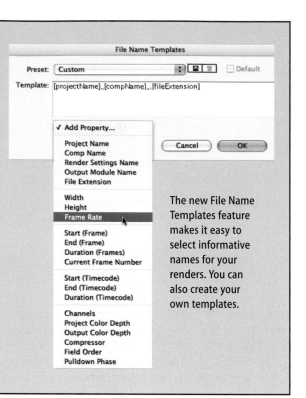

The new File Name Templates feature makes it easy to select informative names for your renders. You can also create your own templates.

Proxy Time

If you have a render-intensive background that is used as a precomp in several other comps, first queue the background to render, and use Post-Render Actions (previous chapter) to assign the result as a proxy for itself. The remaining comps will use the proxy, speeding their own renders.

Also less than obvious are the various proxy options. Proxies were discussed in the previous chapter, but to recap: If you are using proxies as low-resolution or still-image placeholders, definitely disable the Obey Proxy Settings option when you're collecting. This way, both the original sources and their proxies will be copied. However, if you prerendered some comps and set proxies, and are now collecting files simply to render on a separate machine, you might consider checking Obey Proxy Settings. This will copy the currently enabled proxies, but *not* the source material used in the comps that the proxies are standing in for. This means fewer files will be collected, but you won't be able to turn off the proxy later, as the sources that created it would not have been copied.

Network Rendering

"Network" or "distributed" rendering can be as simple as setting up a second computer (or even a second copy of After Effects on your main computer) to render a project while you continue to work, or as advanced as having a render farm of multiple machines all pitch in to crank through a time-intensive set of comps.

As an overview, to set up a distributed render you need a copy of the Professional edition installed on each computer you want to enlist as a render slave. Another option is to perform a Custom install of After

Effects and install the Render Slave version of After Effects on your other computers. You need to set up and share a central Watch Folder that the render slaves look at. At your main computer, queue up the comp you need rendered. Then use the Collect Files feature to place a copy of this project and its source materials in the Watch Folder, as well as create a Render Control File: This tells the slaves the status of the project (whether or not it has already been rendered).

If you select an output format of a sequence of still images, multiple computers can work on the same comp, each taking a different frame to work on. If you render to a movie-based format, only one computer can work on a comp, because there is no way for multiple computers to insert frames into the middle of a movie file. Only one computer can work on an individual frame.

Cloning

As mentioned, Collect Files does not copy fonts, effects, or codecs. Therefore, you need to make sure matching sets of fonts and effects are installed on your render slaves, as well as any codec your files may be compressed with or that you want to write to.

When you install the Render Engine, it installs all of the After Effects' plug-in effects, so you're covered there – but you have to remember to install third party effects yourself. If a particular effect needs a hardware key or is serialized to a single machine, you'll need multiple keys, or you'll need to prerender out those sections so you no longer rely on this effect.

Setting up a Distributed Render

Create a folder that will act as Grand Central Station for your distributed render, and mount it on the computers that will be using it. This is referred to as your Watch Folder. In the slave copies of After Effects, use File>Watch Folder to select this folder. The slave copies will start checking this folder every 10 seconds for new or updated Render Control Files.

Next is queuing up a comp to render. When you're network rendering, there are a couple of settings you need to pay additional attention to. If you want more than one render slave to work on the same composition, in Output Settings you must choose an output file format that is a sequence of still images. Once you have set this up, go to the Render Settings and enable "Skip existing files" in the Options box at the bottom. This prevents multiple computers from trying to render the same frame – they will look to see which frames have already been rendered, and start on the next one that hasn't been rendered. After Effects provides Multi-Machine templates for the Render Settings and

Media Encoding

The Windows version of After Effects supports enhanced rendering to MPEG2, RealMedia, and Windows Media formats, including pre- and post-encoding options such as noise reduction and deinterlacing.

Luminance Ranges

Some codecs – such as Avid and Aurora – have switches that determine how to treat the luminance range of your footage (see Chapter 24) when they retrieve and save files. Make sure these switches are set the same on all of your rendering machines.

When a render slave has been assigned a File>Watch Folder, it will look inside it every 10 seconds for a new Render Control File.

Merging Projects for Render

If you import a project (File>Import>Project), not only will it add all the comps and source material to the current project, it will also merge all of the items in the imported project's Render Queue into the current project's queue.

If we are working with several different project files but want to render them as a batch, we'll set up their respective Render Queues the way we want, create a new project, import all the projects we want to render, open the Render Queue, and hit Render to do the entire batch.

Render Settings

Composition "00_D1 render"

Quality: Best	Proxy Use: Use No Proxies
Resolution: Full	Effects: Current Settings
Size: 720 x 486	Solo Switches: Current Settings
Disk Cache: Read Only	Guide Layers: All Off

Time Sampling

Frame Blending: On For Checked Layers   Time Span: Work Area Only
Field Render: Lower Field First
3:2 Pulldown: Off   Set...   Start: 0:00:00:00
Motion Blur: On For Checked Layers   End: 0:00:09:29
                                                   Duration: 0:00:10:00
☐ Override shutter angle: 180   Frame Rate
                                         ⦿ Use comp's frame rate (29.97)
                                         ◯ Use this frame rate: 29.97

Options
☐ Use storage overflow
☑ Skip existing files (allows multi–machine rendering) ⟵

Cancel   OK

To have more than one computer work on the same comp, render to a sequence of stills, and enable "Skip existing files" in the Render Settings.

Output Module which set this up for you; change the Format in the Output Module to the file type you prefer.

Rendering comps as a sequence of stills may not be optimal for your situation if, for example, you require an embedded audio track or you need to reimport the files into an editing system that does not support sequences. An alternative is breaking a longer render into segments such as 10- to 60-second increments. This will allow the job to get distributed while still writing movies, and it is a good practice even with a single machine so that one bad disk sector does not trash many minutes worth of frames.

Next, you need to decide where the rendered files are written to. This must be a shared disk or folder so all the slaves can access it as well. Either mount the shared drive and aim the Output To pointer in the Output Module to a subfolder in this shared folder or drive, or enable the option "Change render output to" in the Collect Files dialog, which creates a subfolder inside the one used for your collected project. We prefer the latter approach, as it creates a new folder with each render; this eliminates potential confusion with overwriting or skipping an already-rendered version of the project.

Speaking of File>Collect Files, this is your next step. Check the option Enable "Watch Folder" render; this is what writes the all-important Render Control File. To save on the amount of data that is collected, select For Queued Comps in the Collect Source Files popup. Then click Collect. You will be prompted to choose where to write the collected files; choose your Watch Folder. Note that Collect Files will not allow you to overwrite folders; you must give each collected project a new name. After Effects will then write the sources, project, and Render Control File into this folder.

When the slave renderers check the Watch Folder and find a Render Control File that points to a comp that has not yet been rendered, they will open the collected project and start rendering it. Each slave renderer also updates an HTML file in the Watch Folder called **watch_folder.html** that details its history and progress – open this in any web browser to check its status or perhaps to see why a render failed.

There is no limit to the number of machines that can pitch in on a network render; the bottleneck tends to be network activity as multiple machines work on the same project.

Recovering from Failure

Once a render engine records a failure (such as from a missing file), the entire project will be tagged as failed. This means that none of the render engines will start work on the remaining queued items. If one machine has already started to render an item and a second machine gets an error, the currently rendering item will finish rendering, but subsequent items won't. Open the HTML log file created to see what went wrong and fix it – these problems unfortunately don't disappear on their own.

Your collected project has not been damaged or changed; however, its Render Control File now thinks there's a problem with it and won't allow it to be rendered. To start rendering a previously collected project that didn't complete rendering:

Step 1: Open the copied project (*not* the original!).

Step 2: Select File>Collect Files with the Collect Source Files popup set to None.

Step 3: Save the new project; this will create a new collect folder.

This process allows you to create a new project with the path to already collected source files intact. You should delete all partially rendered files to save disk space and remove any potential confusion as to which files are the "real" ones.

To Collect Files for a distributed render, make sure you check the option Enable "Watch Folder" render. For efficiency, collect sources just For Queued Comps; for safety, check the option "Change render output to".

Network Rendering with the Standard Edition

After Effects has long supported a simple form of distributed rendering. It requires having a copy of After Effects on more than one computer and duplicating the project files and sources to each of these machines. Network the computers together, and have them all render to the same shared folder. If you render to a sequence of still images rather than to a movie and select the Render Setting option "Skip existing files", each computer will look at this folder, figure out what was the next frame number that had not been rendered yet, write a placeholder for that frame, then render it.

Network of One

Some users don't bother setting up a network; instead, they set up render engines on the same multiprocessing computer. Users have reported up to 80% faster rendering times because the operating system is using the computer's resources more efficiently.

It is not uncommon to need to render a project again, perhaps to accommodate a client correction. If you had to copy a large amount of source material to the Watch Folder, you may understandably want to avoid doing this again. Just collecting files again will either copy all of the sources again, or create a project that doesn't point to the old sources. Users have come up with different techniques to hack the Render Control File to force a rerender; sometimes they just manually reload the render on the slave machines. Here's the technique we suggest for re-rendering a project without having to recopy the sources:

Step 1: Collect Files – sources included – to a shared folder, *without* checking the Enable "Watch Folder" render option.

Step 2: Then Collect Files to the Watch Folder with Collect Source Files set to None (Project only) and with Enable "Watch Folder" render checked.

Step 3: If you need to rerender, repeat Step 2.

Other Network Solutions

There are other solutions for network rendering with After Effects. For example, After Effects 6.5 Professional users can take advantage of an offer from GridIron to download a "basic" two-CPU license of their X-Factor system for free (www.gridironxfactor.com/download).

X-Factor gives you the option of handing off RAM Previews to other networked computers, known as the "grid." You can continue to work in After Effects on your own workstation while the grid processes frames. When the processing is done, the RAM Preview will start to play back. You can then use Composition>Save RAM Preview to save the results to disk. Keep in mind that RAM Previews cannot currently field render; however, X-Factor *can* render an alpha channel for its preview (enable Retain Alpha Channel under the Settings tab in Window> GridIron X-Factor), working around an important limitation of RAM Previews.

You can employ more CPUs with the Basic license, but the cached frames will have a large watermark over them. Alternatively, you can buy a Plus 6-Pack license to employ an additional six CPUs, or an unlimited workstation license which allows one workstation to employ an unlimited number of CPUs to form the grid. Both allow you to send items in the Render Queue out to the grid – not just RAM Previews.

X-Factor allows you to build a "grid" out of CPUs on your network (above), then gives you the option of having a RAM Preview performed by the grid while you continue to work on your main computer (right).

The free X-Factor Basic license has the ability to speed up your workflow if you tend to perform long previews, use a single-CPU computer for your workstation and can enlist two more fast single-CPU computers (such as P4s) for your grid, and are able to multitask (continue working on something else) while a preview is cooking. It is less useful if you tend to perform RAM Previews that take under a minute to compute, want to see the results of your preview before moving onto another task, or have dual CPU computers both for your workstation and grid (such as dual G5s). In these cases, the overhead imposed by moving files between computers over your network means it would probably be faster to perform a local RAM Preview instead.

If you've tried X-Factor and set it aside, know that in early 2005 version 1.5 was released, which is simpler to install and use. As with virtually any piece of software, it is always good to periodically check back with the manufacturer, to take advantage of new features and bug fixes they've cooked up.

Although we have not used it ourselves, we know many high-end users are fans of the cross-platform Rush Render Queue (www.seriss.com/rush/) to manage render farms. Rush uses scripting – added in After Effects 6.0 – to initiate and run the process. (No, you won't spend all of your time in a command line interface; there is a friendlier graphical Rush After Effects Submit user interface, as well as a web-based graphical front end.) In addition to After Effects, Rush works with a variety of other programs, including Maya, Softimage, 3ds max, LightWave, Houdini, Shake, Mental Ray, and Renderman. As of early 2005, Rush costs $150 per "host" with discounts if you order more than 100 hosts.

Network Tips

The single most cost-effective thing you can do to speed up your network renders – whether you are using the Watch Folder, X-Factor, or Rush – is to upgrade the speed of your network. Many computers now feature gigabit ethernet; 8-port gigabit switches can be had for well under $200; higher-quality ethernet cable (such as Cat6) – which also makes your network more stable, and able to continuously operate at a higher speed – has come down in price as well.

Beyond creating a stable network, more than half of the remaining battle is setting up multiple computers to all look at the same folder or folders on a shared drive, with privileges so all can read from and write to those folders. These instructions will vary depending on what type of network you have; don't be afraid to ask around in an online forum to see if someone has a similar setup (or problem) as you do. Certainly one important point is making sure you use naming conventions that are compatible with all parts of your network: Keep the name short and avoid colons, slashes, or any extended characters in the names. Some additional network hints are also included in the After Effects Help (hit F1 to access).

Proxy Time

If you have a render-intensive background that is used as a precomp in several other comps, queue the background to render first, and use Post-Render Actions (see previous chapter) to assign the result as a proxy for itself. The remaining comps will then use the proxy, speeding their own renders, rather than render the background precomp from scratch each time.

The Watch Project

If you open an After Effects project file named **Watch This Folder.aep**, it will automatically launch After Effects into Watch Folder mode, looking at the folder this project was in. Place an alias of this project file in the **Startup** folder, and your render slaves will automatically start up in Watch Folder mode.

Connect

RAM Previewing was discussed in a sidebar at the end of Volume 1, Chapter 2.

The Render Queue and Output Module settings were the subject of Volume 1, Chapter 29.

An overview of scripting was presented at the end of Chapter 6.

Creating and managing proxies were discussed in this volume's Chapter 29.

What's Your Preference?

Setting preferences to optimize your workflow.

After Effects features a variety of settings that control importing files, opening multiple compositions, previewing audio, the appearance and interactivity of the program, plus numerous other details. In this chapter, we'll explain what these settings mean and what they do, highlighting those settings that we find aid our efficiency.

There are 11 individual Preferences windows. To access them, select the main Preferences item under the Edit menu Windows, or under the After Effects menu in OS X. You can also open the General preferences by typing Command+Option+; on Mac (Control+Alt+; on Windows). Once you have one Preference window open, you can access any of the others either through the shared popup or by clicking the Previous and Next buttons. To accept your changes to Preferences, click on OK (which is also the default if you hit Return); to ignore them click on Cancel. You cannot do anything else in After Effects while Preferences are open.

We'll go through each Preferences pane, discussing what the options control and how we personally set them. If you want to learn more about a specific preference, the Help file that comes with After Effects contains thorough documentation on each one.

The Text Prefs

Additional preferences are hidden in the text-based Preferences file. See Bonus Chapter 31B for more info about editing this file, plus a few common prefs to modify.

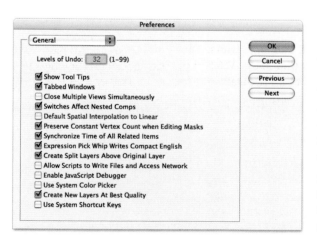

General

Levels of Undo: This controls how many of your last steps After Effects remembers. More Undos take up more memory, leaving less for RAM Previews or handling large source images. Some actions are *not* stored in the Undo buffer, such as – ironically – editing the Preferences.

Show Tool Tips: Ever wonder what a funky icon does? Enable Show Tool Tips, place your cursor over it, wait a few seconds, and After Effects will tell you.

Tabbed Windows: If these are enabled, opening more than one comp results in their going into the same Timeline and Comp windows, appearing under their own tabs. Same goes for Effect Controls and Layer windows. We leave this on, as you can always drag tabbed windows out to new windows. Close your Comp and Timeline windows before changing this.

Close Multiple Views Simultaneously: If you opened multiple Comp windows (View>New View), enabling this means that closing one Comp window closes all associated ones. We leave this off, as we like to be selective about opening and closing alternate views.

Switches Affect Nested Comps: Also known as recursive switches. Setting the comp-wide switches for Resolution, Wireframe Interactions, Draft 3D, Frame Blending, and Motion Blur cause the corresponding switches to be set the same way in any nested comps. Also, changing the Quality of a layer that is a nested comp sets the Quality the same for all layers in that nested comp. We leave this enabled.

Default Spatial Interpolation to Linear: If this is disabled, spatial interpolation between Position keyframes defaults to Auto Bezier, which we prefer. This subject is discussed in detail in Volume 1, Chapter 3.

Preserve Constant Vertex Count when Editing Masks: If this is enabled and you add or delete a mask point for one keyframe on an animating mask shape, that point (or one After Effects thinks is like it) will be added or deleted from all other keyframes.

Synchronize Time of All Related Items: Enabling this means that as you move the time marker in one comp, the time marker is moved to a corresponding point in any nested comps. You may experience odd behavior when the same comp is nested more than once with the copies offset in time, or when a layer has been time remapped. In general, though, this is a hugely useful feature worth the slight slowdown it entails.

Expression Pick Whip Writes Compact English: When enabled (the default), expressions are created using wording that can be transferred across multiple language versions of After Effects.

Create Split Layers Above Original Layer: This option decides if the second half of a split layer appears above or below the first half.

Allow Scripts to Write Files and Access Network: Allows scripts to write files, create folders, and access the network. Disabled by default for security.

Enable JavaScript Debugger: An essential tool when creating scripts. See the After Effects 6.5 Scripting Guide (a PDF file found in the AE6.5 Documentation Folder on the program installer CD) for more details.

Use System Color Picker: As of version 6.5, After Effects defaults to using the powerful Photoshop color picker. Enable to use the System Picker.

Create New Layers at Best Quality: If you have a very slow computer, disable for new layers to default to Draft. Remember to render using Best.

Use System Shortcut Keys (Mac only): When enabled, Command+M, Command+H, and Command+Option+H are taken away from After Effects for use by the system; add Control to them for the normal After Effects use. (You may need to toggle it a couple of times for it to work.)

To lock a window from accepting tabbed items, double-click in the area just above a tab.

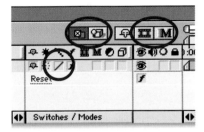

Switches Affect Nested Comps applies only to the comp-wide Wireframe Interactions, Draft 3D, Frame Blending, Motion Blur, and (not pictured here) Resolution switches for nested comps, plus the Quality setting of layers that are nested comps.

Segments and Blocks

Segmenting movies with embedded audio can have strange sequences of white frames at their end, as the segment is padded out to fill an audio block. If you anticipate segmenting your movies, render the audio out separately.

Under the OpenGL Info button (top) is an important Quality preference determining whether to render OpenGL previews Faster, or More Accurate (above). We use More Accurate, as it allows OpenGL to render blending modes and other features.

Previews

The subject of previewing your work – and the associated preview settings – was discussed in depth at the end of Volume 1, Chapter 2. We recommend you read it for a better understanding of how these parameters interact. Here is a quick overview of the Previews Preferences settings:

Adaptive Resolution Limit: If you have Adaptive Resolution enabled in a composition's Fast Previews popup (found along the lower right edge of the Comp window), After Effects is constantly sensing if any action you are taking is going to take a long time to render. If that's the case, it will temporarily switch to a lower resolution to make the program more responsive. How low the Resolution goes is determined by the Adaptive Resolution Limit popup in the Previews Preferences pane.

Enable OpenGL: A global switch of whether to use OpenGL acceleration. Unless you're experiencing problems with OpenGL, leave this enabled, and select OpenGL on a per-comp basis through the Fast Previews popup.

Effects use Adaptive Resolution when OpenGL is enabled: As of version 6.5, OpenGL cannot render effects. Enable this option to use Adaptive Resolution when scrubbing effect parameters.

OpenGL Info: Opens a dialog where you can see what type of OpenGL acceleration your video card offers, tweak the card's Texture Memory allocation (we use the default), and – most importantly – we set the Quality popup to More Accurate to render blending modes and the like.

Audio Preview: The Duration setting controls the length of audio playback when you press the numeric keypad's period key. Of course, the longer you set it, the more time and RAM it will take. Use the popups below Duration to set the Sample Rate, resolution (Sample Size), and number of Channels for the preview. For the fastest, highest quality previews, set these the same as the audio layers you have in a comp.

Display

Motion Path: Determines how many keyframes of a selected layer's motion path are displayed in the Comp window. We prefer to see the entire path (the All Keyframes option), but you can opt for less to cut down on visual clutter when you're focusing on a complicated path.

Disable Thumbnails in Project Window: Normally, After Effects displays a thumbnail of the selected footage file at the top of the Project window, which can slow down the responsiveness of the program, particularly with high-resolution sources. It also creates thumbnails for comps – but it needs to render the first frame to do so. If we are familiar with our sources, we leave this off to buy extra speed.

Auto-zoom When Resolution Changes: If this is enabled and you change a comp's Resolution, its Magnification changes to match. For example, if you switch from Full to Half Resolution, the Magnification changes from 100% to 50%. We find this quite distracting, so we leave it off.

Show Rendering in Progress in Info Palette: This can be handy to tell you what's taking so long (such as a slow effect) each time you move to a new frame. There is a slight render hit, though, so turn it off on slower machines.

Default Height of Timeline Graphs: Affects how tall the Velocity and Value curves are drawn when you first twirl them open. We're fine with the default of 4 cells; you can always drag individual graphs taller or shorter.

Import

Still Footage: When you add a still to a comp, does it default to the comp's length, or a predetermined length? We prefer the former, as it is easy to trim the duration of individual or multiple stills in a comp.

Sequence Footage: Not to be confused with Sequence Layers, this sets the default frame rate of an image sequence when you import it. To save on headaches later, you usually want to set this to equal your working frame rate (such as 29.97 frames per second for NTSC video).

Interpret Unlabeled Alpha As: We set this to Ask User. It's always safest to have After Effects ask you how you want your alpha interpretation set when you import footage, because it sometimes guesses wrong. However, if you drag and drop items to the Project window, it will always Guess regardless of this preference (see Chapter 1 for details).

Default Drag Import As: When you drag a still image (such as a Photoshop or Illustrator file) into After Effects rather than go through the normal Import dialog, do you want After Effects to assume you want these left as individual footage items, or placed in their own comps? The Comp option is handy for layered files, but clutters up the Project window fast if you have it create a comp for every single-layer still.

Output

Overflow Volumes: If there is a chance your render may exceed your drive space, you can set up a chain of additional drives for the render to spill over to. This is a good safety net for those overnight renders you don't want to fail, but be warned that it will split movies into multiple pieces, and complain when removable drives are dismounted. We tend to leave this off.

Segment Sequences At: Some computers really…slow…down when there are too many files in a single folder. If you encounter this problem when you're rendering long image sequences, enable this option and set it to a few hundred or so. It's faster to merge together the files later.

Segment Movie Files At: If you know your render will be transferred to CD-ROMs later, you don't want to create a QuickTime movie that is larger than your media can hold. You can prevent that from happening by enabling this option and setting a size limit a few megs smaller than your media.

Minimum Diskspace Before Overflowing: This is self-explanatory; see also the earlier discussion of Overflow Volumes.

Audio Block Duration: Audio data is typically not saved for every frame of video, as it is usually so tiny compared with the video data in a frame. Realtime playback often works better if audio is saved into larger blocks, such as every half or full second.

Use Default File Name and Folder: When you queue up a comp to render, do you want After Effects to automatically make a file name out of the comp's name, and save it to the last place you saved a render? If not, disable this option, and After Effects will ask for the file name and destination every time you add an item to the Render Queue.

Grids & Guides

Grids, Rulers, and Guides were discussed in detail in Volume 1, Chapter 2, so we're going to deal with them very briefly here. You can toggle the display of these on and off by using the options in the View menu while the Comp window is forward. Note that objects can snap to Grids and Guides, but not the Proportional Grid.

Grid: This is an overlay for the Comp window that can consist of lines, dashed lines, or dots, spaced by the number of pixels specified.

Proportional Grid: An overlay for the Comp window that does the math for you, automatically spacing out lines depending on how many divisions you want for the comp, regardless of its size.

Guides: This controls the color and drawing style of the guide lines you can drag into the Comp window from the rulers. You can add Guides only when Rulers are visible (View>Show Rulers toggles Rulers on and off).

Safe Margins: This is another Comp window overlay, this time telling you where the Action and Title Safe areas are. The defaults are for standard definition video; hi-def uses smaller (albeit, undefined) margins.

Label Colors

Quite simply, this is where you get to change the colors available to be assigned to layers in the Timeline window, footage items in the Project window, and comps in the Render Queue. You can also rename them.

Label Defaults

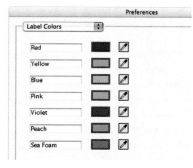

In this panel you get to line up the Label Colors you defined in the previous window with the default colors that layers, footage items, and comps are assigned in the Timeline, Project, and Render Queue windows. Remember you can change the color assigned to these items after they are created or imported by clicking on the swatch next to them – a great way to help visually organize a complex Timeline in particular.

Memory & Cache

After Effects attempts to hold as many source and rendered comp images in memory as possible, planning to save time when you go back to look at them again by not needing to retrieve the sources from disk or rerender the frames of a comp. We've had no problems using the defaults.

Maximum Memory Usage: This controls how much memory After Effects will grab for itself if needed. As modern operating systems support shared and virtual memory, the default value is over 100%, meaning After Effects can dip into virtual memory as needed. Quit other programs or increase this number if you still get Out of Memory errors while you're working or rendering (Adobe does not suggest you go over 200%); decrease it if rendering seems much slower than it should be, as you may be wasting time accessing virtual memory.

Image Cache: As discussed at the end of Volume 1, Chapter 2, After Effects has two strategies to speed up previewing frames in a comp. One is to save images in RAM; Maximum RAM Cache Size determines how much RAM to grab for this purpose. If you need to eke just a few more frames out of your previews, and installing more RAM is not an option, raise this number, although it may cause more trips into virtual memory, which slows the program down.

The second (introduced in version 6.5) is to temporarily save frames to disk: not as fast as RAM, but often faster than re-rendering a frame. Check Enable Disk Cache to use this feature, set the Maximum Disk Cache Size, and use Choose Folder to decide where the frames are cached (pick your biggest, fastest drive).

Video Preview

These settings are discussed at length at the end of Volume 1, Chapter 2 as well as this volume's Chapter 21, so we won't go over them again here. The most common gotcha: When you're previewing through a video card such as AJA Kona, Blackmagic DeckLink, or Digital Voodoo, you need to set Output Mode to RGB, not the 8-bit or 10-bit YUV modes you would normally render to.

User Interface Colors

This new window exposes some previously hidden preferences and allows you to tweak the user interface's appearance.

Use Label Color for Layer Handles and Paths: Makes it easier to relate paths and outlines in the Comp window to layers in the Timeline window.

Cycle Mask Colors: Enable for each mask outline to be a different color; disable for them all to be yellow. (You can always change them later.)

Highlight Entire Row in Timeline: When enabled, causes the Sources, Switches, and other Columns to be a darker gray when a layer is selected.

Pasteboard Color: This defines the color of the border around the Comp window. The default is a light 75% gray; some prefer a neutral 50% gray.

Hot Text Color: The definition of Hot Text is any value you can click and edit, such as parameters in the Timeline and Effect Controls window. Highlighted values or those controlled by expressions are always red.

User Interface Brightness: For those who have always yearned for After Effects to have a darker gray interface, here's your chance…

Connect

Previewing preferences were covered at the end of Volume 1, Chapter 2.

Spatial Interpolation and the Velocity/ Value graphs, see Volume 1, Chapter 3.

Comp and Layer switches are detailed at the end of Volume 1, Chapter 6.

Masking, see Volume 1, Chapter 11.

Rendering was discussed in detail in Volume 1, Chapter 26 and in this volume's Chapters 29 and 30.

Alpha channel types and interpretation were dissected in Chapter 1.

Photoshop and Illustrator files were covered in Chapters 2 and 3, respectively.

Audio concepts were sounded out in Chapter 11.

Time Remapping, see Chapter 13.

Video issues such as safe areas and Video Preview were discussed in Chapter 21.

Bonus Chapter 31B explains how to edit the text-based Preferences file.

Bonus Tutorials

How the tutorials are organized and other useful information…

The DVD-ROM that accompanies this book contains six Bonus Tutorials for you to explore. These focus on teaching skills you will find useful in actual work, including giving you a thorough overview of Particle Playground.

The unifying theme behind these tutorials is that they bring together multiple skills learned throughout this series. A list of those skills, plus the chapter they are introduced, is included on the first page of each tutorial.

Each tutorial is graded for **Style** and includes:

- *Step-by-Step* – shows you how to build the project from scratch.

- *Guided Tour* – dissects an already-made project layer by layer.

The **Difficulty Level** is also noted and is based on a hiking guide theme of Easy through Challenging. The exact levels are *Easy, Easy–Moderate, Moderate,* and *Challenging.*

This icon is used if the tutorial requires the Professional edition of After Effects.

The **Trail Head** description inside the PDF that accompanies each tutorial will give you an outline of what will be covered, and which, if any, of the free plug-ins from the DVD or bundled with After Effects are being used.

We hope you enjoy these bonus tutorials. The following folders on the DVD are used by the Tutorials:

▶ Bonus Tutorials

Each tutorial folder contains a PDF file of the tutorial itself (.pdf suffix), an After Effects project file (.aep suffix), and a QuickTime movie of the final result (.mov suffix). These folders also may contain an additional subfolder with extra source material used just by this tutorial. Note that you will need Adobe Reader to open the PDF file; an installer is included on your After Effects CD, and may also be downloaded from www.adobe.com, if you don't already have it.

The final movies can be played from any Quick-Time player utility or from within Adobe Reader.

Opening Projects: The tutorials can be run directly from the DVD by opening the After Effects 6.5 project file. If you copy the Tutorial folder to your hard drive, you may need to relink the source material to the master Sources folder on the DVD, or a copy of it on your drive. (Alternatively, you could open the project file from the DVD, and then do a File>Collect Files to your hard drive.)

If files become "unlinked", they will appear in *italics* in the Project window. Simply double-click the first missing item, which opens the Open dialog, and navigate to it on the DVD or your drive. Select this item and After Effects should relink to all other missing items.

▶ Sources

The Bonus Tutorials use the movies, music, mattes, objects, stills, and text elements from this folder. Each footage item has a two-letter prefix that identifies its creator; a key to the companies, artists and musicians who provided the footage and audio sources is on page 408.

TUTORIAL 1

Dotcom Zoom

Continuous rasterization of vector-based art from Adobe Illustrator opens up a few neat tricks, such as being able to "zoom" through sections of text or a logo while keeping your shapes completely sharp.

This tutorial comes in two parts. First, we step you through how to set up Illustrator text for continuous rasterization, using the Professional edition's Exponential Scale keyframe assistant to keep a consistent speed through the zoom. We also show you how to animate the anchor point to zoom through the center of the "dot" in dotcom. Then, we guide you through a tour of how we applied the result as a track matte to create an interesting animation where the inside and outside of the text are related but different.

Techniques

▶ keyframe animation ▶ animating scale
▶ animating the anchor point ▶ exponential zoom (optional)
▶ motion blur (optional) ▶ continuous rasterization

Footage credits
Artbeats/Digidelic and Digital Web

Music by
Chris Meyer

EASY-MODERATE

STEP-BY-STEP +
GUIDED TOUR

TUTORIAL 2

Enhancing 3D

3D animation programs allow you to create your own virtual worlds, right down to the surface textures and lighting. However, we tend to be so busy creating our models, keyframing realistic animation moves, and worrying about rendering times that we rarely have the chance to get those lights and colors exactly the way we like.

The secret to great-looking 3D is to post-process it in a program like After Effects. A combination of layered, multipass renders, color correction, blurs, and blending modes allow you to perk up – or grunge down – any 3D render. In this project, we'll walk you through our standard procedure to add sex appeal to our renders.

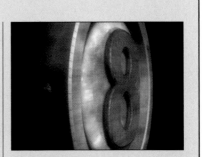

Footage credit
CyberMotion/Countdown animation

Techniques

▶ creating compositions ▶ altering opacity ▶ blending modes
▶ applying effects ▶ adjustment layers (optional)

EASY

STEP-BY-STEP

TUTORIAL 3

Pro Projected Text

We're very fond of the interplay of light on moving objects, such as projecting an image or text onto blowing cloth or flowing water. To create this digitally, you might think you need a 3D program to model these dimensional objects. However, it is possible to fake these "projected" effects in a 2D program like After Effects through use of its Displacement Map effect.

This tutorial shows you how to project text onto the rippling muscles of a body builder. In addition to using displacement mapping, we will also use blending modes to alter the coloration as well as the shapes of the characters. Central to this tutorial is also a lesson on animating type using the new Text engine introduced in After Effects 6.0.

Footage credit
Photodisc by Getty Images/Fitness

Music by
Keith Snyder/Flow of Soul

MODERATE

GUIDED TOUR

Techniques

- ▶ animating position, motion paths ▶ blending modes
- ▶ nesting compositions ▶ applying and animating effects
- ▶ compound effects ▶ text animation

TUTORIAL 4

Revealing Type

One of the most challenging (and potentially tedious) tasks is simulating a word being handwritten onto the screen. In After Effects, you can use the Write-On effect or the new Paint engine to accomplish this – but not to actually write on the text; you use it to *reveal* lines and strokes of text that have been specially prepared ahead of time in Photoshop.

This multipart tutorial will lead you by the hand (so to speak) on how to prepare your text, and then reveal it in a fluid motion to simulate handwriting. This technique will then be used in the context of creating an opening title for a documentary about the Irish famine, set to the music of Troy Donockley. The guided tour will also cover animating text precisely, and using masks to reveal lines of text quickly and easily.

Footage credit
Corbis Images/Irish still images
Getty Images/World Flags

Music by
Troy Donockley

CHALLENGING

**STEP-BY-STEP +
GUIDED TOUR**

Techniques

- ▶ animating paint strokes, effect points, and mask shapes
- ▶ animating text along a path ▶ nesting compositions
- ▶ compound effects ▶ blending modes

TUTORIAL 5

Pro Particle Playground

This bonus tutorial comes in four parts, all focusing on Particle Playground: a complex particle physics simulation effect that can toss text, dots of color, and even other layers around a frame based on a set of rules you can control.

In the first two documents, **JJ Gifford** helps demystify Particle Playground, and shares numerous tips to better control it as well as reduce its rendering times. He follows this up with a simple Playground project to make the individual characters of a word fall away and bounce around the screen.

In the next two documents, **Richard Lainhart** of O-Town Media provides further context on how to approach Particle Playground, and then shows you how to approximate the look of the opening title of the movie *The Matrix* (originally created by Animal Logic).

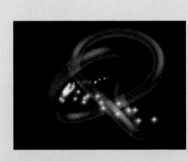

Footage credit
Richard Lainhart/O-Town Media

CHALLENGING

STEP-BY-STEP

Techniques
▶ animating position and scale ▶ masking ▶ composition hierarchies
▶ applying and animating effects ▶ compound effects
▶ rendering stills ▶ prerendering and comp proxies (optional)

TUTORIAL 6

Expressive Particles

In this tutorial, **Dan Ebberts** of MotionScript.com will show you how to create a 3D expression-based particle system where the particles – which can be any layer you choose or create – follow a path defined by animating the position of a target layer. You will create a custom user interface for it employing Expression Controls, and then apply the expressions Dan has created for the task (which are also dissected in detail at the end of the tutorial).

We'll look at a couple of different flavors of this particle system: one where the particles are generated in a single burst, and another where the particles form an endless stream. This type of particle system can be useful for simulating flocking behavior similar to that exhibited by birds or bees. It can also be useful for creating "particle beam" effects.

Footage credit
Dan Ebberts/MotionScript

CHALLENGING

**STEP-BY-STEP +
GUIDED TOUR**

Techniques
▶ animating position in 3D, using multiple views ▶ null objects
▶ animation presets ▶ expressions ▶ expression controls
▶ roving keyframes ▶ auto-orienting layers towards a 3D camera

THANK YOU

Only two names end up on the cover, but in reality, scores of people are involved in the creation of a book like this. We greatly appreciate everyone who worked with us on this revised edition of **Creating Motion Graphics***, including:*

▶ Everyone on our team at CMP Books, including Matt Kelsey, Dorothy Cox, Paul Temme, Gail Saari, Meg McCalmon, and Sachie Jones, who gave us the tools we needed to realize the book we wanted to make.

▶ Numerous people have provided technical edits for various sections of this book through the years, including Steve Tiborcz and Beth Roy. Most recently, Dan Ebberts added his touch to the chapters on expressions, including writing about scripting.

▶ A special nod to JJ Gifford, Richard Lainhart, and Dan Ebberts, who all donated bonus tutorials.

▶ Our wonderful motion graphics clients who have waited patiently while we immersed ourselves in yet *another* book.

▶ Everyone who bought the previous editions of *Creating Motion Graphics* and its companion book *After Effects in Production* – your overwhelmingly positive response is what has encouraged us to keep writing.

▶ The numerous companies, studios, and artists who created the source material used throughout this book. A special thank you to Artbeats and 12 Inch Design for donating D1 NTSC & PAL stock footage. (See a full list of contributors on page 408.)

▶ The companies who contributed free effects for you to use: Digital Film Tools, Fnord Software, and Walker Effects. A special thank you to Jens Enqvist for writing a custom plug-in just for this book (and to Bruce Bullis for porting it to Windows).

▶ All of our fellow users who so willingly shared their knowledge with us through the years – especially when we were just starting out. Thanks also to everyone who participates in the email lists and web forums we frequent – the ongoing sharing of knowledge in these venues is simply amazing.

▶ And of course, the After Effects team, for crafting this wonderful piece of software from which we derive our livelihood. You changed the motion graphics industry, and our lives as well. Be sure to check out *CoSA Lives* on the DVD to see how it all started…

PRODUCTION CREDITS

▶ The book layout, cover, and DVD art were designed by Trish Meyer.

▶ Our manuscript was translated into proper English by copyeditor Mandy Erickson.

▶ The text was proofread by Sam Molineaux, and indexed by Ken DellaPenta.

▶ Typesetting and page layouts were performed in QuarkXpress by Stacey Kam and Trish Meyer, with assistance from Dreyers Grand Light Ice Cream and Bewleys Irish tea.

▶ The Tip, Factoid, Gotcha, and Connect icons were designed by Trevor Gilchrist.

▶ Printed by RR Donnelley, Salem, Virginia, USA.

INDEX

Note: BT = Bonus Tutorial
BC = Bonus Chapter

Effects (alphabetical)

F

G

H

I

BC refers to Bonus Chapters. Example: BT4B = Bonus Chapter 4B.
BT refers to Bonus Tutorials. Example: BT1 = Bonus Tutorial 1.

masks (*continued*)
   creating, BT4
   interpolating between, 82–85
   moving object, 327
   multiple, BT4
   outline colors of, 403, BC31B
   as paths, BT4
   render order position, 202
   Smart Mask Interpolation, 82–85
   stabilized footage, 219
   vertex count when editing, 399
match clip, 374
Matrix title effect, BT5D
mattes. *See also* 3D mattes
   alpha, BC10B
   edge cleanups, 256
   Matte Choker effect, 124, 169
   partial, BC10B
   Simple Choker effect, 124, 169, 256
Maximum Memory Usage setting, 403
Maxon Cinema 4D, 268–70, 280
Maya, 18, 20, 262–64, 277
Media 100 844/X
   exporting to, 244
   importing from, 243–44
Media 100 i/HD, importing from, 241–43
media encoding, 393
memory requirements, 372
memory usage, maximum, 403
methods
   expressions and, 94, 99
   scripts and, 114–15
Minimum Diskspace Before Overflowing setting, 402
MoCon, 270
modes. *See* blending modes
monitoring results, 306–7
monitors
   calibration of, 339
   televisions vs., 307
morphing shapes, 82–85
Most Recently Used settings, BC31B
Motion (Apple), 129, 248–49
Motion Blur, 228, 266, 292, BT1
Motion Math, 89
Motion Path setting, 400
Motion Stabilization
   advice on, 221
   basics, 212–15
   defined, 212
   examples illustrating, 220–23
   masking and, 219

Motion Stabilization (*continued*)
   options, 215–17
   Process Before Match option, 215, 222
   reviewing results, 217–20
   setup, 212–17
Motion Tracking. *See also* Motion Stabilization.
   3D, 232
   Adapt Feature on Every Frame option, 216
   Affine Corner Pin, 228
   Apply Motion To options, 215
   Attach Points, 224–25
   choosing a Type, 224
   defined, 224
   effect points, 226
   examples illustrating, 224–27, 229–33
   Extrapolate Motion option, 216
   Options dialog, 225
   Perspective Corner Pin, 228, 274–75
   removing/cloning objects, 70–72
   setup, 212–16
   Tracking Regions, 213–14, 222–23, 225
   types of, 226–28
movies
   converting interlaced, for computer display, 321
   projects embedded in, 247
   scaling interlaced, without separating fields, 318
multimedia resize, 305
multipass compositing, 285–86

N

name templates, 392
nesting compositions, 3
nesting layers, 97
network rendering
   with AE Standard edition, 395
   basics, 392–93
   failure recovery, 395–96
   other solutions for, 396–97
   with Particle Playground effect, BT5A
   setup for, 392–95
   single-computer, 396
   tips for, 397
NewTek LightWave 3D, 270–72, 281
Noise & Grain effects, 124–27
Non-Drop Frame timecode, 297, 349

nonsquare pixels, 30, 299–301, 342–43, 350–51
NTSC video. *See also* frame rates
   field order, 310, 342, 348
   field rate, 308
   real frame rate, 297, 317, 348
null objects, 98–99, BC31B
numbers
   random, BC6B
   rounding, BC6B
   to text, BC6B

O

objects
   cutting, from backgrounds, 25–26
   null, 98–99, BC31B
   removing or duplicating moving, 70–72
   scripting and, 114–15
"old movie" effect, 80
OMF files, 235, 247
onion skinning, 64
Opacity. *See also* alpha channels
   alphas and, 5–7
   animating, 80, BT4
   changing, BT2
   displaying, 5
   rotation controlling, 92–93
OpenEXR, 374
OpenGL, 276, 400
output
   multiple streams, 19
   preferences, 401–2
   rendering with alpha channel, 16–18
   testing, 314
Output Module Settings, 247
Overflow Volumes setting, 401
oversampling, 255
overscan system, 303

P

Paint and Clone
   animating strokes, 60–64
   blending modes, 57
   Brush Tips palette, 53, 63
   Brush tool, 53
   Channels popup, 56
   Clone Presets, 67
   Clone Source Overlay, 68–69
   Clone Stamp tool, 66–67
   Custom Duration, 62

   editing existing strokes, 54–57
   effects and, 54, 65
   Eraser tool, 58–59
   interpolating strokes, 63
   keyboard shortcuts, 52–53, 62, 67, 73
   Modes popup, 57
   motion tracking with, 70–72
   Paint on Transparent option, 55
   Paint palette, 52–54, 56
   removing/duplicating moving objects, 70–72
   rotoscoping, 62
   Source Time Shift, 69
   straight line stroke, 73
   tablets, using with, 63
   tips for, 73
   transforming strokes, 56
   Write On mode, 61
PAL video. *See also* frame rates
   field order, 310, 355
   field rate, 308
   frame rate, 298
   pixel aspect ratio, 351
   pulldown, 328
pan and scan, 364–65
PAR. *See* pixel aspect ratios
parenting, 97, 108
partial mattes, BC10B
Pasteboard Area size setting, BC31B
Pasteboard Color setting, 403
paths, copying and pasting, as masks, 48
pedestal, 337–39
Photoshop
   alpha channels from artwork, 24
   books recommended, 32, 35
   cell-type animation, 32
   color management, 34
   color picker, 399
   equivalent features of, in After Effects, 28
   Extract tool, 27
   importing from, 27–29, 32–33, 35–36, 234
   layer effects, 36
   Layer Sets, 33
   Layer Styles, 35–36
   layer types, 23
   pixel aspect ratios, 30
   saving layered files, 17, 25
   Styles palette, 35

BC refers to Bonus Chapters. Example: BT4B = Bonus Chapter 4B.
BT refers to Bonus Tutorials. Example: BT1 = Bonus Tutorial 1.

BC refers to Bonus Chapters. Example: BC6B = Bonus Chapter 6B.
BT refers to Bonus Tutorials. Example: BT1 = Bonus Tutorial 1.

CREATING MOTION GRAPHICS WITH AFTER EFFECTS, 3RD EDITION
VOLUME 1: THE ESSENTIALS
TRISH & CHRIS MEYER

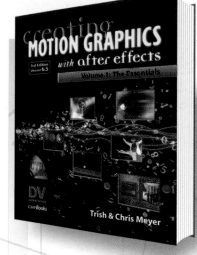

Get the most out of After Effects 6.5, with the 3rd edition of the bestselling After Effects book. This full-color guide covers the core concepts and tools you need to tackle virtually every job, and do it with artistic and technical flair. Features new chapters on dynamic text animation and animation presets, as well as hundreds more new shortcuts and enhancements.

$59.95, 4-color softcover with DVD, 482 pages, ISBN 1-57820-249-3.

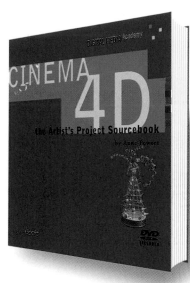

CINEMA 4D
ANNE POWERS

Realize your artistic vision with this treasure chest of instructional projects. Each project introduces new concepts and techniques that move you along to mastery of CINEMA 4D. Perfectly suited for classroom use, as well as the self-guided learner, each project is a discrete lesson complete with media supplied on the companion DVD. Plus—download a free update for V9 from www.cmpbooks.com/cinema4d.

$39.95, Softcover with DVD, 337 pages, ISBN 1-57820-242-6.

COLOR CORRECTION FOR DIGITAL VIDEO
STEVE HULLFISH & JAIME FOWLER

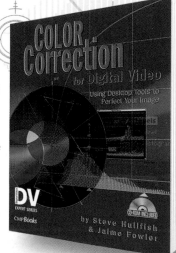

Use desktop tools to improve your storytelling, deliver critical cues, and add impact to your video. Beginning with a clear, concise description of color and perception theory, this full-color book shows you how to analyze color correction problems and solve them—whatever NLE or plugin you use. Refine your skills with tutorials that include secondary and spot corrections and stylized looks.

$49.95, 4-color softcover with CD-ROM, 202 pages, ISBN 1-57820-201-9.

CMP**Books**

www.cmpbooks.com

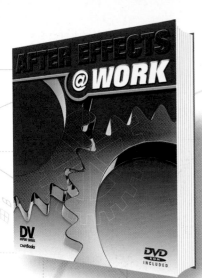

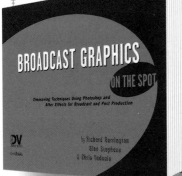

AFTER EFFECTS IN PRODUCTION, 2ND EDITION
TRISH & CHRIS MEYER

"By showcasing a variety of artistic techniques, After Effects in Production is a natural follow-up to Creating Motion Graphics."
— Steve Kilisky, Senior Product Manager, Adobe After Effects

Take your After Effects skills to a new level! Twelve step-by-step tutorials, designed by industry professionals, explore a variety of creative approaches as they teach useful design concepts and production techniques.

Updated for After Effects 6.5, this new edition covers the most significant Version 5 and 6 features including 3D space, cameras, lights, parenting, text, animation presets, paint, and expressions. Each carefully structured project presents the "why" behind the steps, so you can adapt these techniques to your own designs and motion graphics work. All contain timeless concepts that will be of use for many years to come.

After Effects in Production also contains six case studies of commercial projects created by award-winning studios such as ATTIK, Belief, Curious Pictures, The Diecks Group, Fido, and the authors' own studio, CyberMotion. These detail the integration of After Effects, 3D programs, live action, and a variety of animation techniques, revealing the artistic concepts behind the spots as well as the inventive techniques used to execute them. The enclosed DVD contains QuickTime movies of each of the final animations, allowing you to step through them frame-by-frame so you can examine them in detail.

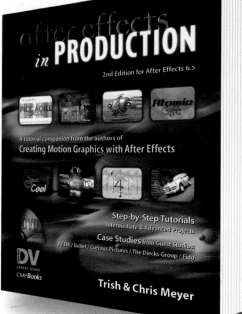

$49.95, 4-color softcover with DVD, 354 pages, ISBN 1-57820-264-7

USER Level: Intermediate to Advanced. *Topics include*:

- Mastering 3D space features, including cameras, lights, shadows, and orientation

- Employing parenting, precomposing, and expressions to group layers

- Refining animations with keyframe assistants, expressions, and velocity curves

- Universal design concepts that can be applied to any version of After Effects

CMP**Books**

www.cmpbooks.com